THE
BOSWELL
PAPERS

THE
GLADSTONE
DIARIES

VOLUME I · 1825–1832

Edited by

M. R. D. FOOT

PROFESSOR OF MODERN HISTORY
IN THE
UNIVERSITY OF MANCHESTER

CLARENDON PRESS · OXFORD
1968

Oxford University Press, Ely House, London, W.1

GLASGOW NEW YORK TORONTO MELBOURNE WELLINGTON
CAPE TOWN SALISBURY IBADAN NAIROBI LUSAKA ADDIS ABABA
BOMBAY CALCUTTA MADRAS KARACHI LAHORE DACCA
KUALA LUMPUR HONG KONG TOKYO

MADE AND PRINTED IN GREAT BRITAIN BY
WILLIAM CLOWES AND SONS, LIMITED, LONDON AND BECCLES

PREFACE

This book has been long in preparation, and the editor's debts of gratitude are many. First among them he must place those to the last and present archbishops of Canterbury, successive owners of the main Gladstone diary, who have made it available for publication and have helped to cover the editorial costs; to Mr. Charles Gladstone, the diarist's grandson, for limitless forbearance; and to the late Arthur Tilney Bassett, the Gladstone family archivist, but for whose persistence the main diary would have slumbered in a deed-box to this day.

The edition has been prepared under the direction of an *ad hoc* committee at Oxford, composed of Sir Kenneth Wheare, Sir Arthur Norrington, Mr. A. L. C. Bullock, Mr. R. N. W. Blake, Mr. A. F. Thompson, and Mr. E. G. W. Bill; to which Mr. C. H. Roberts has acted as secretary. Individually and collectively, the editor owes the members of this committee his very warmest thanks; to the secretary above all. Moreover, he now understands why scholars who have had the good fortune to be published by the Clarendon Press write of it in terms of such respect.

The staffs of Lambeth Palace Library and of the Public Record Office, and those both of the Library and of the Department of Manuscripts at the British Museum, have shown great courtesy and helpfulness; without special facilities provided in the Museum's north library, the edition could hardly have been prepared at all.

Equally, it could hardly have been prepared without the generous support of the Wolfson Foundation, the Calouste Gulbenkian Foundation, All Souls College, and Christ Church, Oxford; all of whom contributed, with the archbishop, to the salaries and expenses of the editor and to his research assistance. The funds they provided were handled by St. Catherine's College, Oxford, which thus undertook the academic sponsorship of the project. The Institute of Historical Research has made available, from October 1967, precious working space near the Museum.

To Miss Mary Sullivan, his senior research assistant, the editor is particularly indebted, both for undertaking much bibliographical research and for her general readiness to watch out for, and correct, his mistakes. He is grateful to Dr. M. A. Clarke, also his research assistant, for her sensitive help with research and translation. Needless to say, such errors as remain are his responsibility alone. He pays tribute also to the practically faultless typing of Mrs. Nicole Mott; to the helpful patience of hundreds of friends and former pupils or colleagues at Oxford and Southampton, who have listened to his queries and discussed them with him; and to his own family, who have endured for years without complaint his preoccupation with a character many years dead.

The copyright of the text below cited from Lambeth MSS belongs, as they do, to the archbishop of Canterbury; of the text cited from British Museum Additional MSS, to Mr. Charles Gladstone. They have been so kind as to authorize publication of the copyright material they hold; and acknowledgement is also due to Lord Kilbracken for the extract from J. A. Godley's letter on page xxv.

M.R.D.F.

Department of History
University of Manchester
24 January 1968

CONTENTS

VOLUME I

List of Illustrations ix

Abbreviated proper names in diary text of Volumes I and II. x

Abbreviated book titles, &c xiii

Other abbreviations xvii

Introduction xix

DIARY TEXT:

16 July 1825 1

1826 27

1827 92

1828 157

1829 220

1830 278

1831 337

1 January 1832 402

1 February 1832, abroad 407

[29] July 1832, 'In England again' 564

VOLUME II

List of Illustrations vii

DIARY TEXT:

1833 1

1834 80

1835 146

1836 215

1837 273

1 January 1838 333

11 August 1838, abroad 390

1 January 1839, abroad 545

31 January 1839, in England again 575

Addenda and Corrigenda 649

Dramatis personae, 1825–39 655

LIST OF ILLUSTRATIONS

Eton. June 1826 . . . . . *facing page* 56
    facsimile of diary in Lambeth MS 1416

Seaforth House, Lancashire 64
    drawing by J. P. Neale

Anne Mackenzie Gladstone, 1828 218
    miniature by T. Hargreaves

ABBREVIATED PROPER NAMES
in diary text of Volumes I and II

A.	Anne Mackenzie Gladstone, *sister*; *or* Joseph Anstice
A., Ld	Lord Aberdeen
Abn, Ld	the same
A.H.H.	A. H. Hallam
A.K.	A. Kinnaird
A.M.	Anne Mackenzie Gladstone, *sister*
A.M.G.	the same
Anne	the same
B., Ly	Lady Braybrooke
B.B.	Bartholomew Bouverie, *pseudonym*
B.H.	Archdeacon Harrison
Bob	Robertson Gladstone, *brother*
C.	Catherine Gladstone, *née* Glynne, *wife*
C., Uncle	Colin Mackenzie *or* Colin Robertson
C.G.	Catherine Gladstone, *née* Glynne, *wife*; *or* Carlton Gardens
Cg.	Canning
C.O.	Colonial Office
Colin, Cousin	C. C. F. Robertson
Colin, Uncle	Colin Mackenzie *or* Colin Robertson
D., Aunt	wife of next
D., Uncle	David Gladstone *or* Divie Robertson
D.G.	David Gladstone *or* deo gratia
D. of N.	duke of Newcastle, *patron*
D. of W.	duke of Wellington
D.R.	Divie Robertson, *uncle*
E., Aunt	Elizabeth Robertson
E.K., Sir	Sir E. Kerrison
F.	Fettercairn
Fa.	father
Far.	father

F.E., Ld *or* Ly	Lord *or* Lady F. Egerton
F.H.D.	Sir F. H. Doyle
G., Lady	Lady Glynne, *mother-in-law*
G., Mr	(Sir) John Gladstone, *father*
G., Mrs	Anne Gladstone, *mother*
G.A.S.	(Bishop) G. A. Selwyn
George	Lord Lyttelton
G.L. Comm.	Glasgow Lotteries Committee
H.	A. H. Hallam *or* (Bishop) W. K. Hamilton *or* Helen Jane Gladstone (*sister*)
H., Mr.	Henry Hallam
Helen	Helen Jane Gladstone, *sister*
HG	the same
H.G.	Henry Glynne, *brother-in-law*
H.J.G.	Helen Jane Gladstone, *sister*
Hn	Hawarden Castle
H.T.	(Sir) Henry Taylor
J.	John Neilson Gladstone, *brother*
J., Aunt	Johanna Robertson
J.M., Lord	Lord John Manners
J.M.G.	James Milnes Gaskell *or* John Murray Gladstone (*cousin*)
J.M.G.(R.)	J. M. G. Robertson, *cousin*
J.N.G.	John Neilson Gladstone, *brother*
J.R.	J. M. G. Robertson (*cousin*) *or* Lord John Russell
K.	A. Kinnaird
L.	Lincoln
L, Ld *or* Ly	Lord *or* Lady Lincoln *or* Lyttelton
Ln	Lincoln *or* London *or* Lyttelton
Lpool	Liverpool
L.S.	*Liverpool Standard*
M.	Archdeacon Manning
M., Aunt	Mary Robertson
M., Uncle	Murray Gladstones
Mamma	Catherine Gladstone, *wife*
Mary	Lady Lyttelton, *née* Mary Glynne, *sister-in-law*
Mary, Aunt	Mary Robertson
Mary Ellen	Mrs. Robertson Gladstone, *née* M. E. Jones, *sister-in-law*
M.E.	the same
M.E.G.	the same
M.E.J.	the same

M.G., Mrs	Mrs. Milnes Gaskell
Mo.	Anne Gladstone, *mother*
Murray, John	John Murray Gladstone, *cousin*
Murray, Uncle	Murray Gladstones
N., D. of	duke of Newcastle, *patron*
Nina	Helen Jane Gladstone, *sister*
Nk	Newark
O. and C.	Oxford and Cambridge Club
O.B.C.	O. B. Cole
O.F.	Oak Farm
Oky	(Provost) Richard Okes
P.	Sir R. Peel
P., Ly	Lady Peel
P., Sir R.	Sir R. Peel
R.	Robertson Gladstone, *brother*
R.G.	the same
R.I., Sir	Sir R. H. Inglis
Rn (G.)	Robertson Gladstone, *brother*
Robert, Uncle	Robert Gladstone
Robn	Robertson Gladstone, *brother*
R.P., Sir	Sir R. Peel
S.	A. P. Saunders *or* (Bishop) G. A. Selwyn *or* Sir Stephen Glynne (*brother-in-law*)
S.G.	the last-named
S.H.	Sidney Herbert
S.R.G.	Sir Stephen Glynne, *brother-in-law*
T.	(Sir) Thomas Gladstone, *brother*
T., Mr.	W. E. Tallents *or* (Bishop) J. M. Turner
T.G.	(Sir) Thomas Gladstone, *brother*
Thomas, Aunt	wife of next
Thomas, Uncle	Thomas Gladstones
Tom	(Sir) Thomas Gladstone, *brother*
T.S.G.	T. S. Godfrey
W., D. of	duke of Wellington
Walter	Sir W. R. Farquhar *or* (Bishop) W. K. Hamilton
W.I.	West Indies
W.K.H.	(Bishop) W. K. Hamilton
W.W., Sir	Sir Watkin Williams Wynn
Xt	Christ

ABBREVIATED BOOK TITLES, &c

Add MS(S)	Additional Manuscript(s), British Muesum
After Thirty Years	Herbert, Viscount Gladstone, *After Thirty Years* (1928)
Argyll	Eighth duke of Argyll, *Autobiography and Memoirs*, 2v. (1906)
Arnstein	W. L. Arnstein, *The Bradlaugh Case* (1964)
Balfour	Lady Frances Balfour, *Life of Earl of Aberdeen*, 2v. [1923]
Bassett	A. Tilney Bassett, ed., *Gladstone to his Wife* (1936)
Bassett, *Speeches*	A. Tilney Bassett, ed., *Gladstone's Speeches: Descriptive Index and Bibliography* (1916)
Battiscombe	Georgina Battiscombe, *Mrs Gladstone* (1956)
Bell	H. C. F. Bell, *Palmerston* (1936)
BFSP	*British and Foreign State Papers*
Blake	R. N. W. Blake, *Disraeli* (1966)
Bright	*Diaries of John Bright* (1930)
Buckle	W. F. Monypenny and G. E. Buckle, *Life of Benjamin Disraeli*, new ed., 2v. (1929)
Cecil	Lady Gwendolen Cecil, *Life of Robert Marquis of Salisbury*, 4v. (1921–32)
Chamberlain	C. H. D. Howard, ed., Joseph Chamberlain, *A Political Memoir* (1953)
DLFC	J. Bailey, ed., *Diary of Lady Frederick Cavendish*, 2v. (1927)
DNB	*Dictionary of National Biography*, 71v. (1885–1957)
EHR	*English Historical Review* (from 1886)
Esher	M. V. Brett, ed., *Journals and Letters of Reginald Viscount Esher*, i. (1934)
Fitzmaurice	Lord E. Fitzmaurice, *Life of Earl Granville*, 2v. (1905)
4sH	*Parliamentary Debates*, fourth series (1892–1908)
Gardiner	A. G. Gardiner, *Life of Sir William Harcourt*, 2v. (1923)
Garvin	J. L. Garvin and J. Amery, *Life of Joseph Chamberlain*, 4v. (1932–51)

Gleanings	W. E. Gladstone, *Gleanings of Past Years*, 7v. (1879)
Greville	Lytton Strachey and R. Fulford, eds., *The Greville Memoirs*, 8v. (1938)
Guedalla, *P*	P. Guedalla, ed., *Gladstone and Palmerston* (1928)
Guedalla, *Q*	P. Guedalla, ed., *The Queen and Mr. Gladstone,* 2v. (1933)
Gwynn and Tuckwell	S. Gwynn and Gertrude M. Tuckwell, *Life of Sir Charles Dilke,* 2v. (1917)
H	*Hansard's Parliamentary Debates,* third series (1830–91)
Hamilton	E. W. Hamilton, *Mr. Gladstone* (1898)
Hammond	J. L. Hammond, *Gladstone and the Irish Nation* (1964)
Hanham	H. J. Hanham, *Elections and Party Management* (1959)
Holland	B. Holland, *Life of Duke of Devonshire,* 2v. (1911)
Hutton and Cohen	A. W. Hutton and H. J. Cohen, eds., *Speeches and Public Addresses of Gladstone,* 2v. (1892–3)
James	R. Rhodes James, *Rosebery* (1963)
Kilbracken	*Reminiscences of Lord Kilbracken* (1931)
Kimberley	Ethel Drus, ed., earl of Kimberley, *A Journal of Events during the Gladstone Ministry 1868–1874* (Camden Miscellany, xxi. 1958)
Lathbury	D. C. Lathbury, *Correspondence on Church and Religion of W. E. Gladstone,* 2v. (1910)
Longford	Elizabeth Longford, *Victoria R.I.* (1964)
LQV	A. C. Benson, Viscount Esher, and G. E. Buckle, *Letters of Queen Victoria,* 9v. (1907–32), in three series each of 3v.: 1s., 1837–61; 2s., 1862–85; 3s., 1886–1901.
Lucy, *D*	H. W. Lucy, *A Diary of Two Parliaments: The Disraelian Parliament 1874–80* (1885)
Lucy, *G*	H. W. Lucy, *A Diary of Two Parliaments: The Gladstone Parliament 1880–1885* (1886)
Lucy, *S*	H. W. Lucy, *A Diary of the Salisbury Parliament 1886–1892* (1896)
Lucy, *HR*	H. W. Lucy, *A Diary of the Home Rule Parliament 1892–1895* (1896)
Magnus	Sir Philip Magnus, *Gladstone* (1954)
Mallet	Sir Charles Mallet, *Herbert Gladstone* (1932)
Martin	(Sir) Theodore Martin, *Life of the Prince Consort,* 5v. (1875–80)

Masterman	C. F. G. Masterman, ed. and abridged J. Morley, *Life of Gladstone* (1927)
Maxwell	Sir Herbert Maxwell, *Life and Letters of Earl of Clarendon*, 2v. (1913)
Medlicott	W. N. Medlicott, *Bismarck, Gladstone and the Concert of Europe* (1956)
Migne, *PG*	J.-P. Migne, *Patrologiae Cursus Completus, series Graeca*, 161v. (1857–66)
Migne, *PL*	J.-P. Migne, *Patrologiae Cursus Completus, series Latina*, 221v. (1844–64)
Mirror	J. H. Barrow, ed., *Mirror of Parliament* (1828–42)
Morley	J. Morley, *Life of William Ewart Gladstone*, 3v. (1903)
Morley, *Cobden*	J. Morley, *Life of Richard Cobden*, new ed. (1883)
NSH	T. C. Hansard, ed., *Parliamentary Debates*, new series (1820–30).
O'Brien	C. C. O'Brien, *Parnell and his Party* (1957)
Ornsby	R. Ornsby, *Memoirs of J. R. Hope-Scott*, 2v. (1884)
Parker	C. S. Parker, *Sir Robert Peel*, 3v. (1899)
Ponsonby	A. Ponsonby, *Henry Ponsonby* (1943)
PP	*Parliamentary Papers*
PRO	Public Record Office
Purcell	E. S. Purcell, *Life of Cardinal Manning*, 2v. (1896)
Ramm, I	Agatha Ramm, *Political Correspondence of Mr. Gladstone and Lord Granville 1868–1876*, 2v. (1952)
Ramm, II	Agatha Ramm, *Political Correspondence of Mr. Gladstone and Lord Granville 1876–1886*, 2v. (1962)
Reid, *F*	(Sir) T. Wemyss Reid, *Life of W. E. Forster*, 2v. (1888)
Reid, *G*	Sir T. Wemyss Reid, ed., *Life of W. E. Gladstone* (1899)
Robbins	A. F. Robbins, *Early Public Life of Gladstone* (1894)
Selborne, I	earl of Selborne, *Memorials Family and Personal*, 2v. (1896)
Selborne, II	earl of Selborne, *Memorials Personal and Political*, 2v. (1898)
Seton-Watson	R. W. Seton-Watson, *Disraeli, Gladstone and the Eastern Question* (1935)
Shannon	R. T. Shannon, *Gladstone and the Bulgarian Agitation 1876* (1963)
Stanmore	Lord Stanmore, *Sidney Herbert*, 2v. (1906)
Stansky	P. Stansky, *Ambitions and Strategies* (1964)
Stephen	(Sir) L. Stephen, *Life of Henry Fawcett* (1885)

Thomas	I. Thomas, [*Henry*] *Gladstone of Hawarden* (1936)
VCH	*Victoria History of the Counties of England*
Vidler	A. R. Vidler, *The Orb and the Cross* (1945)
Walpole	S. Walpole, *Life of Lord John Russell*, 2v. (1889)
West, *PD*	H. G. Hutchinson, ed., *Private Diaries of Sir Algernon West* (1922)
West, *R*	Sir Algernon West, *Recollections* (1900)
Wolf	L. Wolf, *Life of Marquis of Ripon*, 2v. (1921)

OTHER ABBREVIATIONS [1]

ab.	about	deb.	debate
abp.	archbishop	div.	division
abt.	about		
acct.	account	eccl.	ecclesiastical
aft(n).	afternoon	ed.	edited *or* edition *or* editor
agst.	against		*or* educational
agt.	against	evg.	evening
amdt.	amendment		
appt.	appointment	f.	father *or* folio
apptd.	appointed	fa.	father
		ff.	folios *or* following
b.	book *or* born *or* brother	1⁰	first reading
bart.	baronet		
B.B.	black book	gd.	granddaughter
bkfst.	breakfast	gf.	grandfather
Bl.B.	black book	Gk.	Greek
B. of T.	board of trade	gm.	grandmother
bp.	bishop	govt.	government
br.	brother	gs.	grandson
B.S.	Bedford *or* Berkeley Square	H.C.	holy communion
		H. of C.	house of commons
ca.	*circa*	H. of L.	house of lords
cd.	could	Ho.	house of commons
Ch.	church	H.S.	holy scripture
co.	county		
commee.	committee	ibid.	*ibidem*, in the same place
commn.	commission	Int. Calc.	integral calculus
cons.	conservation		
conv.	conversation	k.	killed
cp.	compare		
cr.	created	l.	letter
ctd.	continued	Ld.	lord
cttee.	committee	lect.	lecture
		lib.	liberal
d.	died	Ly.	lady
da.	daughter		
D.Calc.	differential calculus	m.	married *or* mother
		mg.	morning

¹ These are given as they appear in footnotes. The diarist seldom put stops after them. See also p. xxxvii below.

2

nt.	night	tel.	telegram
n.y.n.	not yet numbered	3º	third reading
		tr.	translated *or* translation
p., pp.	page(s)		
pt.	part	Univ.	university
rec(d).	receive(d)		
ref(s).	reference(s)	v.	verso *or* very *or* volume
Rev(d).	reverend	vol.	volume
		vss.	verses
2º	second reading	vy.	very
s.	son *or* series *or* sister		
sact.	sacrament	w.	wife
sd.	should	wd.	would
soc.	society	wh.	which
sp.	speech		
succ.	succeeded	Xtn.	Christian

INTRODUCTION

Morley rightly remarked, in his official *Life of Gladstone*, that his subject was not equipped with 'much or any of the rare talent of the born diarist'.[1] These diaries reveal much about Gladstone's character, and illustrate the religious, political, and social life of his day; yet nobody will find in them either word-pictures of events, or analyses of personality, fit to be compared with Pepys's or with Greville's. Gladstone's diaries were not written with a literary aim. 'You may take', he once said to Balfour, 'the three proverbial courses about a journal: you may keep none, you may keep a complete and "full-blooded" one, or you may keep a mere skeleton like mine with nothing but bare entries of time and place.'[2] The skeleton was not entirely bare of flesh; but primarily it was what Gladstone, a meticulous keeper of accounts, once called 'an account-book of the all-precious gift of Time'.[3]

His own 'fierce regard for the sanctity of time' formed one of his best-known characteristics.[4] From childhood, his elder sister Anne had brought him up to believe that waste of it was sinful, and that at the Last Day he would be called to a reckoning of how he had spent every minute accorded him. Making an entry in this pocket reminder-book of his own deficiencies had taken on, by the end of his teens, the character of a mild penitential exercise: a daily occasion for self-criticism, and for reflexion on how he was expending his 'all-precious gift'. 'Relief from the small grind of the Daily Journal' was how in the end he described giving it up.[5] He found it helpful, in his frequent moods of self-doubt, to have beside him these notes of what he had done and left undone; notes that Herbert Gladstone described as 'a life story of intense introspection in which judgment was almost invariably given against himself'.[6] Ludicrous though it may seem to admirers of Beerbohm's caricatures in the Junior Carlton, entitled 'Mr Gladstone goes to Heaven',[7] this diary has elements in it of an *aide-mémoire* for a future conversation with St. Peter.

[1] Morley, i. 149.   [2] A. J. Balfour, *Chapters of Autobiography* (1930), 79.
[3] Morley, i. 205; recommending his son Herbert to 'keep a short journal of principal employments in each day: most valuable'.
[4] Ibid., i. 186; and see Battiscombe, 36, and Kilbracken, 91.
[5] 17 Dec. 94. All dates below abbreviated in this style—19 Apr. 27, 28 June 40, 8 Oct. 65, etc.—refer to the corresponding entry in the diaries.
[6] Masterman, xxvii.   [7] *Max's Nineties* (1958), plates 35–45.

Gladstone had neither the time nor the inclination to write, like Mrs. Arbuthnot, disquisitions at length about current politics or diplomacy; nor had he any of Greville's talent for gossip. Like Milner, he lived for years at the centre of great events; unlike him, he was too busy making history to record it as it was made. More positively, he wrote for his own eye, and for God's, not for any other reader in his own time or since.

The stylistic evidence on this point is decisive. Readers will see for themselves that Gladstone's inmost journal—the main bulk of what follows—could not have been written with any body of readers in his mind. Its whole tone is that of a purely private document: so private, so intimate, that its privacy alone provides reason enough for the delays that have attended its publication. There is no striving for effect; there is earnest, continual striving after truth. Here he set down what can hardly be found elsewhere: what he thought about himself.

His evidence about himself may be held dubious by those who follow the fashion of accusing him of self-deception; most of them people who have not read Herbert Gladstone's biting comments on that charge.[1] Anyone who still wishes to level it at the father, after reading the son and weighing the evidential value of the pages below, should consider with some care just what the father is supposed to have deceived himself about. Current cant about 'Victorian hypocrisy' needs reconsideration in the light of these painfully intimate self-revelations. Though many passages in the diaries have an unctuous tone that jars, sometimes horribly, on the moderate agnostic or even on the believing Christian today, their whole tone is that of a man making a powerful effort to be honest with himself. In spite of all that has been written, from Demosthenes to MacNeile,[2] onward, about our congenital urge to deceive ourselves, we can acknowledge the sincerity of Gladstone's inward struggle to arrive at the truth.

Most volumes of his diary he sedulously marked 'private'; the only sign that he did not wish it to remain private for good is simply that he did not destroy it. Once or twice in his life he did destroy documents in some quantity: as a schoolboy he often recorded himself as tidying papers—which indeed was a lifetime preoccupation—and rarely as destroying them;[3] and as an old man he burned (at her request) a large pile of letters from a reformed courtesan, including her long blank verse autobiography—'they would lead to misapprehension', he noted at the time.[4] Yet, as a devout Peelite, he did not hold with suppressing the written word: 'Never destroy a letter', Peel said once to Cardwell, 'No public man who respects himself should ever destroy

---

[1] *After Thirty Years*, 70–77.   [2] *Olynthiac* iii, 7, *ad fin.*; *Autumn Journal* (1939), 18.
[3] e.g. 16 Sept. 25, 20 Jan. 27.   [4] 25 Feb. 93.

a letter.'[1] And he needed the diary by him in old age for that process of recollection and self-analysis on which his heart had long been set. 'I deeply desired an interval between parliament and the grave', he wrote, when at last he had secured it,[2] though referring the desire back to his resignation from the liberal leadership over twenty years before. He glanced at his journal no doubt when, at Lord Acton's suggestion,[3] he began a political autobiography.[4] Had he ever written, as he once meant to do, 'a history of the inner life, which I think has with me been extraordinarily dubious, vacillating, and (above all) complex',[5] he would certainly have used the diary, which records many of his doubts, his vacillations, and his surface complexities. But this religious autobiography remained unpenned, as his last illness closed in on him, and his attention moved away from points of wordly wisdom and posthumous reputation into the shadow of approaching death. He could feel, as he looked back on the diary record which he knew had been honestly made, that it was not so disgraceful as to tempt him to put it out of history's way. He could have said, like Kierkegaard, 'Some day not only my writings but especially my life will be studied and studied';[6] and was too fair-minded, and too historically-minded, to want to destroy good evidence for what he had been. As Morley once said, 'what interests the world in Mr. Gladstone is even more what he was, than what he did';[7] and his diaries provide plenty of fresh material on this interesting point.

Two different kinds of diary are intermingled below. The principal one is his daily journal, or jotting-book of how he passed his time; it runs from July 1825, when he was an Eton boy, down to December 1896. Probably the earliest pages of it have vanished; he told Balfour that he had begun when he was fourteen—that is, some time in 1824.[8] The surviving first page is torn, and reads as if it comes in the middle of a spell of rough journalizing, not as the beginning of anything: at that age, one does not begin a day-book without remarking on the fact.

For nearly all of that span of over seventy years, the journal was entered up nightly unless Gladstone was ill. There were four main intermissions: when he was travelling abroad in 1832, 1838–9, and 1850–1, and after his operation for cataract in May 1894. Even during these pauses, he made occasional entries; writing the last one of all on his eighty-seventh birthday, within eighteen months of his death. And

---

[1] Lord Rosebery, *Miscellanies* (1921), i. 187.
[2] In 1897; Morley, ii. 498.   [3] See 8 July 92.
[4] Add MSS 44790–1, unfinished; extensively pillaged by Morley, and now in course of publication by the Historical Manuscripts Commission.
[5] Add MS 44790, f. 19; version in Morley, i. 13.
[6] W. Lowrie, *Kierkegaard* (1938), 28.   [7] Morley, i. 2.
[8] Balfour, *Chapters of Autobiography*, 79. The heading on the diary's first page was added later.

during his three long continental tours, he kept up daily entries in the second kind of diary: traveller's notebooks, more discursively written and much less intimate in tone than his main, private journal. As a child he formed the habit of making a brief record of any tour;[1] as a young adult, he may have started these notebooks as an attempt to provide what he described to Balfour as a 'full-blooded' journal. They show that keeping one was indeed not a task for which he was noticeably well equipped. They were written, moreover, unlike the more private ones, with the prospect that they might perhaps be shown round his family and friends, or even be published for the benefit of later travellers over the same ground.[2] On all his journeys, he kept the current private volume in his pocket, and added to it now and again. The travel diaries have been for years in the British Museum;[3] the main journal, as will be shown, has come to rest at Lambeth.[4]

The diaries' format deserves mention. The main journal is contained in forty-one little volumes, bound as forty; for the first surviving one of all, covering the second half of 1825, was written in a minute printed pocket almanac, on pages measuring only three inches by four. It got torn from its binding in the diarist's lifetime, and was kept inside the cover of the following volume, a crown octavo (seven inches by five) school jotting-book. Volumes iii and iv were also written in soft-covered jotting-books, a little smaller; and volumes v to ix in hard-covered pocket-books a little smaller still (the covers of volumes vii and viii had disappeared by the turn of the century). With his volume x Gladstone at last, in 1838, found a shape that satisfied him, and all the rest of the diary was written on good quality bluish paper in pott octavo pocket-books, measuring six inches by four, bound in cheap black or dark maroon leather; most of them with 130 pages, some with 160 or 180.[5]

All the forty-one volumes have recently been rebound, as forty, at Lambeth Palace Library, in such a way that the inscriptions on the old bindings can still be seen. They will be made available to scholars as they are published: inquiries about access should be sent to the librarian there, not to the editor.[6]

The Lambeth diaries look cramped and crabbed—even more so than the ones in Bloomsbury—and the writing is not always easy to read: even Herbert Gladstone, who knew his father's hand as well as anyone, complained of eyestrain when he settled down to read the diary

[1] See 20 July 25, 31 Aug. 26.
[2] e.g. 25 Sept., 26 Oct. 38.
[3] Add MS 44818. A few travel notes, also printed, for a Welsh tour in 1826, are in the museum as well, in Add MS 44718.
[4] Lambeth MSS 1416–55.
[5] The travel diaries in Add MS 44818 B–E are of the same size as these.
[6] It may be convenient to set out the exact dates covered by each of the Lambeth

through.[1] Nearly all the entries are in black ink, which has faded little; but the handwriting is normally Gladstone's most minute. His passion for economizing paper forbade him to leave any margins; and from September 1847 he wrote in double column. In Masterman's compression of Morley's three volumes into a popular edition in one, several pages of the diary have long been available in facsimile. They give a good idea of the impact of the original on the eye, though they give only a partial idea of the content: carefully though Herbert Gladstone chose the passages for reproduction, discretion compelled one or two visible deletions.[2]

In the diarist's lifetime, no particular precautions were taken to keep the manuscript secret, beyond a little elementary coding in its text. As a boy of sixteen, he sometimes put passages into Greek script, now and then translating into French or Latin first. These were either schoolboy scribblings,[3] or else the few sentences he might not want his mother or his sisters to read accidentally.[4] The current volume lived in his pocket; in an age when gentlemen's pockets were often picked,[5] this

volumes:

Lambeth MS	Gladstone vol. no.	dates	Lambeth MS	Gladstone vol. no.	dates
1416	i	16 July 25–31 Dec. 25	1435	xxi	1 Mar. 59–20 Sept. 60
1416	ii	1 Jan. 26–21 Oct. 27	1436	xxii	21 Sept. 60–30 Apr. 62
1417	iii	22 Oct. 27–22 Oct. 28	1437	xxiii	1 May 62–31 Dec. 63
1418	iv	23 Oct. 28–23 Apr. 30	1438	xxiv	1 Jan. 64–12 Aug. 65
1419	v	24 Apr. 30–10 Sept. 31	1439	xxv	13 Aug. 65–30 Apr. 67
1420	vi	11 Sept. 31–20 July 33	1440	xxvi	1 May 67–31 Dec. 68
1421	vii	21 July 33–24 Mar. 34	1441	xxvii	1 Jan. 69–20 Sept. 70
1422	viii	25 Mar. 34–30 Sept. 35	1442	xxviii	21 Sept. 70–15 June 72
1423	ix	1 Oct. 35–28 Feb. 38	1443	xxix	16 June 72–12 Feb. 74
1424	x	1 Mar. 38–30 Sept. 39	1444	xxx	13 Feb. 74–20 July 75
1425	xi	1 Oct. 39–30 Sept. 41	1445	xxxi	21 July 75–15 Mar. 77
1426	xii	1 Oct. 41—29 Feb. 44	1446	xxxii	16 Mar. 77–31 Dec. 78
1427	xiii	1 Mar. 44–30 June 46	1447	xxxiii	1 Jan. 79–23 July 80
1428	xiv	1 July 46–22 Apr. 48	1448	xxxiv	24 July 80–9 Apr. 82
1429	xv	23 Apr. 48–31 May 50	1449	xxxv	10 Apr. 82–31 Dec. 83
1430	xvi	1 June 50–29 Feb. 52	1450	xxxvi	1 Jan. 84–7 Sept. 85
1431	xvii	1 Mar. 52–31 Aug. 53	1451	xxxvii	8 Sept. 85–11 June 87
1432	xviii	1 Sept. 53–24 Feb. 55	1452	xxxviii	12 June 87–6 May 89
1433	xix	25 Feb. 55–31 Dec. 56	1453	xxxix	7 May 89–28 Feb. 91
1434	xx	1 Jan. 57–28 Feb. 59	1454	xl	1 Mar. 91–30 June 93
			1455	xli	1 July 93–29 Dec. 96

[1] Herbert to Henry Gladstone, 17 August 1917; Lambeth MS, n.y.n.

[2] For an example, cp. Masterman, 176, with 28 Feb. 72. Some light on the objects of Masterman's abridgement of Morley is thrown by letters to him from Herbert (Viscount) Gladstone and Henry (later Lord) Gladstone, on 9 and 12 April 1926 (copies in Lambeth MS, n.y.n.).

[3] e.g. 25 May, 29 June, 1 July 26.

[4] e.g. 16 Mar., 15 July, 8, 11, 23 Aug. 26.

[5] Cp. 3–8 Oct. 31, 6 May 32, 12 Dec. 37n.

perhaps explains why he frequently put entries on sensitive points into Italian.[1] Most of his immediate family, and a few of his servants, could read Italian easily; the precaution could therefore not have been aimed at them, whom in any case he trusted. So natural and complete, in fact, was his trust in his own household, that back volumes of his diary were kept, in the early 1880's at least, in an unlocked oaken box on his sitting-room floor at Hawarden.[2] Later they were no doubt moved into the Octagon,[3] the fireproof annexe to his study where he kept, with hundreds of thousands of other papers, all the letters people sent him marked *please burn*.

He left no instructions about the diaries' disposal.[4] Presumably he was ready, like any other honest political leader in a literate and news-hungry society, to have posterity rummage among his papers for what could be found there. Yet he was a scrupulous man, who hated the very idea of causing unnecessary pain by ill-timed revelations. Near his own day, to publish so intimate a document as his private journal might perhaps have pained many people, his own children above all; and would hardly have been delicate towards his own memory. But now he has been seventy years in his grave; the last of his children died in 1935; a score of his grandsons' grandchildren are growing up. What he was and what he did belong to history; and delicacy need no longer keep his diaries hidden.

Their own history, during these seventy years, bears recording. The travel diaries, seldom much consulted, found their place without difficulty in the 750 volumes of Gladstone papers presented by his family to the British Museum.[5] The private journal did not: for the family could see at a glance how intimate it was; felt themselves bound not to destroy it, because Father had kept it; but certainly did not wish it to become available embarrassingly soon. They might have inclined to keep it locked away in the Octagon, had it not been that Gladstone had never made a secret to his intimate friends of the journal's existence; one of these intimate friends, John Morley, be-came his authorized biographer and asked to see it.

---

[1] e.g. 24 Aug. to 4 Sep. 35, on his feelings for Caroline Farquhar, or 20 Jan. 36 on politics, or 4 Nov. 52 on an important and difficult rescue case.
  As the English-reading educated public's command of languages is not the same now as it was a century ago—the Cyrillic script is becoming better known, for instance, than the Greek—all these lightly encoded passages have been transliterated into the Roman character in the text, or translated in footnotes, or both, as required.

[2] He telegraphed from London to get his son Stephen to look out a particular volume and post it to him: see 23 Mar. 81 and Add MS 48607, bundle 2.

[3] Cp. Morley, ii. 526ff.

[4] None are mentioned in his sons' correspondence about what should be done with them (Lambeth MSS, n.y.n.).

[5] Add MSS 44086–835; cp. Hammond, xxix–xxx. A separate volume of the British Museum's Add MSS catalogue, *The Gladstone Papers* (1953), is devoted to them: an unique distinction.

He saw it; skimmed through it; and, for reasons of overwhelming weight in their day, suppressed most of what he found.

What Morley did with the diary—both what he put in his book, and what he left out—played a part in forming the book's character; from which in turn the modern received view of Gladstone derives. So an excursus on Morley's concern with the journal is necessary, before the rest of the document's history is set down.

After Gladstone's death in May 1898, his family at first proposed to commission two books about him: a sketch of 'character principles & methods', perhaps by Morley, and a 'larger & later historical work' by Bryce, who struck Herbert Gladstone as 'the competent & sympathetic & at the same time judicial historian' who would be needed.[1] Many years later Herbert was again in correspondence with Bryce, viewing a new life of his father; nothing came of either proposal.[2] More immediately, Rosebery and Acton were both consulted; and with their agreement, a definite offer was made to Arthur Godley, later Lord Kilbracken. Godley, who had known Gladstone intimately in the eighties, was one of the ablest civil servants of the day. He replied that he was not in the least anxious to write a life himself, but would readily cooperate with any suitable author; adding, with some asperity, that 'To choose J. Morley to write Mr. G.'s Life is, in my opinion, very much like choosing a man who has been blind from his birth, but is a clever writer, to do the biography of Millais or Burne Jones.'[3]

But Morley was keen to secure this great literary prize, and pressed his claim. He was clearly a livelier author, and one much closer to the subject, than Sir Spencer Walpole, the leading historian at work on the period, who was among those whose claims were also weighed. He seemed, moreover, to have the support of Rosebery, who was later said to have believed him 'the best possible' choice; though at the time Rosebery said to Godley that the thought of Morley as Gladstone's biographer 'gives me a cold shiver'.[4] In any case, it became clear that Morley was indispensable. He persuaded the family that the canvas of a character sketch would not be broad enough for the brush of a former minister;[5] Hamilton's vivid monograph turned out, in any case, to provide what had been envisaged.[6] Little more than three months after his father's death, Herbert Gladstone, in a tactful letter, formally proposed that Morley should undertake a complete biography.

[1] Herbert Gladstone to E. W. Hamilton, 30 June 1898, private; Add MS 48609, bundle 9.
[2] Bryce to Gladstone, 17 July 1914; Lambeth MS, n.y.n.
[3] Godley to Hamilton, 22 August 1898, confidential; Add MS 48616, bundle 8. For some of his reasons for refusal, see Kilbracken, 225–6.
[4] Mallet, 165; Kilbracken, 225.
[5] *After Thirty Years*, 24.
[6] Published late in November 1898.

The proposal was accepted.[1] Morley and the family agreed on one fatal reservation: he was not expected to enter fully into Gladstone's religious life. No other restrictions were placed on him, but neither side thought it desirable that he should attempt any detailed analysis of an aspect of his subject that must necessarily be alien to so dogmatic an atheist as himself.[2] So the choice of Morley imposed a severe handicap on the biography for a start.

Yet in many ways the choice was excellent. Morley's intellect was generally thought one of the keenest of his time, though his career at Oxford was academically undistinguished.[3] He was an accomplished writer, exceptionally widely read. He had not entered parliament till his middle forties,[4] but strode forward at once to prominence, sat in the cabinets of 1886 and 1892–5, and was a competitor for the liberal party leadership at the time of Gladstone's death. (This, as we shall see, handicapped him further as Gladstone's biographer.) Moreover, though he was a radical and an atheist, who lived for years with another man's wife, a decided friendship had sprung up between him and Gladstone. 'I cannot help liking Mr. J. Morley', Gladstone confessed to his diary,[5] and the attraction was mutual; though its unspoken condition had to be that, as Morley reported, 'we never once exchanged a word upon theology or religious creed'.[6] It was indeed powerful enough to draw Morley out of the orbit of Joseph Chamberlain, whose intimate he had been,[7] into that of his prime minister. From the disruption of 1886 to the end, Morley was one of Gladstone's two or three closest friends outside the family circle; indeed, if we may trust a rather lush account of the simple domestic arrangements at Hawarden, a large portrait of him had a place of honour on Gladstone's dressing-table.[8] (This was not necessarily the compliment it was taken to be: Gladstone kept a bust of Disraeli, beside one of Canning, in front of the desk where he did his political work in the 'Temple of Peace'.[9]) He was the trusted lieutenant in the forlorn Irish hope of 1893, figured in the diary a few months

[1] Morley to Hamilton, 7 September 1898, very private; Add MS 48619, bundle 3.

[2] Memorandum by Herbert Gladstone, 3 September and 21 October 1925; Lambeth MS, n.y.n.

[3] Cp. F. W. Hirst, *Early Life and Letters of John Morley* (1927), i. 17.

[4] For the curious circumstances of his first successful election, see *Fortnightly Review*, mlii. 117 (August 1954).

[5] 10 Mar. 77, when they met among 'a notable party & much interesting conversation' at Sir John Lubbock's.

[6] Morley, iii. 471.

[7] Morley and Chamberlain used to tour the continent together; 'for thirteen years we lived the life of brothers', said Morley (*Recollections* (1917), i. 160, 163). Chamberlain concurred: 'I have known him intimately for nine years, we have talked together in private of our dearest hopes and dreams & desires' (quoted from a diary of 7 February 1887 in M. Hurst, *Joseph Chamberlain and Liberal Reunion* (1967), 381).

[8] Hulda Friedrichs, *In the evening of his days* (1896), 150.   [9] *Vidi.*

earlier as 'on the whole . . . about the best stay I have',[1] managed to retain Gladstone's amity in the crisis of 1894, and was one of the last people beyond the household to see him on his deathbed.[2] In fact, as a man of letters, a man of the world, and a man eminent in politics, he could understand more sides of his exceptionally many-sided subject than any other available biographer.

The work that resulted, just 2,000 pages long, was a triumphant success: almost 100,000 copies of the three stout volumes that appeared in 1903 were sold before they went out of print in 1942.[3] The book was bought for the great houses, for the manifest sincerity of its picture of recent controversial history. It was more earnestly read in scores of thousands of poor men's homes,[4] where it was shelved beside the *Pilgrim's Progress* and Foxe's *Martyrs* and hardly less well thumbed than they. For in this book, men thought, was treasured up 'the People's William', that astounding political preacher who could show them 'a World in a Grain of Sand . . . and Eternity in an hour'. The book was an undoubted literary achievement, for it presented a readily recognizable portrait in a powerful and authoritative style. It took its place at once among the principal source-books for the English nineteenth century, and has been quoted ever since as a definitive guide to the inquirer about political or constitutional history.

Unfortunately its reliability in detail does not match its impressive tone. At times its slanting recalls Disraeli's bitter comment on political writers of an earlier day:

> If the history of England be ever written by one who has the knowledge and the courage, and both qualities are equally requisite for the undertaking, the world would be more astonished than when reading the Roman annals by Niebuhr. Generally speaking, all the great events have been distorted, most of the important causes concealed, some of the principal characters never appear, and all who figure are so misunderstood and misrepresented, that the result is a complete mystification.[5]

To start with, Morley's method of composition can only be described as slap-dash. He explained in his preface that while he was preparing the book he looked through something like a quarter of a million documents;[6] sheer quantity overwhelmed him, and he took no trouble, when he quoted any of them, to quote correctly. Nor did Hirst, who

[1] 6 Nov. 92, misdated in Morley, iii. 499.
[2] Morley, iii. 528.
[3] Private information. According to Mallet, 165n, some 50,000 copies of other editions were also sold.
[4] Cp. Hammond, 707–9.
[5] B. Disraeli, *Sybil* (1845), i. 32–33, in Book I, ch. ii; quoted, in the context of French resistance, in *Times Literary Supplement*, 11 October 1963.
[6] Morley, i. [vii].

was his research assistant among those disconcertingly numerous
shelves and boxes in the Octagon, a place which Morley detested.[1]
The nearest approach they seem to have made to a system lay in
marking piles of papers they no longer wanted to see with the symbol
'D.W.' that bemuses researchers on so many dockets in the Museum.
It stands for 'Done With',[2] and seems to have been affixed without
any attempt at checking quotations against the original.

From this haphazard assembly of materials the diary suffered particularly badly. Morley's very first reference to it includes two slight
slips;[3] and there are transcription errors in over half the 500-odd passages he cites from some 25,000 entries. Most of these errors are trivial.
But to repeat trivial errors builds up a misleading effect; it helps to
present Gladstone as Morley envisaged him rather than as he was.
And not all the errors are slight. Only carelessness can have passed the
odd assertion that Lord Clarendon was 'An irreparable colleague'
when Gladstone clearly wrote 'incomparable',[4] and carelessness presumably accounts for many misdatings.[5] Carelessness, again, would
explain such transpositions as 'Lancaster in aft[ernoon] on the
Sac[ramen]t—good. Walk' into 'Lancaster in the afternoon on the
Sacrament. Good walk.'[6]

Slips apart, interpolations in diary passages from other sources are
quite common.[7] The omission of passages in the course of quotations,
with no hint of incompleteness to the reader, is an error so common in
old or popular biographers as to be almost venial; though it is erratic
of Morley sometimes to include, and sometimes to omit, the conven-
tional dots. It was not of course the diary alone that suffered in this
way. He usually re-spelled and re-punctuated Gladstone's thoughtfully
constructed, but to his ear often already archaic, prose; and did not
hesitate to amend the style of others to suit his own taste. Over forty-
five slips, to take an extreme example, are to be found on a single one
of his pages, derived from a manuscript in Gladstone's small but
perfectly legible hand.[8]

[1] F. W. Hirst, *In the Golden Days* (1947), 179n. See ibid. 160–92, 223–9, for some
account of their methods. Hirst was recommended for his post by H. A. L. Fisher, who
refused it (Fisher to Henry Gladstone, Christmas 1926; Lambeth MS, n.y.n.).

[2] Hirst, *Golden Days*, 166–7.

[3] In Morley, i. viii: 'The diaries . . . consist of forty little books in double columns.'
There were forty-one little books; a third of them are in single column.

[4] Morley, ii. 417; 27 June 70.

[5] e.g. 29 Dec. 30, dated a year later in Morley, i. 83; 7 and 8 Apr. 36 conflated—a
common error (i. 35); a sentence from 11 June 74 tacked on to two sentences miscopied
from 15 May 74 (ii. 499); even a compliment to Morley himself, quoted just now, placed
a month too early (6 Nov. 92 and iii. 499).

[6] 19 Jan. 34; Morley, i. 111.

[7] e.g. Morley, i. 75 and 3 to 8 Oct. 31; i. 106–7 and 25 July 33; i. 229 and 30 Mar. to
4 Apr. 40.

[8] Morley, i. 492, on the origins of the Crimean war; miscopied from Add MS 44778,
ff. 169–73.

Clearly no one should cite anything quoted in Morley's *Gladstone* without verifying it, if possible, in a more trustworthy text. Only pedants will want to labour this kind of point long; a more serious charge remains.

In several important cases, Morley's omissions from diary passages he quotes were not made from inadvertence, but from policy; and have distorted the sense of the original, conveying to the reader of the revised version an idea quite unlike that available to the reader of what Gladstone actually wrote. For political as well as religious reasons, the diary was a difficult source for Morley to use; and it is hard not to feel some sympathy with him. Not only was he reluctant, as he put it, to 'violate the sanctuary' of Gladstone's innermost reflexions; he was writing as a member of the country's alternative government, at a time of acute political controversy. His celebrated Manchester speech of 15 September 1899, with its chorus of 'it will be wrong', was delivered—a few weeks before the South African war broke out—when he was already staying at Hawarden, immersed in preparing the *Life*.[1] Party duty alone—all other influences apart—made it imperative for him to present to his readers a Gladstone who was recognizably the Grand Old Man whom all of them had known. Some generations later, people are coming to forget that at the turn of the century Gladstone was worshipped in large areas of Great Britain much as Gandhi is worshipped in India today. Into that atmosphere of reverence Morley felt he really could not inject the diarist's own opinion that he was ἁμαρτωλῶν ὅ πρώτιστος, the very first of sinners.[2] He clearly had reservations of his own: 'Mr. M. wonders', Hirst noted in his diary, 'whether Mr. G. will seem greater or less when all is unfolded.'[3] But the biographer did not feel that he could possibly make whatever revelations needed to be made himself.

What would most have shocked Gladstone's adorers, had his diaries been published within a decade or so of his death, would have been the revelation that in middle life he spent a great deal of time in the company of prostitutes and a great deal of emotional energy in contemplating their problems. Now everyone knew that in the nineteenth century great western cities abounded in women for sale; practically everyone also agreed that it was an indispensable social convention to ignore their manifest existence.[4] The modern degree of freedom of public discussion about prostitution would have been

[1] Hirst, *Golden Days*, 183–4.
[2] 15 Nov. 29, a sentiment often repeated, however little borne out by the rest of the text.
[3] 8 September 1899; *Golden Days*, 180.
[4] Cp. Rudyard Kipling, *Something of Myself* (1937), 87.

wholly inconceivable sixty-five years ago; everyone tacitly concurred that what everyone knew should be ignored.

Everyone in England, that is, save for a few hardened characters who in this respect, if in no other, were radicals, people who cut to the root of the problem and asked new, disturbing questions: a Mayhew or a Stead among commentators, a Josephine Butler or a Lucy Cavendish among gentlewomen, a Stansfeld or a Gladstone among statesmen. Considering the climate of opinion in which Morley wrote, it is hard to see what else he could have done but skate guardedly, as he did, round this patch of thin ice on his subject's reputation;[1] it was no subject for detailed treatment then.

Nor has the moment to treat it in detail quite come yet. These two first volumes contain only a few slight references to the subject, which manifest the diarist's sympathy for women who found themselves entangled in disreputable lives and wanted to leave them;[2] the next two will contain a great many more. As Sherlock Holmes said, 'It is a capital mistake to theorise before one has data';[3] we must leave to a later volume any attempt at analysis of what Gladstone was trying to do, beyond remarking on an apparent connexion between some of his efforts at rescue work and the state of his affections. It was on the very day that he finally admitted to himself that Caroline Farquhar would not have him, that he wrote to his rector, 'wishing to have *one* work of private charity on my hands';[4] shortly after his rejection by Lady Frances Douglas, he was projecting a new religious order, devoted to good works;[5] his understanding with Acland and Hope-Scott, which in the end came to little, began during his wife's first pregnancy.[6] The turning point in this sphere came after his favourite daughter's death in 1850, at the nervous crisis of his middle life.

More of all this in a later volume; one remark to conclude the subject now. Every man needs to judge himself; none needs to judge others, and few can. Nobody is qualified to scorn Gladstone for the pathetic energies he displayed in this field, a field most honest workers in it have found stony to the point of heartbreak.

Just as Morley felt that this prominent aspect of Gladstone's moral character had to be concealed, he had indispensable deletions and reservations to make on politics also. Arthur Balfour once remarked, on being reprimanded for bicycling up to Hawarden from the station while first lord of the treasury, that Gladstone 'is, and always was, in

---

[1] Cp. Morley, i. 99–100, iii. 419.
[2] e.g. 5 and 6 Aug. 28, almost his first nights in Oxford; 24 Oct. 29, 22 July 31, 25 Feb. 37, 30 May 38.
[3] A. Conan Doyle, *A Scandal in Bohemia.*   [4] 13 Feb. 36.
[5] 9 Mar. 38n.   [6] Magnus, 105.

everything except essentials, a tremendous old Tory'.[1] Had he been able to read the journal that follows, he would have found this judgement confirmed on page after page. The political passages in it—not, after all, a great proportion of the whole—are almost all instinct with the Canningite toryism in which the diarist was brought up.[2] Morley was not ten years old when Gladstone last sat in a wholly conservative cabinet, and always thought of him as the liberal leader under whom he served himself; but as late as 1870 Dod's *Parliamentary Companion* was still describing the then prime minister as 'a liberal-conservative', and the label—which Gladstone had chosen—was a fair one.

For the whole of these first two volumes the diarist was in fact a devoted, though not always a black reactionary, conservative; so cases of *suppressio veri* by Morley can more readily be given in later volumes where the reader can appreciate them in context. One such example may suffice meanwhile. Morley quotes[3] a Hawarden villager's remark on the Flintshire election result of 1841: 'I am a great woman for thinking of the Lord, but O! my dear lady, this has put it all out of my head.' He omits the diarist's comment: 'It is seldom that one can see human nature so profoundly and unselfishly moved: & here is one of the best forms of feudalism, still thank God! extremely common among us.'[4]

Let us return to the diaries' history.

It is clear from Herbert Gladstone's comments on Morley's *Life*, in his own book, that he was not altogether satisfied with it.[5] He felt that the result of barring Morley off from religious questions had been to present a lop-sided picture of his father. For Morley had presented the political battles of Gladstone's career—*quorum pars magna fui*, he could after all maintain—as if they had been Gladstone's principal concern; and this, as the family knew best of all, had been far from the case. Hard as it is to remember, this always dexterous and often supremely successful politician had never really felt at home in politics and regarded his forced career in parliament as a second best.[6] 'The pole-star is clear', he wrote once. 'Reflection shows me that a political position is mainly valuable as instrumental for the good of the Church; & under this rule every question becomes one of detail only.'[7] His main interests and his main objects remained religious rather than political; this, combined with his shattering ability, helped to make him so extraordinary a phenomenon, and made his career so fascinating a study. Morley's primarily political book on Gladstone was in

---

[1] Balfour, *Chapters of Autobiography*, 76; dated 1–2 September 1896.
[2] Cp. *H* clxxxiii. 129 (27 April 1866).
[3] i. 239.
[4] 10 July 41.
[5] e.g. *After Thirty Years*, 4, 25–27, 78.
[6] See Kilbracken, 128–9.
[7] 16 Aug. 40.

fact doomed to portray him incompletely, simply because it was primarily political.[1] Probably Herbert, and the rest of the family, came to regret the condition they had had to impose. Probably also they felt that more needed to be said, as it could best be said by one of themselves, about the simple geniality of Gladstone as a family man, and the happiness of Hawarden as a place to live. Anyone who has ever looked into Lady Frederick Cavendish's diary will appreciate at once the distinction between the wholly human and delightful Uncle William of her pages and the thirty-two-bites-to-a-mouthful Titan of Morley.

The family made two more approaches to Godley, one in 1906 and the other, after he had retired with a peerage, in 1910; he again felt himself unable to prepare the sort of book they wanted.[2] Lathbury's two volumes of Gladstone's religious correspondence (1910) filled part of the greatest gap in Morley; but neither this nor his short life of Gladstone[3] seemed to carry the force the family felt the subject deserved.

No more was done for a while. The heir of Hawarden, W. H. Gladstone's son Will, was killed near Laventie in April 1915;[4] and his uncles found themselves the owners of their father's papers. Herbert Gladstone took the diary down to his house at Dane End, near Ware, and went through it carefully in 1917.[5] He prepared a bowdlerized version of it, dictating to a girl typist all those passages he thought fit for a nice girl's ears: this reduced its bulk by about a third. The truncated document was still about as long as the Bible; it, and the original, were deposited in the Octagon.[6]

Reading the diary carefully, he was struck by the intimate tone of many of its entries; and agreed with Henry, his last surviving brother,[7] that if it was ever to see the light at all, it should appear as a whole.[8] Those who read it could thus see all the entries in perspective with each other; no selection, however carefully made, could make this possible. The two brothers saw good reason for excluding the diary from the collection of archives they were preparing to present to the nation as a monument to their father.

Inevitably, it will be asked what this good reason was, and why the diary has been segregated from the mass of Gladstone's papers for so

[1] The diary bears a trace of this slant in Morley's interest. He added to his 'D.W.' on the envelope that then held its eighth volume the significant docket 'Politics very slight'.

[2] Kilbracken, 228.   [3] In a series on 'Leaders of the Church, 1800–1900' (1905).

[4] Viscount Gladstone, *William G. C. Gladstone* (1918), 122, 133; Robert Graves, *Goodbye to All That* (2 ed., 1957), 65.

[5] Mallet, 273.   [6] Private information.

[7] Of W. E. Gladstone's four ss., W. H. died—before his f.—in 1891; Stephen in 1920; Herbert in 1930; and Henry in 1935.

[8] Gladstone to Lang, 23 December 1932; Lambeth MS, n.y.n.

long. The answer is simple. Herbert wrote to Henry Gladstone in 1926, 'What *is* our root difficulty? It is not in the letters and papers. It *is* in the Diary['s] introspections, its spiritual misgivings and self accusations and in the fact that confessions of human weakness are definitely connected with the other sex'.[1] The brothers agreed that many passages in it would be open to misconstruction, especially if quoted out of context, and would give a misleading impression of their father's personality and interests. Most of these passages dealt with his work for reclaiming what his age called fallen women, and with one particular friendship with a courtesan who exchanged physical for spiritual influence; or with self-criticisms of morbid stringency. It did not seem proper to the family that these exceptionally revealing, yet exceptionally private papers should be made available for some considerable time.

How they came to be separated from the rest of the mass deserves an explanation.

In 1925 the Gladstones had been exasperated by a calumny on the dead prime minister. One Peter Wright published that year a book of essays, *Portraits and Criticisms*, of which a few hundred copies were sold. In a digression from a digression, he wrote that it had been the liberal leader's custom 'in public to speak the language of the highest and strictest principle, and in private to pursue and possess every sort of woman'.[2] The brothers, who had long been annoyed about slanderous rumours circulating round the clubs, felt they must not let it be said that they had allowed so iniquitous a comment to pass unchallenged, and wished to take Wright to law. They found, of course, that they could not sue for libel of the dead. Herbert Gladstone therefore drew up and published a letter to Wright in terms so offensive that Wright had himself to sue for libel, or lose his character as a gentleman. The case of *Wright* v. *Gladstone* came on, before Mr. Justice Avory, in January 1927, and lasted five days. Wright did not appear to his own advantage in court; he was unable to substantiate any of the allegations of immorality he brought against the Gladstones' father—they were palpably founded on malicious gossip, and as devoid of substance as he seemed devoid of straightforwardness. A special jury found against him, adding a rider that 'in their unanimous opinion the evidence that has been placed before them has completely vindicated the high moral character of the late Mr. W. E. Gladstone'.[3]

---

[1] Herbert to Henry Gladstone, 9 December 1926, very private; Lambeth MS, n.y.n. He was writing about the disposal of their father's papers in general, not only about the Lambeth deposit. [2] loc. cit. 152–3.
[3] *Through Thirty Years*, 435–6; *The Times*, 28, 29 January, 2, 3, 4 February 1927; and 7 April 1957, Wright's obituary. Many papers bearing on the case are in Lambeth MSS, n.y.n.

Wright sought to cast disagreeable aspersions on Gladstone's attitude to women in general, and relied on stories of much indecency, though of slight evidential value. These tales arose from an utter misunderstanding of Gladstone's motives in spending much time among prostitutes, whom in fact he essayed to convert to another way of life. While preparing for the case, which they did assiduously for many months, the brothers made a careful review of such of their father's papers as bore on this work; and appreciated that numerous passages in his diary might be liable to misunderstanding. For this reason, they did not produce it in court. To do so would have helped them to dispel one of Wright's most ridiculous charges, about Gladstone's activities on the night of Lord Frederick Cavendish's assassination;[1] but it would have laid them open also, they felt, to chance questions that might have arisen from lucky dips in the diary by prosecuting counsel, on entries which would at first appear to tell heavily on Wright's side, and could not be explained without embarrassment.

On reflexion, the brothers decided that the diary, and various other papers bearing on what they called their father's 'rescue work', had better be sequestrated for the time being from inquiring eyes. Reflexion also impressed on them the standing of the diary as a Christian document. Their father, with indomitable tenacity, had set himself to live his life as strictly in accordance with the sermon on the mount as he could: 'From the first, boy and man, he set himself the highest nay, an ideal standard.'[2] Such a task has been undertaken often enough by the hermit or the recluse, but hardly—if at all—attempted, before or since, by one who threw himself with crusading ardour into the great game of government with all its temptations, and who yet added further temptations by undertaking a private work of charity of an especially perilous kind. Gladstone used his diary to explain to himself how he had in fact managed to lay out his time; the assumption that it should be laid out purely for the purposes of a sincere Christian was always implicit, and sometimes directly expressed.[3] Hence the diary's religious interest. Henry Gladstone put this point to Cosmo Lang, then archbishop of York, when Lang was marooned at Hawarden during the general strike of 1926; and Lang suggested the solution that was eventually adopted.[4] All the papers involved were to be handed over for safe custody to the archbishop of Canterbury, to be the absolute

    [1] See 6 May 82, and the fuller accounts in Hamilton's diary for 8 and 9 May 1882 in Add MS 48632, and in Mary Drew to Herbert Gladstone, 29 April 1926, Lambeth MSS, n.y.n.
    [2] Herbert to Henry Gladstone, 9 December 1926, very private; Lambeth MS, n.y.n.
    [3] e.g. diarist's third note after 20 July 33.
    [4] See Herbert to Henry Gladstone, 13 May, Henry Gladstone to Lang, 15 May (copy); and Lang's reply, 17 May 1926, in Lambeth MS, n.y.n.

property of him and his successors. Randall Davidson, who still held office—he retired with a peerage, soon after reaching the age of eighty, late in 1928—readily agreed to the arrangement, which left to the discretion of the archbishop for the time being what access, if any, was to be given to the documents involved. After lengthy discussions, the actual handing over of the papers by Henry Gladstone to Claude Jenkins, the librarian at Lambeth, took place in the presence of both archbishops on 27 July 1928.[1]

Practically speaking, no access was given by archbishops Davidson, Lang, or Temple, though Lang caused a typescript copy of the diary to be made, by H. W. Lawton, later professor of French at Sheffield, whose wife helped him in the task; and from this typescript the Gladstone family archivist, Tilney Bassett, was able to compile a useful forty-page elucidation of many of the diary's abbreviations. Jenkins could not reconcile it with his duty as librarian at Lambeth to leave so important a document unread while it was in his charge, and added acquaintance with it to his extraordinary range of information, that stretched from Noah through Cosmas Indicopleustes and the Anabaptists to Elvis Presley. He was impressed by the diary's historical value, and religious and personal interest; but was unable to secure its publication. When it seemed to be in danger from bombing, during the war of 1939, he moved it from the librarian's room at Lambeth Palace to the wine cellar under his own rooms at Christ Church, Oxford—informing his archbishop after he had done so.[2] Otherwise, the diary has always remained at Lambeth, or in the charge of the editor.

Once or twice, the family at Hawarden made the shortened version of the diary available, in strict privacy, to historians: particularly, to J. L. Hammond, to whom Henry Gladstone lent it in the early nineteen-thirties. This was done without consulting Lambeth, on a condition which Hammond strictly kept: that he told nobody he had used it. Much of the force of his *Gladstone and the Irish Nation*, described elsewhere as 'the most formidable and incisive piece of original research yet published on the history of England or Ireland in the second half of the nineteenth century',[3] derived from his sight of this document, which—truncated as it was—gave him new insights into Gladstone's character and methods.

For twenty years after Henry Gladstone's death, nothing was done with the diary at all. Eventually, in 1955, after Sir Philip Magnus's

---

[1] The circumstances of the transfer are fully described in Lambeth MSS, n.y.n., culminating in Henry Gladstone's letter to his b. of 27 July 1928 giving an account of the final ceremony at Lambeth. For Canon Jenkins, see obituary in *The Times*, 19, 24 January 1959.

[2] Jenkins to Lang, 1 December 1940, Lambeth MS. n.y.n.

[3] Foot introducing the 1964 reprint: Hammond, xxi.

book had revived interest in the diarist, Bassett tackled Archbishop Fisher about it when they happened to meet in the Athenaeum; and after a year's accidental delay,[1] the present writer was invited to report on the diary's publishability. Its enormous interest was apparent, if not at a first glance then at a second. Prolonged study led inescapably to the conclusion that the proper course was to publish it all, if a publisher could be found for so formidable a task. The Clarendon Press took up the diary's cause; Archbishops Fisher and Ramsey agreed in turn; and with this opening pair of volumes, complete publication begins.

Readers may well ask why it is necessary to publish the whole of a document of such inordinate length. There are several reasons. The least is that almost every word in it is likely to be of some use to somebody. Even such apparently wearisome entries as 'H.S. with W. & A.', repeated day after day to record that the diarist read in the Bible with his eldest son and daughter, may interest people working on mid-nineteenth-century family life or systems of religious education. Moreover, the editor found when he tried to establish a line beyond which dullness or (in the earliest volumes) puerility would exclude an entry, that no such line could be drawn. Doubters are welcome to try to do better. But exclusions would involve dots to mark them; and in this work such marks would be bound to lead to misapprehension. (All dots in the text below are Gladstone's own.) Substantial misapprehensions have arisen already: it is time they were allayed.

Besides, part of the interest of the journal lies in its completeness. Gladstone was in many ways a man of superhuman capacities; one of the outstanding figures of his or any other age;[2] perhaps the greatest Scotsman ever born. That such a man as he should keep a day-book, however cursory, for a spell of over seventy years is itself remarkable; some interest attaches to everything that fell from his often busy pen, and special interest to his journal entries, however arid, simply for their part in the total picture of the man that is built up by the journal as a whole. Omissions would detract, however slightly, from that total picture; so there are none that signify. One kind of entry, alone, has been omitted: the page headline, in which the diarist often (though not always) jotted down where he was: 'Liverpool', 'Oxford', 'London—Hawarden—Hagley', and so on.[3] The data in these headlines are included also in the text; and repetition would be needlessly cumbrous, now that pagination has altered.

Otherwise, an attempt is made below to give the entire text; so far

---

[1] Private information.   [2] Cp. Mary Drew, *Acton, Gladstone and others* (1924), 30.
[3] Examples in facsimile at p. 56 below, and in Masterman at 32, 256, 320.

as any nineteenth-century manuscript is transferable into print, and with a few changes which need attention.

The earliest entries, made while he was at Eton and Oxford, were heavily abbreviated by the diarist. The reader's patience would be sorely tried if he had to unravel for himself entry after entry such as this: 'Saturdays busss; notes; readg newsppr—Darwin—Frch exerce —Prive buss (Juvl)—workg at card racks—walk—&c employed me, wt dog a little to Epite of Hooke';[1] while many repetitions of such phrases as 'Priv[ate]e bus[ines]s (Juv[ena]l)' might weary the printer as well. Accordingly, in the first of these two volumes—down to the end of 1832—this text sets down the sense of what the diarist intended, instead of transcribing the symbols that make his intention plain; normally, only abbreviations of time are transcribed. Square brackets are used to convey the editor's interpretation in cases of doubt.

The facsimile at page 56 shows how necessary it has been to do this. But on entering parliament Gladstone dropped these schoolboy mannerisms. Thereafter, his abbreviations are almost all quite obvious, and can be left as he wrote them. It is just worth mentioning his use of a doubled terminal consonant to mean a plural: Univv. for universities, and so on. A very few abbreviations—five—are uniformly printed in full. The most frequent of these is 'find.' for 'finished'; the others are 'anal.' for 'analysis', a simple '-g' for a terminal '-ing', and 'fm' and 'wt' for 'from' and 'with'. None of the rest, it is hoped, will provide occasions of stumbling for readers; square brackets, again, are used in cases of doubt.

If readers are nevertheless puzzled by an abbreviation, it is worth casting back a few days; to see, for example, that 'Ar. Pol.' means Aristotle's *Politics*, or that 'Purg.' is Dante's *Purgatorio*.

The notes are intended to identify, so far as possible, incidents, people, places, books, and documents referred to in the text. Sources are only indicated for unusually recondite fragments of information. As a rule the notes are drawn from the obvious sources—peerages, poll books, local and professional directories, lists of graduates, *Hansard*,[2] gazetteers, bibliographies, biographies, and encyclopaedias (mainly *Britannica, Larousse, Italiana*), among printed books; the Gladstone MSS in the British Museum; and the principal public offices' surviving files in the PRO. It would over-emphasize the task of the editorial staff, which has often been merely routine, and distract attention from the diary text, if detailed references were given for, say, every fragment extracted from Burke's *Landed Gentry*. Nor has any attempt been

---

[1] 15 Oct. 25.

[2] *Hansard* is inferior to Barrow's *Mirror of Parliament*, but is used throughout for references to debates because it has much longer cover and is more readily available. It has been checked where necessary with the *Journals* of each house of parliament.

made to write the history of Gladstone's century in the notes. At the
first mention of each of his main correspondents, the British Museum
reference to their surviving letters is given; first mentions are traceable
through the *dramatis personae* at the end of volume ii.

People are described by their full names, their years of birth and
death, and their occupation, when such particulars are available; this
should facilitate further research in parish or college registers, rate
books, and so on. Any attempt to perfect this edition by such detailed
inquiries into several thousand characters would have imposed an
inordinate delay. Hence numerous queries in the notes: e.g. 'b. 1802?'
for a man whom Foster describes in *Alumni Oxonienses* as 'matriculated 1820, aged 18'. Canons and prebendaries are described alike as
canons; otherwise, it is hoped that correct titles have been given, in
a title-riddled age. Dates of publication of books are given—again,
when available; save for works that can fairly claim to be called
classics. Current issues of the *Quarterly* and *Edinburgh* reviews have
no notes.

Readers are taken to be familiar with the names of the books of the
Bible, of Shakespeare's plays, and of the principal classical authors.
Those who are annoyed at being told Molière wrote *Tartuffe* should ask
themselves who wrote *Le Bon Ménage* or *Monsieur de Pourceaugnac*
before they complain.

Punctuation, use of 'and' or '&', and spelling—sometimes rather
eccentric—[1] follow the original as closely as can be. The diarist was
fond of that common Victorian stop, a short dash placed on the line;
treated here as comma, dash, full stop, or ditto-mark as the sense requires. He often used it also between paragraphs of a day's entry;[2]
a use omitted below, save for the insertion of a paragraph break.
Words underlined are printed in *italics*; and for uniformity's sake, each
entry's date-heading is italicized as well. Double underlinings, rare
enough, go into SMALL CAPITALS.

Marginal entries are incorporated in the text without comment,
when the sense admits them; otherwise they are placed in footnotes.
Late entries are remarked on, when they are known to exist; but as a
rule, these were diaries compiled from day to day. A period of severe
stress, such as his elder sister's death or his first parliamentary canvass,[3] would sometimes force him to suspend nightly entries; once the
excitement of travel did the same, and he only completed the journal
of three weeks of his grand tour some months later;[4] occasionally he
tried entering up his journal week by week instead of day by day.[5]

---

[1] Cp. Ramm, I. i. xvii; and H. W. V. Temperley, *The Crimea* (1936), xxx.
[2] Examples in Masterman at 320, 368.   [3] 21 Feb.–2 Mar. 29; 23 Sep.–8 Oct. 32.
[4] See 18 Apr. and 17, 22 Sept. 32.
[5] e.g. 8 Oct. 30, 31 July 32.

Sometimes he entered up each day's activities on the next: the entry for Christmas Eve, 1829, for instance, admits that he 'walked down to Cuddesdon & dined there very late & forgot to read the Bible at night', a break in a habit already of long standing.[1] But as a rule, he completed each entry last thing at night before he said his prayers and went to bed.

It has been indicated already that such self-deprecatory entries as the one just quoted are common. And not only does the diarist make a point of recording anything that tells against himself: he cannot be relied on to insert points in his favour. While still an undergraduate he noted a 'Discussion long & interesting' at the union, where he carried his motion by a single vote; but omitted to mention that during the evening he was elected president.[2] Attempting a crossing of the straits of Messina on a stormy night, he records the other passengers' panic, and the exact moment at which he felt he could no longer join in their prayers; he adds that he then went on deck, but not that when he got there he and his companion Arthur Kinnaird saved the vessel from shipwreck, one taking the helm and the other the sheet that had been abandoned by the terror-stricken crew.[3] Only on one of the four occasions when he became prime minister did he put the fact down.[4] Almost in fact this seems like an account-book where entries are made on the debit side only; and on most of the occasions when the diarist does rejoice in some achievement or triumph of his own, he remembers to record that 'it comes ἄνωθεν', from above.[5]

Such a tone, as has been remarked already, is barely acceptable in this different age. It may be that today's readers will be more ready to chortle at such accidents as the collocation of the names of Liddell and Scott side by side, before either had written a line of the lexicon that was to bring both of them fame;[6] or to indulge in the opportunities for parody that the diaries' style seems—at a first, deceptive glance—to offer. They might do better to look in the diaries for a solution to Ruskin's difficulty in the eighteen-seventies:

'I have been greatly dismayed by the discovery to me of **Mr.** Gladstone's real character, as I saw it at Hawarden: its intense simplicity and earnestness laying themselves open to every sort of misinterpretation—being unbelievable unless one saw him.

'I must cancel all the attack on him in *Fors*.'[7] For after reading the diaries one can ask, as he does, 'How is it possible for the men who have known him long to allow the thought of his course of conduct now, or

[1] 11 Nov. 25.   [2] 11 Nov. 30.
[3] 5/6 Nov. 38.   [4] 1 Feb. 86.
[5] 14 Aug. 92, after surviving a quarrel with Harcourt.   [6] 24 Jan. 33.
[7] John Ruskin to W. H. Allen, 18 January 1878, in L. March-Phillips and B. Christian, *Some Hawarden Letters* (1917), 21.

at any other time, having been warped by ambition, to diminish the lustre and the power of his name?'[1]

And yet sensible men, or at least *hommes moyen sensuels*, will admit that some aspects of Gladstone were almost too good to be true.

From the time the diary began, he was already an ostentatiously good boy; and he ran into the sort of trouble ostentatious goodness can incur from people who dislike any tone of holier-than-thou. One black-ball was cast against him when he was put up for Pop;[2] luckily for him, one alone did not disqualify. More seriously, he was beaten up by some more boisterous contemporaries at Christ Church; and this incident, of which a few legends survive to the present day, gave the diarist an occasion for self-reproach that does not make agreeable reading.[3]

Good he undoubtedly was; the only item in the normal catalogues of sin that can clearly be laid at his door was some weakness for erotic literature,[4] a failing that only the strictest moralists wholly abhor today. The diary betrays some traces of a private difficulty, that struggle against masturbation through which all young men have to pass;[5] Gladstone seems to have mastered himself before he went down from Oxford. It can hardly have been on this account that he had so strong an inner conviction of sin,[6] or the diary would say more about it.

He suffered from a highly sensitive conscience; his gift for seeing many sides to questions ordinary men saw as plain often led him into tortures of self-doubt and self-reproach about what other people regarded as normal conduct or at worst as peccadillo.[7] The origins of this sensitivity must be sought in his family background, on which the diaries throw a good deal of new light.

His relation with his mother seems to have been thoroughly amicable, but not particularly intense. Her health was clearly not strong: 'Mother ill' are the opening words of the diary's very first mention of her,[8] and subsequent ones often touch on her indispositions. The tone of his comments on her last illness and her death aged 53 in September 1835 can fairly be called respectful but distant; he was of course suffering at the time from a sharp disappointment in love.

He was much closer to his elder sister, also called Anne, who was his godmother as well. She can fairly be put forward as one of Disraeli's principal characters who have never appeared in the history books.

---

[1] Ruskin to Mary Gladstone, same day; ibid., 20.
[2] 27 Oct. 25.   [3] 24 Mar. 30.
[4] There will be more to say of this in a later volume.
[5] 17 Nov. 29, 1 Apr. 31.
[6] For a typical explosion of self-denunciation, see 19 Feb. 30. Many of his entries on his own birthday are similar.
[7] e.g. 7, 20 May 26; 26 Apr. 33.
[8] 17 July 25.

Morley and Magnus each dismiss her in four lines;[1] McCarthy prints a picture of her, but does not mention her directly;[2] other biographers treat her with equal brevity, or ignore her. Yet it was apparently she who encouraged the diarist in many leading characteristics, some of which helped him on his way to greatness; she who made an evangelical of him, and through making him read Hooker showed him also the way out of evangelicalism towards the High Church doctrines he held for most of his life. She died when he was nineteen; he spent much of the rest of his life striving after the almost impossibly severe standards of conduct she had set him.

Two and a half years after her death, after going to communion with the whole family, he prayed: 'may we attain to more than an outward unity. At present I dare not rely much here. I do not feel that [we] are on a sound footing as a Christian family, which is a Christian Church: but the Lord reigneth.'[3] To what threatened disturbances this oracular passage refers is unclear; on the whole the picture of the diarist's relations with his parents, brothers, and sisters gained from the diary is much as Hammond described it, of a lively, close knit, argumentative, yet thoroughly affectionate group.[4]

The most discordant notes in this family harmony were struck by his sister Helen, whose eccentricities will be familiar to readers of Magnus. She was Gladstone's only younger sibling, and he was clearly both very fond of her, and a strong admirer of her intellect;[5] clearly also she was an exceptionally difficult member of any household, capable of shutting herself away for days or weeks in a corner of the great house at Fasque, and in the end she became an exile. The diary fully bears out Hammond's contention that her secession to Rome brought her brother 'more pain than any political disagreement'.[6]

For his eldest brother Thomas he shows mingled affection and respect; mitigated by annoyance when Thomas gets engaged just as he gets jilted himself. He seems to have been fonder of his second brother, the gigantic Robertson who was over two metres tall and whose weight varied from twenty to twenty-five stone;[7] and fonder still of the third, John, who took a spell away from his career in the navy to accompany William on the grand tour (on which, by the bye, they decided that in Lombardy 'The police system seems adequate to nothing beyond administering annoyance to travellers', visited the Vaudois in their

---

[1] Morley, i. 7n and 160–1; Magnus, 7.
[2] Justin McCarthy, *The Story of Gladstone's Life* (1910), 5.
[3] 2 Sept. 32.
[4] Hammond and Foot, *Gladstone and Liberalism* (2 ed., 1966), 8–9.
[5] Cp. 13 June 40.
[6] Hammond and Foot, 8.
[7] McCarthy, *Story of Gladstone's Life*, 6–7; Thomas, 49.

remote valley, met Napoleon's nephew and a friend of Andreas Hofer's, and presented letters of introduction at Lafayette's[1].)

Towering over those and all his other relatives, the Forsyte-like tribes of Scottish uncles and aunts and cousins, there loomed the dominant figure of his father, the self-made Liverpool merchant prince: a ruthlessly efficient man of business of whom his youngest son could yet say, 'None but his children can know what torrents of tenderness flowed from his heart.'[2] John Gladstone directed William's, as he directed all his children's, careers; not always pausing to make sure they wanted to go where he directed.[3] It was he who set aside William's strong desire to be ordained, and dispatched the young man to Lincoln's Inn—and Downing Street—instead.[4] 'For I must not I think', the son noted, 'consider myself as a man exercising the unfettered judgment of a man but as a being not yet competent for self direction nor fitted to act upon his own uncorrected impressions.'[5] This paternal influence remained the strongest force at work on Gladstone throughout his father's lifetime. He took quite literally the biblical commandment to honour his father and mother, and there was hardly a question to be found on which he was ready to cross, or even to contemplate crossing, his father's wish.

John Gladstone was proud of his son, and pleased at the same time to exercise so strong a control over him; and used him without hesitation as a private secretary, long after William had moved not only into parliament but into office. When the two of them were living in the same house, the son's diary was peppered with instances of small tasks he had done for the father, usually copying letters. The son even took occasion to reproach himself for not carrying out such tasks more blithely:

> 'Now it is true that my Parlty duties suffer: but if my Father desires one to do anything, it becomes my duty—& consequently that with wh the service in question may interfere is displaced & ceases for the time to be a duty: so I am to recognize the will of God. . . . and I have often reached this conclusion but in practice I fail to realize it.'[6]

Young Gladstone never felt it a disadvantage to work hard; and there were other, more obvious advantages in being his father's son: of these the principal ones were wealth and position. The family had a strong tradition of Scotch parsimony, which through his influence at the treasury has come to exert an influence on British government spending, at every level, in every field but armaments, down to the

[1] 27 June, 6–8 Mar., 7 Apr., 29 June, 11 Feb. 32.   [2] Morley, i. 19.
[3] e.g. 16 Sept. 27.   [4] Morley, i. 635–41, and 2–12 Aug. 30.
[5] 8 Aug. 30.   [6] 14 Apr. 40.

present day. But except during the Oak Farm crisis of the late forties, he was never short of spending-money himself; and he lived always surrounded by servants, with whom he tried to get on properly friendly terms. His approach would often enough seem ham-handed today: 'started Best [his valet] with his French Grammar; tried to explain how such things should stand, there is *one* more important'.[1] And sometimes he was in a familiar domestic employer's difficulty: 'Obliged to speak about my sugar, which disappears strangely.'[2] Even with all the servants of his father's household, we find him helping to make marmalade,[3] sewing, or marking his own clothes;[4] at Seaforth or Cuddesdon he would help, as everyone else living in the country had done for centuries, at making hay.[5] It is stranger to find him, at Seaforth, 'in orchard watching insects & making experiments',[6] a scientific fit that did not last.

What did last, all through his life, was his overwhelming interest in religion and his incessant preoccupation with religious doctrine; these carried with them a preoccupation with minor good works, with which the diary is also filled. One example, standing for many, can illustrate how unlike Gladstone's life was to that of a boy of nineteen today. He was staying with a school friend in Yorkshire: they went 'to see a poor blind invalid, Mary Clarkson by name. She seemed in a most happy state. We each read her a sermon.'[7]

This was a comparatively light-weight religious item; others were more sombre. He dabbled in the edges of the Irvingite movement, read a few books on the second coming, and once or twice betrayed distinct signs of taking an apocalyptic view of the world in which he lived: 'Surely the actual signs of the times are such as should make us ready for the coming of our Lord', he wrote in the reform crisis of 1831.[8]

His journey to Italy, in the interval between Oxford and politics, enabled him to escape from the darkest corners of evangelical religion and, as is well known, broadened his views of Christianity and set him on the road to being, what he soon became, an ardent high churchman. His friendships at Oxford and his reading after he went down put him in a good position to appreciate the Oxford Movement. He had been influenced, directly, by Bishop Lloyd;[9] he read Jones of Nayland;[10] he tackled Palmer's *Origines Liturgicae*;[11] he read Keble's assize sermon and Newman's earliest tracts, though not quite as soon as they

---

[1] 4 Nov. 34.
[3] 19 Apr. 27.
[5] 26–8 June 28, 8 July 30.
[7] Sunday, 13 Sept. 29.
[9] 10, 16, 17 Aug. 28, &c. See *DNB* xxxiii. 411.
[11] 17 Mar. 33.

[2] 27 June 33.
[4] 25 June 28.
[6] 11 Sept. 27.
[8] 20 Oct. 31.
[10] 10, 14 Sept. 29.

came out;[1] he knew Pusey, and Hope and Manning were for years his closest friends. He told Manning in 1841 that 'were Newman & his friends in intention hostile to the peace of the Church (& they are far otherwise) it is not even within their power to intercept and & reverse the profound comprehension movement towards the true basis of unity in the Church of England':[2] a judgement sadly belied by the result.

People may feel, when they have read all his private diary, that the force of his Christian example is still worth notice and respect; though the most earnest of churchgoers may smile at the punctilious school-boy who notes that 'I must make up in allowing more time to the Bible through the week' when he spends a few minutes on a Sunday revising the proof of the school newspaper he edits.[3] Almost every Lent, moreover, there are details of fastings more severe than con-temporary practice dictated for men out of orders and in society; even as a schoolboy he resolved not to eat his habitual amount of good food in the Lent term.[4]

Yet he was a human being, and no monster either of piety or of priggishness or of industry; the sharpness and genuineness of his sor-row over his disappointment with Caroline Farquhar come forcibly even through the plain style in which he writes, and no one can doubt he felt real anguish. To his own surprise, he was even more thoroughly captivated by Catherine Glynne; and when he had the good fortune to be married to that splendid woman, living with her family relaxed him and brought out his warmest instead of his coldest sides. He soon be-came adept at Glynnese, their private language, and may have contri-buted more to it himself than its lexicographer has allowed.[5]

He seldom uses Glynnese in his diary, of which the vocabulary, unless strained by compression, is the normal literary-theological language of his day. Sometimes he has a ring of Mr. Alfred Jingle—at his first election, for instance, 'Spoke very briefly from the window—stone thrown—thank God missed—man detected. Dinner—papers—whist.'[6] Often he uses words now obsolete—'prog', 'floor', 'an umbra'.[7] And of course many of his phrases now carry different mean-ings; for example, he writes of intimacy and intercourse without any sexual innuendo at all. 'Acted as Bible clerk, ill'[8] means that he acted as Bible clerk badly, not that he was indisposed. 'A murdered day'[9] means a day on which he did nothing that he should have done; 'dies nigerrimus'[10] probably means the same, but might be used of a particularly dense pea-souper.

---

[1] 27 Oct. 33.   [2] 30 Mar. 41.   [3] 25 Nov. 27.   [4] 19 Jan. 27.
[5] Lord Lyttelton, *Contributions towards a Glossary of the Glynne Language* (1851). Gladstone had used 'addle', for instance, on 2 June 30, in a Glynnese sense.
[6] 12 Dec. 32.   [7] 2 Jan. 27, 7 Apr., [14 June] 31.
[8] 19 June 30.   [9] 8 Dec. 28.   [10] 8 Feb. 36.

Obviously, in fact, in a document as long and in places as complex as this diary there will be ambiguities, and difficulties which no amount of scholarship can unravel: 'dined at Benson—(mem. never to dine there again)'[1] may refer to anything, from bad food through a row with a waiter to an over-accommodating landlady. One such complexity, accidentally resolved, is just worth remark.

When the diarist was staying at Cuddesdon in the summer of 1828, with another Christ Church undergraduate, he often wrote down such entries as 'Walk with Puller and giraffe'. The editor toyed with the idea of these two future double firsts wandering among the Oxfordshire hedgerows accompanied—on a lead?—by the tallest of mammals; then observed that there was only one living giraffe in western Europe at the time, and that at Paris; and made the prosaic discovery that 'giraffe' was also a word for an early upright piano. *But does that help?*

Two years later, Gladstone was back at Cuddesdon again, and made several references to 'Spineto'. Musical household; nothing odd, except putting spinet into Italian badly; till the entry 'Spineto & analysing'[2] raised a doubt, and drew attention to the *Lectures on the Elements of Hieroglyphics and Egyptian Antiquities* of the Marquis Spineto who had been the interpreter at Queen Caroline's trial and later became a well known figure in Cambridge, where for many years he was the university's sole teacher of Italian.

Everybody knows that Gladstone could be prolix; all great orators can. Yet he was also capable of an uncanny degree of compression; where he was a *maestro di color che sanno,* he could cram much thought into a very small number of words.[3] Much of the Lambeth diary is so compressed that it reads like a kind of private telegraphese; though a few moments' perseverance almost always suffices to unravel the sense. This compression grew primarily of course from the severe pressure of time under which the diarist chose to pass his political life. Even before he entered parliament, he recorded that 'the time on my hands is little enough, & I am sure it is a duty to husband it'.[4]

Abrupt changes of subject provide a different kind of obstacle to rapid understanding of this text. We have, all mixed together, points he wanted to charge on his conscience, points of pure routine, and points he wanted to charge on his memory: notes of his own shortness of patience or temper, side by side with notes to innkeepers about rooms or postmasters about parcels. As he had always got a volume of his diary handy in his pocket, he occasionally used it simply as a memorandum-book, of peoples' addresses or subscriptions he must

---

[1] 18 Jan. 27.
[3] e.g. Add MS 44648, f. 145.
[2] 14 Sept. 30.
[4] 25 Oct. 32.

remember to pay. Notes to post- and station-masters were commoner when he was out of office, and therefore short of secretaries, than when he was a minister; and may have been due in part, in any case, to his wife's absent-mindedness, which was as well known as her charm.

Gladstone's is not a character one associates first with sport; his abundant physical vigour found its main outlets, in manhood, in walking and in tree-felling.[1] As a schoolboy he sculled a good deal; and as a schoolboy and undergraduate he rode, frequently if not well (he recorded it against himself whenever he fell off his horse; just as he recorded it against himself when he was sea-sick, which he was almost every time he went to sea). He was fond of dogs;[2] he fished occasionally;[3] he could use a bow and arrow;[4] alone on a wet afternoon, he could play billiards, right hand against left.[5] He does not seem ever to have ridden to hounds; but he shot a good deal as a young man. The suspicions of him long cherished by the landed gentry will be confirmed when they read, not only that he shot a sitting rabbit, but that he could shoot—or at any rate shoot at—a fox.[6]

Once the reader has accustomed himself to the style of the diary, in the earlier and non-political passages, what is he going to find about the politics that were a large, if not a wholly preoccupying, element in Gladstone's life?

First, as has been indicated already, a much more strongly tory tone than the bulk of the books so far written on Gladstone would have led him to suspect. For half a lifetime, there has been lurking in the British Musuem—open to public inspection, and unnoticed—the remark of the diarist and his brother John that 'neither of us like liberalism':[7] in a punning context, it is true. Elsewhere in the museum is the diarist's essay on the principles of government,[8] written in his strictest tory phase while he was still up at Christ Church; never in the end discussed with his group of friends there for whom it was written, and undisturbed by historians since. His earliest pamphlet lurks later in the same volume;[9] Hatchard would publish it only at his own expense, his father would not put up the money, and the project dropped. Throughout these early intimations of the toryism that Macaulay correctly assessed, in his over-quoted phrase reviewing Gladstone's

---

[1] W. T. Stead, *Gladstone* (1898), 52–53, explains that he felled trees in order to rest his brain: 'In chopping down a tree you have not time to think of anything excepting where your next stroke will fall. The whole attention is centred upon the blows of the axe'.
[2] 12 Jan. 27, 25 Dec. 31.
[3] 16 Aug. 28.
[4] 29, 30 Aug. 26; 17, 19 Sept. 34.
[5] 7 Sept. 37.
[6] 12 Sept., 11 Oct. 34.
[7] 18 Feb. 32.
[8] Add MS 44721, f. 1.
[9] Ibid., f. 66.

first book, the religious note is always being sounded alongside the political. Even at a Newark election, Gladstone could retain his belief in the providential order.[1]

The electoral material will be useful to psephologists who wish to push their studies back from the twentieth century into the nineteenth; though there will be more about how elections were really conducted, and less about percentage swings, than studies of more recent periods have contained. An account of the riot at Mold on 8 July 1841 bears out Gash's observation that 'The traditional Eatanswill picture of early Victorian elections is in fact not so much an exaggerated as a pale and euphemistic version of the contemporary scene'.[2] There is a great deal about the morality, or immorality, of treating voters at Newark; a subject on which Gladstone had a row with his committee that was prolonged for nearly the whole duration of the parliament elected at the end of 1832. In the end he came to an accommodation with them; and gave his own views on the subject, distinguishing the political from the religious offence (operating as bribery, or making people drunk) in one of the comparatively rare passages of consecutive prose with which he interlarded the diaries' telegraphese.[3]

The sort of minor political point with which the diary is filled is the invitation to him in the spring of 1837 to stand for the county of Middlesex; which he declined, because it would double at least the £1,000 which his father was already putting up to cover his comparatively mild expenses at Newark.[4]

The diary as a whole contains a vast deal of information about the nineteenth-century governmental machine, of which Gladstone was the foremost manipulator; but these two volumes have comparatively little of it, since they cover his education, part of his travels, and his years of early opposition. When they end, he is not yet even on the threshold of his administrative career, which began at the board of trade in 1841. His few weeks each at the treasury and the colonial office in 1834–5 have slight value for the historian; though for him as a politician, that spell under Aberdeen at the colonial office meant a great deal.[5]

In opposition, the most interesting thing he did from the political historian's point of view was to act as a member of a pressure group, the West Indian interest to which his father's commercial operations naturally drew him; but he was never a member of the group's inner

[1] See 21 June 41.
[2] N. Gash, *Politics in the Age of Peel* (1953), 147.
[3] 2 June 41.
[4] 3 and 4 May 37.
[5] Cp. *H* ccciv. 1081 (8 April 1886).

councils, so the diary's evidence about its workings is not extensive. His other main opposition interest was in education; which led him into a number of curious byways, traceable through his reading lists.

For one of the principal interests of these diaries is that in them we can trace a lifetime's course of serious reading by a man with some command of language, insatiable curiosity, and catholic literary tastes. These pages show that his outstanding characteristic, even more than that fantastic fund of energy, was range. From the principal classics of ancient, Italian, and English literature down to the most trumpery pamphlet of the day, nothing of much significance seems to have escaped his attention unless it bore on some highly technical subject or on one of the physical sciences. As a schoolboy, he absorbs Gibbon (six volumes in as many weeks) as an extra during term, Scott and Cervantes in the holidays, while taking in in passing *Star-chamber*, an ephemeral magazine that included some of the earliest published work of his eventual rival,[1] and the *Memoirs* of Harriette Wilson, which he soon seems to have laid down. His rule was to note in his diary anything that struck him, or anything that he felt he ought not to have picked up; either way, his modern reader can acquire a fair idea of the literary influences that worked on him. Dante he did not discover till 1834,[2] but thereafter like Homer he was a constant companion.

His comments, when he makes any at all, are often disappointing: 'read Timaeus (tough)',[3] some years after he went down from Oxford, throws only a limited light on the efficiency with which he had learned either Greek or philosophy, while '(finished) Don Juan (wh cannot be dismissed in a single remark)'[4] is merely tantalizing. In that same week he is reading Archbishop Leighton, Filicaja, *Don Quijote* (in Spanish, which he is learning), Saint Augustine, Moore's life of Byron, Leland's history of Ireland, and a history of buccaneering: a sufficient indication of the variety of the mental fare he laid before himself, and perhaps the start of an explanation of the variety of his speeches.

His written style never seemed to benefit much from his reading; looking back some years afterwards on his work for the *Eton Miscellany*, he found that 'I cannot keep my temper in perusing my own (with few exceptions) execrable productions',[5] and Colburn the publisher would not touch the *Miscellany* for the London market.[6] But in his speeches his capacious memory had full play; and he had as well that mesmeric gift which belongs to great orators and great actors— the gift for getting his audiences to respond to him.[7] Curiously, no one seems to have asked where or how he learned to speak. The answer is

[1] 26 Aug. 26.   [2] 16 Sept. 34.
[3] 6 Sept. 37.   [4] 7 Sept. 37.
[5] 6 May 35.   [6] 20 Feb. 28.
[7] Cp. Kilbracken, 109–12.

clear from the diary: at Eton, and from Dr. Keate—a little direct tuition from the headmaster;[1] a careful reading of the *Lectures on Rhetoric* of Hugh Blair, the Edinburgh don who patronized—in all good faith—MacPherson's plagiarisms from Ossian;[2] and a thorough soaking in Aristotle's *Rhetoric*. The *Rhetoric* he re-read diligently at Oxford, preparing it as a set book with one of his Christ Church tutors; and both at Eton and at Oxford he was an assiduous debater. Some of the most tiresome and pernickety mannerisms of the 'old parliamentary hand' can be foreseen from his behaviour in Pop and at the Oxford Union.

His range extended farther than a miscellaneous acquaintance with literature, good and bad, and a grasp on the attention of audiences large and small. He understood, as few men did, the society in which he lived; even though—for religious reasons—he was disinclined to attempt himself to break up its foundations. The man who launched the canard that it was really Gladstone who wrote Dickens's novels[3] had some understanding of the range and depth of Gladstone's knowledge of English society; which, as will be shown in later volumes, extended from the most rarefied of social circles right down into the pit of Seven Dials. Here in fact is the daily record of the life of a man of no mean capacities, who trod the stage of history and directed the play in which he acted. People who enjoy making fun of the Victorians may enjoy themselves, if they can command the patience to read what follows. People who appreciate the grandeur and the achievements of Gladstonian England, and who see the connexion between Victoria and Amerigo Vespucci, will rather agree with Jenkins, the Lambeth librarian: 'It is extremely doubtful if the diaries ought ever to be allowed to be published except as a whole, but they constitute as a whole one of the most remarkable "human documents" ever composed.'[4]

---

[1] e.g. 23 Feb. 27.

[2] 31 Jan. 26.

[3] *Cornhill Magazine*, xi (NS). 113 (August 1888). The article was by R. A. Proctor—a reference owed to Mrs. Sheila Rosenberg. No attempt will be made below to duplicate the work of the *Wellesley Index to Victorian Periodicals* (1966 ff.); nor will the work of dictionaries of art or architecture be duplicated.

[4] Jenkins to Henry Gladstone, 7 December 1932; from a copy in Gladstone to Lang, 23 December 1932, Lambeth MS, n.y.n.

[VOLUME I][1]

[JOURNALS (NO. 1)]

(Begins July 1825)

[Sat. 16 July 1825]

Read Ovid.[2] Drilled—for 1st time—like it much.[3] Went to Newnham[4] with Mr G.[5] 13 miles from our part of Gloucester. pretty ride—good road. Quaint gardens & ponds on left, about 8 miles [and] ¾ from Gloucester.[6] Saw flood tide come up (called "racers" by country folk,); it filled bed of river very quickly. Day hot.

[Sun. 17]

Tremendously hot. Mother[7] ill from heat at Church. Good funeral sermon at St Johns from Mr. Jones.[8]

[Mon. 18]

Day still hotter. Mother better. With my sisters,[9] she went to Cheltenham. 82 in shade.

[Tu. 19]

Still hotter. one o clock 88 in shade, 124 in sun. four o clock 92 in shade.
    Extreme heat at Paris 89.

[Wed. 20]

See Journal.[10]

[Wed. 27]

Returned from Malvern.

---

[1] Lambeth MS 1416, 11 ff.; see p. xxii above. Bound inside front cover of Volume II. The Gladstone family were living in Beaufort Buildings, Gloucester Spa.
[2] *Metamorphoses*. Notes in Add MS 44717, ff. 122–31.
[3] Under Sergeant Ferry. See 23 Aug. and 7 Dec. 25.
[4] Market town below Gloucester on right bank of Severn.
[5] (Sir) John *Gladstone, 1764–1851, the diarist's f., Scottish-born Liverpool merchant prince, Canningite M.P. 1818–26, cr. bart. 1846; see p. xlii above.
[6] Westbury Court, belonging to Maynard Colchester, local magnate.
[7] Anne Gladstone, 1773–1835, a Robertson of Struan; m. 1800; see p. xl above.
[8] Thomas Jones, 1800–67, rector of Hempstead just outside Gloucester from 1826.
[9] Anne Mackenzie, 1802–29, his godmother, and Helen Jane, 1814–80. See p. xli.
[10] An untraced early travel diary; cp. Add MS 44818.

[*Fri. 29*]

Mr & Mrs Barlow[1] & J. Robertson[2] came; the latter to stay a few days.

[*Sat. 30*]

Went with J. R[obertson] to see County Gaol.

[*Sun. 31*]

Heard Bishop of Gloucester[3] preach a middling sermon.

[*Mon. 1 August*]

Left Gloucester per Mercury [coach], 20 minutes before 7 P.M. Arrived at Birmingham ¼ or ½ after 8 P.M. Slept at Castle—not a comfortable house apparently.

[*Tu. 2*]

Left Birmingham per Bang Up, 20 minutes after 7 a.m. weather variable. From Gloucester to Newcastle [under Lyme] crops ripe generally, & harvest beginning. Crops very fine. Arrived at Liverpool about ¼ after 8 p.m.[4] Aunt J[ohanna][5] & R[obertson][6] well.

met Irish going South.[7]

[*Wed. 3*]

Weather rainy. Mem—This country not *near* so much burnt up as in the south—crops not so generally ripe.

[*Th. 4*]

Weather ditto. Called on Mr & saw Mrs Rawson.[8] Told William I wd pay for W. D[igges]'s schooling.[9] Bought him a Bib.

---

[1] John Barlow of Chorley, Lancashire; his wife was the diarist's aunt.

[2] John M. G. Robertson, d. 1832, a first cousin.

[3] Christopher *Bethell, 1773–1859; tutor to duke of Northumberland; bishop successively of Gloucester, 1824, Exeter, April 1830, and Bangor, October 1830; pronounced high churchman. Over fifty years later the diarist could recollect 'the rolling thunder of the Bishop's voice' (*Gloucester Standard*, 17 January 1880).

[4] Seaforth House, Liverpool, close to the mouth of the Mersey, was then John *Gladstone's principal home. See J. P. *Neale, *Views of Seats* (1819), ii. no. 57, and C. R. Fay, *Huskisson and his age* (1951), 369–70.

[5] Johanna Robertson, b. 1776, Mrs. Gladstone's sister.

[6] Robertson Gladstone, 1805–75, the diarist's 2nd brother, Liverpool merchant; see p. xli above.

[7] See 17 Aug. 25.

[8] William Rawson, 1788–1872, priest at Seaforth from 1815, Gladstone's first schoolmaster; see Morley, i. 14–15, quoting Add MS 44790, ff. 22–23.

[9] A poor Merseyside child, early object of Gladstone's charity.

[*Fri. 5*]

Rode Grey mare to Liverpool. Called on Mrs McCartney[1]—Mrs Conway[2]—Miss Benwell[3]—Mrs McAdam[4], Uncle Hugh[5]—Mrs Smith[6]—& Mr Grant[7] at Cottage in morning.

[*Sat. 6*]

Called on Uncle Murray & Thomas[8]: dined with former. Did some shopping jobs. Mr Finchett not expected to live for any length of time.[9]

[*Sun. 7*][10]

Heard Mr Leigh of Newcastle[11] in morning, Mr Rawson in evening. Wrote home—as I had done on several previous days.

[*Mon. 8*]

Called on Mr Staniforth[12] &c. Heard from home.

[*Tu. 9*]

Mr G. left Gloucester. Rode over & called on Mr Blundell of Ince.[13] Rode thence into town & dined with Mr Conway.[14] Called on Mr Rawson—he & his family flourish. Good old Aunt Mary died.[15]

[*Wed. 10*]

Mr G arrived per Bang Up, looking very well. In town.

[1] See 11 Aug. 25.
[2] d. 1830. See 9 Aug. 25.
[3] Elizabeth, a Liverpool schoolmistress.
[4] Wife of Robert McAdam, merchant, of Seacombe near Birkenhead.
[5] Hugh Gladstone, 1777–1835, sailmaker, one of the six brothers John *Gladstone brought successively from Leith to work with him in Liverpool.
[6] Possibly wife of Charles Smith, professor of music, who lived near the diarist's birthplace, in Rodney Street, Liverpool.
[7] George Grant, junior partner of John *Gladstone's and the diarist's godfather.
[8] Murray Gladstones, 1770–1841, merchant, and Thomas Gladstones, 1772–1844, ship's chandler, also brothers of John *Gladstone's working in Liverpool.
[9] James Finchett, d. 1825, of Liverpool, f. of Murray Gladstones' wife Susanna, who d. 1833.
[10] A few opening words deleted.
[11] Clement Leigh, 1786?–1853, rector of Newcastle-under-Lyme from 1803.
[12] Samuel Staniforth, 1769?–1851, banker; mayor of Liverpool 1812; f. of an Eton friend; called the ugliest man in Liverpool (J. Hughes, *Liverpool Banks* (1906), 150).
[13] Charles Robert Blundell, 1761–1837, son of the collector*, last male heir of an ancient Lancashire catholic family with its seat at Ince Blundell, 4 miles north of Seaforth.
[14] Joseph Conway, d. 1828, Liverpool clothier.
[15] Later note; see 14 and 18 Aug. 25.

[*Th. 11*]

Went into town with Mr G. & Rn: dined at Uncle Roberts.[1] Met Mr Moss[2]—Dr M'Cartney[3]—Mr Conway &c. Bought Pope's Works—Chess illustrated—Middletons Cicero.[4] Mr Finchett died.[5]

[*Fri. 12*]

In town again with Mr G. Mr Blundell came to see him in morning. He was much astonished at the size of 3 pine[apple]s of which our gardener is very proud. Mr G went off by Edinburgh mail. Mrs G's birthday.

[*Sat. 13*]

At home—Cousin Colin came.[6]

[*Sun. 14*]

Excellent sermon from Mr Rawson in morning, & good one from Mr Buddicom[7] in evening. Heard of worthy Aunt Mary's death.[8]

[*Mon. 15*]

Saw Kirkdale house of Correction[9] with Colin. Called on Mrs McAdam & Uncle Murray; heard of Mr Finchetts death on Thursday last.
Dined & slept at Mr Mosses of Otterspool.

[*Tu. 16*]

Called on Mrs Wilson[10]—Sandbach[11]—Rawson—at home; on Mrs Ewart[12]—Mr Jones (clergyman)[13] not at home.
Fraser[14] dined at Seaforth.

[1] Robert Gladstone, 1773–1835, merchant, another of John *Gladstone's brothers.
[2] John Moss, 1782–1858, of Otterspool, 4 miles up river from Liverpool; founder of North-Western Bank, and f. of an Eton friend.
[3] John Macartney, d. 1829; M. D. Edinburgh 1787, practising in Liverpool.
[4] Conyers *Middleton's once celebrated *Life of Cicero* (1741).
[5] Later note; see 15 Aug. 25.
[6] Colin C. F. Robertson, d. 1827, s. of Mrs. Gladstone's brother Colin, who d. 1836.
[7] R. P. Buddicom, 1780?–1846, F.R.S., then priest at Everton, the fashionable Liverpool suburb; principal of St. Bee's from 1840.
[8] See 18 Aug. 1825.
[9] The county gaol, a mile NE. of the city centre.
[10] Wife of John *Gladstone's partner in the merchanting house of Gladstone, Grant, and Wilson.
[11] Samuel Sandbach, a leading Liverpool merchant.
[12] Margaret Ewart, *née* Jaques, widow of the Liverpool merchant after whom the diarist was named and mother of William *Ewart, M.P.
[13] John *Jones, 1791–1889, presented to St. Andrew's, Liverpool by John *Gladstone in 1815, archdeacon of Liverpool 1855–87.
[14] The diarist's other godfather (Morley, i. 7).

[*Wed. 17*]

Rode grey into Liverpool.—started per Bang Up at 8. Rain at times as far as Stone.—made an excellent dinner there. Travelled very well: arrived in Brummagem soon after ½ past 8, thro the Potteries. Cd not get a room at Castle, or Albion; had tea & bed at the Hen & Chickens. Harvest, north of Birmingham general. Met Irishman going north.[1]

[*Th. 18*]

Left Birmingham about 7, per Mercury: breakfasted at Worcester, about which harvest is nearly all got in. Arrived Gloucester before two P.M.: found all as usual—& Aunt Mary among the rest.[2]

[*Sat. 20*]

Went to market for fruit. Mr & Mrs Barlow, with Eliza Robertson[3] called & breakfasted, on their way to Tenby.

[*Sun. 21*]

Went with Aunt Mary & Helen to Gloucester Cathedral. Mr Webb[4] preached.

[*Mon. 22*]

Mrs Larkins[5] & 3 children spent part of the day with us. Went to market again for fruit.
   Wrote to Robertson.

[*Tu. 23*]

Heard from Mr G. & Tom.[6] Marketed again. Drill serjeant. Read Ovid.

[*Wed. 24*]

Market—& drill. Read Ovid.

[*Th. 25*]

Market. Read Ovid. Heard from Mr G.

---

[1] See 2 Aug. 25.
[2] See 9, 14 Aug. 25. Mary Robertson, Mrs. Gladstone's sister, lived at Bath; she d. 1835.
[3] Daughter of Mrs. Gladstone's brother Divie; died young, 1826.
[4] John Webb, 1776?–1869?, minor canon of Gloucester.
[5] Mary Anne, d. 1866?, *née* Gladstone ?, wife of Thomas Larkins, London East India merchant; summering at Cheltenham.
[6] (Sir) Thomas Gladstone, 1804–89, the diarist's eldest brother, tory M.P. Queenborough 1830, Portarlington 1832–5, Leicester 1835–7; 2nd bart. 1851; see p. xli above and Magnus, refs.

[*Fri. 26*]

Market. Aunt Mary left us to return to Bath.[1]

[*Sat. 27*]

Helen & I made places for studying in school room. Heard from Mr G. Wrote to him.[2]

[*Sun. 28*]

Heard Mr Maitland[3] preach in morning—Mr Jones at St Johns in evening —last a good sermon. No rain! but cloudy. Wrote to Aunt E,[4] intending to go to Cheltenham on Monday.

[*Mon. 29*]

Mother ill—cd not go to Cheltenham—Anne ill with sore-throat—Rain— wrote to & heard from Aunt E. Read Ovid—&c—Day cold.

[*Tu. 30*]

Market—1st lesson on Piano Forte. like it much. Read Ovid. Mrs & Miss G. better. Day very hot.

[*Wed. 31*]

Market. Dear Father returned. Day extremely hot. Mrs G. ill—self not well, from the heat & relaxation. Mr G. looking well, but fatigued.

[*Th. 1 September*]

Read Ovid & Racine. 2nd lesson on Piano. Still went on with drilling, 3 lessons a week. Read some Racine—Mr Reid[5] dined with us. wish to finish Ovid Metamorphoses before going back to Eton. Day very hot.

[*Fri. 2*]

Read Ovid. Drilled. played Chess. went to Cheltenham with Mrs G. Saw Aunt E & Mrs Larkins & 3 youngest [Larkins] children. Day hot, but not oppressively. Returned to Gloucester before nine P.M.

---

[1] Add MS 44801, a commonplace book of religious and introspective jottings, bears this date inside its cover and against the verses copied on to ff. 4–5.

[2] Ibid., ff. 6–12 copied this day; ff. 16–18 a day later.

[3] Samuel Roffey *Maitland, 1792–1866, historian, then of Christ Church, Gloucester; librarian at Lambeth 1838–48.

[4] Mrs. Gladstone's sister Elizabeth Robertson, d. 1834.

[5] Alexander Reid, Liverpool merchant and agent.

[*Sat. 3*]

Read Ovid. Left Gloucester for Cheltenham about ½ past eight a.m.—breakfasted with Aunt E at Cheltenham. Bought at a book sale Goldsmith's Works,[1] & Breton's China;[2] Dined with Mrs Larkins; returned to Gloucester about six, & arrived soon after 7.

Day pleasantly warm. Much pleased with purchases.

[*Sun. 4*]

Christ Church in morning—no sermon—St Johns in Evg—a good sermon from a Mr Hawkins, on Ahab & Elijah.[3]

[*Mon. 5*]

To leave home tomorrow for a few days. Dear Anne much as usual.

[*Tu. 6*]

Left Gloucester for Ross &c. See Journal.[4]

[*Sat. 10*]

Returned from Ross &c. Dear Mother & Dear Anne fatigued. Day rainy.

[*Sun. 11*]

Heard a good sermon in morning from a Mr Baillie[5] at Christ Church; in evening from a Mr Hawkins at St Johns. first sermon on, The son of Man is come to seek & to save that which is lost;[6] 2nd (from Matthew Ch 6 v. 31.32.33) Therefore take no thought &c. Uncle Colin came over, & returned.

[*Mon. 12*]

Read Ovid. Mr Mrs & Miss Foy dined here. Mrs & Miss foreigners—not sure whether Mr is or no—good humoured & intelligent people.[7]

[*Tu. 13*]

Not well. Cousin Colin came over; returned before dinner. Dear Anne not feeling well.

---

[1] The works of Oliver *Goldsmith were collected by Bishop *Percy in 1801.

[2] J. B. J. Breton de la Martinière, *China: its costume, arts, manufacturers &c*, illustrated English tr., 4v. (1812 or 1824).

[3] William Hawkins, 1776?–1849, master of Cheltenham grammar school; on 1 Kings xxi. 17–24.

[4] Untraced; cp. 20 July 25 n.

[5] Francis Turner Bayly, b. 1774?, rector of St. John Baptist, Gloucester.

[6] Luke xix. 10.

[7] Perhaps Louis Foy, clerk administering Jesuit estates in Lower Canada, and his family.

[*Wed. 14*]

Dear Mother unwell. Self better. Finished 10th book of Ovid. Went to Cheltenham—bought Burns in Morocco. 2 letters from Dear John.[1] Letters from India. Saw Mary Anne.[2] Packed up & took place [on coach].

[*Th. 15*]

Left Gloucester by the Veteran at 7: a good deal of drizzling rain; arrived at Oxford about ¼ before one; dined; left it at ½ past 1, & got to Slough (by the Worcester Sovereign) soon after 6, safe & well, thank God. Veteran best conveyance of the two. Came down to Eton before 7. Found Mrs Ragenau[3] & Ingalton the shoe maker had died.

[*Fri. 16*]

Friday's business[4]—a good beginning to inure one. Wrote home, & began to get settled.[5] Began to sort my letters setting apart a great quantity for the flames.

[*Sat. 17*]

Busy—but, thank God, well—paid subscription to Library.
    Saw M. Berthomier.[6]

[*Sun. 18*]

Heard from, & wrote home. Fairish sermon from Mr Plumptre.[7]

[*Mon. 19*]

Settled & comfortable. Out in boat a little. Heard from home. Still went on sorting letters. Reading Johnson's Lives of Poets 2nd vol.[8] & picking up what was lost by going home in Homer & Horace.

[*Tu. 20*]

Boat—source of exercise & pleasure. Day fine. ½ holy day. Sorting letters— doing verses—reading &c.

---

[1] John Neilson Gladstone, 1807–63, his brother, then serving abroad; capt., R.N., 1832; M.P. Walsall 1841, Ipswich 1842–7, Devizes 1852–7, 1859–63; see p. xli above.
[2] Mrs. Larkins.
[3] Wife of the duke of *Wellington's dame, Raguenau.
[4] i.e. worked for and in Friday's classes.
[5] Sketch of his dame's in Reid, *G*, 65.
[6] His French tutor; see W. L. C[ollins], *Etoniana* (1865), 230–1.
[7] John Francis Plumptre, 1781–1864, fellow from 1822, bigoted protestant. 'His sermons in Eton chapel were a perpetual source of amusement to his hearers' (Venn, *Alumni Cantabrigienses, II.* v. 141).
[8] Samuel *Johnson, *The lives of the most eminent English Poets, with critical observations of their works* (1779, &c).

[*Wed. 21*]

Went to Berthomier. Whole holiday. Okes asked for a copy of my Greek verses on the Heathen Gods.[1] Took one to his house—he was not at home. Wrote home.

[*Th. 22*]

Heard from home. Boat—sorting letters—getting up Homer &c employed me.

[*Fri. 23*]

Did a bad copy of Lyrics. Heard from home. Dear Dear Anne had been in bed some time but was better. Boat—French lesson—Friday's business—making notes—writing home & reading Johnson's Lives of the Poets.

[*Sat. 24*]

Making Summary of Johnson[2]—French exercise—notes on Juvenal & Theocritus. Saturday's school business—private ditto[3]—& going up to Surly[4] in my boat occupied me this day.

[*Sun. 25*]

Wrote to T. G. & to Dear Anne; middling sermon from Plumptre—employed at theme[5]—writing—saying Juvenal—reading Bible—Sumner[6]—Young[7]—scribbled a little. Read a little Greek Testament.

[*Mon. 26*]

Mondays business—2 newspapers—boat—French lesson—summary of Johnson—writing over Theme[8]—& doing somewhat to my long neglected card racks[9] employed me.

---

[1] Richard *Okes, 1797–1888, assistant master; later provost of King's College, Cambridge. The verses, written in May 1825, are in Add MS 44717, f. 116.

[2] In Add MS 44802A, ff. 2–12.

[3] 'private business' meant preparing work in a class with a tutor; in Gladstone's case, with Henry Hartopp Knapp, 1782–1846, assistant master 1808–30, rector of Ampthill from 1820, lower master 1830, absconded abroad 1834; for whom see W.L.C., *Etoniana*, appx. D.

[4] Surly Hall, an inn on the right bank of the Thames some 2½ miles above Eton. Later photograph in T. K. Selwyn, *Eton 1829–30* (1903) at 200.

[5] Weekly Latin essay. Most of his themes for 1825–7 are in Add MSS 44717–8; list of subjects at 44717, ff. 263–4.

[6] Probably J. B. *Sumner, evangelical abp. of Canterbury from 1848, *Evidence of Christianity derived from its Nature and Reception* (1824).

[7] Edward *Young, *Night Thoughts* (1742–5).

[8] 'writing over' means making a fair corrected copy.

[9] A piece of schoolboy carpentry; see October 1825, *passim*.

[*Tu. 27*]

Wednesday's business—Translation—Summary of Johnson's Lives of Poets—Boat—French exercise—notes—setting papers to rights, &c. occupied me—but today, as every day, I have wasted much of the time committed to me. May God enable me to make a better use for the future.

[*Wed. 28*]

Thursdays business—Boat—Heard from home—apprized of Roses being here.[1] found him out & had some talk with him. French lesson—a few notes —summary—& a little reading in Johnson also.

[*Th. 29*]

Heard from Mr & T. G. Wrote to Miss G & Aunt E. Gave a mess to Moss[2]— Christie[3]—Skinner[4]—the last did not come. Surly Hall in boat. Newspaper —writing—Reading 3rd vol Johnson—doing Lyrics—writing over verses employed me.

[*Fri. 30*]

Not well. Friday's business—French lesson—(finished Malade Imaginaire,)[5] —Summary & reading Johnson—also going on with card-racks.

[*Sat. 1 October*]

Better, thank God. Saturdays business—French exercise—Private business (Juvenal) notes to Scriptores[6], Horace, Juvenal, & Theocritus—reading Johnson—& doing a little to card-racks employed me— — —3 quarters of this year gone—how little of what is good done by me hitherto! with how much opportunity.

[*Sun. 2*]

Wrote to Dear Mother & Dear John a sheet & a half. Sermon from Plumptre on the Communion—Sacrament being administered. Saying Juvenal— writing—scribbling—Theme—reading—More[7]—Young—Bible—Greek Testament—Sumner—employed me.

[1] Probably John Nugent Rose, 1812–67, of Holme, Inverness, and the Bombay Civil Service.

[2] (Sir) Thomas (Edwards–)Moss of Otterspool, 1811–90, banker, s. of John Moss; captain of the boats 1828; cr. bart. 1868.

[3] George Henry Christie, 1811–87, later head of the auctioneers' in King Street, St. James's.

[4] Allan Maclean Skinner, 1810?–85, Eton and Balliol; county court judge 1859–72.

[5] Molière.

[6] *Scriptores Graeci*, a weak anthology of Greek prose, and *Scriptores Romani*, a collection of Latin prose extracts bearing on conduct in public life, were both current Eton textbooks.

[7] Hannah *More, *Sacred Dramas* (1782, &c).

[*Mon. 3*]

Mondays business—writing over Theme. French lesson (Began Le Bourgeois Gentilhomme)[1] Life of Gesner.[2] boat. few notes. Reading Johnson & [making] Summary employed me. Extemp[ore].[3]

[*Tu. 4*]

Holiday. French exercise—Surly Hall in boat—Beginning Herodotus—reading Crevier[4]—Summary of Johnson—Verses—& doing somewhat to Card Racks, &c—employed me, with a *good deal* of time wasted.

[*Wed. 5*]

Heard from home—Dear Anne had been in the house some days. May God give her relief. Letter from Dear John—not to come home till February or March; by no means glad to hear it, but "All is for the best".[5] Wrote home —which with French lesson—writing over verses—reading Crevier—doing some thing to card-racks—summary—& boat employed me. Wednesdays business &c.

[*Th. 6*]

Thursdays business—Lyrics & writing over ditto—French exercise—reading Crevier—Boat—finishing Card-racks—private business in Tacitus—reading ditto—some notes &c employed me Finished 4th v of Crevier.

[*Fri. 7*]

Fridays business—reading Crevier (5th vol) French lesson—summary (finished today) & notes to various books employed me. Heard from home —Dear Anne better—thank God for these and all his mercies. [Was] Asked to go into the Society for 2nd time.[6]

[*Sat. 8*]

Saturday's business—reading Crevier—Notes—Private business (Juvenal) French exercise—a little walking &c. Called up.[7] Attended meeting of

---

[1] Molière.

[2] A life of Salomon Gessner, the Zürich poet and painter, in his *Works* (tr. 1805?).

[3] i.e. wrote an extempore epigram on a set subject. Several of these are in Add MS 44718, ff. 98–99.

[4] J. B. L. Crevier, *History of the Roman Emperors from Augustus to Constantine*, tr. John Mill, 10v. (1814).

[5] But see 25 Oct. 25.

[6] For the Eton Society (*Literati*, later *Pop*) at this time, see C. M. Gaskell, *An Eton Boy* (1939), 77–81; lists of members ibid. 84 and in Add MS 44717, f. 105; 44718, f. 85. Its officers kindly made its minute books available to the editor.

[7] To construe in class.

Society—Praed,[1] Hervey,[2] & Mundy[3] spoke; two former very well. Much pleased on the whole.[4]

[Sun. 9]

Plumptre preached, on lying. Saying Juvenal—writing home (a long letter to Dear Anne) reading Bible—a little in the Greek Testament—a sermon of Sumner—Theme—Scribbling—& Mrs More's Sacred Dramas.

[Mon.] 10

Heard from home & from Dear Anne who was better—thank God. Wrote to my Dear Mother.—Mondays business—with extempore—boat—French lesson—reading Crevier (got into 6th vol) 2 newspapers—write home—&c. Ordered another book-case. Did also a few notes.

[Tu. 11]

Weather fine. Surly Hall in boat. Holyday. Reading Crevier—French exercise—something to card-racks—moving books &c. Received Hooke[5] a few days ago, today got down Moliere & 10 little books from Dear John.

[Wed. 12]

Wednesday's business.—Translation—French lesson—some notes—reading Crevier (got into 7th vol.) Boat—Walk—doing something to card racks & beginning verses (Greek) employed me.

[Th. 13]

Heard from & wrote to Dear Anne. Sculled up to Surly, sicut meus est mos.[6] Day beautiful. Thursdays business—writing home—doing and writing over Greek verses—some notes—French exercise & reading Crevier. Dear Tom, please God, on his way home. Private business.

[Fri. 14]

Fridays business—French lesson—good number of notes—reading Crevier —(finished Adrians reign—now leave Crevier for Gibbon) going on from beginning of 8th vol with Hooke (Epitome)[7]—doing somewhat to card-

---

[1] Winthrop Mackworth *Praed, 1802–39, poet, was at Eton as private tutor to Lord E. Bruce (see 1 Nov. 27 n); later tory M.P. 1830–2, 1834–9.
[2] For (Lord) Arthur Charles *Hervey, 1808–94, bp. of Bath and Wells from 1869, see Add MS 44207.
[3] Charles John Henry Mundy (–Massingberd), 1808–82, Lincolnshire magnate.
[4] The society voted unanimously for colonial emancipation.
[5] Nathaniel *Hooke, Roman History (1738–71).
[6] 'as is my custom'.
[7] Add MSS 44800, ff. 18–25, and 44717, ff. 73–86 (misbound as epitome of Gibbon).

racks, & boat employed me. To be proposed in "Society" tomorrow; person who stole Dupuis' £62 a few days ago found out; name not yet divulged.[1]

[*Sat. 15*]

Saturdays business; notes; reading newspaper—Darwin[2]—; French exercise—Private business (Juvenal)—working at card racks—walk—&c employed me, with doing a little to Epitome of Hooke. Proposed & received in the Society; fear they will have a bad bargain in me. attended debate again —Doyle[3] spoke. Lovell the criminal.

[*Sat. 16*]

Plumptre preached; having moved up in church,[4] could hardly hear, much less understand him. Letter from dear Bob,[5] who is at Gloucester. newspaper also. wrote home to Dear Anne; principally about Lovell;[6] finished ode on Xmas—read Bible—Mrs More—Sumner—Young—Hemans Heliodorus in temple[7] & did theme.

[*Mon. 17*]

Went to booksale—bid for Bibliotheca Gloucesteriensis—lost it. walk.— boat for a little while. Epitome of Hooke—finishing cardracks—writing over Theme—French lesson &c. Paid Ingaltons bill.[8] Ordered things for Mess—Asked Littledale[9] on Saturday—to-day asked Hervey, Staniforth,[10] & Buckeridge.[11]

[*Tu. 18*]

Gave a mess to Staniforth—Buckeridge—Hervey—Littledale—Canning[12] asked—did not come; heard from Dear Anne & Bob—letter inclosed from

---

[1] George John Dupuis, 1795–1884, assistant master 1819–34, fellow from 1838. For the incident see C. M. Gaskell, *An Eton Boy*, 64–65, and next two entries.

[2] Erasmus *Darwin, 1731–1802, gf. of Charles *Darwin and Francis *Galton, philosophical poet; see Morley, i. 29.

[3] For (Sir) Francis Hastings Charles *Doyle, 1810–88, 2nd bart. 1839, patriotic poet, *Gladstone's best man and latterly his opponent, see Add MSS 44150 and 44791, f. 21. His (maiden) speech supported the motion that Regulus was a greater patriot than Camillus; it was carried by 3 to 2.

[4] Eton chapel was still the parish church of Eton village.

[5] His brother Robertson.

[6] Lovell was not heard of again.

[7] Felicia *Hemans' poem on 2 Macc. iii. 21–9 in her *Tales, and Historic Scenes* (1819), 197–206.

[8] T. Ingalton, Eton bookseller and publisher.

[9] Henry Anthony Littledale, 1810?–59, of Liverpool; at Brasenose; barrister.

[10] Thomas Staniforth, 1807?–87, s. of Samuel; captain of boats 1826; stroked Oxford in first race against Cambridge, 1829; rector of Bolton by Bolland, Yorkshire, 1831.

[11] Arthur Nugent Buckeridge, b. 1809?, of Binfield, Berkshire, later rector of Kennerleigh, Devon.

[12] Charles John *Canning, 1812–62; 3rd s. of George*; M.P. Warwick 1836; 2nd viscount 1837; foreign under-secretary 1841–6; postmaster-general 1853–5; viceroy of India 1856; earl 1859. See Add MS 44117.

Mr Jones,[1] who has lost his father. Read Newspaper also. Finished Book of Epitome of Hooke[2]—did French exercise—did divisions—began verses. After four[3] had some game at Littledales room— &c—T.G. arrived from France at Gloucester.

[Wed. 19]

Wednesdays business. French lesson—finishing verses—Epitome of Hooke (began 9th vol) Translation—few notes—& boat.

[Th. 20]

Play at 4—School business—writing to Robertson—writing over verses— doing Lyrics—French exercise—boat for a short time—walking a little— Epitome of Hooke—& few notes employed me.

[Fri. 21]

Fridays business. writing over Lyrics. walking a little. Notes—Epitome of Hooke (got into 10th vol)—reading "Deaf & Dumb"[4] occupied me.

[Sat. 22]

Saturdays business—Epitome of Hooke—French lesson & exercise—Boat —private business—notes— —Took seat as a member of the Society: Buckeridge, Doyle, & Hervey spoke—comparison between Richard 3 & Cromwell, after debate,[5] 5 bottles of wine & various eatables dispatched, till lock up time (half past 5,) read Hypocrite.[6]

[Sun. 23]

Pope[7] preached—on temptations to which a Xtian is exposed; wrote to dear Mother—& began Letter to Dear John—read Sumner—Blair[8] (for theme) Young Milman[9] & More. Read Bible—did Theme.

[Mon. 24]

Windsor fair began. Mondays business—boat—French lesson—Notes— Epitome [of] Hooke—writing over Theme—reading part of Bold Stroke for a Wife.[10]

---

[1] See 16 Aug. 25 n.

[2] i.e. finished the second of the small school notebooks in which he wrote the summary.

[3] i.e. from 3 p.m. to lock-up time at 5: 'the names have ceased to bear any numerical values' (A. C. *Benson, Fasti Etonenses (1899), 506).

[4] Deaf and Dumb; or, The Orphan, historical drama, tr. by B. *Thompson (1801) from the German of Kotzebue, who tr. in turn J. N. Bouilly, L'Abbé de l'Epée.

[5] *Cromwell was held more odious than *Richard III.

[6] 'A.D.', The accomplished hypocrite . . . a moral tale, 2v. (1822); read perhaps to help with verses on hypocrisy, Medea, and Jason, in Add MS 44717, f. 136.

[7] Perhaps William Law Pope, d. 1879, long fellow of Worcester College, Oxford.

[8] Hugh *Blair, Sermons, 5v. (1777–1801).

[9] H. H. *Milman, later Gibbon's editor and dean of St. Paul's, Belshazzar: a dramatic poem (1822).

[10] Comedy (1718) by Susannah *Centlivre, wife of Queen *Anne's cook.

[*Tu. 25*]

Heard from Dear John off our coast, to my great surprise & pleasure, safe & well, thank God. Heard from Dear Mother & Anne. Wrote to Anne & John. Wednesdays business (save play at 4)—doing verses—French exercise—notes—Epitome [of] Hooke (begun 11th vol)—& finishing Bold Stroke for a Wife—& little walking.

[*Wed. 26*]

Fridays business—notes—writing over Verses—French lesson—Epitome [of] Hooke—reading Life of Gibbon[1] & beginning Lyrics—Greek Anacreontics occupied me; with a walk; Day according to the prediction,[2] fair & frosty.

[*Th. 27*]

½ holiday. French exercise—Epitome [of] Hooke—writing home—(heard from home) boat—beginning Gibbon—writing speech[3]—finishing Lyrics &c. Examined journals &c of Society after 4; find I had a black ball—have a good idea of him. Sorry for it; wd not have gone in but was promised there should be none.

[*Fri. 28*]

holiday—after 12[4] read articles in Quarterly Review &c—after 4, another Society meeting for despatch of punch &c; cannot attend any more such in great measure disgusted. Wrote over Lyrics & speech. had French lesson—finished Epitome [of] Hooke—not sorry for it—& read Gibbon. Heard from Dear John—about to be paid off at Spithead.

[*Sat. 29*]

Saturdays business—French exercise—Notes—reading Gibbon—private business—(Juvenal)—spent [time] after 12 at Society room; after 4 made my 1st or maiden Speech at the Society on education of poor; *funced* less than I thought I should—by much.[5]

[*Sun. 30*]

Wright preached in morning—on Law & Gospel &c.[6] Heard from Dear John—wrote to him, & also to Dear Helen Jane. Did theme—read Belshazzar—Mrs More—Young—Sumner—& Bible in Old & New Testaments

---

[1] Probably the short life prefixed to the 1821 ed. of Edward *Gibbon, *History of the Decline and Fall of the Roman Empire*, 12v.
[2] In the almanac he wrote in: see p. xxii above.
[3] See 29 Oct. 25.
[4] i.e. noon to 2 p.m. (*Benson, *Fasti Etonenses*, 506).
[5] See Morley, i. 35–36. Notes for speech in Add MS 44649, ff. 1–2. No minutes survive.
[6] James Camper Wright, 1774–1838, fellow 1821, rector of Walkern, Hertfordshire, from 1817; probably on Matt. v. 17.

as usual. Dear John intended (by his letter) to come & see me—he will not be unwelcome.

[*Mon. 31*]

Boat—French lesson—reading Gibbon—beginning Chronology of Poets &c[1]—½ holiday. At Society room after 4, reading papers &c—long talk about politics &c at night with Handley minor.[2]

[*Tu. 1 November*]

Got Lpool Mercury—& Berwick paper containing Mr G's address to Burgesses &c.[3] Saw Sir J. McGrigor.[4] Reading Gibbon (finished 1 vol)—wrote over Theme—French exercise—Translation & reading Papal Debates[5] &c & Society room & jogging about occupied me.

[*Wed. 2*]

Heard from Mr G at Berwick & from Sister. Trying sortes Horatianae fell on bibulum liquidi Falerni &c & Aufidius forti &c; bad omens!![6] French lesson a little Epitome [of] Gibbon—wednesdays business—reading papers &c at Society room—walking a little—& beginning to read, or rather look over Martial for purpose of extracting points for illustration of Horace, Virgil & others.

[*Th. 3*]

Day tremendously windy; drops of rain in afternoon. So much for almanack prophecies.[7] Play at 4. did verses—read Gibbon, Martial, taking notes into Horace &c—private business (Tacitus)—jogging about & at Society room —Detect many English epigrammatists sources in Martial—many of whose are very poor.

[*Fri. 4*]

Heard from Mr G at Berwick—where his canvass had been very successful. Fridays business—said [lesson] at 5. Read a newspaper received yesterday —had French lesson—read Gibbon—did a good quantity of notes—& had

---

[1] Untraced notes of his own.

[2] Philip Handley, 1809–84, later a partner in Handley, Peacock & Co., Newark bankers.

[3] *Berwick Advertiser*, 29 October 1825, 1. John *Gladstone was parliamentary candidate for Berwick; see June 1826 *passim*.

[4] Sir James *McGrigor, 1771–1858, director-general, army medical department, 1815–1851; cr. kt. 1816, bart. 1830.

[5] Probably the parliamentary debates of the previous summer on a bill for Roman catholic emancipation, passed by the commons but defeated in the lords.

[6] Horace: 'gulping the flowing Falernian', *Epistolae, I.* xiv. 34; 'bold Aufidius mixed honey with strong Falernian', *Satirae, II.* iv. 24.

[7] This day headed in print: '*Weather*—Fair and Frosty, if Wind at N. or NE.; Rain or Snow, if S. or SW'.

a good deal of walking. Inquired at Slough about coaches to Oxford on account of Dear John whom I expect in about a week.

[*Sat. 5*]

Whole holyday. Private business (Juvenal) & notes thereon.[1] Walk after 12; Society after 4; question—army or navy more useful to a country.[2] Had a long letter from dear Anne; read some Ovid—Gibbon (finished 2 vol containing the obnoxious chapters[3]) & Mr Canning's letter (official) to M. Zea vindicating conduct of Great Britain with regard to recognition of South American States.[4]

[*Sun. 6*]

Heard from Dear John; does not take London in his way, not wishing to detain Bob who had joined him at Portsmouth. Wrote to Mr G. (to be at Gloucester to day)—Miss G. & John. Wright preached, on good seed;[5] read Young—More—Milman—Sumner; had walk after 12; in Bible got into 2 Samuel.

[*Mon. 7*]

Whole holiday.—for the doctor's recovery. Mem. He is *more* savage from his illness.[6] French exercise & French lesson—walk after 12—reading Juvenal &c—beginning Medecin malgré lui[7]—& epitome [of] Gibbon (1st vol)[8] employed me. Heard from dear Father & Dear Tom at Oxford.[9]

[*Tu. 8*]

Mondays business: reading Moliere. French exercise—finishing Epitome [of] Gibbon Vol i, beginning Greek verses with few notes & some reading at Society room employed me. Handley minor ill with fulness of blood & impeded circulation—vessels of heart injured & only probability of his recovery.

[1] Notes in Add MS 44717, f. 138.
[2] He voted for the navy, in a majority of 3 to 2.
[3] Chapters xv and xvi, ironical account of early growth of Christianity.
[4] George *Canning, 1770–1827, then foreign secretary; prime minister April–August 1827. For his influence on *Gladstone see *H* clxxxiii. 129.
*Canning's note of 25 March 1825, sent to Zea the Spanish minister for foreign affairs through de los Rios the ambassador in London, expounded the British case for recognizing the revolted Spanish American colonies. Text in *BFSP* xii. 909–15 or *Annual Register* for 1825, 51*–56*; *Gladstone had been reading the twice translated version in *The Star*, 2, or *The Times*, 3 November. See H. W. V. *Temperley and L. M. Penson, *Century of diplomatic blue books* (1938), 565.
[5] Luke viii. 8 or I Pet. i. 23.
[6] For Dr. John *Keate, 1773-1852, the celebrated flogging headmaster, see Morley, i. 32, 44–46; and 20–27 Feb. 27 below.
[7] Molière.
[8] Add MS 44717, ff. 64–72.
[9] Thomas *Gladstone was up at Christ Church.

[*Wed. 9*]

Wednesday's business—French lesson—Greek verses—*preparing* by reading in Prosody of Morell[1] for doing lyrics; read little at Society room; did some notes & Epitome [of] Gibbon which with little reading Moliere (Medecin malgre lui) & jogging about employed me. Tutor told me to [attempt] Greek anapaestics—which I am not at all up to—confused by the extreme liberty of the metre.

[*Th. 10*]

Weather very rainy & windy—so much for almanacks; had it been changeable it wd have changed for the better.[2] Holiday. Heard from Dear Anne & Bob; Dear John had arrived at Gloucester. Received & read two newspapers. Wrote over verses—read at Society room—did lyrics—French exercise—read Moliere & [wrote] little Epitome [of] Gibbon—Learned that poor Handley minor's illness was such that he would probably not live more than 2 or 3 years, and might take him off at any time.

[*Fri. 11*]

Fridays business. got paper. French lesson—notes—Medecin Malgre Lui—writing to Dear Tom & a note to Mr G.—& Epitome [of] Gibbon—with some jogging about, employed me. Mem—reading Bible a regular thing which however I do not put down every day.

[*Sat. 12*]

Saturday's business—Epitome [of] Gibbon (finished 2nd vol) began 3d reading—notes—private business—Tacitus in morning—Juvenal in evening—French exercise & finished Moliere Medecin Malgre Lui. Question at Society—chivalry beneficial—voted for it.[3] Heard that Mr G. had been reported by a paper to have been unsuccessful at Berwick.[4]

[*Sun. 13*]

Good sermon from Wright—on swearing.[5] Disgusting to see the theatrical airs of Hobbes & another singer while singing anthem—laughing & talking after it. Wrote to Dear Anne—read Sumner—Blair—Bible—Testament: Esther (Racine) lot of K. White[6]—did theme & had long conversation with Handley minor.

---

[1] T. *Morell, *Lexicon Graeco-Prosodaicum*, ed. E. *Maltby, 2v. (1824).
[2] Day headed in print '*Weather*—Changeable'.
[3] In a majority of 6 to 1.
[4] Premature report: see 25 June 26 and 20 Mar. 27.
[5] Matt. v. 34?
[6] Robert *Southey, ed., *Remains* of Henry Kirke *White the evangelical poetaster (1807).

[*Mon. 14*]

Mondays business—notes—French lesson—reading Gibbon & beginning Epitome of 3d vol—walking, reading at Society room, & extempore employed me. Heard from Dear John at Gloucester. writes that he thinks of leaving Gloucester on Saturday & paying Dear Tom & me a visit. Tomorrow dear Bob's birthday.

[*Tu. 15*]

Dear Bob's birthday—God bless him. Holiday—walking little—reading at Society room—writing over Theme. French exercise—notes—reading Gibbon—also read an Elegy in Buchanans beautiful Latin Poetry.[1] Drank Robertson's health.

[*Wed. 16*]

Wednesday's business. wrote over verses for Tutor & for School, did Lyrics & wrote over for Tutor; had French lesson—did notes—read Gibbon—did a little of Epitome of 3d volume—which occupied me, with some walking & reading at Society room.

[*Th. 17*]

Weather cold—very little rain—some sun—little or no wind.[2] Thursdays business (½ holiday)—writing speech for Saturday—reading at Society room—French exercise—writing over Lyrics—reading Gibbon, & Epitome of it—with doing some notes & some walking employed me.

[*Fri. 18*]

Bad headache & blister on tongue. thought of staying out [of school], but did not—Fridays business: reading Gibbon & [making] Epitome finished 3 vol both ways—reading at Society room—learnt speech—had French lesson—hope to do something more tomorrow.

[*Sat. 19*]

Heard from Dear Anne & Dear John—fomer giving a bad account of my Dear Mother's headaches, as a species of ticque douloreux[3]—May God support her. Dear John to be here, please God, next week. Bad headache again all day—consists of a pain in forehead principally felt in turning the head—yet tongue pretty clean. Read a little of Gibbons 4 vol & had Saturdays business, with 2 [periods of] private business—also made an exertion & spoke in the Society on the liberty of the ancient comedy—spoke for its utility—against its being justifiable.[4]

[1] George *Buchanan, 1506–82, Scottish poet and historian.
[2] Printed heading for day includes '*Weather*—Cold Rain or Snow, with high Winds'.
[3] *Tic douloureux*, severe facial neuralgia.
[4] In a majority of 5 to 2.

[*Sun. 20*]

Headache again—with blister on tongue, & uncomfortable feeling in teeth; staid out—took strong dose of Epsom-salts at night. Did theme; wrote to Dear John & Dear Anne; read Prayers &c—Bible—Sumner, 2 sermons—& some of K[irke] White's Hymns & letters on religious subjects.

[*Mon. 21*]

Mondays business. Wrote over Theme—wrote to Dear Anne—read papers at Society Room; The prize Odes (Cambridge)[1]; some of Gibbon; head much better thank God; hope to be right tomorrow. Heard from Dear Anne & from Dear Tom.

[*Tu. 22*]

Whole holiday—heard from Dear Mother Father & Anne—wrote to Mother. Messed with Staniforth. Hervey—Canning—Boscawen[2] there. French exercise & French lesson—read papers at Society room, & read Gibbon. All right again today thank God. Dear John, to my great joy, arrived about seven, staid till past ten, & went up Windsor to sleep at the Castle Inn.

[*Wed. 23*]

Leave to [go out with] Dear John, after eight o'clock school—Breakfasted, dined, & had tea with him, at Castle Inn, Windsor. Wrote to Aunt E a very singular epistle. Accompanied dear John to see Windsor & Eton Chapel—College & our Library—Round tower[3]—bridge—went out on the river with him—& into the Little Park. Parted with him on his way to Slough, between 10 & 11 at night.

[*Th. 24*]

Whole holiday. Did & wrote over verses. Took place per Gloucester mail for the night of Monday the 5th of December, at Slough; read papers &c at Society room: did some notes—French exercise—read Gibbon & began Epitome of 4th volume. Day damp—occasionally rainy. Dear John went to London, from Slough early in the morning.

[*Fri. 25*]

Day fine. Fridays business. Had French lesson; read papers; did notes; finished 4 vol of Gibbon in Epitome & reading; began 5 vol—which with little walking employed me. Have not felt headache lately, thank God; a cold is luxury after it.

[1] If this was *Cambridge Prize Poems*, 3rd ed. (1820), it gave *Gladstone his first reading of *Macaulay, whose 'Pompeii' fills pages 209–97; but it may have been *Musae Cantabrigienses* (1810), a collection of Latin and Greek poems and epigrams by various recent authors including *Keate and Plumptre.

[2] George Henry, Lord Boscawen, 1811–52, 2nd earl of Falmouth from 1841.

[3] The oldest part of Windsor Castle, built by *William I.

[*Sat. 26*]

Saturday's business—Private business twice—Tacitus morning, Juvenal evening—Read newspapers at Society room[1]—did notes—& read Gibbon, fifth vol. The style of his history beautiful, but much sneering at Christian religion, partially disguised.

[*Sun. 27*]

Fairish sermon from Bethell.[2] Beautiful anthem. Wrote home to Dear Anne—Father—Tom—expected to hear, but did not. Said private business —read Bible—one of Sumner's sermons—& Kirke White—revised xxx[3] which employed me, with walking after 12 & after 4. Conduct of the singers in Ch disgusting from levity.

[*Mon. 28*]

Mondays business. Heard from Dear Anne & Dear Helen—Wrote to Smith[4] & prepared parcel to send to him; wrote also to Dear Anne & Dear Helen— did French exercise & had French lesson—wrote over theme—did some notes or rather quotations—and read Gibbon and papers at Society room.

[*Tu. 29*]

A time killing headache, with violent cold. Staid out. half holiday. Sorted some letters, & read a little of Gibbon in the evening, head being better. On getting up in the morning took a strong dose of salts, which hasnt answered as yet.

[*Wed. 30*]

Much better thank God—headache almost entirely gone. Staid out however on account of cold. Whole holiday. Day fine. Did Epitome of 5 volume of Gibbon & finished reading it. Began sixth volume. Did verses—attended the *play* upstairs—in which Jabat,[5] Mansfield,[6] &c are the performers— attended this also last night—Representation did not occupy many minutes.

[*Th. 1 December*]

Day very cold. Fridays business—wrote over verses—read Gibbon (6th volume)—read papers & some things in Etonian[7] at Society room—which

---

[1] At a society debate, he voted in a majority of 5 to 1 that *James II's family had been justified in their attempts to regain the crown.
[2] George Bethell, 1779–1857, later vice-provost.
[3] His commonplace book; now vanished.
[4] Liverpool friend; perhaps s. of Charles Smith (see 5 Aug. 25 n).
[5] Rafael Constantine Domingo Jabat, later in the Portuguese diplomatic service.
[6] John Smith Mansfield, 1813–1905, once Gladstone's fag; Marylebone police magistrate 1860–88.
[7] A school newspaper, comprising three volumes of *belles lettres* edited (1824) by W. M. *Praed.

with some talking about &c employed me. Heard from the servants of some unjust acts of my Dame[1]—refusing character without reason &c.

[*Fri. 2*]

Hope to write the bottom of this page at Gloucester. Slight headache—went off soon—Whole holiday—Collegers & Oppidans prevented from playing by rains having fallen & consequent bad state of the ground. Did French exercise & had French lesson—notes to Horace &c—read paper at Society room—went to Slough—found place was secured for Monday, & read Gibbon.

[*Sat. 3*]

Saturday's business. Keate & Yonge[2] ill—Knapp in [charge of] Upper Division. Wrote French letter to sister—and read Gibbon, & papers at Society room—Question for Debate—Was Elizabeth justifiable in aiding United Provinces in rebellion against Spain? Voted that she was so.[3] Fifth form supper—given by Jabat, Mansfield & Selwyn mi[4]—very good—Selwyn ma,[5] Carruthers[6] & I there. Mem. sine fag.

[*Sun. 4*]

Sermon from Vice Provost—Prepare ye the way of the Lord—very very little of it audible.[7] Wrote to Father & Tom—read Bible—Kirke White—Sumner &c. Learnt K.W.'s Star of Bethlehem & wrote it in book[8]—day cold but fair.

[*Mon. 5*]

Mondays business—Read Gibbon—papers at Society room &c. Finished 6 vol of Gibbon. Packed up—& left Eton about $\frac{1}{4}$ before ten—got into the Gloucester Mail at Slough at $\frac{1}{4}$ before eleven. Bonsor[9] went off, having taken leave yesterday.

[*Tu. 6*]

Got to Glos'ter about nine in the morning—Tom & Dear John waiting at the Bell for me—Dear Mother—Anne & the rest as usual. Weather dull. Aunts dined at Sherborne House.

---

[1] Mrs. Stansmore; see Bassett, 3–4, and Morley, i. 26–27.
[2] Charles Yonge, 1781–1830, assistant master 1803, lower master 1829.
[3] Carried unanimously.
[4] Thomas Kynaston Selwyn, Newcastle scholar 1830, d. 1834.
[5] George Augustus *Selwyn, 1809–78, bp. of New Zealand 1841–68 and then of Lichfield, in whose memory Selwyn College, Cambridge was founded; see Add MSS 44299.
[6] John Robert Carruthers, later of the Bengal Civil Service.
[7] William Henry Roberts, 1795–1843, rector of Clewer from 1827; on Isa. xi. 3.
[8] Kirke *White, *Remains*, ii. 124–5.
[9] Joseph Bonsor of Polesden, Surrey, later a partner in Combe, Delafield the brewers.

[*Wed. 7*]

Went in carriage with Dear Anne, & in gig with Dear John—had Ferry again, & resumed my drilling. Day dull—with John & H. had tea at Aunts lodgings in Beaufort Buildings. Ordered some clothes.

[*Th. 8*]

Day dull again—John out shooting over the other side of the river. Bought gloves &c. Began Boswells Life of Johnson—work appears very able—author abominably vain—Aunt J unwell.

[*Fri. 9*]

Reading Boswell—rise abominably late in the morning—Dear Tom arrived about nine from Oxford looking well, having come by the Mercury coach set up instead of the Veteran—Drilled—went over to Cheltenham with John—saw the Barlows and Larkinses.

[*Sat. 10*]

Reading Boswell—Began Holiday Task from Job—Walked &c as usual—Resolutions to amend in getting up.

[*Sun. 11*]

Mr G's birthday—many happy returns to him. Heard Maitland at Christ Church on repentance—Long walk with J. & HG [*sc.* Helen]. Read Bible—did some of my Task—&c.

[*Mon. 12*]

Walk twice—Bought drawers, gloves &c. Day fine—fog in morning—read Boswell—still lagging in the first vol. New *regulations* about getting up—rose at eight—Tom out shooting—Dear Anne unwell—better in evening.

[*Tu. 13*]

Reading Boswell—finished vol 1—& begun 2nd—walk &c—Regulations about getting up broken—Drilled—instead of yesterday—Dear Anne better.

[*Wed. 14*]

Reading Boswell—2nd vol—Great need of new getting up regulations—Uncle David[1] came per Mail—staid—and slept in reception[2] (the back bedroom upstairs), I shifting.

---

[1] David Gladstone, 1783–1863, John *Gladstone's youngest brother; partner in Gladstone & Ogilvy, Liverpool merchants; retired to Sidmouth.
[2] The word 'receptn' written over the words 'my room'.

[*Th. 15*]

Uncle D went per Birmingham coach between 12 & 1. Day fine, T. & J. shooting, killed nothing—saw only one bird. Reading Boswell—2 vol. Up somewhat earlier in morning. Walked good deal & out in carriage. Father & T dined with Bishop.

[*Fri. 16*]

Reading Boswell—Drilled—T. & J. went to Cheltenham—Cousin Divie[1] came over—dined and returned. (Shopped a good deal in Gloucester— Alarm about banks stopping).[2] T & J returned—revised and added to xxx.

[*Sat. 17*]

Read Boswell. finished 2 vol. Cousin Divie came over from Cheltenham to stay for a little. Shopped &c. Turners bank[3] stopped payment—to go on in a few days.

[*Sun. 18*]

At Cathedral in morning—Bishop preached—Ordination held—staid to see it—much pleased—very idle—shamefully so—Read a little of Father Clement.[4]

[*Mon. 19*]

Read Boswell—3d volume. Consternation prevalent about Turner—his notes sold low.

[*Tu. 20*]

Read Boswell. Cousin Divie went by Champion between two and three. T & J riding—People in better spirits—With J & D[ivie] R[obertson] introduced self to Jimie Wood.[5]

[*Wed. 21*]

Read Boswell—drilled—Rode a hack from Gardiners,[6] which we keep & pay a guinea a week for. Earliest thing I can recollect is seeing Brown standing at top of stairs in Rodney Street.[7]

---

[1] Divie Robertson's s.

[2] This sentence lightly erased.

[3] Turner, Turner, & Morris, Gloucester bankers; John *Gladstone became a partner (see L. Melville, *The Huskisson Papers* (1931), 199–201).

[4] [Grace Kennedy], *Father Clement* (1823), an anti-Roman novel.

[5] A local small shopkeeper and banker.

[6] Livery stable.

[7] Brown was a nurse who died when *Gladstone was eighteen months old (Add MS 44790, f. 6); he was born at 62 Rodney Street, Liverpool. He was fond of referring to this memory; e.g. see Add MS 48631, E. W. *Hamilton's diary for 9 September 1881.

[*Th. 22*]

Read Boswell—finished 3d volume. Rode hack again, about nine miles—
T. & J. went out shooting—killed only a few small birds. Day very beautiful—sunset remarkably fine. Began to make list of the books which I have
read.

[*Fri. 23*]

Read Boswell—4th vol—good deal of walking—discovered a shoemaker to
be an old workman of Ingalton's at Eton[1]—T. & J rode—Dined with Mary
Anne at Cheltenham—Concert afterwards. Miss Paton[2]—Sinclair[3]—
Phillips[4]—Morin.[5]

[*Sat. 24*]

Robertson came at half past two in morning—Dear Anne's birthday—God
bless her—She dined with us all (first time all together for 2 years) tho' not
feeling very well. She gave lots of presents to us all. Read Boswell a little.

[*Sun. 25*]

Christ Church—no sermon on account of communion—read Bible and
Father Clement & had a long walk. *Day beautiful.*

[*Mon. 26*]

Read Boswell. Walked &c.

[*Tu. 27*]

Read Boswell. Rode with J.N.G. nearly to Painswick[6]—thoroughly wet[7]

[*Wed. 28*]

Read Boswell—drilled—&c.

[*Th. 29*]

Mr & Mrs G went to Oxford to meet Miss Farenden, an intended Governess
for Helen. My Birth-day[8]—R. & J went to Cheltenham—Read Bos—

---

[1] See 15 Sep. 25.
[2] Mary Anne *Paton, later Woods, 1802–64, Scottish soprano.
[3] John *Sinclair, 1791–1857, Scottish tenor.
[4] Henry *Phillips, 1801–76; Principal bass for Concert of Ancient Music (cp. 7 Apr.
34).
[5] Unidentified.
[6] Some 7 miles SSE. of Gloucester.
[7] One last word deleted.
[8] Verse birthday reflexions in Add MS 44717, f. 258 (1835 copy).

[*Fri. 30*]

Finished Boswell[1]—Rode with R; T & J shooting—Mr & Mrs G returned
from Oxford, pleased with Miss F. Drilled.

[*Sat. 31*]

Mrs Larkins, Mr & Mrs Barlow, & three boys came over from Cheltenham—
walked &c.

[1] Notes and summary ibid. ff. 172–7.

[VOLUME II]¹

January 1 [1826].

At St Nicholas's & Christ Church—heard a Mr White on "redeeming the time"² & a Mr Buchanan.³

2.

T.R. & J. went to meet the hounds—disappointed, as [hounds] did not go out—they went to Ball at Cheltenham in Evening—walking &c.

3.

Rode hack, in company with Dear R. Dear Father set out for Exeter—did some few notes in Horace & Boethius. R.G. disappointed; not being able to get a place in Lpool Mail.

4. Wednesday.

—R.G. went off per Mercury to Birmingham—thence to go on to Lpool. Saw him off—T. & J. hunting—Cousin John Murray⁴ came to stay a few days—Rode in carriage with Dear Anne.

5.

J.N.G. & J.M.G. went to Cheltenham. Day very cold. Drilled—Dined at Dr. Barons.⁵

6.

Drilled again—T.G., J.N.G., & J.M.G. hunting. Mr G. returned from Exeter.

¹ Lambeth MS 1416, 85ff. Inside the front cover the diarist put his signature and 'Private', adding many years later the months covered—January 1826 to October 1827 —and the note 'No. 2'. Below are three columns of figures and symbols, notes of his sculling during the summer term of 1826; they end with this summary: 'Total 315¼ [miles] 80 times—1s 6d each. £6' (see 9 Mar. 1826).
² Perhaps Charles White, vicar of Tewkesbury since 1818; on Eph. v. 15–16.
³ Dr. Gilbert Buchanan, d. 1833, vicar of Northfleet and rector of Woodmansterne, long chairman of Croydon magistrates.
⁴ John Murray Gladstone, 1803–69, only s. of Murray and Susanna Gladstones; priest in Liverpool; rector of Stoke-upon-Terne, Shropshire, from 1846.
⁵ John *Baron, F.R.S., 1786–1851, physician to Gloucester Infirmary.

7.

J.M.G. went to Cheltenham. J.M.G. Robertson came over—visited old Jimie Wood—his notes remarkably dirty—Dear Anne bilious.

8.

At Ch:Ch: Mr Mutlow[1] in morng, Mr Maitland in Evg. the first on "Take my yoke upon you & learn of me"[2] &c. the second on—"In Christ Jesus neither circumcision availeth anything nor uncircumcision—but a new creature".[3]—Read a little of Father Clement. Struck by the reflection, that inasmuch as the path of the Christian to Heaven is steeper than that of his fellows, inso much it leads to a *higher place*—as in ascending a hill & a mountain. Very applicable to Mother & A. Dear Anne ill.

9.

Dear Anne still ill with bile—J.M.G. Robertson went—Miss Cragg[4] came.

10. Tuesday.

J.N.G's leave prolonged:—copying—J.M.G. backwards & forwards between this & Cheltenham—Reading Breton's China—Dear Anne ill still—as also Dear Mother with headache.

11.

Anne a little better—Mother little better—Reading Breton's China.

12.

Both invalids better—Reading Brethon—walked with brother & J.M.G. towards Cheltenham—Mr Grant came—

13.

Invalids again better. Mr Grant here—Went with brothers to Mary Anne's ball!!! My first—read *vy* little of Breton.

14.

Thermometer at 40. Read Brethon—Copying—sliding &c.

---

[1] T. A. Mutlow, b. 1776?, minor canon of Canterbury.
[2] Matt. xi. 29.
[3] Gal. vi. 15.
[4] Perhaps Mary Anne Cragg, author of *Morning Conversations of a Governess and her Pupils* . . . [on] *Zoology* (1830).

15. Sunday.

At St. Nicholass & Ch Ch: heard Mr Kempthorne[1] on Come now & let us reason together[2] &c—Text at Ch Ch, from 103d Ps. 8 to 13 v. Read Father Clement. Mother & Anne pretty well.

16.

Finished Father Clement—walking sliding &c.

17.

Went to Cheltenham. Bought books—Read Brethon's China.

18.

Dear J.N.G's birthday—God bless him. Finished Brethon's China. Walking &c. Took place per Mercury. Packed up.

19. Thursday.

After a short night's rest got up & went off per Mercury in haste, owing to being called late by a misunderstanding. Got to Oxford before one—left it soon after two—got to Slough safely per Hibernia about half past seven, & to Eton soon after eight safe & well, thank God. Set to to get out my books & got my things into order—Dame &c. flourish—a great change of servants —all but one gone.

20. Friday.

Friday's business—saw Berthomier. Keate very savage—Read Gray's Long Story[3] &c—Wrote home to Dear Mother—did some holiday task.

21. Saturday.

Finished & showed up holiday task. Part of the Bible from wh it is taken[4] difficult to put into the shackles of verse, on account of its extreme sublimity, &, at the same time, simplicity. Saturdays business. Read papers at Society room. Vice President for the next week. Read Gertrude of Wyoming:[5] & read up a little Homer—got things into order, & prepared to start in the old routine on Monday, please God—who I trust will be my guide & my defender.

---

[1] John Kempthorne, 1775–1838, senior wrangler 1796, held among other livings the rectory of St. Michael, Gloucester from 1825.
[2] Isa. i. 18.
[3] A squib of Thomas *Gray the poet's, suppressed by the author but printed in his posthumous *Works*, ed. T. J. *Mathias (1814), i. 325–31.
[4] Job.
[5] Thomas *Campbell, *Gertrude of Wyoming*, a Pennsylvania tale in verse (1809).

22. Sunday

Heard from Dear Anne. Sermon from Vice Provost on "Prove all things" &c.[1] Read Milmans Fall of Jerusalem[2] through—Read Bible O & N Tests, Blair, & Sumner.[3] Mr G. to leave to Gloucester for Lpool.

23.

Read up Homer—Horace & Virgil. & did notes on them—Monday's business. Read Moliere with Berthomier & alone. Meeting at Society room—rules read &c—Wrote out the proceedings, as V.P. Read Papers there—Heard from Dear John—to leave Gloucester today for Portsmouth with J.M.G.

24. Tuesday.

Did notes on Poetae[4] &c—Read Papers & a vy interesting article on the Waldenses in the Quarterly Review at Society room—finished Molieres les precieuses Ridicules—Wrote to Dear Father & Robn at Lpool. Half holiday.

25.

Holiday—Did & wrote over verses—Read Papers at Society room—& some Ovid—I intend to make my French lessons longer & take them only twice a week instead of three times.

26. Thursday.

Whole schoolday. Heard from Dear Mother. Wrote to Sister & Brother John. Read papers at Society room—read & talked a little French with Berthomier—looked over Crevier—ad scribendam orationem de Trajano, Marco Aurelio &c.[5] Private business—Tacitus.

27. Friday

—Friday's business. Composui λόγον demain edendum[6] in the Society. Did & wrote over lyrics—read papers at Society room. Long talk with Carruthers some of it about the prophecies in the Bible concerning Millenium &c.

28. Saturday.

Saturdays business. Read some of Martyns Life of Virgil[7]—& Papers at

[1] Roberts on I Thess. v. 21.
[2] H. H. *Milman, *The Fall of Jerusalem*, verse drama (1820).
[3] Three and a half lines erased illegibly.
[4] Probably *Poetae Graeci*, a school textbook.
[5] 'towards writing speech on Trajan, Marcus Aurelius &c', delivered two days later.
[6] 'Composed speech to be delivered tomorrow'.
[7] John *Martyn the botanist prefaced a life of the poet to his edition of Virgil's *Eclogues* (1749).

Society room. Acted as Vice President there and wrote out the proceedings —spoke also.[1] Did French exercise. Private business—began Medea.[2]

29. Sunday.

Sermon from Grover[3] on obedience—almost inaudible. Said some Juvenal. Wrote long letters to Dear Anne & John. Read Bible O. & N. Testaments— two of Blairs Sermons—two of Sumner's—learnt & copied into scrapbook part of a hymn of Kirke Whites, & read part of Montgomery's Greenland.[4]

30.

Read papers at Society room—French lesson—spoke a little—read the 1st Eclogue of Virgil—with several of Martyns notes—& made a good many quotations to different books. Whole holyday.[5]

31. Tuesday. Holyday.

Read papers at Society room; Mem; so regular in reading the papers *now* because, as Vice President, I am obliged to file them daily. Began Blairs Lectures[6]—Read Macbeth & the Second Eclogue of Virgil, & did a good many quotations.

1st February. Wednesday.

Half holyday. Read "Taming of a Shrew"—a little of Blair's Lectures—& Lord Chatham's Letters to Thomas Pitt.[7] Read Third Eclogue of Virgil, with some notes—Wrote also some quotations in different books, & read Papers & some Speeches at Society room.

February Second.

Holiday again. Read Blair's Lectures which I like very much. Heard from Dear John—a welcome letter—announcing that he had passed in seaman-ship. Wrote to him—to Dear Anne—& to Pulford.[8] Read French & had a long argument with Berthomier on subject of religion. Began verses—Read papers at Society room—& Virgils 4th Eclogue with some quotations. Had also private business (Tacitus).

---

[1] Dated 26 January in Morley, i. 36. *Gladstone proposed, and carried by 7 to 1, a motion that Trajan was not unequalled among the emperors of Rome.

[2] Euripides.

[3] John Septimus Grover, 1766–1853, rector of Farnham Royal 1817; fellow from 1814, vice-provost 1835–51.

[4] James *Montgomery, *Greenland and other poems* (1819).

[5] Anniversary of execution of *Charles I, 1649.

[6] Hugh *Blair, *Lectures on Rhetoric* (1783); a few notes in Add MS 44718, ff. 2–3.

[7] Ed. Lord *Grenville, 1804; advice to an undergraduate of fifty years earlier.

[8] His tailor (Bassett, 6).

6—I.

Feby 3d. Friday.

Fridays business: mem.—only whole schoolday in the week. Finished verses, & wrote over for Tutor & School. Read papers & some old speeches at Society room. Read a little of Blair's Lectures & began (by myself) Molieres Le Festin de Pierre.[1] Did some quotations. Attended, after supper, the rehearsal of a play in my Dames. all the fellows, save self & the three above me, actors. They have provided themselves with swords & shields—have tin helments & some Breastplates—dresses principally made by themselves —scenes of paper, which they have made and painted.[2]

Saturday. Feby 4th.

Saturdays business: Heard from Dear Anne, and from Mr. Rawson. Private business (Medea) & quotations &c to that—to Tacitus, & a good many others. Read some of Molieres Festin de Pierre, & some of Blair's Lectures. Read Virgils fifth Eclogue, & some of Martyns notes. Read papers at Society room & acted as president there—question—Archbishop Cranmer's character—Farr,[3] Hallam,[4] & Selwyn spoke.[5]

Sunday Feby 5th.

Wrote to Dear Anne. Sermon inaudible—preached by Grover. Read Bible O. & N. Testaments. The Brothers & some other poems on religious subjects with notes by Elton—one particularly on the Deists & Atheists.[6] Read a sermon of Blair's & one of Sumner's; said private business (Catullus): Read a Preface on Sacred Poetry & began a poem called the Messiah, translated from the German of Klopstock.[7]

Feby 6th.

Mondays business. Read French with M. Berthomier & part of Le Festin de Pierre alone. Read papers at Society room. Made a book-cover. Read some of the Messiah—many faults, some fine passages in it. On the whole, I should think, very far inferior to Paradise Lost. Wrote over & gave to Okes copy of sent up Greek verses.

7.

Holiday. Read some of the Messiah—the papers at Society room—part of

---

[1] *Dom Juan, ou le Festin de Pierre*, comedy.
[2] See 8 Feb. 26.
[3] William Wyndham Farr, 1808–87; next senior to *Gladstone at Eton; Hampshire country gentleman.
[4] Arthur Henry *Hallam, 1811–33, *Gladstone's closest school friend, subject of *Tennyson's *In Memoriam*. See Add MS 44352 and *Gladstone's article in *Daily Telegraph*, 5 January 1898.
[5] *Cranmer was held admirable by 9 to 2.
[6] (Sir) C.A. *Elton, *The Brothers, a Monody; and Other Poems* (1820), 9–46, 89–96.
[7] Mary *Collyer, tr. F. G. Klopstock, *Messias* (1749), with preface.

an article on the Catholics[1]—a good deal of Le Festin de Pierre. Began the seventh Eclogue, & put down a good many quotations to different books.

8. *Ash Wednesday.*

Wednesdays business & long Church in morning. Finished Le Festin de Pierre & the article on Catholics—Read papers—some of the Etonian & the Messiah. Did French Exercise—& made a book-cover. Present at the representation of Lodoiska by eight of my Dame's fellows—first night of acting.[2]

9.

Holiday. French lesson. Read Messiah—Etonian—papers at Society room: had Private business (Tacitus) & did a long copy of verses.

10.

Friday's business. Wrote over verses. read Messiah & papers at Society room—put down many quotations in different books, & wrote to Dear Mother & Dear Tom.

11.

Saturday's business. Read Messiah (Mem. I have met with several palpable absurdities in it)—Began Molière's Monsieur Porceaugnac—Private business (Medea) & notes thereon; Read papers at Society room—read 6th & 7th Eclogues of Virgil, & put down many quotations &c in Virgil & other books. Richard 3ds Character question at Society—I behind chair.[3] Got Pickering mai[4] fined for taking a paper out of the room without leave, & Doyle for not filing the papers nor entering the question in time.

Sunday Feby 12th.

Sermon from Grover. those that repent shall live.[5] Not much audible. Heard from Dear Father & Mother, line from Anne also. Read Messiah—Sumner—Blair. Did a long Theme—Read Bible O. & N. Testaments & began Racine's Esther. Dined with Mr Moss, Mr Rd Harrison,[6] & Mr Lawrence[7] at the White Hart; several other Eton fellows there—they went off between 7 & 8.

---

[1] Probably *Quarterly Review*, xxxiii. 1 (December 1825).

[2] See 3 Feb. 26. *Lodoiska; or, the Captive Princess*, adapted in Hodgson's *Juvenile Drama* (1825) from the operetta by J. P. *Kemble (1794).

[3] See Hallam to Farr [14 February 1826] in *Bulletin of John Rylands Library*, xviii. 24 (January 1934). *Gladstone's vote was minuted against *Richard III.

[4] Edward Hayes Pickering, 1807–52, captain of the school; assistant master from 1830.

[5] Probably Luke xiii. 3.

[6] Richard Harrison, promoter of the Liverpool–Manchester railway and business friend of John *Gladstone and of John Moss.

[7] Charles Lawrence, d. 1853, the same; mayor of Liverpool 1823; a pall-bearer at *Huskisson's funeral.

13.

Monday's business. Finished L'Etourdi[1] with M. Berthomier, & read some
of M. de Pourceaugnac by myself. Read papers & some Etonian at Society
room; some of the Messiah. Wrote over part of theme; & read Virgil's eighth
Eclogue, putting down a good many quotations to that & other things.

14.

Holyday. Finished writing over theme—Finished First number of the
Etonian—Finished Molières M. de Pourceaugnac. Read also all Swifts
Directions to Servants[2]—some of the Messiah—& part of the Ninth
Eclogue of Virgil, with several quotations. Hoc quoque die orationem
composui ον μεν ενι societate. I mean edere next Samedi.[3]

15.

Wednesday's business. Precensui et partim didici λογον.[4] Began verses;
read papers & Etonian at Society room. Did French exercise; Read Messiah—Read latter part of 9th & whole of 10th Eclogue of Virgil, putting
down quotations in those & some other places.

16.

Half holiday. Finished & wrote over verses; had a long letter from Dear
Anne, a letter from John, & a few lines from Father. Wrote to Dear Anne—
Read papers Etonian & article in fourth vol of Quarterly Rev. "on the
Evangelical Sects".[5] Read Messiah—didici orationem—cui tamen lituram
forsan applicabo[6]—French lesson (began George Dandin)[7]—& read Martyns
preface to the Georgics,[8] with about fifty lines of the first, putting down
quotations to it &c. Private business—Tacitus. Finished Germania.

17.

Fridays business: Read Messiah. very heavy—bears no comparison with
Paradise Lost or Regained. Wrote over speech & made some alterations in
it. Read (by myself) Molieres L'Amour Médecin. Read papers at Society
room & put down quotations to Horace & yesterdays Tacitus.

18.

Saturdays business. Private business (Medea) & notes thereon. Did French
exercise—Read Messiah—First act of Le Tartuffe[9]—about 80 lines of

---

[1] Molière's first comedy.
[2] Posthumous ironical pamphlet.
[3] 'This day besides prepared speech, the one for Society. I mean to speak it next Saturday'.
[4] 'Wrote over and partly learned speech'.
[5] iv. 480 (November 1810).
[6] 'learned speech—in which I shall perhaps make cuts'.
[7] Molière's prose comedy.
[8] John *Martyn edited Virgil's *Georgics*, with a marginal prose translation (1741).
[9] Molière's exposure of hypocrisy.

Virgil's First Georgic & put down quotations to that, Poetae &c—Spoke only a few words at Society as Buckeridge forestalled my arguments— Hallam spoke.[1] Got Wellesley[2] fined.

19. Sunday.

Bishop of Gloucester at our Church & service some 20 min. longer than usual on the strength of it! Sermon preached by Grover on Falsehood. Catechism—after some reading by the Vice Provost, brought in, as usual, his prejudices against the Roman Catholics. Said Catullus (Private business)—Read Blair—Sumner—Racine's Esther—Klopstock's Messiah— besides Bible O. & N. Testaments. Did a longish theme on "vitae praecepta beatae".[3]

20.

Monday with part of Mondays business & Virgil. Notes to do & several other things—French lesson—Read also, alone, a good deal of Le Tartuffe. Read papers & Etonian at Society Room. Wrote over theme. Finished Klopstock's Messiah. Heard from Dear Anne, inclosing a most gratifying letter from Captain Spencer[4] about Dear John.

21.

Play at four—Wrote home—read Etonian at Society room—by myself, Le Tartuffe, a little of the First Georgic (with some notes) & a little of Blair's Lectures. Did Translation & began verses (Greek).

22.

Fridays business. Notes to Horace. Read Etonian at Society Room— finished Le Tartuffe—finished & wrote over verses & began Lyrics. Patteson[5] (being Vice President this week) went out of the Society, leaving his duty undone. I undertook in some way to supply the deficiency, & wrote out some of the last Saturday's debate.

23. Thursday

—half holiday. Finished Lyrics—French Exercise & French lesson (Finished George Dandin)—Finished writing out the debate, filed the papers, entered question &c. Read paper & Etonian at Society room. Read Blair—Epitome of 1st vol of Gibbon—made part of a list of the Emperors & time of deaths

[1] *Gladstone voted, in a minority of 5 to 6, that Virgil was as great a poet as *Shakespeare.

[2] For Gerald Valerian *Wellesley, 1809–82, *Wellington's nephew and *Victoria's confidant, dean of Windsor from 1854, see Add MSS 44339–40 and 48607, 18 September 1882.

[3] 'principles of holy life'. Theme in Add MS 44718, f. 53.

[4] (Sir) Robert Cavendish *Spencer, 1791–1830, 3rd s. of 2nd earl Spencer; J. N. *Gladstone had fought under him in *Naiad* in the near east.

[5] Thomas Patteson, d. 1874, scholar of Eton, later vicar of Hambledon, Hampshire.

or abdications—Read some of the First Georgic & put down quotations to it. Also read a little of Blair Lectures.

24. Friday

—holiday—Read Blair—Etonian at Society room—Began L'Avare.[1] Wrote over Lyrics—had Private business (Medea)—wrote part of a speech on the fall of the Roman Empire—read some of the first Georgic—& scribbled.

Febry 25. Saturday.

Saturdays business. Notes to Poetae, private business (Medea & Catullus) &c. Finished speech & spoke. Made also a short extempore speech at Society in answer to Selwyn. Capital debate on the fall of the Roman Empire.[2] Hervey—Selwyn—Farr—Hallam—Doyle & I spoke—Hervey & Farr, besides myself, a second time. Chessboard introduced—& also John Bull[3]—I opposed them both. 6 Clerks up—glad of it, as the occasion was favourable.[4] Read Blairs Lectures, & L'Avare; attended play in my Dames, & read Etonian at Society Room.

26. Sunday.

Breakfasted with Sir J. McGrigor—Read Bible O & N Testaments—a sermon of Sumners—the first book of Paradise Lost—finished Racine's Esther & began Athalie.[5] Learnt & wrote in scrapbook Ld Byrons Destruction of the Assyrians[6] & read over all the sacred poetry in scrapbook.

27.

Had letters from Anne & John, & wrote to John & Helen. half holiday, Read French & spoke somewhat with Berthomier. Finished Virgils First Georgic; read a *little* of Blair's Lectures—some of L'Avare, & put down a great many quotations in different books.

28.

Wednesdays business. Read Memoirs of Sir Rt Walpole in Biograph. Dict:[7] finished L'Avare: read a speech of Huskissons on Silk Trade. Capital.[8] Began Lyrics (Greek Iambics, instead of usual) & read about 160 lines of the second Georgic, with quotations to them & other places. Read paper also.

---

[1] Molière.
[2] This was held, by 9 to 2, a blessing rather than a misfortune.
[3] Then a somewhat scurrilous Canningite journal.
[4] Thenceforth for some time, up to six boys, not yet quite distinguished enough to enter the society, could attend its debates, retiring before the division.
[5] Also Racine's.
[6] *Byron, *The Destruction of Sennacherib*.
[7] Probably Alexander *Chalmers, *The General Biographical Dictionary* (1812–14), xxxi. 49.
[8] 23 February 1826, *NSH* xiv. 763. See *DNB* xxviii. 326.

March 1.

Whole holiday. Went to Maidenhead—a good stretch.[1] Read Etonian at Society room—at room. Blair's Lectures—about 180 lines of Virgil Georgic 2. with quotations to them & other books. Began (having lost what I had before done) my Greek Iambics & did about 30.

2.

Friday's business. Finished Greek Iambics. Read Blair—Finished the Second Georgic, with quotations to it & to other places. Even worse day's work than usual.

3. Friday.

Whole holiday. Wrote over Lyrics—Read Blair—Etonian at Society room —had private business (Tacitus)—& read about 50 lines of 3d Georgic with quotations to them &c. Worse and worse—Attended play again in Dame's.

4.

Question at Society. Sir Rt Walpole—did he deserve well of his country? Voted against him[2]—like a fool (1827)[3]—Wellesley—Hervey—Farr— Hallam spoke. Saturdays business. Read Etonian at Society room. Read Blair's Lectures & a good deal of the 3d Georgic. Wrote to Hallifax,[4] & put down good many quotations in different books.

5. Sunday.

A letter from Dear John—few lines from Dear Father—who is to leave Gloucester today. Sermon from Grover, as inaudible as usual. Read Bible O & N Testaments—Blair—Sumner—& three books of Paradise Lost. Did theme—said private business.

6. Monday.

Heard from Dear Tom—wrote to him & Dear Anne. Monday's business. did two extempores—read Blairs Lectures—did French exercise & had French lesson. finished 3d Georgic, & began fourth with some quotations.

7.

Whole holiday—this being a regular week. Sent a leaving book to Buckeridge —read Etonian at Society room—finished the 4th Georgic, & read some of Blair's Lectures. Wrote over theme. took place.

---

[1] Six and a half miles upstream.
[2] In a majority of 6 to 3.
[3] These four words added later; see 10 Feb. 27 and Morley, i. 37.
[4] Henry Crawford Hallifax, captain of the boats 1825, had just left Eton; later of the 69th Regt.

8.

Wednesday's business. Read Etonian at Society room—at room—Blair's Lectures—four first Eclogues a second time over—did verses—& Translation.

9.

half holiday. French Exercise & French lesson—wrote over verses—read Blair, & put down many quotations to 4th Georgic—& other places. Chess &c at Society room—I heard from Dear Anne—sent a leaving book (with Hanmer[1]) to Wellesley—Johnsons Works—& agreed for a lock up next term, the same boat as last year—price two pound ten.

10.

Friday's business. Read Blair's Lectures—Etonian at Society room—& second Satire of Juvenal—with quotations to it & to lessons of the day. Sat with Wellesley after four.

11. Saturday.

Question—Sylla or Marius—wh greatest? Mundy spoke for Marius—Farr & I for Sylla—in minority.[2] Read Blair: finished Misanthrope with Berthomier—Etonian at Society room. Dined with my Tutor.[3] Hartopp[4]— Ashley[5]—Farr & Houston[6] also there. Very good turn out. Some plays at cards in Evg—lost—of course.

March 12. Sunday.

Briggs[7] preached—Hosea 10, 12. Bid Wellesley goodbye—who goes to London without taking leave on account of his hand. Sorry to lose him. Read Bible O & N Testaments—Sumner—Blair—5th & 6th books of Paradise Lost, & a good deal of Athalie. Did also, in a way, a shuffling theme. Vice Provost lugged in Ch of Rome for 3d time in the Evening Lecture.

13.

Mondays business—few quotations—finished Athalie—read Blair, & Etonian at Society room. Paid a pound out of 50s. for my boat. Packed up —got into Gloucester Mail at Slough little before 11.

---

[1] (Sir) John, later Lord, *Hanmer, 1809–81, 3rd bart. 1828, later *Gladstone's Flintshire neighbour; M.P. 1832–7 and 1841–72 when he was cr. a baron.

[2] Of 3 to 4.

[3] Knapp.

[4] Edward Bourchier Hartopp, 1809–84, at Christ Church with *Gladstone, conservative M.P. for North Leicestershire 1859–68.

[5] Anthony John Ashley, 1808–67, M.P. for Gatton 1831–2, Q.C., 4th surviving s. of 6th earl of Shaftesbury.

[6] George Houston, 1810–43, tory M.P. for Renfrewshire 1837–41.

[7] John Briggs, 1771–1840, rector of Southmere, Norfolk; fellow from 1822.

14.

Got to Gloucester about 9. Dear John gone to Lpool. Rest at Gloucester pretty well—copied 2 letters. Began The Crisis[1]—out with Dear Anne.

15. Wedy.

Copied 3 letters—read Crisis—out with Dear Anne.

16.

Dear Tom came. Copied 1 Letter—read Crisis—played chess.

17.

Out with Dear Tom—read Crisis—played chess—Drilled—Wrote to Gale.[2]

18. Saturday

Father heard from Uncle D[avid] respecting T.O.[3] Moi quidem δοκει ειναι quelque φρενος aberratio.[4] Wrote to Dear John—Finished Crisis like it much—Began Pierre & his Family.[5]

19. Sunday.

Ch Ch in morning—Mr Maitland preached—St Aldates in afternoon—Mr Kempthorne preached 1st, on Philipp.2.5.—& second on Christ—our high priest—touched with feeling of our infirmities.[6] Read Bible & Pierre.

20.

Finished Pierre & his Family—began Southeys Paraguay[7]—wrote to Gale εσκριβλη[8] &c.

21. Tuesday

—Drilled—went to Cheltenham—read some of Southeys Tale of Paraguay —bought Pindar—copied 1 Letter.

22.

Copied. Finished Tale of Paraguay—dangerous doctrine of human innocence in state of nature. Chess.

[1] Edward Cooper, *The Crisis; or, an attempt to show from Prophecy, the Prospects and the Duties of the Church of Christ* (1825), a visionary anti-romanist work.
[2] John Gale, Liverpool bookbinder.
[3] Thomas Ogilvy, d. 1826; of Poulton, Birkenhead; David Gladstone's partner; had married one of the ten Gladstone sisters.
[4] 'It seems to me to be some aberration of the mind'.
[5] [Miss Grierson] *Pierre and his Family; or, a Story of the Waldenses* (1823), an anti-Roman historical novel.
[6] Heb. iv. 14–15.
[7] Robert *Southey, *A tale of Paraguay* (1825), narrative poem.
[8] 'Scribbled'.

23.

Drilled.

24. *Good Friday*

—read Sophia de Lissau[1]—at Ch.Ch.—read Bible.

25. *Saty*

—read "Adventures of a young rifleman".[2] Chess.

26. *Sunday.*

Ch.Ch twice—read Sophia de Lissau—Bible.

27.

Copied 6 Letters—read Adventures of Rifleman—Chess.

28. *Tuesday*

—Drilled. Chess. Read Adventures of Young Rifleman.

29. *Wednesday*

—saw Judges come in for Assizes—Read Advent. Rifleman—Copied 1 Letter.

30. *Thursday*

—Attended Assizes Criminal Court. Man convicted of horse-stealing—finished Advent. Rifmn. Copied 2 Letters. Drilled.

31 *March.*

At Assizes—Man acquitted of horse stealing, & another of stealing hay—Read part of a speech of Mr. Huskissons on restrictive policy in Trade &c.[3] Heard sentence pronounced (of death) on a boy about 15—with a recommendation to mercy. Chess with Helen. Made up Summary of accounts.

Saturday—1st April.

At Assizes—finished Mr Huskissons speech. Rode. (Mr Huskisson's speech most excellent).

---

[1] [Amelia Bristow] *Sophia de Lissau; or, a Portraiture of the Jews of the Nineteenth Century* (1828), a Christian account of Jewish domestic arrangements, in form of a novel.
[2] *Adventures of a Young Rifleman in the French and English Armies . . . 1806 to 1816*, a Saxon's autobiography (tr. 1826).
[3] 21 and 25 March 1825, *NSH* xii. 1097 and 1196.

2nd April. Sunday

—cold & headachy—Mother—Anne & Tom the same—Talbot[1] came—At Ch Ch twice—read a little of Sophia de Lissau. (Maitland preached both times.)

3.

Talbot went per London Mail. Began Naval Sketchbook.[2] Copied 1 Letter.

4. Tuesday.

Read Naval Sketchbook—chess—ride in gig with J.N.G.

5. Wednesday.

—called on Miss Baron[3]—at Assizes. read Naval SketchBook—poor. Chess, wrote to John Gale for AMG.

6.

Assizes finished—Mother—Anne & Tom still invalided. Chess—Naval Sketchbook—copied 2 Letters—Drilled—wrote to Miss Benwell for A.M.G.

7. Friday.

—read Naval Sketchbook—poor, in many parts. Long ride with J.N.G. a long way thro a beautiful & hitherto unknown part of the country, between Bristol road & Severn. Chess.
    wrote to Robn.

8.

finished 1st vol of Naval Sketchbook, & began 2nd. Invalids better. bought a watch (on trial) pro gulielmo the Poor man.[4]

9. Sunday.

at Ch: Ch: in morng—Maitland preached. Cathedral in afternoon—Bible & Sophia de Lissau. Copied 2 letters.

10. Monday

—read Naval Sketchbook—wrote to Robertson—copied 1 Letter. Chess.

---

[1] George Gustavus Chetwynd Talbot, 1810–96; Eton and Christ Church; brother of 18th earl of Shrewsbury; rector of Withington, Gloucestershire.
[2] *Naval Sketch book*, by an Officer of Rank [W. N. *Glascock], 2v. (1826), nautical chit chat.
[3] See 5 Jan. 26 n.
[4] 'for William' Digges. Last four words in Greek script.

11.

Drilled. rode with J.N.G. to Purton Passage & back, on a hack from Robertson's—35 miles—walked 4 there, to Sharpness.[1] Chess—read Naval Sketchbook.

12. Wednesday.

took place per Mercury—packed up. read Naval Sketchbook—still poor—& Sophia de Lissau. Tired with yesterdays exercise.

13. Thursday.

Left Gloucester at 7 per Mercury—got to Oxford between 12 & 1—left it about 2 per Hibernia, & got to Slough about 7, safe & well, thank God. returned to Eton for the 15th time! pulled out books &c, & did a very little of my holiday task.

14.

Got things in some degree set to rights: Friday's business; wrote to my Dear Mother; finished Blair's Lectures; & did some holiday task.

15.

Became (j'espere,) pretty well settled. Called on Berthomier. Sculled about a little—1st time this year. Saturdays business. Finished holiday task, wrote over & shewed up.[2] Read 1st canto of Darwins Economy of Vegetation[3]—Etonian at Society room—read up Horace & Virgil, with quotations to them.

16. Sunday.

Briggs preached—St John. 4–44.—Read Bible O & N. Testaments—Blair—1 sermon—Sumner—ditto—the 7th book of Paradise Lost—the 39 Articles—& began Corneilles Polyeucte. Heard from Dear Anne & Dear John—wrote to Dear Anne—news of 2 deaths in their letters—Mary Annes servant's, & Mrs Phillipps's son's.[4]

17. Monday.

Began & read a good deal of Les Femmes Savantes[5] with Berthomier. Mondays business—meeting at Society room—moved John Bull should be thrown out—negatived—out in boat—read Etonian—2 & 3 Cantos of Darwins Economy of Vegetation (Partly) & read up Homer.

[1] Purton is on the Severn's left bank, 12 miles SW. of Gloucester; Sharpness is 2 miles farther downstream.
[2] The dying Cyrus to his sons, in Latin alcaics; Add MS 44718, ff. 24–26.
[3] Erasmus *Darwin, *Botanic Garden*, part i (1792).
[4] Unidentified.
[5] Molière.

18.

Holiday. out in boat—read Etonian at Society room—4th canto of Darwin —& begun verses. This will not do.

19.

Wednesdays business. Read 1st Canto of Loves of Plants[1]—finished & wrote over verses—had private business (Tacitus) did French exercise, & wrote to Mr G., T.G, & J.N.G. out in boat.

20.

The first week of the term gone—half holiday—out in boat. Did some vile Lyrics & wrote them over—read Darwin—Etonian at Society room, & Les Femmes Savantes with Berthomier—& some quotations &c to various books. Received dear Johns sword for Montem.[2]

21.

Friday's business. Quotations to various things—heard from Mr G. Wrote to him & to J.N.G.—heard of Ld M.'s promise to provide for him.[3] Read Darwin—looked over Hume[4] & Tytler,[5] & wrote a speech for tomorrow on the Norman Conquest. Out in Boat.

22.

Added to my speech, & looked at Hallam[6] & at Henry[7] in addition to Hume & Tytler. Farr & Hallam spoke against Norman Conquest. I spoke for it; majority for it.[8] Moved John Bull should be thrown out—carried. Good deal of debating after the main speeches. Heard from Mr G. & J.N.G. put down good many quotations in various books.

23. Sunday.

Champnes[9] preached—on the history of Joseph.[10] Long talk with Hallam on subjects of Trinity, Predestination, &c. Read Bible O. & N. Testaments. Made analysis of 4 First Chapters of Genesis. Read 8th book of Paradise Lost—Sermon of Blair on Candour, & some of Corneille's Polyeucte—a fine piece.

[1] Erasmus *Darwin, *Botanic Garden*, part ii (1789).
[2] See 16 May 26.
[3] John Hay *Forbes, 1776–1854, Scottish judge and Edinburgh episcopalian; as a lord of session, 1825–30, and of justiciary, 1830–52, he became Lord Medwyn.
[4] David *Hume, *History of England* (1761).
[5] A. F. *Tytler, *Elements of general history* (1801).
[6] Henry (father of A.H.) *Hallam, *View of the State of Europe during the Middle Ages* (1818), ii. 127–203.
[7] Robert *Henry, *History of England* (1771).
[8] Of 5 to 2.
[9] Thomas Weldon Champnes, 1773–1841, fellow of Eton from 1825, held various preferments including canonries of Windsor and Westminster.
[10] Gen. xxxvii–1.

24.

Whole holiday. Out in boat twice—sculled to Surly after 12—rushes after 6. Read a good & very just article in Quarterly on W. India Slavery.[1] Finished Darwins Loves of the Plants & began the Temple of Nature;[2] he has great talent, me saltem judice,[3] but a great deal of sameness, & a pomposity or affectation or want of taste in his versification. French with Berthomier. Did some of the List of my books, & a little of a sort of Epitome of Boswell Life [of] Johnson—putting down the principal transactions of his Life.

25.

Whole holiday. Dear Tom to go up for his degree tomorrow: hope to have good news by Friday.[4] Out in boat twice. Read Darwin & did some Epitome of Boswell's Johnson. A truly glorious days work. This will not do—again.

26. Wednesday

—part Wednesdays & part Mondays business—some quotations. did French exercise—verses & translation—read Darwin & Etonian at Society room. Chess. Dear Tom, please God, to go up to day, Hope for good news Friday or Saturday. Heard from Mr G. A.M, & J.N.G; J.N.G. to go abroad to S. America, & carry his commission with him.[5] Trevelyan my fag:[6] began on Monday; answered very well indeed.

27. Thursday

—play at four—with part Wednesdays & part Monday's business. Wrote over verses. Did Lyrics. Finished Darwin's Poems. Had French lesson. Wrote to A.M, & J.N.G. Wrote out an abstract of the proceedings on Roman world debate day (Saty Feby 25th) in Society Book.[7] Called up. out in boat. Private business—Tacitus. Tutor told me he would send me up soon. Montems are right.[8]

28.

Friday's business. Wrote over Lyrics. Read little Etonian at Society room; finished 1 vol Epitome [of] Boswell's Johnson: put down a good many quotations in different books. Out in boat. No news of T.G.—hope to hear tomorrow.

[1] xxxiii. 410–29 (March 1826).
[2] Erasmus *Darwin, *The Temple of Nature; or, the Origin of Society: a Poem, with Philosophical Notes* (1803).
[3] 'in my view at least'.
[4] Misunderstanding: see 29 May 26.
[5] He sailed shortly for South America, but was not commissioned lieut., R.N., till 7 July 1827.
[6] James Harington Trevelyan, 1811–75, nephew of 5th and uncle of 8th bart.; lieut.-col. 60th Rifles.
[7] See p. 36 above.
[8] See 16, 19 May 26.

29.

Half holiday. Sculled up to Surly after 12. Cluer[1] after 6; Read Montgomery's Greenland from near the beginning to the end—some pretty po's
in it. Private business—Medea—quotations to it. Began Tom Jones—
faithful picture.[2] Question at Society—Was Queen Eliz. justified in her
persecution of the Roman Catholics? Voted for "not justified"—in a
majority of one! Hallam—Pickering minor[3]—Doyle & Farr spoke—at
considerable length. Debate on whole excellent. Question of mine marked
for Saturday after next. Moved that next room be kept locked—carried—
Selwyn alone opposing it. Moved also that any member throwing about—
striking with, or using in any offensive manner any property of the Society,
or any other property in Society room, be liable to a fine of 2s 6d. Opposed
vehemently by Hervey & Farr—tacitly by Selwyn. Carried however.
Subscription declared—£.1. 10s. Heard from Mr G. & A.M.G.

Sunday, 30 April.

Champnes preached. "For what shall it profit a man, if he shall gain the
whole world" &c.[4]—Read two of Blair's Sermons, & the ninth book of
Paradise Lost. Finished Corneilles Polyeucte—a very good piece—wish we
had talents directed to the same end in the same way, instead of many of
our trash or licentious plays. Read Bible O. & N Testaments; did Epitome
of 5, 6, & 7 Chapters of Genesis. Mem. Epitome laborious & slow, but I hope
useful. Heard from T.G.

May 1.

Whole holiday. Finished Les Femmes Savantes & spoke a little French with
Berthomier; read Etonian at Society room, & Tom Jones. Sculled up to
Surly after 12, & up to the Shallows after 6.[5] Heard from Buckeridge.

2.

Monday's business. had a Letter from Buckeridge, at St John's, Oxford.
Sculled up to Cluer &c after 6. Read Etonian at Society room; & by myself
Tom Jones—Finished 1 vol & began second of it. Wrote several things in
extract book.

3. Wednesday.

Half holiday. Read Etonian at Society room, & 2nd vol. of Tom Jones. Did
Translation & began verses. Wrote to Buckeridge. Read also papers at
Society room. Day cold and uncomfortable.

---

[1] Clewer, on Berkshire bank of Thames, upstream suburb of Windsor.
[2] Henry *Fielding (1749).
[3] Percival Andrée Pickering, later recorder of Pontefract.
[4] Mark viii. 36.
[5] i.e. after 5 o'clock lock-up (A. C. *Benson, *Fasti Etonenses*, 506).

4. Thursday.

Heard from Dear John. Wrote to T.G. & J.N.G. Holiday; French exercise & French lesson; finished verses; had private business (Tacitus); Began l'Ecole des Maris[1] with Berthomier. Finished 2 vol & began 3d vol. of Tom Jones.

5. Friday.

Friday's business—wrote over verses—read Tom Jones: & read a little & fished about a good deal in various books to make a list of the great men of Augustan age. Number immense.

6. Saturday.

Half holiday. Sculled up to Shallows. Finished 1 vol. of Etonian. Finished 3d vol of Tom Jones. Did French exercise: & some quotations in Horace. Debate. Italy greater in literature and arts under Augustus or under Leo the tenth? Voted for Augustus—*solus*. Hallam & Hervey spoke for Leo. I spoke for Augustus—wrote my speech.[2]

7. Sunday.

Heard from A.M. & J.N.G. Few lines from Sister on an excellent letter to her from John Gale; poor Gale obliged to stop. I remember his once speaking to me when I, being in a rage about some charge or other in his shop, asked him why the devil he did so & so. He spoke to me forthwith; & for it I ought always to respect him. Read Blair's Sermon on Submission to the Divine Will. Foster Pigott[3] preached on the sacrament. Wrote to A.M.G. Did theme. Read Leslie on Deism; also his letter to a convert; & began his conversation between a Deist & a Christian.[4] Like all three very much; Hallam lent me the book.

8.

Monday's business. Extempore—French Lesson; few quotations—Read some of Leslie & began fourth volume of Tom Jones. Out in boat twice. Day somewhat summerized, at least comparatively.

9.

Holiday. wrote over theme, & read Tom Jones, vol. 4; also papers at Society room. Sculled up to Surly &c. after 12 & after 6.

---

[1] Molière.
[2] Notes for speech in Add MS 44649, ff. 9–11.
[3] Dr. William Foster–Pigott, d. 1827, fellow since 1790.
[4] Charles *Leslie, *A Short and Easy Method with the Deists; A Letter . . . to a Deist, upon his Conversion;* and *The Truth of Christianity Demonstrated, in a Dialogue betwixt a Christian and a Deist* (1698, &c).

10.

Wednesdays business. A good many quotations in different books. Finished Tom Jones, & Leslies Conversation on truth of Christianity—excellent. Read Etonian at Society room. Out in boat twice.

11. Thursday.

Heard from home. Wrote to J.N.G. Engaged a bed for him for Montem. Happy to think I have had very little botheration about it. Holiday—for the new Bp of Landaff.[1] Out in boat. Private business—Tacitus. Read 1st canto & part of 2nd of Childe Harold,[2] with notes. Like it much. French with M Berthomier. Finished L'Ecole des Maris. Read Etonian at Society rooms, Saw Canning's dress—somewhat like my last Montem dress.

12.

Friday's business. Finished & wrote over my Greek anapaests. Finished 2nd Canto, & read 3d & 4th of Childe Harold. Quotations &c to Horace. Looked over the end of Mitford's 2d volume about Pericles.[3]

13. Saturday.

Half holiday. Heard from A.M. & J.N.G. Engaged bed for Dear Tom. Sculled Hallam up to Shallows after 12. Private business. Medea. Wrote speech & spoke, on the politics of Pericles. said they were neither useful nor justifiable.[4] Pickering minor spoke against me. Hervey for. Acted as V.P. at the Society, & wrote out fourteen pages of debate: Seconded Selwyns most excellent motion for a Subscription for the weavers.[5] Tried my Montem traps on.

14. Sunday.

Foster Pigott preached on—the law by Moses, grace & truth by Jesus Christ.[6] Wrote to Mrs G: stiff arguments with Hallam, as usual on Sundays, about Articles, Creeds &c. Read Bible—10th book of Paradise Lost—finished 2nd vol of Blairs Sermons; did Epitome of several chapters of Genesis, and did even comparatively a most vile and shuffling theme on a bad subject, wh was the cause. Said Private business.

15.

Mondays business. Bustle & consequent idleness, Montem approaching.

---

[1] Charles Richard (brother of J.B.) *Sumner, 1790–1874, current favourite of *George IV, nominated bp. of Llandaff 25 April 1826, translated to Winchester December 1827, resigned 1869.
[2] *Byron (1812).
[3] W. *Mitford, *History of Greece* (1810), xii–xiv.
[4] Notes for speech in Add MS 44649, ff. 6–8. The society condemned Pericles by 5 to 3.
[5] The society resolved unanimously to subscribe for the relief of distressed weavers in manufacturing districts.
[6] John i. 17.

7—I.

Filed papers &c. as V.P. & finished the report in the Journal. French exercise & French lesson; & a few quotations. Sculled up to Shallows after 6.

16. Tuesday.

Montem day—did—*nothing*. Day dwindled away & wasted miserably. Hot. Squash excessive in various places. Several fainted. Turn out of men on the whole smart. Breakfasted in Hall, extremely well, & very comfortably, considering; band playing. Walked three times round schoolyard in about an hour or hour & half. Dear Tom & John here, & many old Eton fellows whom I know. Dined at Salthill,[1] pretty well, but extremely uncomfortably. Idled away two or three hours in the gardens. Came down to College with Brothers—leave to [visit] them in Evening: tea & pleasant Evening with them at White Hart. Bid T. G. goodbye & J.N.G. till Thursday. Phil[2] my guest. Saw amongst others, Parr,[3] Beadon,[4] Phillpotts,[5] Sampson,[6] Fitzroys,[7] Mitford,[8] Blackett,[9] Caldwell,[10] & many whose faces I recollect names forget—also Bonsor—Bullock[11]—Broderick[12]—Kinglake[13]—Young[14]—Booth[15] &c. again. The whole thing a wretched waste of time and money; a most ingenious contrivance to exhibit us as baboons; to most or all Eton fellows a day of fatigue, smothering, idleness—&—a bore in the full sense of the word. Hope twill soon be abolished.[16]

17.

All right again; stowed away my Montem Traps. Read the Belles Stratagem.[17] Phil still my guest—much admired. Did some verses: & a French

[1] At the Windmill Inn, 2 miles north of Eton, at the western end of Slough. Programme in Add MS 44718, ff. 35–36.

[2] (Sir) Robert Joseph *Phillimore, 1810–85; M.P. 1852–7, judge 1867–83; cr. bart. 1881. See Add MSS 44276–8.

[3] Thomas C. Parr, b. 1804?, of Christ Church and Indian civil service.

[4] Probably Frederick Fleming Beadon, 1806?–80, vicar of Burnham, Somerset.

[5] Thomas Phillpotts, 1807–90, b. at Gloucester; scholar of Eton and King's; vicar of St. Feock, Cornwall, 1844–74; canon of Truro 1877.

[6] Probably Daniel Dod Sampson, 1806–91, rector of Kingston, Cambridgeshire.

[7] Henry, 1806–77, Northamptonshire squire, and Hugh, 1808–79, Grenadier lieut.-col., ss. of Lord Henry Fitzroy, canon of Westminster and 3rd s. of 3rd duke of *Grafton.

[8] Probably John Thomas Freeman–*Mitford, 1805–86, from 1830 2nd baron and from 1877 1st earl of Redesdale; chairman of lords' committees from 1851.

[9] Probably Sir Edward Blackett, 1805–85, 6th bart., Christ Church, life guards; four times m.

[10] Henry Barney Caldwell, b. 1805?, of Lacock, Wiltshire.

[11] Either Richard, d. shortly, or James Trevor Bullock, of Debenham, Suffolk; younger bb. of Edward Bullock, d. 1857, common serjeant 1850–5.

[12] Probably George Alan Brodrick, 1806–48, priest, 5th Viscount Midleton 1836.

[13] William Chapman Kinglake, 1807–81; rector of West Monckton, Taunton, 1838.

[14] (Sir) John *Young, 1807–76; Peelite M.P. Co. Cavan 1831–55; junior whip 1841–6; 2nd bart. 1848; Irish secretary 1852–5; governed Ionian Islands 1855–9, New South Wales 1861–7, Canada 1869–72; cr. Lord Lisgar 1870. See Add MS 44237.

[15] (Sir) Williamson Booth, 1808–77; partner in gin distillery; succ. uncle as 2nd bart. 1850.

[16] Extracts in Morley, i. 30, and in Bassett, 8; contrast *Disraeli, *Coningsby*, i. xi. *Hawtrey abolished Montem in 1847.

[17] Hannah *Cowley's comedy (1782).

exercise. Wrote a long long letter home about Montem. Filed papers & read a bad account of Montem in Morning Chronicle. Sculled up to Water Oakly [1] after 12, Shallows after 6.

18.

Wednesday's business. French lesson. Did some more verses. Read part of King Lear. Filed papers & read somewhat in them. Sculled up to Shallows after twelve. Wrote to Dear Father & Dear Tom—both very briefly. John came a little before eight, got tea at my room & sat with me, went over before 11, to sleep at Christopher. [2] Called up.

19.

Fridays business saying at 5. Breakfasted with J.N.G. at Christopher after 8 o clock school nearly & sculled him to the rushes afterwards. He bathed at Upper Hope, on the way. Left him to go to 11 oclock school; he [had] gone when I came out. Finished a tremendous copy of verses about Montem; abusing it vehemently; as I think properly. [3] Tutor much pleased—said twould not do to send up, for I had taken the unpopular side of the question. Read great part of King Lear. Sculled Hallam up to Shallows after 6.

20.

Sculled Hallam up to Shallows after 6. holiday. Wrote over my tremendous copy of verses; compared by some to an Epic poem. Mem, I remember once when I had done 34 stanzas of Alcaics for a holiday task that a fellow said he did not know "whether he would sooner go to hell or write over Gladstones holiday task." Heard from Mr & R. G. Quotations to Horace & other things. Saw Mr Staniforth—gave me a pound—not sure about propriety of the practice. Read about 200 lines of 10 Satire of Juvenal; excellent; with quotations &c. Finished King Lear. Read Miltons beautiful Epitaphium Damonis—exquisite; & several other of his Latin poems. My Dames servant got a 16th of a 30,000 £ prize in the Lottery. a lie! [4] How many made miserable . . . [5] Question at Society—did the Whig Ministry deserve well of their country? Hallam & Doyle spoke & said Yes; Farr ditto. & said no. Excellent debate, but not such as to make one acquainted with the subject. Hervey—Hallam—Doyle—voted for—Selwyn—Farr—Pickering minor against them; I being President, & the numbers equal, obliged to vote; did so against them; but not very decided on the subject. [6]

---

[1] About 3 miles upstream.
[2] The Christopher Inn was opposite his dame's.
[3] Add MS 44718, f. 28.
[4] These two words interlineated later.
[5] Diarist's dots.
[6] 'Did the Whig Ministry in Queen *Anne's reign deserve well of their country?'

21. Sunday.

Breakfasted with W. India Mr McDonald.[1] Champnes preached very poorly
—& of all subjects, on the Trinity! Read Bible O. & N. Testaments, & did
some Analysis: read the 131st Psalm in Buchanans Version[2]—the 11th
book of Paradise Lost, & the 3 first sermons in Blairs 3d vol; with a little
of the Apocrypha.

22.

Holiday. [Sculled to] Lower Hope, &c after 4—Shallows after 6. Read
French &c. with Berthomier. Read some of the Spectator[3], & the sketches
of the characters,[4] & some of Boswell's Johnson; put down also some of the
facts &c.

23. Tuesday.

Mondays business; heard from J.N.G. & wrote to him: had a long letter
from A.M.G. Shallows after 6 in boat. Read Etonian at Society room—at
room—Spectator & remainder of 10 Satire of Juvenal; with quotations to
it & several others.

24.

Wednesdays business. Called up again. Did verses, & wrote them over; read
Spectator, & Etonian at Society room; did French exercise, & put down
quotations to Virgil &c. Day rainy, consequently no boating. Father
Mother, Anne, John & Helen, please God, to set off for Seaforth today; may
it be for good to all.

25. Thursday.

mes amici ἄλλαμος τε καὶ ἀνμηρος moi showed leurs carminδοις.[5] French
with Berthomier: read Spectator; did Lyrics; put down quotations in
sundry books; read a little of Hogg.[6] Great agitation here on account of the
Derby being run at Epsom. Hope they[7] are all now safe at Stone.

26.

Hope they are all now safe at—home[8]—after an absence of more than a
year & a half. Friday's business. Quotations to Horace & other books.

---

[1] Alexander *Macdonnell, 1798–1835, chess master; secretary to London committee
of West India merchants.
[2] *Paraphrasis Psalmorum Davidis poetica*, 1590 &c.
[3] *Steele and *Addison's early eighteenth-century daily, not the once radical weekly
founded in 1828 which survives as a conservative one.
[4] *Sketches of character, or specimens of real life*, a novel, 3v. (1815).
[5] 'my friends Hallam and Hanmer showed me their joint verses'.
[6] James *Hogg, 'the Ettrick Shepherd', *Poetical Works*, 4v. (1822).
[7] His family.
[8] At Seaforth House.

Read papers, Spectator; wrote over Lyrics. Private business—Tacitus. Wrote out a good deal in Album. Shallows after 6.

27.

Sundays business—Private business—Medea—Quotations to sundry books packed off a whole lot to be bound by Mr Ingalton—31 vols. Sculled Hand-mer up to Boveney[1] after 6. Viewed books at Bartons to be sold on Monday. Read Spectator—Les Deux Billets—a little piece by Florian.[2] Johnson's "Taxation no Tyranny"[3]—as far as I have read, a poor performance in-deed. Did French exercise—Debate at Society (very good;) Mathematics or Metaphysics—wh most useful in forming the mind? Hallam—Hervey—Selwyn—Pickering minor spoke. Voted for Metaphysics—in the sense of—the philosophy of the human mind.[4]

28.

Champnes preached—on forgiveness of one another.[5] Read Bible O & N Testaments; read Blair; he has, or seems to have formed too high an esti-mate of our character as "men"; read 12th Book of Paradise Lost, & some more of Buchanan's Psalms. Did also the Epitome of 3 chapters of Genesis, & wrote to H.J.G. $\epsilon\sigma\kappa\rho\iota\beta\lambda\eta\delta$ &c paulum.[6]

29.

Holiday for the Restoration.[7] Day very rainy—attended Booksale—bid for eight or nine lots,—got none. Had French lesson; (finished L'Ecole des Femmes.)[8] Read the Spectator—and two of Florians plays; Le Bon Menage, & Le Bon Pere; very pretty pieces—especially the latter; he brings about his plan naturally & prettily, & yet makes all his characters amiable. Dear Tom took his degree—or rather passed his examination.[9]

30. Tuesday

—Mondays business. Read over in school Greek copy on Heathen Gods. Keate did not seem to like it much. Heard from Mr G of their safe arrival at Seaforth; & from T.G. even better news that he had taken his degree. Thank God. Wrote to T. G. Read Florians Jeannot et Colin; finished Taxa-tion no Tyranny—an able piece written to justify a bad cause. Read Spec-tator, & Etonian at Society room. Day very wet.

[1] Two miles upstream.
[2] Jean-Pierre Claris de Florian, 1755–94, Voltairean author and dramatist; *Gladstone was reading vol. iv (*Théâtre*) of his collected works (Paris 1824).
[3] Samuel *Johnson's pamphlet (1775) in favour of taxing American colonies.
[4] *Hallam gave his casting vote on the same side.
[5] Probably Matt. vi. 14–15.
[6] 'scribbled, etc., a bit'.
[7] Of *Charles II, 1660.
[8] Molière.
[9] He took an ordinary degree in classics.

31.

Wednesday's business. Day middling only. Did verses & French exercise. Read Florians Les Jumeaux de Bergame; Spectator; & an article on the Long Parliament in Knights Quarterly.[1] Wrote over verses.

June 1.

Sculled up to Monkey Island[2] after four; river very high—consequently hard work. About two hours & ten minutes in doing it—impeded by barges. Heard of the death of Ld M yesterday.[3] Half holiday. Did & wrote over Lyrics; had French lesson; began La Critique de l'Ecole des Femmes.[4] Read Florians "La Bonne Mere". Like his pieces very much. Read Spectator & Etonian at Society room. Locked up at ¼ before nine.

June 2.

Fridays business; sculled up to Surly after 6. Read Etonian at Society room; also read Spectator, & Florians Le Bon Fils. Heard from & wrote to Dear Anne: put down quotations to Horace &c; & had private business—Tacitus. Mr G, I suppose, to set off for Berwick today.

June 3.

Saturdays business: read Florians "Idylle de M. Gessner" & "Myrtil et Chloe". Read Spectator. Quotations to Poetae. Private business—Medea. Acted as V.P. at Society—& wrote out the debate, a very long one—on a Standing Army—whether, in a monarchical Govt, dangerous or no? Majority of 1 that it was not. Farr—Hallam—Doyle spoke—that it was—Hervey—Pickering minor—that it was not; I wd have spoken, but prevented by question being called very quickly. Had Doyle fined 5s., unanimously, for not bringing book back & not reporting debate in time &c. Sculled up to Surly after 6; heard from J.N.G.

4. Sunday.

Foster Pigott preached; inaudible. Mr G, I hope now at Berwick. Did a little Epitome [of] Genesis & read Bible O & N: Blair: Cowpers Tirocinium;[5] & some of Buchanans Psalms; scribbled moreover a little.

5.

Holiday. 4th of June kept.[6] Finished my V.P.'s duty, save filing the papers daily till next Saturday. Heard from R.G.: saw account of meeting at

---

[1] By Joseph Haller, in *Knight's Quarterly Review*, ii. 369 (April 1824).
[2] Four miles upstream.
[3] A false report. Cp. 21 Apr. 26.
[4] Molière.
[5] William *Cowper, *Tirocinium; or, a Review of Schools*, a defence in heroic couplets of private education, usually printed with his *The Task* (1785, etc.).
[6] *George III's birthday.

Lpool where Mr G. was called for in Morning Chron.[1] Read Florians Hero
et Leandre, & Le Baiser. Read Russel[2] & part of Smollett[3] on the Forty
five, & wrote part of speech for Saturday the 17th; Sculled Handmer to
Locks, Lower Hope &c &c. after four; sculled from Upper Hope to Surly, &
Surly down to Eton &c. after 6, very comfortably & enjoyed the whole
thing. Saw Young, Hood,[4] Stanhope[5]—Sir J. MacGregor—Micklewham[6]
from Oxford & others. Fire works excellent.—the best, I think, I ever
remember.

June 6.

Mondays business. Finished 1st vol Spectator. Finished Theatre de Florian:
did French exercise & had French lesson. Did a few Gk verses—read
Etonian at Society room. Saw by papers account of meeting at Lpool—
agst Mr Huskisson.[7] Bathed at Upper Hope after 6; first time this year.
Sculled up to Upper Hope, & a good deal about besides.

June 7.

Finished & wrote over my verses. Wrote a little more speech; did French
exercise. Began 2 vol of Spectator; read Etonian at Society room, and about
half of Ben Jonson's Poetaster.

8.

Holiday—consequence—as usual, scarce anything done. Cricket after 12,
with Wright;[8] wine after dinner, with Hervey; Boat after 4, walk after 6
with Hallam. French lesson; read Spectator; got thro' about 60 lines of
Pindar; 1st Olympian; & did some Gk Anapaestics. A very easy & very
nice metre.

9.

Fridays business. Wrote to Dear Robertson; read Election news[9] in papers,
& Etonian at Society room; played chess with Hallam; sculled down to
Locks[10]—up to rushes &c. after 6; bathed; went to see Staniforth, who has
been ill; finished my Lyrics; had private business—Tacitus; read Spectator, & a little Pindar, with quotations.

[1] *Morning Chronicle* that day, 3. John *Gladstone had been called to chair the meeting
that invited *Huskisson to continue to contest *Canning's former seat at Liverpool.
[2] W. A. Russel, *History of England* (1777), 704–10.
[3] Tobias *Smollett, *History of England . . . designed as a Continuation of Mr. *Hume's*,
(1790), iii. 156–90.
[4] Francis Grosvenor Hood, 1809–54; 3rd viscount's brother; col., Grenadier Guards;
killed at siege of Sebastopol.
[5] Charles Wyndham Stanhope, 1809–81, 7th earl of Harrington 1866.
[6] Unidentified; nickname?
[7] A street demonstration on 2 June protested at the Canningite faction's dominance in
local politics.
[8] Thomas Wright, d. 1827, a scholar of King's College Cambridge.
[9] Parliament had been dissolved on 2 June; voting in the general election had in some
places already begun (writs returnable 25 July).
[10] By Romney Island, opposite the main college buildings.

10. Saturday.

Fifth form supper—given by Mellish:[1] fellows got their removes. Supper very good; & nobody intoxicated. Canning took 8 places; saw Mr Canning[2] here—not to speak to. Question at Society Aristocracy or Democracy, wh best? Farr & I spoke—both for Aristocracy; Society unanimous. Doyle fined. I President. Toasts drunk at supper. Wrote speech; half holiday business, & private, Medea; read Spectator, Etonian, papers, & review of Etonian in Quarterly[3] at Society room. also read some more of Ben Johnson's Poetaster; Sculled up to Rushes after 6; to Surly, turn about with Antrobus,[4] after 12.

11. Sunday.

Wright preached well on sin against God, direct, as opposed to sin against man, indirect: from, I think, Samuel 1.2.25. Walk with Farr. Read Bible O & N Testts, & put down some marginal references; read Blair, & some of Buchanan's Psalms; also some of the [39] articles.

12.

Had a long letter from Dear Anne, with much news. Read papers Lpool & London, for Election news. Election at Windsor. No contest.[5] Sculled up to Surly after 6; took Staniforth & a dog of his up above the shallows, where landed them. Met Oxford boats at Surly. Saw Parr—on his way to town. Mondays business. Upper Division full—large new remove. Berwick Election, I suppose, to begin. Did French Exercise; did & wrote over theme. read a little Spectator, & Etonian at Society room: & put down some few quotations; finished Pindars first Olympian. A fine fellow.

13.

Holiday. Masters off to Cambridge.[6] Anxious about the Berwick Election. Read Smollett's account of the 45, & wrote some more of my speech. Read Election news in papers. Bathed. Had French lesson. Began L'Impromptu de Versailles.[7] Seeing match of Junior versus Upper [school] after 12. Read some Spectator, & put down some Quotations. Sculled to Surly—took Hallam—left boat at Upper Hope coming down.

---

[1] William Leigh Mellish, 1813–64, once Gladstone's fag; Nottinghamshire gentleman.
[2] George *Canning, 1770–1827, orator; Eton and Christ Church; M.P. from 1794, incl. Liverpool 1812–22; foreign secretary 1807–9, 1822–7; prime minister April–August 1827; f. of C.J.*
[3] April 1821, xxv. 95.
[4] Edmund Antrobus, 1811–84, curate to his f. at Acton, Middlesex, 1835–53; Northumberland gentleman.
[5] John Ramsbottom, d. 1845, brewer and banker, whose family shared with the crown the ownership of the borough, was again elected; M.P. for Windsor from 1810 (see *EHR* liv. 653ff.). His colleague this time was Sir R. Hussey *Vivian, 1775–1842, cavalry brig. at Waterloo, cr. Baron Vivian 1841.
[6] To vote in the university election.
[7] Molière.

14.

Holiday. A miserable failure—forgot to take key to Upper Hope—boat sunk. Bathed after absence & with help, got it set to rights again. Brought it down after 12; & sculled up to Lower Hope &c. &c. after 6. Read papers & Etonian. Did French exercise; put down some quotations. Did some verses. Read Goldsmith's Deserted Village. Hervey drank wine with me— as does sometimes Farr, sometimes Hallam, after dinner.

15.

Wednesdays business; after 11 o clock school, cut to Hattons;[1] thunder-struck by the state of the Berwick poll; Beresford[2] 60—Blake[3] 53—Glad-stone 36. Hope that it is owing to Mr Gs voters being principally non resi-dent, & therefore not so much at hand: as also I consider that the poll had then only just begun. Very anxious for a letter. Had French lesson; finished a vy long copy of verses; improved them in writing over by cutting out some 30. Took Hallam out in boat, Man drowned above Clewer. Read papers at Society room; read Goldsmiths Traveller,[4] & Spectator: also put down some quotations.

16.

Fridays business. Glorious news! Poll at Berwick on Tuesday at half past one—Beresford 222—Gladstone 195—Blake 191. Famous & rapid change indeed. Hope for a continuance tomorrow. Letter from Dear Tom. Heard also from Mrs G. Wrote to Aunt E & to Miss G. both long letters; read papers & Spectator. Put down a few quotations. began Odes[5] in school. Wrote some more speech; corrected & wrote over some of it. Boat after 6. up to Surly—& down millstream thence to Clewer.

17.

Saturdays business. More good news. Letter from J.N.G. dated Berwick. Beresford 403; Gladstone 381: Blake 357. they[6] have coalesced. Hope a day or two will announce the conclusion. Private business—Medea. Put down some quotations & read Spectator; read also papers & Etonian at Society room. Made two Latin Versions of the little thing in Theocritus about the bee.[7] Boat & walk afterwards, after 6. Question at Society—disarming of Highlanders laudable? Opened—spoke very *longly* & tediously against it.[8]

---

[1] Newsagent's and pastrycook's; the Eton Society met in the room above the shop.
[2] Captain Marcus Beresford, tory M.P. for Berwick till 1832.
[3] Sir Francis Blake, 1774–1860, 3rd bart. of Twisel Castle, Northumberland; whig M.P. for Berwick 1820–6, 1827–35.
[4] His first successful poem, 1764.
[5] Horace.
[6] Beresford and Blake.
[7] *Idyll* xix, Eros' complaint to his mother at being stung; no longer thought to be by Theocritus (A. S. F. Gow, *Theocritus* (1950), ii. 362). Versions untraced.
[8] Notes for speech in Add MS 44649, ff. 17–20. The society supported him by 4 votes to 2.

Farr & Doyle spoke on the same side; Hallam against; Selwyn voted with Hallam, Mundy & Pickering major with us. Finished my speech. Moved Doyle shd be fined—carried: moved Hallam ditto. negatived—they say.

18. Sunday.

News from Berwick pretty good; rascally coalition, & business consequently run fine. Wright preached on—weighed in the balance & found wanting.[1] Said private business; took solitary walk in Evening; did part of my theme, read Bible O. & N. Testaments, Blair, Buchanan Psalms, the Articles &c.

19.

No post from London. Morning Herald said contest was between Mr G. & Sir F. B; very near, & termination uncertain. Hallam told me a lady told him she had had something to do with a Berwick Election, & that it was the most corrupt place possible. Perhaps she had been unsuccessful.—Sculled up to Shallows &c. after 6. Finished & wrote over Theme. French exercise & French lesson; Began Regnard's Le Distrait.[2] Read Spectator. Etonian Papers—finished Poetaster; not over good. Put down some quotations.

20. Tuesday.

Holiday: Boat before absence in morning: sculled up to Surly Hall after 6. Looking at match between Hawtreys & the School after 12, & reading the papers. Finished the Etonian. Read Spectator: put down a few quotations. Hervey now become Lord Arthur, his father Marquis of Bristol.[3] Berwick Poll by papers—Beresford 505; G. 463; Blake 459. Vy close.

21.

Wednesdays business. Eton fellow drowned at the Oak Tree, named Dean;[4] could not swim—in water 40 min; all endeavours to recover him unavailing. Such accidents rare here, thank God. Our days are indeed but as grass.[5] Read Papers & Spectator. Much surprised at not hearing from Berwick, & no news in papers. Did Translation & French exercise. Wrote to dear Mother. Put down some quotations. Father elected for Berwick.[6]

22.

Sculling sweepstakes. Bankes[7] 1st; Selwyn second. Read papers. Boat with Hervey after 6, to see the match. Heard from Berwick—contest tremen-

---

[1] Dan. v. 27.
[2] Jean François Regnard, 1655–1709; slave at Algiers 1678–81; French novelist and playwright.
[3] Frederick William Hervey, 1769–1859; 5th earl, cr. marquess of Bristol 30 June 1826.
[4] Ralph Deane of Pinner; in his fourteenth year.
[5] Ps. ciii. 15.
[6] Later entry; see 25 June 26.
[7] Meyrick Bankes of Winstanley Hall, 1811–81, Lancashire coal-owner.

14. Holiday. A miserable failure — forgot to take key to upper Hope — boat sunk. Bathed after absence. Hart help, got it set to rights again. Received it soon after 12. Sculled up to home & Hope &c. after 1. Read papers & Eton? Did French exercise; put down some quotns. Did some verses. Read Goldsmiths Deserted Village. Heavy drank wine at me — as does sometimes pass. sometimes Hallam. after dinner.

15. Wednesdays business; after 9oclock school, out to Hallows, thence 200 struck by the state of the Berwick poll. Beresford 60. Blake 53. Gladstone 36. Hope that it is owing to Mr G's voters being principally non-resident, & therefore not so much at hand. as also I consider that the poll had then only just begun. Very anxious for a letter. Read Fch lesson; found a verse long copy of verses; improved them in writg over by cutting out some. By book Hallam out in boat, then dressed above Clewer. Read papers at Socy room; read Goldsmiths Traveller, & Spectator; also put down some quotns.

16. Fridays business. Glorious news. Poll at Berwick on Tuesday at half past one — Beresford — 222 — Gladstone 195 — Blake 194. Famous & rapid change indeed. Hope for a continuance tomorrow. letter from Tom Heard also from Mrs G. Wrote to Aunt E & to Miss G. both long letters; read Jap & Spectator. Put down a few quotns. began odes in school. Wrote some more Spch; corrected & wrote over some of it. Boat after 6. up to Surly & down the stream thence to Clewer.

17. Saturdays business. More good news. letter from J.N.G. asked the result. Beresford 603; Gladstone 381; Blake 357½ they have coalesced. Hope a day or two will announce the conclusn. Pink busts — Medea. Put down some quotns & read Spect; read also prospect & Eton? at Socy room. Made two latin versions of the little thing in Theocritus about the bee. Boat fresh afternoon. after 6. debate at Socy — disarming? Highlanders laudable? Opened — spoke very longly & tediously against it. Law & Doyle spoke on the same side; Hallam against & Selwyn voted with Hallam, Hanbury & Pickering were with us. find — my speech. Moved Doyle shd be fined — carried. moved Hallam be reprimanded — they say.

18. Sunday. News from Berwick pretty good; rascally coalition & business consequently uncertain. Tonight peevish — weighed in the balance & found wanting. Said Spirit busts; took solitary walk in evening; did part of my theme; read Bib. & Th. Locke, Blair, Buchanans Psalms, the Articles &c.

19. No post from London. Morning Herald sd contest was between Mr G & Sir F. B: very near, & all doubtful. nil cert & Hallam told me a body told him he had had something to do with a Berwick Electn, & that it was the most corrupt place possible. Perhaps he had been unsuccessful. Sculled up to Shallows &c. after 6. Fin & wrote over Theme. Fch Exercise & Fch lesson; Began Repond & did it exact. Read Spect? Eton? Papers — find Portaster; wrote good. Put down some q. Stations.

dous; depending almost entirely on whether London voters arrive in time
or no. Bd. 509; G. 464; B. 462. Close indeed—owing to the rascally coalition. Began B. Jonsons Fox; did & wrote over verses. Fridays business;
had French lesson.

23.

Half holiday. Boat after 6; seeing Aquatics (after 4,) playing at cricket;
after 12, reading papers &c. Read good part of Ben Jonsons Fox. rather a
good days work: Private business. Medea.

24.

Holiday. Bathed. Sculled up to Surly after 6. Staniforth spoke for first time.
Put down some quotations; finished B.J.'s Fox—excellent: Began The
Silent Woman.[1] Read papers at Society. Question—man who rebels agst
long established usurper—traitor or patriot? Spoke for his being a patriot—
for the first time (I think) extempore almost entirely. Debate good. I in
majority.[2] News from Berwick (per Morning Chronicle) very good Mr G.
478, Blake 469.

25.

Heard that Father was elected for Berwick on Wednesday. Tom's letter,
announcing it, indeed welcome. Wrote to congratulate.[3] Wright preached
very well—agst giving selves up to sensual pleasures. Said private business.
Walk with Farr. Did great part of theme; read Bible O & N. Testaments, &
Blair.

26.

Day extremely hot. Finished theme. did French exercise & had French
lesson. Read papers—part of an article on Kemble in Quarterly, & a good
deal of Ben Jonson's Silent Woman. After 4 & after 6, with Gaskill,[4] at his
room at Reeves's, wh is very comfortable. He is to be proposed on Saturday
next. He is a great politician, but, as far as I have seen, a very pleasant
fellow, & I shd think likely to make an excellent Member.

27.

Heard from Dear Mother; wrote to her. Day extremely hot; thunderstorm
about 3 o'clock cooled it most pleasantly; wrote over theme; finished article
on Kemble &c. in Quarterly. finished Ben Jonson's Silent Woman. Sculled
up to Surly after 6. Wednesdays business. Put down some quotations.

---

[1] Another comedy of *Jonson's.
[2] Of 3 to 1.
[3] The figures were Beresford 512, *Gladstone 479, Blake 473; but see 20 Mar. 27.
[4] James Milnes Gaskell, 1810–73, M.P. Wenlock 1832–68; a lord of treasury 1841–6;
see Add MS 44161.

28.

Dear Helen's birthday, God bless her; drank her health. Heard from Aunt E. half holiday. Surly after 6. Called up; got off ill. Did Translation & some verses. Finished 2 vol of Spectator; & read papers. Walk after 4. Most tremendous thunderclap I ever heard; Christopher struck; man injured: in a storm about half past two.

29.

Holiday. French exercise & French lesson. Finished & wrote over verses; Tutor told me he thought he wd send them up. Put down some quotations. Match between Eton & Uxbridge; Eton (proh pudor!) beaten, & that by a poor eleven! With Hallam after 12, Gaskill after 12—as mihi dokei einai υυ youth φορτ βουυς.[1] Tea with him after 6, & took him out in my boat.[2] Mr. Canning here; inquired after & missed me.[3]

30.

Fridays business. Did Lyrics. Read papers, & part of an article on Culloden Papers in Quarterly.[4] Put down many quotations, & began Juvenals 3d Satire, with quotations: tea & talk after 6 with [Charles] Canning & Gaskell, at latter's room.

July 1st.

Saturdays business: Private business—Medea—wrote over Lyrics, put down some quotations; read papers & began Massingers Fatal Dowry. Debate at Society on Rebellion in 1745. voted for the Stewarts, the case not being made out clearly against them. I am not however very decided.[5] Gaskell elected with one black-ball; ιδ μοί δοκει ειναι το σελωινου.[6] Wine & fruit (wh last Gaskell had sent me) with Gaskell & Canning at my room; tea with ditto at G[askell]'s. Sculled Hanmer up to Surly after 6. (Soon decided agst Stewarts P.S. W.E.G.).[7]

2. Sunday.

Wright preached *extremely well*: introduced poor Dean's death.[8] Heard from & wrote to Dear Father. Read Bible O & N Testaments; & Apocrypha. Did some of my theme, and read Blair.

---

[1] 'as he seems to me to be a very good youth'.

[2] Gaskell wrote next day to his mother 'I was out all yesterday evening on the water with Gladstone, who is one of the most sensible and clever people I have ever met'.— *An Eton Boy*, 79.

[3] Version of this sentence in Morley, i. 34.

[4] *Quarterly Review*, xiv. 283 (January 1816).

[5] By 5 to 2, the society upheld the view that a conscientious Briton ought not to have rebelled in 1715 or 1745.

[6] 'I think Selwyn's'.

[7] Later entry.

[8] See 21 June 26.

3.

Mondays business. Finished & wrote over Theme: did French Exercise, put down some quotations; wrote out the Society Debate for Pickering major; read part of Fatal Dowry—wh I like very much; & of the article on Culloden Papers in Quarterly. Also did extempore. tea with Gaskell, as last night; sculled him up to Boveney after 6.

4.

Holiday. Tea with Gaskell again; sculled him up to Boveney after 6. He & I pretty much alike in our ideas of politics, ancient & modern. I rather getting a new light on subject of Stuarts, 1745 &c. French lesson. Finished Massingers most excellent Fatal Dowry; with notes & critique. Read papers & spoke in 2 private debates at Society room, on Milton's political character, & on James 2nd. Messed with Carruthers—involuntary but forced.[1]

5.

Wednesdays business. Did & wrote over verses. Put down quotations. Had private business. Sculled up to Surly after 6. Read Part of the Maid of Honour.[2] Wine & fruit with Gaskell & Hallam after 4 at my room; tea with ditto at Gaskell's.

6.

Half holiday. Tea & talk with Gaskell. Sculled Hallam nearly up to Surly after 6. Read & talked French—finished Le Distrait. Did some vile Lyrics, & wrote them over. Finished The Maid of Honour; good—not equal to the splendid Fatal Dowry. Copied out of latter into scrapbook. Read Cambridge Odes &c. Greek & Latin, & Epigrams got by Selwyn, formerly maximus.[3] Read some speeches papers &c.

6 [sc. 7]

Fridays business. Sculled up to Surly after 6. Wrote to Mr G. began the Alchemist[4]—put down some quotations; read paper. Frere[5] came back. run over in boat by a man in a wherry. Bathed.

7 [sc. 8]

This week I have done the vilest exercises I have done for a long time; wh is saying a good deal: & have no excuse, for I have done very little else. Read Alchemist—several lives in Biographical Dictionary: put down some

---

[1] *Gladstone usually messed—that is, breakfasted—with *Hallam; though they lived at opposite ends of the school (*Daily Telegraph*, 5 January 1898).

[2] *Massinger.

[3] William *Selwyn, 1806–75, elder brother of G.A.*, canon of Ely from 1833, Lady Margaret professor from 1855.

[4] * Jonson.

[5] John Frere, d. 1851, rector of Cottenham, Cambridgeshire, from 1839.

quotations; had private business. Medea. A change for better lately; instead of 60 & construed, we do 100 & are not.[1] Tutor called me up—& actually seemed to expect I should have looked at it. Got thro' 45 lines "as well as might be expected". Question at Society. Athens or Lacedaemon most deserving of celebrity? Spoke & voted for Athens: as, of celebrity. Gaskell made an excellent maiden speech; Selwyn also spoke well.[2] Moved Pickering major shd be fined, for not filing papers: carried unanimously.

8 [sc. 9]

Sunday. Heard from Mrs G & J.N.G. who is returned from Scotland. Walk with Gaskell. Read Bible: O & N Testaments. Read one of Massillons Sermons—very eloquent[3]—& finished 3d vol of Blair. Said private business, & did theme. Wright preached on Free Agency—too difficult a subject I think for him—better let alone than ill handled.

July 10, 1826. Eton.

Mondays business. Some quotations. Finished Alchemist, a most excellent play, but Face comes off too well. Sculled to Boveney &c after 6. Wrote over theme. French exercise & French lesson; began Le Joueur.[4] Wrote to Miss G. did extempore. Bathed. Happy to have been, I hope, useful, in taking a man nearly drowned to shore in boat.

11.

Walk with Gaskell & Canning after 6. Boat up nearly to Water Oakley after 4. Bathed. Read paper; private debate with Gaskell about Sir R. Walpole— am now decidedly for him on the whole. Read part of Attorney general's Speech agst T. Hardy &c.[5] Heard from T.G. & Mrs G: heard of my poor dear Uncle Colin's suspension. May God bless it to him, & draw good out of seeming evil—also for the first time of Mr Larkins's arrival.

12.

Wednesdays business. Some quotations. Wrote to J.N.G. Made up accounts for last quarter, and found a deficiency of three pence. Read more of Attorney Generals speech agst Hardy; & finished article in Quarterly on Culloden Papers. did French exercise & Translation, & sculled Hanmer up to Rushes after 6. Mem. I now frequently wake at half past five or so; if I could but get over the other half, & get up when I wake, it would do.

---

[1] That is, the boys prepare 100 lines instead of sixty but are not expected to get up in class and translate what they have prepared.

[2] Athens was supported by 8 votes to none.

[3] J. B. Massillon, 1663–1742, court preacher to Louis XIV and XV, bp. of Clermont from 1717.

[4] Regnard.

[5] Sir John *Scott, lord chancellor as 1st Lord Eldon 1801–6 and 1807–27; as attorney general unsuccessfully prosecuted Thomas *Hardy, radical, for treason in 1794.

13.

Half holiday. Did Greek Anapaests on Athens. Put down some quotations, did some verses for Gaskell, who was in a great hurry. Walk with Farr & Hallam—caught in rain—Day rainy—read papers—a little of Burke[1]— more of Attorney Generals speech agst T. Hardy—had private business— & 2 private debates, with Hallam, Pickering, & Gaskell. On duelling— Hallam and I vehement against it—Gask. & Pick. for it being *beneficial*— & on Queen Elizabeths internal policy, on wh also I spoke—wh was adjourned.

14.

Fridays business—pleasant enough now, as we do so much Horace. Sculled up to Surly after 6. Sculled Colvile[2] down. Finished Attorney Generals speech &c. began Erskine's.[3] Read article on Iron Mask in Quarterly. Wrote home. Chess with Selwyn minor: some quotations put down. Heard from Dear Father. Very poor news concerning health, May God send better! & Dear John going away in the beginning of next week. Wrote over Lyrics.

15.

Saturday's business. Some quotations—private business—finished Erskines splendid speech for Hardy. Walk with Gaskell after 6. Question—Polish Govt justified in excluding Protestants? voted—no.[4] Hallam—Farr— Pickering minor—Gaskell spoke—all on same side. Selwyn only behind chair. Moved Fine on Hallam—carried—met Uncle & Aunt Divie & Edward,[5] who is to come here after Election.

16. Sunday.

Good sermon from Wright—on God is a spirit.[6] Wrote to Mrs G. giving account of yesterdays rencontre with Uncle & Aunt &c. Did nearly all my theme. Read a sermon of Massillon, translated & retranslated a little. Read 2 sermons of Blair: & Bible. Walk alone after 6.

17.

Mondays business. Sculled up to Surly after 6 in 34 minutes & a half; down, after an interval, in 24 minutes. Put down quotations, Finished theme and began writing over. Hervey asked me to breakfast on Wednesday. French exercise & French lesson. Heard from Dear John. He hopes to be here on

[1] Edmund *Burke, political philosopher.
[2] (Sir) James William *Colvile, 1810–80, judge.
[3] Thomas (Lord) *Erskine defended *Hardy.
[4] None voted for, and 6 against.
[5] Edward Lovell Robertson, *Gladstone's first cousin, later a Pall Mall wine merchant.
[6] John iv. 24.

Wednesday week, on his way to join the Ganges.[1] Read Massinger's "City Madam", & began "The Old Law".

18.[2]

Wrote over Theme, & read part of Massinger's Old Law before breakfast. Then received a letter from Dear Anne, with one from Mr G. to my great surprise desiring my immediate return home, & inclosing letter for Keate; on account of Dear Annes late severe illnesses, & Dear Johns contemplated departure in a week. Went to Keate: he kind; gave leave; Tutor very kind; Dame too. Sorry for this summons itself; sending up, any other things, done away with by it: but far, far more anxious as to the cause. Packed up in great hurry; paid bills &c. In School at 11 &c. Sent leaving book to Farr, —bid him & many of my friends goodbye; arranged to write to him, Hallam, & Gaskell. I had expected, or rather hoped to do much between this day & the Vacation. God grant the cause of my being sent for may be a futile one. Tea with Dame. Got into Prince at Slough between 6 & 7. Travelled all night.

19.

Got to Birmingham between 7 & 8 A.M. Breakfast & wash; left it per Aurora at ¼ before 9; very fast coach; too much so. Got to Lpool at 25 min. before 8; came home to Seaforth in Gig; got there about 25 before 9. Found nothing so immediately evil as I had feared. Dear Anne however thin & weak, & Mother especially very anxious. Father conceals it more.

20. Thursday.

Made resolutions. Looked about me. Began Caelebs;[3] got my things in some degree put to rights. We are again all together here. &c . . .[4]

21. Friday.

Read 3d book of Horace Odes: Euclid definitions, Axioms & postulates. also got things to rights, & prepared for carrying resolutions into effect. I degenerate in getting up; at Eton I got up before 7: now scarce before 8.

22.

Copied a long letter. Wrote to Hallam; & in French to Berthomier to discontinue my pupilage; sent Vale to Carruthers; proved two 1st propositions of Euclid. Read Caelebs; wrote part of an ideal speech; made up accounts & diary from 18th.

[1] H.M.S. *Ganges*, 84; see 25 July 26.
[2] Late entries till 22 July.
[3] Probably [Hannah *More] *Caelebs in search of a wife*, 2v. (1809), moral tale; possibly Harriet Corp, *Caelebs deceived* (1817), the same.
[4] Diarist's dots.

23. *Sunday.*

Read Bible & Caelebs. John Murray [Gladstone] preached in morning on parable of marriage-supper,[1] in evening extremely well on "Cease to do evil, learn to do well". Is.1.[2] Cousin Robert[3] down here. Quick, but forward.

24.

operation on dear anne.[4] Read Caelebs. Rode Helens Poney into Lpool. Bought books there—saw sundry relations & friends.—&c.

25.

Dear Johns last day. He is to go tomorrow to Portsmouth; thence to go in the Ganges to South America, for about two years. Looking forward, how shall we be situated then? Tom query?[4] Robn nearly out of his Clerkship: John Lieutenant; William—please God, at Oxford. Helen a big girl: Dear[5] Anne, please dieu restored to health.[6] Tried to draw—found I had lost what little [skill] I ever possessed. Read Caelebs &c. Rode to Lpool. Aided John in Packing. Copied 4 things for Mr G.

26.

Dear John went per Umpire at 1. Extremely sorry to lose him; but have seen more than had reason to expect of him. In Lpool, & rode. Read Caelebs—Byron—&c. Drew Anne in her chair, as several evenings before.

27.

Last term was, independently of state of health at home, by far the happiest I ever spent at Eton. The termination was different for a wise purpose. ne nimium sperare velim.[7] Rode into Park, breakfasted with Uncle Murray. Called on Uncle Thomas. Did Jobs—Read Caelebs &c.

28.

Read Caelebs. Finished 1st, began 2nd vol. Did 3d Proposition. This rate will not do. Rode grey in Evening. Drew Anne in chair.

29.

Read Caelebs. Heard from, & wrote a long letter to Berthomier; endeavoured therein to remove an erroneous impression produced on his mind, of my having been offended by him. Anne, I hope, better. She walked a

---

[1] John ii. 1–11.
[2] Isa. i. 16–17.
[3] Robert Gladstone, 1811–72, Manchester merchant; 4th s. of John *Gladstone's brother Robert.
[4] These sentences in Greek script.
[5] Rest of this entry, and all but last sentence of next, in pencil.
[6] Last four words in Greek script.
[7] 'Lest I should wish to hope too much'. This sentence in Greek script.

8—I.

little in Evg, wh she has not done before since I have been here. Great day at Eton.

30. Sunday.

John M. little Murray,[1] & Stewart[2] at breakfast. 2 former at dinner. Walk & talk with J.M.; latter with Anne. Read Bible & a little Caelebs, also scribled[3] a little. J.M. preached extremely well on Free Agency in Morning, very well on Sabbath in Evening. Heard from J.N.G. I heard from Hallam. Mother ill.

31.

Wrote to John. In Lpool. Called on Mrs McCartney & jobs. Drew Anne in chair in Eveng. Read Caelebs. Breaking up day at Eton—had it been so that I could have staid—Diis aliter visum.[4] Looked at different vessels. Did 4th proposition. Mother better thank God.

1st August.

Copied great part of a very long letter. Wrote a long one to Gaskell, & a short one to Aunt E. Finished Caelebs. Walk with R.G.: as sometimes before. Caelebs might have been, I think, much better as a tale, & is left rather unfinished or unsettled; but its religious views most sound & excellent; temperate yet zealous; truly, me judice, Christian.

2nd August.

In Lpool. Called on Mrs Wilson, Mrs Conway, Miss Benwell, Mrs Smith; & roked[5] about in Book Shops. Began Woodstock;[6] & crossed the Pons Asininus—5th Proposition. Must however give him[7] another benefit soon. Drew a plan of an Inn—an old propensity of Mine.

3d. Thursday.

Rode into Lpool in Evg with Letters. Copied a long letter from Mr G. to Clunie,[8] & one from Clunie to a Mr Dudgeon;[9] on the disgusting subject of the Berwick Election—Read Woodstock; finished 1st, began 2nd vol. Read a little Cicero.

---

[1] Murray Gladstone, 1816–75, Manchester merchant; 6th s. of John *Gladstone's brother Robert.

[2] Probably Thomas, d. 1832, a first cousin; s. of John Stewart, manager of the Gladstone sugar estate in Demerara.

[3] Word in Greek script.

[4] 'the gods saw it otherwise'.

[5] Evidently a portmanteau combination of raked and poked.

[6] *Scott's latest novel.

[7] Euclid.

[8] Unidentified.

[9] Unidentified.

Drawn by J. J. Doyle

SEAFORTH HOUSE,

LANCASHIRE.

Engraved by T. Barber

4th. Friday.

Went against my will to hear a Charity Sermon in Lpool at the new St Michaels, for benefit of schools; preached by Dr Trevor;[1] sincere tho' not able—apparently. Object most excellent. Read Woodstock—Rode with T.G. in Evening.

5th.

Wrote to J.N.G. Read Woodstock—began & read most of 2d vol. Drew plan of a house. Rode in with T.G. & dined with Uncle Robert: a bouncer of the name of Harrison[2] there; party in all only 7. &c. &c. Journal now very defective; somewhat irregularly kept. Wrote to John.

6th. Sunday.

A Mr Fearon[3] preached indifferently as to ability, sound enough in principle. Matheson[4] down here. Read Bible & part of an article in Quarterly Review about Ch of England—Missions. Heard from Gaskell.

7th August. Monday.

Finished Woodstock: very good, me judice. Also finished article in Quarterly Review—rode in in Evg with Letters. Wrote at length & at considerable length to Hallam; copied a long letter to Henry Joy.[5] Helen renewed her proposals about Latin. I acccdc, the higher powers being willing. Heard from Dear John. Probably to sail today. Meikle[6] drudgery entre moi et moi meme falls to my lot. There are some things wh happen every day wh I leave out. Family Prayers & reading Bible—walking, wh I do much in the garden. Singing, with R.G., frequently, after prayers: &c.

8. Tuesday.

Cousin John here. Walk &c. Copied several things. Read great part of the Bride of Lammermoor. A beautiful tale indeed.[7]

9. Wednesday.

Finished Bride of Lammermoor—Read Bernardi on swimming & began article on English Industry in Quarterly.[8] On this & several other days I amused myself by reading different curious books in the Library—several

---

[1] Dr. Thomas Trevor, formerly Humphreys, 1771?–1827, vicar of Eastham from 1797 and rector of West Kirby from 1803; both Cheshire parishes near Liverpool.

[2] Possibly George Harrison, silk merchant.

[3] John Fearon of Liverpool academy; perhaps vicar of Painswick 1802–23.

[4] F. Matheson, perhaps s. of William Matheson, Edinburgh merchant.

[5] Henry Hall Joy, 1786?–1840, at Christ Church; K.C. 1832; a connexion of the diarist's stepmother, Jane Hall Gladstone (d. 1798).

[6] Rest of this sentence in Greek script.

[7] *Scott; see *DNB* li. 93.

[8] xxxiv. 35 (June 1826), reviewing O. di Bernardi, *Lehrbegriff der Schwimmkunst*, and 45.

lives—Jenny Cameron[1] &c. Wrote to some solicitors in London about a bill to Gale.

Thursday 10.

drew plans &c. Finished article on English Industry & Prospects: a good one—Heard from & wrote to Aunt E. Bathed, & out in carriage. Walk with R.G. at night & singing down towards the shore. Called at Parsonage. Mr & Mrs Rawson not come back from Harrogate. My Father said to me—You shall be my biographer, Wm.

Friday 11th.

Wrote a long letter to Gaskell[2]—et, de plus, un epitre pour le liverpool kourier,—an extraordinari undertaking—suspect tha will not insert it.[3] Went to Ince with Mr G; dined with Mr Blundell. Fair allowance of talk, indeed conversation. Read a little about Phrenology, & other things there. Also some Latin with Helen. Do not expect to do much; do however what we do, in accordance to her wishes. Began "Disappointment" by Mr G's Recommendation.[4]

12.

korrected & wrote over part of letter.[5] Finished Disappointment—very unequal in merit. Began Legend of Montrose.[6] Drew Anne in chair—&c. &c.&c.—for 2nd time.

13. August. 1826. Sunday.

Mr Rawson preached morng & eveng not very well, & in desultory way. Read Bible; an article in Westminster Review on Mr Irving;[7] several Lives of Divines in Encyclopoedia;[8] &c. Drew Anne in chair—copied 2 letters.

14. Monday.

konkluded letter to the kourier.[5] Rode grey mare into town, & delivered it. Finished Legend of Montrose, began Waverley,[9] for 2nd time. A little Latin with Helen. Walk with R. G. drew Anne in chair—Dear John off, probably for 2 years some days ago—

15.

Latin again. Read Waverley. Called on Mr Rawson—missed him again—

[1] A. Arbuthnot, *Jenny Cameron* (1746), a picaresque anti-Jacobite tale.
[2] Rest of sentence in Greek script.
[3] Rough draft in Add MS 44718, ff. 61–65. See 23 Aug. 26.
[4] A poem by John Williams (1814).
[5] Sentence in Greek script.
[6] In *Scott's *Tales of my landlord.
[7] i. 27 (January 1824), reviewing Edward *Irving, *For the Oracles of God* and *For Judgment to Come.*
[8] Perhaps *Encyclopaedia Britannica*, 6 ed. (1823–4).
[9] *Scott.

(in Evg.) Hard at work getting the Library into some kind of order, nearly all day, bearing off lumber, reading &c . . .[1]

16. *Wednesday.*

"A Friend to Fair Dealing come to hand—postponed, on account of pressure of Assize Matter, tho' in part prepared for the press". Lpool Courier. Aunts expected—went into Lpool to meet them; they did not come: headache; did a little to books; read Waverley.

17.

Read Waverley. Wrote to Dear John, directed to Madeira; Drew Anne in chair. Rode into Lpool—there caught & kept by the rain.

18. *Friday.*

On these days finished Library—finished Waverley. Rode—Drew Anne. Bathed.

19. *Saturday.*

Dined at Mossley Hill; Mrs Ewart, J.B. & W. Ewart, & Mr & Mrs Gott, with Tom & I formed the party.[2] Read sundries. Journal worse & worse.

20. *Sunday.*

Mr Rawson preached twice; better. Read Bible, lives of some Divines, and began Evans's Sketch of Religious Denominations.[3]

21. *Monday.*

Read Article in Westminster Review on Edinburgh Review.[4] Severe; in some cases justly so. Drew Plans, &c. &c.

22.

Wrote a long letter to Hallam: Read article in Westminster Review on Quarterly Review.[5] Drew Plans.

23.

In Lpool, walked out. First decent exercise for some time. Read Westmr Rev. on Travels in United States.[6] Bought two or 3 books in Lpool. Aristotle—& read part of it. de plus, je lisois a part de chef d'oeuvre

---

[1] Diarist's dots.
[2] Mossley Hill, the Ewart mansion 5 miles SE. of the centre of Liverpool; William *Ewart, 1798–1869, radical M.P.; Joseph Christopher Ewart, 1800–68, Liverpool merchant, his brother, M.P. Liverpool 1855–65; Margaret Gott, his sister.
[3] John *Evans, *A Sketch of the Denominations of the Christian World* (1795).
[4] i. 206 (January 1824)
[5] Ibid. 250.
[6] Ibid. 101, reviewing J. M. Duncan, James Flint, and W. Faux.

d'aristote.[1] os mihi paroit to be pas turpis, nescio an χρησιμος.[2] My letter in Courier.[3] Highly amused by the conjectures. Style voted somewhat obscure —Sense strong according to Mr G. R.G.[suggested] Sandars[4] perhaps the writer; Mr G[replied] no: have not the most distant idea who it is; attack very severe, but just; must draw a reply, if Egerton[5] can manufacture one; T.G.: a well written letter. Anne—fair.[6] Mr G. I must ask Kaye[7] on Saturday who it is—That will betray me; Kaye will show the letter, & my Father know the handwriting.

Thursday. Aug. 24.

More conjectures. Let Anne, Mother, Robn into secret. Tom out at dinner —did not hear it—At Ince with Tom—Tom recommended Mr Blundell to send for the Courier. Read Westminster Review—&c.&c. Singing at night generally with my Brothers &c.&c.

Friday.

Wrote a letter abusing [Liverpool] Mercury for mutilating Mr Cannings Shooting Breeches.[8] Finished the articles I wished to read in Westminster Review. Called on Mr Rawson. Archery—Heard from Gaskell.

Saturday 26.

Archery—Long day of calls in Lpool & Park with Tom—Otterspool, Mossley Hill, Miss Benwell, Mr Wilson, Mrs Sandbach, Mrs Staniforth &c. Read a little in the Starchamber,[9] lent me by Mr Blundell. Drew Anne in chair: Wrote to Gaskell. Wrote over & corrected part of my letter.

Sunday.

Mr Rawson preached pretty good sermon morng, & better Evening. Morng for Jews. Said what could be said. Bad case, as far as I can judge. Read Evans's Sketch; some lives—Drew Anne in chair—copied 1 Letter.

Monday.

In Lpool. Black mare fell down dead from slavers in stomach. A Faithful

---

[1] This sentence written in Greek script and scored through. Aristotle's Master Piece had been for over a century the principal popular handbook in English of sex physiology.
[2] 'It seems to me not bad; whether useful or not I do not know'.
[3] Half a column on p. 3, signed 'A Friend to Fair Dealing'.
[4] Joseph Sandars, Liverpool corn merchant.
[5] Egerton Smith published the Liverpool Mercury.
[6] Substituted for 'pretty good'.
[7] Thomas Kaye published the Liverpool Courier. See Morley, i. 32, and 26 Sept., 6 Oct. 26.
[8] Draft in Add MS 44718, ff. 66–67; again by A Friend to Fair Dealing. See 30 Aug. 26.
[9] A few squibs in this short-lived magazine, run by Peter Hall, were by *Gladstone's eventual rival, Benjamin *Disraeli, 1804–81; novelist; prime minister 1868 and 1874–80; cr. earl of Beaconsfield, 1876.

Servant, & a great loss. Began Tomlines Memoirs of Pitt,[1] & Epitomized a few pages of them. Talk with Jones, Bookbinder;[2] a civil & apparently sensible man. Finished writing over Letter, & sent it. Archery. Cousin the Revd J.G. at Seaforth. Walked from Lpool.

Tuesday. August 29.

Archery. Read Tomlines memoirs of Pitt &c &c.

Wedy Aug. 30.

Read Tomlines' Memoirs of Pitt. Archery—got on better alone, as does Tom. Heard from Hallam, & from Solicitors in London. Wrote to Solicitors & to Jones bookbinder. Fair Dealing in the Courier.[3] To go to the Menai tomorrow, please God.

31.

Read some European Magazine[4] on board steamboat: read also Ciceros first Catalinarian, & began the second. See Separate Journal of Tour.[5]

Thursday. Aug. 31. 1826.

Left Seaforth 20 m. before 8, A.M.: L'pool, by Prince Llewellyn, Steam-packet, soon after 9. Fast sailing vessel. Engine 70 horse power. Water pretty smooth—therefore escaped sickness. T.G. with me. dined on board, pretty well, ½ crown a head. Delightful Sail; along the Cheshire, & then the Welch coast; the latter becomes very bold & fine; passed Ormshead[6]—bold & fine projecting rock: sailed up the Menai straights, past Pen Maen Mawr;[7] arrived off Beaumaris[8] about 4; beautiful place of Lord or Lady Bulkeleys[9] above it; landed passengers at Beaumaris, & at Bangor;[10] sailed on to Bangor Ferry, just by the bridge. Landed there; got on ricketty & poor coach, called "Pilot", for Caernarvon;[11] about 10 min. before 5 P.M. Arrived safely at Caernarvon (for which we had much reason to be thankful) between six & seven after a nine mile ride thro', in general, a beautiful country. Set down at the Uxbridge Arms; a *very good* Inn, & moderate enough. Looked about town (the walls thereof curious & fine—) & castle of Caernarvon; the latter a most magnificent, extensive, & imposing

[1] George Pretyman *Tomline's *Memoir of William *Pitt* whose tutor and secretary he had been, and on whose advice he became bp. of Lincoln (1787).
[2] John Jones of Kirkdale Road.
[3] On p. 3, quoting *Canning's verses in full.
[4] A monthly magazine of *belles-lettres*, July 1824–June 1826.
[5] The following account is in Add MS 44718, ff. 68–71.
[6] Great Ormes Head, 35 miles west of Liverpool.
[7] Six miles SW. of Great Ormes Head.
[8] The county town of Anglesey, near that island's eastern corner.
[9] Thomas James Warren–Bulkeley, 1752–1822, 7th and last viscount, cr. Lord Bulkeley of Beaumaris 1784; his widow, Elizabeth Harriet, née Warren, d. February 1826.
[10] Three miles SW. of Beaumaris, on landward side of Menai strait.
[11] Nine miles SW. of Bangor, also on the Menai strait.

building. Fine view. A royal castle; Marquess of Anglesea[1] constable. A neat town; very prettily situated. Slept at Uxb[ridg]e Arms. Left Caernarvon about 6 A.M. (1st Septr) by water; embarking place leads down from a fine terrace walk, commanding seaview. 4 oars down the Straits 10 or 11 miles—sailed under Bridge—fine Echo—. Beautiful scenery in some parts down the Straights; Marquess of Anglesey's place fine;[2] some others pretty. Navigation in some parts dangerous for Vessels of much size. Beautiful view of the Bridge; I think the best point for seeing it, & recommend coming from Caernarvon by water.

Breakfasted at Bangor Ferry House; a comfortable Inn; went over Bridge, a most wonderful, stupendous, & also beautiful thing.[3] White paint, however, glaring. Dimensions enormous; about 536 tons of iron; chains fixed in the earth; span of suspension Bridge, 540 feet; height above high watermark, 100 feet to platform, 153 to top of towers. Bridge well parapetted; stonework of towers &c. beautiful.

Left Bangor Ferry by car before ten: thro' Bangor & Aber[4] to Conway;[5] 17 miles; Bangor a nice town; Cathedral neat tho not to be compared with Engl[ish] Cathedrals; Passed Penryn castle:[6] the grounds inclosed immens. Revenue, arising from slate quarries, said to be enormous. Pretty or grand scenery for most of the way—picked up some rather curious stones—terrible hills. Road under Pen Maen Mawr awful—nearly three hours on the way—walked many hills—arrived at Conway about ¼ before 1 P.M. The Inn very full, & therefore the people not able to attend well; dinner however good, & very cheap. Two shillings a piece. A good Inn, I should think, when not so crowded. We were quartered in the travellers room. Castle a fine & most interesting ruin, & extensive.[7] One tower hangs over in an awful way. Bridge[8] not so fine as the Menai, but still fine, & prettier; architecture agreeing with that of the castle; into which the chains at one end are fastened. Long & solid causeway joins the bridge & confines the stream, which is very swift, & I should think, dangerous. Town dirty. Beautifully situated; the whole thing—the tout ensemble—town—river—bridge—castle—country around form an exquisite scene. Entrance curious, thro' the town gates. Left Conway soon after three, in a machine called an outside car, wherein the passengers sit with their legs over the wheels, back to back. A real Irish car, I believe. Pleasant ride of twelve miles to Abergele;[9] road pretty, & hilly; in one place ascends to a great elevation;

[1] Sir Henry William *Paget, 1768–1854; earl of Uxbridge 1812; commanded cavalry at Waterloo, where he lost a leg; cr. marquess of Anglesey 1815; lord-lieutenant of Ireland 1828–9 and 1830–3.
[2] Plâs Newydd, on the Anglesey shore midway between Carnarvon and Bangor.
[3] Road suspension bridge, designed by Thomas *Telford, begun 1819, opened January 1826.
[4] Village 5 miles east of Bangor.
[5] Four miles south of Great Ormes Head, on left bank of River Conway.
[6] On the eastern side of Bangor; seat of the *Guest family, iron-masters and slate-miners.
[7] Built, like Beaumaris and Caernarvon, by *Edward I; *Richard II here agreed to abdicate.
[8] Also a newly opened suspension bridge by *Telford.
[9] Due east of Conway, close to the Denbighshire coast.

passed a mountain with a curious cave, extending, we were told, a quarter of a mile (!!) inwards, & a large castellated pile on the right.[1] Got to Abergele about five. Pay for cars a shilling a mile, besides gates & drivers.— Apparently comfortable Inn at Abergele; went on direct thro', generally, a fine country, to St Asaph.[2] Passed a noble place belonging to Col. Hughes on the left.[3] Amusing to remark how few names are to be met with in Caernarvonshire. Williams, Roberts, Jones, Hughes, Evans, & some few more form the whole nomenclature of the county. Got over the eight mile stage, with a good, but rather hilly road, pretty quickly, & got into St Asaph between six & seven. House comfortable enough, but very full; very moderate in charge; 18 pence for tea—a shilling a bed. Went to see Cathedral; a neat & pretty building; but we see Welch Cathedrals to great disadvantage after having seen English. Slept at St Asaph. Left it per chaise some time after six in the morning for Bagillt.[4] Road hilly—passed thro Holywell[5]—a dirty manufacturing place, prettily situated—stage thirteen miles—got to Bagillt before nine; intending to take the boat to Liverpool; by great luck, discovered that a steamboat was just setting off for Chester, & that we could breakfast on board. Went down immediately & embarked on board the St David; 24 horse power, but a good boat—sailed well up to Flint— fine ruin there:[6] rather unfairly, the steamboat took two vessels in tow, captain intending to take them up to Chester. Obliged to let one go; towed the other fairly up, which delayed us an hour. Navigation very difficult; at low water those who know the fords may easily walk across. River very wide. Got to Chester about twenty min: to twelve. A very curious & respectable city. Took place for Liverpool. Breakfasted (not having been able to do so on board) at the Royal Hotel; an excellent house, & moderate enough, apparently. Walked on the walls[7] & saw the cathedral, a venerable building after breakfast; left Chester at 20 min. past one P.M.: got to Tranmere ferry[8] about half past three; great delay in embarking and landing, the latter especially very ill arranged Got ashore in Liverpool about half past four. Nothing waiting, owing to a mistake. Waited sometime. T.G. rode R.G.s horse out, I walked. Got home, safe & well, thank God, about six; much fatigued, but much more delighted. Dinner & a good nights rest set me pretty nearly to rights.—

2nd Septr 1826.

1 September[9].

Finished 2nd Catilinarian & began third.

[1] Gwrych Castle, near Abergele, seat of the Bamford-Heskeths.
[2] Seven miles ESE. of Abergele, 5 miles from the mouth of the River Clwyd.
[3] Kinmel Park, midway between Abergele and St. Asaph but on the right or southern side of the road; seat of William Lewis Hughes, 1767–1852, cr. Lord Dinorben 1831.
[4] A dozen miles due eastward, on the Dee estuary.
[5] Two miles west of Bagillt.
[6] Two miles upstream, SE. of Bagillt; ruin of *Edward I's castle, where *Richard II surrendered to *Henry IV.
[7] Erected by the Romans in the second century.
[8] On the Mersey, 1½ miles south of Birkenhead.
[9] The diary here resumes (Lambeth MS 1416).

2 Septr.

Too much fatigued on getting home to do any thing.

3. Sunday.

Read the Roman Catholic Mass, & part of Evans's Xtn denominations. Mr Rawson preached mony[1] & log; well save a piece of bigotry & I grieve to say[2] untruth; il disoit que les Roman catholics ask pardon of their saints & angels. Inconsistent with Christian principle & practice. Mr Finlay dined here. Drew Anne in chair.

4. Monday.

Drew Anne in chair. In Lpool, doing sundries for Mother Anne. &c. Read a little of the life of Pitt: wrote, copied off & sent a long letter to the Courier,[3] I hope my last. &c.

5.

Read Tomlines Life of Pitt—Indian Chief launched.[4] Beautiful sight: &c. &c. Wrote catalogue of books.

6.

Read Tomlines Life of Pitt; copied a Letter, longish. Wrote account of tour &c.

7. Thursday.

Wrote to Pickering; finished 1st vol of Life of Pitt; began Nicholl's Recollections.[5] Wrote to Jones, bookbinder; wrote in Cousin Helens Album.[6] Archery. Wrote part of a letter to Hallam. T. Ogilvie & Stewart dined here.

8. Friday.

Archery—Read Nicholls—continued Letter. Dear Anne ill with sore throat. Journal worse & worse.

9. Saturday.

Dear Anne still ill. Read Nicholls—finished letter to Hallam, & sent it. Also heard from him. Wrote Catalogue of books, alphabetical as I find no other way answers. Read 6th Proposition &c.&c. Wrote to John.

[1] Scots variant of 'many'; use obscure.
[2] Rest of sentence in Greek script.
[3] Draft in Add MS 44718, ff. 72–74.
[4] A large ship built for the Gladstones in Wilson's yard.
[5] John Nicholls, M.P., *Recollections and reflections . . . during the reign of George III*, 2v. (1822).
[6] Either Helen Neilson, 1801–81, younger da. of Thomas Gladstones, or Helen, 1810–1869, 2nd da. of his brother James, 1775–1832, Liverpool iron merchant.

10. Sunday.

Mr Rawson preached, well: morng on Thanks be unto God for his unspeakable gift;[1] Evg on Looking unto Jesus.[2] Copied 3 Letters. Wrote by Mother's desire, to Aunt E. Read a little of Evans's Sketch, & Simeons two first sermons on the Liturgy.[3] Excellent. Read Bible. I do not put down in my diary my nightly reading of Bible during the week. Dear Anne had a blister on.

11.

Dear Anne a little better. In town for a short time, doing shopping work. Copied a Letter. Heard from Pickering. Read Nicholls. Wrote up Journal.

Tuesday.

Dear Anne still ill. In Lpool. Wrote to Hallam. Finished Nicholls's first volume. An independent & clever man, apparently. Read Mr Cannings speech on the admission of the Catholic Peers;[4] both sound & brilliant. Copied a Letter & a case.

13. Wednesday.

Dear Anne's sore throat still very bad. In Lpool. Fair Dealing published in Courier.[5] Father appeared to like it; asked me what I thought of it. "Middling" I said. Began the 2nd vol of the Life of Pitt; wrote to Gaskell; & read part of 4th Catilinarian.

14.

Dear Tom to go to Harrogate tomorrow with J. Finlay.[6] Dear Annes throat still bad. Read Tomline; finished 4th Catilinarian—4 brilliant speeches— read part of Mr Huskissons Speech on Navigation Laws;[7] & wrote up Journal. Archery.

15.

Anne still ill. Finished Mr Huskisson—not convincing if Mr G's assertion be correct that they [i.e. foreign exporters] *must* have our market & cannot do without it. *Nothing* made out save on score of necessity & question not quite fairly met. Nothing in Mercury. Read article in Edinburgh Review on W. India Question. Read part of 2 vol of Tomlines—a heavy work tho on a most interesting subject. Tom went to Harrogate with J. Finlay. Heard from Aunt E & Berthomier—very satisfactory letter.

[1] 2 Cor. ix. 15.
[2] Heb. xii. 2.
[3] Charles *Simeon, *The excellency of the Liturgy, in four discourses* (1812).
[4] 30 April 1822, *NSH* vii. 211, 273.
[5] Half a column on p. 4.
[6] John Finlay, Liverpool gentleman.
[7] 12/13 May 1826, *NSH* xv. 1144.

16.

Anne considerably better in aftnoon. At Ince. Mr B[lundell] thought little
of Fair Dealing's first. Wrote to Tom & John. Copied 1 Letter, did 10
Propositions. Read Tomline &c. Long, miscellaneous & heterogeneous
conversation with Mr Blundell.
              Place taken.

17. Sunday.

Sermon in morng for Infirmary—in afternoon text out of Revelations. Read
Bible—Simeons 3d & 4th Sermons, & finished Evans. Anne still better.

18.

Made 14 calls—on Uncles Murray—Hugh—David—& at Laverock Bank;[1]
Mr Jones; Miss Benwell; Mrs Conway; Mrs Smith; Mrs Wilson; Mrs Mac
Cartney; Mrs Traill;[2] Messrs Ewart; Mr Staniforth & Mr Sherborne.[3] also
went to see Athenaeum Library[4]—& shopped. Copied a good deal—& read
Tomline—finished 2 vol. & read a few pages of 3d.

19. Tuesday.

Called on Mr Rawson. Read Tomline, 3d vol. Wrote up Journal—got things
put away—wrote in Cousin Helens Album—Packed chief part of my things.

20.

Up at half past seven instead of half past five—so unable to finish Tomline
—read a little. Finished packing & getting things put by. Drew Anne in
chair. Dined at $\frac{1}{2}$ past one; left Seaforth 20 m. past 2.—& Liverpool per
Express at half past three. Tobin[5] the only inside passenger besides myself,
for the night. Tea at Norton Gate.[6] Good coach. Travelled all night.

21. Wednesday.

Got to Birmingham about a quarter to five. Left it, by Hibernia, about $\frac{1}{4}$
past six; breakfast at Leamington; dinner at Benson;[7] good coach; full,
many Eton fellows; got safe to Eton, thank God, soon after seven. Got tea,

---

[1] A house on the edge of the sea, a furlong west of Seaforth House.
[2] Wife of Thomas Stewart Traill, physician, associated with John *Gladstone in various local good works.
[3] Perhaps Charles Robert Sherbourne, 1755?–1836 of Hirst House.
[4] Opened 1799; John *Gladstone, whose portrait is there, was a prominent member.
[5] John Tobin, 1810?–74, schoolfellow; incumbent of Liscard, near Birkenhead, 1833;
s. of Sir John Tobin, 1762?–1851, mayor of Liverpool 1819, *Huskisson's electoral
manager.
[6] At Norton-on-the-Moors, a village 4 miles north of Stoke-upon-Trent.
[7] In south Oxfordshire, 2 miles NE. of Wallingford.

& began to get things to rights, pull books out, &c. Found Coleridge[1] & Okes had been married in holidays; to Miss Keate[2] & Miss Sibthorpe.[3]

22.

Met my old Eton friends again. Walk & tea with Hallam. Friday's business; called up. Getting to rights. Wrote home to Mrs G. Berthomier called on me. Read part of Burkes Appeal from New to Old Whigs.

23.

Saturday's business. Got things to rights, & *did out* my old study—read papers—Walk with Hallam & Gaskell. Robinson[4] my fag. Saw Cousin Edward Robertson—likes Eton much. read part of Burkes Appeal. But a poor beginning to the Christmas term, wh is generally, with me, the most sapping.

24. Sunday.

Plumptre preached; well, as far as I could hear him, on rendering selves a living sacrifice.[5] Breakfasted with Hallam. Walk with Hallam. I esteem as well as admire him. Perhaps I am declaring too explicitly & too positively for the period of our *intimacy*—which has not yet lasted a year—but such is my present feeling. Did Theme. Read Bible; & 5 of Blairs Sermons. Not enough of them on Gospel, I think, the practice is excellently recommended & principle is not discouraged, but only not enough mentioned. Read a little of the Roman Catholic Prayer Book & Waterlands Commentary on Athanasian Creed;[6] answers to Objections,[7] Latin Version &c.

Monday. 25.

Mondays business, with Virgil. Doubtful whether or not shall be in the sixth form—depends on Hervey's coming back, or no; hope however that he will. Saw Edward Robn again not well—but likes Eton & behaves well. Finished Burke's Appeal; read his Speech on American Taxation[8] & began that on India Bill;[9] &c. Meeting at Society: proposed Wentworth;[10] elected unanimously. Pickering proposed Wilder,[11] elected unanimously &

[1] Edward Coleridge, 1800–83, assistant master 1825, lower master 1850, fellow 1857–1883; vicar of Maple Durham, Berkshire, from 1862. See Add MS 44137.

[2] Mary, eldest daughter of the headmaster; great-granddaughter of the Young Pretender.

[3] Mary Elizabeth, da. of late Thomas Sibthorpe of Guildford; she bore *Okes three das. and died long before him.

[4] William Frederick Robinson of Markham Grange, Newark.

[5] Rom. xii. 1.

[6] Daniel *Waterland, *A Critical History of the Athanasian Creed* (1724).

[7] Either Daniel *Whitby, *A reply to Dr *Waterland's objections*, about the nature of the Trinity, or *Waterland's *Answer to Dr *Whitby's reply* (both 1720).

[8] 19 April 1774.

[9] 1 December 1783.

[10] William Charles Wentworth-Fitzwilliam, 1812–35; whig M.P. for Northamptonshire from 1832; styled viscount Milton, 1833, when his father became 5th Earl Fitzwilliam.

[11] Charles Wilder, 1808–38, later an assistant master.

Law,[1] rejected by one blackball: wh I am sorry for. Made several motions for alterations in rules; all of them (I believe) passed.

26.

Holiday for Miss Keate's marriage. Wrote over Theme; walk with Hallam; finished Burke's Speech on Fox's India Bill; began that on Nabob of Arcot.[2] read up Homer: and wrote a long letter to Mr G, signed "A Friend to Fair Dealing" wh I thought a good way of letting him into the Secret. Heard from Miss G. Heard debate on Reform after 4.

27.

Finished Nabob of Arcot: began Charles XII:[3] read up Horace; Fridays business; did Translation; walk with Hallam. Tutor told me he wd give me an exercise to be sent up in [at] end of week; not to be counted for this term:—&c.&c.

28.

Thursdays business. Read Memoir of Richard Roberts Jones,[4] wh Gaskell gave me. Read Charles XII. Did verses; read Tacitus for private business. Read a little Spectator. Called on Berthomier. Saw Cous. Andrew;[5] very kind. I see Ed. Robn generally once or twice a day. Gaskell drank wine with me.

29.

Holiday. Walk with Hallam. Mounted new bookcase. Hallam drank wine with me. Read some of Charles XII. Wrote speech for Saturday in favour of Richard.[6]

30.

Saturdays business. Walk with Gaskell. Private business: Tacitus in morng, & began Oedipus Tyrannus[7] in Evg; Nicholl & Buller[8] now with me. No exercise made its appearance. Read Irene;[9] the argument to Cicero pro Milone: altered & wrote over speech; added to it considerably in speaking.[10]

---

[1] John Halsey Law, 1809–77, barrister, bursar of King's College Cambridge.

[2] 28 February 1785.

[3] Voltaire, *Histoire de Charles XII roi de Suède* (1731).

[4] A short appeal by William *Roscoe and others on behalf of 'Dick of Aberdaron', R. R. *Jones, 1780–1843, self-taught Welsh philologist (1822).

[5] Andrew Robertson.

[6] Next day's debate was to compare *Richard I of England and Charles XII of Sweden.

[7] Sophocles.

[8] Henry Iltid Nicholl, 1809?–1845, advocate, and John Richard Nicholl, 1809–1905, rector of Streatham 1843–1904, were both in Gladstone's form; so was Anthony Buller, 1809?–81, rector of Tavy St. Mary, Tavistock, from 1833.

[9] Samuel *Johnson's tragedy.

[10] Notes for speech in Add MS 44649, ff. 12–13.

Hallam, Gaskell, & Pickering also spoke; Pickering converted; Hallam alone voted for Charles. Moved Gaskell shd be fined; carried; Courier shd be taken in; carried. Pickering elected Vice Chairman: Hallam alone voted for me.

Sunday. October First.

Plumptre preached. on "a living sacrifice".[1] Inaudible; not from weak voice, but from his very indistinct utterance. Pickering drank wine with me. Walk with Hallam & Gaskell after 4. Read Bible; more of Catholic Prayer book; Johnson's Prayers;[2] & 2 of Blair's Sermons: did a poor Theme.

Monday.

Wrote over Speech & also minor speeches for Gaskell to report from as Vice President. Monday's business. Hope to hear from home tomorrow. Read life of Burke, prefixed to his works; Canning's Speech in 1812 on Catholics:[3] & the Preface to Clarendons Rebellion.[4]

Tuesday. Octr. 3.

Holiday. Walk with Hallam. wrote over Theme—Read Clarendon; wrote Speech for Saturday week; poor enough—walk with Gaskell; did punishment set by Keate to all the fifth form, for being late in Church.[5]

Wedy. Octr. 4.

Wrote to A.M.G. & to Jones, Bookbinder. Walk with Hallam & Gaskell: read Clarendon, did verses; read Bethell's Squib book.[6] Called up.

Thursday.

Holiday. Walk with Hallam; read paper. Wrote over verses for Tutor: had private business—Tacitus. Put down some quotations to various books. Read a little Clarendon, & about 120 lines of Pindar. Had Cousin Edward to breakfast with me. Private debate on Pitt & Fox after 4. I spoke for Pitt—not giving opinion on Revolutionary War, but defending him in toto up to that time. Pickering, Gaskell & Hallam also spoke: Hallam well; Gaskell very cleverly, tho' not meeting the question in a very fair way.

Friday.

Short walk with Gaskell: one also with Pickering. Breakfast with Gaskell. wrote over verses: finished 2 Olymp. of Pindar: learned Sophocles for to-

---

[1] Rom. xii. 1.
[2] Samuel *Johnson, *Prayers and Meditations* (1785).
[3] 3 February 1812; *NSH* xxi. 514.
[4] Edward *Hyde, 1st earl of Clarendon, *The True Historical Narrative of the Rebellion and Civil Wars in England*, 3v. (1702–4).
[5] In Morley, i. 42.
[6] Perhaps *Bethell's Life in London, and Liverpool Sporting Register* (1826).

morrow. Put down sundry quotations. Read a few pages [of] Clarendon, & did an Abstract of about 100 pages. Wrote speech for tomorrow in favour of Caesar. Heard from Dear Mother & A.M.G: Father glad to hear I was "Fair Dealing": so am I, I am sure.[1]

Saty Octr 7.

Got up speech & spoke for Caesar agst Alexander.[2] Moved Gaskell be fined, carried. moved Courier be brought in, on Morning Heralds being turned out. Saturday's business. Private business, & quotations. 2 propositions of Euclid: walk with Gaskell: read a little Herodotus & a little of the Pro Milone.[3] Attended play in Mansfields room: tedious & poor, tho' ludicrous.

Sunday. 8th.

Private business—Catullus. Walk with Hallam & Gaskell; made list of characters ancient, modern, & divines. Read characters of Luther & several others.[4] Read Bible; 3 sermons of Blair; several Psalms in Buchanan's Translation. Did Theme. Put into play.[5] Construed it for tomorrow.

October 9th.

Monday's business. Play; & some annotations thereto; (Play nominally; it really being now the Funeb. Orats)[6]—quotations to sundry books. Walk with Pickering; did extempore. Read part of an article in the Quarterly on Burke: breakfast with Hallam; read Clarendon; & a good number of parliamentary Speeches of the last century. Also corrected some copies of the Rules, pro bono Societatis.

10th.

Holiday. Walk with Gaskell after 4; melon chez lui after dinner. Did some verses; read Clarendon; added to Milton Speech; formidable opposition to be expected. Heard from home; extremely satisfactory letter from Mr G. on "Fair Dealing". Wrote over Theme.

11.

Wednesday's business. Walk with Hallam: Pickering, Hallam, & Gaskell drank wine chez moi after dinner. Wrote to Mr G: & to Jones Bookbinder. Meeting at Society about a question of mine. Whether W. Hastings behaved

---

[1] Version of part in Morley, i. 42. Cp. 11, 23 Aug., 26 Sep. 26.
[2] Caesar was held a greater character than Alexander by 5 to 3.
[3] Cicero.
[4] Probably in *Chalmers' *Biographical Dictionary*.
[5] *Keate took a class called 'play', made up of the sixth form and the clever senior boys in the fifth, through most of the classical dramatists; see next entry.
[6] A textbook collection of Roman funeral speeches.

ill towards Rohillas;[1] declared Illegal by Pickering, Wilder, Wentworth, & Gaskell; declared legal by Hallam, Selwyn, Doyle & me; we however ready to exchange it on other grounds. Carried agst us by Pickerings casting vote. Finished verses & wrote over for Tutor: turned speech in As you like it into Gk Iambics for Lyrics: added to & wrote over part of speech on Milton; read a few pages of Clarendon.

12.

Half holiday. Wrote over verses; did some Lyrics for Gaskell, he being in a hurry, & giving me Hecuba[2] for them!! Wrote over Iambics for tutor. Walk with Gaskell. Hallam had wine chez moi—Read a little Clarendon; & wrote over the rest of speech, adding & altering. Spoke on Pitt & Fox in private debate after 4: ill.

13.

Friday's business. Walk with Hallam. Spoke over & altered a little my speech. Read a most violent article on Milton by Macaulay in Edinb. Rev;[3] fair & unfair; clever & silly; allegorical & bombastic; republican & anti-episcopal; just & absurd. A singular composition indeed. Wrote to R.G. Wrote over Lyrics: read a little Clarendon; some Herodotus; some quotations; & learnt Gk play for tomorrow morng.

Saturday, Octr 16 [sc. 14][4].

Finished 1 vol of Clarendon. Walk with Gaskell. Got up Speech & spoke on Milton; rather too violent.[5] Acted as Vice President & wrote out nearly seventeen pages of the debate. House did not adjourn till near $\frac{1}{4}$ before six; I fined, on Selwyn's motion, for putting down question about Warren Hastings; Hallam & Doyle opposing it. *Very much fatigued.*

Sunday 15th.

Plumptre preached on mystery of religion.[6] Headache. Read Bible, & Blair. Did Greek Theme. Read Mr Wilberforces admirable speech & several more on the Slave Trade in 1791;[7] breakfast chez Gaskell, & walk with him. Also wrote out about 4 pages & a half of yesterdays debate, wh I considered right, it being moral. But may God teach me what is right.

Monday.

All right again: copied out about 18 pages of the debate: had Monday's business, & play: breakfast with Hallam; walk with Gaskell. Read part of

---

[1] See C. C. Davies, *Warren *Hastings and Oudh* (1939), 41–61.
[2] Euripides, a current school text.
[3] xlii. 304 (August 1826).
[4] This entry was written below the entry for Sunday 15th.
[5] *Milton's political conduct was deplored by 4, including *Gladstone, to 3.
[6] 1 Cor. ii. 7?
[7] Commons debate 19 April 1791.

a preliminary discourse to poems of Ossian.[1] Got almonds & raisins from Handley[2] & Pickering, who were put into the 6th form on Saturday Evening.

Tuesday.

Half holiday. Heard from Anne & Tom: Dear Ma & cousin Eliza[3] had been ill, but thank God better. Wrote over theme. Wrote out Doyle & Wentworth's speeches, finished debate: covers 44 pages. read 3d & 4th Olympics; breakfasted with Hallam; walk with Gaskell after 12: wrote to Farr; also to Buckeridge; & read a little about Ossian.

Wednesday.

Finished duty as V.P. save filing the papers. Walk with Gaskell after 12; with Pickering & Gaskell after 4. Handley spoke—very fairly. Breakfasted with Gaskell. Read Dissertation on Ossian.[4] Wrote to A.M.G. did verses & Translation, & read some copies in the Musae Etonenses.[5] Also wrote a song on Gaskell, abusing him: to be sent to him.

19th.

Wednesdays business. Gaskell's birthday! Walk with Doyle. Wrote over verses for Tutor, did Lyrics & ditto. Read a little more about Ossian: breakfasted with Hallam, &c.&c. Saw Uncle Divie after 12, who told me that on Tuesday my Cousin Eliza Robn was given up by Sir H Halford[6] who said she cd hardly live 3 hours, but that last night she was much better, & tho danger still remained, in a fair way to recover. God be praised, & spare her!

20th.

Friday's business. Wrote over verses; also Lyrics for Tutor. Read 5th Olympic; a little Spectator; a little on Ossian: finished article on Priors Life of Burke: & sundry copies in Musae Etonenses; also relearnt private business. Selwyn read over a good copy of verses. Walk with Doyle. Tutor promised exercise to be given tomorrow.

21.

No exercise: to be looked over tomorrow. Saturday's business. Called up. Wrote over Lyrics: read a little Cicero; finished Blair on Ossian; walk with

[1] Prefixed by *Blair to James *Macpherson's *Fingal* (1762).
[2] John Handley, 1807–80?, brother of Philip; banker; liberal M.P. for Newark 1857–1865.
[3] See two entries later.
[4] Hugh *Blair (1763).
[5] Two volumes of Latin and one of Greek verse by Eton boys, collected by William *Herbert, brother of 2nd earl of Carnarvon, in 1795.
[6] Sir Henry *Halford, formerly Vaughan, 1766–1844, fashionable physician; cr. bart. 1809.

Hallam & Gaskell after 12, Pickering & Doyle after [6]. Question—Ossians Poems: Selwyn & Pickering spoke: I voted agst authenticity, not believing them either entirely MacPhersons or authentic.[1]

22.

Kind letter from Farr. Went to Tutor: made an alteration in exercise for him; Private business. Read Bible; Blair 2 serm; Buchanan; a Sermon by Chalmers on mote in brother's, beam in own eye, excellent.[2] Plumptre preached. did Theme. &c.

Monday 23.

Mondays business. Read Spectator. Musae Etonenses; Herodotus; & did 4 propositions of Euclid. Wrote to A.M.G. & T.G.: read part of an article on Hamiltons Education in Edinburgh Review, & did Epitome of a little Clarendon. Walk with Pickering.

24.

Half holiday. Wrote over Theme. Read Spectator, heard from A.M.G. Read Gray a little.[3] Heard thro' Edward that Eliza was better; thank God. Walk with Hallam; & with Hanmer up to the fair after 6. Finished article on Hamilton-system; very good. Pickering had wine chez moi: did verses; wrote song *at* Gaskell; read a little Cicero, & did a little Epit. Clarend.

25.

Wednesdays business: wrote over verses for Tutor: & copy to be sent up, produced at last. However, I ought to be thankful. Read Spectator; walk with Gaskell. Wrote to A.M.G. made some more plans of book-cases. Read about 60 lines of Εκαβη:[4] & did some Epit. Clarend.

26.

Friday's business. read paper; did bad Lyrics: wrote over Verses. Bought Sophocles; read First 200 lines of [his] Electra, & wrote quotations &c. to them, & other books. Read Spectator. Finished Epit Clarend of 1st vol.

27.

Wrote over part of my bad Lyrics; the shorter the better. Read Spectator: & odd lines of Electra; learnt & did Œd. Tyran. with Tutor; quotations &c to both these. Half holiday. Read Musae Etonenses; papers, & began an article in Ed. Rev. on Icon Basilike.

---

[1] The society voted against the poems' authenticity by 6 to 3.
[2] Thomas *Chalmers, 'The doctrine of Christian charity applied to the case of religious difficulties' (1818), on Matt. vii. 3–5.
[3] Thomas *Gray the elegist.
[4] Euripides' *Hecuba.*

Saturday 28.

Holiday. Heard from A.M.G. Read about 100 lines of Electra; some Herodotus; some Cicero; Spectator; & did two propositions. Walk with Doyle: read papers. Question Hannibal or Epaminondas, wh greatest character? moved to read "finest" for "greatest", ill received: so I went behind chair; cd not vote the question being put so.[1] Did a very foolish thing, & very unaccountable; interrupted Pickering when talking about Blackwood, for wh he had just moved, because the motion had not been seconded! Play in Evening: rather poor acting—Love a la mode.[2] fellows not knowing their parts. Breakfasted with Lady McGrigor.[3]

29.

Fair sermon from Bethell on Prayer. Walk with Hallam; said private business: & construed play. Read Bible; Buchanan; Blair; a Letter from Wharton, a Roman Catholic on leaving that faith;[4] did a long theme; wished it to be a good one; fear it is not.

30.

Mondays business. Called up: an idle day. Theme not to the purpose; but Tutor otherwise liked it. Did a few verses, on an excellent subject— Admonitu locorum.[5] Anxious to do a good copy this week, if I can. Play. Read a little Spectator, & Edinburgh Review; read paper. Walk with Hallam. Began 2nd vol of Clarendon, & Epitome; &[6] read about 100 lines of Electra, with quotations &c.

31.

Half holiday. Breakfast with Gaskell. Walk with Doyle. Heard from H.J.G, & also letter from J.N.G. to R.G. Wrote to Mr G, & to Farr. Wrote over theme; read some Herodotus; Spectator: about 140 or 50 lines of Soph. Electra; Life & some poems of Gray; & a little Clarendon with Epit. Antrobus, Selwyn, & Hervey, put into 6th Form. I Captain of Fifth.

First November, Wednesday.

Holiday. Walk with Hanmer. E. Robn breakfasted with me. Did Translation, & Verses; long, but not near so satisfactory a copy to myself as I was anxious to do. Read about 140 lines of Electra; read Spectator; & Edin. Rev.

---

[1] The society preferred Epaminondas to Hannibal by 7 to 4.
[2] Charles *Macklin's farce (1759).
[3] Née Mary Grant of Lingeistone, Morayshire; m. 1810.
[4] C. H. Wharton, *Letter to the Roman Catholics of the City of Worcester* (1784).
[5] Cicero, *De Finibus*, v.2; on the power of suggestion exercised by places.
[6] 'did' deleted.

2.

Almonds & raisins from Antrobus, Selwyn, & Hervey. Wednesday's business. Wrote over verses for Tutor. Read Spectator. Breakfasted with Lady MacGrigor. Good natured & kind. Read a little Electra. Walk with Doyle: made Speech on Strafford; long & poor;[1] read Horace; & did a good many rudiments of rum Alcaics.

3.

Fridays business. Wrote over verses: finished Lyrics—Heard thro Edward, that Eliza was worse again: but a little better when the account was sent. Hope for good accounts tomorrow. Wrote over & partly learnt speech. Wrote to A.M.G. Learnt private business. Called up: read about 100 lines of Electra; & an attempt at answering Mr G. on Reciprocity Treaties.[2]

4.

Saturdays Business; wrote over Lyrics. Private Business. Read full two hundred lines of Electra. Did two propositions; & read Spectator. Got up speech & opened debate. Question; Were the proceedings of the Commons against E[arl of] Strafford deserving of censure? Wilder absent; Durnford[3] & Selwyn behind the chair; rest of the House with me—that they were not. Gaskell, Law, & Wentworth spoke; W. very well, & others by no means amiss.

5. Sunday.

Bethell preached fairly on obedience to higher powers:[4] Hallam called out of Church, on account (I believe) of his grandmother's sudden & dangerous illness at Windsor.[5] Said private business; & construed Play. Read Blair; 2 numbers of Spectator; some of Johnsons Latin Poems; & some of Buchanan's Psalms; & Bible.

6.

Heard from T.G; no hope of Dear Eliza—Aunt Fanny,[6] & Mr Ogilvy—May God take them all to himself: the latter in the course of Nature; & may He support & bless Uncle Colin. Holiday. Finished Electra; a beautiful play. Did verses. Walk with Doyle. Read Spectator & Clarendon a little. Read also a little Herodotus. Did 3 propositions.

7.

No letter, I am happy to say; as had there been news it wd in all probability

---

[1] i.e. prepared speech delivered two days later. Notes in Add MS 44649, ff. 27–28.
[2] *Huskisson inaugurated in 1824 a series of reciprocity treaties with other states.
[3] Edmund Durnford, 1809–83, rector of Monxton, near Andover, from 1846.
[4] Rom. xiii. 1.
[5] *Hallam's father's mother died there that day, aged 90.
[6] Mrs. Gladstone's m.'s s.; née, and m. of Colin, Mackenzie. See 12 Nov. 26.

have been news of death. Monday's business. Walk with Gaskell. Read Spectator, Clarendon, (& did Epit) Herodotus—newspaper & sundries: did 2 propositions. Must get more'n this out of tomorrow.

8.

No letter. glad. Wednesday's business. Finished 3d vol of Spectator; read a little Clarendon, & Herodotus; wrote to T.G.; walk with Doyle; wrote over verses for Tutor; did Lyrics & wrote over for tutor. Keate began to read me over at 5; fellows made a row; he left off, & went on with the lesson.

9.

No letter again—Half holiday. Walk with Hanmer. Wrote over verses. Read Clarendon & did Epitome read Herodotus; learned & had private business.

10.

Still no letter. Friday's business. quotations; called up; wrote over Lyrics. read paper; walk with Doyle. Hallam still absent. Read Clarendon & did Epit; also began Trachiniae;[1] read argument accounts in Classical Diction-ary &c: & read 200 lines of the play: with quotations.

11.

Still no letter. Saturdays business. Play. Private business: learned also: & quotations. Read 230 lines of Trachiniae with Quotations; did 2 proposi-tions; read Cicero; & a little Clarendon, with Epit. Walk with Doyle & Pickering. Read papers. Debate on Wolsey; was Henry 8 justified in de-posing him? Voted Yes. Gaskell & Doyle spoke "No"; Wentworth "Yes".[2]

12. Sunday.

Had a long letter from A.M.G. Eliza still, by their last accounts alive; had rallied again, & issue uncertain. This gives hope again. Aunt Fanny dead; aged 79. Said private business; construed Play: breakfast with Hallam, who is just come back: walk with Gaskell. Read Bible, O & N. Testts, Blair, & Buchanan's Psalms: & did a long Theme.

13.

Mondays business & extempore. Play. Breakfast with Hallam. rainy day—Wrote to Mr G, & a vy long letter to J.N.G. read a little Clarendon; read over 10th Satire [of] Juvenal: & 5th making quotations to it & some other places. Did a few verses.[3]

[1] Sophocles, *The Women of Trachis*, in Thessaly.
[2] *Wolsey was held unjustly dismissed by 5 to 4.
[3] Morley, i. 42.

14.

Holiday. Wrote over Theme; did verses; walk with Hallam & Doyle; read papers & debate at Society; heard from Mr G, & from Farr; read 200 lines of Trachiniae; a little Gil Blas in French: & a little Clarendon.[1]

15.

Read papers &c at Society. Breakfast with Hallam. Wrote over verses for Tutor; turned Shakespeare into Greek Iambics for Lyrics; Lady Anne & Richard.[2] Wednesdays business. Wrote to Mr G. Learnt & had private business; read 100 lines of Trachiniae. Walk with Hallam & Gaskell, & again with Pickering. Sent 2 Pine Apples to Tutor, just received from home. Dear R.G's birthday.

16.

Half holiday. Wrote over verses; & Lyrics for Tutor. Heard from T.G; & also from Mr G who says there is no hope of poor dear Eliza. May she be removed to a better place; & my Uncle & family be supported under their heavy trials. Walk with Hallam & Gaskell, & again with Hanmer. Read Clarendon; papers; about 260 lines of Trachiniae; & did 3 propositions.

Friday. 17.

Wrote to Mr G and a few lines to H.J.G. & A.M.G. Wrote over Lyrics. Friday's business. Construed play. Read paper &c. Hallam breakfasted with me. Walk with Gaskell. Finished 2nd vol of Clarendon; did 2 propositions; & read about 160 lines of Trachiniae. Quotations to sundry books.

Saturday. 18.

Saturday's business. Play. Read papers &c. Finished Blair's dissertation on Ossian. Finished Trachiniae. Did 3 propositions of Euclid. Learned & had private business. Question. Deposition of Richard II justifiable? Voted —no: Hervey, Hallam, Law, & Doyle voted Yes. rest no. Good debate.[3] Moved 2 fines. Finished the delightful Oration "pro Milone".[4]

Sunday. 19.

Heard from A.M.G. Said private business; & construed Play. Hallam breakfasted with me. We generally mess together now. Read Bible, O & N. Testts; did a long Theme, on Speech; read Blair, his Life,[5] & Buchanan's Psalms.

[1] A. R. Le Sage, *Histoire de Gil Blas de Santillane*, picaresque novel.
[2] *Richard III*, I. ii.
[3] See *Hallam to Farr [21 November 1826] in *Bulletin of John Rylands Library*, xviii. 24 (January 1934). The deposition was held unjustifiable by 7 to 4.
[4] Version in Morley, i. 42-43.
[5] A short life of Hugh *Blair by James Finlayson was prefixed to the 1807 edition of *Blair's *Sermons*.

20.

Mondays business. Play. read papers. Walk with Hallam. Read over 3d book of Horace's Odes. Did extempore. Read part of a Radical Pamphlet, calld "Appendix to the Black Book".[1] Began 3d vol of Clarendon, & did some Epitome of Second.

21.

Holiday. Wrote over theme. Read papers; part of Article in Edin. Rev. on Icon Basilice. Read Herodotus; Clarendon; did 3 Propositions; & some verses. Scrambling & leaping expedition after 12, with Hallam, Doyle, & Gaskell.[2]

22.

Short walk with Gaskell. Wednesday's business. Read paper. Wrote to Farr; read Clarendon; did verses; & read a little Herodotus: also read two or 3 copies in Musae Etonenses.

23.

Dined with Hervey after 4 at Christopher: Canning & Gaskell also there. Half holiday. Heard from Mr G, A.M.G. & J.N.G.: thank God well. Mr Ogilvy released from this world. tranquil & without pain. Walk with Hallam & Doyle: wrote over verses for Tutor, & in part for school. Had private business; read Clarendon; finished Epitome of 2nd vol: & read a little Herodotus. Wrote to A.M.G.

24.

Friday's business: called up. 7th time this term, I think. Finished writing over verses—read Clarendon—paper—wrote to take place—read Herodotus, & did 3 propositions—Walk with Hanmer.

25.

Saturday's business & Play—read paper, & finished 3d Vol of Clarendon. read Herodotus; did 3 propositions; & read argument of 1st Philippic,[3] & greatest part of the oration itself. Also learned & had private business. Walk with Doyle. heard from R.G: debate on George 2's execution of the rebel Lords: voted that he was justified, in a majority.[4] Lots of jaw afterwards.

26.

Staid out with a cold, caught yesterday in Church, my place being much

---

[1] [John *Wade] 'New Parliament. An appendix to the Black Book', a fifty-page hostile analysis of the newly elected house of commons.
[2] Version in Morley, i. 43.
[3] Demosthenes.
[4] Of 8 to 5.

exposed in a draught. Read Bible, Blair, Buchanan; did Theme, & read a few pages of Cicero de Natura Deorum.

27.

Monday's business & Play: dreadfully cold. Walk with Doyle. Wrote to Mrs G. & Aunt E. Read Clarendon & Herodotus (beginning 4th vol of Clarendon) & did 3 propositions.

28.

Holiday. wrote over theme—heard from Mrs G—read Clarendon—papers— saw Colleger & Oppidan match—Oppidans won—did 2 propositions—read Charles XII & Herodotus.

29.

Half holiday. read Clarendon. Walk with Doyle & Gaskell—Hervey drank wine with me after four—read Charles 12—& Herodotus. Did 2 propositions.

30. *Thursday.*

Holiday. Read Clarendon—began Vol 5th: read Herodotus. Breakfasted with Gaskell. He & Canning drank wine with me after 4. Walk with Hallam. Did verses. Finished 1st book of Euclid; & read a little Charles 12.[1]

1.

Friday's business. Sent leaving book to Hervey: wrote over verses for Tutor—called on Berthomier. Walk with Pickering—read Clarendon— Herodotus—Charles 12—wrote to Mr G: & made speech for tomorrow.

2.

Saturday's business. Wrote over verses—read Clarendon. wrote over & got up Speech in favour of modern writers against ancient—Gaskell & Hallam spoke on same side—Wentworth for ancients. Majority for moderns—8 to 3. Election of chairman afterwards. I chosen. I voted for Hallam—Selwyn (I think) for Wentworth—Pickering[2] & Wilder for Pickering—& Hervey, Hallam, Durnford, Law, Wentworth, Doyle & Gaskell for me. Read Herodotus; & supped[3] with Carruthers—he getting into the 5th form today.

3. *Sunday.*

Hervey took leave—a great loss—Bethell preached well—Short walk with Pickering—did short theme—read Bible. Buchanan. Blair. &c. Heard from Buckeridge.

---

[1] Version in Morley, i. 43.
[2] This name interchanged in the MS with Durnford's.
[3] Instead of 'attended'.

4.

Monday's business. Bid Hervey good bye—read Clarendon—& a little Herodotus—Doyle & Hallam drank wine with me—arranged about Society carpet—got things into order & packed up in part—finished article in Edinburgh Review on Icon Basilike. Berthomier called on me.

5.

Finished the first book of Herodotus & packing. Read a little Dryden. Half Wednesdays business. Went up to Windsor to arrange about Society carpet. Left Eton soon after 12 with Hanmer, for Uxbridge. Dined there. Came on in Evening by the Union, a slow coach. Travelled all night—tea at Oxford.

6.

breakfast at Birmingham—left it by Aurora—Day foggy & journey not over pleasant—almost all night travelling at this season. dined at Newcastle. Got to Lpool before ten; & to Seaforth before eleven—Found all pretty well there. heard of Dear Eliza's death, yesterday at three a.m.

7. Wednesday [sc. Thursday].

Tired—having slept very little on the road. getting books in the Library to rights. Read part of the Confessions of Ireland[1] & went on with Tomline's Life of Pitt.

Friday. Decr 7 [sc. 8].

Out & about the place—finished Tomline. began Brambletye House.[2] Tomline heavy—strong on subject of Revolutionary War.

Saturday.

Wrote to J.N.G. read Brambletye House—in Lpool shopping—wrote up Journal. &c.

Sunday. 10.

Church—read 2 of Chalmers's Astromical Discourses[3]—& Bible. Copied a short letter.

Monday 11.

in Liverpool, buying books &c. Walked thence to Seaforth. read Brambletye House—copied a letter.

---

[1] *Confessions* of W. H. *Ireland, literary forger (1805).

[2] [Horatio *Smith] *Brambletye House, or, Cavaliers and Roundheads*, 3v. (1826), historical novel.

[3] Thomas *Chalmers, *Discourses on the Christian Revelation, viewed in connection with the modern Astronomy* (1817).

12. Tuesday

—two Finlays[1] dined here—read Brambletye House.

13.

finished Brambletye House—heard from J.N.G. read Confessions of Ireland &c.

14.

In Lpool—walked out. read Confessions of Ireland—heard from Hallam &c.&c.&c.

15. Friday.

Mr G. ill—Walk with T.G.—called on Mr & Mrs Rawson—Finished Confessions of Ireland—began Hume[2]—wrote to J.N.G. & a long letter to Hallam.

16. Saturday.

Read Hume—Iconoclastes[3]—& a long debate on probable war with Spain, with some fine speeches[4]—Iconoclastes abominable.

17.

Church. read a manuscript account of death of Miss C. Buchanan[5]—Bible with some commentary—and 2 of Chalmers's discourses. Copied 1 letter—walk.

Monday.

Copied 2 letters—In Lpool & walked out—read Hume—a delightful history —barring the religious principles.

19. Tuesday.

Read Hume—& began a kind of Epitomized Epitome of him. Walk with T.G.

20.

Finished First Vol. of Hume—Mr G. & T.G. dined with Mr Bolton.[6] Did 2

[1] Thomas Kirkman Finlay, of Alston, Finlay & Co, Liverpool merchants.
[2] David *Hume, *History of England*, 6v. (1754–62).
[3] G. *F[ox], *Iconoclastes: or a Hammer to break down all invented Images* (1671).
[4] *NSH* xvi. 350–98, commons debate on royal message, 12 December; including *Canning's celebrated 'called the New World into existence' speech. See H. W. V. *Temperley, *Foreign policy of Canning* (1925), frontispiece, 379–81, and 579–85.
[5] Untraced.
[6] John Bolton, 'the doyen of Liverpool commerce, the West India merchant prince' (Fay, *Huskisson*, 381).

propositions in 2d B. of Euclid—but not thoroughly. Read paper. Catholic Address &c—walk.

21.

Shortest day—went to Ince. saw Mr Blundell—Read Hume—paper. read Eng. Bards & Scot. Rev.[1] partly over again.

22.

Read a little of "Royal & noble authors"[2] & Hume; also a letter of Mr G's on W. India Question.

23. Saturday.

—walk—read Hume—get on miserably—partly from a habit of miscellaneous & desultory reading in the Library. heard from Hallam—Dined with Mr Conway. Joe Ewart, H. Harrison,[3] Headlam,[4] Tom, Robn & I composed the party, with the host & hostess. All the guests Etonians.

Sunday. 24.

Dear Anne's birthday. Walk. Copying. Read 2 of Chalmers's Discourses— & Bible.

Monday—Christmas day.

Our Christmas times are not now what they used to be. Sic visum supero[5]— Not well. Took medicine. Read the last of Chalmers's Discourses (most powerfully & beautifully written—perhaps too copious in style) & a few pages of Hume.

Tuesday.

Wrote to Hallam; heard from Gaskell. Took medicine again. Walk. Read Antijacobin[6] &c. read a little Hume. Must somehow make up for my miserably slender doings hitherto since I came home.

Wednesday 27.

Out leaping a little. read a little Hume—Cousins Colin and John came to dinner. time much taken up with them in Eveng.

---

[1] *Byron, *English Bards and Scotch Reviewers* (1809).
[2] Horace *Walpole, *A Catalogue of the Royal and Noble Authors of England, Scotland, and Ireland*, 5v. (1806); perhaps in enlarged ed. by T. *Park.
[3] Henry Harrison, at Eton in 1811, s. of Richard Harrison.
[4] Thomas, probably a nephew of John Headlam, 1769–1854, archdeacon of Richmond, Yorkshire.
[5] 'So one above ordains'.
[6] Pro-government satirical weekly by *Canning and others, published in the session of 1797–8.

Thursday 28.

Copying—leaping, with Cousin John—Backgammon with John, & with Colin. Little time now left to me, ESPECIALLY as I do not rise near as early as I ought. Mother ill with headache. &c.

29.

My birthday—aged seventeen—retrospect does not give me much reason to congratulate myself on great industry in any branch of improvement. Trust that another year, if granted, may afford a somewhat fairer prospect! A birthday in name—Anne McKenzie[1] came in—leaping & backgammon with John. Wrote to Aunt M. Finished 2nd vol of Hume.

30.

Began 3d vol of Hume—Copied—walked into Lpool with John Robn— shopped, & dined with Uncle Robert—T.G, R.G, C.C.F. Robn[2], J.M.G. Robn, T. Ogilvie & self there. Uncle very kind. No very bright beginning of my new year. Backgammon.

31. Sunday.

Church twice—Cough—Began Tomlines Elements of Theology[3]—& read Bible.

---

[1] His sister.
[2] Cousin Colin Robertson.
[3] G. P. *Tomline, *Elements of Christian Theology*, 2v. (1799).

Seaforth. January.

1827.

1.

The New Year not signalized in its beginning by any great improvement in me—read Hume a little—& a volume called German Popular Stories[1]. Nursed for Cough. Backgammon & Billiards. Cousin Colin detained by contrary winds.

2.

Read Hume. Walked into town & did business there. Went to Indian Chief to see Colin's books & Cabin—very comfortable. Also saw T. Watson[2]. Went down the river in her & returned in the steam-boat wh had towed her. Prog[3] in the Cabin. Captain Gill[4] very civil. Walked back with Cousin John in a snow storm—very wet.

3.

Read Hume—played billiards & backgammon—Cousin Colin sailed for India. John remains with us a few days—began a letter to Hallam. Heard from him & Gaskell. Read Arabian Nights a little.[5]

4.

Finished letter to Hallam—copied—read Hume—& began an Irish Tale—Crohoore of the Bill Hook.[6] Walk in snow—unjolly.

5.

T. & R.G. dined with T. Staniforth—Copied a good deal. Wrote to Gaskell. Finished Crohoore—an interesting tho wild tale. Poor Ireland. Read Hume. Walk again partly in snow. D. of York died.[7]

6. *Saturday.*

Walk—read Hume—copied a good deal—& occupied for several hours in

---

[1] The Grimm brothers' famous tales.

[2] Thomas Watson, Liverpool master mariner.

[3] Food.

[4] Henry Gill, the same.

[5] Several more or less bowdlerized English versions, derived from Galland's translation into French, were available.

[6] The first volume and a half of [John and Michael *Banim] *Tales by the O'Hara Family* (1825), melodramatic Irish novelettes.

[7] *Frederick Augustus, 1763–1827, duke of York and Albany; field-marshal 1795; nursery rhyme hero.

going through Henry Joy's letters to find some particular passages, for Mr G.

7. Sunday.

2 good Sermons from Mr. Rawson. read Bible—Article in Edin. Review on Church of England—& a little of Tomline's Theology.

8.

In Lpool—jobbing—called on Mrs Conway, Miss Benwell & Mr Staniforth. Walked out. Finished 3d & began 4th vol of Hume. Mr Grant dined at Seaforth.

9.

Copied more than three sheets of letterpaper full; walk; day very boisterous; read Hume: & some parts of "Paris as it was & as it is".[1]

10. Wednesday

—Copied again: a good deal more; read Hume—played billiards & backgammon with Cousin J. Robertson.

11.

John Robertson went per Umpire. Finished a great copying job, begun on Tuesday—ten or twelve sheets in the last three days—to account for little else being done—Heard from & wrote to Hallam: read Hume.

12.

Walked into & out of Liverpool; did some small jobs there; dodged old Pincher in with me; he was heartily tired coming back[2]—read a good deal of Hume.

13.

Rode to Uncle Murray & breakfasted with him: detained by rain: called on Aunt Thomas;[3] at Otterspool, & Mossley Hill; rode with P. Ewart[4] as far as Vauxhall[5]—compared, to prove the correctness, what I copied in the beginning of the week; & read Hume; finished 4th & began 5th vol.

14. Sunday.

Tide, driven up by a tremendous gale, did much damage, & encroached—a

---

[1] [F. W. *Blagdon?] *Paris as it was and as it is*, 2v. (1803); tourists' guide.
[2] Perhaps the Newfoundland dog that impressed Arthur *Stanley (R. E. *Prothero, *Life of Stanley*, i. 22); d. 1831.
[3] Janet Strong of Orkney, m. Thomas Gladstones 1799; d. 1846.
[4] Peter Ewart, d. 1853, William *Ewart's brother; rector of Kirtlington, Oxon.
[5] About half a mile north of Liverpool town hall.

fine sight, however. 2 fair sermons—read Bible,—with Mants Compilation of Notes[1]—& Tomline a little.

15.

Copied one letter. Went to Lpool—shopped, & called on Mrs Bolton[2] Wilson—Sandbach—Traill—McCartney—& Woode[3]—read Hume.

16.

Read Hume, & a speech of Lord Liverpools on the Queen's Business[4]—In town in the morng, with Dear Tom, who went off to Shropshire—bound thence for London—Walked out to breakfast. Aunt Johanna came— Packed partially—& made up accounts for the last six months.[5]

17. *Wednesday*

—Read Hume—finished 5th vol. copied one letter. Finished packing—bid goodbye—left Seaforth soon after 2—Liverpool at half past three, by Express coach—Travelled all night.

18.

Dear John's birthday. God bless him. Got to Birmingham before 5 a.m. left it about 6. Breakfasted at Lymington—dined at Benson—(mem. never to dine there again)—& got to Slough $\frac{1}{4}$ or $\frac{1}{2}$ past seven—to Eton about eight —seventeenth time of returning—Did a few stanzas of holiday Task[6]—but a good deal fatigued.

19. *Friday*.

Friday's business: a dreadful beginning. got things partially to rights— read a few pages of Clarendon & paper. Wrote to Mrs G. & did holiday task— Walk in morng & up Windsor after 12[7]—socked at Leightons—mem. not to sock[8] this half, unless really hungry, & then the plainest.

20.

Saturdays business. Hallam & I again commenced messing together. wrote over holiday task—read a little Clarendon—& paper—walk. & up Windsor. —rooted up many old papers in eveng & cleared bureau: destroying much rubbish & perhaps keeping much.

[1] G. *D'Oyly and Richard *Mant, *The Holy Bible, . . . with Notes, explanatory and practical; For the Use of Families*, 3v. (1814).

[2] Cp. 20 Dec. 26 n.

[3] Possibly the wife of J. M. Woode, vicar of Stoddenden, Shropshire, who was a burgess of Liverpool.

[4] On the bill against Queen *Caroline; house of lords 3–4 November 1820; reprinted in *NSH* iii. 1574–1619, from the pamphlet edition.

[5] See Add MS 44804A, ff. 2–3.

[6] On Panthea, in Latin alcaics; Add MS 44718, ff. 86, 147–8.

[7] See 21 Jan 27 n.

[8] 'sock' is the Eton word for what many schools call 'tuck'.

21. Sunday.

Provost[1] preached—weather most bitterly cold, especially in Church, especially in my seat there.—wrote to Mr G.[2] Pickering come back: & Selwyn.—read Bible, O. & N. Testaments; began Mant, reading the Introductions, Notes &c: therefore slow work. Read Tomline, & a sermon of Blair: did Theme.

22.

Monday's business. Heard from Aunt Mary, with a few lines from Mr G. Mem. henceforward to label my letters. read Clarendon. began 2nd book of Herodotus—wrote over Theme—walk with Hallam—Meeting at Society— much confusion & little business.[3]

23.

Wednesdays business. Have been expecting to be called up for some days. Weather still very cold: read paper—Clarendon—a little Herodotus—did Translation—& a few verses, on Satire—called on Berthomier—he said he had heard an excellent account of John from Mr Tennant.[4]

24.

Half holiday. Walk with Hallam. read papers—Clarendon—finished 5th vol—did verses—read a little Herodotus—read also Preface & Introductory Letter to Pursuits of Literature.[5]

25.

Holiday. Tutor tells me there is to be a confirmation here next week— notice just received. Had Edward Robertson & McKay[6] to breakfast—up Windsor with Hallam—wrote over verses for Tutor & for school—did some Lyrics—read Baviad & Moeviad, with the notes &c. Both excellent.[7] Writing Society accounts also.

26.

Fridays business. Finished & showed up a hodge podge lot of hendecasyllabics[8]—wrote them over for school—wrote to Miss G. & to T. G. Weather still very cold. Walk with Hallam. Read Clarendon began 6th vol. read

[1] Joseph *Goodall, 1760–1840, headmaster 1801, provost 1809.
[2] In Bassett, 10–12; with an account of the duke of *York's funeral at Windsor on the 19th.
[3] Choosing a rug and newspapers.
[4] Probably William Tennant, Staffordshire gentleman, whose s. Charles Edmund was John Gladstone's junior in the navy.
[5] Satirical poem by T. J. *Mathias on the British literary scene (1794).
[6] William McKay, a new boy.
[7] William *Gifford, editor of the *Anti-Jacobin* and the *Quarterly Review*, ridiculed in these parodies of Persius the affectations of London literary society (1794–5).
[8] Version of this phrase in Morley, i. 33.

10—I.

Heredotus—& 3 first propositions of 2nd book of Euclid. Hope to take lessons next vacation.

27.

Saturdays business. Learned & had private business. Heard from A.M.G. Walk with Doyle. read Clarendon—Herodotus—mem: the second book extremely stupid & heavy for the most part—2 propositions—quotations to sundry books—finished reading up what had been done in the holidays of those things wh I think worth reading up. Question: conduct of England to Ireland from Revolution to 1776 justifiable? Voted, no; Hallam spoke well on that side; as did Gaskell;[1] Law & Wentworth also spoke.

28. Sunday.

Grover preached—could not hear him at all. read Bible—with Mant's Compilation of Notes—will call them for brevity, Mant's Notes. They are bulky, but excellent. Read a few of Buchanan's Psalms—1 of Blair's Sermons, & some Tomline: also endeavoured to prepare myself for the sacred & awful rite of Confirmation. May it please the Giver of all good things, for the sake of His Dear Son, our Adorable Redeemer, to give unto me & my fellows the grace of His Holy Spirit, and to grant efficacy to the means which have been ordained for our assistance, in working out our Salvation. May He have compassion on our weakness, and remove our corruption; may He give us both the power to promise, and the strength to perform; and when we take upon us our Baptismal Vows, may we do it with a stedfast resolution to fulfil them, and an humble hope that God in His mercy will be pleased to grant to us that without which we cannot attain unto so great a glory. Tutor read to all his pupils to be confirmed, a most excellent sermon in a most impressive manner. Walk with Pickering & Doyle. Wrote to A.M.G. & J.N.G.

29. Monday.

Holiday for the Accession.[2] Read Clarendon. Walk with Doyle: heard from & wrote to T.G. He kindly sent me a box of Le Mann's biscuits—read Herodotus—& 2 propositions of Euclid—also read Nelson's book[3]—Catechism —parts in the Bible relating to Confirmation, with Notes & part of Serm. on Mount, with Notes. read paper.

30. Tuesday.

Holiday for the Martyrdom.[4] Read Clarendon: breakfasted with Went-

---

[1] See Gaskell, *An Eton Boy*, 84, 111–19. Nine members voted no, none aye; *Selwyn abstained.
[2] Of *George IV, 1820.
[3] Perhaps Robert *Nelson, *The great duty of frequenting the Christian Sacrifice*, prefixed by *Instructions for confirmation* (1707). Among other possibilities, such as numerous lives of the admiral, may be mentioned *Memoirs of the late John *Nelson . . . Written by Himself* (1807), autobiography of a colleague of John *Wesley's.
[4] Of *Charles I, 1649.

worth; heard from Mrs G. Walk with Doyle after 12; sat with Gaskell and Wilder after 4; former gave us coffee at his room. read Herodotus & 1 proposition. Tutor read us another very good sermon on Confirmation—and—Read more of Sermon on the Mount.

31. Wednesday.

Monday's business. The only whole school-day this week. Walk—read paper—Clarendon—part of Pursuits of Literature—wrote to R.G. did a few verses on "books". A most vile subject—or as Chapman[1] would say, a most *bald, insufficient, jejune, & tame one.* Copied a few references in Hecuba —unpacked wine &c. Read more of the Sermon on the Mount—A long account of a very short day's work.

February First.

Holiday for the Confirmation.

This day, with upwards of two hundred more, I, most unworthy of so great a privilege, was confirmed according to the apostolical rite preserved in the Church of England. O God, my Heavenly Father, look down in mercy on thy sinful creature, and grant unto me that these ordinances of thy Church may not be to me unmeaning ceremonies, and formal rites; Grant that I may indeed go forth strengthened by Thy Holy Spirit; do Thou, who hast given the power to promise, give also the power to perform; having given the outward symbol, O let me feel and believe and find that I have the inward and spiritual strengthening & refreshing of the soul. Purify my thoughts, my words, and my deeds; confirm the mercies of Thy Covenant of Grace, and enable me *to govern myself—to love my neighbour—and to serve my God*; not crying Lord Lord, but doing Thy Will; not seeking after vain things, but making the One Thing Needful the great, the supreme, the paramount object of my pursuit and my desire; using and improving my one talent, that by Thy Grace I may be enabled to make it two; feeling that I must die, trusting that I shall live; knowing that I am sown in corruption —praying—hoping—believing that I shall be raised in Incorruption. And not unto me alone, O Most Merciful God, but unto all thy people, especially unto those who have this day gone through the solemn rite of Confirmation, grant a participation in the Blessing of Redeeming Love; guard us from temptation; support us under what seems to us evil; excite us unto Virtue, strengthen us in Faith, confirm us in Penitence, and lead us to the mansions which are prepared for those who are washed in the blood of the Lamb. For the sake of his worthiness be so great mercies vouchsafed to our unworthiness. Amen! Amen!

Bishop[2] not dignified in appearance—but went through the service apparently with great feeling and piety—gave an exhortation after the Blessing.

---

[1] Charles Chapman, b. 1807; priest at Lindsey and Kersey, Suffolk, 1836; vicar of Prescot, Lancashire, 1848; suicide 1849.

[2] George *Pelham, 1766–1827, bp. in turn of Bristol 1803, Exeter 1807, and Lincoln 1820.

—Dined with Wellesley after four—still gentlemanly, good-natured, and unaffected. Hallam & Pickering also there. Hallam's birthday. Finished Clarendon—a beautiful History. Finished verses: and read some Herodotus.

February 2nd.

Holiday for the Purification. This easy week of easy weeks getting to an end. Breakfasted with Wellesley at the Castle Inn, Windsor. Went up again to him after 12, and walked with him, Hallam, & Pickering to Bells of Oosley,[1] on his way to Egham:[2] finding he had time, he accompanied us part of the way back: promising to come down, if possible, tomorrow week. Began 4th vol of Spectator, & went on with Charles 12—& Herodotus. Wrote to H.J.G. Wrote over vile verses on a vile subject—made them 4 better by making them 4 shorter—cut off the end—better if they had never had a beginning. 1 Proposition; & learnt private business for tomorrow. May it please God to render me more worthy of the blessings I receive, & more able to keep the vows I have taken upon me.

3. Saturday.

Debate on character of Augustus. Gaskell—Hallam—Law—Durnford—Pickering—spoke all against: Doyle said a few words almost neutral, but rather favourable. Voted against him.[3] Moved vote of thanks to Ld A. Hervey— —which I am to concoct. Moved a fine on Wentworth—carried—both unanimously. Read Spectator & Herodotus—a good deal of. Began Persius for private Business. & had Greek also. Persius hard but good: & Keate gave me a job—three fresh copies of verses to write over—as I forgot them at 8 & 11, from Yonges hearing in pupil room & my not going in to school—a job & a jaw too. I am certainly not in his good books.

4. Sunday.

Could not hear sermon at all connectedly. read Bible & Notes—1 sermon of Blair's: he is more flowery than solid;[4] near 100 pages of Tomline's Theology: & a few of Buchanan's Psalms. Did theme; & said Private business. Walk with Pickering.

5.

Monday's business. Not called up yet. Walk with Doyle—read paper—wrote to Ld A. C. Hervey, conveying the Vote of Thanks of last Saturday—walk with Doyle—read the First Volume of Coxe's Life of Walpole[5]—save the Appendix.

---

[1] Inn on right bank of Thames some 3 miles SE. of Eton, beyond Windsor Great Park.
[2] West of Staines, and 5 miles SE. of Eton.
[3] In a majority of 7 to 1 on the motion that Augustus deserved well of Rome; *Doyle abstained.
[4] Cp. Morley, i. 33.
[5] Archdeacon William *Coxe, *Memoirs of Sir Robert *Walpole*, 3v. (1798).

6.

Holiday. Walk with Doyle—read the greatest part of the Appendix to V.1. of Coxe—some of the Drapiers Letters[1]—and above half of 2nd vol of Coxe; Berthomier called on & interrupted me in Eveng. Working at nothing else, in order to make up my mind on Sir R. Walpole by next Saturday.

7.

Wednesday's business. Still not called up. Did a long copy of verses on Memory. Finished 2d & Appendix & began 3d v. of Coxe. Heard from Mr G. —going to Gloucester given up for the present. a letter from J.N.G. also sent me—walked with Hallam. Heard of Dr Foster Pigott's death.

8.

Still not called up. Friday's business. A very satisfactory letter from Hervey: read Coxe—about 250 pages—wrote a longish letter to Mr G: and wrote over verses. Heard an account wh I sincerely hope is not, but much fear is true, that the Bp of Lincoln is dead—who confirmed us only a week ago.

9.

Holiday. Report confirmed.[2] Our confirmation, I suppose, was his last labour. Walk with Hallam: Gaskell, Wentworth & Canning drank wine with me after four. Read paper—finished 3d & read good part of 4th v. of Coxe.[3]

10. Saturday.

Read Coxe: & paper. Saturday's business. Still not called up. Gk play private business in morng. Debate on Sir R. Walpole; Hallam, Gaskell, Pickering, & Doyle spoke. Voted for him—last time, when I was almost entirely ignorant of the subject, agst him: there were sundry considerable blots,—but nothing to *over*-balance, or to equal, the great merit of being the bulwark of the Protestant Succession—and his commercial measures— & (*in general*) his Pacific Policy.[4] Persius private business in evg. on coming back, agreeably surprised to find T.G. & T. Stewart here. about half past seven; T.G. got me leave; tea & walk with them at the White Hart.

11. Sunday.

Read Tomline—went up & breakfasted wt T.G. & T.S.—had long & most excellent & pious Letter from my Beloved Sister—unworthy am I of such an one. Went to St. Georges;[5] very fair & practical sermon—went with

[1] *Swift's anonymous pamphlet on Irish coinage (1724).
[2] The bp. died on the 7th.
[3] *Coxe's fourth volume, *Memoirs of Horatio, Lord *Walpole* (1802), dealt with Sir Robert's next younger brother.
[4] Version in Morley, i. 37. See also 4 Mar. 26. *Walpole was held to deserve well of his country by 8 to 2.
[5] The chapel of Windsor Castle.

Stewart thro' the Castle—wrote shortly to J.N.G. dined & spent the evg till half past ten—bid them goodbye, not being certain of seeing them again. Read Bible.

12.

Monday's business—ran up after saying at 8, & sat with them till near a quarter to nine. they were to go off by the nine o'clock coach—obliged to come down to Play. Still not called up; finished Coxe—read a little Swift—finished 2nd book of Herodotus—much better latterly—read a little Charles 12—did theme, & a few verses. Meeting at Society after 4: various motions brought forward with different fates. contentions ran very high.[1] Hallam & I much together—pretty much beaten.

13.

Breakfasted with Doyle—Wentworth & Hallam there—Walk with Wentworth—read paper—wrote over theme—Doyle & Hallam drank wine chez moi after dinner. Read Spectator; wrote to A.M.G. & to Farr. had Greek private business; did about 170 lines of Hippolytus,[2] & the Argument, with quotations to sundry books, & read a little Charles 12. Holiday.

14.

Wednesday's business. Still not called up; he [Keate] has taken his time about putting me in—read about 100 lines of Hippolytus.—Spectator—Walk with Doyle—did a good many verses; and put down a great many quotations to two lessons of Persius—also some to 2 of Greek Play. (the Cast). & some other books.

15.

Half holiday. I do not think I have ever been before so long a time, in the Upper Division, without being called up, as the month wh has now elapsed since the holidays. Wrote over verses for Tutor & for School—read papers & article in Edin. Rev. on Culloden Papers.[3] Walk with Doyle—E. Robertson drank wine with me—read Spectator—a little Charles XII, & about 340 lines of Hippolytus, with et ceteras.

16.

Friday's business. Called up at last in Scriptores, which I love not. Wrote to T.G. Lonsdale elected Fellow.[4] Walk with Gaskell. read Quarterly on Gertrude of Wyoming[5] & Edinburgh on Birkbecks Notes on America.[6] read

---

[1] Private society business.
[2] Euripides.
[3] xxvi. 107 (February 1816).
[4] John *Lonsdale, 1788–1867, bp. of Lichfield 1843; said to write the best Latin since the age of Augustus.
[5] i. 239 (May 1809).
[6] xxx. 120 (June 1818), on Morris Birkbeck, *Notes on a journey in America* (1817).

papers—& Lpool paper—read Spectator—& about 450 lines of Hippolytus. —did not do quotations however for much of that. Read a little Charles 12.

17.

Saturday's business. Walk with Hallam & others. read Spectator—a little Euripides & had private business—(Persius)—read paper—Debate on accounts of Cyrus by Herodotus & Xenophon. Voted for Xenophon as more credible—more consonant with Scripture accounts.[1] Moved a Vote of Thanks (ironical) to Pickering for saying hold your tongue to Hallam during a discussion, & spoke at considerable length—voted agst it. had other *fun* there—but what was no fun, Tindal[2] proposed & black-balled by Pickering & Selwyn.

18. *Sunday.*

Staid out [of church] for cold—weather bitter. & my place particularly exposed.[3] Read 2 of Blair's Sermons (having no others at hand) Mants Bible for about 1 hour & half—above 100 pages of Tomline's Theology— apocrypha—a little Yonges Night Thoughts, & Buchanan's Psalms—and wrote briefly to Mrs G.

19.

Monday's business. called up again. Tutor again asked twice about my being put in, & seemed surprised.[4] Play. read Spectator. Finished the debate for Doyle, entering &c: put down quotations to Persius. Read Edin: Rev on Burgh Reform:[5] & paper; finished Hippolytus, & put down some of my arrear notes—very few, as most anticipated, to Hippolytus itself, but put down in the places referred to.[6] Had Gk private business.

20.

Half holiday. Keate put me into the sixth form. told me to take pains &c. be careful in using my authority &c. &c. He was very civil indeed, & said he was going to put me in, asking if I had any objection.[7] He set me a speech. Wrote to Mr G. read Spectator. finished quotations for play. Did translation —read paper—did some verses, & sapped at speech.

21.

Finished learning Speech, & spoke to my Tutor. *Called up in Homer.* Keate looked over my Translation—awfu' parteeclar. Construed too at my Tutors

---

[1] The eight other members voting agreed.
[2] John William Warre Tyndale, b. 1811?, barrister and manager of Scott's bank.
[3] 'to draught' deleted.
[4] See next entry.
[5] xxx. 503 (September 1818).
[6] Notes in Add MS 44802D, ff. 2–6.
[7] Version in Morley, i. 34.

for the first time. Wednesday's business—finished verses & wrote over for Tutor & Keate: ordered Almonds & Raisins & sent them round—30 packets. read Spectator—Charles 12—better than 200 lines of Hecuba.

22.

Spoke again to my Tutor. Fridays business; somewhat different to what it is in the 5th form. Read a little Hecuba, Charles 12., & Spectator. did Lyrics—Sapphics. Wrote to Aunt J., A.M.G., & T.G. Walk with Pickering, Doyle, & Wentworth.

23.

Half holiday. Time much cut up in the morning by going to Keate. Long walk after 12 with Doyle. Finished 4th vol. of Spectator; read paper, Charles 12—Walker's Elements of Gesture[1]—& about 120 lines of Hecuba. Had private business—Persius—and spoke to Keate at night. The action I found very difficult. He was very goodnatured, for I was intolerably stupid —& recommended practice.

24. Saturday.

Holiday. Question—Lord Bute's conduct laudable? Voted, no.[2] Motions afterwards—& ballot. Ld Selkirk[3] elected. Read Hecuba—near 200 lines. Charles 12th—paper & Lpool paper. Heard from Mr G. Read the First Philippic.[4] Practised my speech & more particularly gesture: spoke to my Tutor—& to Keate at night. Not quite so bad as last night—he very civil & patient. Wrote over Lyrics.

25. Sunday.

Bethell preached. Notice of Sacrament. Said private business: finished Vol. 1 of Tomline's Theology: read Young—Buchanan—Blair—Secker's 5 first lectures on the Catechism[5]—and several Chapters of Matthew with the Notes. Wrote to Mrs G. Went in at two—almost the first time for 2 or 3 years.

26.

Often in chambers in the morning now without being looked over. Mondays business. *Called up in Homer.* Spoke to Keate for the 3d & last time; to perform in school tomorrow. Read Charles 12—1st Canto of Lay of L.M. & 3

[1] Essay prefixed to John *Walker the philologist's *Academic Speaker* (1801).
[2] John *Stuart, 1713–92, 3rd earl of Bute, was first minister of *George III 1760–3; the society deplored his conduct by 8 votes to none.
[3] Dunbar James Douglas, 1809–85, 6th earl of Selkirk from 1820; F.R.S. 1831; minor office 1852 and 1858–9.
[4] Demosthenes.
[5] Abp. Thomas *Secker, *Lectures on the Catechism . . . with a Discourse on Confirmation* (1769).

first of Lady of L;[1] finished Hecuba & began Alcestis.[2] Heard from Mr & Mrs. & Miss G.

27.

Holiday. Finished the Lady of the Lake; dressed & went into school with Selwyn: found myself not at all in a func; & went through my performance with tolerable comfort. Durnford followed me; then Selwyn, who spoke well; then Sivewright,[3] then Wethered.[4] Horrors of speaking chiefly in the name.[5] Walk with Pickering; read Paper; review of Monks Hippolytus;[6] Charles 12; Alcestis; with sundry quotations to other books. Wrote to A.M.G.

28. Ash Wednesday.

Church & Wednesday's business; some time now taken up in writing quotations and preparing for school. Rain—so very little walk—read Charles 12th—paper—Alcestis; (near 300 lines without quotations)—& did a good many verses, but not all to the purpose.

Thursday. March 1.

Holiday. did some verses. Had Leycester[7] to breakfast. Walk with Hallam read London & Lpool paper. Dined with Gaskell & Canning after four at Christopher: expensive abominably: & not an advisable practice. Private business. Finished Œd. Tyran.: read Charles 12th; wrote quotations to 2 lessons of Horace on; & read a little Alcestis, with quotations to some of what I read before, &c.[8] A few lines from Mr & R.G.

2.

Friday's business. Finished—abbreviated—& wrote over verses for Tutor & for School. Walk with Hallam; finished Charles 12th; read paper. Alcestis—& did quotations—read part of Gibbon's account of Mahomet[9]— did quotations to Persius—&c.&c.

3.

Saturday's business. learning Testament & Poetae included wh take much more time now—breakfasted with Gaskell; read paper; & Thursday Nights

[1] Walter *Scott, *The Lay of the Last Minstrel* and *The Lady of the Lake* (1805, 1810).
[2] Also by Euripides.
[3] Charles Kane Sivewright of Cargilfield, near Edinburgh; then in sixth form.
[4] Florence James Wethered, 1807–67, vicar of Hurley, Berkshire, from 1838.
[5] Version in Morley, i. 43.
[6] Perhaps *Quarterly Review*, viii. 215 (Sept. 1812), on J. H. *Monk's edition of Euripides' *Hippolytus* (1812).
[7] Ralph Gerard Leycester, 1813?–51, of Toft Hall, near Knutsford, Cheshire; a new boy.
[8] Add MS 44802D, ff. 6v—8.
[9] *Decline and Fall of the Roman Empire*, l.

Canning Speech on Corn Laws,[1] &c—read more Gibbon on Mahomet & in the Society gave my vote agst him in a large majority.[2] Moved a fine—good debate—Doyle spoke remarkably well—walk with Hallam—had private business—Persius. & put down many quotations to it; skimmed the Remedia Amoris[3]—and read 2 Sermons of St Johns on Sacrament,[4] wh I am to take tomorrow. May God hallow it to me. Read also some of the passages in Scripture with the Mant Notes.

4. Sunday.

Bethell preached; & administered sacrament to me and the rest—sixth form—masters—some of their families &c. It is a blessed institution indeed; a work worthy of the Divine Grace; may we, seeing his wonders not be like Capernaum & Bethsaida, lest it be more tolerable at the great day for Sodom & Gomorrah than for us.[5] Wrote to Mother—in Prose—construed Play—read Secker's Lectures on the Sacraments & several others; and Bible with Mant Notes. Made out a list of some of the Authors & their ages—declined an invitation to breakfast with Sir J. McGrigor.

5.

Mondays business. Play—and learning it (what I had not been construed &c) Walk with Doyle. read paper. began 6th vol of Gibbon—read nearly 200 lines of Alcestis: and a great deal of Ovid (Heroides & Amores)[6] putting down quotations from it. Heard from my Dear Sister. Almonds & raisins from Law.

6.

Holiday. Walk with Doyle. Finished Alcestis: a delightful play: but character of Admetus not good. read Ovid: a little Gibbon; & the paper: a short article in the Quarterly on the Translation of Persius:[7] did a few verses.

7.

Wednesday's business, quotations &c: read Gibbon; and Ovid. Walk with Doyle. Received the horrible news of the defeat of the Catholics. I trust it is all for the best; but the prospect is awful. Read a considerable part of an immensely long debate.

8.

Holiday. Finished the debate. Splendid speeches; Plunkett's & Brougham's

[1] *NSH* xvi. 758–72.
[2] Mahomet's character was deplored by 6 votes to 3.
[3] Ovid.
[4] In T. J. St. John, *52 Original Sermons* (1790).
[5] Matt. xi. 20–24.
[6] More mildly erotic poetry.
[7] i. 355 (May 1809).

particularly; men of amazing talents; Canning's very good too: But the result dreadful.[1]—Speeches. did verses, & wrote over for Tutor and for school. read Paper—Martial—Gibbon. learned Horace for tomorrow.

9.

Friday's business: read a little Gibbon; Porson's Preface & Part of Supplement;[2] wrote to T.G. & A.M.G. read paper; did quotations: read Potter[3]— private business (Persius)—& learned some of the play for tomorrow.

10.

Saturdays business—Play—& remainder of learning it—*Called up in Poetae* —Walk with Hallam—debate on Wat Tyler—whether justified in rising agst Poll Tax—Voted no: in a majority.[4] Many speeches—Chairmanship adverse to speaking—Private Business. began Iphigenia in Aulis; began Supplices[5]—& read Gibbon—

11. Sunday.

Bethell preached; Briggs[6] read Lecture in Evg, after Catechism, read Secker's; said private business; sat & talked with Hallam & Hamilton[7] after four; construed Play; in Prose—finished Table of Authors[8]—read Mant's Bible—read fewer things now & more of them on Sundays. Heard from T.G. Nothing important as yet.[9]

12.

Mondays business. Learned & was *called up in Play*: I construed at my Tutors this week. Sat with Hallam after 12: read paper. Finished the 6th vol of Gibbon—& there the history of Rome. Hume, me judice a greater historian. Gibbon's style diffuse; sometimes very beautiful, sometimes too highly ornamented—much. Read Supplices.

13.

Holiday. Selwyn to be sent up for play. Heard from Farr. Breakfasted with

---

[1] The commons defeated *Burdett's motion for considering relief to Irish catholics, by 276 to 272, after debate on 5 and 6 March. *Plunket's, *Brougham's, and *Canning's speeches are in *NSH* xvi. 928, 981, and 993 respectively. William Conyngham *Plunket, 1764–1854, cr. Baron Plunket 1827, whig lord chancellor of Ireland 1830–4, 1835–41; Henry Peter *Brougham, 1778–1868, cr. Baron Brougham and Vaux 1830; lord chancellor 1830–4, radical; see Add MS 44114.

[2] In *Euripidis opera omnia*, 1821 ed., i. cliii–cxciii.

[3] Probably John *Potter, later abp. of Canterbury, *Archaeologia Graeca, or the Antiquities of Greece*, 2v. (1697–8).

[4] Wat *Tyler, d. 1381, leader of the peasants' revolt. Majority against him of 6 to 4.

[5] Both by Euripides.

[6] Substituted for 'Grover'.

[7] Walter Kerr *Hamilton, 1808–69, bp. of Salisbury 1845. See Add MS 44183.

[8] Add MS 44718, ff. 195–6.

[9] See 19–20 Mar. 27.

Gaskell: walk with Doyle after 12; sat with Hallam after four. Read papers; began seventh vol. of Gibbon; read Ovid; & Supplices. Hallam ill.

14.

Wednesday's business, quotations &c. *Called up in Homer.* Sharp work. Taken unawares & looked over my vile holiday Task by Keate! He very good natured, considering the utter badness & inapplicability. Did quotations to some of what I had read in the Supplices; read papers; walk with Doyle; sat with Hallam; read a little Gibbon; Measure for Measure; and did some verses. Keate's subjects do not suit me & I seem to get worse as I go on.

15.

Half holiday. Thursdays business: finished[1] verses, & wrote over for Tutor: walk with Doyle after 12; with Pickering & sat with Hallam, after four. Wrote to Farr (at night); read paper; Gibbon;[2] a little Supplices; & learned Horace for tomorrow.

16.

Friday's business; saying at five. *Called up in Horace* at eleven. said to Keate at five. Looked over my 6th Form Exercises; Keate civil & apparently rather pleased. Walk with Doyle. Wrote over verses. Sat with Hallam —read paper—wrote to Mrs & T.G. Had private business—Persius—read Gibbon & a little Supplices: altogether a hardish day's work, but very satisfactory.

17. Saturday.

Holiday. Greek Private business; read paper; short walk with Doyle. Finished 7th vol: of Gibbon—except a considerable part of the notes— which are rather an incumbrance in many places: his account of Belisarius[3] very fine. Read a little Cicero, & Supplices; wrote some of my arrear quotations to Persius &c: made enquiry about Question—about the men who lived in each age—Elizabethan & Annes: voted for Elizabeth, in a majority of one: putting Locke out of the scale.[4] Motions & afterwards vote of censure on Wentworth.

18.

Walk with Doyle; sat with Hallam a little; he better now. Said Private Business; construed Play. Wrote to T.G. in answer to a letter received from

---

[1] Substituted for 'did'.
[2] 'with' deleted.
[3] Ch. xli.
[4] John *Locke, 1632–1704, philosopher. *Elizabeth's reign was held more fertile in literary figures than *Anne's by 5 to 4.

him yesterday. Vice Provost preached; Briggs read lecture in Evg. Read Bible: & Secker for several hours. Finished his Lectures.

19.

Monday's business. Had a most excellent Letter from My Dear Father; but the news alas! public & more particularly private, very bad. Dr Baron to be at Seaforth today![1] May God bless his attempts—but I dare not look upon the worst. But whatever it shall be, may we cry Gods will be done.— Did theme; read Gibbon: skimmed the notes of 7th, & began 8th vol; read paper; sat with Hamilton after 12; Hallam part of after 4; quotations to Persius, Supplices &c.

20.

Heard from T.G: my Father has lost his seat: and Berwick a representative ten times too good for it. Wrote to my Father; no longer M.P. When we have forgotten the manner, the matter is not so bad.[2] Wrote over theme; walk with Doyle; read paper—Gibbon—& Supplices—received some wine &c, sent me by T.G. from London.

21.

Wednesdays business. Virgil quotations tiresome & troublesome; read a little Gibbon; read paper; walk with Hallam; finished Supplices; a very beautiful play: a few quotations to it; did some Greek anapaests.—read Selwyns Play Exercise, which is good.

22. Thursday.

Holiday. Finished Anapaests; wrote over for Tutor & for school. read paper; walk with Doyle; finished quotations to Supplices &c:[3] read again The Tempest; Gibbon.

23.

Friday's business—Learned Horace. *called up in Scriptores.* Heard from Farr. Read papers. Walk with Hallam. Read Gibbon—had Greek Private business—did part of a copy of English verses on Palmyra, set by Tutor, instead of Persius.

24. Saturday.

Half holiday: Play, & learning it. Walk with Hallam; read papers; Hallam drank wine with me after dinner. Finished 8th vol of Gibbon; read account of Palmyra in 2nd; did more verses on it; began 3d book of Herodotus.

[1] To operate on Anne Gladstone.
[2] John *Gladstone was unseated on petition. Extract in Morley, i. 43.
[3] Notes in Add MS 44802D, ff. 8v–13.

Read payments as Chairman, made up accounts &c—much jaw about nothing at Society and absurd violence.[1]

25. Sunday.

Expected letter, but did not receive one. Walk with Hallam: Vice Provost preached & Briggs read lecture in aftn. Old Spier[2] buried. Wrote part of a letter to A.M.G. Read Bible—finished Buchanan's Psalms—& read Herbert's Life, Country Parson, and some of the Poems.[3]

26. Monday.

Holiday. Finished and wrote over verses on Palmyra; numerous enough, but I fear not very good. Went to Burnham[4] with Doyle & Hallam after 12, & back by Dorney[5]—a good stretch. Read paper; began the ninth volume of Gibbon; and read over again Much Ado about Nothing; learned Play to construe for tomorrow. Pickering drank wine with me after dinner.

27. Tuesday.

Monday's business; Play & quotations &c. *Called up in Burnet.*[6] Finished Letter to A.M.G: Expecting to hear, but no letter. Read paper; wrote over again my Palmyrenians, & showed them up. Read Gibbon; and did a good many verses.

28.

Wednesday's business: quotations to Virgil &c. Holidays now drawing very near. Walk with Pickering, and Hanmer. Finished verses, & wrote over for Tutor; he pleased with the English ones; read papers; Herodotus; & Gibbon; bid Gaskell good bye—he goes tomorrow morning, as does Wentworth. Read Ovid Heroides. Still no letter.

29.

Holiday. Walk with Hallam & Doyle to Burnham Abbey[7] & round by Salthill. Heard from home, & dear Anne, thank God, considerably relieved. Wrote to Mrs G. & to Farr. Doyle drank wine with me after dinner. Read Gibbon and Herodotus, & wrote over verses. Read paper.

[1] A debate on whether the Greeks excelled most in history or drama degenerated into a series of wrangles. Version in Morley, i. 43.
[2] He kept a sock-shop; *Shelley called his daughter 'the loveliest girl I ever saw' (Cust, *Eton*, 169).
[3] George *Herbert, 1593–1633, metaphysical poet. His poems, his essay on *The Country Parson*, and an abridgement of his life by Isaak *Walton were collected in one volume in 1824.
[4] Four miles NW. of Eton.
[5] Two and a half miles west of Eton.
[6] Perhaps Thomas *Burnet, *Telluris Theoria Sacra* or *Archaeologiae philosophicae . . . libri duo* (1694), good late Latin, if bad sense, and odd reading for schoolboys.
[7] Three miles NW. of Eton.

30.

Friday's business, and learning Horace &c. Walk with Hallam—he also drank wine with me—heard of place being secured. Read Gibbon & Herodotus fiercely—wishing to finish 9th vol. of G. & 3d book of H. before I go home.

31.

Saturday's business, learning &c. Walk with Hallam after 12 & after debate. Read Gibbon, & Herodotus, fiercely again: Berthomier called inopportune, and interrupted me grievously. Read paper. Debate on York & Lancaster. Voted for York.[1] Elected Chairman & refused to accept. Selwyn elected. I gave my Vote for him: vote of Thanks to Gaskell; Canning proposed & elected.

First of April. Sunday.

Walk with Hallam. Tea with Doyle. In Prose; holiday Task set. Hallam dines with his Tutor.[2] Vice Provost & Briggs again; the latter good—the former inaudible. Finished Blair's Sermons; not very substantial[3]—read Herbert; did short Theme; and finished the Gospel of St. Matthew in Mant with the notes &c.

Second.

Monday's business. *Called up in Homer*, & cleared off in Exercises. Finished 9th vol. of Gibbon & 3d book of Herodotus. read Paper—packed up &c. Tea after four—& started at six for St. Albans[4]—reached it soon after 9—got into Mail at ½ past ten—Travelled all night.

3.

Breakfast at Coventry. Mail travelled capitally. Lunch at Newcastle. Read some of the Beauties of Sheridan[5]—arrived at Liverpool soon after seven—Seaforth about eight. Found Dear Anne fully as well as expected. Not much tired.

4. Wednesday

Unpacked & arranged &c. Walk. Got Letter from J.N.G. & wrote to him. heard from Gaskell—read sundries—Began Acts in Bible.

---

[1] The Yorkists' revolt against *Henry VI was held justified by 4 to 3.
[2] Edward Craven *Hawtrey, 1789–1862, later headmaster and provost; for his influence on Gladstone see Add MS 44790, ff. 1–3.
[3] This phrase in Morley, i. 33.
[4] Twenty two miles NNE. of Eton, on main road from London to Liverpool.
[5] *Sheridaniana,* a recent collection of Richard Brinsley *Sheridan's *bons mots.*

5. *Thursday*.

Began Don Quixote—never having read it through before—Walk—Backgammon with Aunt E. & Chess with Helen Jane.

6. *Friday*.

In Liverpool—ordered Books &c. Walked out—Drew Anne in chair—Backgammon with Aunt E—Chess with Helen—read Don Quixote—Browne's Poems.[1]

7th.

Wrote up Journal—Drew Anne in Chair—called on Mr Rawson—Finished 1st Vol. of Don Quixote. Lazy all this week.

8th. *Sunday*.

Copied. Drew Anne in Chair. Mr Rawson preached in morng, Lectures & Catechized in Evening. Began Martyn's Life[2] & read Bible.

9th.

Drew Anne in chair. Read Paper—Walk—read Don Quixote—Chess.

10th.

Drew Anne in Chair—went into town & walked out—read paper—& Don Quixote—Backgammon.

11th. *Wednesday*.

Read Don Quixote. Finished Second Volume. Drew Anne in Chair.

12th.

Copied. Read Don Quixote—paper—went with Mr G. to Kirkdale—went thence into Liverpool, & walked out. Chess.

13th. *Good Friday*.

Read Martyns Life—&c—Church morng & afternoon—To be no service on Sunday—had intended to receive the Sacrament then, but in consequence of this notice I received it today—from Mr Rawson—70 communicants or upwards. May God make me a worthy partaker in so solemn & so healthful a feast.

---

[1] Probably Isaac Hawkins *Browne, *Poems upon various subjects, Latin and English* (1768).

[2] [John *Sargent] *Memoir of the Rev. Henry *Martyn* (1819), 1781–1812, missionary in Asia.

14th. Saturday.

Read paper—now very interesting[1]—wrote to Gaskell. Read Don Quixote —Heard from Hallam—Drew Anne in Chair—Journal very imperfect, as usual during the holidays, when I have not my goods and chattels "handy".

15th. Sunday.

Mr Bold[2] officiated—fair sermons—Read Bible & Martyn's Life—Drew Anne in Chair, in part.

16th. Monday.

Copied. Finished 3d vol. of Don Quixote—stopped there, 4th being lost. Began the sixth of Hume; resuming from last Vacation. Wrote to Hallam: heard from Farr. Mrs G. very unwell—Read paper &c.

17th. Tuesday.

T. G. went to Bath to drink the waters, which I hope may do him good. Read Hume. Read paper; drew Anne in Chair; copied. Draughts with Aunt J. Mother a little better.

18th.

Read Hume—paper—in Liverpool—I get the grey mare again now, save when my Father rides—Backgammon with Aunt E. Copied two Letters.

19th.

Copied one Letter—wrote to Tom—in Liverpool—read Hume & paper— assisted in making marmalade—Draughts with Aunt J.

20th. Friday.

Read Hume—read paper—walked into town—dined with R.G. in Slater Street.[3] Went to concert in the Eveng with him, Kelso[4] & Robt G. Heard Braham[5]—Phillips,[6] Monsieur Mont Gresin[7]—& a Lady—very good. Phillips glorious. Slept in Slater Street.

21st.

Breakfasted with R.G.[8] who entertains famously. Heard from Hallam—

---

[1] On 10 April the king had asked *Canning to reconstruct the administration, left headless by *Liverpool's seizure on 17 February.
[2] Probably Hugh Bold, 1798?–1883, of Eton and Christ Church, rector of Tal-y-llyn, Breconshire.
[3] Robert Gladstone's house.
[4] Probably Archibald Kelso, later partner in Gladstone & Co.
[5] John *Braham, 1777–1856, tenor and composer.
[6] See 23 Dec. 25.
[7] Unidentified.
[8] Robert, not Robertson, Gladstone.

11—I.

walked home—copied letter—Finished 6th vol. of Hume & the reign of James 1st.

22. Sunday.

Mr Rawson preached, morng & Evg. Weather cold. Read Martyn's Life, which I do not like as entirely as I had expected. Read Bible.

23. Monday.

Intended to go & make my calls—but prevented by the storminess of the weather. Read Hume—began seventh vol. Wrote a longish letter to Hallam —played backgammon with Aunt E. Read papers.

24.

Again detained at home by the weather: a regular December or January day, very stormy & very cold. Backgammon with Aunt E. Read Hume. T. Ogilvie breakfasted here. Read also in the Library Forsyth's Italy, parts.[1] Read papers.

25. Wednesday.

Still detained by the weather. Draughts with Aunt J. Read Hume (vol 7) & began Kings Anecdotes of his own times.[2] I am now deputy teamaker, & Helen's Journeyman Gardener. Read papers.

26.

Read papers—Hume—finished Kings Anecdotes. played backgammon with Aunt E. Wrote to T.G. Rode into Liverpool—did sundry jobs—& called upon Mrs Smith, Miss Benwell, Mrs Conway, Mrs Wilson, Mrs McCartney, Mrs Sandbach, Mrs Traill, Mr Staniforth. Met an old Etonian, of my "remove"—Ld. A. Chichester,[3] now in the army.

27. Friday.

Read papers: went to Jones[4] again: read Hume; (finished 7th vol;) played chess with Helen Jane; copied a letter.

28.

Read Hume: wrote to T.G. informing him that the plan of my going by Bath was decided on. Rode into the Park—called on Uncle Murray, the

[1] Joseph *Forsyth, *Remarks on Antiquities, Arts, and Letters . . . in Italy*, 2v. (1813).
[2] Dr. William *King, *Political and Literary Anecdotes of his own Times* (1818), mid-eighteenth-century gossip by a Jacobite don.
[3] Lord Arthur Chichester, 1808–40, 3rd s. of 2nd marquis of Donegall, whig M.P. for Belfast 1882–4.
[4] Owen Jones of Litherland, the local surgeon.

Mosses, & Ewarts: did business also in Liverpool.—Labelmondier[1] dined with us; played backgammon with him in the Evening; a very pleasant young man. (Began eighth vol. of Hume). (On Wednesday the 25th I went to consult Jones about a rash broken out on my chest. He gave me ointment, which did it good.)

29. Sunday.

Mr Rawson preached morng & afternoon. Drew Anne in Chair; read Martyn's Life—& Bible.

30. Monday.

In Liverpool: finished my business. Labelmondier went; Steuart[2] dined with us; to commence business tomorrow. Read Hume—to the end of Charles 1sts reign. Read papers; & finished my gardening work.

May First.

Packed up & put away my things. Read papers. Wrote a long letter to J.N.G: bid goodbye to all; Bob took me in in the gig; & I came off by the Birmingham Mail. Pace very good. Travelled all night. Rainy.

2.

Arrived at Wolverhampton between five and six. washed there, and went by coach to Worcester—arrived there instead of a little after ten, a little before eleven: in consequence obliged to start immediately by a Bristol coach & catch a Bath one just going out of Gloster where it had dined. Missed, ergo, my dinner. Beautiful ride thro' the vale of Rodborough.[3] Arrived at Bath before eight—found Tom waiting, & my Aunt Mary's tea ready. Slept at her house.

3.

T.G. lionized me in Bath; with its beauty I was much delighted. The rooms very fine. Went almost over it with him, & on the river in the evening: my Aunt fed us very well, & has many comforts in a very nice house, & a very beautiful situation. Wrote to Mrs G. and read papers.

4. Friday.

Went to see the Abbey. Read paper. Walked about Bath, which I know a little now. Heard from Gaskell. Went in the evening to the theatre with

---

[1] Douglas William Parish Labalmondiere, 1815–93, then at Eton; passed out senior from Sandhurst; capt., 83rd Regt.; assistant commissioner, metropolitan police 1856–84.
[2] Thomas Steuart Gladstone, 1805–82, Robert Gladstone's eldest s.; later of Capenoch, Dumfriesshire.
[3] This vale runs westward from Stroud into the Vale of Berkeley, on the Severn's left bank below Gloucester.

T.G. performance over about eleven. White Lady's Secret[1]—Duel[2]—performed very respectably.

5. Saturday.

Weather wet put off going till evening: read papers: played Backgammon with T.G.: made up accounts & put my things away: after an early tea left my kind & hospitable Aunt, & dear Brother: left Bath in the Shamrock before seven. A very good coach. Travelled all night.

6. Sunday.

Set down at Slough at ¼ past five: came down—lay on my bed & slept till between 8 & 9, dressed &c. as well, thank God, as after a regular night's rest. Met my old Eton friends———wrote home, to Mr G.—Wright preached—began the second vol of Tomline—Gospel of St Mark in Mant—read Jeremiah; did 3 stanzas of holiday Task. Began again to mess with Hallam.

7.

Half holiday. Read the papers for some days back & today. Walk with Hallam. Called on & sat some time with Berthomier. Began 4th book of Herodotus—10th vol. of Gibbon—and did 10 stanzas of holiday task.

8. Tuesday.

Wednesday's business: quotations &c. CALLED UP IN VIRGIL.[3] Read paper, but the debate too long to get through in the time I had[4]—read Gibbon—and Herodotus—did about 8 stanzas of Task. read up &c. I have made as usual a very poor beginning since the holidays. Walk with Hallam. Meeting at Society after 12. Thanks to me—made a miserable reply—Gaskell a very good speech, in answer to his vote.

9.

Walk with Hallam—tea with Gaskell—read papers—and two articles in the last Edinburgh Review on the Catholics.[5] read Gibbon—and did a good many verses. Subject bad.

10. Thursday.

Finished verses. Wrote over for Tutor and for School. Finished holiday

---

[1] Probably based by S. *Beazley on Eugène Scribe's *La dame blanche* (1825), which derived in turn from *Scott's *Monastery* and *Guy Mannering*.
[2] Probably Richard Brinsley *Peake's comedy *The Duel, or My Two Nephews* (1823).
[3] For the rest of his time at Eton, *Gladstone twice underscored each of his notes of being called up.
[4] On 7 May parliament debated the new administration and the catholic question: *NSH* xvii. 564–71, 578–91.
[5] xlv. 423 and 513 (March 1827), both strongly in favour of catholic emancipation.

Task. Read Gibbon. Heard from Mrs G. Read papers: the debates long now & take a good deal of time.[1] Read the lives of Clarendon & Hambden[2] in the Biographical Dictionary. Walk with Hallam after 12—Hallam & Doyle after 6.

11.

Friday's business. Learning Horace &c. Called up in Scriptores. Walk with Hallam. Wrote over part of holiday Task. Wrote to my dear Mother. Wrote a longish speech unconnectedly for tomorrow. Read a little Gibbon—papers —a good speech of Earl Greys[3]—relooked over Clarendon.

12. Saturday.

Saturdays business. Keate away—said at two. read a Lpool paper—wrote a longish letter to T.G. Read Gibbon, Cicero, and Herodotus. Voted the written speech a bore—put down heads & an ending, & got on for near half an hour by dint of the systematic cheering of what they call the Treasury Bench. Divided eight to four.[4] Gaskell—Hallam—Doyle—and Law spoke. Moved expunction of an illegal question about the Test Act—author unknown.

13. Sunday.

Wright preached. Received from William Ewart his father's picture, very neatly framed—wrote to thank him for it, briefly. Short walk with Gaskell. Did a Theme. read Locke's First Letter on Toleration[5]—Tomline—and 5 Chapters of Mark with Mant Notes.

14.

Monday's business. Keate away—Walk with Gaskell after 12—Hallam after 6—read Gibbon and Herodotus—wrote to Buckeridge. bought a large paper Heyne's Virgil[6]—read paper—did extempore.

15. Tuesday.

Holiday. Read Gibbon—finished 10th vol. Read papers—wrote to Farr— had Greek private business—began Greek Sapphics, & read Clarke about Marathon[7]—Walk with Gaskell after four & after six. Two rival plans com-

---

[1] Long commons debate on corruption at Penryn, *NSH* xvii. 682–703, 8 May.

[2] John *Hampden, 1594–1643, parliamentary statesman.

[3] In the lords, opposing the ministry, on the previous day (*NSH* xvii. 720–33; dated 7 May in G. M. Trevelyan, *Grey*, 203).

[4] On a motion that *Clarendon's conduct was more praiseworthy than *Hampden's.

[5] John *Locke's four *Letters on Toleration* were collected in vol. v of the latest (1812) ed. of his *Works*.

[6] There were several printings of the edition of Virgil by C. G. Heyne, 1729–1812, Saxon classicist.

[7] E. D. *Clarke, *Travels in Various Countries*, 6v, (1810–23), ii. iii. 1.

municated to me of revivals of the Etonian—one by Gaskell—the other by Hallam.[1]

16.

Wednesday's business. Did Greek Sapphics—read Gibbon—11th vol—, paper—& Liverpool paper, with letters about Mr G.[2] Heard from T.G. also from R.G. finished writing over holiday Task—& wrote over theme. called up in Virgil, by Yonge—did the whole lesson—engaged in gobetween negociations between the two rival intended publications—wishing to effect a coalition.

17.

Half holiday. Did Lyrics. Wrote over Greek Sapphics—read paper—and a little Gibbon—and Microcosm[3]—had private business—walk with Pickering—read Liverpool paper with much about Mr G.—Coalition effected—good. Hallam Doyle Hanmer Skirrow[4] & Wentworth to come in on their side—I was elected Chairman of both the general committee—to consist, probably of 12—& the select—of four. Name chosen &c. Wrote some stuff wh I may perhaps offer as an introduction.

18. Friday.

Friday's business—saying at five. Wrote over Lyrics. Read Liverpool paper, with account of meeting, & my Father's excellent speech—wrote to Mr G. and to Pulford—read Gibbon—& part of an article in Edinburgh Review on Machiavel. Meeting after four—Gaskell, Selwyn, & Hallam elected for the Select Committee—& other arrangements made—Selwyn & I to write introduction—sat together in the evg, but made out very little —had however a pleasant conversation—Berthomier too came in & sat some time.

19.

Holiday. Read Gibbon—& lives of Leo and Lorenzo in Biographical Dictionary. Voted for Lorenzo.[5] Acted as Vice President and wrote out the debate—12 pages—Walk with Hallam—Selwyn sat with me in the Evening—a pleasant hindrance—perhaps I a hindrance to him, without being pleasant—Moved two fines—Day wretchedly dribbled away, I do not get up as I ought.

[1] Genesis of *Eton Miscellany*.
[2] A town meeting in Liverpool on 9 May, at which John *Gladstone spoke at length, resolved to congratulate *George IV on the formation of *Canning's government; there was some opposition to *Gladstone's participation.
[3] The first of school papers; by *Canning, Hookham *Frere and others, 1786–7.
[4] Walker Skirrow, 1809–90, barrister.
[5] Lorenzo de' Medici, 1449–92, and his 2nd s., Giovanni, 1475–1521, Pope Leo X 1513; patrons of the Italian renaissance. By 7 to 4, the fine arts were held to owe more to Lorenzo than to Leo.

20. Sunday.

Worse still in rising—a change is necessary—Plumptre preached—Said private business—Walk with Gaskell—wrote a few lines—read Lockes 2nd Letter on Toleration—Tomline's Elements—and six chapters of Mark in Mant.

21.

Holiday. up Windsor—read Gibbon—breakfasted with Durnford major—very agreeable and good natured—read paper—heard from A.M.G. My Mother had been very ill, but thank God better. Finished Article on Machiavel—very clever—and read one on Anne Boleyn[1]—Wrote my part of the introduction & a piece, in part, on pronunciation—received sundry contributions—Selwyn sat with me in Evg, & we reviewed ourselves & others. Walk with Doyle.

22.

Monday's business, with Virgil—heard from and wrote to Farr—walk with Gaskell—read paper—quotations—Legh,[2] Bacon,[3] & Dowell[4] put into the sixth form yesterday appeared so to day. Wrote over my part of the introduction—reading contributions & fellows in my room for the same purpose took up much time. Read Gibbon. Selwyn with me at night.

23.

Half holiday. Did Translation—and verses—poor, on Painting—read paper —read Gibbon—& contributions—walk with Hallam after 12, & after 6, a short one—met Seale,[5] Mundy, & Marsham.[6]

24.

Holiday. Read Gibbon & up Windsor in the morning. Walk with Hallam after 12—read paper—wrote some verses (English) learned & had private business—did Lyrics—wrote to my Brother Robertson.

25.

Friday's business. Finished & wrote over Lyrics, Wrote over & added to verses. Learned Horace. Called up at eleven & at three; so had plenty of it. Keate told me he would send me up for Play (for last week) for an old exercise on hands.[7] Select Committee after 12; framed rules &c. General

---

[1] Also in current *Edinburgh Review*.
[2] William Price Legh, s. of Windsor banker, later in South-Western Railway.
[3] Robert William Bacon, 1810–62, rector of Ewhurst, Sussex, from 1854.
[4] James Wanklyn Dowell, 1809–79; fellow of King's College, Cambridge 1830–79, though insane from about 1833.
[5] (Sir) Henry Paul Seale, 1806–97, 2nd bart. 1844, Devonshire magnate.
[6] Charles, viscount Marsham, 1808–74, M.P. for Kent 1841–5 when he became 3rd earl of Romney.
[7] Printed long afterwards by *Okes in *Musae Etonenses*, new series, ii. xcii (1869).

Committee after 4—read compositions, fixed name, ratified rules &c.—
Parleyed with Ingalton after 6.—read Saltbearer[1]—Selwyn sat with me
after lock up time—Hallam & Sanford[2] put in.

26. Saturday.

Wrote over Lyrics. Wrote a few sentences towards a speech, but did not
get up. Finished an Epilogue which I began yesterday in a great hurry—&
wrote it over—finished 11th vol of Gibbon—Saturday's business—read
Herodotus—quotations to Persius—Debate on Montrose—voted for him—
Clerks, & wishing not to have a very long debate, kept me from speaking[3]—
Wright proposed & elected—General Committee met after 12—read compositions &c. Rogers[4] admitted—as was Shadwell[5] yesterday. Select Committee after debate & after 6—got thro the corrections, & delivered to
Ingalton material for No. 1. of the Eton Miscellany.

27. Sunday.

Read Tomline. Breakfasted with Mrs Christie[6]—much pleased with her—
Plumptre preached—said private business—construed Play—wrote to
Miss G. & to T.G.—did Theme[7]—read a little of Locke's 3d on Toleration,
finished St Mark in Mant—read introduction to St Luke—walk with Pickering part of after four.

28.

Monday's business. Play—learning it—began 12th of Gibbon—walk with
Doyle after 12—short with Pickering after 6—read paper—Article in
Edinburgh on Shipping Interest[8]—read a little Herodotus—wrote over
Theme—Selwyn with me after dinner & part of the Evening.

29.

Holiday. Ingalton returned—the printers at work—read Massingers Old
Law—read paper—walk with Hallam after 12—Doyle after 6—read Gibbon
—Selwyn with me after dinner, marking for correction—with Ingalton
giving directions after 4—wrote a character of Selwyn[9] &c—Notice up in
Ingalton's window—dunning—inquisitiveness—& almost all in the dark.

30. Wednesday

—no proof sheet—at Ingalton's after 12—subscription gets on famously—

[1] A previous Eton magazine, published anonymously in 1820–1.
[2] John Bracebridge Sanford; b. in India; barrister; Northamptonshire gentleman.
[3] *Montrose's conduct was approved by 7 to none.
[4] (Sir) Frederic *Rogers, 1811–89, fellow of Oriel; permanent head of colonial office
1860–71; cr. Lord Blachford 1871. See Add MS 44107.
[5] John Aemilius Shadwell, 1809–43, rector of All Saints, Southampton, from 1835.
[6] G. H. Christie's mother.
[7] Add MS 44718, f. 96; on avarice.
[8] xlv. 446 (March 1827), reviewing *Huskisson's commons speech, 12 May 1826.
[9] As 'Antony Heaviside', in *Eton Miscellany*, i. 49.

Wednesday's business—quotations—did some Greek Iambics—read Gibbon
—wrote to my Mother. read newspaper—walk with Hallam after six.

31.

Thursday's business—finished Iambics—wrote over for Tutor—played
Cricket in the Upper Club, & had tea in Poets walk[1] wrote a few lines—had
private business—busy long in correcting proof sheets with Selwyn, after
dinner & at night.

June One.

A busy day, but little done—Wrote over Iambics—finished & wrote over
Introduction to No. 2—and a letter for it. Fridays business—learned
Horace—learned private business—heard from Mr G.—had leave, after
4 till night, dined with Mr Moss at Salthill—sat up a little, and wrote some
verses.

June 2. Saturday.

half holiday—learned play but had none—Walk with Doyle after 12—
Selwyn drank wine with me after dinner—Question—Govt of Athens—
spoke, & voted in a large majority agst it[2]—Bacon proposed—Heard from
Mr G. Reported some of the debate after 6—meeting for approval of contributions after four—correcting with Selwyn from half past 8 for 3 hours—
writing to Jelf[3] &c.

June 3. Sunday

—Plumptre preached. The Eton Miscellany occupied too much of my mind,
which I hope & pray will not be the case again. Walk with Hallam—with
Selwyn after 6—read Tomline—a little Locke on Toleration, but found
much Repetition, so began Reasonableness of Christianity.[4] Wrote to my
Father—read the Bible—with Mant Notes—Began St Luke.

4. Monday.

An Eventful day. Up soon after five; corrected &c. with Selwyn: slow and
tedious work. Up to Ingalton's with S. B.B.[5] published a little before eight
—sale very great and very rapid—opinions of course various.—Finished
reporting the debate. Hallam spoke in school. Wrote a long letter to J.N.G.
Had leave to Uncle Divie; dined with him at Salthill, went to Surly in his
carriage, and saw fireworks &c. They were very kind. A good fourth of
June. Selwyn max. down here— —& many others.

[1] In Morley, i. 43.
[2] By 10 to 1 the society rejected a motion that the government of Athens was admirable.
[3] William Edward *Jelf, 1811–75, theologian and grammarian.
[4] Also *Locke's (1695).
[5] Bartholomew Bouverie, *Gladstone's pen-name as editor of the *Eton Miscellany*.

5. Tuesday.

Holiday—rainy—writing for Eton Miscellany—and working in correction &c arranged the second number, & gave it into Ingalton's hands. read Gibbon—wrote to A.M.G. heard from her—Selwyn sat with me at night.

6. Wednesday

Monday's business—with Virgil—quotations—learned & had Play—called up in Play—walk with Hallam—did some verses—called on Berthomier—learned & had Greek private business—Selwyn sat with me part of the night—wrote good part of an article on Fashionable Follies.[1]

7. Thursday.

Play at 4—finished verses, & wrote over for Tutor—played cricket in Upper Club; tea in Poets Walk. Finished article on Fashionable Follies. Read Gibbon.

8. Friday

—Friday's business; learning Horace &c—wrote over verses—walk with Hallam—read papers—had private business—read Westminster Review on Truth a novel; the article a wretched mass of sophistry & delusion.[2] Finished Persius—Selwyn sat with me at night.

9. Saturday.

half holiday. Called up in Scriptores. Wrote some verses; read papers: & an article in Westminster Review on Education of People.[3] Read Gibbon. Cicero—quotations to Persius—walk & tea with Gaskell at Salthill—Hallam drank wine with me—so happy as to argue Wood[4] over & propose him—elected unanimously. Voted for Peter preferably to Charlemagne; fines: Wrights maiden speech. good.[5]

10. Sunday.

Received the Sacrament again from Keate and Carter:[6] reading &c. Would that I had a fit and deep sense of the immense importance, and inestimable value of the Holy Supper. But may God give it me: and all the requisites: repentance—faith—gratitude—resolution—charity—Walk alone after four. Did a Theme on Friendship—read Locke—Tomline—& Mant.

---

[1] Later scrapped: see 13 June 27.　　　　[2] xiv. 341 (April 1827).
[3] Ibid. 269.
[4] Probably Samuel Francis Wood, 1809–43, barrister; younger br. of (Sir) Charles*.
[5] By 11 to 3 the society held that Peter the Great conferred more blessings on his country than Charlemagne did on his.
[6] Thomas Carter, 1775–1868, lower master; vicar of Burnham from 1833, vice-provost from 1857.

11. *Monday*.

Holiday. Read Gibbon—read paper—wrote an Epilogue for Number 2nd—meeting after dinner—sculled up to Surly after six—bathed coming down—Selwyn with me at night—proof sheet work &c. &c.

12. *Tuesday*.

Monday's business. called up in Homer—wrote over Theme—read Gibbon —read paper—wrote to T.G.—went to Theatre after six—wretched—Selwyn with me after 4, & part of the night—wrote and wrote over for the Miscellany.

13.

Wednesday's business—some quotations—did Translation—read Gibbon—Selwyn with me at night—correcting &c. Sculled up to Surly after six—finished writing for Miscellany—one article rejected.

14. *Thursday*.

Holiday—Learned & had Greek private business—walk with Hallam after 12—meeting after dinner—read paper—Pitts letters to George 3 on Catholic Question &c:[1] Keate set me Sinon's speech[2]—sculled to Surly after 6—learning speech—finished Gibbon. Elegant and acute as he is, he seems to me not so clear, so able, nor so attractive as Hume: does not impress my mind so much. Selwyn with me part of the night.

15.

Friday's business, quotations &c. Finished learning my speech & spoke to my Tutor—read papers—read Milner's 6th Letter[3] &c—learned & had Gk private business—Walk with Hallam after 12 & after 6.

16.

Saturday's business—called up in Poetae. Finished reading for question—spoke for Catholics—majority for them[4]—walk with Hallam—called on Berthomier, heard from Farr—spoke to Keate—supped with Selwyn minor on his getting into 5th Form—read part of Massingers Great Duke of Florence—boat in evening.

17. *Sunday*.

Briggs preached—said private business—spoke to Tutor—construed Play

---

[1] Reprinted in the current *Quarterly*, xxxvi. 285.
[2] Virgil, *Aeneid* ii. 57–194, the double agent's tale of the wooden horse.
[3] John *Milner, *Letters to a Prebendary* (1800), 139–91, a defence of the English catholics' conduct under *Elizabeth.
[4] The penal laws against catholics enacted under *Elizabeth were held unjust by 8 to 6.

—read Luke in Mant—Locke's Reasonableness—and Tomline. Walk with Hallam. Selwyn with me part of night—so sat up later.

18. Monday.

No 2 published—apparently liked better than No. 1.—Play, and Learning it—Monday's business—did Odes—sculled to Surly &c &c in Evg, & bathed coming down—working in Club after dinner, Committee after 4[1]— Had Gk private business—finished Great Duke of Florence & began Parliament of Love[2]—spoke again to Keate—Selwyn with me at night—working in corrections.

19. Tuesday:

finished Parliament of Love—spouted speech—dressed—and spoke in school. Sanford 1st—Durnford 2nd—Farquharson[3] 3d—& I last. My speech on the whole a very agreeable one. heard from Mr & A.M. & wrote to A.M.G. Walk with Hallam: read paper: Select Committee work after 4: did some verses: began the Bondman.[4]

20.

Wednesday's business—quotations &c—read Massinger—finished verses— wrote over for Tutor—read paper—Select Committee work after dinner, part of after 4 & after 6, and walk with Selwyn till lock up time. He sat with me at night. Read contributions to be carried on for No 4. No. 3. at length with much trouble, sent up to Ingalton. wrote over part of Doyle's Prediction.

21. Thursday.

Half holiday: wrote over verses: did Lyrics: & wrote them over for Tutor; read paper; walk with Pickering after four, with Hallam after six: finished Bondman—began Renegado in Massinger—and wrote about 30 lines (heroics) on Richard Coeur de Lion.[5]

22.

Friday's business—learning Horace &c—wrote over Lyrics—walk with Hallam after 6—construed Play—learned & had Greek private business— read papers—translated a chorus & wrote a letter to B.B.—& finished the Renegado.

---

[1] i.e. in general and then in select committee on *Eton Miscellany;* see 17 May 27.
[2] Another comedy of *Massinger's.
[3] Robert Farquharson, 1810?–81, rector of Long Langton, Wiltshire, from 1855, prebend of Salisbury from 1865.
[4] *Massinger.
[5] This poem eventually filled six pages of the fifth *Eton Miscellany*: i. 199–205.

23. Saturday.

half holiday—Learned & had Play—read Porson—read paper—read "The Grand Vizier Unmasked"[1]—debate on English Drama—spoke & voted for its being superior to any other[2]—moved fine on Gaskell. Cavendish[3] elected—Club business afterwards—Hanmer went out[4]—afraid what I said accelerated it—read over &c. Boat match after 6—boat with Hallam—walk afterwards—Read Massinger's Roman Actor.

24. Sunday.

Read Tomline—breakfasted with Gaskell—said Private business—read Reasonableness of Christianity—walked alone to Iver,[5] after four—construed Play—did Theme—read some of St Luke in Mant's Bible.

25.

Monday's business—learned & had Play (by having I mean writing quotations &c) Read papers—with Ingalton about Miscellany accounts—heard from T. & H.J.G; wrote to H.J.G: went to see a match part of after four—sculled up to Surley &c—after six; bathed coming down: Selwyn with me at night—Began Racine's Iphigénie.

26.

Wednesday's business, with play at four: wrote over Theme—read Iphigénie—called up in Homer: proof sheets came—read paper—some things in Knight's Quarterly, Athenian Revels[6] &c. wrote an introduction for No. 4., wrote over the chorus, & some other things—sculled Hallam to Surly after 6—went to see a cricket match after 4.[7]

27. Wednesday

—Friday's business—wrote a good deal—some poetry or rather verse, and some prose. Learning Horace &c. Doyle with me after 12—read papers—read Herodotus—& Racine—did Translation—went to see match after 6 between the Aquatics & the eleven who played the seven.

28. Thursday.

Half holiday. Wrote some verses (heroics) on Richard First—wrote part of an Epilogue, and a letter signed Philophantasm[8] after 12 & in morng—

[1] An anti-Canningite pamphlet by 'A Protestant Tory' (1827).
[2] Pop was unanimous.
[3] (Lord) Richard Cavendish, 1812–73, brother of the 7th duke of *Devonshire; see Add MS 44124.
[4] See *Doyle, *Reminiscences and Opinions*, 44–45.
[5] Some 6 miles NE. of Eton.
[6] Tristram Merton, 'Scenes from Athenian Revels', a comic prose drama, in *Knight's Quarterly Review*, i. 17.
[7] Morley, i. 43.
[8] Untraced; unless re-signed 'Philomathes', in *Eton Miscellany*, ii. 92–96.

reading over after dinner. Boat dinner after 4 & after six—Bouverie's health drunk—I returned thanks for my worthy friend—a short walk after it—Selwyn & Devereux[1] with me at night. Dear Helen's birthday—God bless her.

29. Friday.

Holiday. Did my Verses. Learned & had Greek private business: finished Racine's Iphigenie which I like much. Finished Epilogue: Select Committee work after dinner. Got my exercise after 4—seeing matches with Nicholl after 6—wrote over 2 copies of my exercise at night. Selwyn sat with me till twelve.

30.

Saturday's business: wrote over Verses: also another copy of my Play Verses—read paper—account of Strafford in Biographical Dictionary—spoke, & voted in a majority, for him.[2] Club business after debate, which was long. Hallam—Wentworth—Gaskell—Canning spoke—Sculled to Boveney &c. &c. after 6, & worked at corrections with Selwyn at night, till a quarter to twelve.

July the First.

Breakfasted with Doyle's Father, Col. Doyle: a very gentlemanly & apparently sensible man[3]—said Lucretius for private business after 12—finished Locke's Reasonableness of Xtianity, which I like very much indeed[4]—read St Luke in Mant, & Tomline—had a speech set after 4—walk with Hallam afterwards—construed Play after six—Did Theme.[5]

July Second.

Monday's business—Called up in Horace's Odes—wrote over another copy of my Play Verses for College—corrected my things for the Miscellany & wrote one over—wrote to Mrs G—read Pursuits of Literature, and paper—strawberries at Salthill with Gaskell after 6—Worked after 12 & dinner, & again at night in correcting &c. for the Miscellany—Got ready No 4.

3. Tuesday

—Holiday—Hallam to be sent up—Sent No. 4. to Town early in morning—walk with Colvile before absence—walk with Hallam after 12—read Pursuits of Literature—settling pecuniary matters with Ingalton after 4

---

[1] Probably Robert Devereux, 1809–55, canon of Durham, 15th Viscount Hereford from 1843; possibly his elder brother Henry Cornwall, 1807–39.

[2] Notes for speech in Add MS 44649, ff. 27–28. *Strafford was upheld by 11 votes to 5.

[3] (Maj.-Gen. Sir) Francis Hastings Doyle, 1783–1839, cr. bart. 1828.

[4] Cp. Morley, i. 33.

[5] Add MS 44718, f. 101; on devotion to virtue.

about No 1—also read paper—learning speech—in Upper Shooting-fields after 6 with Law—read Phillpotts' 2nd to Canning[1]—& Herodotus—& wrote to Farr. 11 & 22 match—I did not play.

4.

Wednesday's business—finished learning speech—spoke to my Tutor—wrote over Theme—read 2nd Dialogue of Pursuits of Literature—& notes, by far the best part—read papers—& part of an article in Quarterly—with Sanders[2] in Upper Shooting fields after four—walk with Gaskell after 6—did Translation.

5. Thursday.

Half holiday—Learned & had private business—played cricket in Upper Club after 12—heard from my Dear Sister—read paper, Quarterly &c. after 4—walk with Hallam after six—Read Ford's Lover's Melancholy—much of it good—the end remarkably beautiful.[3]

6.

Friday's business. Read Ford's horrible but powerful play Tis pity she's a whore. Learned Horace &c. Read Cambridge Prize poems. Read papers; finished Article in Quarterly on Home's Works, & began that on Milton: wrote to A.M.G.—with Hallam after 6—Selwyn with me part of Eveng.

7.

Saturday's business, and Play—Began Pindar in private business—spoke to Keate—walk with Gaskell—went to see match of the two tens after six—sculled about a good deal. Read Ford's beautiful Broken Heart: like it much better than either of the others, tho' scene before last very unnatural[4]—Began Æschylus Septem contra Thebas[5] with Hallam—Spoke a few words in favour of Sylla agst Marius[6]—proposed Sanders—unanimously elected—Pickering proposed Handley minor—elected with one Black Ball.

8. Sunday.

Walk after six. Construed Play—spoke to my Tutor—said Lucretius for Private business. Read St Luke in Mant, & Young's Night Thoughts—Finished Tomline's Elements of Theology—as far as I can judge a very good & useful work.

[1] Henry *Phillpotts published two letters to *Canning, dated 23 February and 7 May 1827, protesting against catholic emancipation.
[2] Thomas Sanders, 1809–52, barrister; fellow of King's College, Cambridge 1831–45.
[3] See Morley, i. 33.
[4] See Morley, i. 33. *Ford's act v, scene ii, included various incidents of superhuman Spartan stoicism.
[5] 'Seven against Thebes'.
[6] Sulla was held less odious than Marius by 6 votes to 3.

9.

Mondays business. Learned & had Play (began Demosthenes.) Did Theme. Called up in Scriptores Romani. Read papers—Read a pretty long pamphlet called Life of Ld Eldon[1]—sculled up to Shallows &c. & called [on] Berthomier after 6—writing notice to Correspondents &c. part of the night.

10. Tuesday

—Turned part of speech in Macbeth into Greek Iambics—Bathed after absence—match with the King's men—seeing it after 12 for the most part, after dinner, & after six—reading paper &c. after 4. Selwyn with me part of the night—Read Humes History of Richard First.[2]

11.

Wednesday's business—wrote over Theme—Began Massinger's Duke of Milan—read paper—finished Article in the Quarterly on Milton—very good —spoke to Keate—finished Greek Iambics, & wrote over for Tutor—wrote for Miscellany—after 6 with Gaskell & Doyle, seeing a skiff-pulling match, & in boat.

12. Thursday.

Holiday. Wrote more verses on Richard, and a good deal of prose for the Miscellany. Breakfasted with Gaskell. Spoke in school; not much to my own satisfaction or that of anyone else. Meeting after four. Walk with Gaskell, Canning, & Pickering after six. Heard from T.G. Learned & had private business. Read a little Massinger—& paper.

13.

Fridays business. Learning Horace &c. Wrote over Greek Iambics. Wrote a little for the Miscellany. Learned & had private business—Pindar—Finished Massinger's Duke of Milan. Read the papers—wrote to T.G. Sculled to Surly after 6. Prospects for No 5 of Miscellany not as yet good.

14.

Saturday's business—Learned, & had, & was called up in Demosthenes— Read papers. Wrote a few notes for a speech—and spoke at the Society agst Elizabeths conduct to Mary Queen of Scots.[3] Select Committee business after the debate, & at night. Long walk with Gaskell after 6, beyond the top of the Long Walk—sat up late to finish my concern on Richard Coeur de Lion.

---

[1] *The Life, Political and Official, of John, Earl of *Eldon* (1827), anecdotal and critical.
[2] D. *Hume, *History of England,* I. x.
[3] The society agreed with him by 17 votes to none.

15. *Sunday*.

Briggs preached—said private business—construed Play—Heard from A.M.G. With Gaskell & Bruce[1] after 6—Fellows in my room some part of the day—impeded me—Read St Luke in Mant—& Quarterly Review on Progress of Dissent,[2] & an excellent Article (apparently) on Ch in Ireland.[3]

16.

No IV published—Monday's business—learned & had Play—wrote over Richard Coeur de Lion—did Theme[4]—read papers—sculled up to Surley after 6—Hard at work till between twelve and one with Selwyn—got the fifth number ready to go up in the morning—Hanmer angry about Epilogue[5]—but conciliatory notes passed in the Evening—of which I am, God knows, extremely glad.

17. *Tuesday*.

Holiday. My proportion of No 5. will be very great. Hanmer at my room after dinner—all set to rights, & hopes of aid from him for next term. Read Papers—conversation between Cowley & Milton in Knight's Quarterly[6]— the Quarterly on Biddulphs operation of the Spirit[7]—& Massinger's Virgin Martyr. Sculled up the river &c. after six, and bathed. Election Speeches set after four. Made up accounts for last quarter.

18.

Wednesdays business. Wrote over Theme—read papers—speech fixed on. do not much like the sort—seeing Cricket Match part of after 12—up at Ingalton's with Selwyn after four, about Miscellany, & worked in corrections &c. of matter to carry on, at night. Read part of Massinger's Unnatural Combat. In boat after six.

19. *Thursday*.

Holiday—Match with Epsom rain—concluded with Ingalton for No 2— & gave him No 3—read paper—Canning & Gaskell with me after dinner— wine &c. seeing match &c. Wrote to A.M.G. finished Unnatural Combat[8]— read the Advertisement, Introduction, & Essay on Massinger.[9]

---

[1] James *Bruce, 1811–63; 8th earl of Elgin 1841; governor-general of Canada 1847–1854; had Pekin summer palace burnt 1860; viceroy of India 1862.
[2] xxxi. 229 (December 1824).
[3] xxxiii. 491 (March 1826), mainly on church property and tithes.
[4] Add MS 44718, f. 102; on telling the truth.
[5] *Eton Miscellany*, i. 191–2, the 'Epilogue in Quindecasyllabics', which closed no. 4, burlesqued *Hanmer in the character of David ap Rice.
[6] iii. 17–33. (August 1824).
[7] xxxi. 111, reviewing T. T. *Biddulph, *Divine Influence*.
[8] Instead of 'Virgin Martyr'.
[9] In *Gifford's edition of him (4v., 1805).

12—I.

20.

Friday's business. Called up in Horace's Odes. Finished learning speech, & spoke to my Tutor. Began reading the Antiquary.[1] Had Greek Private business—Walk with Gaskell after six—Tutor gave a subject for English Verses.

21. Saturday.

Saturday's business—read Antiquary in Morng—spoke to Keate—read paper—Spoke in the Society on the War against Charles the First.[2] Walk with Pickering after six—Correcting proofs &c at night, with Selwyn. Again to receive the Sacrament tomorrow—4th time.

22. Sunday.

Late, too late in getting up: read &c. in preparation—received the Sacrament—Provost administered it—Wrote a Summary of Facts about the Irish Church—Finished Acts in my daily readg, & St Luke in Mant. Read Quarterly on Scott & Newton's Memoirs[3]—on Reason & Revelation,[4] & Reformation in England.[5] Rain—wrote to Mr G.

23. Monday.

Learned & had Demosthenes—no more play this time—Monday's business —read a good deal of the Antiquary—wrote notice to Correspondents &c— seeing match between Hallam & Doyle, & Cowper[6] & Bernard[7] after 12: in boat with Colvile after 6. Society meeting after 4. I moved votes of Thanks to Hallam and Gaskell—both great losses to us, & I fear not soon or easily to be repaired.[8] Put off Selwyn's by his own desire. Law elected Chairman, and Doyle President for next Term.

24. Tuesday.

Half holiday—Finished Antiquary—read a little more of Septem contra Thebas with Hallam, & put down quotations—Spoke to Keate—read papers—at the Opidan Dinner part of after 4, & after 6. Toasts &c. Miscellany among others, & W.E.G. with it, drunk.

---

[1] *Scott.

[2] Notes in Add MS 44649, ff. 21–26. Unanimously, the war was held unjust.

[3] xxxi. 26 (December 1824), on memoirs of two Anglican priests, Thomas *Scott and John *Newton.

[4] xxxiii. 356 (March 1826), reviewing James *Nicol of Traquair on *Scripture Sacrifices*.

[5] xxxiii. 1 (December 1825), reviewing among others *Lingard *History of England* iii and iv and *Cobbett *History of the Reformation*.

[6] William Francis *Cowper(-Temple), 1811–80, whig politician and *Palmerston's heir.

[7] Francis Bernard, 1810–77, tory M.P. for Bandon 1831 and 1842–56, styled Viscount Bandon 1830; succ. as 3rd earl of Bandon 1856.

[8] See *Bulletin of John Rylands Library*, xviii. 5–6 (1934) for Gaskell's account.

25. *Wednesday.*

Dear T.G's birthday—may God bless him & if it be His will, restore him to health—played cricket in morning with Sanford—sent leaving books—read papers, & some Æschylus with Hallam—read Herodotus—and Spectator—tea with Gaskell—[who had] wine with me after dinner—Wrote to T.G.—& to London to take my place for Monday.

26. *Thursday.*

Friday's business. Read paper. Read Spectator. Spoke to my Tutor, and to Keate. Read a little Aeschylus—Worked at night at English Verses for my Tutor—did about eighty.

27. *Friday.*

Holiday for the Provost's return! Spoke to Keate at night. read Spectator. breakfasted with Gaskell[1]—read papers—wrote over my English verses. Walk with Gaskell after six—finished Septem contra Thebas & read Herodotus. Heard from Mr G—& also that my [coach] place was secured—Took [place in] chaise.

28. *Election Saturday.*

Half holiday—Finished Vol. 5 of the Spectator—made up accounts—read Herodotus—wrote out for Gaskell to report my speeches about Votes of Thanks—tea with Gaskell in Trotmans garden—Gudgeon fishing with Sanford after 12—Speeches after 4—Selwyn generally judged best (in Greek) Devereux next. No 5 of Miscellany published—very sorry that my name is—Boats fireworks &c after 6. Called on Durnford—he was not in.

29. *Election Sunday.*

Sorry to lose my friends. An excellent sermon preached by Lonsdale—much pleased & I hope something better—Walk with Hallam after six—Began St John in Mant—Read Young's Night Thoughts—& Quarterly Review on Revelation of Soeur Nativité,[2] & on "an Improved Version of the new Testament".[3]

30. *Monday.*

Got up at 5. read Herodotus—but did not get quite to the end of Book Four. Packed up—Shopped—put my things away—Went into School about ¼ before 11—Speeches went off pretty well—Hallam & Selwyn spoke well—Went in chaise to Uxbridge with Hanmer & Warner[4]—dined there with them—got into the Union before six, & travelled all night.

---

[1] See C. M. Gaskell, *An Eton Boy*, 107–9.
[2] xxxiii. 375 (March 1826), on popish impostures.
[3] xxx. 79; see 11–12 June 29.
[4] Henry James Lee-Warner, 1809–86, of Walsingham Abbey, Norfolk.

31. Tuesday.

Got to Birmingham about half past six—Breakfasted &c.—walked about—
Left it about 9 per Aurora—travelled well—got to Liverpool about nine
o'clock—Seaforth about ten—Found all pretty well.

First August—Wednesday.

—Not up very early—Unpacked & put my things out of the way—read
papers—and the Saltbearer—wrote to J.N.G.

2nd. Thursday

—read paper—archery—Began King & No King (Beaumont & Fletcher)[1]
& read various books idly in the Library—Drew Anne in Chair.

3d.

In Liverpool. Read Saltbearer—7th & 8th Numbers—went to settle with
Mr Marrat[2] who is to teach me Mathematics—shooting a little in Evg—but
walked in—out—& about Town, so tired.

4th. Saturday.

In Liverpool—walk'd out—call'd on Mrs Wilson & Miss Conway—saw T.
Ogilvie & congratted him on his approaching nuptials[3]—wrote to Gaskell—
Draughts with Robn & Aunt J.

5th. Sunday.

Went to Bootle Church in morng[4]—sat with Anne a good deal—read Bible
& Memoirs of Martyn & drew Anne in Chair—Mr Grant & Uncle Robert
dined with us.

6th. Monday.

In Liverpool. Took my first lesson in Algebra & a little Euclid from Mr
Marrat—who is very civil—went in with Mr G. Read paper. Drew Anne in
Chair. Draughts with Aunt J. John Murray [Gladstone] dined with us.
Wrote to Dear John. made two or three calls.

7th.

Staid at home—Drew Anne in Chair—Walking—read Edinburgh Review on
W. India Mulattoes—Ellis's original Letters—G.3. & the Catholic Question
—& Present Administration—heard of Mr Canning's alarming illness—
Played bowls—& draughts in Evg—Heard from Gaskell.

[1] Romantic drama about incest.
[2] Charles Marratt, Liverpool mathematics tutor.
[3] See 9 Aug. 27.
[4] Bootle was then a hamlet, south of Seaforth House on the way to Liverpool. (See
Morley, i. 21.)

8.

Mr Canning worse by the accounts, on Monday night & Tuesday morning. May God spare him to the country & his friends. Wrote great part of a letter to Hallam, & heard from him. Read Edinburgh Review on Society for diffusion of Useful Knowledge—read paper—in Liverpool—lesson from Marrat—learned the 3 first Propositions [in Euclid] for & did them with him & went on with Algebra. Made one or two calls—Aunt Johanna ill.

9. Thursday.

Mr Canning still alive. At the wedding breakfast of Mr & Mrs T. Ogilvy.[1] They started for the North afterwards. Called on Miss Benwell. Finished letter to Hallam. Read papers—& finished "A King & No King". Stewart dined at Seaforth. Drawing Anne a little—shooting & Bowls.

10. Friday.

In Liverpool heard of Mr Cannings death at 10 minutes before 4. on Wednesday morng. It has pleased God to remove him—and I trust to a better place —but the recollection of the past, and the anticipation of the future involve us in sorrow, and in uncertainty. Personally, I must thankfully remember his kindness and condescension—especially when he spoke to me of some verses, wh H. Joy had, at least injudiciously, mentioned to him:[2] all is for the best: and I trust in God this has been to him a happy release. Read the Accounts in the papers. Read his glorious speech on the Lisbon business[3] —& some of those at Liverpool. Rode—learned 4th 5th & 6th Propositions, & did them & Algebra with Marrat. Drew Anne in Chair. Wrote part of a letter to Gaskell. Mr G. T. & R. G. had intended to go to Dublin—prevented by a westerly gale. Aunt J. set right again, I hope.

11. Saturday.

Rode to Liverpool with Tom—Finished letter to Gaskell—Drew Anne in Chair—Began the vol. of Cannings Liverpool Speeches, and read the Introduction & some of the first.

12. Sunday.

Mr Rawson absent—a stranger officiated—Drew Anne in Chair—read 2nd & third Chapters of St John with Mant Notes, & read Memoir of Martyn— sat with Anne a good deal.

13th.

Learned 7th, 8th, 9th, & 10th Propositions, & did them & Algebra with Marrat. 4th lesson—went on with Cannings Speeches—rode into & out of Liverpool. Trip put off again.

[1] Thomas Ogilvy married Elizabeth, only da. of John Wilson of Rodney Street, Liverpool.
[2] Version in Morley, i. 34.   [3] See 16 Dec. 26 n.

14th. Tuesday.

Heard from Hallam—read Cannings Speeches—Day rainy—Draughts with Aunt J.—Rode into town & ordered a black coat—Father & Tom went by William Huskisson[1] to Greenock in afternoon.

15. Wednesday.

Learned the four next propositions for Marrat—& did them & Algebra with him. Went with R.G. to & from town. Wrote to Hallam. Drew Anne in Chair—Draughts with Aunt J. Read Cannings Speeches. Called on Mrs Wilson.

16.

Mr Cannings funeral day: and Manchester Anniversary![2] Heard from Gaskell. Wrote to J.N.G. Drew Anne in Chair—In Liverpool—Put on mourning —Finished Canning's speeches—in Evg, began Old Mortality[3]—2nd time of reading. Rode.

17.

Learned 5 propositions & did them & Algebra with Mr Marrat—Rode— Drew Anne in Chair—Draughts with Aunt J—Read Old Mortality.

18. Saturday.

Finished Old Mortality—in the first rank of Waverley Novels, me judice. Drew Anne in Chair—Wrote to Gaskell—played draughts with Aunt J. & chess with H.J.G.—Began Miss Edgeworth's Love & Law.[4]

19. Sunday.

Mr Rawson preached, morning & evg.—Drew Anne in chair—Read Mant, & a little of Scott,[5] for comparison—read Martyn's Life.

20. Monday.

Learned 5 propositions for Marrat & did them & Algebra with him. Finished Love & Law—began the next[6]—Draughts with Aunt J. Went to see Uncle Murray; called on Mrs Staniforth.

21. Tuesday.

Heard from Hallam—draughts with Aunt J. Went to see Mr Rawson.

---

[1] One of three steam packets run between Liverpool and Glasgow by James Allan.
[2] Eleven people were killed at the 'massacre of Peterloo', a meeting in St. Peter's Fields, Manchester, on 16 August 1819.
[3] *Scott.
[4] The first of Maria *Edgeworth's *Comic Dramas* (1817).
[5] Thomas *Scott's annotated *Family Bible* (1788, &c).
[6] 'The Two Guardians'.

Finished Miss Edgeworths Comic Dramas[1]—& began Black Dwarf[2], 2nd time. Drew Anne in chair.

22. Wednesday.

Learned the five next propositions, & did them & Algebra with Marrat—finished Black Dwarf—Drew Anne in Chair—Draughts with Aunt J.—call'd on Mrs Traill—read paper—

23. Thursday.

Wrote to Mr G. Sorted and labelled some packets of letters—Began Rob-roy[3]—second time (at least) Drew Anne in chair—I spend some time in the garden about the place.

24.

Learn'd the five next propositions. & did them & Algebra with Marrat. Wrote to Aunt E. Just past the Lodge, the grey mare came completely down with me; & as she was going pretty fast, pitched me clear over her head a considerable distance *on the pavement*—thanks be to God, I was not hurt beyond a slight bruise—turned back & changed, & rode in safely. Took Complete Angler[4] in in my pocket, & read it in town to employ the time. Din'd at Slater Street & went to Theatre with Robn & Kelso: C. Kemble[5] acted Hamlet very beautifully. Came away before the 2nd piece, & rode home—rather fresh gale on the shore in our faces.

25. Saturday.

Matheson came down in Evg—Draughts with him & Aunt J.—Read Rob Roy—drew Anne in Chair—shot a little—Busy in getting fruit ready to send out.

26. Sunday.

Church morning & Evg. Read two next Chapters & Notes in Mant, besides Evg reading. Drew Anne in Chair. Finished Martyn's Life—it might be called with a slight variation, Martyrs Life. Read Buddicom's 3d sermon (in his Exodus)[6] aloud to A.M.G.: & read Faber's First[7]—which seems to me very able.

27. Monday.

Learned six propositions for Marrat, & did them & Algebra with him. Went

---

[1] The volume also contained 'The Rose, Thistle, and Shamrock'.
[2] *Scott, in *Tales of my Landlord*.
[3] Also *Scott.   [4] Izaak *Walton.
[5] Charles *Kemble, 1775–1854, actor.
[6] R. P. Buddicom, *The Christian Exodus*, 2v. (1826), sermons on the flight from Egypt as a precursor of Christ's coming, i. 46–65.
[7] G. S. *Faber, *Sermons on various subjects and occasions*, 2v. (1816–20), i. 1–21, 'The Universal Profitableness of Scripture'.

to the meeting about Mr Canning's monument—late, in consequence of my Mathematics Lesson. Dined with Dr M'Cartney—Mr Stewart M'Kenzie[1] & others there. Read Rob Roy.

28. Tuesday.

Read Rob Roy, and paper. Drew Anne in Chair. Draughts with Aunt J. Mr & T.G. returned. Rode over to Ince & saw Mr Blundell & a Dr Maxwell,[2] who is staying with him. Poor Tom looking no better.

29. Wednesday.

Finished Rob Roy—resumed Hume. Draughts with Aunt J. drew Anne in chair a little—learned 6 Propositions, & did them (skimming two) & Algebra with Marrat—Bathed.

30. Thursday

—read Hume—rain—draughts with Aunt J.—busied in arranging my old letters for some time—& began a comparison between ancients & moderns for the Miscellany.[3]

31. Friday.

Read paper—read Hume—Learned Propositions for Marrat—(got into book Second) & did them & Algebra with him. Draughts with Aunt J. Rode grey into & out of town.

1 September. Saturday.

Read Hume, & newspaper. Resumed "Ancients & Moderns"—finished what I mean for the first part—worked at arranging my letters. Read in Evg for Sacrament.

2. Sunday.

Received the Sacrament—forty or more communicants—Mr Rawson offici-ated. Read Bible & Notes on the Sacrament, &c. Read Fabers 2nd Sermon —and one of Buddicom's Exodus aloud to Anne—very able—Read Quarterly on Bible Society—very strong[4]—but audiam alteram partem[5]— Read two Chapters in Mant & Notes—Heard from Gaskell: & wrote to him to catch him leaving England; he desiring it: his letter very kind.

---

[1] James Alexander Stewart-Mackenzie, 1784–1843; m. 1817, Mary, widow of Sir Samuel *Hood, chieftainess of clan Mackenzie; M.P. for Ross and Cromarty 1831–7.
[2] One of several Maxwells who held Edinburgh medical degrees.
[3] Published next term, ii. 7–16, 52–64.
[4] xxxvi. 1–28 (June 1827); alleging bad finance and worse translations.
[5] 'I should hear the other side'.

3. Monday.

Read the remainder of the Identical Propositions, & learned two more, & did them & Algebra with Marrat. Rode brown mare—a nice animal. Read Hume—& paper—Bathed. Mother ill—seized with spasms after I had come home. Mr Jones sent for & found immediately. They soon went off, thank God, & left her quiet, but with headache.

4. Tuesday.

Mother better—read Hume—and paper—Wrote to J.N.G.—began an endeavour to demonstrate a proposition—interrupted & did not proceed far. Mr G, T.G. & I went over to Ince—dined with Mr Blundell. returned in Evg—he not very well.

5. Wednesday.

Learned to the end of the 2nd book, & did Propositions & Algebra with Marrat. Like him well. Wrote to W.W. Farr—Finished 8th & began 9th vol. of Hume. Rode grey into & out of town.

6th. Thursday.

Near two hours measuring walls with Mr G. Read Hume. Put down some Mathematical trifles. Went out & swam dogs—read paper—Mrs G. much the same. Finished arranging letters, bills &c.

7th.

Copied a few small things. Began [Euclid] Book 3, learned 7 Propositions, & did them & Algebra with Marrat. Read paper—read Hume. Went in [to Liverpool] & out with R.G. My Mother in bed with cold & headache.

8. Saturday.

Wrote about six or seven more pages on Ancient & Modern Genius. Swam dogs—read paper—read Hume. My Mother in bed still.

9. Sunday.

Mr Tattershall[1] preached in morning: Mr Simpson (I believe)[2] in afternoon. Read Bible—Notes only to one Chapter that I might get thro' a good deal of Faber. Read about 140 pages—& read out one of Buddicom's sermons to Anne—both very able. Mother better.

[1] Thomas Tattershall, 1795?–1846, wrangler 1816; worked with *Simeon; D.D. 1838; priest in charge of St. Augustine's, Everton, 1830.
[2] James Simpson, 1787?–1870, in charge of Great Sankey, 14 miles east of Liverpool, 1814.

10.

Learned seven propositions, rode into town & did them & Algebra with
Marrat. Came out with Mr G—Read Cobbetts last[1]—very clever—read
Hume. T. & R.G. dined at Mossley Hill[2]—I was asked but did not go.

11. Tuesday.

Copied two letters—short—read Hume—in orchard watching insects &
making experiments—rewrote & added to part of ancient & modern writers.
Mr Rawson had tea with us.

12.

Read papers—read Hume—learned 6 Propositions—went in in gig with
heavy rain—did them & Algebra with Marrat. Wrote a little Ancients &
Moderns—Heard from Farr—read Miniature.[3]

13. Wednesday [sc. Thursday]

—Finished 9th (& last) of Hume's beautifully written & most valuable
History.[4] Read Quarterly on Wolfe Tone, & began it on State of Universities. Wrote to Doyle. Mrs T.G. & D.G. with daughters[5] called, wh interrupted me much—so I could write only a little—Read papers—Went to
Jones about a, thank God, very slight ailing—swam dogs, in garden &c.

14. Friday.

Learned six propositions & did them and Algebra with Marrat—Wrote to
Farr—Wrote out Mr Cannings Epitaph on his Son[6] for my father—read
paper—drove Bolton into Town.—read on the article on Universities.

15. Saturday.

Went into town early with Mr G. and staid some time waiting for Tom—
to go into Park—he did not come on account of weather—walked out.
Wrote to J.N.G. read papers, finished Quarterly on Universities, & my own
concern on Ancients & Moderns.

16. Sunday. Sept. 16th

Mr Rawson preached morning & Evg—read Bible—a good deal more of

[1] *Cobbett's Weekly Political Register*, lxiii. 641–93, for 8 September.
[2] The Ewarts'.
[3] Another Eton school magazine, published in 1804–5 by Stratford *Canning and
others.
[4] *The ninth volume was *Smollett's continuation.
[5] Janet, wife of Thomas Gladstones, had two das. Janet Forrest, 1801–50, and Helen
Neilson; so had Emmeline Ramsden, d. 1885, wife of David Gladstone: Anne Ramsden,
1817–1906, later Mrs. T. F. Bennett; and Harriet Emmeline, 1821–1905, later Mrs.
William Woodhouse. (The David Gladstones' 3rd da. was not b. till 1830.)
[6] *Canning's eldest s., George Charles, b. 1801, an invalid all his short life, d. 1820;
epitaph in L. T. *Rede, *Memoir of George *Canning* (1827), 97.

Faber, & one of Buddicom's Sermons aloud to Anne. Settled that I am not
to reside at Oxford till October; which I trust is for the best: but my own
wish had been to go for a term previous to Long Vacation.

17. Monday.

Learned 7 Propositions, & did them & Algebra with Marrat. I like the mas-
ter, and also the business, very well. Draughts with Aunt J. Called on Mrs
Moss & the Sandbaches, where we saw Mrs Parker;[1] called also at Aunt
Thomas's & Aunt David's. Began 1st part of Henry 4th: heard from
Pickering. monsr. bickersteth[2] dit que ma soeur anne etoit better.[3] May
God be thanked & praised for it.

18. Tuesday.

At home. Went to Jones's twice & missed him. In garden—swimming dogs
—walking—drew Anne in chair—copied one letter—finished First part of
Henry the Fourth (not the first time, of course) began making a fresh copy
of one part of Ancient & Modern Writers.[4]

19. Wednesday.

Wrote to C. Canning. Learned the 4 last propositions of Book 3, & did them
& Algebra (near the end of simple equations) with Marrat. Paid him his
Bill, & bid him goodbye. I hope to see more of him. Went to the meeting
for a requisition to Mr Huskisson: Mr G. spoke.[5] Did a good deal of business
in Liverpool: called on Mrs M'Cartney: went to Exhibition:[6] & walked
about it a great deal on different matters. Walked out. Read part of 2nd
part of Henry 4. The Goalens[7] dined with us. Read papers.

20. Thursday

read more of Henry 4th, but had not time to finish it. Wrote to Pickering.
Wrote to Hallam. & finished writing over Ancients & Moderns. Long conversation with Tom. Called on Mr Rawson to bid him good bye. Put my
things in order & away, & packed up. Bid them goodbye.

Thursday. 20.

[second entry] Up pretty early. Wrote to Pickering—& a long letter to Hallam. Finished writing over the 1st sheet of Ancient & Moderns. Called on
Mr Rawson. Put things away, & pack'd. Letter from J.N.G. received. read
more of 2nd part of Henry the Fourth. Bid goodbye to Mother Anne &c.

---

[1] Wife of Charles Parker, gentleman, of Aigburth, near Otterspool.
[2] Robert Bickersteth of Rodney Street, senior surgeon to the Liverpool Infirmary.
[3] This sentence in Greek script.
[4] The pagination of the rest of this volume is confused, because the writer here turned
over two pages at once.
[5] Town meeting to request *Huskisson to stand for *Canning's seat.
[6] Fourth exhibition of works by living artists at Liverpool Royal Academy.
[7] Thomas Goalen, Liverpool ironfounder, and his wife, a sister of John *Gladstone's.

21.

Up at 5, called by Mr G. Breakfasted before six; H.J.G. up to see me off, very kindly. R.G. meant it, but I did not awake him. Left Liverpool at 7 by Alliance: travelled all day & all night. Good coach. Weather cold. I inside.

22. Saturday.

Escape in morning, thank God. All but upset. Arrived at Lad Lane[1] before ten: dressed, breakfasted &c. went to Davisons[2] &c. in hackney coach to West End. Went to York Place;[3] Uncle Colin out; to Wimpole Street; found Mrs Larkins & Miss Nan; lunch &c there: left about 3: went down to Westminster Abbey, to see poor Mr Cannings burial place.[4] Left London at 5. arrived at Eton before 8, by Mat. Milton [coach]. Found my Dames band assembled. Unpacked &c. in part. Somewhat tired.

23.

Champnes preached. I wrote to T.G.; read Mant, Notes only to one Chapter: read Faber, & did Theme.[5] Eton almost desolate, so many have left. Finished unpacking &c.

24.

Monday's business, quotations &c. Called up in Scriptores Romani. Meeting at Society—made many motions: & reported the whole.[6] read papers. began Hallam's Const.Hist: & a book of Facts &c. from it.[7] Heard from Selwyn, with Articles. Sat up late to write an Introduction, wh I did. Offers from Hanmer, & consultations. Wrote up Journal.

25. Tuesday.

Wrote over Theme. Stated Hanmer's proposals, with the pros & cons, at a meeting at my room: unanimous opinion that we cannot accept. With Law and Rogers, prepared, after 12, after dinner & after 4, the sixth number for the printer—sent it up. Walk with Rogers for near an hour till lock up time afterwards—After tea, wrote a long letter to Selwyn, & part of one to Mrs G.—also began an article—arm aching at night, having held the pen for seven or eight hours, or more, today. Half holiday.

26

Wednesday's business. Law's resignation came. Did verses at night.[8] Read

---

[1] Swan-with-two-necks, Lad Lane, Cheapside, a coaching inn.
[2] Probably Davison & Simpson, Broad Street merchants.
[3] Off Portman Square; Colin Robertson lived there.
[4] See 7 Oct. 27 and Bassett, 12.
[5] Add MS 44718, f. 104, on corruption of youth.
[6] Private business.
[7] Henry *Hallam, *Constitutional History of England*, 1485–1760, 2v. (1827).
[8] Add MS 44718, f. 105; reflexions on death, in Latin hexameters.

papers: & did several little things for the Society. Did translation. Finished writing to Mrs G. Meeting of Library Directors after dinner. Sat singing at night. Worked a little at Algebra, & a little at Horace for tomorrow.

27.

Wrote over verses for Tutor. Friday's business. called up in Scriptores Graeci. Private business—finished Iphigenia in Aulis. Quotations to Horace &c. Read paper. Walk with Jelf. Sent Law a leaving book. He came & sat with me at night. Breakfasted with Hamilton. Finished Henry 4—Book 4 of Herodotus—dull and tedious. Began Schlegel's Lectures on Dram. Lit., lent by Tutor.[1]

28. Friday.

Friday. Breakfast with Doyle & Hamilton. Wrote over verses. Heard from A.M.G. T. & R.G. to leave home, I suppose, today. Walk with Doyle after 12. read papers. Doyle with me after dinner—of the general opinion about Hanmer. Called on Berthomier. Putting study &c. to rights. Began 5th of Herodotus. read a little Schlegel, & Hallam on Queen Annes reign &c.[2] for debate tomorrow.

29. Saturday

—holiday—heard from home—Wrote to T.G. read paper—read Schlegel— walk with Doyle—Handley sat with me part of Evg—learned & had Private business (Pindar)—read Cicero a little—began to report the Debate. Debate on Tory Ministry of Queen Annes reign—voted in a majority agst them.[3] Proposed Lyall,[4] who was elected. Armstrong[5] also elected. Moved a Vote of Thanks to Law. Doyle & Jelf spoke. To receive the Sacrament tomorrow. Read &c.

30. Sunday.

Went up to Salthill in morng with a parcel to send to Tom to Oxford. Plumptre preached—received the Sacrament: few communicants. Finished Faber's First vol: he is very able, but his subjects above me, in general at least. Walk with Doyle. Did Theme[6]—began Paley's Evidences of Christianity[7]—Read Bible, & Notes. Reviewed my past employments, reading &c. which has not been very great.

---

[1] A. W. von Schlegel, *Lectures on dramatic art and literature*, tr. J. *Black, 2v. (1815); romantic criticism. Knapp was a keen playgoer: see W. L. *C[ollins], *Etoniana*, appx. D.
[2] *Constitutional history*, ii. 549ff.
[3] He spoke also; motion defeated by 4 to 2.
[4] John Edwardes Lyall, advocate-general of Bengal; d. 1845.
[5] John Armstrong, d. ca. 1865; canon of Wells, rector of Dinder, Somerset.
[6] Add MS 44718, f. 106; on conquest of temptation.
[7] Archdeacon William *Paley, *A View of the Evidences of Christianity* (1794), long a prop of the anglican faith.

October First.

Monday's business. Called up in Scriptores Romani. Canning with me after dinner—wine. Walked with him after four. Read papers. Finished reporting debate. Morning, part of after 12, & part of Evg, correcting proof sheets. Wrote part of an article (intended) on eloquence. Did Extempore. Sat with Handley minor part of Evg.

October 2. Tuesday

Holiday. Wrote part of different verse things. Read paper. Sent back proof sheets. Walk with Doyle after 12. Wrote over Theme. Read Schlegel. Read Musae Etonenses. Did some verses. Read Georgics. Correcting Miscellany accounts &c. part of after 4.

3.

Wrote to my Father. Heard from Pickering. Finished verses; wrote over for Tutor & for School.[1] Read paper—Schlegel—Herodotus: did some Alcaics: walk with Rogers part of after four. Keate told me he wd send me up for Play for last week's exercise on Mr Canning's death.[2] I ought to be thankful. With him part of after 12.

4.

Half holiday—read paper—walk with Doyle after 4—after much alteration, and waiting with Keate all after 12, took it up to Plumptre's. This sort of sending up does not trouble one much by delay. Finished Lyrics, & wrote over for Tutor & school—wrote in all four Copies of the Sent up Exercise. Read Schlegel. Sat with Handley after supper.

5. Friday.

Friday's business—learning Horace &c—quotations—wrote to Pickering— read paper—read Schlegel—walk with Doyle after four. read Herodotus— corrected &c. my second Part of Ancient and Modern Genius—wrote some letters &c. to make a conclusion for Number Seven.

6. Saturday.

Called up in Poetae. read paper: walk with Canning. Saturday's business. Began Phoenissae[3] in private business. Question—Execution of Sir Walter Raleigh. I spoke, & voted unjustifiable.[4] Hamilton, Taunton,[5] & Bruce elected. Wrote nearly sixteen pages in the debate book. read a little Herodotus: & began turning some of Sampson Agonistes into Greek Anapaests.

---

[1] Add MS 44718, f. 107.
[2] Eventually printed by *Okes, *Musae Etonenses*, new series, ii. xcvi.
[3] Euripides.
[4] By 10 to none the society agreed.
[5] Thomas Henry Taunton, captain of boats 1827, Bond Street wine merchant.

7. Sunday.

Lonsdale preached another *good* sermon. He may I hope do good here. Said private business (Lucretius). Construed Play. walk with Rogers. read Paley, 3 Chapters in Mant & Notes—did Theme[1]—wrote a thing on Canning's death purporting to be in Westminster Abbey[2]—remiss somewhat.

8.

Monday's business. Called up in Scriptores Romani. Wrote to Law. Finished Debate. Wrote over Fragment, & Reflections on Westminster Abbey. Walk with Doyle. Had Play, learning &c.—not long. Did Extempore. Read papers. Sir J. M'Grigor came & sat with me at night. Correcting & getting ready things for No. 7. Wrote an Introduction. Altering too an old exercise for which Keate told me he would send me up for Play this week again. May I be thankful and humble.

9. Tuesday.

Holiday—but a hard day's work. Up pretty early—working with Rogers at No 7—breakfasted with Sir J. & Lady McGrigor at White Hart—heard from Hallam—Worked after 12—except a short part of it in altering my verses for Keate—worked part of after 4, & took the number up with Rogers. Read papers—wrote to A.M.G.—read a little Schlegel—did Greek Iambics on the Sun.

10.

Wednesday's business. Wrote over Theme—& Iambics for Tutor—read papers—Selwyn down here—with him part of after 12, after dinner, & part of after 4—few pages of Schlegel—finished what is now a long article on Eloquence[3]—writing all but the 1st 2 pages—Handley minor came & sat in my room. Did 4 stanzas of Greek Sapphics.

11.

Half holiday. Wrote over Greek Iambics for School. Finished Greek Sapphics—wrote over for Tutor and for school—read paper—few pages of Schlegel—letters from home—Mr G., A.M.G., J.N.G., &c. walk with Doyle —sat with Handley &c. part of Evg. Finished Greek Anapaests for Canning, wh I am doing because he lately got a punishment thro' me. Breakfast with Hamilton—Moss & Canning "wined" with me after dinner.— Sent up for Play. Wrote over for College and for Keate.

12.

Friday's business. Called up in Horace. Wrote two more copies of sent up Exercise—one for Tutor—Private business (Phoenissae)—read papers—

---

[1] Add MS 44718, f. 110; the wise man is free.
[2] *Eton Miscellany*, ii. 79–81.   [3] Ibid., ii. 107–15.

wrote to Mr G. Hamilton & Doyle had wine with me after two—read Schlegel; & Hallam[1] & Hume[2] on Vane's Execution. Handley sat with me part of Evg. Corrected my thing on Eloquence.

13.

Saturday's business—learned play, but had a run. Heard from Gaskell & Law. read papers—walk with Canning—finished Vol First of Schlegel. Debate on Vane's Execution—voted agst it—shd have spoken, had there been a deficiency,[3] wrote out the debate, Proposed Rogers—elected. unanimously—Chisholm[4] & Snow[5] proposed—elected with one black ball. Private business (Pindar) & learning it.

14. Sunday.

Lonsdale preached; very well. Walk with Rogers. Said Lucretius for Private business. Sat part of Evg with Handley. did Theme:[6] read 2 Chapters & Notes in Mant: read Paley's Evidences—& 2 of Dodwell's Charges in Vindication of Athanasian Creed.[7]

15.

Monday's business. Play; called up—up the whole time. Walk with Doyle— read papers—correcting proof sheets after dinner—part of after 4, & in Evg. Wrote over & altered Theme. Sat with Handley part of Evg—tired with proofsheet work. Reading letters from correspondents &c. Finished Debate & V.P's business, save filing papers.

16. Tuesday.

Wednesday's business—Quotations &c. Began 2nd Vol of Schlegel. Walk with Hamilton—read paper—at Society after 12, wrote some verses and some prose, and sat talking with Handley minor in Evening.

17. Wednesday.

Half holiday. Walk with Doyle: with Ingalton about Miscellany—did Translation—read Schlegel—after much doubt about a way of doing them, did my Verses[8]—and read a little Herodotus. I have been shamefully idle. Meeting at Library—making out list of books.

---

[1] *Constitutional History*, ii. 186–7.
[2] In *History of England*, lxiii.
[3] *Vane's execution was held unjustified by 12 to none.
[4] Alexander William, The Chisholm, 1810–38, of Erchless Castle, Inverness-shire; M.P. for that county 1835–8.
[5] Either William Snow, afterwards Strahan, a London banker; or Henry Snow, 1811?– 1874, vicar of Bibury, Gloucestershire, 1843.
[6] Add MS 44718, f. 112; on not wasting time.
[7] W. *Dodwell, *The Athanasian Creed indicated and explained, in three charges* (1802).
[8] Add MS 44718, f. 113.

18. Thursday.

Holiday. Wrote over verses for Tutor—did some Lyrics—read papers—walk with Doyle—read Schlegel—called on Durnford, who was out. Sat in Evg. part with Handley minor: & another part with Carruthers.

19. Friday.

Took medicine & staid out. Walk with Handley, pretty long. Sat with him some time, he staying out too. Wrote to Miss G—part of a letter to Gaskell—read papers—finished Lyrics—wrote over verses for school—read Schlegel—& Shakespeare's Richard 2nd. How hard is Johnson upon it![1]

20. Saturday.

Staid out. Finished letter to Gaskell & wrote part of one to my Brother R.G. Walk with Handley. Read Schlegel: & a little of Herodotus. read paper: & reported nearly 21 pages in the Society book—in 5 hours. Debate on Caesar's passing Rubicon: Hamilton, Doyle, Taunton, spoke for; Snow, Bruce (very well), Jelf, Canning, & I agst it. Canning not bad. In a huge majority.[2] proposed Chisholm, mi.[3] Elected. Scarlett[4] also proposed & elected.

21. Sunday.

Bethell preached. Said private business. Read Dodwell's 3d Charge. They seem able & good. Read Mant (finished St John) & Paley. Finished letter to R.G, which I totally forgot yesterday. walk with Handley for an hour. Dined with Durnford to meet Gooch, my brother's friend.[5] Both very kind. Like them much.

[Inside the back cover of vol. II Gladstone twice signed his name, and wrote below:]

Was the deposition of Richard II justifiable?[6]

[1] Samuel *Johnson, *Works*, ed. R. Lynam (1825), v. 151–2.
[2] Of 13 to 3. Part of minutes reproduced in *Strand Magazine*, viii. 75 (July 1894).
[3] Duncan Macdonnell Chisholm, The Chisholm from 1838, d. 1858.
[4] Robert William Scarlett, b. Jamaica 1810, d. an undergraduate of Trinity College, Cambridge 1832.
[5] Frederick Gooch, 1804?–87, fellow of All Souls 1828–53, rector of Baginton, Worcestershire, from 1833.
[6] Draft motion for society; see 27 Oct. 27.

[VOLUME III][1]
(*No. 3*)

William Ewart Gladstone.
Private.

October 22, 1827 to Oct, 1828.[2]
Eton, October, 1827.

22.

Monday's business, & Play. Finished Debate. read papers. Did Theme & Extempore. Called up in Scriptores Romani. Wrote over last week's Lyrics. Out for a very short time with Hamilton. Read correspondents &c. Finished Introduction & a piece of poetry for No 8. No 7 published.

23.

Wrote over Shipwreck.[3] Finished a Chorus from Euripides—wrote it over. Holiday. Working for the Miscellany, with Doyle. Got all ready except Rogers's pieces after four, and took it up to Ingalton's. Walked with Doyle after it. Read Schlegel: sat with Handley: wrote over Theme; wrote some verses: had a speech set[4] & began to learn it.

24.

Wednesday's business. Learn'd more of speech. Agreed to mess with Handley minor till holidays.[5] Walk with him part of after 12, with Doyle part of after 4. Keate told me he wd send me up again. This is a great accumulation, which I trust may not do me harm. Occupied much in alterations &c. of the Exercise. Did Translation—sat with Handley minor.

25.

Did verses. Wrote over for Tutor & for school. Wrote to Aunt Mary & to Buckeridge. Private business (Phoenissae) Read paper—read Schlegel—at fair with Handley after 4. At the theatre—*disgusting*—Sent up for Play. wrote over for College & Keate. Heard from home—several letters.

26.

Friday's business. Read papers. Learning Horace &c. Walk with Doyle.

---

[1] Lambeth MS 1417. 23 ff.
[3] *Eton Miscellany*, ii. 115–17.
[5] *Hallam was in Italy.

[2] These four lines inside front cover.
[4] See I Nov. 27.

Spoke to my Tutor. Read Schlegel. Wrote to Mr G. Handley sat with me part of Evg. Read Hume & Hallam on Richard 2nd's reign;[1] for tomorrow.

27. Saturday.

Play & learning it. Half holiday. Read papers at Society after 12, having missed any one to go out with me. Heard from home. Had Private business (Pindar), & learning it. Finished Schlegel, whom I like much. Read a curious letter of Mrs Canning's[2] given me for G[askell] for the purpose. Spoke for 15 or 20 minutes at Society against Deposition of Richard 2.[3] Much *noise* and *fun*. Proof sheets at night.

28. Sunday.

Much rain. Mr Lonsdale preach'd. Said private business. Construed Play. Sat some time with Handley. Did Theme. Read Paley's Evidences. Remarks on the Gospels &c. in Mant, & 2 Chapters of Acts with Notes &c.

29. Monday.

Finished proofsheets & sent them back to Town. Monday's business. Called up in Scriptores Romani. Read papers—spoke to Keate—walked with Handley after dinner. Spoke again in Society (Adjourned Debate) after 4. Doyle converted. Great majority.[4] Proposed Nicholl—elected. Wrote over Theme—Wrote to Selwyn. *Finished " The Ladder of the Law "*.[5]

30. Tuesday.

Wednesday's business. Walk with Canning before breakfast. Spoke to my Tutor. Copied parts of Mrs Canning's letter to G[askell]—G had wine with me after dinner—walk with Handley part of after 4. Began 6th Vol of Spectator—Did Translation—Looked over revises of 8. Eton Miscellany at night—wrote & corrected &c.

31. Wednesday.

Half holiday. Walk with Hodgson[6] in morning to Slough—with Doyle after 12. Read papers after dinner—spoke to Keate—at Society & wrote to A.M.G.—did verses—talked with Handley minor—finished (& writing over) Guatimozin's Death Song.[7] Heard from Gaskell—A.M.G.—Selwyn. A.M.G's letter contained news of Dr Munro's death.[8] He is, there seems much reason for hoping, in a far happier place.

[1] *Hume, *History of England*, xvii; *Hallam, *State of Europe*, ii. 263–90.
[2] Joan Scott, heiress, m. George *Canning 1800; cr. viscountess 1828; d. 1837. Her sister Henrietta m. 4th duke of Portland 1795.
[3] Debate adjourned to 29th.
[4] Of 12 to 4 against deposition of *Richard II.
[5] *Eton Miscellany*, ii. 149–55.
[6] Probably Edward Tucker Hodgson, then an Eton boy, who d. 1832.
[7] *Eton Miscellany*, ii. 159.
[8] Perhaps a Munro of Dingwall, friends of Mrs. Gladstone's family.

November First, Thursday

Breakfast with Hamilton & Doyle—read Spectator. Spoke the peroration for Coelius[1] in school—read papers—& a Liverpool one—walk with Hamilton, Doyle, & the Bruces[2] after twelve—wrote over verses—sat with Handley minor—wrote to Farr—corrected & wrote over (no trifle) Ladder of the Law.

2.

Friday's business. Learning Horace &c. Called up in Horace. Sat with Canning—who has sprained his arm & stays out. Walk with J. Bruce after 12 (part of it) Rogers after 4. Read papers. Had private business (Phoenissae). Read Spectator, & wrote for the Miscellany at night. Not very successful, I fear.

3.

Saturday's business. Walk with Bruce after 8 o'clock school—with Handley after twelve—read papers—read Spectator—sat with Canning—wrote a good deal for the Miscellany till very late at night—Read all Canning's papers in the Microcosm. Debate on Elizabeth's character—Spoke against it—to help out the debate[3]—Cowper proposed & elected.

4.

Bethell preached. Wrote to Mr G. & sent a copy of the Miscellany by his desire. Said Lucretius. Asked for a holiday—in vain, I fear. Walk with J. Bruce after prose—Hodgson after 4—with Handley in Evg—Read Bible & Paley.

5. Monday.

Holiday. Looking over and preparing matter for No 9, except walk with Moss and reading paper after twelve. Handley with me part of night—part with Mellish,[4] eating some sock of his—part writing for Miscellany.

6.

Finish'd my things for No 9. Got it ready, (partly with Doyle & Rogers) and sent it off—Monday's business. Heard from Mr G. Walk with Lyall— read papers—read Spectator—Had Play—called up in Scriptores Romani —did some verses—set my bureau &c.&c. to rights in Evening.

---

[1] Coelius Antipater, Roman historian, late second century B.C.
[2] Besides James *Bruce, later Lord Elgin, Lord Ernest A. C. B. Bruce, 1811–86, M.P. for Marlborough 1833–78, 3rd marquess of Ailesbury from 1878.
[3] *Elizabeth's character was deplored by all sixteen members present.
[4] William Leigh Mellish, 1813–64, Nottinghamshire landowner; Sherwood Foresters, 1833–46.

7. Wednesday.

Half holiday. Finished verses. Wrote over for Tutor and for School. Rain—read papers—sat with Bruce (Ld E.)—did some Alcaics—with Handley—read Spectator—went out at night—first to Denton's[1]—then to Ingalton's—got the Triumvirate[2]—(to be published tomorrow) & read it.

8. Thursday.

Wednesday's business—Walk with Doyle after 12—Finish'd Lyrics—wrote over for Tutor and School—read papers—sat at Society—read Spectator—wrote to Gaskell—sat with different fellows in Evg.

9.

Friday's business. Read Spectator—learning Horace—construe at Tutors a good deal now—Read papers—walk with J. Bruce—seeing match between Dame's & Hawtrey's after 12 at football, & hollowing for Dame's, as in duty bound. Construed Play—had private business & learning it. Wrote somewhat.—sat with Jabat.

10. Saturday.

Called up in Poetae. Learned & had Play. Learned & had private business. Sat with Canning after 12. Read papers. Saturday's business. Question on propriety of putting a Sovereign to death. Made few observations & voted agst.[3] Proposed Rickards[4]—elected—& Hodgson, rejected—4 black-balls. Read Spectator—a little Herodotus—corrected in part the proof sheets—went out with Handley to sup with Bruce—he was found out—also went to speak to Hodgson &c.

11. Sunday.

Said private business (Lucretius) Construed Play—Heard from home. Walk with Rogers—saw Canning & Taunton—Hodgson with me—wrote to H.J.G. No Theme. Sat with Handley—Read a good deal of Mant & Paley.

12. Monday.

Play & learning it—Resumed Demosthenes—called up in Play. Monday's business. Finished proof sheets &c. & sent up the Number. Up Windsor after dinner—Walk with Doyle after 4 & read paper. Read Spectator. Handley with me—thought a good deal & at last wrote somewhat, for Miscellany.

---

[1] A bookseller.
[2] A vanished competitor of the *Miscellany*; described by Charles *Canning as 'the most despicable thing I had ever heard of, seen, or read' (Gaskell, *Records of an Eton Schoolboy*, 99).
[3] The society disapproved tyrannicide by 6 to 5.
[4] (Sir) George Kettilby *Rickards, 1812–89, Balliol and Trinity; professor of political economy 1852–7; counsel to speaker 1851–82; K.C.B. on retiring.

13. Tuesday.

Holiday. Not very well. Up Windsor in morning seeing O'Reilly.[1] Read papers. Bruce (Ld E.) breakfasted with me. At Salthill with him, Handley, & Canning, after 12. After dinner & 4 seeing the row, & with Keate &c. Wrote to Selwyn—sat with Handley—cleared away more of my rubbish &c.&c.—did some verses.

14. Wednesday.

Staid out, by O'Reilly's desire. Finished verses, & wrote over for Tutor. Heard from Hallam. Doyle & Canning sat with me after 12. Wrote to Mr G—& a very long letter to Hallam—sat with Handley—read Spectator—Quarterly on London University[2]—wrote a good deal more of Metempsychosis.[3]

15.

Having been dosed with calomel last night, very sick & uncomfortable for half the day. Eat a little partridge after 4 with Handley—who had also Canning & E. Bruce. O'Reilly came—sat with Handley—Read nearly 2 vols of Heart of Midlothian.[4] Better in afternoon thank God. R.G's birthday.

16. Friday.

More pills—went out & read papers—sat with Handley minor—read Heart of Midlothian—finish'd Conclusion—& wrote for Miscellany during the evening.

17. Saturday.

Staying out—on an allowance of three doses daily. Wrote a great deal for the Miscellany—finished Metrical Epistle.[5] Wrote on Punctuality[6] &c. Heard from Selwyn & A.M.G. Wrote List of Contributors & worked a good deal alone in getting up the Number. Disappointed by Doyle & Rogers, who are not ready. Ballot repeated—Hodgson got in—Voted for Phocion[7] agst. Demosthenes.

18. Sunday.

Grover preached. Said private business. With Handley &c. Wrote a short letter to Mrs G. & a line to Jones. Read Mant & Paley, & Quarterly on American Mission to Burmese[8]—but sick & unwell at night, & could not do much.

---

[1] A local doctor.   [2] xxxiii. 260 (January 1826).
[3] Concluding essay in *Eton Miscellany*, ii. 257.   [4] *Scott.
[5] *Eton Miscellany*, ii. 194–200.   [6] Ibid. 217.
[7] Athenian general, fourth century B.C.; the society unanimously held him a greater patriot than the orator Demosthenes.
[8] xxxiii. 37 (January 1826).

19.

Monday's business.—Demosthenes &c—Called up in Homer—Working at Number 10, which will be long & I think pretty good. Made Index &c. Did Theme & reported the Society debate in the Evening. Sent up No. 10. Hurra, Hurra, Hurra!

20.

Letters from R.G.—Mr G—Mrs G—A.M.G. &c—very kind & satisfactory. Holiday. Read papers. Walk with Handley, 2 Bruces, & Canning after 12. Jaws—sat at Society after four. Finished Heart of Midlothian. Wrote over Theme, & last weeks verses. Got my fram'd picture of Mr Canning.

21.

Wednesday's business. Called up in Virgil—DID WHOLE. read Spectator—read papers—wrote to Mr G. a longish letter—sat with Taunton & at Society—walk with Doyle—read a little Herodotus—got out at night, & supped with Bruce—in before 11.

22. Thursday.

Walk with Canning, Handley, & 2 Bruces, after 12, & sock at Salthill. Ran to milestone with Doyle—after absence. Setting Bouverie papers to rights. Heard from Selwyn. Read Spectator—at Society after 4—had private business—read up Phoenissae—& on. Received, as B[artholomew] B[ouverie], some lithog[raph] drawings with the delineator's respectful compliments! He is very civil indeed. Sat singing.

23.

Friday's business. Rogers with me after 12—read papers—sat with Hamilton—wrote to Mrs G.—play'd chess & cards with Handley minor—read Spectator—& Phoenissae—snow on ground. Expecting proof sheets all day. Sat singing.

24.

Saturday's business. Called up in Testament. Read papers—Finish'd Phoenissae—read Spectator—Voted for Charles 2. against Cromwell[1]—propos'd Kinglake,[2] who was elected—Chess and cards at night while expecting proof-sheets—they came down & I corrected them. Wrote a letter to Law.

25. Sunday.

Gave some time, on the emergency, to revising the corrected proofsheets, &

---

[1] *Cromwell was held more detestable than *Charles II by 18 to none.
[2] Alexander William *Kinglake, 1809–91, historian of the Crimean war; wrote *Eothen.*

took them up to Ingalton's. I must make up in allowing more time to the Bible thro' the week. Grover preached—sat with Handley &c. after 4—did a long Theme—read 3 Chapters in Mant; & a good deal of Paley. Heard from Farr.

26. Monday.

Play and learning it. Walk with J. Bruce. Wrote list of Contents of No 10, for Ingalton to advertise. read papers. Sat at Society. Look'd over my last theme. Chess with Handley minor. read Spectator—wrote letters to Selwyn & Farr—notes to Law & Frere[1]—ask'd by tutor to dine with him on Friday.

Novr 27. Tuesday.

Holiday. Bid Canning goodbye—no more to see him as a fellow Etonian— received a leaving book from him with a very kind note—walk with him, Handley, Doyle, 2 Bruces, & Hodgson, to Salthill &c. & sock. Read papers wrote over Theme—finished Vol 6. of Spectator—began Life of Petrarch[2]— did some verses on Laura's death—set by Tutor—Up town after 4 with Handley—he sat with me part of Evg.

28. Wednesday.

Friday's business. walk with Moss—learned Horace—read papers—sat at Society—read Life of Petrarch—Wrote to H.J.G., and to Cartwright[3]— did a good deal of my Vale, I am afraid poor enough—received leaving books, very handsome, from Moss, Rogers, Robertson—put up a good many books for packing, carefully.

29. Thursday.

Rec'd leaving books from Handley, Chisholm minor, Mansfield major, Carruthers major, Jabat, Mellish major & Mellish minor,[4] White,[5] Robinson, Buller major.[6] I am now very well off—Finished Vale—immensely long. & poor—curtailed it—still very long. Chess & cards with Handley, at night, after work—wrote note to O'Reilly to go with Mr Canning's bust— walk with Handley in morning—after 12 with Doyle—read paper—put up a good many more books. Football match to have been played, between Society & 2nd eleven—not so however.

<hr>

[1] John Frere, 1807–51, rector of Cottenham, Cambridgeshire, from 1839.
[2] Probably A. F. *Tytler's (1810).
[3] Possibly Richard Aubrey Cartwright, 1811–91, of Aynhoe; eldest s. of W. R. Cartwright, M.P. for Northamptonshire 1806–54.
[4] Sir George *Mellish, 1814–77, younger brother of W. L.; Q.C. 1861, judge and kt. 1870.
[5] Samuel George Booth White, 1812?–80, vicar of Boughton-under-Bean, Kent, 1854– 1869, chaplain to duke of Marlborough.
[6] James Buller, b. 1813, Devonshire gentleman.

30. Friday.

Holiday—Putting up books—packed one large box—read part of Prometheus Vinctus[1]—a little Petrarch—wrote over part of Vale—read paper—pack'd desk, Miscellany papers &c. wrote to A.M.G. Leaving books from Selwyn major[2] and Nicholl major.[3] Dressed & went to dine with Tutor.

December 1.

Leaving books from Jelf by hand [?] and J. Bruce. Saturday's business. Packing—with Ingalton, &c.&c. Finished writing over Vale—at Scotch breakfast—worked hard, & finished Prometheus Vinctus, putting down words to be explained. Handley with me. Spoke at Society[4]—received Vote of Thanks—spoke in return for some little time—proposed Moss—elected unanimously. At Robinson's 5th form supper at night, part of Evg. Mr Berthomier called.

Decr 2. Sunday.[5]

I sit down with a heavy heart, to write an account of my last Eton day, in all probability. Would that it had been a more tranquil one. May God make my feelings on leaving Eton—my feeling, that the happiest period of my life is now past,—produce the salutary effect of teaching me to aim at joys of a more permanent as well as a more exquisite nature—and to seek humbly, penitently, constantly, eagerly, after an eternal happiness which never fades or vanishes. But oh! if any thing mortal is sweet, my Eton years, excepting anxieties at home, have been so! God make me thankful for all I have enjoyed here.[6] I am perhaps very foolishly full of melancholy.

Received Sacrament—finished Paleys Christian Evidence—read Bible—called on Durnford to bid goodbye—& on O Reilly. Continued packing—which after all I shall have hard work to get through. Wrote to A.M.G.[7]—& to Canning.

Decr 3. Monday

—& 11 o clock Schools, my last at Eton. Finished packing, & settled bills &c. Took leave of Keate & my Tutor after 12—at Society room as an Honorary Member. Left my kind and excellent friends, my long known and long loved abode at three. Finished & gave up my Petrarch Verses on Laura. Reached London about 6—tea at Hatchett's[8]—went to Covent

[1] Aeschylus.

[2] T. K. Selwyn, now that G.A.* had left for Cambridge.

[3] H.I. and J. R. Nicholl (see 30 Sep. 26) each had a younger brother at Eton, and so were both known as Nicholl major.

[4] The society deplored the peerage bill of 1719, by 19 to none.

[5] This and following entry in facsimile in Masterman, at 16.

[6] Short deletion.

[7] Extract in Bassett, 1.

[8] John Hatchett's coaching inn at the New White Horse cellars, 67 Piccadilly.

Garden—saw Kemble as Falstaff, Young[1] as Hotspur—Madame Vestris[2] in Don Giovanni, wh I do not like. [5½ lines erased.] Slept at Hatchett's.

4.

Went to call on Uncle C. & Mr Larkins in morng—missed both—meals at Hatchetts—went to Parkinson,[3] who advised me not to do anything about my teeth—walked about to various places—bought books & read—read papers—called on & sat some time with Mr & Mrs Larkins.

5. *Wednesday.*

Breakfasted with Uncle Colin—anniversary of poor Eliza's death. He was in low spirits. Saw Mrs Larkins & bid her goodbye—left London by the Umpire—Travelled all night.

6. *Thursday.*

Weather not very good. Arrived at Liverpool, safe & well thank God, at 6. Went to Seaforth—there by 7. Found all doing pretty well—Dear Anne looking better.

7. *Friday.*

Unpacked & put things away. Sat talking &c. long. Mr Turner now seems likely to be my private Tutor.[4] Began Chronicles of Canongate[5]—Mr G. went to Scotland. I was comfortable enough at Hatchett's, & enjoyed the variety.

8. *Saturday.*

In Liverpool—shopping, & called on Uncle David. Rode in. Heard from Gaskell. Chess with H.J.G. Read Chron. of Canongate—finished Tale 1— which I like. Sitting with A.M.G. &c.

9. *Sunday.*

Walk alone—Church morning & Evening—reading Bible—began Paley's life[6]—read Platt's Facts, in answer to Quarterly Review.[7] not *quite* satisfied

[1] Charles Mayne *Young, 1777–1856, comedian.
[2] Lucia E. Bartolozzi, 1797–1856, wife of A. A. Vestris (d. 1825) and later of Charles James *Matthews, stage singer.
[3] Parkinson & Son, dentists, 36 Sackville Street, Piccadilly.
[4] John Matthias Turner, 1785?–1831; servitor at Christ Church; tutor to marquesses of Donegal and Londonderry; rector of Wilmslow, Cheshire, 1824–9, then bp. of Calcutta. See 24 Jan.–11 Apr. 28 for *Gladstone's spell as his private pupil.
[5] 2v. of tales by Sir Walter *Scott, who admitted in the preface his authorship of *Waverley* (1827).
[6] Short lives of *Paley were prefixed to the editions of his works by Alexander *Chalmers and by Robert *Lynam.
[7] T. P. *Platt, 'Facts . . . in reply to . . . the Quarterly review', a pamphlet defending the Bible Society. (See 2 Sep. 27.)

either way. Read a sermon of Eyton's[1] aloud in Evg—sitting with Mrs &
A.M.G. &c.

10. Monday

—rode into Liverpool—read papers—and Chronicles of Canongate—chess
with H.J.G. Draughts with Aunt J. &c.&c. Weather mild but windy.

11. Tuesday.

Ride—and walk—Finished Chron. of Canongate—last tale improbable but
interesting, me judice—resumed Don Quixote, wh I left off from not having
a 4th vol. wh. is now supplied. Wrote to Colburn[2] about Miscellany—to Mr
O'Reilly. read papers. Mr G's birthday.

12. Wednesday.

Mr G. returned from Scotland, most unexpectedly—reports I hope on the
whole favourable. Read Don Quixote—called on Mr Rawson—walk—wrote
a long letter to T.G.

13. Thursday.

Read Don Quixote—read paper—chess with H.J.G.—wrote to Doyle—
copied a letter—walk—& out leaping—unpacking part of my luggage,
arrived from Eton.

14. Friday.

Copied two letters—read papers—and Don Quixote—walk, swimming dogs
&c—C. Canning fifteen today. Helen's chicken pox much better—I am
vilely idle; & short of matter for my diary.

15. Saturday.

Read paper—& Don Quixote—walk—in Liverpool, riding—wrote to
Pickering—chess with H.J.G.—unpacking things from Eton—hope to begin doing a little work on Monday or Tuesday.

16. Sunday.

Stewart breakfasted with us—walk with him &c, after morning Ch. Ch.
morning & evening. letter from Ingalton—Mr G. read one of Buddicom's
Sermons in Evg—read Bible, Paley's Life, & a Sermon of St Johns—&
looked thro' a little book of a Miss Grays Memoirs.[3]

---

[1] Probably from John Eyton, *Sermons on various Subjects*, 2v. (1815).
[2] Henry *Colburn, d. 1855, publisher.
[3] [Samuel Hey, her uncle] *Some account of the Personal Religion of Margaret Gray,
1808–26.*

17. *Monday.*

Rode over to Ince, & saw Mr Blundell. Unpacked a large box of books—read paper—and Don Quixote—letter from my Dame. with Anne &c.

18. *Tuesday.*

Drew Anne in Chair—out with Helen—copied a Letter—chess with Helen—read Don Quixote; & Edinburgh Review on state of Parties.

19. *Wednesday.*

Out a long time watching &c. a very high tide—water very rough, & a magnificent sight. out with H.J.G.—read papers—and Don Quixote—Chess with H.J.G. Mrs G. ill—better in Evg. Made some additions to my book Catalogue.

20. *Thursday.*

Out to see the Tide—not so fine as yesterday's, from there being little wind. Finished Don Quixote—copied—got things put away, & established self in T.G's sitting room—Mrs G. better—heard from Doyle—read Edinburgh Review on Natural Theology &c., & part of Article on Burke & Laurence.

21. *Friday.*

Letter to H.J.G. from J.N.G.—rode mare—draughts with Aunt J. Wrote a long letter to Gaskell—wrote to Aunt E—& to Durnford on the subject of Oxford reading, at Mr G's desire—finished Edinburgh Review on Burke & Laurence, & read it on Taxation, Retrenchment, &c. absurd.

22. *Saturday.*

Rode into Liverpool—shopping &c—Wrote to OReilly. Chess with H.J.G. read in Liverpool about American War, while detained waiting for Jones. Read argument & began Œdipus Coloneus.[1] Read Edinburgh Review on Private Theatricals & on O Driscol's History of Ireland. Heard from **Farr**. Read paper.

23. *Sunday.*

Went with Mr G. into Liverpool to hear Mr. Jones on the reopening of St Andrew's.[2] A most excellent & appropriate sermon. He is a good servant of his Heavenly Master. Ch at Seaforth in afternoon. Day much cut up—read Bible, & Paley's Life.

24.

Dear Anne's birthday. Thank God for her passing it in better health than

---

[1] Sophocles.
[2] John *Gladstone built this church in Renshaw Street in 1815; it had just been enlarged.

the last. May it please Him to grant a further amendment. Above all, let us thank Him for the good gift which he has bestowed upon her of a true & fervent Christian spirit & heart. She dealt about presents, as usual. Began "Sure Methods of Improving Health & prolonging Life"[1]—read a good deal. Read paper—Walk &c—Sitting with A.M.G.

25. Tuesday.

Christmas day. Read Paley's Life—Church in morning, & Sacrament—Drew Anne in Chair, & walk. Chess with H.J.G. Draughts with Aunt J. read "Sure Methods".

26. Wednesday.

Read papers—Draughts with Aunt J. Read Sure Methods. Rode into town —shopped—& made calls—on Mesd[ames] M Cartney & Conway, at home —Mrs Wilson, Mr Jones, Mr Hugh G., & the Ewarts.

27. Thursday.

Walking—with H.J.G. &c. Read Sure Methods. Draughts with Aunt J. Wrote to Doyle, to congratulate him on his Father's being made Bart[2]—& also a letter to Ingalton.

28. Friday.

Read paper—walk with H.J.G., leaping, &c. Read Sure Methods. Draughts with Aunt J. Chess with H.J.G. Vaccinated. read old Liverpool election papers, received in a bundle from Mr G. & sorting some. Another lazy day—& so ends my 18th year.

29.

My birthday: & accompanying retrospect—a retrospect of time misapplied or lost, advantages neglected—I am sorry to say, that I cannot perceive any great improvement (too much I fear of the contrary) to have taken place in any respect as regards my disposition & conduct—my temporal or spiritual duties. Idleness in the one, & neglect of the other are but too prominent. May God give the time and the grace for a better life: and if it be his will that another year shall pass & leave me living, may I be able to look back on it with less of regret on many (on all as regards self) accounts, than the last. Amen, for Christ's sake.—Presents from Mrs., A.M. & H.J.G. Walk & Chess with H.J.G. Went on reading & endorsing the old papers: Finished Sure Methods, & read papers.

30. Sunday.

Ch morning & Evg—walk. T. Finlay dined with us. Frost. Read Bible—

[1] A treatise on diet by T. J. Graham (1827?).
[2] Baronetcy formally cr. 18 February 1828.

Paley's Life—St John—& Christian Guardian[1]— —tho not very much of any of them.

31. Monday.

T. Finlay went. Weather rainy or uncertain. Walking &c. long. Wrote to Selwyn, & to Colburn. Read papers—& went on with the bundle of old ones. Chess with H.J.G. Began Tales of a Grandfather.[2]

[1] A protestant monthly.
[2] *Scott's just-published tales from Scottish history.

January. 1.

May this year, or any part of it which God may give, be better spent than the last: as regards God, man, & myself. Copied over a letter of Mr G's to Mercury.[1] Took it into town—shopped—walk—Miss Benwell came—a kind letter from Durnford—Read Tales of Grandfather. Chess with H.J.G. —Draughts with Aunt J. read paper.

2. Wednesday.

Heard from Hallam—went on reading & sorting papers—very interesting. Wrote a note to P. Ewart—not sent—weather bad—some walk however— read papers—& Tales of Grandfather. Long conversation with A.M.G.— Chess with H.J.G. Draughts with Aunt J.

3. Thursday.

A. Fraser dined at Seaforth. Went on reading & sorting old papers. Read Tales of a Grandfather & papers—walked to the Alt & back[2]—rain & hail— draughts & backgammon in evg—letter from T.G.

4. Friday.

Read papers—Tales of a Grandfather—Christian Observer—Chess with H.J.G.—In Lpool—at meeting of Mar[ine]rs Ch Society[3]—subscribe from henceforward—Bishop,[4] Mr G., Mr Buddicom, Mr Scoresby,[5] &c. spoke— very much delighted—shopped, & walked out.

5. Saturday.

Walked &c—heard from Gaskell—finished reading & marking the papers, & arranged them. Read Tales of a Grandfather, & paper—Sat with A.M.G. —Copied 2 letters—not over well, as also yesterday evening.

6. Sunday.

In Liverpool with Mr G. to attend Mariner's Church. Congregation admirably & beautifully attentive & devout. Ch at home in afternoon. Walking.

[1] Untraced.

[2] Probably to the mouth of the river, 5 miles north of Seaforth.

[3] John *Gladstone was a vice-president of this local charity, intended to protect seamen from the usual moral perils of a port.

[4] Charles James *Blomfield, 1786–1857, bp. of Chester June 1824, of London August 1828.

[5] William Scoresby, F.R.S., chaplain of the Mariners' Church, priest at Exeter 1832.

Read Bible, & by reading a good deal finished Paley's Life, in wh. I had been slack. The Life certainly defic[ien]t in many things wh ought to attend an account of such a man.

7. Monday.

Read Tales of a Grandfather—read paper. Revd Mr Scoresby, & T. Moss, called. read Antijacobin &c.&c. Drove over to Mossley Hill. (N.B. lost my way, & went thro Wavertree[1]) Dined there—met Mrs & P. Ewart, also two Miss Leghs.[2] Slept there—Read verses of Wm Ewart's at Caen—very good at least to me.

8. Tuesday.

Called on the Mosses, Sandbaches, & Parkers. Breakfasted at Mossley Hill —came home—dressed & went off with Mr G. to Ince—dined there, with Mr Blundell. Met Mr Silvertop:[3] a most agreeable & polished man, very well informed.

9. Wednesday.

Letter from Dean.[4] I am I believe to matriculate next term. Heard from Doyle. Read papers. Read Tales of Grandfather. Chess with H.J.G. Walking &c—at Mr Rawsons—wrote a long letter to R.G.

10. Thursday.

Left home at 2. Called on Stewart Gladstone, & Mr Staniforth—shopped— Drove out with Moss in gig to Otterspool—dined there & remained for the night. Met Headlam. most hospitably received. Billiards—read Tales—& "Dissent justified".[5] Out with H.J.G.

11.

Breakfast at Otterspool. Much snow. Waited some time. went, in snow, with T. Moss to town. Called on Mrs Trajll, & Mr Jones: with whom I sat long. Drove out to dinner. Mr & Mrs Rawson dined with us—read papers & Tales of a Grandfather.

12. Saturday.

Finished Tales of a Grandfather wh I like very much. Walking &c. read papers—draughts with Aunt J.—Began an Article in Quarterly, reply to Butler's reply to them on Soeur Nativité.[6] Wrote a note to Colburn.

---

[1] Suburb 2½ miles east of Liverpool's centre.
[2] Several Cheshire families called Legh had unm. das.
[3] George Silvertop, 1774–1849, Tyneside proprietor.
[4] Samuel Smith, 1766?–1841, dean of Christ Church 1824–31.
[5] Perhaps S. Lowell, *Reasons for Dissent* (1825).
[6] xxxvi. 305 (October 1827), violently anti-romanist; on *Bibliothèque Chrétienne*.

13. Sunday.

Ch morning & afternoon. Walking.—Began to read, & make notes & marginal references, in my new interleaved Bible. May God guide & enlighten me in studying it. Read some Mant—& three of St John's Sermons.

14. Monday.

Day fine. Walking, & running, wh I now often do for exercise. Finished Quarterly on Bibliotheque Cretienne, & began it on Agriculture & Rent.[1] Read papers. I now intend to read & make a few references, as they occur, in my interleave Bible every night. Chess with H.J.G. Read some Œdipus Coloneus.

15.

In Liverpool. Paying Bills &c. Breakfasted (leaving home early) with Uncle Murray—called on Mr & Mrs Bolton, the Ewarts, Mrs Smith, Miss Benwell, Mrs Conway, Mrs Wilson, Mrs Staniforth, Mrs Traill, Mrs M'Cartney. Came out in gig. Mrs G. unwell. Copied a letter—read paper—finished Article on Agriculture & Rent.

16. Wednesday.

Went over more bundles of papers, for most part cursorily. Read part of Quarterly's Article on Hallam's History[2]—& some Œdipus Coloneus. Read papers. Draughts with Aunt J. Snow—got out however & had a run for a little.

17. Thursday.

Walk. read paper—letter from T.G. to H.J.G. By Mrs G's desire, I am not to go till Monday. Draughts with Aunt J. Finished Quarterly on Hallam—read article on Literary Souvenirs, & began one on United States. Read some Œd. Col. On Hallam they are very severe—I agree in many things.

18.

Dear John's birthday. May God bless & preserve him, & soon bring him home in safety. Chess with H.J.G. Backgammon with Mr G. Called on Mr Rawson. Walk. drew Anne in Chair. Finished Quarterly on United States. Read papers, & Œd Coloneus.

19. Saturday.

Read Quarterly on New South Wales. read papers—& some Œd. Col. Went to the Alt to see the high tide, which was there extremely fine. Remained some time. Wrapped up & packed nearly all my books, & some of my clothes. Very much tired.

[1] Ibid. 391.
[2] xxxvii. 194 (January 1828), acrimonious.

14—I

20. Sunday.

Ch morning & afternoon. Walk a little, & with Anne who was out in Chair. Cousin Rob. G. & the Ewarts down here, so time unavoidably occupied. Read Bible, & British Review on Dissent;[1] very long conversation with A.M.G. on many interesting subjects. The more one sees, the more one *must* admire.

21. Monday.

Finished packing books & clothes, & put things away. Wrote to T.G. read two days papers—early dinner—bid goodbye to all—left home at 4, & Liverpool at 5, by Aurora; a very good coach. travelled all night. Matthie[2] & Morrall,[3] Oxonians, my companions.[4]

22.

At Birmingham early—left it before 6, per Oxonian. Got to Oxford soon after 2. Dressed &c. taking up my quarters at Angel. Dinner, tea, & bed there. Called on Mr Biscoe[5] twice & saw him. He seems a very pleasant man. Walked about. Read papers, University Calendar &c—& a good deal of Œd. Col. at night up in my room.

23. Wednesday.

Breakfast with Mr Biscoe—introduced to his brother.[6] Walk with Morrall & Hone[7]—also alone—made a writing day of it, & wrote letters, pretty long, to my Mother, to Hallam, Gaskell, Farr, Doyle, Handley. Went to the Dean with Mr Biscoe—then to the Vice Chancellor, & matriculated, taking the oaths, & subscribing to the Articles & Statutes.[8] Lunch at Angel— dined in Brazennose Hall, taken in by Lawrence[9]—wine with Morrall afterwards—tea with him—put up my things & left Oxford at 12—travelled thro' the night. Read papers.

24.

At Birmingham between 8 & 9. Left it by Traveller, about 9. Posted from

[1] *British Review, and London Critical Journal*, xxiii. 200 (1825), reviewing J. A. *James *Christian Fellowship* and S. Lowell *Reasons for Dissent*.
[2] Hugh Matthie, 1805?–42, of Greenock, rector of Worthenbury, Flintshire, from 1831.
[3] Cyrus Morrall, 1804?–82, s. of Liverpool merchant; priest there 1833–56; vicar of North Leigh, Oxfordshire, 1856–61.
[4] This entry and next in pencil.
[5] Robert Biscoe, 1802?–70, student of Christ Church; rector of Whitbourne, Herefordshire, from 1833.
[6] Frederick Biscoe, 1808?–80, also a student; vicar of Turkdean, Gloucestershire, from 1837.
[7] Richard Brindley Hone, 1805?–81, Brasenose; rector of Halesowen, Worcestershire, from 1836.
[8] Certificate by Richard *Jenkyns, 1782–1854, Master of Balliol from 1819, in Add MS 44719, f. 2.
[9] Charles Washington Lawrence, 1805?–61, s. of Charles; priest in Liverpool.

Congleton[1] to Wilmslow,[2] & arrived there, thank God safe & well, about seven in Evg. Found Wood[3] there. Mr & Mrs Turner very kind. A Miss Sumner, sister to the Bp & John Bird Sumner, on a visit to them.[4]

25.

My first Wilmslow day. Breakfast at 9—lunch at 1—dinner at 5—tea at 8 —supper at 10! Plenty of food, at any rate. Unpacked my clothes & books —read paper—long walk with Wood. Powys[5] not returned yet. Preliminary discourse with Mr Turner, & reading settled. Wrote to Mr G. Letters from home, & an excellent one from dear John. Read Greek Testament with Bible at night, & endeavouring to work at it with my interleaved copy. Made up accounts & wrote up Journal.

26. Saturday.

Read Testament—Homer, beginning Il[iad] 1—Cicero—beginning de Officiis—& Euclid's Definitions c. & 15 propositions & did them with Mr Turner. Not full time with him, so obliged to leave 10 propositions undone. Began Prior's Burke, putting down some chief facts. Read paper—made an inventory &c. Long walk.

27. Sunday.

Walk alone, & again with Wood. Ch morning & afternoon. Mr Turner preached. We have family prayers & reading every morning (save Sunday) & every Evening.—Read Bible. Began Gisborne's Survey of Christian religion[6]—& read six short but good printed discourses of Mr T[urner]'s on Infidelity, wh he was so good as to give me.[7]

28. Monday.

Learned Homer, & Cicero. Did nothing but Testament with Mr Turner: went to Macclesfield[8] in his carriage with him & Miss Sumner. Introduced with Wood to the Cruttendens[9] of Macclesfield. Went to see the powerloom & improved French loom factories.[10] Returned to a late dinner. Read paper —sat with Wood—learned Greek Testament.

[1] About 20 miles south of Manchester.
[2] Midway between Congleton and Manchester.
[3] (Sir) Charles Alexander Wood, 1810–90, emigration commissioner; see Add MS 44350.
[4] Marianne (Mrs. J. B.) *Sumner and Mrs. Turner were both das. of Capt. George Robertson, R.N., of Edinburgh.
[5] Atherton Legh Powys, 1809–86, 4th son of 2nd lord Lilford; rector of Titchmarsh, Northamptonshire, 1842–61.
[6] T. *Gisborne, *Familiar Survey of the Christian Religion* (1799), for young people.
[7] Shortly published, as *Six discourses on the evils of unbelief.*
[8] Silk manufacturing town, 6 miles SE. of Wilmslow.
[9] William Cruttenden Cruttenden, 1776–1863, parish priest of Macclesfield 1811–47, local notable.
[10] He said many years later that on this occasion he first contemplated free trade. (Cp. 29 Oct. 90 and Robbins, 79–80.)

29. Tuesday.

Walk with Wood. Mr Stanley,[1] Mr D'Arcy,[2] & Mr Reid, dined here. Wrote to A.M.G., Mr G. & T.G., H.H. Joy I am happy to say has returned to right. Sat with Wood. Did Testament & Euclid with Mr Turner—learned to end of Iliad 1 but did not do.

30. Wednesday.

Learned Euclid—but, after much waiting, the rector being ill, did nothing but Greek Testament with him. Wrote to Pickering. Began to make diagrams &c. read a paper—read Prior. Long walk to Alderley Edge[3] &c.&c. Powys returned. Mr M'Caw,[4] an Independent preacher, clever & agreeable, dined here.

31. Thursday.

Did Homer, Euclid, Greek Testament, & Cicero—learned Greek Testament —Long walk—met young Arthur Stanley.[5] Wrote to Mrs G. Heard from Gaskell. Went with Powys & Wood to Alderley Park,[6] to dine with Sir J. & Lady Maria Stanley.[7] Met also 3 Miss Stanleys[8]—Rector & Mrs Stanley[9] —young Mrs Stanley[10]—Miss Leigh[11] &c.—cards.

February 1.

Learned Homer, Cicero, & Euclid. Did Homer Euclid & Greek Testament. Read 2 days' papers. Walk with Wood. Read Prior & learned, in part, my Milton for tomorrow—also Greek Testament.

2.

Walk with Wood. Alderley Edge &c. Read papers. Learned Cicero, Milton, Euclid, solved an easy problem, did a Translation. did Euclid, Cicero, & Greek Testament, & said Euclid. Read part of Troilus & Cressida. Bad cold.

3. Sunday.

Bad cold. Ch only in morning—received Sacrament—not many above 20 at it. Did not go out afterwards—read Gisborne, Bible, & Greek Testament. Heard from Mrs G.—& had a letter about Miscellany.

[1] Edward *Stanley, 1779–1849, bp. of Norwich from 1837.
[2] John Darcey, b. ca. 1769, priest at Marton, Cheshire, 10 miles south of Wilmslow, 1806–44.
[3] Wooded hills to the south of Wilmslow.
[4] Possibly Duncan McCaig, priest at the Gaelic Chapel in Edinburgh.
[5] Arthur Penrhyn *Stanley, 1815–81, dean of Westminster 1864. See Add MS 44318.
[6] Four miles south of Wilmslow.
[7] Sir John Thomas *Stanley, 1766–1850, 6th bart., cr. baron Stanley of Alderley 1839, and his wife Maria Josepha Holroyd, 1771–1863.
[8] Rianette, 1797–1882, and Louisa, 1799–1877, unm. das. of the house, and one of their five younger sisters. (See Nancy Mitford, Ladies of Alderley [1938], xxxi.)
[9] Née Catherine Leycester; 1792–1862.
[10] Ellin Williams, wife of Edward's twin William, 1802–84.
[11] Miss Leigh of Twemlow, a neighbour.

4. Monday.

Cold better, I having taken treaclewhey last night. learned Euclid & Homer—did Euclid & Greek Testament with the rector. Read papers. Worked in vain, in Evg, at a problem he has given me—got a lesson in [wood] turning from Powys—who took the trouble to give it, kindly.

5. Tuesday.

Cold better, after another bason of whey. Heard from Farr—wrote to A.M.G.—learned Euclid & more Homer & did them with the rector—read part of Troilus & Cressida—parts of the religious periodicals for the month —another lesson in turning from Powys. Invited to dine with Rev. E. Stanley, but did not, on account of cold.

6. Wednesday.

Read paper—heard from Handley—learned some Homer, Euclid, & a little Cicero for rector. Did Greek Testament & a little Cicero. Another lesson from Powys—in his shop in afternoon. Finished Troilus & Cressida—read Pericles—this is a play wh one can neither wholly attribute nor absolutely deny to Sh[akespeare], I think.

7. Thursday.

Learned Homer & Euclid. Did Greek Testament, Homer, & Euclid, with Mr T. Read papers. Frisking on a rope with Wood, & turning in Powys's shop—Managed a lignum vitae box, thro' his former teaching.[1] Read Prior. Powys sat with me. Learned Greek Testament.

8. Friday.

Learned Homer & Euclid. Did Greek Testament with rector—turned somewhat—read paper—at the rope &c. Read Prior's Burke—& part of King John—did part of a Translation into blank verse from Euripides—& read over Turnus's speech once or twice.[2]

9. Saturday.

Out—at the rope & sawing wood &c.&c. for turning. Read some papers, with Mr Huskisson's Liverpool speech, (very able indeed) &c.&c.[3] Learned Homer & Euclid & finished my translation—read King John—did Testament, & Euclid, & said Tur*nus* to Tur*ner*. Went out with Wood & Powys to Henbury, 8 miles off,[4] to dine with the Jodrells; found Mr & Mrs J., Miss J, a sister of Mrs J., the son, my old schoolfellow,[5] & Lady Louisa Grey, Ld

---

[1] Noted in Bassett, 1.   [2] Virgil, *Aeneid*, ix. 128–58 or xi. 378–444.
[3] 5 February 1828, on re-election, explaining why he took office under *Wellington (*Times*, 7 February, 3).
[4] To the southward; it lies 2 miles west of Macclesfield.
[5] Francis Jodrell, ca. 1776–1829, m. 1807 Maria, da. of Sir William Lemon, bart.; their s. John William Jodrell, 1808–58, at Eton and in grenadier guards. His aunt, also Maria, later m. John Stratton.

Stamford's sister.[1] Very kindly received. Found out, as I hope, the bisection of a triangle.

10. Sunday.

Tired last night, so not up early. Church morning & afternoon—out a little, with Wood. Looked over the Oxford Statutes de Moribus Conformandis[2] &c; read Bible, and Gisborne. With Powys.

11. Monday.

Learned Homer & Euclid. Did Greek Testament with Rector, also Euclid. Letters from Mr G. & A.M.G. also from J. & R.G. to read. Wrote to H.J.G. Turning & out a little. Endeavoured to find out the 2nd Demonstration of the bisection of triangle. Read Greek Testament.

12. Tuesday.

Learned Homer & Euclid—did Greek Testament & Euclid in morning— Homer in Evg, getting up the arrears. Out & also turning. Snow &c. Read papers. Finish'd King John—Learned Greek Testament.

13.

Learned Cicero & Euclid—did Greek Testament, Euclid, & a little Cicero. Read paper. Heard from Pickering—out—turning—and on the rope— Learned Greek Testament—Read in "Holland Tide"[3] "the Aylmers of Bally Aylmer" & "The Hand & Word".

14. Thursday.

Gale of wind & drifting snow tremendous. With Powys & Wood out heaping up & condensing a great mass of snow, clearing walks &c.&c.—Learned Homer—did Greek Testament & a sort of retrospect in Euclid with Mr T. Finished Holland Tide, nothing particular, me judice, save Hand & Word, perhaps. Read paper—a very interesting debate in Lords.[4]

15. Friday.

—Out—turning—& at the rope—read papers—wrote to Mr G.—Wood sat with me—began a letter to P. Handley—learned Homer—& at night Greek Testament—did Greek Testament with Rector. Read Prior.

16. Saturday.

Learned Homer—& a long Ode of Horace to repeat. Did Greek Testament,

[1] Louisa, d. 1830, sister to George Harry Grey, 1765–1845, 6th earl of Stamford and lord lieutenant of Cheshire from 1819.
[2] Notes on behaviour presented to undergraduates on matriculation.
[3] Irish short stories by Gerald *Griffin; his first popular success (1827).
[4] NSH xviii. 260–305, 11 February; ministerial explanations about Navarino and the fall of *Goderich's government.

Euclid, & said Horace with Rector. Finished writing to Handley. Heard from Doyle. read paper—turning, & at the rope—&c. Read Prior, & Broad Grins.[1]

17. Sunday.

Ch, morning & afternoon. Wrote to Doyle, on his Mother's death,[2] &c. Walk with Wood, & alone. Wasted some time, as usual. Read Bible (making notes) & Greek Testament; also Gisborne, & Robert Hall's splendid & excellent sermon on Infidelity.[3]

18. Monday.

Did a translation from Demosthenes. Learned Homer—read Euclid. Did Greek Testament & Euclid with Mr T. Miss Sumner went. Read papers. Walked—& in the turning shop. Went with Wood & Powys to dine at Alderley Rectory. Met Mr & Mrs S., two Misses S. from the Park, & two Miss Tattons.[4]

19. Tuesday.

Learned Homer & Euclid—twice with rector—did Greek Testament & Euclid, & got up arrears in Homer. read papers. Heard from Mr G. Labelling letters &c. Out—turning—& at the rope, with Powys & Wood. Finished Broad Grins. Read Greek Testament.

20. Wednesday.

Learned Cicero & Euclid—did Gk Testament & Euclid with Mr T. Out leaping &c. with Powys. Turning—& at the rope. Read papers. Heard from Colburn—who will have nothing to say to us.[5] Read Prior. Greek Testament—& Bible as usual, but made some notes.

21. Thursday.

Learned Euclid & Homer—did Greek Testament & Euclid with the rector —Walk with him on his visits to the poor. Saw one miserable case.—Read Greek Testament, & Prior's Burke. Wrote to Mr G. Debates now very interesting—today's particularly so.[6] worked away at it, nearly through.

22. Friday.

Box arrived from home. Letters from A.M.G. & H.J.G., long & very kind.— Learned Euclid & Homer—did Greek Testament, Euclid, & Cicero—

---

[1] Comic poems by George *Colman the younger (1815).
[2] Diana Elizabeth, née Milner, d. 31 January 1828.
[3] *Modern Infidelity Considered* (1800); see *DNB* xxiv. 86.
[4] Two of the seven daughters of T. W. Egerton Tatton of Wythenshawe, Cheshire. Morley, i. 46, dates this on 5 February.
[5] That is, refuses to republish *Eton Miscellany*.
[6] 'Ministerial explanations' in the commons, 18 February, on fall of *Goderich's government: *NSH* xviii. 449–562.

Finished the last debate, & read part of the day's paper &c. Hit on the 2nd way of bisecting the triangle—read Greek Testament—out with Wood & Powys jumping &c. over Alderley Edge.

23. Saturday.

Out from half past 11 to near 5 with Powys & Wood, on horseback—rode to Macclesfield—shopped—rode to Henbury—called—thence to Alderley Park—call'd—thence home. Learned parts of Vanity of Human Wishes,[1] & Homer—did Greek Testament, & repeated the lines, to rector. Read Prior, read paper. Wrote hurriedly to A.M.G.

24. Sunday.

Ch morning & afternoon.—out a little besides going. Had a long & kind letter from Selwyn. Mr T. preached well on the Lord's Supper in the afternoon. Read Bible, not doing so much to it as I had hoped; read Gisborne; Robert Hall on the Peace, & part of Sermon on the Fast.[2]

25. Monday.

Read papers for two days. Learned Homer, & did part of a translation from Plato. Finished Prior's Life of Burke. Did Greek Testament, & Homer with rector: looked over Book 6 of Euclid, & [was] examined in it. Walk with Wood, rope, & turning. Reading Eton old copies—melancholy. Read Greek Testament.

26. Tuesday.

Rope, & turning a good deal—did some translation from Plato & learnt Cicero. Did Greek Testament & some preliminaries to Algebra with Rector. Heard from Mr G. Powys & Wood dined out. Read Greek Testament &c. Read London Magazine on Appx to Black Book—Pere la chaise[3]—& Eliza Evanshaw, wh seems to me a most dangerous book.[4]

27. Wednesday.

Rope—& a chase to Alderley Edge, with Wood, Powys, & a younger brother of his,[5] come over from Mr Horden's.[6] Heard from R. G. Read paper. Read Mr Stanley in London Magazine on French Charity Schools.[7] Wood sat with me. Learned Homer, definitions to B.II, & some Algebra. Did Greek Testament & Algebra with Rector. Read Greek Testament & Homer again.

---

[1] *Johnson, imitating Juvenal.
[2] 'Reflections on War', preached in thanksgiving for the peace of Amiens; 'Sentiments proper to the present crisis', preached on 19 October 1803, day appointed for a fast.
[3] vi. 450, 464 (December 1826).
[4] x. 84 (January 1828), reviewing an anonymous novel (1827).
[5] Either Henry Littleton Powys (-Keck), 1812–63, or Charles Powys, 1813–97; both regular officers.
[6] Joseph Hordern, 1784?–1876, vicar of Rostherne, 6 miles west of Wilmslow, 1821–55.
[7] x. 14 (January 1828), signed 'A.Y.'

28. Thursday.

Powys's Brother went. Rope, turning shop, & walking, with Wood & Mr Turner. Learned Homer & did some sums in fractions—Did Greek Testament & some little in Mathematics with him—Read papers—Mr Stanley's article in Retrospective on British Insects[1] & began Parry's Account.[2]

29. Friday.

Learned Homer—did some sums—did Greek Testament & Fractions with the Rector. Read Capt. Parry; Channing on Buonaparte; frothy;[3] & the long debate on Tuesday on Corporation & Tests Acts—closed by a division of 193 for to 237 against them.[4] Rope, turning, & out. Read Greek Testament.

March 1. Saturday.

Out with Powys & turning. Read papers. Read Mr T's pamphlet on Phrenology, wh I like.[5] learned Algebra & Homer—did Greek Testament & Algebra with rector. My classics are in a poor way. Heard from A.M.G. & from Doyle—Wrote to Doyle. Made up accounts &c &c.

2. Sunday

Church morning & afternoon. Received the Sacrament—few communicants. Wilmslow Church in the forenoon service is dismal. May God make it otherwise. Read Bible; Gisborne; "Plain & Short instructions on the Sacrament";[6] & finished Robert Hall's Sermon on the Fastday. Wrote to A.M.G. Walk with Wood, after lunch, & between Ch & dinner.

3. Monday.

Learned Cicero, Algebra, Homer: did Greek Testament & Algebra with rector. Read papers—& good part of Capt. Parry's narrative. Turning, rope &c. My room has long been in a very bad state with soot, & much incommoded my reading. I hope my Father & the rest are now on the way [to Scotland].

4. Tuesday.

Learned Algebra (a good deal) Homer—did a good part of a translation—Finished Capt. Parry—read paper—began a long letter to my brothers & wrote a good deal—read Greek Testament—Greek Testament & Algebra with rector—Rain—rope & turning.

[1] Untraced.
[2] One of several accounts of the Arctic expedition in 1827 of H.M.S. *Hecla*, Capt. William Edward *Parry, R.N., a relative of the Stanleys.
[3] Review of *Scott's *Life of Napoleon* in *Christian Examiner* (Boston) iv. 382, by William Ellery Channing, the New England unitarian pacifist.
[4] *NSH* xviii. 676–784.   [5] Untraced.
[6] Anonymous, undated pamphlet.

5. Wednesday.

Out—turning a little—& rope—Mr Garratt[1] dined here—a very pleasant man—prepared Homer & Algebra—finished my translation—finished writing to Robn & wrote to Tom. Heard from Gaskell & Handley. Read papers. Read Greek Testament. Testament & Algebra with Mr T.

6. Thursday.

Walk, rope, digging. Learned Homer, & Eclogue 1. of Virgil. did Testament & Algebra, & said Virgil to Rector. Read papers. Read Homer & Greek Testament. Heard from Hallam—Wrote to Mrs G. to meet her, please God, at Edinburgh—also a long letter to Selwyn.

7. Friday.

Rain. Mr Turner ill. Nothing done with him. Rope, turning, &c. Read papers. Preparations for setting up poles &c, Powys being workman. Read a Letter of Mr T's on Catholic Question;[2]—a good deal of Homer—wrote out some Algebra sums in my book—began a translation.

8. Saturday.

Out, turning—preparing for poles &c. read paper. Read London Magazine on Loss of Kent.[3] Heard from Mr G. & H.J.G. on their way—date, Langholm.[4]—Read Cicero—wrote a long letter to Gaskell. Did Testament & Algebra with Rector—finished my translation.

9. Sunday.

Heard from Doyle. Walk with Powys & Wood between Church [services], alone after afternoon Ch. Ch morning & afternoon. Mr T. preached very well in afternoon—Congregation better than I have yet seen it. Read & worked at Bible—read Greek Testament—Gisborne—Hall on Mr Robinson's Character, & on the advantages of Knowledge.[5]

10. Monday.

Walk with Wood—rope & poles. Read papers up. Wrote to Handley. Read Cicero & Homer—& did a good many examples in Algebra. Did Greek Testament & Algebra with the rector. Miss H. Greig din'd here.[6]

---

[1] Thomas Garratt, 1796–1841, Turner's curate at Wilmslow for part of 1828–9.
[2] Untraced; Turner's views in favour of emancipation are clear from Garratt's *Appeal to Protestants* [1829], a controversial pamphlet.
[3] v. 335 (July 1825); on an east Indiaman burnt in the Bay of Biscay, 1/2 March 1825.
[4] Twenty miles north of Carlisle on the Edinburgh road.
[5] Robert *Hall on 'The character of the late Rev. Thomas *Robinson', Leicester Auxiliary Bible Society (1813), and on 'The Advantages of Knowledge to the Lower Classes' (1810).
[6] A *Greig of Quarry Bank, 1½ miles NW. of Wilmslow.

11. Tuesday.

Did sums in Algebra, & read a good deal of Homer. Did Greek Testament & Algebra with Mr T. Wrote to Farr. Read Oxford Prize Poems—Palestine is most beautiful indeed.[1] Out—walk alone & with Wood—turning a little —bowls. Weather beautiful.

12. Wednesday.

Restor'd to my room, from sitting in wh I have for some time been prevented by the chimney discharging soot, wh has hindered me somewhat. Rode to Alderley Rectory. Staid some time with Mr & Mrs Stanley. Learned Homer & Algebra. Read Greek Testament. Did with Mr T. Cicero, Greek Testament & Algebra. Read paper.

13. Thursday.

Learned Homer, & did Questions in Algebra as usual. Began learning the 10 Satire of Juvenal. Said Juvenal, & did Greek Testament & Algebra with Mr T. Walked—with Wood to call on the Greigs at Quarry Bank. They appear most kind & worthy people. Rope a little. Read papers—Oxford Prize Poems—& (+) Talisman.[2] Read Greek Testament &c.

14. Friday.

Out, & turning. Read paper—wrote to Mr G. on the subject of Mr Turner's intended departure from Wilmslow. Read The Talisman—& Homer—did Algebra sums. Did Greek Testament & Algebra with Rector.

15. Saturday.

Did translation from Plato—read Cicero—Algebra sums. Testament & Algebra with Rector. Read paper. Long walk with Wood to Alderley Edge &c. &c. met Revd E. Hanley.[3] Read the Talisman—wh is really fine.

17 [sc. 16]. Sunday.

Church morning & afternoon. Heard from A.M.G. & H.J.G. Walk with Powys between services, Wood & Powys after Evg. Service. Mr Turner preached well & boldly in afternoon on the state of religion in the parish. Read Bible: making some notes & references; Gisborne; & Robert Halls Sermon on the Work of Holy Spirit,[4] Address to a Christian Minister's Comforts & Discouragements,[5] & Speech at Bible Society Meeting.[6]

---

[1] *Oxford Prize Poems*, 7 ed. (1826), included 'Palestine' (1803) by Reginald *Heber, later bp. of Calcutta; on which see *DNB* xxv. 356.
[2] *Scott.
[3] Edward Hamley, 1764?–1835, rector of Cusop, Herefordshire.
[4] Baptist circular letter (1809).
[5] 'On the Discouragements and Supports of the Christian Minister' (1812).
[6] To Leicester Auxiliary Bible Society (1812, 1817).

18 [sc. 17]. Monday.

Sums in Algebra. Cicero—learning some Juvenal. Greek Testament & Algebra with Mr T. Turned—walked to Quarry Bank with Wood & Powys, & dined there. Read paper—wrote to Mrs G. Finished Talisman, wh I like better than ever.

19 [sc. 18]. Tuesday.

Homer—sums in Algebra—Greek Testament & Algebra with the Rector. Read paper—read Greek Testament—walk with Powys—& alone—turning —wrote to Doyle—& to Pickering. Sundry domestic jobs.

20 [sc. 19]. Wednesday.

Turned a little. 8 miles walk with Wood. Read papers. Homer & Algebra— did Greek Testament & Algebra & said Juvenal to Rector. Read part of an Article in Quarterly—Palestine again—& began writing some of a projected piece.

21 [sc. 20]. Thursday.

Turning—rope—walking. Read Homer & Algebra. Did Greek Testament & Algebra with Mr T, & Homer at night. Read paper. Finished Quarterly on Hebers Journals, & began it on Reformation in Italy. Read Greek Testament.

22. [sc. 21]. Friday.

Heard from Mr & Mrs G, wrote to Mr G. Bad news I fear concerning the Edinburgh hopes: may God grant it may not prove so. Learning Homer & Algebra—did Greek Testament & Algebra with Mr Turner. Read paper— interesting—on Corporation & Test Acts.[1] Walk with Wood. Turning. Finished Quarterly on Reformation in Italy, & Oxford Prize Poems. Read Greek Testament.

22. Saturday.

Read Cicero, a little Homer—did part of a translation—working at Algebra Problems in vain. Greek Testament & Algebra with Rector. Read papers. Walk with Powys & Wood. Began Mill's Crusades.[2] Wrote to Hallam. Mr Neill, intended new Curate, arrived.[3]

23. Sunday.

Church morning & afternoon. Mr Neill read prayers in morning, & preached in afternoon: seems a good & agreeable man, with good abilities, at least.

[1] Commons debate on their repeal, 18 March, in NSH xviii. 1180–1208.
[2] Charles *Mills, History of the Crusades, 2v. (1820).
[3] Possibly Frederick Neale, 1806?–72, vicar of Wotton near Bedford from 1852.

Weather bad, so walk but short, with Wood. Read Bible & Greek Testament: & half a vol. of Warton's (Wood's) Deathbed Scenes,[1] wh occupied most of my time.

24.

Mr Neill returned to Liverpool. His preaching seems much liked among the people. Read paper—10 Satire Juvenal (in part)—finished Translation—at Algebra—Testament & Algebra with Mr T.—Read Greek Testament—Warton—& Mill's History of Crusades. Out—rope—&c. Learning some Juvenal.

25. Tuesday.

Homer—Algebra—learned Juvenal. Greek Testament, Algebra, & saying Juvenal with Mr T. Read Greek Testament. Read paper—Mill's history—out. turning [wood] a little, & leaping, with Powys & Wood. Mrs & Miss Robertson, Mrs T's sister in law & niece, came for a visit.[2]

26. Wednesday.

Homer & Algebra—Greek Testament & Algebra with Rector. read paper—walk with Wood. Read Greek Testament—Warton, & Mill. Wrote a few lines too. It appears now that we must leave Wilmslow in less than three weeks.[3]

27. Thursday.

Homer & Algebra—Greek Testament & Algebra with Rector. Read paper—Deathbed Scenes—Mill's Crusades—Greek Testament. Wrote to A.M.G. Out—turning—rope. Weather cold & rainy.

28. Friday.

Homer & Algebra. Greek Testament & Algebra with Rector. Read paper—Dr Warton—Mill's Crusades—Greek Testament. Turning—and out walking alone.

29. Saturday.

Juvenal Finished Sat[ire] 10—Algebra, a good deal—part of a translation—Greek Testament & Algebra with Mr T. Walk with Wood, &c. Read Mill, Johnson & Goldsmith's Poetry. Read papers—tried to write some lines.

30. Sunday.

Church morning & afternoon. A little walk with Wood—& again with Powys. No home accounts now for nine days. Read Bible, putting down

[1] John Warton, *Death-Bed Scenes and Pastoral Conversations*, 4v. (1826), in Wood's copy.
[2] Wife and da. of one of Mrs. Turner's elder brothers.   [3] Mrs. Turner was ill.

references &c. & more than half Vol. 1. of Deathbed Scenes, wh together occupied me pretty fully.

31. Monday.

A poor close to the month—Translation—Algebra—a little learning Juvenal. Greek Testament & Algebra with Rector. Read Greek Testament. Read up papers. Walk to Alderley Edge &c. with Powys & Wood—a kind letter from Mr Moss. Potter'd in the Evg. and [visited] Powys's room. Walk after dinner.

1. April. Tuesday.

Homer—learning Juvenal & Algebra—Greek Testament, Algebra, & said Juvenal with Rector. Walk with Wood. Wrote to Mr Moss. Read a good deal of Mill, having lost yesterday. Heard from Mr, Mrs & A.M.G., Handley, & Farr. Began a letter to Mrs G. Read Greek Testament.

2 April. Wednesday.

Homer—Algebra—finished letter to Mrs G. read papers—Greek Testament & Algebra with Rector. Read Mill. Out, walking & running. Mr Stanley din'd with us. I should much like to see more of him. Drew up a statement of the Eton expenses for him.[1] Read Greek Testament.

3. Thursday.

Homer—Algebra—Greek Testament, Algebra & read over Translation with Rector. Read paper—debate on Corn Laws[2]—Read Mill. Mr Hayes[3] had tea with us. A long walk, 11 or 12 miles perhaps, alone.

4. Good Friday.

—scantily observed in this country, it appears & by myself too. Ch in morning—Read Bible. Testaments—Warton. Walk with Powys & Wood. Read paper—& a little Mill. Finished Homer's Iliad.

5. Saturday.

Rain. Finished Mill, & my notes for Richard [Coeur de Lion] from him. Did part of a translation—learned a little Juvenal—read paper—Greek Testament & Algebra with Mr T.—Wrote a note to Mr Stanley—a kind answer. Read Cicero—Goldsmith on Richard[4] &c. Mr Robertson from India[5] & Miss R. came. Much waiting & wasting time.

[1] See Morley, i. 47.
[2] In the lords, 31 March; NSH xviii. 1364–76.
[3] Perhaps Thomas Hayes, d. 1887, then vicar of Bracewell, Yorkshire; Master of Colne grammar school 1842–79.
[4] In Oliver *Goldsmith, History of England (1771).
[5] Thomas Campbell *Robertson, 1789–1863, Indian civil servant, Mrs. Turner's youngest brother; unm. till 1830.

Easter Sunday. 6.

Church morning & afternoon. Sacrament in the morning. Upwards of 40 Communicants; wh is an improvement. Walk with Powys & Wood—& with Wood. Heard from Mr & Miss G. & from Doyle. Wrote to Mr G. Read Bible —Gisborne—finished Warton. Read Greek Testament.

7. Monday.

Began to pack my books, a troublesome & timekilling business. Bid good bye to Powys. Read Gisborne—Cicero—Greek Testament. Read paper. Out with Wood—called on the Greigs. Did some translation. Wrote some Richard—not much. Greek Testament & Logarithms with Rector.

8. Tuesday.

Packing. Money letter from Mr Grant—wrote to him—& to H.J.G. Sent to take my place for Friday—went to bid farewell to Alderley Edge. Wrote some Richard. Finished Gisborne—I like it very much. Read Cicero—Greek Testament—Logarithms—did some translation. Learning Juvenal.

9. Wednesday.

Mr Robertson went, Mr Bayne,[1] master of the Warrington School, came. Read Greek Testament—Cicero—did translation—began Mayers[2]—read paper—Greek Testament, said Juvenal: & Logarithms: & read over Translation with Rector. Out with Wood—wrote Richard.

10. Thursday.

Finished Plato's 2nd Dialogue in Translation—St Matthew in Greek Testament with Rector—did Logarithms—Finished Cicero de Officiis 3. Finished my concern on Richard. Sat a good while with Mr Turner. Carpentering & packing work. Read paper—Mayers—out. Up late.

11. Friday.

Very busy. Wrote over & corrected Richard somewhat—& packed up my things. All being settled, bid farewell to friends & went off by Mail to Manchester—thence on—Travell'd all night.

12. Saturday.

Carlisle in morning—thence on to Edinburgh—Mail a capital conveyance— arrived before six, safe thank God. Found all much as before. Some of the road very beautiful—between Longtown[3] & Langham—some between

---

[1] Thomas Vere Bayne, 1803?–48, Warrington master 1828, priest in Manchester 1842.
[2] W. M. Mayers, 'A critical examination of our Saviour's Discourses', Hulsean prize essay (1827).
[3] In Liddisdale, 9 miles north of Carlisle.

Hawick[1] & Selkirk.[2] Edinburgh magnificent. Bad cold. Wrote a few lines to my brothers.

13. Sunday.

Unable to get to Ch in morng. Went to hear Mr Craig[3] in afternoon at his Episcopal Chapel. Out a little too. Read Bible—& Olney Hymns.[4] I seem likely to get little out of my time here I fear. Copied 1 Letter—wrote to T.G.

14. Monday.

Read paper—&c &c. Time wasted. Out with Mr G. called on Mr Craig—not at home. Out about the town a good deal, at Shops &c. Read a Correspondence on Mr Canning's Monument,[5] &c.

15. Tuesday.

Mr G. went to London. Read Edinburgh Review on Sir H. Moncreiff, & State of Parties.[6] Aunt Ogilvy here.[7] Called on Mr Craig—out. Mrs Fraser[8] —out—Lady Moncreiff[9]—at home. Out shopping also, & initiating myself in finding way about the town. Made up accounts.

16.

Call'd on Mr Craig—out. Mrs Fraser—in. Read papers, & part of Answer to Dr Philpott's Letters.[10] Out shopping &c. Read out of Dr Warton to A.M.G.

17.

Finished Answer to Dr Philpotts. Began a book of Dr Kitchiner's on health.[11] Found Mr Craig at home—sat long with him—then went out to Libraries, Parliament House: & High School—he kindly piloting me. 3 Miss Frasers had tea with us. Shopping &c.

18. Friday.

Read papers & Dr Kitchiner—Out in carriage & also walking. Wrote to Mr

[1] In Teviotdale, midway between Carlisle and Edinburgh.
[2] Nine hilly miles north of Hawick.
[3] Edward Craig, priest at St. James's, Broughton Place; controversialist.
[4] By John *Newton and William *Cowper (1779).
[5] Untraced.
[6] xlvii. 242 (January 1828), reviewing funeral sermon on Sir Henry *Moncreiff Wellwood, and 100, reviewing trial of Edward Gibbon *Wakefield.
[7] Mrs. David Ogilvy, John *Gladstone's sister; lived at Leith.
[8] Wife of James Fraser, Bank of Scotland.
[9] Ann Robertson the wife of Sir J. W. *Moncreiff, 1776–1851, whig judge, the 2nd s. of Sir H. *Moncreiff Wellwood, divine.
[10] A sixty-page pamphlet by 'Clericus' (1828).
[11] Dr. William *Kitchiner, *The Art of invigorating and prolonging Life, ... and Peptic Precepts*, full of cheerful advice on sleep and diet (1821).

G. Read Dr Warton to A.M.G. & sat with her—at figures in Evening with H.J.G. a little. I now get a good deal of walking.

19. Saturday.

Call'd on Mr Craig—& on J. Moncreiff [1]—sat some time with both—began Paterson's Prize Essay [2]—read papers—out walking—wrote a little Algebra in my book—a bad & idle day, but a very long [3] conversation with A.M.G. at night, wh may God render useful to me a miserable sinner.

20. Sunday.

Mr Craig's in morng. Went in afternoon to Dr Gordon's [4]—but a Mr Ritchie [5] preached. Walk. Read Valpy's notes to the end of Matthew. [6] Began to read Mark with A.M.G.—sat with her &c.

21. Monday.

Read paper—debate on Corporation & Test Acts. [7] Out with young Moncreiff—went to see the Academy. Read Bible with A.M.G.—read Paterson. Wrote to Mr Turner. Out in old Town—buying stationery, a stock—& again in Evg. Lazy & doing little since I came to Edinburgh.

22. Tuesday.

Rain—read paper—& Paterson. Bible with A.M.G. in Evg. taking Greek text & Valpy's Notes at same time. Out—sat with A.M.G. Sir W. Arbuthnot called. [8]

23. Wednesday.

Mr Brown, a dissenting Minister [9] breakfasted with us. Apparently an agreeable man. Read paper. Finished Paterson's Essay & Appendix: very clever, & erudite. Out in the town, & walked to Mr Goalen's [10]—back with H.J.G. Bible as usual with A.M.G. & Valpy's Notes.

24. Thursday.

Algebra in book—out; over the Princes Street Gardens. Read paper—Dr

---

[1] James*, 1811–95, s. of Sir J. W. *Moncreiff; lord justice clerk 1869–88, Lord Moncreiff 1875.
[2] J. B. *Paterson, 'On the National Character of the Athenians and the Causes of those Peculiarities by which it was distinguished', Edinburgh prize essay (1828).
[3] The words 'and most interesting' here deleted.
[4] Dr. Robert Gordon of Lauriston, priest at Hope Park.
[5] Three Ritchies, Dr. David, professor of logic; Dr. John; and Dr. William, professor of divinity, were in orders in Edinburgh.
[6] Edward *Valpy, *The Greek Testament, with English notes* (new ed. 1826).
[7] Lords' debate on their repeal in *NSH* xviii. 1450–1520.
[8] Sir William Arbuthnot, 1766–1829, cr. bart. 1822 while lord provost of Edinburgh; east India merchant.
[9] Probably John Brown of Rose Street.
[10] Alexander Goalen, banker.

Kitchiner—part of Mr Craig's "Respectful Remonstrance"[1]—Bible & Valpy in Evg. Mrs & 2 Miss Frasers came for the evening. Asked to Mrs Massie's[2]—but did not go.

25. Friday.

Took Epsom Salts. Read Kitchiner—& papers—debate on Corporation & Test Acts &c. in them.[3] Out in carriage with Mrs G. & A.M.G. Invited to dine at Mrs Frasers & to go to Concert in Evg: declined. Miss Augusta M'Kenzie[4] having tea with us. Invited to Lady Moncrieff's for Tuesday: accepted. Out in afternoon & after dinner. Heard from Uncle Colin of dear Cousin Colin's death in Bombay, on 8th Decr. May God support & bless this trial to his parent: & may the change be a blessed one to the poor departed. Wrote to Mr G.—& part of a letter to T.G. Heard from Mr Turner—& from T.G.

26. Saturday.

Out—in carriage at Mrs Ogilvy's. & ordering mourning &c. Sent excuse to Lady Arbuthnot[5] for not going in Evg. Called on Mr Craig & sat with him. Sent letter to T.G. Tried Algebra—read paper & Kitchiner. Bible &c. with A.M.G.

27. Sunday.

Mr Craig's Ch in morning: dined between services: Dr Thomson's[6] in afternoon. Mr Craig preached on the temple of Christ's body & resurrection. Dr T. on Judas's repentance & repentance in general.[7] Read Bible & Testament —part of Mr Knight's prayers.[8] Sat a good many hours in[9] conversation with A.M.G.

28. Monday.

Up in better time & out—wrote a note to Mr Turner, meaning to send it by Mr Craig, but missed him. Read Bible &c. with A.M.G.—papers—& Kitchiner. Out in bookseller's shops, &c. Wrote to Aunt Johanna—Miserable day! as usual: o when will exclamations of regret for lost & wasted time be followed by measures of amendment!

29. Tuesday.

Read paper—Kitchiner—Quarterly Review—out: looking over a stock of

---

[1] A pamphlet on his dispute with the local bible society.
[2] Wife of W. W. Massie of Charlotte Square.
[3] Lords' debate, resumed, in *NSH* xviii. 1571–1610.
[4] D. 1856; 5th da. of Lord *Seaforth.
[5] Anne, née Alves; m. (Sir) William Arbuthnot 1800; 10 c.; d. 1846.
[6] Dr. Andrew M. Thomson, priest at St. George's, Charlotte Square.
[7] John ii. 21; Matt. xxvii. 3.
[8] S. *Knight, *Forms of Prayer, for the use of Christian Families* (1791).
[9] The word 'interestg' here deleted.

books: made a considerable purchase. Out again—shopping. Dressed & went at 5 to dine with Lady Moncrieff. Met a Mr Stoddart[1] &c. They are very kind. Bible alone.

30. Wednesday.

Read papers—Finished Kitchiner: began Brougham's Preliminary Treatise.[2] Out twice: ordering books for A.M.G. &c. Read Bible &c. in Evg with A.M.G. Mr Graham[3] breakfasted with us. At the Bp's Chapel in afternoon. He[4] preached a very good sermon on behalf of Naval & Military Bible Society. So ends a very idle month.

May First. Thursday.

Out in carriage with Mrs & A.M.G. Shopping, on Calton Hill[5] &c. Weather now warm—but season not forward. Finished Brougham's Prelim. Treatise —read papers—and began Philpott's Letter to Canning.[6] Bible &c as usual.

2. Friday.

Bible &c—papers—Philpotts—& Useful Knowledge Society's Life of Wolsey[7]—Walked down to Aunt Ogilvy's[8]—sat with her some time— returned by the Old Town &c. after dinner out again. Heard from Pickering & Gaskell.

3. Saturday.

Bible &c—papers—finished Philpott's very able letter. Out with J. Moncreiff—on the top of Arthur's seat—in Duddingstone[9] &c. &c.—out again on a fruitless quest. Sacrament tomorrow.

4. Sunday.

Bible &c—Finished Mr Knight's Prayers—read Barrow's Doctrine of the Sacraments—& again that of the Eucharist, with part of a Sermon, aloud to A.M.G. Read "Some Account of his Life".[10] Mr Craig's Ch in morng. Mr. Golding[11] preached very well on Lord's Supper—of wh I partook. God bless

[1] John F. Stoddart, advocate.
[2] Henry *Brougham, 'A Discourse of the Objects, Advantages, and Pleasures of Science' (1827), prefixed to the *Natural Philosophy* volumes issued by the Society for the Diffusion of Useful Knowledge.
[3] John Graham, portrait painter. Cp. 10 May 28.
[4] Daniel *Sandford, 1766–1830, bp. of Edinburgh from 1806; preaching at St. John's, Princes Street.
[5] The hill beyond the eastern end of Princes Street.
[6] Henry *Phillpotts' lengthy pamphlet opposing catholic relief (1827).
[7] [By Katharine *Thomson] (1824).
[8] Seacot House, Leith, close to the sea to the east of the port.
[9] Then a hamlet, south of Arthur's Seat and SE. of the city.
[10] By A[braham] *H[ill], in Isaac *Barrow's works (1683).
[11] Perhaps Joseph Golding, 1756?–1848, vicar of Newbold Pacey, Warwickshire, 1803.

it to me for Christ's sake.—Dr. Gordon's in afternoon—He is a very able preacher—on Christ as suffering Redeemer.[1]

5. *Monday.*

Rain. Out a little. Finished Life of Wolsey. Read part of "The System".[2] Read paper. Bible with A.M.G. Yesterday we heard of reconciliation effected with Uncle Divie. Today confirmed. Thank God. Wrote to Farr—part of a letter to Handley.

6. *Tuesday.*

Mr G. returned. Out—weather very cold. Finished letter to Handley. Bible & finished System—read papers—debate on Canada in it[3]—A.M.G. not very well.

7. *Wednesday.*

Out—shopping. With A.M.G. she less well than usual, so Bible alone. Made up my accounts for some time. Read papers—Harrovian, No. 1.[4]—Began Conversations on Natural Philosophy[5]—finished Mr Craig's Remonstrance. Wrote to Mr Turner & to Doyle.

8. *Thursday.*

Copied a letter & another document—read papers—heard from Selwyn— Mrs G. unwell—Bible alone—read conversations on Natural Philosophy— & in Blackwood, writing later—Public men &c—& Causes of Change of Ministry[6]—out—wrote a few lines to Aunt Mary. Chess with H.J.G.

9. *Friday.*

Copied a paper for Mr G. Read Bible &c. with A.M.G. Harrovian—Blackwood (Siege of Bhurtpore & Letters from Peninsula)[7] & papers. Wrote part of a letter to Selwyn. Went with Professor Hope,[8] Mr G. & H.J.G. to the Botanic & Experimental gardens,[9] very well worth seeing. Again out, jobbing.

---

[1] Titus ii. 14.
[2] Charlotte Elizabeth [Phelan, later *Tonna], *The System: a tale of the West Indies*, strongly anti-romanist (1827).
[3] *NSH* xix. 300–44; the commons agreed on 2 May that a select committee should inquire into the civil government of Canada.
[4] A school magazine, published monthly for Harrow from March to August 1828.
[5] [Jane *Marcet] *Conversations on Natural Philosophy* (1824), elements of science for children.
[6] *Blackwood's Edinburgh Magazine*, xxiii. 520 and 504 (April 1828).
[7] Ibid. 445 and 431.
[8] Dr. Thomas C. *Hope, professor of chemistry and chemical pharmacy.
[9] In Inverleith Row, in the northern part of the city.

10. Saturday.

Out—at Graham's, who is painting Mr G [1]—at the Academy exhibition: much pleas'd. Heard from Mr Turner. Bible &c with A.M.G. Read Harrovian & part of Quarterly on Collingwood. Finished letter to Selwyn & wrote to Pickering—both at some length.

11. Sunday.

St Paul's in Morning. Mr Morehead preach'd, on "Leaving us an example".[2] St George's in afternoon—a Mr Gregory preachd, on the things which make for peace.[3] Walk alone. Read Bible &c. Barrow's Exposition of Lord's Prayer, & part of that of the Decalogue. read a long but excellent sermon of his aloud to A.M.G. on honouring God.[4] We both like him exceedingly. Thanks be to God, I have had great pleasure on this & last Sunday—but must not be too bold or presumptuous.

12. Monday.

Out &c. read a long debate on Catholic Question [5]—& finished Quarterly on Collingwood. began it on Leigh Hunt. Wrote to Aunts E. & J. & copied, for Mr G. Went out in Evg to Sir W. Arbuthnot's, & passed a pleasant Evening. Met Mrs Hagart, the beauty; & a very clever & fascinating woman. [6]

13. Tuesday.

Mr & Mrs G. went North to look at Estates. Read the 2nd long debate on Catholic Question—again adjourned. Out in the town. Went down in afternoon to Mr Goalen's—saw him & my Aunt. Meals with A.M.G. now— Finished Quarterly on Leigh Hunt—read [its] Article on Maynooth. Called on Ja's Moncrieff & Mr Craig.

14. Wednesday.

Wrote to Mr G.—Read Bible &c—Conv. on Nat. Philos. and paper—heard from Mr G.—Mr Hagart call'd—out with A.M.G.—Breakfasted early, & went with James Moncrieff to Old Town—thence by coach to Loanhead— thence to Roslin—saw the Abbey & Castle—went up Hawthornden—back, thro' Roslin to Eldon, Sir J. Moncrieff's—thence home—perhaps 16 miles walk in all. The Abbey is a beautiful & curious ruin—the situation of Castle fine—Hawthornden (all, we did not see) lovely.[7]

---

[1] Untraced portrait.
[2] Robert Morehead, on 1 Pet. ii. 21.
[3] James Gregory, on Rom. xiv. 19.
[4] On 1 Sam. ii. 30 (1683).
[5] See 15 May 28 n.
[6] Elizabeth, née Stewart, m. 1813 Thomas Campbell Hagart, 1774–1868, of Bantaskine, Co. Stirling.
[7] An excursion to the middle Esk, south of Edinburgh.

15. Thursday.

Read paper—wrote to Mrs G—Read Bible—Valpy—Conv. on Nat. Phil.—
out with A.M.G.—Called on Lady Arbuthnot—out. Mrs Fraser—in—Mr
Hagart—out. Wrote a little in Algebra book. Catholic Question carried in
Commons. *272 to 266*.[1] This is good.

16. Friday.

Read debate on Catholic Question &c. Letter from J.N.G. an excellent one,
even more than usual. Date 15 Decr. had not heard of his promotion! Mr &
Mrs G. returned. Hagarts breakfasted with me—very nice boys.[2] Read
Bible—Valpy—Conv on Nat. Phil. Wrote to Mr Turner, & some sense[3] &c:
for the Hagarts—out—called on Lady Moncrieff, Professor Jameson,[4] Miss
Augusta M'Kenzie & Mrs Massie.

17. Saturday.

Up Arthur's seat &c. with H.J.G. before breakfast. At Mr Hagarts—wrote
sense for the sons &c. Went with them to see Archery in the Meadows—
bowling—& the Riding School. Walked down to Seacot—dined & had tea
with Aunt Ogilvy (who is now a grandmother)—returned in Evg—read
Bible—papers—Conv. on Nat. Phil. much walking.

18. Sunday.

Mr Craig's morning—Mr C. preached. He shall feed his flock like a shepherd.[5] Mr Shannon's[6] afternoon. Mr Gregory preached—Quench not the
Spirit.[7]—Out with A.M.G. Read Bible, Valpy, & Barrow. Began a book of
Collections, which may God make useful. Long converse with Miss Farenden & Helen.

19. Monday.

In morning copying letter &c for Mr G.—sewing—read papers. Called on
young Aspull[8]—out. Mr Craig—at home. Began copying Inventory of
Dunottar[9] furniture. Out. Went to see Mr Wood's School.[10] Dressed & went
to dine with Mrs Hagart—spent a pleasant Evg there. Very kind.

---

[1] See *NSH* xix. 375–680 for debate on 8, 9, and 12 May on *Burdett's motion favouring
catholic emancipation. Sir Francis *Burdett, 1770–1844, 5th bart. 1797, fox-hunting
radical; M.P. Westminster 1807–37, then tory M.P. Wiltshire; advocate of free speech.
[2] Charles, 1814–79, and James McCaul Hagart, 1815–95?, ss. of T.C.; Charles commanded a cavalry brigade in the Indian mutiny, and was made general in 1877.
[3] Bare prose passages for translation into Latin verse.
[4] Robert *Jameson, regius professor of natural history.
[5] Isa. xl. 11.
[6] R. Q. Shannon, clergyman at St. George's, York Place.
[7] 1 Thess. v. 19.
[8] George *Aspull, 1813–32, pianist and composer.
[9] A house on the outskirts of Stonehaven, Kincardineshire, which John *Gladstone
contemplated buying.
[10] John Wood of Great King Street; cp. 1 Jan. 35.

20. Tuesday.

Read Bible—part of "Statement" in favour of Bible Society by Editor Corresponding Board. Read papers. Heard from Pickering—long & kind letter from R.G. Went to College—saw Museum, Library, Lecture rooms &c. The first beautifully arranged. Library in confusion at present.

21. Wednesday.

Read Bible—papers—finished "Statement"—Finished copying Inventory —Attended Deaf & dumb meeting—exceedingly interesting. Went to see Parliament House &c. Mr Graham, Mr Hodgson,[1] & a Mr Robertson,[2] breakfasted here. Read Valpy.

22. Thursday.

Saw procession to Ch (commencement of General Assembly)—in Ch for some time. Called on Mr Craig—Hagarts—Mrs Fraser—Sir W. Arbuthnot— shopping. Out with young Hagarts. Read Bible—Conv. on Nat. Phil.— papers—Wrote Algebra—People breakfasting & having tea with us.

23. Friday.

Algebra book—papers—Conv. on Nat. Phil. Read Bible—wrote to T.G. & some letters of introduction for the Hagarts. Breakfasted with Mr Ainslie, W.S.[3] He kindly went with me to the Courts &c. & Register Office. Saw many curious papers there. Called on Hagarts. Out with Mr & Mrs Hagart. Frasers had tea with us.

24. Saturday.

Finished preparing 4 letters of introduction for the Hagarts—called on them & on James Moncreiff. Went to see Mr Woods school—& then to Aspull's concert. He & his brother played & sung—Miss E. Paton[4] likewise. Dined at Mr Sutherland M'Kenzie's[5] read Bible, paper &c—& wrote in Algebra book. Cold.

25. Sunday.

Out—Mr Craig's morning—Sermon on being in the Spirit—Sacrament— near 150 Communicants. Bishop's in afternoon—Mr Ramsay[6] preached on the Spirit. Heard from Pickering—Bible, with A.M.G. & H.J.G.—Valpy— Barrow—Copied a note—and looked over Liverpool Mariners' Ch. Report.

[1] Perhaps John Hodgson, barrister of Lincoln's Inn.
[2] Perhaps Robertson of Stornoway. (See 26 May 28.)
[3] Robert Ainslie of Messrs. Ainslie & McAllan.
[4] Sister of M.A.*; da. of George Paton, Edinburgh writing-master and violinist.
[5] Cousin and next-door-neighbour of Lady Seaforth in Charlotte Square.
[6] Edward Bannerman *Ramsay, 1793–1872, dean of Edinburgh 1841; became a close friend; see Add MSS 44283–4.

26. Monday.

Read up papers—Mother very unwell with cold & headache. Packing & disorder. Heard from Wood. Dined with Mr Craig—met Mr Golding— pleasant Evg there—called on Mr Robertson [of] Stornaway,[1] Mr Hagart, Mr M'Kenzie [of] Applecross.[2] Attended General Assembly: heard Chalmers.[3] Read Bible.

27. Tuesday.

Called on Hagarts—Mr Sutherland M'Kenzie. Shop business &c. Called on Mr Craig & sat with him some time. He has treated me with great kindness, as have the Hagarts & others. Mother better thank God. Wrote in Algebra Book. Read Bible. Began Chronicles of Canongate 2 Series.

28. Wednesday.

Out, alone & with H.J.G. Mother a little better, still considerable pain. Finished Vol 1 of Chronicles of Canongate. Began Jerusalem destroyed.[4] Wrote in Algebra book. Read Bible. Letter from R.G. arrived. Read paper. Invited to theatre by Sir W. Arbuthnot—but did not go.

29. Thursday.

Mother better. Out—in bookshops &c—& with H.J.G.—wrote in Algebra book. Read paper—& Jerusalem destroy'd. Looked over Tait's Catalogue &c.[5] We do not go till next week. At Millers[6] &c. reading.

30. Friday.

Out—& with H.J.G. Looked over Tait's books—bought some. Read Bible —Jerusalem destroyed—Wrote in Algebra book. Mrs Ogilvy called. Din'd at Ld M'Kenzie's.[7] Very kind & agreeable people. Mother better.

31. Saturday.

Read Bible—Jerusalem destroyed—papers—wrote in Algebra book. Out. A bad day with my Mother. (Omitted writing Journal in Evg—record therefore imperfect.)—Copied two letters.

June 1. Sunday:

Mr Craig's morning—Sermon on Trinity, & the Creeds. Received the Blessed

[1] Presumably a cousin; Stornoway, Isle of Lewis, the largest town in the Hebrides.
[2] Thomas Mackenzie of Applecross, near Lochcarron, on the SW. shore of Wester Ross; M.P. for Ross and Cromarty 1837–47; cousin to the Mackenzies of Seaforth.
[3] Thomas *Chalmers, 1780–1847, preacher; professor of morals, St. Andrews, 1823; of divinity, Edinburgh, 1828, till the disruption of 1843; free church leader.
[4] Tasso (1592); presumably in translation.
[5] William* and Charles Tait, booksellers.
[6] Manners and Miller, also Princes Street booksellers.
[7] Joshua Henry Mackenzie, d. 1851, a lord of session from 1822; m. Helen Anne, Lord *Seaforth's sixth da., in 1821; she d. 1852.

Sacrament. At Mr Grey's[1] in afternoon—heard a Mr Logan[2] preach, on the Atonement. Mother easier thank God. Read Bible—Mr Craig's Christian Circumspection & Two Tracts called "Public & Private Means" & "The Coronation". All very good. Wrote to Aunt Johanna.

2. Monday.

Called at Mr Craig's—dined with him, went to a prayer meeting of communicants, spent the evg with him—Met Mr Golding &c. Went with Mr G. to General Assembly & Courts, & made some calls. Read Bible—Jerusalem destroyed—& papers.

3. Tuesday.

Went to breakfast with Dr. Hope—saw young Aspull. Walked home with Mr G. Called on Mrs Hy M'Kenzie, Miss Augusta M'K., Mrs Massie & Sir W. Arbuthnot. In booksellers' shops. Tea & walk with Mr Craig. Read Bible—Jerusalem destroyed—paper. Long & interesting conversation with A.M.G. but sat up too late. Asked to breakfast at Lady Seaforth's[3]—unable to go.

4. Wednesday.

Eton Reminiscences[4] arrived—packing & disturbance. Read Bible—Jerusalem destroyed—paper—Went to St Paul's in morning—heard Mr Ramsay preach very well on rightly dividing the word of truth.[5] Called on Mrs S. M'Kenzie & Ld M'K's lady—&c. Wrote in Algebra book. Packing &c.

5. Thursday.

Packing &c. Call'd on Mr Craig, Mrs Fraser & James Moncreiff. read Jerusalem destroyed. Read Bible—& papers—Wrote a pretty long letter to J.N.G. Heard from Aunt Johanna. Mother pretty well.

6. Friday.

Read Bible—finished Jerusalem destroy'd—read papers—began New Tory Guide.[6] Called on Mr Craig to bid him goodbye. Left Edinburgh in forenoon—by Fusie Bridge,[7] Torsonce[8] & Selkirk to Hawick, where we slept at the Tower—good inn. Weather at first rainy—afterwards fine. Journey pleasant.

[1] Henry Grey, clergyman.
[2] Unidentified.
[3] Mary, née Proby, d. 1829, widow of the Lord Seaforth and *Mackenzie, 1754–1815, who raised the Seaforth Highlanders, was regarded by John *Gladstone as head of his wife's clan, and died under an ancient curse.
[4] Possibly James *Lawrence, *Etonian out of bounds*, 3v. (1828).
[5] 2 Tim. ii. 15.
[6] Squibs reprinted from the *Morning Chronicle*, 1815–18.
[7] Ten miles SE. of Edinburgh.
[8] The seat on Gala Water, some 20 miles SE. of Edinburgh, of Sir John Pringle, 1784?–1869, 5th bart.

7. Saturday.

Read Bible. papers. new Tory Guide. Went by Mosspaul[1] Langholm & Longtown to Carlisle, where we slept, at the Bush, excellent Inn. My Mother not well—journey otherwise very agreeable—went to see Langholm Lodge[2] on the way.

8. Sunday.

Cathedral in morng—Mr Fawcett's Ch.[3] in aftn—no Sermon—went on to Penrith[4] slept at the George—good Inn. Read Bible—Parley the porter (+) Tis all for the best[5] (+) & Mr Craig's Foundation of Christian Hope. Mother ill. Good news from J.N.G.

9. Monday.

Went on to Shap, Kendal, Burton,[6] & Lancaster—where we slept, at the Royal Oak—comfortable Inn—Weather very fine. My Father & I outside passengers. The journey a great struggle for my Mother. Went to see the old Castle at Penrith.[7] Read Bible—papers—new Tory Guide.

10. Tuesday.

Read Bible—papers—new Tory Guide—on thro' Garstang,[8] Preston & Ormskirk[9] homewards. Arrived safely thank God in the evening. Found Seaforth in its best dress.

11. Wednesday.

Unpacking, moving books &c. & endeavouring to get things in some degree arranged in the large upper wing room, which is now to be my domicile. My Mother better. Out & about. All things looking well. Read Bible &c.

12. Thursday.

Copied a letter—Read Bible—finished new Tory Guide—read paper. At the same employment as yesterday's, chiefly, & a very wearisome one—now however pretty well closed.

13. Friday.

Rode into town. Saw Uncle David & with him some time—did shopping business. Wrote up my journal since leaving Edinburgh—read Bible—

[1] Hamlet 10 miles north of Langholm.
[2] A palace of the duke of *Buccleuch's.
[3] John Fawcett, 1769?–1830, in charge of St. Cuthbert's, Carlisle, 1801.
[4] Twenty miles south of Carlisle.
[5] Two cheap repository tracts, signed Z, by Hannah *More.
[6] Nine, 25, and 35 miles south of Penrith on the Lancaster road.
[7] Dismantled in civil war.
[8] Ten miles south of Lancaster.
[9] Twenty-seven and 14 miles NE. of Liverpool.

paper—& Liverpool Christian Knowledge Society's Report over. Called on Mr & Mrs Rawson.

14. Saturday.

Out. Read Bible—papers, containing two debates on Catholic Question.[1] Copied a short letter. Weather fine. Hope to begin bathing in a day or two. Began V.2 of St Valentine's Day.[2]

15. Sunday.

Ch. morning & evg. Mr Rawson preached in morning—a stranger in Evg. on "My Son, give me thine heart".[3] Stewart G. & Robert came down. Out. Read Bible—began Porteus's Life[4]—& read Dr Walker of Edinburgh's sermon on "the Gospel Commission".[5] Tomorrow please God I hope to begin to "redeem the time"[6] in some small degree, & be up pretty early.

16. Monday.

T.G. & R.G. arrived between 9 & 10 at night anticipating our expectations, to our great joy. In Lpool shopping—walked out. In Garden &c. Read Bible—papers—St Valentine's Day. Copied a long letter & compared it &c. &c.

17. Tuesday.

Read Bible—papers, including Specimen of the "Argus"[7]—finished Vol 2 of St Valentine's Day. Out with R.G. & with A.M.G.

18. Wednesday.

Read Bible as usual. Papers—& began 3d vol of St Valentine. Began, but alas! only just began, the Odyssey. Weather wet. Now pretty well settled; some things still to arrive from Edinburgh.

19. Thursday.

Bible as usual. Papers—finished St Valentine's Day. Wrote in Algebra book —Read Odyssey. Out with A.M.G. & with R.G. Up earlier, but not right yet.

20. Friday.

Bible as usual. Papers. In Lpool with T.G. Opening & unpacking Edin-

---

[1] The lords resolved by 181 to 137, after debate on 9 and 10 June, that it was inexpedient to consider the catholics' claims: *NSH* xix. 1133, 1214.
[2] Better known as *Scott's *Fair Maid of Perth*.
[3] Prov. xxiii. 26.
[4] Dean Robert Hodgson's life of his uncle Beilby *Porteus (1811).
[5] James *Walker, later bp., on Matt. xxviii. 18–20.
[6] Eph. v. 16.
[7] London evening newspaper unsuccessfully projected by J. S. *Buckingham.

burgh packages. Wrote in Algebra book—read Odyssey. Out in Evg. Cousin J. Murray dined here. Weather still unsettled. Uncle Murray down here.

21. Saturday.

Algebra—Euclid—Homer—but little: went into town & did shopping work. Detained & delayed by rain. Heard from Gaskell. Read Bible. Read papers. Began Heber's Journal.[1] Out in Evg. Had a long talk with Jones the Book-binder & much pleased.

22. Sunday.

Church morning & Evg. A.M.G. there in Evg. We should be thankful. Out. Bible & notes with A.M.G. Greek Testament alone. Finished Hodgson's Life of Porteus: I like it very much. Read the Notes to Dr Walker's Sermon. &c.

23. Monday.

T.G. went to Leamington[2] in morning. Wrote a long letter to Gaskell. Read Bible &c. with A.M.G. & H.J.G. & alone (wh I shall not make particular mention of for the future—as it is brief & ordinary.) With Mr & Mrs Rawson about two hours. Read paper. Made up my list of books read for three months—very unsatisfactory. Much out.

24. Tuesday.

Went down to bathe, but could not get a machine. Young Stanley & Myers[3] came to breakfast, & for the forenoon. The former a very fine & a remarkable boy.[4] Read paper—& Conversations on Natural Philosophy. Wrote letters to Hallam, Farr, & Pickering. Out with A.M.G.—with R.G. At marking work.

25. Wednesday.

The Egertons[5] came to breakfast, & remained for the forenoon. Bathed before breakfast. Out with A.M.G. &c. &c. Read Bible—paper—& Conversations on Natural Philosophy. Heard from Handley. Marking clothes &c.

26. Thursday.

Making hay & getting in during the afternoon. Wrote in Algebra & Euclid

[1] Reginald *Heber, *Journey through India*, 2v. (1828).
[2] This year the Gladstones took a house at Leamington, by Warwick.
[3] Son of John Myers, priest at Wavertree?
[4] See R. E. *Prothero, *Life of A. P. *Stanley*, i. 22.
[5] Probably William Tatton Egerton, 1806–83, conservative M.P. for Cheshire 1832–58, cr. Lord Egerton of Tatton 1859; and his younger brother Thomas, d. 1847, rector of Dunnington, Yorkshire, from 1835; both Eton acquaintances.

—read Arthur Stanley's poems, which are wonderful, I think. Bible &c. with A.M.G. & H.J.G. read paper. Out with R.G. Slight headache in Evg., Bible alone.

27. Friday.

Headachy—Bathed—worked at the hay &c—Out too in Evg. Read Bible &c. with my sisters. Read papers including some debates.[1] Singing with R.G.

28. Saturday.

Festivities for H.J.G's birthday. Bible &c. with Anne & Helen. Read paper, & Conversations on Natural Philosophy. Very hot. Out at hay &c. &c. Read a little Odyssey. A bad week. Strawberries &c. in the arbour in Evening. May God bless my dear Sister, & make her to grow in every grace.

29. Sunday.

Mr Rawson preached for Church Missionary Society a very good sermon. Ch morning & Evg. Bible with A.M.G. & alone. Conversation with her. Looked over again Mr Craigs Respectful Remonstrance—read Dr Walker's Serious Expostulation[2]—Began Mr Craig's Reply. Began a book of "Opinions of Eminent divines".[3]

30. Monday.

Out—garden &c. Bible &c. with my sisters—Algebra—a little Odyssey— papers—finished Conversations on Natural Philosophy: which I think are very ably done: but I am a wretchedly incompetent judge. Read part of Quarterly Review on Baptismal Regeneration—Wrote down Jewel & Hammond's opinion.[4]

July First. Tuesday.

Read more of Quarterly Review—Wrote Bradford & Hooker's opinions. Algebra—a little Odyssey—Bathed—drew A.M.G. in chair—called on Mr Rawson—working at the hay—in garden—Mr Conway din'd here—read paper, & Heber's Journal. Bible &c. &c. with A.M.G. & H.J.G.

2. Wednesday.

Finished Quarterly on Baptismal Regeneration. Wrote more opinions. Algebra—went to Town & shopped. Got tracts &c. on Confirmation for

[1] Commons debates on misappropriation of public money on 23rd and on emigration from Ireland on 24th, *NSH* xix. 1476, 1501.
[2] A pained attack on Craig (1828).
[3] Add MS 44803B; on baptism, and on fasting.
[4] xv. 475 (July 1816). *Gladstone collected numerous opinions on the subject from Anglican divines: Add MS 44719, ff. 126–86.

H.J.G. Read Hale's Method of Preparation for Confirmation.[1] Wrote an anonymous letter to Bp of Chester—wrote to Doyle—read paper & a little Heber.

3. Thursday.

Made up accounts—Wrote opinions—Algebra—read papers—& Heber. Wrote to T.G. Bible &c. with A.M.G. Rain. Drew Anne in chair a little.— The debates are pretty stiff now.[2] Lookd over Christian Observer for the last month.

4. Friday.

¼ before 7.[3] Wrote opinions—also in Evg Texts. Algebra—a little Odyssey —papers—Bible &c. with sisters. Wrote to T.G. Getting together &c. things for him—took them to town—called on Mrs M'Cartney, Mrs Wilson & Miss Benwell. Mr Rawson's boys came to strawberries &c. &c. in Evening.

5. Saturday.

7.—Wrote out texts. Algebra—a little Odyssey—a little Heber—papers— Bible &c. with A.M.G. & H.J.G. Conversation afterwards with A.M.G. Called on Mr Rawson. Heard from Wood. Wrote to Mr Turner: did a good deal of copying—read. Drew Anne in Chair. Busy, yet little done.

6. Sunday.

7. Read Pott's Discourses for people after Confirmation.[4] Bible with A.M.G. Ch. morng & Evg. Attended the Lord's Supper—above 30 communicants. Out with Anne, & in garden. Wrote out opinions. Began Life of Secker[5]— read Quarterly on Alison, & on Bp of London v. Belsham.[6]

7. Monday.

past 7. Late last night.—Wrote out opinions—read Heber's Journal—Went to Lpool—saw F. Matheson—walked out—read papers—Clare Election Speeches &c[7]—Heard from C. Hagart—out with R.G.—read a little Odyssey.

8. Tuesday.

½ past 6. Read Heber. Went down & bathed. Algebra—wrote to C. Hagart

---

[1] Short devotional handbook by W. H. *Hale (1827).
[2] The commons had debated on the disfranchisement of East Retford for excessive corruption (27 June), Portugal on 30 June, and on 1 July the claims of the baron de Bode, a French émigré, against his own government. NSH xix. 1530, 1545, 1563.
[3] Times of getting up noted for next ten days.
[4] By J. H. *Pott (1792).
[5] By Beilby *Porteus (1770).
[6] xiv. 429 (January 1816), on the 2nd vol. of canon *Alison's sermons; and xiv. 39 (October 1815), on a controversy between *Howley and the unitarian Thomas *Belsham.
[7] Torrents of oratory accompanied the by-election in Co. Clare, decided on 5 July, in which Daniel *O'Connell defeated Vesey *Fitzgerald.

—& to Wood—did some copying, an hour or so. in garden. Read papers. Drew Anne in Chair twice. Bible &c. with my sisters. Began working at "Guide to French Conversation".

9. Wednesday.

Not called. Slept till 20 m. past 7. Got a better bit of Algebra than usual—read Bible with my sisters Testament & Notes &c. with Bible alone, a little of course as usual—Read Odyssey—Guide to French Conversation—Heber —papers—drew Anne in Chair—out. Rainy day in part.

10. Thursday.

7. Algebra. Read Bible &c. with A.M.G. & H.J.G.—read a little Odyssey—& Heber. 3 cousins call'd. Out, Drew Anne in Chair. Sorting a number of old magazines, reports &c. &c. Edward's child died.[1]

11. Friday.

Bathed—Read Heber. Algebra—wrote to T.G. read papers—sorting—Bible with A.M.G. & long conversation on W. Indies &c. Wrote letters (3) to the Mercury & Albion[2]—drew Anne in Chair. Out. (20 before 7 in morning.)

12. Saturday.

Papers. Heber. Algebra—in Lpool. getting books &c. &c.—Bible—came out of town on foot. John arrived: and we now find we have to thank God for having preserved him from the very jaws of death. In January he had a fever, & was *given over*—now he is here, strong, healthy, & fearless! ($\frac{1}{2}$ past 6).

13. Sunday.

Past 7. Read Bp Bradford on Regeneration[3]—part of Mr Craig's Reply—and finished Porteus's Life of Secker. Read Bible &c. with my sisters. Searched out & wrote Opinions on Baptism. Ch morning & evg—2 very good Sermons from Mr Le[i]gh of Newcastle. With A.M.G. Long conversation at night with John, on his illness, confirmation &c. till 20 m. to 1.

14. Monday.

$\frac{1}{2}$ past 7 to 12— —Brothers R. & J. long with me. Read Bible &c. with A.M.G. & H.J.G. Read papers. Finished Vol. 1. of Heber. Read Thomas's Protest & Wilson's answer.[4] Finished setting the pamphlets & reports &c. to rights. Weather extremely wet still.

[1] Probably a servant's child.
[2] Untraced letters to Liverpool newspapers.
[3] S. *Bradford, *Discourse concerning Baptismal and Spiritual Regeneration* (1709).
[4] Josiah Thomas, *An Address . . . with a Protest*; and Daniel *Wilson, *A Defence of the Church Missionary Society*, against it; an acrid quarrel of ten years before.

15. Tuesday.

Read Bible &c. with my sisters—Heber—papers—Odyssey a little—Wilmot Horton's letter to Bp of Rochester.[1] Out—& with J.N.G. calling on Mr Rawson. Weather fine—John's being here affords some palliation to idleness, wh wd probably have existed without, had he been absent.

16. Wednesday.

Read Bible &c. with sisters—Heber—Algebra—papers—Wilmot Horton's Letter to Oxford University—& a little Odyssey. Heber can now get only a short time, as my Mother is reading the same vol. Unpacking for J.N.G.—Out—Heard from Gaskell. Cousins Stewart & Robert G. here—Bowls &c in Evg.

17. Thursday.

Heber—Algebra—Bible &c—paper—W. Horton's Appendix—Odyssey—wrote to T.G. Drew Anne in Chair—out with my Brothers. Read a Tract called Dialogues on Confirmation, of Bristol Ch. Tract Society.[2]

18. Friday.

Drew Anne in Chair—out with J.N.G. &c—Read Heber—papers with debates—finished Wilmot Horton—Algebra—no Bible with sisters today—spent some time in scheming & making an article to hold my watch.

19. Saturday.

With J.N.G.—went with him into town & saw him off for Leamington—brought back the gig—did jobs in town—tea with A.M.G. & a long conversation—could not get Heber—Read Bible with sisters, Quarterly's very able & excellent Article on Jews[3]—paper—Odyssey—did Algebra—wrote a note to T.G.

20. Sunday.

Read Mant on Regeneration & Conversion.[4] Ch morning & Evg. Mr Le[i]gh again preached an excellent sermon in morning—Weather very wet —read Bible—collected & wrote out opinions &c—Read Bp of Chester's Sermon before Soc[iety for the] Prop[agation of the] Gospel—& Report, with part of Appx.[5] With A.M.G.

---

[1] (Sir) R. J. W. *Horton (see 16 Apr. 30) prefixed a letter to the bp. of Rochester to his 'Protestant Securities suggested, in an Appeal to the Clerical Members of the University of Oxford' (1828); see next entry.

[2] (1827).

[3] xxxviii. 114–45 (July 1828), reviewing Peter Beer, *Geschichte, Lehren, und Meinungen der Juden* (Leipzig 1825).

[4] Richard *Mant, *Two Tracts, intended to convey correct notions of Regeneration and Conversion* (1817).

[5] C. J. *Blomfield on Matt. xxiv. 14, bound with the society's *Report* for 1826.

21. Monday.

Heber—Algebra—Odyssey—read papers—which were in arrear. Began a letter to Aunt E.—consultations about going to Oxford or remaining at home—Drew Anne in Chair. Examining a Catalogue of books & writing to T. Ogilvy about them, for Mr G., A.M.G. & self.

22. Tuesday.

Out—swimming dogs—gathering fruit, &c—with A.M.G.—wrote to Aunt E.—& to T.G. Read paper. Algebra—a good deal of work, but little fruit—Heber—Quarterly—Odyssey. It is now I believe nearly settled that I am to go to Oxford.

23. Wednesday.

——7. Read Heber. Algebra—went into town—did business there, called on Mr Moss & F. Matheson, read papers, wrote to Hallam & Handley, also a letter to Kaye on King's College—went over & dined with Eliza Ogilvy at her cottage, & spent the evg.[1] Returned to Lpool about nine. Today we hear Abp of Canterbury[2] is dead: & trust he is gone to peace & joy.

24. Thursday.

Read Propagation [of] Gospel Society (to wh I have become a subscriber) Report—Heber—the papers—Odyssey. Did Algebra Bathed—out gathering fruit—with R.G. in evg—getting boxes for packing &c—to go to Oxford.

25. Friday.

Heard from Doyle—wrote to T. Ogilvy—packed most of my books, Helen & Aunt J. folding for me. Read Bible &c. with sisters—Heber—papers—Odyssey—did Algebra—rain—out in evening. Letter from Tom—who thank God heartily for this good letter on his birthday is doing well.

26. Saturday.

Rain & thunder great part of day. Out: & called on the Rawsons. Read Bible with Valpy &c. with sisters—finished St Luke. Did Algebra—read Heber, papers, Odyssey—finished packing books &c. (3 large boxes) & nailing up—with A.M.G.—up late—heard of Bp of Chester's translation to London.[3]

27. Sunday.

J.N.G. returned from London—Finished Appx to Propagation [of] Gospel Society's Report—Ch morning & Evg—Mr Rawson & Mr Le[i]gh—out

---

[1] The Ogilvys lived at Poulton, just NW. of Birkenhead.
[2] Charles *Manners-Sutton, 1755–1828 (d. 21 July), abp. since 1805.
[3] *Blomfield's formal nomination to London was made on 15 August, when *Howley was translated thence to Canterbury.

with J.N.G.—Read Bible—Began Bp Wilson on the Lord's Supper;[1] wrote out opinions &c. on Baptism. J.N.G. with me at night. Late.

28. Monday.

Read the remainder (near the whole) of Wilson on the Sacrament, wh I like exceedingly. Read papers—wrote to the Albion[2]—& to Mr Rawson—conversation with H.J.G.—Out. Drew Anne in Chair—read Heber. Preparing to pack. Up late.

29. Tuesday.

Read Heber—Drew Anne in Chair—packed up my things & "cleared out" —went with John to Lpool & left by Aurora at 5. Travelled all night.

30. Wednesday.

Upset, 7 miles from Walsall[3] between 3 & 4 in the morning. The hedge, being very high & thick, supported the coach, & most providentially no one was hurt—Arrived at Birmingham at 6, & at Leamington soon after 9 —Found Tom stronger in stomach, thank God, than when he left Seaforth —out in gig & walking with him—read papers & part of "The Election", a comedy of Joanna Baillie's.[4] Wrote home faithfully.

31. Thursday.

Out—& in gig with T.G.—yesterday to Stoneleigh Abbey, today to Bagginton[5]—the country *most beautiful*. Much with T.G. A letter of mine on Kings College in Courier received today.[6] Read papers—& finished the Election—bad, I think, for many reasons—did Algebra.

August First.

Out—& drove with brother to Kenilworth—saw the magnificent ruins[7]— Heard from Pickering. Euclid—Algebra—Odyssey—read papers—& "The Second Marriage"[8]—poor indeed, I think. Heard Sumner was made Bp of Chester, for wh we shd I think be thankful.[9] Wrote to A.M.G.

2. Saturday.

Rain—out—went to Warwick in gig—saw the splendid castle, & vase, the

[1] An S.P.C.K. tract by Thomas *Wilson, 1663–1755.
[2] Untraced.
[3] i.e. some 16 miles NNW. of Birmingham.
[4] (1811).
[5] Chandos *Leigh's and Davenport Bromley's seats, on the Avon some 4 miles north of Leamington.
[6] *Liverpool Courier*, 30 July: a lush appeal for funds for the new London College.
[7] Kenilworth castle, 5 miles north of Warwick, twelfth and fourteenth centuries, famous from *Scott's novel.
[8] Comedy by Joanna *Baillie (1828?).
[9] J. B. *Sumner was formally nominated on 23 August.

armour, &c.[1] Walked back. Got a peep too at St Mary's Church. Walked back to Leamington—Odyssey—Algebra—Euclid—all a *little*. Forenoon taken up by deliberations about going to meet Mr Saunders.[2] Afternoon in part by getting memoranda & information from T.G. Read papers—& part of "Two Gentlemen of Verona" (+).

3. Sunday.

Rain—out with T.G. walking & in gig—Ch in morning—received Sacrament in the parish Ch—near 80 communicants. A Dr Breare[3] & the curate administered it. Read Bible—Wilks's Essay on Conversion[4]—& Society [for] Propagation of Gospel's Address for 1826. Marginal references, notes in Greek Testament &c. Note from A.M.G.

4. Monday.

Read papers—finished 2 Gentlemen of Verona—packed—walk with T.G.— left Leamington at half past 11—a pleasant ride to Oxford—arrived safely —put up at Angel[5]—met Mr Saunders—he examined me slightly—very kind to me—read papers at Angel. Bed early. Wrote a note to A.M.G.

5. Tuesday.

Euclid in morng—Meals at Angel—walking about, & at sundry places jobbing—wrote to T.G. & to R.G.—read papers—wrote some verses & worked Algebra at Saunders's rooms—read Odyssey—Newdigate Prize for this year[6]—out at night—met a woman & had a long conversation with her.[7] Up late. Bible as usual.

6. Wednesday.

Euclid—read papers—out—in bookshops &c—at night met the poor creature again, who is determined to go home—turned some Spectator into Latin & into Greek—finished Book 4 of Odyssey & read good part of book 5. reading at Saunders's rooms.

7. Thursday.

Euclid & Odyssey in morning—breakfasted at Angel & went by coach to

---

[1] Warwick castle, fourteenth and seventeenth centuries, included among other splendours a marble vase from Hadrian's villa at Tivoli. Cp. 23 Nov. 32.
[2] Augustus Page Saunders, 1801–78, one of *Gladstone's tutors at Christ Church; headmaster of Charterhouse 1832; dean of Peterborough 1853.
[3] William Thomas Bree, b. 1787?, rector of Allesley, 12 miles north of Warwick, 1808–63.
[4] S. C.* Wilks, *On the Signs of Conversion and Unconversion in Ministers of the Church* (1814).
[5] Coaching inn in the High, below University College.
[6] W. W. Tireman 'Trajan's Pillar'.
[7] See pp. xxix–xxx above.

Wheatley—thence to Cuddesden[1]—met Puller, old Etonian, who is reading here.[2] Saunders extremely kind—I am to lodge here for the present—worked at Mathematics. Read papers—out.

8. Friday.

Heard from T.G. & A.M.G. Out—fishing with Puller—a long day of Algebra & Trigonometry—papers—& a little Homer. As yet unsettled & fidgetty. Newton Don to be sold today.[3]

9. Saturday.

Sewing &c—Trigonometry—wrote to Mr G—read Odyssey—paper—went out fishing in afternoon. A large party—Gooch,[4] Phillimore,[5] Freemantle,[6] Kynaston,[7] Baring,[8] came down from Ch Ch to fish—day thereby in great measure consumed & cut up.

10. Sunday.

Church morning & afternoon. Bp[9] preached a powerful Sermon on Ps.130, 7. Taught at Sunday School before morng & after Eveng. Ch. Out, Finished Mr Craig's Reply—& read Bible, making references. Company increased. Still unsettled. Altogether a Sunday but little employed, & that little but ill.

11. Monday.

A good deal of Trigonometry, & some Algebra—read Odyssey & Horace, wh I am now beginning in Bentley.[10] Read papers. Out a little: but weather still rainy. Please God it must soon now settle. Unpacking books &c. arrived from Seaforth per canal. Read "Every Day Occurrences"[11]— Backgammon with Puller.

12. Tuesday.

Out fishing—& out—Trigonometry &c—read Odyssey, Horace, & a little

[1] Wheatley lies 6 miles east of Oxford; the bp's palace at Cuddesdon is 2 miles south of Wheatley. Saunders was acting as vicar in the village.

[2] Christopher William (Giles–) Puller, 1807–64; double first 1828; M.P. Hertfordshire from 1857.

[3] The place near Kelso, Berwickshire, of Sir Alexander Don, d. 1826; not in fact sold till 1845. (See *DNB* xv. 206.)

[4] Frederick Gooch, d. 1887, rector of Bagington from 1833.

[5] Probably (Sir) Robert Joseph *Phillimore, 1810–85; or perhaps his elder brother John George*, 1808–65, also a jurist.

[6] William Robert Fremantle, dean of Ripon 1876.

[7] Herbert *Kynaston, 1809–78, high master of St. Paul's School 1838–76.

[8] Charles Thomas *Baring, 1807–79, double first 1829; bp. of Gloucester 1856–61, and then of Durham.

[9] Charles *Lloyd, 1784–1829, bp. of Oxford from 1827 and inspirer of the Oxford movement.

[10] Edited both by the great Richard* and by Thomas *Bentley.

[11] Romantic novel, 2v. (1825).

of "Every Day Occurrences" (+). Algebra—Bible as usual—weather better, thank God: & promising to be fine.

13. Wednesday.

Rain, out little. Wrote to J.N.G. & to Hallam. Trigonometry—Odyssey—Herodotus—recapitulating those parts of what I have read which have any difficulties. Began today. Every Day Occurrences. Paper, Met Bode, a young Etonian,[1] who gave me some Eton news. Up ½ past 6. Read an Ode of Horace.

14.

Past 7. Trigonometry & questions in it. Herodotus—construed some to Saunders—Horace. Much rain. Out a good deal in Evg. Read paper—heard from A.M.G. Finished Every Day Occurrences—Bode & his brother[2] breakfasted with us.

15. Friday.

¼ past 7. Bad. Trigonometry—Herodotus—going through some parts & looking at the heads of the rest—out fishing—read Horace—& Part of Laurent's Introduction[3]—& paper—Out in Evg—Mr Lloyd, Bp's Brother, dined with us.[4]

16. Saturday.

20 m. past 6. Odyssey—about 430 verses. Questions in Trigonometry, wh require time & care as I have not regularly gone through the rules. Read paper—heard from home: a long letter from H.J.G. & very good—Horace—Fishing, & with Puller—Dined with the Bishop of Oxford—he seems a remarkably kind man. A family party. Prayers at night in his chapel.

17. Sunday.

Church & teaching in Sunday School morning & afternoon. Weather wet—little out. Heard from Hallam—read Bible, made references. Read Budd's Ch. Miss. sermon,[5] & part of Report, about Bp. Heber &c.—Heber's Hymns[6]—Burgess's Short Catechism[7]—& Gray's Serious Address.[8] Wrote up my list of books read—wh. is humiliating.[9] "Redeem thy misspent moments

---

[1] John Ernest *Bode, 1816–74, don.
[2] Another, and still younger, s. of William Bode of Marylebone.
[3] P. E. *Laurent's Introduction to his recent translation of Herodotus.
[4] Edward Lloyd, d. 1850, priest.
[5] Henry *Budd was a constant preacher for the Church Missionary Society.
[6] Reginald *Heber and others, *Hymns written and adapted to the Weekly Church Service of the Year* (1827).
[7] In Bp. Thomas *Burgess, *First Principles of Christian Knowledge* (1804).
[8] Robert *Gray, *A Serious Address to Seceders and Sectarists* (1812).
[9] Add MS 44719 ff. 188–9.

past ". Not up till near 8—Bishop of Oxford preached ably on " For many are called, but few are chosen ".[1]

18. Monday.

Horace—Herodotus—Trigonometry—busy with a question which could not be brought to right—Walk to Wheatley &c. with Puller. Wrote to A.M.G. & to Doyle. Read paper.

19. Tuesday.

½ past 6. Writing out Trigonometry expressions, Theorems &c. read Herodotus—Horace—read paper—finished Laurent's Preface. Out. Walk in Evening with Saunders & Puller to Garsington.[2] Construing Herodotus with Saunders.

20. Wednesday.

10 m. before 7. Read Odyssey—Horace—newspapers several—wrote a long letter to Gaskell—& one to Albion about Methodists[3]—walk to Wheatley with Puller—wrote out Trigonometry Rules & questions &c. [Working on] Preliminaries to Conic Sections in Evg.

21. Thursday.

Out—in Evg walk to Garsington with Puller. Not up till 7. Odyssey— Herodotus—Conic Sections—& questions in decimals—Horace—read papers—Isaac Walton's Angler. Conic Sections Propositions begun today. Marginal ref's to Bible, a few, usually now at night. Heard from home.

22. Friday.

Spent early part of day at Herodotus—did some with Mr S. Out fishing with Puller—read Horace—Read Conic Sections—read papers—Algebra— Read papers.

23. Saturday.

7. Read Odyssey—Conic Sections—[worked on] Conic Sections & Herodotus with Saunders. Out with him & Puller—read papers & Isaac Walton— Horace—(about an Ode, or little more, each evening)—wrote to Farr—Mr Vesey[4] & Mr Williams[5] of Ch Ch, & Mr Newman of Oriel,[6] dined here. Draughts at night.

---

[1] Matt. xxii. 14.
[2] One and a half miles west of Cuddesdon, and 5 miles ESE. of Oxford.
[3] Untraced.
[4] Daniel Veysie, 1799–1866, censor 1828–33; proctor 1831; priest at Daventry 1833.
[5] John Williams, 1798?–1873, student 1816–42; vicar of Spelsbury, Oxfordshire, 1841.
[6] For John Henry *Newman, 1801–90, anglican divine and Roman cardinal, see his *Apologia* (1864).

24. Sunday.

¼ past 7 nearly. Church Morning & Afternoon—School morning & after-
noon—a long walk alone, & short one with them—read Bible—Leslie's
Method with Deists (+) & Craig—Wrote a very long letter to H.J.G. on
Baptism.

25. Monday.

Conic Sections—little Algebra—Odyssey—Horace—a little Herodotus—
papers—Isaac Walton—wrote to T.G.—a long walk with Puller, 8 miles
probably—out besides a little—Weather beautiful.

26. Tuesday.

Conic Sections—Herodotus (finished Euterpe[1])—a little Algebra—Horace
—Isaac Walton—papers—Conic Sections & Herodotus with Saunders. Out
—after dinner walked into Oxford, & did shop business there. Lost my way
miserably.

27. Wednesday.

Tired & late last night—late this morning—Conic Sections—Odyssey—
papers—Horace—Isaac Walton—wrote to Pickering—Out—& out fishing.
Conic Sections with Saunders.

28. Thursday.

Out—in Evg a 10 mile walk (or so) to Nuneham.[2] Heard from home—& a
batch of newspapers—read them—Conic Sections—Algebra—Odyssey—
turned a little Spectator [into Latin]—read Horace—part of a pamphlet on
Indian Ch Establishment.[3]

29. Friday.

Odyssey—Horace—Conic Sections—looked over & then wrote out without
book an Analysis of Clio[4]—read papers—heard from Hallam—finished Mr
Shepherd's pamphlet—walk with Puller—wrote notes to H.J.G. & Jones.

30. Saturday.

Out—in afternoon, walked nearly to Newington,[5] partly with Puller—read
paper—Isaac Walton—Horace—Odyssey (finished Vol. 1.)—finished Conic

---

[1] Book ii of Herodotus' *History*; the nine books were long named after the muses.
Notes scattered in Add MS 44719, ff. 16–87.
[2] The Harcourt family had a palace on the Thames at Nuneham Courtenay, some 4
miles SW. of Cuddesdon.
[3] Henry Shepherd 'On the inefficiency of the ecclesiastical establishment of India'
(1827, 2 ed. 1829) recommended the appointment of a second anglican bp. east of the
Cape.
[4] Herodotus, book i.
[5] Four miles south of Cuddesdon.

Sections—writing Analysis of Herodotus & Odyssey—Phillimore dined with us.

31. Sunday.

Church & school morning & afternoon—walks between services & before dinner—Read Bible, Craig, Gray's Dialogue between Churchman & Methodist—Sikes's First Dialogue—& Gibson's Caution agst Enthusiasm.[1] Heard from Doyle.

September First—Monday.

Read papers—a little Odyssey—Horace—Looking over Conic Sections again—worked at Analysis of Odyssey—writing out from Conic Sections & Algebra—read Isaac Walton—out—& a good walk in Evening—moved again for a day or two.

2. Tuesday.

A basket of fruit from home—letter from A.M.G., R.G., & J.N.G. read Odyssey—finished Analysis to B.14 inclusive—read papers & Isaac Walton —Began Wood's Mechanics[2]—read Horace—walked to Oxford after dinner.

3. Wednesday.

Early part of day at Odyssey—read B.15—Isaac Walton—papers—heard from Hagart & T.G.—wrote to T.G. & a long letter to Hallam—giraffe[3] & walk with Puller—Rev. A. Short[4] & Baring came down—Horace—Wood's Mechanics—Questions—translated a little Herodotus.

4. Thursday.

Heard from A.M.G. & H.J.G.—also from [C.A.] Wood—a batch of papers— wrote to C. Hagart & a letter (of introduction) to Jabat. Walked into Oxford with it after dinner—Read another book of Odyssey—Horace—papers— Isaac Walton (Finished his portion)—worked at Wood's Mechanics.

5. Friday.

Moved back.—Out—& fishing with Puller—a guest came in Evg. Read a book of Odyssey—& did Analysis—a little Translation of Herodotus— Wood's Mechanics—Horace—Isaac Walton—papers—(the guest Mr Rowlandson,[5] a relation of S.)

[1] Three S.P.C.K. tracts.
[2] James *Wood, dean of Ely, *The Principles of Mechanics* (1796), a standard textbook.
[3] An early piano: see p. xiv above.
[4] Augustus *Short, 1802–83, student of Christ Church 1820–36; 1st bp. of Adelaide 1847–82.
[5] Possibly Edward Rowlandson, 1803?–64, priest; fellow of Queen's College Oxford 1826–9.

6. Saturday.

Read about the same rate of Odyssey—Horace—Compleat Angler—& worked at questions from Wood's Mechanics. Read paper. Out fishing. Giraffe. Rev. J. Ley[1]—Gooch—Freemantle—two Pages[2]—came down to dine &c. Draughts in Evg.

7. Sunday.

Ch. morning & afternoon—[Sunday] School morning & afternoon—walk between services, & before dinner—people here—read Record—Craig—Leslie—Sikes. In Evg, Bible with many refs—time much broken up. Bp preached an excellent sermon, in my poor opinion.

8. Monday.

Read, same rate—Wood—and Horace. A very bad day—Saunders sent for by express to come to his mother ill, at Brighton.[3] He went immediately, in great agitation—Giraffe—went over in afternoon with Puller to Cowley[4] to a sort of feast given by Rev. J. Ley. S. was to have been there. Only 5 in all. Walk back in the dark. Wandering &c.

9. Tuesday.

Wrote to A.M.G. & to Doyle—read paper—finished Compleat Angler. Read another book of Odyssey—Wood's Mechanics—and began Œdipus Coloneus, part of wh I have read before. Long walk, most of it with Puller.

10. Wednesday.

Read paper—began Paley's Natural Theology.[5] Read more Odyssey than usual—Wood—Œdipus Coloneus. Heard from T.G. & J.N.G. Read Scholarship Questions &c. Walk with Puller.

11. Thursday.

Read Odyssey & work'd at it the greater part of day—i.e. day's labour—read Œdipus Coloneus—Paley's Natural Theology—wrote to G. North[6]—translated Herodotus. Giraffe—walk with Puller & alone—Wood's Mechanics. Draughts.

[1] Jacob Ley, 1804?–81, student of Christ Church 1822–59, vicar of Staverton, Northamptonshire, from 1858.
[2] Charles William, 1806?–73, student of Christ Church from 1823, and William Emanuel, 1808?–68, physician; ss. of William Page, headmaster of Westminster 1814, d. 1819.
[3] His mother, widow of Robert Saunders of Lewisham, d. that day at Brighton.
[4] Cowley, then a village 3 miles west of Cuddesdon, now the main manufacturing suburb of south-eastern Oxford.
[5] By W. *Paley (1802).
[6] Perhaps a younger s. of John North, Liverpool gentleman, whose eldest s. Thomas was up with *Gladstone at Oxford.

12. Friday.

Paper—worked much at Odyssey & finished the reading it & made analysis —wrote to R.G.—Wood's Mechanics—walk with Puller—Herodotus Translation—Oedipus Coloneus—Paley's Natural Theology.

13. Saturday.

Weather rough—walk little—giraffe—draughts—did near 60 Greek verses in forenoon &c. Read Oedipus Coloneus (a larger portion)—Paley's Natural Theology—Council of Ten on Bp. Marsh's Questions[1]—Herodotus & began re-translation—Odyssey Analysis & recapitulation finished[2]—Wood's Mechanics.

14. Sunday.

Church & school morning & afternoon. A Mr Bishop[3] preached. Walking &c with Puller. Read Bible & Greek Testament (little)—Craig's Sermons— Leslie—& Sikes's Third Dialogue.

15. Monday.

Read Œdipus Coloneus. papers—Herodotus (began book 3. +.) Wood's Mechanics—Paley's Natural Theology—Equations. Making list of words &c. to Herodotus. Giraffe & out with Puller.

16. Tuesday.

Saunders returned, very melancholy[4]—heard from J.N.G. poor Mr Conway died on Saturday—now I trust happy. Received & read papers—Paley— Herodotus—Œdipus Coloneus—(these with notes of hard passages, &c. as usual) & Wood's Mechanics—Equations a little—& writing out from Wood's Mechanics. Walk beyond Nuneham. It is a pleasure to me even to walk on the road which leads to Eton, as renewing associations of memory, & connection in imagination.[5]

17. Wednesday.

Giraffe & walk with Puller. read papers. Herodotus—Œdipus Coloneus— Paley—Wood's Mechanics & Questions on lever—worked time enough, but did little.

18. Thursday.

A bad day. Out with Puller & giraffe—many papers—read Œdipus Coloneus

---

[1] *Council of Ten*, a tory monthly, ii. 312–34 (1823), protesting at the eighty-seven questions levelled by Herbert *Marsh, 1757–1839, controversialist and scholar, bp. of Llandaff 1816, Peterborough 1819, at candidates for ordination.

[2] Add MS 44719, ff. 7–10.

[3] Probably John Bishop, d. 1838, minor canon of Gloucester.

[4] Cp. 8 Sep. 28.

[5] This sentence in Bassett, 1.

—Herodotus (finished Thalia[1])—Paley's Natural Theology—Wood's Mechanics & Questions.

19. Friday.

Walk with Puller & giraffe—paper—wrote to Mr G. read Paley—Œdipus Coloneus—Herodotus (began Melpomene[2]) Wood's Mechanics—& did a few equations.

20. Saturday.

Walk with Puller. Giraffe. read Paley, & papers. Worked at Herodotus, Œdipus Coloneus, Wood's Mechanics, & Bland.[3]

21. Sunday.

Church & School morning & aftn. Received Sacrament. Bp & Saunders officiating. Communicants 34. May we be participators indeed. Walk between services: & before dinner. Bible. Finished Natural Theology. read Walton's Life of Sanderson[4]—& Craig. Conv. on diff[eren?]t texts &c. in evg. with S. & P.

22. Monday.

Sweet weather—walk & giraffe. Acland (Sir T.D's son[5]) came down to work & dine here; liked what I saw.—read papers—worked at Œdipus Coloneus —Bland—Wood's Mechanics—Greek Testament—Herodotus.

23. Tuesday.

Walk with Puller, as commonly, & giraffe. Sundry newspapers. Began Gray's Letters.[6] Worked at Herodotus—Œdipus Coloneus—Wood's Mechanics—& Bland: the latter much, but effected very little.

24. Wednesday.

read papers—wrote to J.N.G.—read Gray's Letters, wh though very clever I do not altogether like. Walked to Oxford & had haircut, got books &c. Work at Wood's Mechanics—Bland—with Saunders (as commonly) Sophocles Œdipus Coloneus—Herodotus—finished Melpomene, began Terpsichore (partly +).[7] Two sons of Ld. Amherst came.[8]

[1] Book iii of the *History*.
[2] Book iv.
[3] M. *Bland, *Algebraical Problems* (1812).
[4] Isaak *Walton's life of Robert *Sanderson, bp. of Lincoln (1678).
[5] (Sir) Thomas Dyke *Acland, 1809–98, 11th bart., agriculturalist, politician, and west country magnate; eldest s. of Sir T. D. *Acland, 1787–1871, philanthropist; lifelong friend of *Gladstone's; see Add MS 44092.
[6] *Letters* of Thomas *Gray the elegist (1814).
[7] Book v.
[8] William Pitt, 1805–86, later 2nd earl, and Frederick Campbell, 1807–29, ss. of William Pitt *Amherst, 1773–1857, 1st earl 1826, governor-general of India 1823–8.

25. Thursday.

Letter from Farr, with invitation. Wrote to him & declined. Acland & Hussey[1] came down. Walk with Puller & Acland to Great Milton.[2] Much interruption, of course, with a party. Giraffe—papers—Gray—Wood's Mechanics—Bland—Sophocles Œdipus Coloneus—& Herodotus Terpsichore. A bad day—up pretty early for once in morning.

26. Friday.

Papers—Gray's letters—Equations—Wood's Mechanics—Sophocles Œdipus Coloneus—& Herodotus. Walk with Puller, Giraffe & other games: Gooch, Ley, & Freemantle came to dine. Idle days, now I hope over.

27. Saturday.

Guests went, much to my regret, were we not here to work. Walk & giraffe with Puller. Heard from A.M.G.—papers—Wood's Mechanics—Bland—Gray's Letters—Sophocles Œdipus Coloneus—& Herodotus—a long day.

28. Sunday.

Church & School morning & afternoon: & received the Sacrament. An *excellent* sermon from Mr Pusey.[3] Out between services & before dinner—read Bible, Craig, Leslie—worked at texts &c. H. H. Dodgson[4] came. Much conv. with Puller.

29. Monday.

Saunders went—& Dodgson—Walk with Puller &c. Greek Testament—Sophocles Œdipus Coloneus—Herodotus[5]—Wood's Mechanics—Questions Bland—papers—Gray's Letters.

30. Tuesday.

Walk with Puller—giraffe—paper—wrote to A.M.G.—Herodotus—Sophocles Œdipus Coloneus—Wood's Mechanics, & $\alpha\nu\alpha\kappa\epsilon\phi\alpha\lambda\alpha\iota\omega\sigma\iota\varsigma$[6] thereof—Bland—& Questions in Mechanics—Gray's Letters.

October First. Wednesday.

Finished Œdipus Coloneus & finished my list of words &c. Some of it very fine. Giraffe & walk with Puller—Wood's Mechanics—Questions—$\alpha\nu\alpha\kappa\epsilon\phi$ (wh brings reperusal with it)—Bland—Herodotus. began Polymnia[7]—paper—wrote to Wood—Gray's Letters.

---

[1] Edward Hussey, 1807–94, Christ Church undergraduate; high sheriff of Sussex 1844.
[2] Two miles east of Cuddesdon.
[3] Edward Bouverie *Pusey, 1800–82, led the Oxford movement. See Add MS 44281.
[4] Hassard Hume Dodgson, b. 1804?, student of Christ Church 1822–33.
[5] Presumably book vi, Erato.
[6] Summary.   [7] Book vii.

2. Thursday.

Walk giraffe &c. with Puller. Gray's Letters—Heard from T.G., J.N.G. & Farr—Wood's Mechanics—αvακεφ—Questions—Bland's Praxis[1] & Herodotus—Behind still.

3. Friday.

Walked out part of way to Oxford with Puller—who left to go home, meo damno.[2] Wood's Mechanics—αvακεφ—Questions—Equations—Herodotus —finished Gray's Letters—wrote a note to Mr Hagart who is in Oxford.

4. Saturday.

A dirty morng—walked (after a little work) into Oxford. breakfasted with Mr & Mrs Hagart at Star—went to Ratcliffe,[3] Bodleian &c. With them & returned in afternoon to an early dinner. A long day's walking—14 to 15 m. I think. Paper—Gray's Life[4]—wrote to Mrs G.—Wood—αvακεφ—Bland— Herodotus.

5. Sunday.

Church & school morning & afternoon. Bp preached on Sabbath. Out—went to see the old Sanders's. Din'd with the Bishop & remained till half past nine nearly—read Bible, Leslie & Craig.

6. Monday.

Walk—read paper—Bp. came down & worked at Bland, catching me at it —Wood—αvακεφ—Bland—Gray's Life & Poems (+) & a longish day at Herodotus. finished Polyhymnia.

7. Tuesday.

Walk to Toot Baldon[5]—papers—letters from home, & from Pickering—Bp came down again—Gray's Poems & Notes—finished Wood. Worked at Herodotus (Urania[6])—Bland—αvακεφ. of Wood—Questions—.

8. Wednesday.

Out—began to pack books—paper—wrote to J.N.G.—read Gray—Bland —Woods αvακεφ—Questions—another pretty long day of Herodotus.

---

[1] The last quarter of *Bland's *Algebraical Problems* (1812), devoted to exercises on the text; cp. Add MS 44719, ff. 249–73.
[2] 'to my loss'.
[3] *Gibbs's Radcliffe Camera, then a museum, now part of the Bodleian Library.
[4] J. *Mitford, *Life of Thomas *Gray* (1814).
[5] Two and a half miles SW. of Cuddesdon, 5 miles SE. of Oxford.
[6] Book viii.

9. Thursday.

Walk short—packing—read paper—finished Gray's (English) Poems & Notes—worked at Bland—αvακεφ—Questions in Mechanics—& Herodotus —got into Polymnia—packing—made up my accounts.

10. Friday.

Packing—Questions in Algebra &c—reading Useful Knowledge Society's Treatise[1]—& a little Herodotus—paper—went into Oxford—called on Short—got put into rooms[2]—met the Todds at Angel—tea with them— spent Evg in conversation with Todd mi.[3] Wrote to Selwyn. Slept in Ch Ch.

11. Saturday.

Appeared in Chapel in cap & gown—about shopping &c. Breakfasted with Acland—Wrote home—& to G. North—called on Biscoe, Saunders, & Veysey who is to be my Tutor. Fell asleep over my Herodotus.

12. Sunday.

In great measure destitute of books—read Bible & Craig—wrote out texts —Chapel morng & aftn—at St Mary's in afternoon. At Staniforth's rooms at lunch & in Evg to wine & dine him, but did not suit me.

13. Monday.

Read a little Herodotus—worked at Bland—wrote to Hallam, & to Gaskell —Wine with Puller in Evg—a very pleasant party. Sat with Egerton[4] some time. Out.

14. Tuesday.

A day spent chiefly *in expecting to be turned out*—at length migrated from Horner's[5] to Kenyon's[6] rooms—Out—Bland—& began Thucydides—had my first Lecture with Short jun.[7] Began Macintosh's Vindiciae Gallicae.[8]

15. Wednesday.

Moved again into Chaplain's Quadrangle—rooms wh I believe I am to

[1] Probably [T. F. *Ellis] Outlines of general history, part i (1828).
[2] See 14, 15 Oct. 28.
[3] James Frederick Todd, 1808–63, vicar of Liskeard, Cornwall, from 1839, s. of a London merchant; had an elder brother Horatio, d. 1868, rector of Occold, Suffolk, from 1845.
[4] Thomas Egerton, of Tatton.
[5] Thomas Strangways Fortescue Horner, 1808?–43, of Mells, Somerset.
[6] Edward Kenyon, 1810–94, 2nd s. of 2nd Lord Kenyon; landowner.
[7] i.e. Augustus,* see 3 Sept. 28 n; his senior was Thomas Vowler,* 1790–1872; student 1809; double first 1812; tutor 1816–29; rector of St. George's, Bloomsbury, 1834–41; bp. of Sodor and Man, 1841–6, St. Asaph, 1847–70.
[8] (Sir) James *Mackintosh's whig defence of the French revolution (April 1791).

keep.[1] Very dirty indeed, but I suppose very fair first rooms. Idle day. Out. Bland & a little Thucydides.

16. Thursday.

Read some Thucydides & had Lecture in it. Out. & seeing about rooms &c. Heard from Selwyn. Worked at Bland &c, & looked a little at Introduction to Differential Calculus. My last week I may reckon as vacation.

17. Friday.

Read a little Boucharlât[2]—wrote a long letter to T.G.—read part of "Friendship in Fashion"[3]—read paper—a long day of unpacking books, china, glass &c. In Evg wine at Baring's rooms—met Paget,[4] Puller, Glynne,[5] Mordaunt,[6] Acland, Sneyd,[7] Duncombe,[8] Cholmondeley,[9] Egerton,—afterwards coffee at Pagets—a very pleasant Evg.

18. Saturday.

Workpeople &c. about me: & unpacking—these things afford excuse to my laziness—heard from T.G. & from Biscoe that I am to be his pupil, for wh I ought to be thankful. Call from a Mr M'Kenzie.[10] Read a *little* Herodotus & a great deal of Otway—Venice Preserved I think magnificent.[11] Wine with Glynne—met chiefly as before—with the addition of Anstice[12]—Weather favourable to R.G.[13]

19. Sunday.

Chapel & St Mary's morning & Evg. Out a little with Skinner—breakfast with Kynaston—heard from home—prepared for & had Divinity Lecture in St John with Biscoe—Bible. Finished Craig, read Barrow on infidelity[14]— also Arminian Skeleton.[15]

---

[1] This quadrangle stood to the SE. of the cloisters, where Meadow Buildings now are. Photograph in H. L. Thompson, *H. G. *Liddell* (1899), at 16.

[2] Probably J. L. Boucharlat, *Mort d'Abel* (tr. from Salomon Gessner), and *Sacrifice d'Abraham* (both 1827).

[3] Comedy by T. *Otway (1678).

[4] Edward James Paget, 1811?–69, student of Christ Church 1828–42; rector of Smithland, Leicester, 1841–58.

[5] Sir Stephen Richard *Glynne, 1810–74, 9th bart. of Hawarden 1815, later *Gladstone's brother-in-law.

[6] (Sir) John Mordaunt, 1808–45, 9th bart. 1823, M.P. for Warwickshire from 1835. At Christ Church like all the others. Cp. 15 June 39.

[7] Walter Sneyd, 1810?–88; of Keele Hall, Staffordshire; priest.

[8] Adolphus Duncombe, 1809–30, 4th s. of 2nd Lord Feversham.

[9] Hugh Cholmondeley, 1811–87; Welsh county M.P. 1840–8; 2nd Lord Delamere 1855.

[10] Charles Mackenzie, 1806?–88, of Pembroke College; founder of City of London College; canon of St. Paul's from 1852.

[11] Tragedy by *Otway.

[12] Joseph *Anstice, 1808–36, professor of classics at King's College London 1831–5.

[13] Robertson Gladstone was to visit America.

[14] Perhaps W. *Barrow, *Familiar Sermons* (1819), i. 101.

[15] W. *Huntington, *The Arminian Skeleton; or, the Arminian dissected and anatomized* (1787), a violent anti-calvinist book.

20. Monday.

Read part of "Caius Marius".[1] Dined with a Pembroke man named M'Kenzie—read Differential Calculus & worked at Bland. Lecture at 11—& again at 7 p.m.—an hour & half in Evg—read a little Herodotus. Out in a boat &c.

21. Tuesday.

Finished Caius Marius. heard from A.M.G. & Gaskell—wrote somewhat long letters to each. Thucydides & Lecture—Bland Differential Calculus—a little Herodotus. walk with Puller, & out a good deal, my rooms in confusion, & the walls being today distempered. odour *not good*.

22. Wednesday.

Began "Orphan".[1] Unpacked & put away contents of a large box from Wilmslow. Bland—& a good deal of time at Differential Calculus—Math. Lecture. a little Herodotus. Wine at Sneyds—met nearly same party. Out. Coffee with Staniforth.

[1] Tragedies by *Otway.

[VOLUME IV][1]

Private. Oct. 1828–Ap. 1830.

πρώτιστος ἀμαρτωλων.[2]

W.E. Gladstone
Ch Ch.

(*No 4*)

1829[3]

Society for Promoting Christian Knowledge	1.1	+ 1.1.
Society for Propagating Gospel. – – – – – – –	1.1	+ 1.1.
_____ Church Missionary – – – – – – – – –	1.1	
_____ Mariner's Church – – – – – – – – –	1.1	
_____ Church Building & Enlarging – – – –	1.1	
_____ Conversion of Jews – – – – – – – – –	1.1	
_____ National School – – – – – – – – – – –	1.1	
_____ Slave Conversion		
Liverpool Infirmary		

Charge for W.D[igges]	1.10
Sacraments £1 Collections 10s.	1.10

Opp to Eggs.
Jan 27.   9d.
Feb. 6 11d.[4]

Ideas[5]
subj.   obj.

Ideas.

sens.perc.   *refl.*

modif sens perc.)   (pure refl.

Feb. 15.

Not to eat more than one dish at any dessert except [illegible].[6]
Exclude from conversation devil, defile, 'whoring rant', 'infernal'.[6]

[1] Lambeth MS 1418. 32 ff.
[2] 'The very first of sinners'. Cp. 15 Nov., 29 Dec. 29.
[3] Notes of charitable subscriptions follow.
[4] These three lines in pencil.
[5] These rudimentary notes on theory of knowledge are jotted down at right angles to the rest.
[6] These sentences heavily deleted.

Ch Ch—Oct–November. 1828.

23. Thursday.

Wrote to Hallam—out with Hill,[1] & jobbing.—preparation & Lecture in Thucydides—attended Prof. Cardwell's[2] first Lecture on Romans in 2nd Century. Finished Orphan—Bland & Differential Calculus. Began Clinton's Introduction &c.[3]

24. Friday.

Began "Soldier's Fortune"[4]—out—wine with Paget, & nearly the old party. Read Differential Calculus & had Lecture—questions—Bland too. & had a Juvenal Lecture—partial preparation—Whist in evg (at Hill's)—a little Herodotus.

25. Saturday.

Paper: Finished Soldier's Fortune. Wrote a long English Theme—worked at Bland—did a little Herodotus—called on Rogers, out with him & had him at my rooms in Evg—unpacked a large box of wine—went to hear music at Magdalen. Wrote over Greek verses for Tutor.

26. Sunday.

Chapel morng & aftn. St Mary's morng—Rogers breakfasted with me—out with him—Divinity Lecture & preparing for it—read Testament & made notes—read St John's Sermons, & Huntington[5]—& Valpy's commentary.

27. Monday.

Differential Calculus & questions—Drew a table of numbers & powers. Bland—a little Herodotus—also Thucydides—began Atheist[6]—read paper —worked at Bible quotations—Mathematics Lecture morng & Evg. Parr came to see me—Dined with him at Angel—out—called on Mr Ratcliffe.[7]

28. Tuesday.

Thucydides & Lecture—Cardwell's Lecture—heard from home—finished Atheist. Otway is as mean in principle, in his plays, as great in talent. Out with Puller. Bland—Clinton—a little Herodotus.

---

[1] Edward Hill, b. 1810?, student of Christ Church 1827–50, canon of St. Albans from 1872.
[2] Edward *Cardwell, 1787–1861, Camden professor of ancient history 1826; principal of St. Alban Hall 1831.
[3] H. F. *Clinton, *Fasti Hellenici*, a chronology of ancient Greek history (1827).
[4] *Otway.
[5] *Arminian Skeleton*.
[6] *Otway.
[7] Perhaps James Radcliffe, d. 1836, at Christ Church 1807–11; headmaster of Kirkham grammar school, near Preston, from 1816.

29. Wednesday.

Thucydides—Clinton—Public Lecture in Diff. Calc.—reading it & Questions—private Lecture in Evg—wine with Beach[1]—walk—wrote to Farr—wrote out from Diff. Calc. Bland.

30. Thursday.

Thucydides & Lecture—Cardwell's Lecture—out—call'd on Skinner—Bland—Juvenal—read papers—Corsaire![2]—part of Harriette Wilson[3]—wrote home.

31. Friday.

Read Juvenal all the morning—(save that I now read a few verses of Greek Testament the first thing)—finished Clinton's Introduction—Bland—questions Diff. Calculus—table of powers—out with Skinner—began Bacchae.[4] Dined at Oriel with Tucker[5]—wine & tea with him afterwards.

Saturday November First.

A great day—Latin speech in Hall &c. called on Bernard & several more at Oriel. Out. read a little Thucydides & Bacchae—Bland—Rape of the Lock. Attended Cardwell's Lecture &c.

Sunday Nov. 2.

Read Bible—[Greek] Testament—Barrow—St John's Sermons—Arminian Skeleton—commentary to Testament &c. Wrote notes & texts. Lecture in St John. Out. Part of evening at Staniforth's rooms—had wine. Quiet but query. Heard Mr Short preach very ably on Corruption.

3. Monday.

Papers—wrote home—Diff. Calc—Math. Lecture—walk with Anstice—wine with him—afterwards with Tobin—read Bacchae—Thucydides—Bland—quotations to Bible & Gk Testament.

4. Tuesday.

Thucydides—heard from home—Lecture in Thucydides—& at Cardwell's Lecture. Out with Rogers, &c. Bland—Bacchae—Pope—Wine at Pusey's[6]—Skinner had tea & sat with me afterwards.

---

[1] Michael Hicks Hicks-Beach, 1809–54, 8th bart. 1834.
[2] *Byron on Aegean piracy (1814).
[3] *Memoirs of Harriette *Wilson, written by Herself* (1825), adventures of a regency courtesan.
[4] Euripides.
[5] Benjamin Wadham Tucker, Eton and Oriel; read for bar; retired to Cornwall.
[6] William Bouverie Pusey, 1810–88, a brother of E.B*.; Eton and Oriel; rector of Langley near Maidstone from 1842.

5. Wednesday.

Breakfasted out, with Hill. paper—wrote to J.N.G. & to Gaskell. Drew up a scheme of reading! Thucydides—Bacchae—Clinton—translating Thucydides—out. Made some calls.

6. Thursday.

Thucydides & Lecture—Prof. Cardwell's Lecture—Gooch called on me—out with Skinner—read a good deal of Thucydides.

7. Friday.

Juvenal & Diff Calc. Finished Juvenal. Lecture in Calculus—in Juvenal—& Prof. Cardwell's Lecture—out—read Greek Theatre[1]—Gifford's Introduction[2]—Oppidan No 1[3]—did some verses for my theme—Anstice with me in Evg, & Tobin. Breakfast with Gooch.

8. Saturday.

Theme—Gifford—Greek Theatre—G.T.—out with Rogers—&c—read Oppidan—paper—Bacchae—Thucydides—did Translation from both. Little of all & a bad day.

9. Sunday.

Chapel & St Mary's, morng & aftn. Mr Burton of Ch: Ch:[4] preached two particularly able sermons. Out—Anstice sat with me. Gk. Test. Lecture & preparation—notes—read St John. Mosheim's Sketch of Ch in Cent. 18[5]—Arminian Skeleton—Bible.

10. Monday.

Breakfasted at Courtenay's.[6] Gk. T. Notes—Diff. Calc. & Lecture. Out. In the Schools hearing exams for 4 hours or more with Anstice. Read pt of Othello (+) Gk. Th. —a little Bacchae, & do. of Thucydides. Translated some Thucydides.

11. Tuesday.

Out. heard from Hallam: from home. Wrote home. heard Puller's examina-

---

[1] P. W. Buckham, *The Theatre of the Greeks*, subsequently rewritten by J. W. *Donaldson (1825, 1827).

[2] William *Gifford introduced his translation of Juvenal's *Satires* (1802) with a brief autobiography, a life of Juvenal, and 'An Essay on the Roman Satirists'.

[3] Ephemeral successor to *Eton Miscellany* (October 1828).

[4] Edward *Burton, 1794–1836, regius professor of divinity 1829.

[5] J. L. Mosheim, tr. A. *Maclaine, *Ecclesiastical History* (1765), vi. 1–44 (last chapter).

[6] William Reginald *Courtenay, 1807–88, lately elected to All Souls; 11th earl of Devon from 1859 ('the good earl'); Peelite and philanthropist; chancellor of duchy of Lancaster 1866–7.

tion nearly through.—Thucydides—Bacchae—Gk. Theatre—finished Othello—translating sundries—Blackstone[1] sat with me, a very bad day.

12. Wednesday.

G.T.—Bacchae—D. Calc. Lecture—& private Lect. in Evg. Wine with Tancred[2]—out with Anstice—Gifford on Roman Satirists—& a good deal at Thucydides, at wh I am slow.

13. Thursday.

G.T.—Thucyd—Heard from Farr—Breakft with Moncrieff[3]—Thucyd. Lect—Giffords Introd. to Pers[ius][4]—paper—walk—Gk Theatre—Bacchae —translating—Calculus Questions.

14. Friday.

G.T.—Gk. Theatre. Diff. Calculus—Lecture in it—reperusing Juvenal— Bacchae—Gifford's Juvenal—paper—began a Letter to R.G.—translating—walk—Anstice sat with me part of evg—heard from Gaskell.

15. Saturday.

G.T. Gk. Theatre. Heard from Mr Turner & wrote to him. R.G's birthday— God bless him—finished a long letter to him & stupid—did an En[glish] Theme—read Bacchae. breakfast with Hill. Wine with Tancred after Hall. Walk with Puller, who is out of the Schools. Wine after Tancred's at Hanbury's[5] in St Mary Hall—who had kindly invited me—I was introduced to him by Moncreiff on Thursday. A new party—hearers apparently of Mr Bulteel[6] at St Ebbes.

Mr Q.	Have you heard Mr Bulteel yet?
W.E.G.	No Sir I have not.
Mr Q.	Miss B[enne]ll wd recommend him to you.
W.E.G.	Yes Sir she did.
Mr Q.	You do not attend his Church then?
W.E.G.	No Sir. It seems to me right to attend our own Church.
Mr Q.	Then you go to hear University Sermon?
W.E.G.	Yes Sir; it seems to me right to do so.
Mr Q.	You will go & hear Dr B[arne]s[7] tomorrow?
W.E.G.	Yes Sir.

[1] William Seymour Blackstone, 1809–81, gs. of the lawyer; conservative M.P. for Wallingford 1832–52.
[2] (Sir) Thomas Selby Tancred, 1808–80, 7th bart. 1844.
[3] (Sir) Henry Wellwood *Moncreiff, 1809–83, then at New College; 10th bart. 1851; minister of St. Cuthbert's, Edinburgh, from 1852; moderator of the Free Church 1869.
[4] William *Gifford, Satires of . . . Persius translated (1821).
[5] Alfred Hanbury, 1807?–59, vicar of Wickhambrook, Suffolk, from 1855.
[6] Henry Bellenden* Bulteel, 1800?–66, curate of St. Ebbe's, Oxford, from 1826 till the bp. revoked his license to preach, 1831; joined Plymouth brethren.
[7] Frederick Barnes, b. 1781?, sub-dean of Christ Church.

Mr Q.   Do you feel edified & instructed?

W.E.G.   I feel in my duty; & I think there is much to be gathered: I have heard 3 sermons from wh it appeard to me a great deal was to be gathered.

Mr Q.   Who were the preachers?

W.E.G.   Dr W[hatel]y[1] & Mr B[urto]n. (Here I forgot one. Mr Sh[or]t).

Mr Q.   Dr W[hatel]y is considered a very clever man, one of the cleverest men here, a very clever man.

W.E.G.   Yes Sir a man of an original mode of thinking.

Mr Q.   I should like you to come & hear Mr Bulteel, & will at any time find you a seat.

W.E.G.   Thank you Sir, you are very kind.

Mr Q.   Come & hear him once & judge for yourself.

W.E.G.   You are very good Sir, I daresay I shall have opportunities.

Mr Q.   Unless I am disappointed in your name, I think you would like him.

W.E.G.   In my name, Sir?

Mr Q.   Yes, Sir, in the name of your family & principles.

W.E.G.   Pray Sir, what time do Mr Bulteel's services begin and end?

Mr Q.   The morning at eleven, & ends soon after one.

W.E.G.   I have Univ. Sermon to attend, & a Divinity Lecture at one.

Mr Q.   Now should not you feel justified in missing that, if you are not obliged to attend.

W.E.G.   No Sir I am not obliged to attend but I should not wish to miss it.

Mr Q.   Put in the balance what you wd get there & what you wd get at St Ebbes.

W.E.G.   I believe I should get a good deal there.

Mr Q.   In the afternoon service is at 3.

W.E.G.   We have Chapel at four, which precludes my attendance then.

Mr Q.   Oh I am very sorry. I hope you can come at some time & I shall be happy to get you a seat.

W.E.G.   You are very kind Sir, & I hope for an opportunity when my Lectures do not interfere.

Sunday Nov. 16.

Chapel & Sermon morng & aftn. out little. Lecture & preparation for it. Bible—wrote out texts &c—read Barrow, St John, Valpy's Commentary. Breakfast with Hill—Tea with Anstice, & a conv. of 3 hours with him by which I was much delighted & I hope instructed too.

Monday 17.

G.T. Gk. Theatre. Notes & Quotations to Bible—Long conv. with old Mrs Halbert[2]—Diff. Calculus—Lecture—Bacchae—paper—wrote part of a

---

[1] Richard *Whately, 1787–1863, principal of St. Alban Hall 1825; abp. of Dublin 1831.
[2] Mrs. Albutt; the 'old egg-woman' in Morley, i. 54. Perhaps Rachel Jones's mother; see Add MS 44719, f. 110 v.

letter to A.M.G.—Thucydides—translating some of him—out—at Book sale—call'd on Hanbury & Pusey.

Tuesday 18.

Heard from T.G. & Doyle—Thucydides—Lecture in ditto—heard Sir S. Glynne examined[1]—Bacchae—G.T.—Gk. Theatre—working at T.G's books, dusting &c.—out—papers—finished letter to A.M.G. Began Andria[2] —doing translation.

Wednesday 19.

G.T. Gk Theatre—paper—Diff. Calculus—Lecture—much unpacking books, cleaning &c. Out with Rogers—read Thucydides—T.G. arrived in Evg—had tea with Gooch—a ruinously spent day.

Thursday 20.

Thucydides all the morng—& G.T.—my Brother breakfasted with me— saw him off at 9. Thucydides—& Lecture—read Bacchae—& Andria— papers—Miscellany Calculations[3]—out with Rogers—wine with Seymour.

21. Friday.

Terence—worked a good deal at Equations—Differential Calculus Lecture —& in Andria—Wrote to Selwyn. Papers. did some verses. Wine with Neale.[4] Out:—with Puller &c.

22. Saturday.

G.T.—Bacchae—Theme & verses—wrote a letter to T.G.—Thucydides— out—worked at packing books &c—breakfast with Hill. Wine with Buller at Oriel[5]—Equations—Made up accts.

23. Sunday.

Chapel & St Mary's morng & aftn—heard a Mr Blackstone[6] preach a most excellent sermon—& Dr Whately. Out—reading Bible & Testament—Lecture & prep—read Barrow, Mant, St John, & Arminian Skeleton—Sacred Poetry.

24. Monday.

Gk. T.—Quotations to Bible & Testament. D. Calculus questions &c. & equations. Thucydides—part of Summary prefixed to Hobbes[7]—Bacchae

[1] He took a third in Greats.
[2] Terence.
[3] See 27 Jan. 29.
[4] Edward Vansittart *Neale, 1810–92, of Oriel; Christian socialist.
[5] Antony Buller, 1809–81, rector of Tavy St. Mary, Devon, 1833–76.
[6] Frederick Charles Blackstone, b. 1795?, vicar of Heckfield, Hampshire, from 1824.
[7] Thomas *Hobbes, 1588–1679, philosopher, published his translation of Thucydides, 1629.

—heard from A.M.G. Wrote to J.N.G.—wrote over some things for Tutor
—translating Thucydides & Bacchae—read paper—walk with Anstice—
work at books.

25. Tuesday.

Gk T. all day till 2 (save talk with Mrs Halbert) at Thucydides—at
Glynne's—he went off—walk with Puller & Baring—dined with Skinner at
Balliol & wine with him—wrote to Doyle—worked at Books—Gk Theatre
—Potter[1]—Fell's Ex[hibition] Questions &c.[2]

26. Wednesday.

G.T. Gk. Theatre. Potter. Thucydides. D. Calculus &c. out shopping—
working at books—wrote a note to H.J.G., T.G. came, had tea & wine with
me, & sat till 12, talking on several things, at last on profession. Left me
then.

27. Thursday.

G.T. Thucydides & Lecture—Potter, & papers on those subjects—Pusey
called on me—worked at books—out with Skinner & he took wine with me
—read paper—wrote to Gaskell—read Bacchae, & Andria—Adam Rom.
Ant.[3]

28. Friday.

G.T.—Terence—finished Andria—& Lecture—Egerton sat with me—
finished packing the large box—called on Moncreiff & Hanbury; sat some
time with both. Out: read Thucydides a little, & Bacchae. Gk. Theatre &
worked at papers. Wine with Dean. Horace [de] Arte Poetica.

29.

Thucydides—a theme—Hall at two—out with Anstice—wrote to Pickering
—wine with Bernard—and with Hanbury—finished Bacchae—translating
Thucydides—G.T.—Potter.

30 Sunday.

Chapel &[4] Sermon morng & aftn—Out—lecture & reading for it. Bible—
book of texts—Barrow—Paley—Arminian Skeleton—St John's Sermons.
Heard from J.N.G.

---

[1] Abp. John *Potter, *Archaeologia Graeca* (1697–8).
[2] Old papers for a college prize founded by Dean John *Fell; the diarist won it next
year (29–30 Oct., 2 Nov. 29).
[3] Alexander *Adam, *Roman Antiquities* (1791).
[4] 'St Mary's' lightly erased.

December First. Monday.

G.T.—worked at T.G's books—out with Rogers—he had wine & tea with me—Potter—D. Calculus & book—Thucydides. Translating do—Wrote to my Mother—newspapers.

Decr. 2. Tuesday.

Thucydides the early part of the day, and Lecture. Finished repacking T.G's books. Out. Translating Thucydides, & working at papers. Read Potter, & began (+) Mitford.[1] G.T.

Decr 3. Wednesday.

Thucydides—G.T.—Equations—Differential Calculus. Questions—talk as usual with Mrs Halbert—out—Censor's speech. read Mitford—Lecture in Bacchae—work at boxes—Gk. Theatre—translating Thucydides & at papers.

Dec. 4. Thursday.

G.T. Mitford. visit from Mrs Halbert. finished box work—walk with Rogers wrote to Mrs G. Tea with Rogers. Thucydides—Terence—& classical papers—newspapers.

Dec. 5. Friday.

G.T. Thucydides & Terence. Lecture in both—heard from home & from Selwyn—wrote to Ingalton—read Mitford: tea with Hanbury. Scriptures & prayer afr.

Dec. 6. Sat.

Puller has got his double [first], at wh I rejoice greatly. He sat with me some time. Equations—Mitford—G.T.—Finished my Herodotus—out with Anstice—Lecture in Bacchae—censor's speech—wrote to T.G. Wine & tea with Cole.[2]

7. Sunday.

Chapel & St Mary's morng & aftn—out with Cole. Received the Sacrament; few, too few Communicants.—Barrow—Tomline—finished Arm. Skel. Finished St John Vol.1.—Gk T. Lecture & Preparation. Bible—Testament—Hymns—part of Walton's Hooker.[3]

8. Monday.

B[ible]. Mitford. Heard from A.M.G. Accts &c. Out. Wine with Puller—

---

[1] William *Mitford, *History of Greece*, ii (1790).
[2] Owen Blayney Cole, 1808–86, high sheriff of Co. Monaghan 1843; see Add MS 44137.
[3] Isaak *Walton's life of Richard *Hooker (1665).

after, with Moncreiff. Thucydides—papers—Bible notes. Newspaper—a murdered day.

9. Tuesday.

B[ible]. Mitford—Thucydides. Potter—Equations—D. Calculus. wrote to J.M.G. R[obertson]. got books ready & packed them to go to him. Wine with Neale. Pusey had tea with me. read Tomline. Out.

10. Wednesday.

B[ible]. Mitford—looking over &c. for Collections—a little Thucydides—& Adelphi.[1] D. Calculus. Out—jobbing. called on Skinner. At Mr Charrière's[2] in Evening. Hanbury, Moncreiff &c.

11. Thursday.

B[ible]. Mitford. Finished Vol.1. Finished Book 5. of Thucydides. worked at Chronology—also Calculus. Finished Adelphi—Out—paying Bills &c. & endeavouring to get things set straight. Wrote to A.M.G. took place for tomorrow night.

12. Friday.

B[ible]. Fasti Hellenici & Chronological Table. Collections at 9. in till 3½. Examined (not *grievously*) in Differential Calculus Herodotus Thucydides Odyssey Juvenal Bacchae & Terence. also put a bit of English into Latin. Wrote & delivered my letters for leave of departure—made payments—pack'd up. wine with Pusey—he had tea with me—wrote to Selwyn. left Oxford past 12 by Rocket—travelled all night.

13. Saturday.

At Birmingham by 8. Left it by Aurora. Egerton a fellow passenger—weather wonderfully mild & agreeable—arrived safely, thank God, at Seaforth between 10 & 11. Found Mother & T.G. much improved—but Dear Anne, I much fear, weakened.

14. Sunday.

Ch morng & aftn. Out with J.N.G. Bible & Hannah More's Essay on St Paul,[3] begun.

15. Monday.

Began reading St John's Gospel with A.M.G. & H.J.G. to which an hour a day is to be allotted, & from wh I hope to receive benefit. In Lpool with

[1] Terence.
[2] Just possibly Ernest Charrière, 1805–65?, French writer, translator of Gogol and Turgenev.
[3] *Essay on the Character and Practical Writings of St. Paul* (1815).

J.N.G. shopping. Read Christian Observer &c. &c.—Heber—paper—with A.M.G.

16. Tuesday.

Bible — up early — Mitford — Thucydides — Equations — Heber — paper walked into & out of Town with J.N.G. With A.M.G.

17. Wednesday.

In town—walked out—Bible—unpacking &c. a number of my Father's books—Heber—Equations—Thucydides.

18. Thursday.

Equation—Bible—Heber—Mitford—paper—called on Mr Rawson—with A.M.G. At Meeting in Lpool in evg, to form an Auxiliary Naval & Military Bible Society. Finished Vol 2 of Heber. Aunt moved. Heard from Wood.

19. Friday.

J.N.G. went to Ingestre.[1] Went to see Aunts. Walk with T.G. Bible—began Heber Vol.3. papers. Equations & copying them out. Wrote to Hallam. Mitford. Backgammon with T.G.

20. Saturday.

Made up Accounts. & wrote up Diary. much rain—out. Equation &c—re-wrote letter to Hallam—Mitford—papers—Heber. Bib. & Commentary—wrote on Baptism.[2] Backgammon with T.G.

21. Sunday.

Ch mg & aftn. School aftn. Bible &c. wrote on Baptism. Out. Read H. More on St Paul, & began Grimshaw's Life of Legh Richmond.[3] Finlay dined with us.

22. Monday.

Bible—Equations. Heber (finished his portion of the tour). papers—out—saw Aunts &c. Heard from J.M.G. R[obertson]. wrote a very long letter to Ed:s Merc.[4] Sat with A.M.G.

---

[1] Ingestre Hall, near Stafford, restored Elizabethan seat of the earls of Talbot. Henry John Chetwynd-Talbot, 1803–68, viscount Ingestre 1826, 3rd earl Talbot of Hensol 1849, 18th earl of Shrewsbury 1856, served in navy 1817–37—he commanded *Philomel* at Navarino and brought home the dispatch.
[2] Add MS 44719, ff. 126–86, includes *Gladstone's reflexions on baptism in 1828–30.
[3] T. S. *Grimshawe, *Memoir of Legh *Richmond* (1828).
[4] The *Liverpool Mercury* did not publish it.

23. Tuesday.

Mr Hargreaves[1] here to proceed with A.M.G's portrait. Bible—paper—Equations—Heber—Out—Mitford—Copied a long letter—rode into town with T.G. &c.

24. Wednesday.

Dear Anne's birthday—(26th) & may God bless her—Bible—Equations—Heber—romping at night—papers—heard from Doyle—J.N.G. returned. &c. &c.

25. Christmas Day.

Church & Holy Sacrament. Bible. Moss called. (near 60 communicants) read Life of L. Richmond & Heber—walk with J.N.G. Festivities.

26. Friday.

Equations—Mitford—Heber—Bible—Arithmetic &c. with H.J.G. (as on Wednesday). Walked to town & back with J.N.G.—papers—backgammon.

27. Saturday.

Equations—Mitford. Heber—Bible—Arithmetic &c with H.J.G. Walk—papers—backgammon—&c. &c. Made out my estimate of expenses for 1829.

28 Sunday.

Church & school morng & aftn. out with Brothers. Read Bible—Legh Richmond's Life—& More on St Paul. Heard from Gaskell.

29 Monday.

This day by God's mercy I close my 19th year. Would that in looking back I could discern any decided features of improvement. Would that I did not on the other hand see many grievous crimes, many unlawful fears & defections. Should I most blame[2] myself for these, or bless God for his infinite mercies? May those mercies provided for us relieve me: & may a melancholy retrospect of the past bring forth good fruits in prayer & watchfulness for[3] the future. Amen, for Christ's sake.—I have been brought in contact with many individuals previously new to me—from some I hope to derive great benefit. Some whom I had known have been called to their account. O may my day of birth bring to my mind the consideration of my day of death—& may it become habitual & abiding.

Equations—a good deal of Heber—with A.M.G.—out—working at books

---

[1] Thomas *Hargreaves, 1775–1846, Liverpool miniaturist.
[2] Instead of 'grieve'.   [3] Instead of '& prayer'.

Anne Mackenzie Gladstone, 1828

for Mr G.—Aunts din'd here—play & backgammon with T.G. in Evening—Bible &c.

Tuesday. 30.

Equations—Heber—papers—wrote over part of letter to Egerton Smith. Rode to Lpool Mossley Hill & Uncle Murray's. Arithmetic with H.J.G. Chess with T. Finlay who dined here. Bible as usual.

Dec. 31. Wednesday.

Papers—finished Bp Heber's book with Appx &c. Equations—arithmetic with H.J.G. Out with J.N.G.—Bible. T.G. began Chess with me—with A.M.G.

Thus ends the old year. Praise be to Him who gave it, & pardon to us who have abused it.

A. D. 1 8 2 9.

January—Seaforth.

Thursday. 1.

Equations—Mitford—Began 2nd Series of Tales of a Grandfather[1]—Bible with A.M.G.—made an Estimate—a little copying—out with J.N.G. colds prevalent—worked most of day at the books—papers. & Chess with J.N.G.

Friday. 2.

Bad cold. Equations. Tales of a Grandfather. Chess—Arithmetic with H.J.G. Bible—rode into Lpool, & did business there—&c. Wrote to Gaskell. papers.

Saturday 3.

Cold continuing. Bible—Equations—Arithmetic with H.J.G.—out—Chess —papers—finished V.I of "Tales of a Grandfather". Accounts. Missionary Register &c. &c.

Sunday 4.

Ch morng & aftn. No [Sunday] school, on account of cold. read Bible—a sermon of Bp's[2]—Mr G. read another—out with T.G. & J.N.G. read a good deal of Legh Richmond. At Aunts. Missionary Register &c.

Monday 5.

Copied—Bible—Equations—Tales of a Grandfather Vol 2. Walked into & out of Lpool with J.N.G. Wrote over &c. my long letter to Egerton Smith & delivered it. At Aunts.

Tuesday 6.

Out. At Aunts—Bible—with A.M.G.—worked at a long butcher's Bill— wrote to R.G.—read "Tales of a Grandfather"—wrote a little on Baptism —Chess with J.N.G.—went to see poor T. Parr,[3] dying of a consumption— (at A.M.G's request, I am bound to add).

Wednesday.

Bible—A.M.G. & H.J.G.—Tales of a Grandfather. finished vol 2nd.

[1] *Scott, 3v. (1828).
[2] J. B. *Sumner.
[3] Thomas Parr, Liverpool painter and glass stainer.

Algebra. Walked into & out of Town with J.N.G. Wrote an anonymous note to Mr Brooks[1] on Christian Knowledge matters. Newspapers.

Thursday 8.

Bible with A.M.G. & H.J.G. Walked into town to Christian Knowledge meeting. Tales of a Grandfather—Mitford—wrote on Baptism—papers. &c. &c. Journal defective as usual in vacations.

9. Friday.

Thucydides—Tales of a Grandfather—Bible & commentary as usual—out with J.N.G.—wrote on Baptism—read a sermon to A.M.G.—papers—heard from Gaskell—Arithmetic with H.J.G.

10. Saturday.

Mitford—Tales of a Grandfather—Bible &c as usual—out with J.N.G.—called on Mrs Conway—wrote on Baptism a good deal—Arithmetic with J.N.G.—papers—settled my accounts.

11. Sunday.

Church & school morng & aftn—out—read a good deal of Legh Richmond to finish him—read Bible—& More on St Paul.

12. Monday.

Bible with A.M.G. & H.J.G. Tales of a Grandfather—Mitford—newspapers —Out—at Aunts &c. &c. Saw Mr Rawson & T. Parr.

13. Tuesday.

Went in to consecration of St Martin's—& heard Bp preach an excellent sermon on "it is good for us to be here".[2] In town afterwards—papers—finished Tales of a Grandfather—at Aunts. Miss Moss married.[3] Dined at Uncle R's.

14. Wednesday.

Went in to the Confirmation & after some waiting & difficulty got in & just managed to see H.J.G. confirmed. The scene was very interesting but order destroyed by the immense number. Called on T. Moss—walked out—papers. &c. &c. A conv. with H.J.G. at night.

[1] Jonathan Brooks, 1775–1855, rector of Liverpool 1829; archdeacon 1848.
[2] Luke ix. 33.
[3] Margaret, eldest da. of John Moss of Otterspool, m. Walker Ferrand, 1780–1835, of Harden Grange near Bingley-in-Airedale; M.P. for Tralee 1830–2. She d. 1846.

15. Thursday.

Packed. set things in order—dined early—finished V.1. of More on St Paul
—Finished St John with sisters. Bid goodbye & left Lpool by Aurora at 5.

16. Friday.

A rather cold journey but thank God arrived safe. Got to Oxford about 6.
Had tea & unpacked—sat with Anstice & Hill.

17. Saturday.

in chapel as usual—saw Saunders & Biscoe—Doyle who has just come up a
good deal with me, also Gaskell, come for matriculation, whom I am very
glad indeed to meet again. Sat talking with them most of the day—wrote
home, to J.N.G. Sent things away &c. Doyle & Hill had wine with me.

18. Sunday.

Chapel & St Mary's morng & aftn—Mr Cramer[1] & Mr Girdlestone[2]—the
latter I thought very good. read Bible—had convs with Doyle & Gaskell—
read Burrows[3]—dined at the Bishops—met Mr Lyall,[4] Mr Buckley,[5] &
Howley[6] there. J.N.G's birthday, whom may God bless & prosper.

19. Monday.

heard from J.N.G. Finished Burrows—read Mitford—with Hill—out with
Doyle—Anstice, Doyle, & Hope[7] had wine with me—wrote up accounts &
journal—algebra (fruitless)—&c. &c.

20. Tuesday.

Bible as yesterday. began Burton on Metres[8]—Mitford—Algebra—Still the
weather bitterly cold. Out. &c. &c. &c.

21. Wednesday.

Mathematics Lecture. Began & read some of Carr's Newton.[9] Mitford—
Romeo & Juliet—out with Doyle—Translating—wrote to Mrs G. finished
Burton on Gk Metres. Things now in order.

[1] John Antony *Cramer, 1793–1848, then a don at Christ Church; principal of New
Inn Hall 1831–47; regius professor of history from 1842; dean of Carlisle from 1844.
[2] Charles *Girdlestone, 1797–1881, then fellow of Balliol; rector of Alderley 1837–47
and of Kingswinford, Staffordshire, 1844–77; wrote biblical commentaries.
[3] Robert Burrows, dean of Cork, *Sermons* (1817).
[4] William Rowe *Lyall, 1788–1857, archdeacon of Colchester 1824, of Maidstone 1841,
dean of Canterbury 1845.
[5] Henry William Buckley, b. 1800?, fellow of Merton 1821–32.
[6] William Hamilton Howley, 1810–33, then at Christ Church; only s. of William *Howley, 1766–1848, bp. of London 1813, abp. of Canterbury 1828.
[7] James Robert *Hope(-Scott), 1812–73, Q.C. 1850, convert to Rome 1851; see Add
MSS 44214, 44440 ff. 43–59; contrast Morley, i. 55.
[8] [E. *Burton] 'Introduction to the Metres of the Greek Tragedians' (1814).
[9] John Carr ed. *The first three sections of *Newton's Principia* (1821).

22. *Thursday.*

Recapitulation of Thucydides for Lecture in wh we only began L.5. Began Antigone.[1] Successful in Equations at last. Out with Anstice. Read Romeo & Juliet. Translated. wrote out equations. Began Eunuchus.[2] Mitford.

23. *Friday.*

Very cold. out little. Doyle sat with me. Newton[3]—Notes—Lecture—Terence, & Lecture—Translation—Antigone—finished Romeo & Juliet (+) read Mitford. began Logic.

24. *Saturday.*

Logic Lecture. Sat with Rogers, raising doubts on his Iambics. Equations—Mitford (finished Vol 2)—Antigone—Rogers had wine with me—out. Classified my verses &c.

25. *Sunday.*

Chapel & St Mary's morning & afternoon. Mr James[4] & Mr Cramer. Walking with the Coles[5] twice. Gk T.—Notes—Lecture. Bible—Warton—Morehead's S.[6]—finished Waltons beautiful Life of Hooker.

26. *Monday.*

Reading Newton & Carr—Mathematical Lecture—paper—out with Doyle —wrote to Farr. Mitford—Antigone—began the Georgics with Rogers—spent a good deal of time in answering questions given me by my Tutor.

27. *Tuesday.*

G.T.—Logic—Lecture—a little Thucydides—& Lecture—Bland—Mitford —Sophocles—wrote a few Iambics—heard from J.N.G., Pickering, Selwyn —wrote to Pickering—settlement with Doyle & Rogers about Miscellany— a wretched day—but little of anything done.

28. *Wednesday.*

Antigone—Carr's Newton—Equations—Lecture—Gk Testament—out—wrote to A.M.G.—T.G. & J.N.G. arrived before 5. Dined with them at Angel. spent Evg in my room. had a long letter from H.J.G. writing memoranda to go to Town—Paper—Missionary report.

---

[1] Sophocles.

[2] Terence.

[3] (Sir) Isaac *Newton, *Principia Mathematica* (1687); probably in Carr's introductory version.

[4] William James, 1787–1861, fellow of Oriel 1810–37, rector of Bilton, Warwickshire, from 1853.

[5] Francis Burton Cole, d. 1833, O. B. Cole's brother; also at Christ Church; later of Lincoln's Inn.

[6] Robert Morehead, *Sermons* (1816).

18—I

29. Thursday.

Long service. Gk Testament—paper—Equations—Thucydides—Lecture in do—Puller sat with me—out with Hill—read Antigone—put into Gk some of the Translation—Terence—Georgics & Mitford with Rogers—wrote to Selwyn.

30. Friday.

Church morng & afternoon. Finished Eunuchus. Lecture—Equations—walk with Walter[1]—paper—turning into Iambics—Antigone—Gave a wine party—Puller, Baring, Sneyd, Anstice, Howley, Doyle, Rogers—tea with Anstice.

Saturday. 31.

Doyle went away—with him, calling &c in forenoon—Made up accounts—Logic & Lecture—read papers & Antigone—out a little with Pusey—Cole's & Rogers spent the evening with me: read Barrow on Sacrament &c.

Sunday. Feb. 1.

Chapel & St Mary's morng & aftn. Sacrament—six undergraduates—Ld Grimstone,[2] Baring, Harrison,[3] Anstice, a servitor,[4] & myself. A very excellent sermon from Mr Girdlestone. Walked twice, & sat with Coles. Began a letter to H.J.G. read Bible, & Gk Test. Began Rowland Hill's village Dialogues.[5]

Monday Feb. 2.

No Math Lect, Saunders being absent on account of the death of his sister. Read Rowland Hill—Long service—Antigone—conv. with Mrs Albutt. Shopping, buying prayer book &c. out—finished letter to H.J.G. Read Georgics—Equations—wine with Riddell[6]—after with Warter.[7]

3. Tuesday.

Village dialogues—Logic Lecture—heard from T.G.—Thucydides and Lecture—Equations—Antigone—had two little Jones's to me, questioning &c.[8]—out—Mitford—Georgics—wrote to T.G.—putting English into Iambics.

---

[1] W. K. *Hamilton.

[2] (Sir) James Walter Grimston, 1809–95, styled viscount Grimston 1815, conservative M.P. 1830–45, then 2nd earl Verulam.

[3] Benjamin *Harrison, 1808–87, archdeacon of Maidstone 1845, a reviser of Old Testament. See Add MS 44204.

[4] Christ Church was the last college to maintain this class of inferior undergraduates—there were still a dozen in 1829—who, instead of paying fees, waited in hall.

[5] Popular tracts (1810).

[6] Sir Walter Buchanan Riddell, 1810–92, judge; 10th bart. 1819.

[7] John Wood *Warter, 1806–78, vicar of West Tarring, Sussex, from 1834; son-in-law and editor of Robert *Southey.

[8] Children of Rachel Jones, who lived in the poorhouse.

4. Wednesday.

Village Dialogues. paper—wrote to Mr Turner—Mitford—Equations & writing them out—Newton—finished Antigone—translations—Georgics—walk—shopping—examined the two Jones's in Testament—wrote out some Logic for Williams.

5. Thursday.

Village Dialogues—wrote to Gaskell—Logic Lecture—Thucydides & Lecture—Equations & writing them out—Mitford & Georgics with Rogers—Translating Sophocles—Began Phormio[1]—went to Convocation House—heard Anti-Catholic petition discussed &c.—and Mr Peel's letter of resignation read.[2]

February 6. Friday.

Village Dialogues—finished Vol. 1.—heard from J.N.G. & wrote to him[3]—heard from Mr Craig. Began Head on Early Rising.[4] read Newton—Terence—and Thucydides. Lectures in Mathematics & in Terence. Out. Mitford & Georgics with Rogers. Read Parliament proceedings on opening session, long & interesting.[5]

7. Saturday.

Head—papers—wrote to Mr G—out with Cole. Logic & Lecture—Equations—Thucydides—Began 2nd Georgic with Rogers—Paley's Sermons.

8. Sunday.

Head—heard from Doyle—walking with the Coles—they also sat with me—and Seymer in Evening—Chapel & Sermon morng and aftn. Short in morng—most excellent. Girdlestone afternoon. Began compiling opinions on Baptism in another form & on a fresh plan. Wrote also concerning it. Read Moore on Baptism[6]—Bible—Barrow—May God vouchsafe to sanctify and direct all my few and poor studies.

9. Monday.

Had a most affectionate letter from H.J.G. but sad accounts of Anne. "Sad"!—Walk & much conv. with Cole, on such subjects as yesterday. Had

---

[1] Terence.
[2] *Stanhope and *Cardwell, Memoirs by . . . Sir Robert *Peel, i. 312–15. Government announced that day that a catholic relief bill was about to be brought in. (Sir) Robert *Peel (1788–1850, then home secretary and leader of the commons; 2nd bart. 1830; prime minister 1834–5, 1841–6) wrote to the vice-chancellor that he must therefore resign as M.P. for Oxford University. And see Morley, i. 53; and Add MS 44275.
[3] See ibid.
[4] H. E. Head, Observations on early rising and on early prayer (1828).
[5] NSH xx. 1–102, 5 February 1829, mainly on catholic relief.
[6] Thomas Moore, A Brief Discourse about Baptisme (1649)?

Adam Merton[1] talking to me &c. Newton—Equations & writing out—Mathematical Lecture—Thucydides—finished Head—Georgics & Mitford with Rogers—Translating, writing answers to questions. &c.

10. Tuesday.

Papers—Logic Lecture—Equations—Thucydides—Lecture in ditto—Old Wm Harris[2] with me. Out. Georgics and Mitford with Rogers. translating English into Greek—Ajax[3]—wine with Skinner. Gk. T.

11. Wednesday.

paper—Newton & writing out. Equation—Thucydides—Ajax—out—Georgics & Mitford with Rogers. wine with Childers—putting Thucydides into Greek.—Gk T.

12. Thursday.

Letter from Mr G. & alas a melancholy account of dear Anne.—Gk. T. Thucydides—Logic Lecture—read Short's pamphlet[4]—papers—Lecture in Thucydides—Equations—Ajax—Georgics & Mitford with Rogers—wrote to A.M.G. Terence. Out & jobbing.

13. Friday.

Gk. Testament. Terence—finished Phormio. Newton—Mathematical Lecture—out with Seymer—called on Nicoll, Buller, Pusey, Puller &c. prepared for & gave a wine party to Tancred, Hill, Kynaston, Nicoll, Buller, Pusey, Seymer—Georgics & Mitford with Rogers. Equation—translating—Thucydides—Ajax.

14. Saturday.

Gk. Testament. heard from J.N.G. & Gaskell. wine with Neale—out with Seymer—Logic & Divinity Lectures—Began Whately's Logic[5]—Thucydides—Equations—Georgics—wrote a few lines—paper—little of all, & a bad days work.

15. Sunday.

Chapel & Sermon morng & aftn—Mr Short & Mr Blackstone. went also to Mr Bulteels, with Seymer & both Coles. Heard between the three, a great deal of admirable matter.[6] Walk with Cole & Harrison—again with both

[1] Adam Morton, blind mat-maker, of St. Thomas's, west of St. Ebbe's; see Add MS 44719, f. 109.
[2] Of Friar Street, St. Ebbe's, then as now a working-class district, just west of Christ Church. [3] Sophocles.
[4] T. V. *Short, 'A Letter ... on the ... Public Examinations in the University ...' (1822, reprinted 1829).
[5] R. *Whately, Elements of Logic (1826).
[6] Cp. last entry on p. 207 above.

Coles—sat with them in Evg & had a sermon read—read Bible—part of Walton's Life of Donne—Morehead—worked at opinions on Baptism &c.

16. Monday.

Gk. Testament—papers—Equations & writing out—Newton—Mathematical Lecture—Bible quotations—Thucydides—Ajax—Mitford & Georgics with Rogers. Debates now steal time.[1] Out—called on Moncreiff, & others.

17. Tuesday.

Greek Testament—papers—letters from H.J.G. & from Farr. Whately—Logic Lecture—Thucydides & Lecture—calling—out—preparing dessert—wine-party—much of evening consumed—read some Ajax—Equations & writing out.

18. Wednesday.

Gk Testament. Equations—Newton—Mathematical Lecture—Thucydides—out—papers—wrote to H.J.G.—Georgics & Mitford with Rogers—Ajax—Dearest Anne alarmingly ill at night.[2]

19. Thursday.

Gk Testt. Thucydides. Logic Lecture—Thucydides Lecture. paper—equations—began Heauton Timorumenos.[3] Wine &c with Rogers—& conv. with Grice[4] &c. then on to Byron, 39 Articles &c. Thoughts for Lent Verses.

20. Friday.

Greek Testt. Heauton Timoroumenos. Responsionibus in Parviso per integrum tempus interfui.[5] Solaced during aftn with a little copy of Legend of Montrose.[6] Out. paper—Georgics & Mitford with Rogers—Equations & Questions—a little Ajax.

Thursday.[7]

At 20 m. to 3, A.M., our dearest sister Anne breathed her last without a struggle or a groan. Present. Father & Mother—Tom & Helen—Aunts E. & J. Mr Bickersteth—& Janet.[8]

---

[1] *NSH* xx. 103–344, 6–13 February 1829, almost entirely preoccupied with Irish and catholic questions.
[2] Last six words a later entry.   [3] Terence, 'The self-avenger'.
[4] Joseph Hill Grice, 1809?–67, Eton and Christ Church; priest at Upton-on-Severn.
[5] 'Was present throughout at Responsions in the Chamber': certificate of due attendance in the schools, a necessary preliminary to passing the examination (Add MS 44719, f. 111).
[6] *Scott.   [7] Later entries till 2 March.   [8] A maid?

Saturday 21 February.

Greek Testament—papers—between 8 & 9 got a letter from my Father, announcing the sad & unexpected decease of my beloved sister. Took place —called on the Dean—wrote notes to Biscoe—to Childers,[1] with whom I was engaged to breakfast, &c. Packed up things necessary, & left Oxford at two by Triumph. Travelled all night. At first much dismayed: but afterwards unable to *persuade* myself of the truth of the news.

22. Sunday.

Arrived in Liverpool between 11 & 12 by Magnet, & went down to Seaforth —found all in great grief, especially my dear Mother, but looking to the High and Mighty One for support. Saw the pale remains of dearest Anne, but felt in weeping over them, that my tears were entirely selfish. Blessed & praised be God's Holy Name for thus calling to Himself first from among us one who was so well prepared, so thoroughly refined, so weaned from earth, so ripe for Heaven. Out with H.J.G. Began Sumner's Apostolical Preaching.[2] Bible. Listened to the accounts given of Dearest Anne's deathbed scenes, with an interest which must be felt under such circumstances even by those whose feelings are as little tender and as much abstracted as my own.

23. Monday.

Sumner—papers. Wrote a long letter to Robertson—copied a letter—out with Helen. Dear Anne's remains still were open. I felt a wonderful apathy, considering how many opportunities I had enjoyed of conversation & intercourse with my dear deceased sister: of knowing her character: of estimating her powers of mind and her tenderness of heart and her numberless Christian graces; how unworthy I had been of the love, and the attention, with which the departed saint had honoured me, as well as others more worthy.

If this comparative apathy was the result of a *just* view of the case, it was well: if it arose from that estimate which Christianity teaches us to form of time and eternity, life and death, earth & heaven; and from—not a careless belief—but a deeprooted conviction that *she* was happy, and that *our* first & highest duty, after suffering the tribute of tears to be paid, was to seek what she had sought, and to honour her memory in following (by God's grace) her footsteps. But it was not so. It was from a torpor of mind & habitual selfishness, which she [who] is gone was freed from, & from which "Good Lord deliver us".

24. Tuesday.

paper—Sumner—out—copied a letter—made extracts on Baptism—John

[1] Charles Childers, 1806–96; anglican chaplain at Nice, 1843–84; canon of Gibraltar, 1884–8.

[2] [J. B. *Sumner] *Apostolical Preaching considered in an Examination of St Paul's Epistles* (1815).

arrived at night from Plymouth, anticipating even our hopes—at night he enjoyed the melancholy pleasure of weeping over Anne's cold remains.

25. Wednesday.

Sumner—papers—extracts—out. This day the remains of dearest Anne were inclosed in their last earthly house. The lead was soldered over the shell, and all placed in the outer coffin—which then remained on the bed where she breathed her last. Read burial service &c. to Mother.

Thursday 26.

Breakfast early—we were all now in regular mourning—then clad in mourning cloaks—about 10 m. past 10 we left Seaforth in the following order (I believe)—

Mutes.

Hearse.

1st Coach. Father, Tom, John, & myself.
2nd. Mr Rawson, Mr Jones, Mr Bickersteth, Dr M'Cartney.
3d. Uncles Murray, Thomas, Robert, David.
4th. Uncle Hugh—Cousins T. Ogilvy, T. Murray G., W. Goalen.[1]
5th. Cousins Steuart, Robert—Thomas G—Mr Grant.

Soon after 12 we heard the bell of St Andrew's, and the burial service was read by Mr Rawson. The coffin was placed in a vault in the Church, by my Grandmothers. Surely never could mourners receive the glorious consolations which that sublime service is intended to impart, with better or surer confidence.—The day was very rainy & seemed as we left home to suit our occupation. Sumner &c. Extracts.

27. Friday.

Sumner—papers—extracts. copying—made (with H.J.G.) an Inventory of dear Anne's books—out.

28. Saturday.

Sumner—papers—extracts on Baptism—much copying—out.

Sunday March 1.

Bible—Sumner—out. Extracts on Baptism—much copying—sermon read at night. Mr Rawson preached a Funeral Sermon in the morning. text "Enoch".[2] much admirable. I trust it might do good. Mr Fearon preached well in the afternoon. Sacrament—Mr G., J.N.G., H.J.G., Aunts &c. near 50 communicants.

[1] Walter Mitchell, s. of Thomas, Goalen; later clergyman at Laurencekirk, Co. Kincardine.
[2] Gen. v. 24.

Monday March 2.

Copying parts of T.G's recollections [of their sister]—finished Sumner—read papers—made up accounts—in Liverpool with J.N.G., paying Bills &c. wrote up journal since February 21—conv. with H.J.G. &c.

3. Tuesday.

Copied a long letter. wrote one to my Mother. papers—packing up—J.N.G. drove me into town & I set out for Oxford at 5 by the Aurora. Travelled all night.

4. Wednesday.

At Birmingham soon after 6. Oxonian gone. had to wait till half past nine —read paper—& Ch. Missionary Association report. read two tracts in coach—arrived about 20 m before 6.—could not get housed from having forgotten to give notice, till past 8—tea—letters—unpacking &c.—things in much confusion, from the presence of my subtenant.

5. Thursday.

Gk Testament—unpacking &c—out—Cole & Doyle sat with me—Rogers came to tea—Logic Lecture—Thucydides & Lecture—arranging all my letters from dear Anne & other papers. read Paley.—Labelled the letters & read a good many: it is delightful to dwell on what Tom beautifully calls "the sweetening recollections of that spirit which was but too pure for an impure world".

6. Friday.

Gk Testament. walk. wrote to J.N.G.—Quarterly Review—Terence— finished Heaut[ontimoroumenos] & began Hecyra.[1] Thucydides—Newton —Mathematical Lecture & Terence Lecture. Adam—& at night with Rogers—Horace's Odes.

7. Saturday.

Gk Testament. long walk with Cole. wrote to my Father. Theme on the mutability of human affairs. Thucydides—Horace's Odes—Equations— Whately & Logic Lecture—Dr. Walker—paper—made a list of divines to seek opinions from—read Quarterly on Sumner's Records of Creation.[2]

8. Sunday.

Walk after morning sermon with Harrison—Evg, with Moncreiff—Out mg & after sermon. but only mg chapel, being late, so read prayers alone. A good deal of conv. with Doyle at night & much on religious subjects. Baptism

[1] 'Mother-in-law', also by Terence.
[2] xvi. 37 (October 1816).

Extracts—Walton. finished life of Donne—Divinity Lecture. Quarterly Review. Progress of Infidelity,[1] very able—Paley's sermons on Spiritual influence[2] &c.

9. Monday.

Gk T. Horace. Began Hydrostatics.[3] Mathematical Lecture. Newton's Principia. Thucydides. Letter from home, pleasing. wrote part of a letter to Canning & read part of Quarterly Review on Ld Selkirk.[4] Juvenal with Rogers—Beloe's Herodotus.[5] Out. Puller (very kind) called on me—also Ward of Wadham[6]—called on Dr. M'Bride.[7] Answers on Gk Drama questions. little tho' much seeming.

10. Tuesday.

Letter from J.N.G. a most kind & excellent letter. wrote to Canning. Finished Quarterly on Ld Selkirk. Out. paper. called on Mrs Charriere, & Price[8] of Worcester. Juvenal with Rogers. Gk Testament. Thucydides & Lecture—Algebra &c. Horace—wrote a few lines. Logic Lecture.

11. Wednesday.

Gk. Testament—paper—called on Dr. M'Bride—out with Childers. read London Review[9] & Quarterly on Bp. Watson.[10] Vince Hydrostatics— Newton—Mathematical Lecture—Thucydides. Juvenal: little of any.

12. Thursday.

Gk Testament—Logic Lecture. Equations. Finished Thucydides. Began Hellenics.[11] Lecture [on] Thucydides—Cole sat with me. paper—out with Cole. Quarterly on Ice & Passage into Pacific.[12] Horace's Odes. Dined & sat with the Coles. Juvenal in Evg.

13. Friday.

Gk Testament. Hydrostatics. Math. Lecture. Terence Lecture. Hellenics. Horace. Juvenal. Gk. Theatre. Gk History &c. wrote to Hallam—paper—

[1] Perhaps xi. 144 (April 1814), reviewing C. Lacretelle, *Histoire de France*.
[2] R. *Lynam, ed. William *Paley, *Complete Works*, iv. 172–93, on 1 *Cor.* iii. 16.
[3] Samuel *Vince, *Principles of Hydrostatics* (1796), in James *Wood's Cambridge Course of Mathematics.
[4] xvi. 129 (October 1816), reviewing the 5th earl of *Selkirk's *British Fur Trade in North America* (1816).
[5] William *Beloe tr. *History of Herodotus* (1799).
[6] Edward Langton Ward, 1809?–81, rector of Blandworth, Hampshire, from 1834.
[7] John David *Macbride, 1778–1868, orientalist; principal of Magdalen Hall from 1813.
[8] Bonamy *Price, 1807–88, Drummond professor of political economy from 1868.
[9] First (February) number of a new quarterly.
[10] *Quarterly Review*, xviii. 229 (October 1817); on the life of R. *Watson.
[11] Xenophon.
[12] Probably xvi. 144 (October 1816), reviewing L. F. Maldonado, *Voyage de la Mer Atlantique à l'Océan Pacifique par . . . la Mer Glaciale* (1812). See 26 Mar. 29 n.

long walk with Harrison. My name put down for Scholarship: in going in I question whether I am right, as Short seems to dislike it, & my Tutor not much to like it.[1]

14. Sat.

Logic Lecture. Horace. Xenophon a little. Gk Testament. Paper. Out. Gooch & Price called on me. Juvenal with Rogers. Latin Theme & Verses. Part of London Review on Ch Reform.[2] Wrote to T.G. & to J.N.G. Worked at Gk Theatre & trying to get up a general smattering of History & Chronology.

15. Sunday.

Chapel & St Mary's morng & aftn. Mr Burton preached his 1st Bampton Lecture on Heresies in Apostolic age.[3] Walk with Coles & with Moncreiff, Seymer, & also Harrison, with me part of Evg. Bible. Testament Lecture—finished "Church Reform"—finished Walton's Lives—began Horae Paulinae[4] & Whish.[5] Wrote an anonymous sketch.

16. Monday.

Gk Testament. Adams—Chapel. Burton's Metres (cursory of course)—Scholarship Examn at 9. in till 12 putting English into Latin prose. In again at one & till 4 with English into Gk Iambics. Walked &c.—also after dinner. Doyle came to me in Evg. very little done.

17. Tuesday.

Gk. Testament. History &c. Scholarship Examn—9 to 12 Latin (Pliny) into English. 1 to 4 Roman History Questions—with which I got on very poorly indeed. Mr Crook's[6] Lecture in Evg. paper—heard from T.G. Gk History.

18. Wedn.

G.T. heard from J.N.G.—Chronology &c. English into Greek in morning—Greek History questions in Evg. 9 to 12 & 1 to 4. Walks—paper—London Review on Pollok[7]—Puller & Doyle sat with me—Horace's Odes at night.

19. Thursday.

Gk T. Gk Theatre. Chronology Metres &c in morng. 12 to ¼ before 2. Gk into

[1] Dean *Ireland's scholarship; see 16–21 Mar.
[2] i. 44–85 (February 1829).
[3] E. *Burton, *An Inquiry into the Heresies of the Apostolic Age*, lectures delivered on the endowment bequeathed in 1751 to the university of Oxford by John *Bampton, canon of Salisbury.
[4] W. *Paley (1790).
[5] M. R. Whish, 1792?–1852, prebendary of Salisbury; published several sermons.
[6] Perhaps Henry Simon Charles Crook, 1806?–84, B.A. from Lincoln 1828; vicar of Upavon, Wiltshire, 1840–70; inspector of schools 1860–70.
[7] i. 233–51 (February 1829), on Robert *Pollok's poem *The Course of Time* (1827).

Latin & English. 2 to 5 Critical Questions—walked after dinner—tried to begin Whately on St Paul[1] but did little—headach in Evening. Finished L4 of Horace Odes.

20. Friday.

Gk T. 9 to 12 Chorus into Alcaics. 1 to 4 an Essay English on Taste. heard from Hallam—began v.2 of Village Dialogues—walking with Rogers—& in Evg.—Sundries—Headachy.

21. Saturday.

Borrett of Magdalen[2] declared successful candidate. Out with Childers & with Harrison &c. About in forenoon looking out for the news. papers— heard from Canning—read Whately—& a good deal of Rowland Hill, v.2.

22. Sunday.

Chapel & St Mary's morng & aftn. Walked with Cole—aft[erwards] with Moncreiff. Bible—Whately's Essays[3]—Rowland Hill v.2—Extracts &c. on Baptism—Tea with Childers.

23. Monday.

Finished Rowland Hill v 2 & L.1 of Hellenics. Analysis [of] Mitford—wrote to Hallam—out with Harrison—Newton, Hydrostatics & Mathematical Lecture &c. Montgomery.[4] Sat with Doyle & Harrison & Rogers in Evg.

24. Tuesday.

Mitford—Whately—papers—Hellenics & Lecture—Mrs Albutt with me— heard from T.G. & H.J.G. wrote to H.J.G. read Montgomery—Walk with Cole—wine with Bernard, 1st accepted since my return—headachy—wrote a few lines. Sat with Doyle.

25. Wednesday.

Montgomery—Whately—Saints' day[5]—Hydrostatics—Newton—Mathematical Lecture—Quarterly Review. Moncreiff calld on me—walk with Doyle—wine with Pusey—went with Doyle & Hope to hear Rowland Hill.[6] Long conv. chiefly on religious subjects with Doyle till 12.

---

[1] R. *Whately, *Essays on some of the Difficulties in the writings of the Apostle Paul* (1828).
[2] Charles William Borrett, b. 1810?, fellow of Magdalen 1834; of Lincoln's Inn.
[3] *Letters on the Church by an Episcopalian* (1826). See *DNB* lx. 425.
[4] Probably Robert *Montgomery's notorious *Omnipresence of the Deity* (1828).
[5] Lady Day: i.e. long morning service.
[6] Rowland *Hill, 1744–1833, itinerant preacher; author of *Village Dialogues*; uncle of the general.

26. Thursday.

Finished Montgomery—Whately—papers—heard from J.N.G.—out with Cole—at Wheeler's[1] &c. finished Hellenics L 2, & had Lecture. Read Quarterly again on North Pole Voyages &c.[2] & fear I must give up the subject.[3] read Middleton.[4]

27. Friday.

Whately—Gk Testament—Turned Ps 137 [into Latin verse]. Hydrostatics & Lecture. Hecyra. Walk with Seymer. Record &c. Wine with Nicholl. Wrote a paper on Oxford—&c.

28. Saturday.

Gk Testament & Lecture. Whately—2 copies of Lent Verses. walk with Harrison—wine with Neale & Tancred—Quarterly on Parry & Weddell.[5] A Theme. Some Hecyra. Sat with Harrison—worked a little at Divinity in Evening.

29. Sunday.

Chapel & St Mary's morng & aftn. St Ebbe's—Mr Bulteel on "I know that my Redeemer liveth"[6] &c & on rejoining our relatives in heaven! It was suited well to my circumstances, and touching. Meadow with Cole—in aftn with Harrison—finished Whately & also Whish. Bible—read various sermons & made Extracts on Baptism & Spiritual influence—wrote on Baptism.

30. Monday.

Wrote to Farr—out with Childers—Hydrostatics &c. began to read St John for Collins—began Tusculan Disputations[7]—wine with Ward—& with Beach—talked to my Tutor about Latin prizes—read Carne [?] Quadragesimalia.[8] finished Hecyra—a long talk on religion with my old man.[9]

31. Tuesday.

Bible. Tusc. Quaest, Middleton Cicero. paper. did a kind of copy of Lent

[1] James Luff Wheeler, bootmaker.
[2] xxxvii. 523 (5 March 1828), on *Parry's attempt.
[3] 'Voyages of discovery to the Polar Regions' was the subject for the *Newdigate prize.
[4] Conyers *Middleton, *Cicero* (1741).
[5] xxxiv. 378 (September 1826).
[6] Job xix. 25, familiar as preface to burial service.
[7] Cicero, *Tusculanarum Quaestionum libri v*, moral philosophy. See 13 Apr. 29.
[8] Perhaps sermons by R. H. *Carne on Lenten observances (1810).
[9] William Harris, cottager in St. Ebbe's.

Verses. read Bp Butler's Charge[1]—Close's Sermon[2]—wrote to Mrs G. & to J.N.G. Called at various places. Harrison had tea with me. Made up monthly accounts.

April 1. Wednesday.

A wine party. Moncreiff Hanbury Coles Childers Skinner Ward—out—Cic Tusc. Quaest. Whately's Logic. heard from J.M. Gaskell. did some verses. Bible. with Saunders.

2. Th.

Bible. Breakfast with Seymer. paper. Whately. wrote over &c. Theme. corrected Lent verses. Whately—Analysis of Logic begun.—out with Harrison. Tupper[3] had wine with me—wrote to Pickering—Cic. Tusc. Quaest.—&c.

3. Fr.

Bible. Whately. Analysis. wrote over Lent verses. read out in Hall. Tusc. Quaest. Doyle walked, has wine & tea with me. Talk on religion a good deal, but not very direct. Letters from T.G. & H.J.G.—much misunderstanding: God grant it may be set to rights—wrote a long letter to him. paper.

4. Sat.

Greek Testament & Divinity Lecture. Whately. Analysis. read Arnold on Catholic Claims.[4] Out. wrote to Canning. Finished Tusculan Disputation 1 & read part of 2.

5. Sunday.

Bible &c. Mg chapel & communion—5 undergraduates. Ld Grimstone, Acland, Madan,[5] a servitor & myself. Chapel evg. St Marys mg & aft. Mr Ogilvie[6] in aftn—cd not hear him well, & fell asleep.[7] Walking with the Coles. Sat with them & Harrison for the Evening. Read Barrow—D. Wilson's Essay before Wilberforce[8]—Horae Paulinae—2 serm. of Shuttleworth[9]—Extracts on Baptism. Heard from J.N.G.

[1] Joseph *Butler, 'A Charge delivered to the Clergy at the Primary Visitation of the diocese of Durham in the year 1751'.
[2] Francis *Close, later dean of Carlisle, 'The Christian's Duty in the Present Crisis', preached at Cheltenham on 15 February on 1 Tim. ii. 1–2.
[3] Martin Farquhar *Tupper, 1810–89, author of *Proverbial Philosophy*; see Add MS 44336.
[4] T. *Arnold, 'The Christian Duty of conceding the Roman Catholic Claims' to political equality with protestants (1829).
[5] George Madan, b. 1808?, canon of Gloucester 1851.
[6] Charles Atmore *Ogilvie, 1793–1873, theologian; then fellow of Balliol; regius professor of pastoral theology from 1842.
[7] And see *Doyle, *Reminiscences*, 125–6.
[8] Daniel *Wilson prefaced an essay to William *Wilberforce's *Practical View of the prevailing religious system of Professed Christians, . . . contrasted with Real Christianity* (1797).
[9] From P. N. *Shuttleworth, warden of New College 1822, later bp. of Chichester, *Sermons on some of the leading principles of Christianity*, i (1827).

6. Monday.

Bible &c. Public Formularies on Baptism.[1] Extracts—a conv. with my old man W. Harris—walked with Seymer &c. Whately—& Abstract of Logic.[2] wrote to Selwyn—Tusc. Quaest—finished 2nd & began 3d—&c.

7. Tuesday.

Bible. Thank God, received a most kind & satisfactory letter from T.G.— Whately—finished my Abstract of Logic—Tusc. Quaest. finished 3, read 4, began 5. out with Harrison. papers—wrote to Mr G. &c.

8. Wed.

Bible. Horace. Began Wilberforce. Walk. sat with Doyle &c. finished Tusc. Quaest. *Roked* for information & tried to concoct rudiments. read Quarterly on Britton's Cathedral Antiquities[3]—Middleton's Cicero.

9. Thursd.

Bible. Wilberforce.—A Bold Stroke for a Wife (+)—out—occupied most of the day with Thucydides History, Vince's Hydrostatics & Carr's Newton —of wh I know little or nothing. Also with other matters for Collections.

10. Frid.

Xenophon Hellenics &c. Bible. Collections—examined in St John, Logic, Thucydides & Xenophon, Cicero, Sophocles, Horace, Mathematics—slightly —not at all in Terence. out between 3 & 4. read Record[4]—at Hanbury's. Harrison sat with me—heard from Wood—called on Mrs Charriere— talked with Biscoe on Latin Verse prize Poem—took place & packing &c. &c.

11. Saturday.

Finished Packing &c. Left Oxford after breakfast by Leamington coach & arrived about 3 p.m. found all as well as I had hoped—Mother much re- duced.—Out with H.J.G.—read papers—unpacked—accounts—read letters —Christian Observer.

12. Sunday.

Ch morng & aftn. Rector's[5] sermon seemed to me good. Out with T.G. & H.J.G.—Read Bible with H.J.G. (began Romans)—began Sumner's Sermons on the Festivals.[6] Notes to Gk Testament &c. &c.

[1] In the prayer book; see Add MS 44719, ff. 128–34.
[2] Ibid. ff. 106–7.
[3] xxxiv. 305 (September 1826), reviewing the first 10 vols. of J. *Britton, *Cathedral Antiquities and Life*, 14v. (1814–35).
[4] Anglican weekly.
[5] Robert Downes, 1795?–1859, vicar of Leamington Priors from 1826.
[6] J. B. *Sumner, *Sermons on the principal Festivals of the Christian Church; to which are added three Sermons on Good Friday* (1827).

13. Monday.

Began Æneid. (+) Bible with H.J.G. 10–11 a.m. referring to Simond's [?] It[1] & began Cicero at Tusculum[2]—papers—containing debates &c. Chess with H.J.G. Rode over to Baginton with T.G. Read various.

14. Tuesday.

Æneid—Bible 10–11. Cicero at Tusculum with Middletons Cicero. wrote to J.N.G. Rain. Gooch dined here. papers. Copied two letters. &c.

15. Wed.

Æneid. Bible with H.J.G. 10–11. Cicero at Tusculum with Middleton 11–1. Copied 3 or 4 letters. papers—memoir of Mr. Canning in Constable's Misc.[3] &c.—Out—alone & also with H.J.G. Notes to Gk Testament.

16. Thursd.

Æneid. Bible with H.J.G. 10–11. Out—with H.J.G. & alone. Read Quarterly on Elementary teaching (very able, I think) & part of Art. on Paley.[4] Cicero at Tusculum. verses & newspapers. Conv with T.G. on Ch Ch matters.

17. Good Friday.

Sumners 3 Sermons—Ch morng & aftn. Sacrament in morng—60 or 70 I think. sermon from Rector in aftn. Bible 10–11. Out—finished Quarterly on Paley—began on Ireland.[5] read papers.—heard from Dr Turner.

18. Saturday.

Virgil Æneid. Bible 10–11 with H.J.G. Out with H.J.G. Cicero at Tusculum —wh I take easy, bestowing a conven[ien]t time daily on it. papers— finished Quarterly on Ireland. Mr. Larkins arrived in Evg.

19. Easter Sunday.

Sacrament in morng: about same number of communicants. Rector preached in aftn. Out alone & with H.J.G. Bible 10–11. Read nothing else but Sumner's Sermons on Festivals wh I wish to finish.

20. Monday.

Virgil finished Æneid 3—reading superficial—a good deal of copying. Bible

---

[1] L. Simond, *A Tour in Italy and Sicily*, tr. (1826)?
[2] University Latin verse prize subject.
[3] Prefaced to *The General Registry for 1827* in *Constable's Miscellany of Original and Selected Publications in the various departments of Literature, Science, and the Arts.*
[4] xxxix. 99 (January 1829); and xxxviii. 305 (October 1828), reviewing W. *Paley's Works.*
[5] xxxviii. 535 (October 1828), a long article on Irish catholicism.

10–11. Out alone & with H.J.G. Cicero at Tusculum &c. newspapers. Began a Sketch of old England by a new England man.[1]

21. Tuesday.

Virgil Æneid. Bible 10–11. Cicero at Tusculum—trying to make some show or order in my chaos—out alone & with H.J.G.—Mr Larkins laid up—newspapers—Sketch of old England—copying—chess with H.J.G.—conv. with Mrs G & H.J.G. on West Indian matters &c. &c.

22. Wednesday.

Virgil Æneid. Bible 10–11. W.I. matters & many other such again. Out. Mr. Larkins better. Chess with H.J.G.—newspapers—"old England"—Cicero at Tusculum.

23. Thursday.

Anniversary of Grandmother's death.[2] Virgil Æneid. Bible 10–11. Wrote to J.N.G.—also to R.G. Chess with H.J.G. Out—finished "Old England". Began Granby.[3] Cicero at Tusculum. copied a letter. Came under Dr J[ones] for an ailing ear.

24. Friday.

Virgil Æneid. Cicero at Tusculum—a good deal.—Chess with H.J.G. Newspapers—Granby—out alone & with H.J.G. Saw Mr Larkins as usual. Bible 10–11.

25. Sat.

Virgil Æneid. Bible 10–11. Cicero at Tusculum—newspapers—Chess with H.J.G. Granby. Wrote to Gaskell—saw Mr Larkins—out with H.J.G. &c. Conv. with Mrs G.

26. Sunday.

Bible 10–11. Sumner's Sermons on the Festivals finished. Church morng & aftn. Mr Staunton,[4] a very young man preached an able sermon in aftn. Out. Headache & unwell.

27. Monday.

Bible 10–11. finished Romans with Mant. Attempted Verses. A day of sickness—with me unusual, & ought to be useful. Copied a letter & read a little Granby.

---

[1] By J. K. Paulding; published anonymously, 1822.
[2] His mother's mother, Anne Robertson, née Mackenzie.
[3] Novel by T. H. *Lister, 3v. (1826).
[4] William Staunton, 1806–60, Warwickshire gentleman; curate of Bishop's Tachbrook from 1852.

28. *Tuesday.*

Better thank God, & able to work a little at my Cicero at Tusculum—finished Granby. read newspapers &c—packed up. Extracts from Adult Baptismal Service—&c.

29. *Wednesday.*

Left Leamington about 12 & arrived in Oxford past 6.[1] I ought to be thankful for leaving all so well. I myself very nearly so, thank God. Papers. Wrote over &c. a good part of Cicero at Tusculum. read Herbert.[2] Unpacked &c.

30. *Thursday.*

Out with Cole & seeing Books at Wise's.[3] Record. read Wilberforce & began Rowland Hill V.3. wrote to Mrs G. & to J.N.G. Finished my Cicero at Tusculum. *cut him* down, & finished writing out the roughish copy. May God grant that such things may not engross my heart, for Our Saviour's sake. So ends April.

May First. Friday.

Wrote over the fair copy, made up & sent in my packet.[4] Out—Long chapel—at Univ. Sermon at Merton Chapel preached by Mr Dennison[5]—Record—Rowland Hill—reading & sorting letters of A.M.G.s—wrote to Bp of Calcutta—breakfast with Tancred.

2. *Saturday.*

Rowland Hill—out with Moncreiff—wrote to Wood—read Æneid L.1—sat with Cole—Doyle had tea & sat with me at night—called on Biscoe & Saunders. Short arranged with me to go in for the Craven.[6] Tomorrow if it please God, to receive the sacrament. read Bible.

3. *Sunday.*

Received the blessed Sacrament. Harrison—Anstice—Madan—I did not observe whether the servitor. Sermon morng & aftn. Mr. James in aftn I thought good. Read Bible—Barrow—G. Herbert—& finished Rowland Hill—a day of a discontented & morbid state of mind—but I trust one not so utterly dead as most, & a happy one if there has been vouchsafed any humiliation & sense of sin.

4. *Monday.*

Gk Testament. Chapel at 7. Doyle breakfasted with me—round meadows

---

[1] Cf. Morley, i. 53, where this journey is put on the next day.
[2] George *Herbert's poems (1633, etc.).
[3] John Wise, 1809?–77, Rugby and Wadham; vicar of Lillington, Warwickshire, 1833–74; or bookseller in St. Clements.   [4] Add MS 44720, ff. 218–22, on Cicero.
[5] Edward *Denison, 1801–54, dean of Merton 1827–33; bp. of Salisbury from 1837.
[6] University classical scholarship: see 5–9 May 29.

with him—& walk in aftn. Heard from & wrote to H.J.G. Gaskell came. read Gk. Theatre. Vince Hydrostatics. 2nd Book of Æneid. heard more about lectures—wrote a few lines. read Wilberforce.—Latin Pr[ize] Poems.

5. Tuesday.

Gk Testament. Breakfasted & sat with Gaskell. He had tea with me. round meadows with Doyle. out with Gaskell. read Æneid 3—Vince's Hydrostatics—accounts & paying Bills—Greek Theatre—Record—wine with Hanbury. Craven Scholarship I find [begins] tomorrow.

6. Wednesday.

Gk Testament. Gk. Theatre—Chronology &c. & history.—Scholarship examn—9–12 English into Latin. 1–4 a piece of Odyssey into Latin hexameters. Walk with Rogers before dinner—alone after it. Wilberforce—sundries.

7. Thursday.

Gk Testament. Left off my draught by way of experiment. Gk Theatre—chiefly getting a little Roman history & dates. Examn again—Shakespeare into Gk Iambics & Pliny into English & Gk, with notes—did not finish this latter. Walked in evg a good deal—altogether from 2 to 3 hours. Wine & tea with Gaskell. Acland there. read a little Ajax.[1]

8. Friday.

Gk. Testament. Greek Theatre & metres—a little Juvenal with Gaskell, & a little Sophocles. 9–12 Historical questions &c. 1–4 Andocides[2] into English, with notes. 8 or 9 mi. walk with Harrison & Childers in Evg (besides &cs) tea & sat with them & the Coles at night. read paper—got Hallam's Timbuctoo.[3]

9. Saturday.

9–1. Critical Questions. Thomas & Rogers declared victors in Evening[4]—in mg read metres & canons. With Doyle, who is to be sent down today[5]—out with Gaskell—He & Doyle had wine with me & tea—at Cole's rooms till late—bid Doyle goodbye—began a letter to Mr G. Talk on Athanasian creed &c.

[1] Sophocles.
[2] Attic orator.
[3] *Hallam's entry for the Cambridge prize poem of that year.
[4] John Thomas, 1811?–83, of Wadham; vicar of All Hallows, Barking, from 1852; canon of Canterbury from 1862. William Henry Johnson, 1810?–77, of Worcester, vicar of Witham, Lincolnshire, from 1835, was awarded a *Craven scholarship as well as Thomas and *Rogers.
[5] Only rusticated for a few days: see 14 May 29.

10. Sunday.

Breakfast with Gaskell. Divinity Lecture—out a little with Gask[ell]—
finished letter to Mr G. read religious meetings, Jerram (excellent)[1] & Soc.
Conv. Rep [2]—tea with Coles & Harrison—Chapel & St Mary's mg & aftn.
Kennington[3] in Evg—Mr Cramer & Mr Sibthorpe[4] very good.

11. Monday.

—paper—pamphlet on Convocation—out, walking, shopping &c. Pusey sat
with me. Heard a most gratifying account from my Tutor about the Scholarship, for wh thanks be to God. read Æneid 4—some Ajax—began Wood's
Optics,[5] & had Lecture in do—wine with Littledale—calling—Gk Testament—Conv. Soc. Report.

12. Tuesday.

Rhetoric—& Lecture. Sophocles—& Lecture—Virgil—Record—ordering
& preparing dessert & inviting—wine party to Gaskell Rogers Pusey Neale
Tancred Graham[6] Bernard Price Seymer—tea with Gaskell—out with him
& alone—Puller sat with me at nt. Gk. T.

13. Wed.

Out, with Gaskell, Seymer, & alone—went to see Puller—wine with
Moncreiff. Gk Testament—Virgil Æneid—Slave Conv. Soc. Rep—Wood's
Optics & Lecture—Sophocles Ajax. Began Livy.

14. Thursd.

Gk Testament. Rhetoric, & Lecture. Sophocles (Finished Ajax) & Lecture.
walk with Doyle (who has just returned) Virgil. Slave Conv Rept. Christian
Student (skimmingly).[7] dined at Angel & spent evg with Father, Mother &
H.J.G.—walk with H.J.G.—showed her my rooms.

15. Friday.

Gk. Testament after Morning Chapel. went to Angel—walked with H.J.G.
before breakfast & lionised afterwards—Bodleian, Theatre Ratcliffe &c.
&c. read Clissold—Record—Christian Student—they went about one—
Wood's Optics—& a little Virgil—Gaskell had wine with me—walked with
him—tea with him & conv. till midnight 12 with him Hope & Doyle on
religious subjects.

[1] C. *Jerram, *Conversations on Infant Baptism* (1819).
[2] Annual report of the society for the Conversion and Religious Instruction of the
Negro Slaves in the British West Indian Islands.
[3] Hamlet 2 miles south of Oxford.
[4] Richard Waldo *Sibthorp, 1792–1878, brother of M.P.; evangelical preacher; fellow
of Magdalen 1818–41; thereafter alternated between Roman and anglican churches.
[5] James *Wood, *Elements of Optics* (1799).
[6] William Graham, b. 1808?, of Southampton.
[7] By Edward *Bickersteth the evangelical (1829).

16. Sat.

Gk T. Record—Rhetoric—Lecture—& private Lect. with Biscoe—Theme & a few verses—long walk with Harrison—wine & tea with Gaskell—sums &c there—a little Virgil.

17. Sunday.

Chapel & St Mary's mg & aftn. Kennington after dinner—Mr Sibthorp very good indeed on the gift of the Spirit[1]—Seymer Childers &c there—tea & conv. with Childers afterwards. walked with Coles & Harrison—Gk T. & Lecture. "Christian Student" and Wilberforce.

18. Monday.

Christian Student—Wood's Optics—walk with Childers—Virgil & Sophocles —began Electra—Evg with Gaskell, part [with] Doyle & Hope. Mathematical Lecture. Very idle day.

19. Tuesday.

Rhetoric & Lecture—Sophocles & Lecture—round meadow with Seymer— out alone—wine with Gaskell—another long conv. with him—in wh I behaved, God forgive me, very badly—read papers—sat with Rogers— Gibbon Beloe &c. with a view to Scythia, which it is now very late to begin.[2] G. Testament.

20. Wednesday.

Heard from home & T.G.—letter too from R.G. out alone & in company— paper—Mathematics & Lecture—Virgil reading for Scythians—wrote a few verses—Gk T.—Xtn Student—wrote to T.G.

21. Thursday.

Gk. T. paper. Rhetoric—writing for Williams—& lecture. Electra & Lecture. a little Livy. wine with Pusey. Gibbon & sleepy attempt at Scythia. walk with Doyle & Rogers. boat with Doyle.

22. Friday.

Gk T. Mathematics & Lecture. papers—Livy & Lecture—read Herodotus for Scythians—out with Gaskell—wine with Kynaston—Gaskell sat with me &c. &c.

23. Sat.

Gk. T. Rhetoric—public & private Lecture—sat with Gaskell & Doyle—

[1] 1 Cor. xii or xiv.
[2] For University Latin prose prize.

did Theme—paper—heard from T.G.—dined & up Cherwell with Pusey. Adam. Geog.[1]

24. Sunday.

Chapel & St Mary's mg & aftn. An excellent sermon from Mr Clarke.[2] out with Childers—sat with him—tea with Gaskell—writing in G.T.— Divinity Lecture—Wilberforce—Christian Student—extracts from Jerram.

25. Monday.

Gk. T. reading for Scythian & did a little—paper—out with Gaskell, Doyle, Joyce[3]—tea with Gaskell—read Christian Student—Mathematics & Lecture—Sophocles—wrote to Hallam—in schools a little—pottered.

26. Tuesd.

Gk T. papers. heard from & wrote to T.G. Wrote to H.J.G. out with Harrison—Rhetoric & Lecture—Sophocles & Lecture—a little Livy—Scythians, wh get on wretchedly—Heard of the Bp's being most alarmingly ill.[4]

27. Wed.

Gk T. paper. Math & Lect. Livy. Justin[5] & Scythians. went with Seymer to see cricket match. with Williams about theme a good while & seeing rooms—I do not wish to change just now. Wine with Monteith. read Philoctetes.[6] called on Puller.

28. Thursd.

Out with Gaskell & D[oyle] &c.—paper—Gk T. Breakfast with Puller— heard my Tutor preach his 1st University Sermon—sat with Gaskell &c. & accompanied to [Union] Society, where he & D[oyle] made their debuts.[7] Sophocles—Livy—Scythians—Xtn Student.

29. Frid.

Gk. T. Livy & Lecture. Mathematics. papers: Long service as yesterday. out with Gaskell—Scythians—verses on Theme subject—Sophocles— Christian Student. &c.

30. Sat.

paper. Gk T. Rhetoric—public & private Lectures—did Theme—out, wine,

[1] A. *Adam, Summary of Geography and History* (1794).
[2] Charles Carr Clerke, 1798–1877, 3rd s. of 8th bart.; archdeacon of Oxford 1830; canon of Christ Church 1846.
[3] James Wayland Joyce, 1812–87, author; rector of Burford 1843.
[4] See 1 June 29.
[5] Roman historian, flourished ca. 200 A.D.
[6] Sophocles.
[7] Both opposed a motion against annual parliaments, which was lost without a division.

& tea with Gaskell. sat with Harrison Coles & Seymer till very late—
Scythians Sophocles.

31. Sund.

Christian Student—Wilberforce—Christian Year[1]—notes in Bible. Chapel
morng & aftn. walked to Abingdon & heard Bp of Calcutta preach an
admirable Sermon. New Coll Chapel in Evg—walking, & tea with Moncreiff
afterwards. I like him exceedingly.

1 June. Monday.

Gk Testament. Notes in ditto—gave a breakfast to Puller, Harrison,
Childers, two Aclands,[2] Doyle, Gaskell, after went to hear Baring. Heard of
the Bp's death with great regret.[3] Bp of Calcutta called on me—out with
Childers—with Gaskell. he read a Charge of the late Bp's to me—papers—
Sophocles—Livy—made up monthly accts.

2 June. Tuesday.

Out with Harrison—wine with Childers—paper—sat with Doyle—Gk
Testament. Rhetoric—Breakfast with Bp of Calcutta. Moncreiff there.
Sophocles & Lect—Livy—Scythians—& commenced writing over a cleaner
copy.

3. Wedn.

Gk T. out with Doyle—in schools—paper—breakfasted again with Bishop
[of Calcutta]—Coddington[4] & Wood—Lecture. read Shuttleworth's consecration sermon—tea with Gaskell—finished Scythians & writing over 1st
copy—Livy & Sophocles. Wrote to H.J.G.

4. Thursd.

Gk T. out with Seymer. Breakft with Bp [of Calcutta]. wrote over Scythians,
wrote Notes &c. & showed it up[5]—Rhetoric & Lecture—Sophocles & Lecture—Wrote to Pickering & Selwyn—began Anne of Geierstein[6]—heard
Palk[7] in the schools.

5. Frid.

Gk T. out with Doyle. hunting for lodgings for T.G. heard from & wrote to

---

[1] John *Keble's celebrated pious poems (1827).
[2] Both (Sir) T. D. *Acland and his brother Arthur Henry Dyke Acland, 1811–57; surname changed to Dyke-Troyte 1852; Devonshire gentlemen.
[3] Bp. *Lloyd died in London on 31 May.
[4] Christopher William Codrington, 1805–64, conservative M.P. for east Gloucestershire
from 1834.
[5] Add MS 44720, ff. 231–4.
[6] *Scott.
[7] Arthur George Palk, 1807?–35, curate at Owston, Yorkshire, 1830.

him—hoped to have seen Bp [of Calcutta], but missed. Wine with Seymer. Tea with Gaskell. Livy a good deal & Lecture—paper—Heard from H.J.G.

6. Sat.

Gk T. Rhetoric—Public & private Lectures—paper—shopping—out—speeches in Hall & aftn Surplice Prayers—Farr came & had wine with me, as had Gaskell & Doyle—Tea with Doyle—Sophocles. Horridly spent.

7. Sunday.

Barrow on Sacrament. Chapel & St Mary's mg & evg. Sacrament—a great increase thank God! 12 undergraduates. Lds Grimston & Selkirk, Acland, Grimston jun.,[1] Drake,[2] Harrison, Anstice, Madan, Lindon,[3] Gill,[4] Tupper, & myself. Bible—& Comment[arie]s. Wilberforce. Bickersteth. Wrote to Mrs G. having received in a frank a note from her & beautiful letters written by Robertson on hearing of dearest Anne's removal.[5]—Out. Farr & Gaskell had tea with me—but an unsatisfactory conversation on "saints" &c. nothing being defined.

8.

Surplice prayers. Christian Student—paper—Sophocles—Livy—dinner & wine with Warter—out—engaged lodgings for T.G. Wrote to him & to C. Hagart. Prize poems reading &c—many reports flitting.

9.

Christian Student—Record—wine & tea with Gaskell—long walk with Harrison—Surplice prayers—Sophocles (finished Trachiniae +) and Lecture—began Æneid 8 +, and read some Livy.

10. Wed.

Christian Student. Breakf. with Tancred. Livy.—at Doyle's—left Oxford for Henley 10 ¼: arrived about 1: spent day chiefly at Childers's. Mrs & Miss very agreeable.[6] saw Selwyn. dined with party there—went in boat with Seymer & Tancred—saw race[7]—tea at Mrs Childer's—left about 9. & returned safely before 12—after an exceedingly pleasant day. Childers very kind. Harrison & Joyce made up the party, with Seymer Tancred & me.

[1] Edward Harbottle Grimston, 1812–81, fellow of All Souls 1834–42, conservative M.P. St. Albans 1835–41, then rector of Pebmarsh, Essex.

[2] Octavius Samuel Drake, b. 1809?, of Chard, Somerset; servitor.

[3] Abel Seyer Lendon, b. 1808?, later curate of Sutton and Upton, Northamptonshire.

[4] John William Gill, b. 1810?, of Sherborne, Dorset; servitor.

[5] Robertson Gladstone was in America.

[6] Charles Childers's mother and sister, Selena, 3rd da. of Sampson, Lord Eardley, and Selina, who m. George Burroughs, R.A.

[7] The first boat race between Oxford and Cambridge; Oxford won. See Bassett, 14.

11. Thursd.

Surplice prayers. Paper—Sophocles a good deal. Lecture—Livy—put my name down for Responsions[1]—out—tea with Gaskell. read part of Belsham's letters to Bp of London:[2] Christian Student. Sat with Rogers.

12. Frid.

Finished Belsham: began Animadversions on his Version.[3] Wine with Pusey—tea with Gaskell—out with Doyle, seeing cricket match. Livy and Lecture—Mathematics & Lecture—paper—began to write over a theme.

13. Sat.

Finished writing over Theme & read over. out with Harrison. paper. heard from H.J.G. wrote to Mr G. wrote English Theme. Rhetoric & Lecture. Sophocles & Livy a little. Finished Animadversions &c. wh I think very able.

14. Sund.

Chapel & Sermon mg & aftn. Mr Crotch[4] & Dr. Whately; each good in their ways. Sat with Gaskell. Walk to Cumnor[5] &c. N[otes] to Gk Testament. Finished Christian Student. Read Wilberforce. began Le Bas, Vol 2nd.[6]

15. Monday.

Le Bas. Mathematics & Lecture. T.G. came. shopping and sundries. with Gaskell—Sophocles—Livy—Virgil finished 8 Æneid. gave in my list for littlego.[7] unpacked a box of wine. Sat in Evg with T.G. a good deal.

16. Tuesday.

Le Bas. Rhetoric and Lecture. Livy. Sophocles and Lecture. Virgil Æneid —paper—wine with Hill. Out with T.G. & sat with him.

17. Wed.

Le Bas. Sophocles—Livy—Æneid—Mathematics & Lecture—paper—rain —got back Cicero at Tusculum. read Anstices & Doyles.[8] Conv with Gaskell & with T.G. &c.

---

[1] Preliminary examination, essential before proceeding to an Oxford degree.

[2] Thomas *Belsham, controversialist, *Letters to the Bishop of London, in Vindication of the Unitarians* (1815).

[3] Perhaps *Quarterly Review*, xxx. 79 (October 1823).

[4] William Robert Crotch, 1799?–1877, fellow of New College 1818–32, vicar of Catherington, Hampshire, 1872.

[5] Four miles west of Oxford.

[6] C. W. *Le Bas, *Sermons on various occasions*, 2 ed. (1828), 2v.

[7] Responsions.

[8] Their versions on the same subject. The prizewinner was (Sir) John Eardley Eardley-*Wilmot, 1810–92, of Balliol; 2nd bart. 1847; judge 1854–74; M.P. south Warwickshire 1874–85.

18. *Thursd.*

Le Bas. Rhet & Lect. Logic & Lect. Livy—Soph—Virgil—none to any great extent. Papers—out alone & with T.G. wine with Moncreiff—went to debating society.[1]

19. *Frid.*

Le Bas. Math & Lect. Livy & Lect. Sophocles—Virgil—papers—out, alone & with T.G. Doyle & Hope sat with me.

20. *Sat.*

Le Bas. Rhetoric—public & private Lectures. Theme & Verses—Sophocles & Virgil—walk with Doyle—wrote to my mother—papers—wine with Bernard & Ward. Shuffled dreadfully about Sunday.

21. *Sun.*

Chapel mg & aftn. St Mary's aftn.—& heard part of Mr Newman's sermon. Dinner & walks with T.G. Bible—Le Bas—finished Wilberforce—& Barrow on Faith—writing notes &c & reading in Mant. &c.

22. *Mond.*

Le Bas. Logic. Mathematics & Lecture. Sophocles and Virgil, working hard at both. Out. Wine with Doyle. paper. College prize decided for Kynaston.

23. *Tues.*

Le Bas. Finished Æneid. Read some Sophocles over again. Passed my littlego.[2] Did English into Latin. Chorus & some Virgil into English &c. Out between 2 & 3. papers. Out with T.G. tea with Gaskell &c.

24. *Wed.*

Le Bas. Mathematics. Rhetoric. Heard Theological Prize Essay read.[3] Out shopping: rode to Cuddesdon—walk &c: & a splendid dinner there: Saunders, Dennison of Oriel,[4] my Brother, Anstice, Tancred, Selkirk, Hill &c.

25. *Thursd.*

Le Bas. Rhetoric & Lecture. Horace beginning Satires. Livy. papers. wrote

---

[1] Oxford Union Society: *Moncreiff was president. Debate compared *Cromwell with Napoleon, to the latter's advantage.

[2] Certificate in Add MS 44719, f. 112.

[3] William *Jacobson, *What were the Causes of the Persecution to which the Christians were subject in the first Centuries of Christianity?*; *Ellerton prize essay.

[4] George Anthony *Denison, 1805–96, fellow of Oriel 1828–39, archdeacon of Taunton 1851; see Add MS 44140.

to Canning. wine with Rogers. Out with T.G. Gaskell had tea with me. Sophocles Lecture. Letter from Mr G. on Mr Huskisson's conduct &c.

26. Friday.

Le Bas. Livy a good deal & Lecture—papers. Horace Satires—Wood's Optics—wrote to H.J.G. Out with Gaskell & also with T.G., neither long—wine with Buller & Hanbury. Livy Lecture.

27. Sat.

Gaudy Day. Le Bas. Livy. Horace. Rhetoric. Mathematics. none very much. papers. wrote to J.N.G. a long letter. Gave wine party—had Hanbury, Coles, Menteaths,[1] Seymer, Gaskell, Ward, Moncreiff, Childers.

28. Sunday.

Bible—notes—& to Gk Testament. Le Bas—Ch. Missionary [Society] Sermons & Reports. Chapel mg & aft. St Ebbe's—& heard pt of Mr Newman's [sermon] in aftn—dinner with T.G. sat with him & tea with Gaskell —letters from home. Tomline on evidence of Scripture &c. a poor Sunday.

29. Monday.

Le Bas. Began Rhetoric Abstract,[2] collecting from self, Rev. I.W.,[3] Hobbes, Harrison. Wine with Harrison. Supper with Seymer. Out with T.G. walk with Doyle & Gaskell. Notes to Bible & quotations. Up late.

30. Tuesday.

Wine party. Le Bas. Abstract of Rhetoric. Heard from Canning & Bp of Calcutta: wrote to Mrs G. Calling &c. Horace. Heard Bp of Llandaff[4] preach. Read Quarterly Review on Phillips[5] &c. Monthly accts.

1. Wednesday.

At Commemoration.[6] Called on Moncreiff. Much conv. with T.G. Out with him. Wine party. T.G., Doyle, Gaskell, Anstice, Warter, Egerton &c. &c. Read Doyle & Claughton's English Poems.[7] Rhetoric Abstract—Horace— wrote to Mr Craig. Quarterly Review. Le Bas.

---

[1] Francis Hastings, 1807–75, vicar of Thorpe Arch, Yorkshire, from 1834; and Granville Wheler, 1811–87, rector of Morcott, Rutland, 1868–72; 5th and 7th ss. of Charles Granville Stuart–Menteath, cr. bart. 1838; both at Magdalen Hall.

[2] Abstract of Aristotle in Add MS 44808.

[3] Perhaps Isaac *Williams of Trinity.

[4] Edward *Copleston, 1776–1849, bp. of Llandaff and dean of St. Paul's from 1828.

[5] xvi. 27 (October 1816), attacking the verses and speeches of Charles *Phillips.

[6] Of the benefactors of the university.

[7] Thomas Legh *Claughton, 1808–92, *Newdigate prize 1829; fellow of Trinity 1832–1842; bp. of Rochester 1867–77, of St. Albans 1877–90.

2. Thursday.

Le Bas. Notes to Bible &c. Worked a good deal at Rhetoric Abstract. Had
T.G., Harrison, Moncreiff, & Gaskell to wine. papers. Out with Harrison.
Breakf. with T.G.

3. Friday.

Le Bas. Rhetoric Abstract. very slow work. Breakf. with T.G. A party of
Tutors. Paper. Out. Horace. Letters from home & brothers. dined with
Mr Pusey—he was very kind.

4. Sat.

Le Bas. Finished Rhetoric Abstract at last. Out with Cole. tea with Gaskell
Sat with T.G., Doyle—heard from home. Bid T.G. goodbye—talking over
our journies as projected. Newspapers. Livy & some dates to him.

5. Sund.

Sacrament. Sat at a breakfast of Aclands—Walking with Harrison & Cole
—again Doyle & Gaskell—sat & talked much with Doyle Gaskell & Hope
on different religious subjects. Only Grimstone Junior & myself at Sacrament. Sermon mg & aftn. Dr. Burton exceedingly good. finished Le Bas.
read Dealtry's Sermon for Christian Knowledge & Prop[agation of] Gospel
[Societies].[1] Acts History & Barrow.

6. Monday.

Mathematics &c. Collections—out before 3. Took up Acts—5 B of Livy—
—Sophocles—Æneid—Optics—Rhetoric B.1.—afterwards paid Bills &c.
Out with Cole. Packed up. Tea & sat with Gaskell, Harrison—Doyle—Left
Oxford between 12 & 1 by Rocket.

7. Tuesday.

Arrived safely at Birmingham thank God: our load was terrific. Relinquished my walking plan, went on direct with Seymer to Lpool—arrived
about 9. Slept at Talbot.[2]

8. Wednesday.

Walk out to Seaforth—Breakfast—returned to Lpool. went about with
Seymer seeing lions—drove him out to dinner—Mrs Twemlow[3] & Miss
Hamilton[4] dined there. R.G. we hope, to sail.

[1] William *Dealtry, 'The Excellence of the Liturgy', sermon preached for S.P.C.K. and
S.P.G. on 22 April 1829.
[2] An inn near the town hall.
[3] Elizabeth Twemlow lived near Birkenhead.
[4] Mary Ann Hamilton kept a ladies' boarding school in Liverpool.

9. Thursday.

In town with Seymer. Saw Botanic Gardens. Tunnel[1] &c. The same party.
Heber's Sermons.

10. Friday.

Seymer went, by steamboat to Glasgow. Billiards with him—took him in
after lunch & returned in Evening. Anne of Geierstein—paper.

11. Saturday.

Mrs & Miss Ridewood[2] came—Anne of Geierstein—Cotton's Poems[3]—
Heber at nt—Walking about, seeing Church &c.

12. Sunday.

Letter from R.G. Went to St Andrew's to Ch. Walked out. Heber—Life of
Wesley[4]—Hooker's Eccl. Pol.[5] (Preface &c) &c.

13. Monday.

Hooker—Anne of Geierstein—Onania[6]—in town buying books—&c. &c.

14. Tuesday.

Copied a short letter—Anne of Geierstein—Footes Memoirs &c.[7]—Walk.

15. Wednesday.

T.G. returned. Anne of Geierstein. made up accounts and wrote up journal.
read papers—& plays.

16. Thursday.

read Anne of Geierstein—wrote to J.M.G.—newspapers—in Lpool shopping.

17. Friday.

Finished Anne of Geierstein wh I like much. papers. Copied a letter. Began
Mac Laurin's Algebra.[8]

---

[1] The botanic garden lay off Oxford Street, at the south-eastern edge of the town; the
tunnel of the Liverpool and Manchester railway ended near the King's Dock.
[2] Unidentified.
[3] Charles *Cotton, Isaak *Walton's friend.
[4] Robert *Southey, *Life of John *Wesley*, 2v (1820).
[5] Richard *Hooker, *Laws of Ecclesiasticall Politie* (1594–7).
[6] An early eighteenth-century work deploring masturbation; usually attributed to
Dr. Beckers.
[7] William Cooke, *Memoirs of Samuel *Foote*, 3v. (1805). Some alteration in MS.
[8] Colin *Maclaurin, *Treatise of Algebra* (1748).

18. Sat.

Heber's 30 Sermons.[1] Notes to Gk Testament. In Lpool. walked out & bathed. papers—Hooker's Preface—Wood's Algebra—and MacLaurin's—Ch, in garden &c.

19. Sunday.

Ch at St Andrew's. Mr Bickersteth again. read &c. with H.J.G. Walked out from Liverpool—sermon read at night as last Sunday. Read Hooker's Eccl. Pol. & Southey's Wesley.

20. Monday.

In Lpool for Mrs G—Walked out—Hooker—Life of Wesley—papers—Maclaurin's Algebra & Wood's. In a bad state. Began Laurence on Baptism.[2]

21. Tuesday.

Hooker E.P.—Mrs Ridewood went—copied a letter—Equations—Wood—MacLaurin—a little Livy—papers—out, at Church &c—Life of Wesley. Letter from R.G.

22. Wed.

Hooker E.P.—Copied a little—Life of Wesley—Capt. Proby[3] dined here—Equations[4]—Wood—a little Livy—out, at Church &c.

23. Thursd.

Hooker E.P. Livy. Drove Capt. Proby into Lpool—walked with him there. Life of Wesley. Bathed. Equations—Shopping in Lpool for Mrs G &c.

24. Frid.

Hooker E.P. began book 2. Out in carriage. Life of Wesley—papers—tremendous thunderstorm—equations—Wood—Livy.

25. Sat.

Dear Tom's birthday. May God bless & keep him. It passed with little notice, for we are but thin at present. Eccl Pol.—Life of Wesley—paper—Equations—Wood's Algebra—& Livy a little.

---

[1] Reginald *Heber's sermons were collected after his death by his widow in 2v. (1829).
[2] Roger *Laurence, *Lay-Baptism Invalid* (1710).
[3] Granville Leveson *Proby, 1781–1868; fought at Nile and Trafalgar; capt. R.N. 1806; whig M.P. Wicklow 1816–29; 3rd earl of Carysfort 1855; admiral 1857.
[4] M. *Bland, *Algebraical Problems, producing Simple and Quadratic Equations* (1812).

26. Sunday.

Church reopened. There morng & evg. At School aftn. Bible with H.J.G.
&c.—Heber's Sermons—Eccl. P. began Book 3—& Life of Wesley.

27. Monday.

Eccl. Pol—Breakfasted with Aunts. Life of Wesley—Livy—Equations—
Wood's Algebra—papers—wrote to Farr—out, in garden, at church &c.

28. Tuesday.

Eccles. Poll. T.G. went to Knutsford.[1] Poor Dr McCartney died 3½ a.m. A
long & unpleasant discussion with my Aunts. Equations—Wood's Algebra
—Life of Wesley—Livy—out &c.

29. Wed.

Eccl. Pol. Livy. Equations. Life of Wesley.—papers—& sundries—worked
much at the library &c—Another very painful discussion with Aunt J.—
she & my Mother much agitated—writing notes to go to her, but did not
send. Mrs & Miss Wadd came.[2]

30. Thursd.

Eccl. Pol. Life of Wesley. Equations, pretty successful. Drove in in gig &
brought out R.G. arrived from America safe & well, thank God. MacLaurin
—Livy—papers.

31. Fr.

T.G. returned. Eccl. Pol. Life of Wesley—paper—at Aunts'—Equations—
MacLaurin—Livy—out &c.

August 1. Saturday.

Eccl. Pol. Paper—Life of Wesley. Wrote to J.N.G. Equations a good deal—
MacLaurin little—Livy—Drove into town—walked out—, &c.

Aug 2. Sunday.

Ch mg & aft. Sacrament—30 to 40—School in aftn—notes in Testament
&c—Hooker's Eccl. Pol. & Life of Wesley—Sat with H.J.G.

3. M.

Eccl. Pol. made up accts. Equations. MacLaurin—Livy—paper—Life of

---

[1] Some 14 miles SSW. of Manchester; the Egertons lived there at Tatton Park.
[2] Caroline Mackenzie, Mrs. Gladstone's cousin, m. William *Wadd 1806; and her da.
Caroline, b. 1810. See 23–24 Aug. 29, 3 Dec. 30.

Wesley. Out—Backgammon with cousin Divie. Dr Rutter[1] & Mr Bicker-steth here for Mrs G. & H.J.G.

4. T.

Eccl. Pol. Equations. Maclaurin. paper. American Souvenir. Life of Wesley. Livy. Equations copied out as usual. Notes to Testament & reading Improved Version.[2]

5. Wed.

Eccl. Pol. Equations. papers sundry. Out: at Aunt's. Backgammon with Divie. Livy. Life of Wesley. Bow & arrows with Divie.

6. Th.

Life of Wesley. Eccl. Pol. Wrote to Canning. Laying in stock of scribbling paper. Livy. Equations—paper—at nt, singing a little.

7. Fr.

Eccl. Pol. Livy. Equations. papers. Life of Wesley. Backgammon—singing —walked to town—saw Regatta, with Robertson & Cousin Divie.

8. Sat.

T.G. & Divie went to Scotland. Eccl. Pol. Livy—Equations. papers—Life of Wesley—wrote to Gaskell—went down to bathe, but missed Johnnie.[3]

9. Sunday.

Ch mg & aftn. School in aftn. Sat with H.J.G. Notes to Bible. Hooker's Eccl. Pol. Finished Life of Wesley (reading a good deal)—Heber's Sermon.

10. Monday.

Eccl. Pol. Finished Notes to the Life of Wesley. The book I think very interesting, & the subject of it wonderful. Livy—Equations—Wood's Algebra—Quarterly on Ch in India & Bp Heber[4]—at Mr Rawson's & Aunts'. Papers. Out with H.J.G. Notes to Testament.

11. Tuesday.

Eccl. Pol. Equations—Livy—Life of Martinus Scriblerus[5]—heard from Canning—paper—prepared my receptacle for 'Selections'—went into

---

[1] John Rutter, M.D., Liverpool physician.
[2] [T. *Belsham ed.] *The New Testament, in an Improved Version* (1808).
[3] Bathing-machine attendant?
[4] xxxvii. 100 (January 1828).
[5] Possibly 'An Heroic Epistle to the Rev. Richard *Watson' (1780), a jeu d'esprit published in 1780 by 'Martinus Scriblerus', a common pseudonym.

Town—heard Mr Hesketh[1] preach, & the Bishop deliver an excellent charge to the Clergy.

12. Wed.

Eccl. Pol. Equations. Livy. Began my 'Selections'.[2] paper. Martinus Scriblerus. A dinner party—Messrs Staniforth, Brooks, Horsfall,[3] Porter,[4] Littledale,[5] J. Ewart, Dr Traill &c.

13. Thursd.

Dined at Mossley Hill. Walked into town. Eccl. Pol. Equations—Livy— Selections—paper—Martinus Scriblerus—heard from Gaskell.

14. Friday.

Eccl. Pol. Martinus Scriblerus—Livy—Equations—Selections—papers— out with father & mother &c.

15. Sat.

Eccl. Pol. Finished Martinus Scriblerus—Equations, a good deal—Selections—papers—Livy—Kelso & G. Fraser dined here—Rain—read Fable of Bees,[6] Burtons Anatomy of Melancholy[7] &c.

16. Sun.

Eccl. Pol. Ch morng & aftn. School aftn. Sermon read at nt. Notes to Bible —& began the "Christian"[8] wherein God enlighten me. Life of Gilpin[9]— Heber's Sermons—I know now that a high mental *standard* of sanctity not without desires for reaching it, can exist together with wallowing in sin: for the heart is deceitful above all things. For holiness the desire is (to one's self) avowed but not efficient: for sin, efficient but not avowed. God deliver us!

17. Mon.

Eccl. Pol. Bland's Equations & entering, as usual. began life of Horne Tooke[10]—papers—Livy—went to Ince. game called "Secretaire" at nt. Out with R.G. &c. Notes to Bible.

---

[1] William Hesketh, 1795?–1858, priest at Toxteth Park, Liverpool.
[2] Add MS 44807, a commonplace book, mainly religious.
[3] Charles Horsfall, Liverpool merchant, mayor 1832–3.
[4] William Field Porter, merchant, of Aigburth.
[5] Probably Anthony Littledale, Liverpool gentleman, father of H.A.
[6] B. *Mandeville, The Fable of the Bees, or Private Vices Public Benefits (1714).
[7] (1621).
[8] Sermons by Samuel *Walker (1755).
[9] William *Gilpin, Life of Bernard *Gilpin (1753; but see 23 Aug. 29 n).
[10] Alexander *Stephens, Memoirs of John Horne *Tooke, 2v. (1813).

18. Tues.

Eccl. Pol. Bland's Equations &c. Life of Horne Tooke—papers—Livy—out—dinner party—Mr. Huskisson, Mayor of Lpool,[1] Sir J. Tobin, Messrs Moss, Lawrence, Tennyson,[2] Ewart, E. Ewart, Bird[3] &c.

19. Wed.

Eccl. Pol. Bland's Equations—wrote to T.G.—papers—Life of Horne Tooke—Livy—weather still very rough. Heard from Pickering.

20. Thursd.

Eccl. Pol. Bland's Equations. papers. Life of Horne Tooke—Livy—Singing at nt—Selections—& notes to Testament &c. at Aunts'.

21. Fr.

Eccl. Pol. Selections. Bland's Equations—papers—Livy—Lucretius—Life of Horne Tooke—music at nt. Mr & Mrs Grant, Mr D. Armstrong,[4] Mrs Dirom,[5] here.

22. Sat.

Eccl. Pol. Selections—Equations—papers—Livy—Horne Tooke—Hume's Essays[6] (cursorily) &c &c   as on a rainy day meus est mos.

23. Sun.

Ch morng & Evening. A long & able sermon from Mr Saunders[7] for the Jews & a very good one from Mr Rawson in Evg. Gilpin's Life—Irving's Introductory Essay[8]—Heber—Hooker—Selections—Christian—School in aftn—up late.—Received the awful account of poor Mr Wadd's death.[9] O may God comfort the widow & the fatherless, and turn even this to their unspeakable & everlasting benefit. & may we hence learn how great is the mercy of God towards ourselves, & how wonderful his tenderness.

24. Monday.

Eccl. Pol. Finished Book 5. Bland's Equations—papers—Livy—Life of

---

[1] Sir George Drinkwater, of Rodney Street.
[2] Charles Tennyson (*D'Eyncourt), 1784–1861, uncle of poet; M.P. Grimsby 1818–26, Bletchingley 1826–31, Stamford 1831 (fighting duel with fellow-member), Lambeth 1832–52; changed surname 1835.
[3] Perhaps Nehemiah Bird, Liverpool merchant.
[4] David Armstrong, Wavertree wine merchant.
[5] Unidentified.
[6] David *Hume, *Essays, Moral and Political*, 2v. (1741–2).
[7] Samuel Walker Saunders, of Liverpool, priest at Dale, Pembrokeshire, from 1832.
[8] Edward *Irving wrote an introductory essay to the 1824 ed. of William *Gilpin's life of his ancestor Bernard *Gilpin.
[9] William *Wadd, 1776–1829, surgeon and author; d. in carriage accident in Ireland on 20 August.

Horne Tooke—wrote to T.G.—copying—company went early—the painful news communicated to the Wadds. I saw them in the evening—in very deep, but not impatient nor I trust inconsolable affliction.

25. Tues.

Eccl. Pol. began B.6. Selections—Equations—Livy—Life of Horne Tooke finished V.1. Mr Huskisson[1] here at breakfast & in forenoon. Mr. Blundell also. In Lpool—called on Mrs MacCartney but did not see her—read Davys's Vill. Conv. on Ch. Offices.[2]

26. Wed.

Weather still tremendous. Mr Stewart Mackenzie dined here. Eccl. Pol. Equations—Livy—Selections—papers—Life of Horne Tooke.

27.

Mr. S. Mackenzie still here on account of the weather, wh was tremendous. Eccl. Pol. Selections. Livy—Equations—Horne Tooke—papers—heard from & wrote to Saunders—read London Review on Bp. Heber.[3]

28.

Mr S. Mackenzie went. In Lpool—saw Mrs MacCartney. Eccl. Pol. Selections—Equations—Livy—Horne Tooke—papers—sat some time with Mrs Wadd.

29.

Eccl. Pol. Equations—Livy—Selections—Horne Tooke—papers—out with Mrs Wadd & with H.J.G.

30. Sunday.

Eccl. Pol. Selections—notes to Testament &c. &c. read Gilpin's Sermon—finished the life of that most holy man—read a sermon of Heber's—Ch. morning & evg. School in aftn.

31. Mon.

Eccl. Pol. Equations—Livy—papers—Horne Tooke. made up accounts. Rode into park & made calls. In Lpool & had a tooth drawn. Mr Graham dined here.

September 1.

Eccl. Pol. Selections. Equations—Livy—wrote a longish letter to J.N.G.

[1] William *Huskisson, 1770–1830; saw Bastille stormed; M.P. from 1796, for Liverpool from 1823; at board of trade, 1822–8, liberalised economy. Cp. 17–18 Sept. 30.
[2] George *Davys, *Village Conversations on the principal Offices of the Church* (1824).
[3] *Quarterly Review*, xxxvii. 100 (January 1828).

In town—at Perry's[1]—teeth filed &c. dined with Mr. Staniforth—particularly pleased with Mrs S.—called on Mrs Traill &c. Also very much pleased with Mr R. Hughes.[2]

2. Wed.

Eccl. Pol. Selections & notes—Life of Horne Tooke—papers—Equations—Livy finished Book 10—rode out with H.J.G. & alone. Graham still here. out with R.G. &c. wrote some stanzas of a kind of hymn.

3. Th.

Eccl. Pol. Notes—with Mr. Graham—papers—Christian Observer, sundry articles.—Life of Horne Tooke—Equations.

4. Fr.

Eccl. Pol. Equations. wrote to T.G. & J.M. Gaskell—papers—Horne Tooke—very long conv. with Mrs G. In Town during the early part of the day, shopping.

5. Sat.

Eccl. Pol. Notes to Gk Testament—Note from Aunt J. answered it—Equations—Livy—finished Life of Horne Tooke a very poor book, I think; papers. out with Mr Graham. Sorting books &c.

6. Sun.

Ch morng & aftn. School in aftn. Sacrament—near 50, I think. Selections—Notes to Gk Testament—out with H.J.G. & alone. Finished B.7 of Eccl. Pol. read Serm. on Perseverance & several of Heber's.

7. Mon.

Livy little—Packed up—rode with H.J.G. Paper—sundries. Pope—Left Lpool at 5 for Manchester. Slept there. Out & conv. Equations.

8. Tuesday.

Went to Collegiate Church.[3] began Life of Alexander.[4] Left Manchester at 2 & arrived at Thornes House[5] between 8 & 9.

9. Wed.

Billiards with Gaskell. Read paper & sundries—out, in Wakefield &c. Re-

[1] William Perry, Everton surgeon and dentist.
[2] Probably Robert Hughes, the S.P.C.K.'s Liverpool agent.
[3] Became cathedral, 1847.
[4] Archdeacon John *Williams, *Life and Actions of Alexander the Great* (1829).
[5] The seat near Wakefield, Yorkshire, of J. M. Gaskell's father Benjamin, 1781–1855, whig M.P. for Maldon 1812–26.

began "The Inheritance".[1] A murdered day or nearly so. Began to get a little acquainted with Mr & Mrs Gaskell.[2]

10. Th.

Rain. Out little. Billiards—paper—Inheritance—Jones's Letter to Common People[3]—wrote to Mrs G., Wood, &c. Hagart. Convss. with J.M.G. Draughts.

11. Fr.

[Read] Ld Palmerston's Portugal Speech.[4] Began Gurney on Quakerism.[5] Went to see the Lunatic Asylum with J.M.G.—very interesting indeed. paper—sundries. Billiards.

12. Sat.

Wrote a long letter to Hallam[.] Billiards & out with J.M.G. arranging Steph. Lexicon[6] with Mr Gaskell. Singing at night. Inheritance—& Gurney's "Society of Friends". Dr Gilby[7] dined. Wrote a few lines.

13. Sunday.

Parish Ch. in mg. New Ch in aftn. A good sermon by a Mr Kilby.[8] serm. read in Evg. Went with J.M.G. to see a poor blind invalid, Mary Clarkson by name. She seemed in a most happy state. We each read her a sermon. At Dr Gilby's. Conv. in Evg. on War &c.[9] read Jones on Trinity & Gurney.

14. M.

The history of my connection with _____[10] is as follows.
It began late in 1824, more at his seeking than mine.
It slackened soon: more on my account than his.
It recommenced in 1825, late, more at my seeking than his.
It ripened much from the early part of 1826 to the middle.
In the middle, [Farr?] rather took my place.
In the latter end [of 1826], it became closer & stronger than ever.
Through 1827, it flourished most happily, to my very great enjoyment.

[1] Novel [by Susan E. *Ferrier], 3v. (1824).
[2] Mary, d. 1845; eldest da. of Dr. Joseph Pilkington Brandreth of 68 Rodney Street, Liverpool; m. 1807.
[3] Printed from 1767 at the back of William *Jones of Nayland Catholic Doctrine of a Trinity Proved (1756).
[4] NSH xxi. 1643–70, 1 June 1829.
[5] J.J. *Gurney, Observations on the . . . Society of Friends (1824).
[6] Henricus Stephanus (Henri Estienne), Thesaurus Graecae Linguae, 5v. (1572) was being re-issued in parts.
[7] Perhaps William Robinson Gilby, 1787?–1848, wrangler 1809; vicar of Beverley, Yorkshire, 1823–33.
[8] Thomas Kilby, 1784–1868, perpetual curate of St. John's, Wakefield, 1825.
[9] See Magnus, 8.
[10] A. H. Hallam. (WEG. S[eptember] 8.71).

Beginning of 1828, [Hallam] having been absent since he left Eton, it varied but very slightly.

Middle of 1828, [Hallam] returned, and thought me cold. (I did not increase my *rate* of letters as under the circumstances I ought to have done.)

Early in 1829, there was friendly expostulation (unconnected with the matter last alluded to) and affectionate reply.

Illness in [spring and summer of 1829].

At present, almost an uncertainty, very painful, whether I may call [Hallam] my friend or not.

Wrote a few lines—billiards with J.M.G. Inheritance. Finished Jones on Trinity—a most admirable book—Gurney—papers. Profr Smyth[1] & Mr & Mrs P. Ainsworth[2] came.

15. Tuesday.

Wrote to Canning. Inheritance—paper—chess—billiards—drove to see ruins of Sandall castle[3]—a pleasant excursion—Selections.

16. Wed.

Recd a very gratifying letter from Hallam—Selections—paper—Gurney— Dr Parr's Memoirs[4]—Life of Alexander—billiards. Went to Templenewsam, 10 miles off, a most beautiful place. Saw picture gallery; a very pleasant day.[5]

17. Th.

Wrote to H.J.G. Billiards much—went to Lupseth[6]—Selections—Ld Palmerston on Cath. Quest.[7] Inheritance—Life of Alexander. paper.

18. Fr.

Billiards much, weather being rainy—Selections—Inheritance—a good deal of singing, & trying to learn a catch, wh escapes me as soon as I have got it. paper—Life of Alexander.

19. Sat.

Billiards a long time—Inheritance—singing—paper—Life of Alexander— finished Vol 1. of Inheritance—Gurney.

[1] William *Smyth, 1765–1849, s. of Liverpool banker; wrangler 1787; tutor to R. B. *Sheridan's s. 1793–1806; regius professor of modern history at Cambridge 1807.

[2] Peter Ainsworth, 1790–1870, Lancashire magnate; M.P. for Bolton 1835–47; m. 1815 Elizabeth Byrom, Liverpool heiress.

[3] Norman castle close to Wakefield.

[4] John *Johnstone, *Works of Samuel *Parr . . . with Memoirs of his Life and Writings* (1828), i.

[5] The dowager Lady Hertford's palace at Temple Newsam near Leeds, which has since swallowed it up.

[6] Daniel Gaskell, 1782–1875, Benjamin's b.; reforming M.P. Wakefield 1832–7; lived at Lupset Hall, close to Thornes House.

[7] *NSH* xx. 1238–53, 18 March 1829.

20. Sunday.

Ch morng & aftn—out—sermon of Paley's read in evening—& music. read hard at Gurney's Society of Friends—Scripture.

21. Monday.

Life of Alexander—Billiards—finished Gurney's Society of Friends—paper—music—walked with J.M.G. to Heath[1]—in Evg bid good bye with great regret. Packing.

22. Tuesday.

Up soon after 5. J.M.G. kindly up too—breakfasted with me—left at 6. arrived in Lpool at 6. Staid some time in Manchester—read Life of Alexander by snatches. Walked out to Seaforth—found all pretty well—Aunt Divie there.

23. Wednesday.

Edward Robn came. Collected & reperused Hallam's letters to me. read papers—Quarterly on Progress & Prospects of Society—Life of Alexander.

24. Th.

At Aunts—discussion—no appearance of good. Selections—Life of Alexander—began the Nubes [= Clouds] of Aristophanes—rode with Edward—paper—read part of Quart. on Portugal.

25. Fr.

At Aunts—gleams appearing, for wh we shd be thankful. Billards with Edward—began B.8. Eccl Pol—Life of Alexander—collected Gaskell's letters & reperused many—paper—Nubes—finished Quart on Portugal. read Ed. on Pestalozzi.[2]

26. Sat.

Eccl. Pol. Billiards with Edward—Equations—Nubes—Life of Alexander—paper—part of Ed. Rev. on Catholic Question[3]—out with Edward & in [—] wrote to Gaskell & to Canning.

27. Sunday.

Church morng & aftn—School in aftn—out—read part of Hooker on Justif.[4] Clissold—Heber's Sermons—one aloud at night—wrote notes & selections.

---

[1] A mile east of Wakefield; cp. 17 Oct. 32.
[2] *Edinburgh Review*, xlvii. 118–31 (January 1828).
[3] xlix. 218–72 (March 1829).
[4] Richard *Hooker, *A Learned Discourse of Justification* (1612).

28. Monday.

Finished Hooker on Justification—Equations—Aristophanes—finished Life of Alexander—wrote a long letter to Hallam—billiards & out—read Sadler's speech at Whitby.[1]

29. Tuesday.

In Town, riding. Selected books from the Christian Knowledge [Society's] List for a servants' Library, & arranged with my dear Mother about them. Finished Hooker's Eccl. Polity: began Analysis of do.[2] papers—Niebuhr[3]—Nubes—billiards—made out monthly list—& accounts.

30. Wednesday.

Rode with H.J.G. Analysis of Hooker—paper—Niebuhr—Nubes—billiards—Selections—Scraps—MacLaurin.

1. Thursday.

Rode with H.J.G. A Sermon of Heber's. Selections—Scraps—Nubes—Niebuhr—paper—dined at Uncle Robert's—billiards—wrote part of letter to J.N.G. Analysis [of Hooker].

2. Fr.

A Sermon of Heber's—on Shipwreck of St Paul—very beautiful & original, & quite a model of composition, I think.[4] finished letter to J.N.G. Niebuhr—Nubes—paper—Ed. Rev. on Signs of Times.[5] Young Moss called here—Selections—Brought out Uncle Divie.

3. Sat.

A Sermon of Heber's. Analysis of Eccl. Pol. Billiards—out—rode with H.J.G.—read papers—singing at night—Ed. Rev. on Utilitarians[6]—Nubes—Selections.

4. Sunday.

Ch mg & aftn. School in aftn. Sacrament—Aunt D. & Jane, Mrs G. & H.J.G., Mrs & Miss Wadd, Miss Maurice[7]—altogether I dare say near 50—read a Sermon of Heber's—Clissold—& part of "Conversations on the Parables"—Selections & Notes.

[1] M. T. *Sadler, 1780–1825, tory radical; M.P. for Newark 1829–31, Aldborough 1831–1832; spoke at Whitby on 15 September 1829 against free trade.

[2] Add MS 44720, f. 86.

[3] J. C. *Hare and Connop *Thirlwall tr. B. G. Niebuhr, *Roman History*, 2 ed, i, (1828).

[4] In R. *Heber *Sermons preached in England* (1829), 298, on Acts xxvii. 23–24.

[5] xlix. 439 (June 1829).

[6] xlix. 159 (March) or 273 (June) or l. 99 (October 1829), a controversy with James *Mill and the *Westminster Review*.

[7] Elizabeth, 1795–1839, eldest sister of F. D. *Maurice; companion to Helen Gladstone.

5. M.

T.G. returned. Uncle R. & T. Steuart dined here. Billiards—papers—finished Heber's Sermons—Equations—analysis of Eccl. Pol. wh is very substantial. Nubes—Ed. Rev. on "Sadler on Ireland".[1]

6. Tuesday.

Analysis Eccl. Pol. Selections—began V.2 Inheritance +. billiards—Nubes—Equations—walked to Town—dined at Otterspool—back late—Mr. Lock,[2] Mr. Lawrence, Mr. W. W. Caine,[3] Mr Saunders &c. there—Mr G, R.G., Ed. Robn & I. Uncle & Aunt D. went. Clissold.

7. Wed.

Selections. Clissold. Inheritance V.2—part of Ed. Rev. on Drama[4]—papers—looking over Catalogue & went into town early with Father to a booksale—there long—a very bad day—read some Nubes, & began Analysis of Second Book [of Hooker] in the Evening.

8. Th.

Notes. Clissold. Inheritance V.2. finished Ed. Rev. on Drama. paper. Nubes—Analysis of Hooker. In town, at book-sale &c—at Christian Knowledge Society Quarterly meeting.

9. Fr.

Clissold. Selections. little Analysis—little Aristophanes—paper & V.2 Inheritance—called on Mrs Conway, Mrs Grant, Mrs Jones, Mrs D. Gladstone, Mr Staniforth, Mrs M'Cartney & did sundries in town, in great haste. young Moss dined here.

10. Saturday.

Clissold. Selections—analysis—papers—Inheritance—wrote briefly to Aunt Mary & Hallam—called on Mr Blundell & Mr Rawson—billiards—wrote in & made a list of the books for the servants.

11. Sunday.

Ch mg & aftn. School in aftn. Clissold—Selections—finished Conversations on Parables, a very pleasing book—out with H.J.G. sat with her & at night wrote a long letter to her.

12. Monday.

read much at Inheritance—finished it—paper—pack'd up &c. bid goodbye

[1] xlix. 300 (June 1829).
[2] John Lock, Liverpool customs officer.
[3] Perhaps William Cain, master mariner.
[4] xlix. 317 (June 1829).

to Aunts—left home between 3 & 4—saw Tam O Shanter & Souter Johnnie[1]—admirable. Travelled all night, by Aurora.

13. T.

at Birmingham before 6. thence to Worcester—got a peep at Cathedral— went on to Malvern & joined Hallam—Walk with him—I remain with them in day, & sleep at Inn—began Law's Call.[2] Had to unpack part of my portmanteau, for breaking of a jar within. Met an apparently religious stage coachman.

14. W.

read more of Law—much sitting talking & walking with Hallam. read Channing on Fenelon[3]—Wordsworth[4] &c. Dr Card,[5] Mitford of Ch Ch[6] &c. at Mr Hallam's.

15. Th.

wrote home—repacked—& came with Hallam to Oxford thro' Worcester & Cheltenham. finished the Christian Knowledge Abridgment of Law. arrived at Oxford past 11 at night.

16. Fr.

Hallam breakfasted with me, & with me most of the day—read the Cambridge Prize Poems at nt—Tennyson's[7] sundry times in order if possible to understand it—liked it exceedingly—out with Hallam & Doyle—they had wine with me—making inquiry about rooms—saw my tutor.

17. Sat.

Had Hallam, Gaskell, two Coles, & Seymer to wine—out with Hallam &c. pottering about—wrote up Journal & accounts—began Cowper's letters— some conversation with old Wm Harris—tea with Doyle, Hallam & Gaskell, & a long conversation on the nature of Poetry & of beauty. H. & D. defined poetry, after much discussion [, as] "the attempt to produce the impression of the beautiful by the mental faculties". To me it seemed better "the image of the beautiful" or simply "beauty" or "the beautiful".

[1] James *Thom's life-size statues illustrating *Burns's poem. See *DNB* lvi. 156.

[2] William *Law, *A Serious Call to a Devout and Holy Life* (1728), abridged for the S.P.C.K.

[3] William Ellery Channing, 'Remarks on the Character and Writings of Fenelon', in *Christian Examiner*, vi. 1–35 (Boston 1829).

[4] Probably poems by William *Wordsworth; possibly his brother Christopher *Wordsworth's *Ecclesiastical Biography* or *Sermons* (1810 or 1814).

[5] Henry *Card, 1779–1844, vicar of Great Malvern 1815.

[6] John Reveley Mitford, 1807?–38, vicar of Manaccan, Cornwall.

[7] Alfred *Tennyson, 1809–92, poet laureate 1850, cr. baron 1884; his 'Timbuctoo' won the chancellor's prize in 1829.

18. Sunday.

Breakfast with Doyle, Hallam, Gaskell—in which I hope I was right. It is difficult to draw line between a private breakfast & a party. Chapel & sermon. Dean preached in morng: in aftn Mr Palmer of Brasen-nose,[1] an able & excellent sermon—walking with Harrison, & again with Moncreiff. read Bible—Mant notes—wrote notes a good deal—Dodwell's 3 Charges[2] (+) & Laurence on Baptism[3] partially.

19. M.

Cowper's Letters—& Niebuhr—routing, sorting, & arranging—walk with Moncreiff—reading put off another day—breakfast with Rogers—Hallam, Doyle, Gaskell there—Hallam & Doyle with me during the evening.

20. T.

Cowper's Letters—sat with Doyle &c. out in bookshops &c. Gaskell had tea with me. Harrison & Seymer there too—much conversation chiefly on projected Society.[4] Anstice also sat with me, conversing chiefly on that.

21. Wed.

Heard from & wrote to T.G. Breakfast with Harrison. He, Seymer,[5] Childers, Gaskell, wined with me. Lecture in Polybius—read a little—Cowper's Letters—Hooke—killed time reading sundries at Parker's [bookshop].

22. Th.

breakfast with Seymer. At Mr Cardwell's Lecture. A delightful letter from H.J.G. Had also a very kind one from Mr Craig. Spent most of morning in talking to Acland & Anstice on Essay[6] Soc. also to Cole, & arranging for a meeting tomorrow. At Deb. Soc. in Evg—elected—1 Black Ball.[7] Farr with me, & Rogers—sat at Gaskell's—Cowper & a little Polybius—out a little while with Anstice. Wrote somewhat.

23. Fr.

Div. Lect. Polybius—Cowper—out shopping—day again spent, in great measure in (idleness, or else) canvassing for the projected Essay Society. Its prospects very dark during the early part of the day—Acland & Anstice refusing even to attend the meeting—Rogers uncertain, Harrison backing out in consequence of this bad news, Seymer & Gaskell lukewarm. In the

[1] William Jocelyn Palmer, 1778–1853; rector of Mixbury, Oxfordshire, 1802; f. of Roundell*.
[2] W. *Dodwell, *Three Charges on the Athanasian Creed* (1802).
[3] R. *Laurence, *Doctrine of the Church of England upon Baptism* 2v. (1818).
[4] See 22, 23 Oct. 29.
[5] Henry Ker Seymer, 1807–64, fellow of All Souls 1831–5, Peelite M.P. Dorset 1846–64.
[6] Substituted for 'Debatg'.
[7] The Oxford Union Society; by courtesy of its officers notes of its debates are taken from its minute books. This evening it carried by 45 to 17 Gaskell's motion approving *Pitt's conduct as minister.

evening however we met at Jim Gaskell's rooms—rules were agreed upon—
a President chosen (Harrison), Secretary (Gaskell) & arrangements made
for our first meeting tomorrow week, when Anstice opens. All went off in
the most satisfactory manner, to my great delight. I trust it may work well,
& that nothing in it may be displeasing to our Heavenly Father, but all in
strict subordination to his will. Acland—A. Acland—Anstice—Cole—
Doyle—Leader[1]—Harrison—Gaskell—Moncreiff—Seymer—Rogers—&
myself made up the full complement.[2]

24. Sat.

Polybius—Rhetoric & Lecture—began Book 2. some conv. & business with
two persons both really, I believe, in great distress.[3] Cardwell's Lecture—
did an English Theme—walk with Harrison—read Blackwood—wine tea &
talk at Gaskell's for most of evg with him & Doyle—partly on religion—
finished Vol 1. of Cowper's Letters—Pindar—shopped.

25. Sunday.

Chapel & St Mary's. Dr Burton preached ably on Creeds in general, &
Athanasian in particular. Doyle sat with me after dinner—we had much
conv. on these subjects—also at Gaskell's a little having tea there. Walking
with Coles—Mant's 1st Bampton [Lecture].[4] Stanhope's Prayers & Medita
tions—Stonehouse's Admonitions[5]—G.T.—Paley—Nares—Selections.

26. Mon.

Pindar—Polybius little—MacLaurin & Wood on Cubic Equations—papers
—at reading room—wrote to Pickering—Gaskell had tea with me—Lect.
in Divinity, Mathematics, and Polybius—conv. with Mrs Albutt. Potter
&c.—walking with Joyce.

27. Tuesday.

Two letters, 1 from Mrs G, 1 from H.J.G. Wrote to Mr G.[6] Paper. Cowper's
Corresp—began V.2. Rhetoric & Cardwell. MacLaurin—notes to Bible—
Polybius—& getting up Rhetoric—paper—at booksale & walk with Doyle.

28. Wednesday.

Gk T. Long Church. Pindar and Polybius—MacLaurin—at book sale & out
—papers—sat with Gaskell—Cowper's Letters—wrote part of a letter to
Hallam. At nt crammed a little—Gk Theatre &c.

---

[1] John Temple *Leader, 1810–1903, radical M.P. Bridgewater 1835–7 and Westminster
1837–47; retired to Cannes, 1844, and Florence, 1850. Cp. Jan. 1888.
[2] This college essay society was known, from *Gladstone's initials, as the 'WEG'. Its
minute book now forms Add MS 44809. Morley, i. 59–60, summarized its activities.
[3] More rescue work; see pp. xxix–xxx.   [4] R. *Mant, *An Appeal to the Gospel* (1812).
[5] Sir J. *Stonhouse, 'Admonitions against swearing' (1773), a tract.
[6] On the essay society; in Bassett, 15–17, dated a month early.

29. Thursday.

Gk Theatre dates &c—also Integral Calculus in morng. In the Fell's Exhibition Examination from 9 to 12, & from 1 to 4. Debate on Portugal[1]—tea & sat in Evg with Cole—met his old Tutor Mr Roberts a very agreeable & superior man apparently[2]—finished letter to Hallam. read Peel's June speech on Portugal,[3] &c. Gk. T.

30.

Six hours of Fell again. Out with Tancred. He had tea with me. newspapers —reading room—Gk Testament, Gk Theatre. Fasti Hellenici & Chronology. read Cowper—Gaskell sat with me.

31. Sat.

Five hours [at work]—2 a paper—near 3 construing & pottering. Out with Doyle—paper—calling—Tancred sat with me—Cowper—Fasti Hellenici &c. First meeting [of essay society] at 8½ in Anstice's rooms—he read a very good Essay[4]—business after. Rogers had tea with me—sat late. monthly accts. Gk. T.

Nov. 1.

Sacrament. Drake, Anstice, Harrison, Ld Grimstone & his brother, the two Aclands, Tupper—& perhaps the servitor—I did not observe. Chapel & St Mary's mg & aftn. Walk with Harrison—again with Moncreiff. Extracting passages—sat with Doyle—[read] Mant—Laurence—Nares—A Tract called "Lives of Bp Wilson & Hildesley".[5]

2. T. [sc. Monday.]

Gk. T. Div. Lect. Pindar, and Lect—notes to Gk T—sat with Gaskell, & he with me—wrote to H.J.G. read papers—out with Moncreiff—gaudy & all its nuisances—day miserably spent—declared first of the Fell candidates— little credit, so not much food for vanity, thank God. Slave Conv. Soc. Rep.[6]

3. Wed. [sc. Tuesday.]

Lecture in Rhet & Integral Calculus—also [worked on] those subjects out of Lecture—Polybius—Cowper—papers—wine with Neale—sat with Gaskell—tea with Doyle—out with Pusey—Cardwell's Lecture.

4.

Sore throat & hoarseness in mg—missed chapel & Div. Lect. Gk. Test &

[1] *Doyle's motion against govt. policy with regard to Portugal was carried, 25–21.
[2] Perhaps Arthur *Roberts, 1801?–86, rector of Woodrising, Norfolk, from 1831, author.
[3] NSH xxi. 1624–36, 1 June 1829.
[4] On the connexion between the moral and intellectual faculties.
[5] (1821).
[6] Cp. 10 May 29.

notes. Pindar & Lecture—Polybius little—integral calculus &c. Cowper's Letters—writing—and sundries. Out little. Wine with Tyndale. Tea with Gaskell.

5. Th.

Gk. Testament. Cowper. Polybius & Lecture. Integral Calculus. Pindar—part of sermon—out with Harrison—Jelf had tea with me—interesting evening at Debating Society[1]—&c.

6. Fr.

Gk. Testament. Div. Lect. Began Cicero's Select Orations, some of wh I have read before. Lect. in them.—Rhetoric—Integral Calculus—papers—out with Harrison—wine with Rogers & a pleasant Evg there—began Theme.

7. Sat.

Gk Testament. Rhetoric & Lecture. Integral Calculus and Lecture. Cardwell's Lecture—finished Theme and verses—finished Cowper's correspondence—calling &c. wrote to Mr G. Essay meeting at New Coll—satisfactory.[2] I was chosen Secretary. A little Pindar.

8. Sunday.

Chapel. Evg Sermon. read Mant a good deal. finished Laurence on Baptism. read two first homilies—Bible—extracts & writing. out with Moncreiff and alone—heard from T.G.

9. M.

Gk T. Div. Lect. Pindar & Lect. Notes and quotations to Bible, and other books—Integral Calculus—out with Doyle—a little Polybius & Rhetoric—Wine with Gaskell—papers—began Shelley's Posthumous Poems; read Alastor, wh is astonishing.

10. T.

Papers. At Wise's. Gk. T. Integral Calculus & Lecture. [Aristotle's] Rhetoric & Lecture. Cardwell's last. wine with Gaskell. Polybius—at Jelf's reading Rickards's verses &c. Part of Shelley's Prometheus unbound.

11. W.

G.T. & Div. Lect. with Biscoe about Theme—Pindar & Lect. Int. Calc. At Wise's long—dinner, wine & tea at New Coll. with Moncreiff—read part of

---

[1] Mainly spent in discussing books and periodicals for the library, and the rate of subscription.

[2] Essays were read to the society at two successive meetings, and discussed at the second. This time, *Anstice again; and *Moncreiff on natural and political freedom.

Oppidan No II.—with Rickards—Seymer with me too—wretchedly spent day, God forgive me.

12.

No improvement. Gk T. Int Calc & Lect. Rhet & Lect—both little. Polybius and Lect. At Wise's—booksale—[Union] reading room—debate—sundry motions[1]—finished No 2 of Oppidan & Prometheus Unbound.[2]

13. Friday.

G.T. Div. Lect. Cic. Orat. and Lecture—wrote over & altered a Latin Theme—did verses to it in English—paper—wrote to Robn—walked from 5 to 7½—Rhetoric—part of Cenci & preface.[3]

14. Sat.

Heard from Childers. G.T. Rhet & Lect. Int Calc Lect. paper. wrote Theme —worked at verses ineffectually, a little. read over last week's Theme in Hall—Dean gave me a book—wrote to Childers—& to J.N.G. Essay meeting in Evg—Moncreiff & Rogers—spirited discussion—all went off well again—wrote out the proceedings[4]—coffee with Rogers afterwards—a little Pindar—Moncreiff came to me for a little after dinner.

15. Sunday.

Dear Robertson's birthday. May God bless and keep him. How can I hope otherwise for him when I think of what is done for *me*: when in spite of my deep, inveterate, pervading depravity God so far, I believe, deigns to check me as to show me at times that I am ἁμαρτωλων ὁ πρωτιστος.[5] Were I substantially & practically sensible hereof, the first step would be made. Chapel & sermon mg & aftn—Mr Keble[6] (earnest on love & recollection of our Lord) & Dr Whately. Out with Coles—sat with Seymer. Read "Faith & Duty of a Christian"—two homilies—& went on with Mant—Selections —letter from H.J.G.

16. Monday.

Breakft. with Pusey—wine with Nicoll—tea with Hanbury—prayer— Notes to Bible &c—G.T. & Div. Lect—Pindar & Lect. Did some blank verse from him. finished Cenci. made list of Deb. Soc. as to pr[evious] votes on Sporting Magazine.[7]

[1] 'That the Revolt of the American Colonies was justifiable', carried without a division; and much private business.
[2] *Shelley.   [3] *Shelley.
[4] *Moncreiff again; and *Rogers on current English higher education.
[5] 'the very first of sinners'.
[6] John *Keble, 1792–1866, double first, 1811; fellow of Oriel, 1811–23, professor of poetry 1831–41; beloved country priest, vicar of Hursley, Hampshire, 1836; originated Oxford movement 1833; Keble College Oxford founded in his memory.
[7] See 26 Nov. 29.

17.

Gk T. Rhetoric—examples—Lecture—ran round meadow—out with Doyle —Pindar—Cole passed[1]—wrote to Farr—read papers at Deb. Soc. & Record—Polybius—part of "Soldier's Manual".[2] beast, fool, blackguard, puppy, reptile.

18. Wednesday.

Gk T. Div. Lect. Pindar & Lecture—Hobbes's Analysis—finished Soldier's Manual—Polybius—Int. Calc.—papers—out with Harrison. At "Independent Debating Society". scene ridiculous. Heard from T.G. & from Canning.

19. Th.

Gk T. Polybius & Lecture—Rhetoric & Lecture—Int. Calc. &c. paper— Beauties of Dryden—out—at debate[3]—tea & conv. after with Acland— Cic. Orations—wrote to H.J.G.

20. Fr.

Gk T. Divinity Lect. Cic. Orat. Int. Calc. papers. At Cole's concert & supper till between 12 & one—wine & coffee with Anstice—long conversation he & Acland only being there. At Wises—called on Price & sat some time with him.

21. Sat.

Latin Theme and Verses. papers. Rhetoric & Lecture. Essay meeting at Seymer's for two hours.[4] out with Harrison & Wilberforce.[5] Pindar—wrote to Aunt E—& wrote out an account of the proceedings, in the Journal. Letters from Farr & Selwyn.

22. Sunday.

Chapel & St Mary's morng & aftn. heard too an *excellent* sermon at Carfax from Mr Jones, our Precentor[6] on the Resurrection as a proof of our Saviour's claim to character of Messiah & the completeness of his work.— Mant—Began Heber's Life of J. Taylor[7]—writing—and two Homilies— Tupper had wine & tea with me.

[1] In his final examination, without honours.
[2] Indian army drill-book (1827).
[3] Unanimity in juries was deplored; various minor motions discussed.
[4] *Rogers again; and Seymer on application of steam to warfare.
[5] Henry William *Wilberforce, 1807–73; pupil of *Newman at Oriel; became Roman catholic 1850.
[6] John *Jones, 1792–1852, the poet Tegid; chaplain of Christ Church 1819–43; incumbent of St. Thomas's, Oxford, 1823–41; vicar of Nevern, Pembrokeshire, from 1841.
[7] (1822).

23. Monday.

Gk. T. Div. Lect. Pindar & Lect. After Lecture, my Tutor asked me whether I was going into the Church, and whether there wd be any chance of my wishing to remain here & take pupils. Integral Calculus questions & writing them out—out with Hope—papers at reading room—Manfred[1]—Heber's J. Taylor little—quotations to Bible, & to Rhetoric.

24. Tuesday.

G.T. Rhetoric & Lect. Polybius—Pindar—(neither very much or effectually) —Int. Calc.—out with Moncreiff—Record—began Erskine's Freeness of the Gospel.[2] Had Moncreiff, Hanbury, Ross,[3] and Ward, to wine—Hanbury & Moncreiff staid to tea.

25. Wed.

Gr. T. & Divin. Lect. Pindar & Lecture. Int. Calc. questions &c. we get nothing from Saunders now. Biscoe told me I shd probably be made Student for wh I ought to be thankful—Out little—Polybius—at reading room—papers—Erskine—Cain (Byron's)—Mazeppa[1]—& prisoner of Chillon[1] (+). Gratifying letters from R.G., J.N.G., & John Conway[4] . . . all much so.

26. Th.

G.T. Rhet & Lect. Polybius & Lecture—mathematics—Erskine—Shelley debate—Cambridge men came & all spoke—rather astounding to us—voted for Shelley—& against Sporting Magazine, which was carried by 65 to 58. Wine with Price. Supper with Doyle & the Cambridge men after debate— up late[5]—wrote home.

27. Friday.

G.T. & Lecture—Cicero Orat. & Lecture—Milnes & Hallam sat with me part of forenoon—(hot) lunch at Hamilton's—Mathematics—Record— wine with Gaskell—much discussion—sat talking till 12.

28. Sat.

Rhet. little—Had Hallam, Milnes, Hamilton, Gaskell, Doyle, to breakfast,

[1] *Byron.
[2] Thomas *Erskine—the theologian, not the lawyer—*The Unconditional Freeness of the Gospel* (1828).
[3] John Lockhart Ross, 1810–91, of Oriel; gs. of 6th bart; vicar of Fifield, Oxfordshire, 1840, Avebury, Wiltshire, 1852, St. George-in-the-East, London, 1863, St. Dunstan-in-the-East 1873; author.
[4] Of Edgehill, eastern suburb of Liverpool.
[5] A. H. *Hallam, Thomas Sunderland, 1806–67, and Richard Monckton *Milnes, 1809–85, cr. Lord Houghton 1863, dilettante, came over from Cambridge to support *Doyle's motion that *Shelley was a better poet than *Byron. A speech from (Cardinal) H. E. *Manning, 1808–92, of Balliol, the president, brought on defeat by 90 to 33. For *Milnes and *Manning, see Add MSS 44215, 44247–50.

they remained during forenoon—did Theme hurriedly, they not going till past one. heard from Mr Hagart & H.J.G.—paper—Erskine—Essay Soc. meeting[1]—Int. Calc.—Pindar—sat at Acland's till 10 & with Gaskell till 11. With respect to the Cambridge philososphy I am not altogether enchanted—I should like more time to judge—I fear in some more show than substance—Hallam I think the deepest—I cannot help liking Milnes, with whom I had a great deal of conversation, and we scarcely agreed on one point excepting the universality of love; and then on the end not the means.

29. Sunday.

Chapel & St Mary's morng & aftn. sat with Cole after dinner & had tea with Harrison. finished Erskine—an extraordinary book—writing—Jeremy Taylor's Life—Began Erskine on Evidences[2] &c.

30. Monday.

All Saints day.—Pindar a good deal, and Lecture—a wine party—asked very many, got but few—Began Coleridge's Friend[3]—wrote to Mr Hagart —called on Mr Pusey—Polybius. tea with Doyle—some Bible—reading. out with Joyce.

December 1. Tuesday.

heard from Mother & wrote part of a letter to her. Rhetoric & Lecture. Record & papers—Friend—out a little. Wrote out Essay Soc's proceedings —Mathematics a good deal—in Evg with Saunders long—he confirmed Biscoe's news about Studentship—a little Pindar and Polybius. G.T.

2. Wed.

G.T. Div. Lect. Pindar & Lect. quotations to Rhetoric. Friend. finished letter to Mrs G. out, but not very long. wine party. had Gaskell, Doyle, Hope, Price, Lyall, young Grimston, Rogers: asked 2 Bernards.[4] Polybius. censor's speech. monthly accts.

3. Th.

Polybius a good deal—& Lect. Rhetoric & Lect. Friend—wine with Harrison. long debate[5]—Equation—Cic. Orat.—breakfast with Seymer.

4. Friday.

Cic. Orat. & Lect—paper. Friend. Sunday School Reader Soc. proceedings.

---

[1] Seymer again; and A. H. D. Acland on progress of arts and sciences.
[2] T. *Erskine, *Remarks on the Internal Evidence for the Truth of Revealed Religion* (1820).
[3] S. T. *Coleridge's metaphysical periodical, 1809–10.
[4] Charles Brodrick Bernard, 1811–90, Eton and Balliol, bp. of Tuam from 1866, younger brother of Lord Bandon.
[5] A motion of Gaskell's approving Russian policy in the eastern question was lost by 12 to 67.

Wine with Tyndale—afterwards with Cole—Pindar, & Rhetoric. began Abstract—Equations.

5. Saturday.

Record. Pindar. out. pottered talking &c—but it is hardly necessary to mention this since it is as regular an occupant of a portion of my time, as eating or sleeping. Othello, part of (+) Rhetoric Abstract for a long time; but did little. Wine with Buller. Essay-meeting.[1] Censor's speech. Long debate. Wrote out proceedings. Anstice with me some time after. Polybius a little.

6. Sunday.

Sacrament: as cold and unprepared as usual. Ld Grimston & his brother, Acland jun. Tupper, Anstice, Williams (sen)[2] & myself. St Mary's in aftn. Mr Keble, good. Heard a beautiful sermon from Sibthorp in the morning for Ch Miss[ionary] Society. Many Ch Ch men there. May he who ministereth seed to the sower sow it in us all & cause it to spring up & bring forth much fruit. Oh how unworthy am I to put up such a prayer. But there is balm in Gilead.[3] Psalms & notes—Heber's J. Taylor—Mant—Erskine on Evidences —wrote in Selections &c.

7. Monday.

Wrote to T.G. out with Harrison & Rogers—Int. Calc. Rhetoric Abstract, with wh I am miserably slow. Polybius & Friend. Dined at Dr MacBride's— very much pleased with him. Sat with Doyle afterwards.

8. Tuesday.

Heard from T.G. Record—papers—Friend—sat with Ross—Polybius. Mathematics. Pindar—Abstract of Rhetoric & some examples. Wine with Anstice—& with Ward at Wadham.

9. Wed.

Breakfast with Tupper. Polybius. Pindar. tea with Gaskell—he sat with me also. Abstract of Rhetoric & Examples a good deal—Friend—wrote to Mr Craig—killed time, tho' in some want of it.

10. Thursday.

read hard & sat up (a nine years wonder with me) till 3½. Finished Abstract of Rhetoric—V 2 of Friend, and read part of V.1. many examples to Rhetoric —Read Pindar & Polybius—wine with Gaskell after dinner. &c.

[1] A. H. D. Acland on arts and sciences; T. D. *Acland on the theory of beauty.
[2] Penry Williams of Penpont, 1807–86, Brecon magnate.
[3] II Cor. ix. 10, Jer. xlvi. 11.

11. Friday.[1]

Pindar. Collections 9—4. English into Latin—Latin into Greek—Divinity & History papers—*vivâ voce* in Pindar, Rhetoric, & Polybius. History—Math.

Dean told me I should have a Studentship. May I be grateful to him & thankful to the giver of every good & perfect gift. Wrote letters to my Father & Canning—read Record & Heber's Life of J. Taylor. a few English Verses.

12. Saturday.

Walking with Harrison—pottering—read papers—wine with Moncreiff—wrote upon λόγος, παραβολὴ, & παράδειγμα[2]—began Life of Ld Bacon[3]—&c. Wrote a long letter[4] wh I think of sending anonymously to Howley.

13. Sunday.

Ch & Sermon morng & aftn—out with Harrison & Moncreiff, & in evg alone. read Mant—Shuttleworth's Serm. at Festival of the Sons of the Clergy, very able & good[5]—Barrow's on the Crucifixion (admirable)[6]—Heber's J. Taylor—Bible—writing &c.

14. Monday.

Out with Harrison—dined with Moncreiff—wine in New Coll. common room —Pindar with Harrison at nt—heard from T.G. finished Bacon's Life—Mathematics—D. Calc.—Othello—&c. &c.

15. Tuesday.

Canning came, in Evg. heard from home; congratulatory letter. Out. Record. finished Othello. Bacon's Adv. of Learng[7] began. Pindar with Harrison. Wrote to Selwyn. D. Calc. &c. Wrote part of a projected thing, προσραγορευ-ομενου.[8]

16. Wed.

Much with Canning & sometime with Steel[9] too—They, with Anstice & Harrison, had wine with me—sat with Anstice—English Verses. wrote home. Cic. Orat. but little, notes to Bible, Adv. Learning & Mathematics. none much.

---

[1] In the original, this day's entry precedes the entry for 10 December.
[2] Word, parable, and example.
[3] By David *Mallet (1740).
[4] Untraced.
[5] Preached in St. Paul's cathedral 8 May 1828.
[6] Isaac *Barrow, 'A Sermon upon the Passion of our Blessed Saviour' (1677).
[7] Francis *Bacon, *Advancement of Learning* (1605).
[8] 'Greeting'. A second word in Greek script deleted.
[9] Richard Steele, 1812?–31, student of Christ Church 1829.

17. Th.

Out with Canning who had breakfast & tea with me & staid chiefly in my rooms—we both had wine with Wood & staid pretty late—an agreeable evening—sat with Saunders some time—finished Pindar with Harrison—Adv. Learning—& little Cicero. Mathemat. questions.

18. Fr.

Out. Pindar with Harrison—ἀνεδράμομεν[1] some of the difficulties. paper. Adv. Learning. Had Acland senior, Moncreiff, Rogers, Canning to wine. Mathemat. Quest. A little elementary Algebra with Canning.

19. Sat.

Pindar with Harrison. Cic. Or.—Adv. Learning. paper, wrote to Mr G. Math.—some time with Saunders. Made my Latin Epistles, one for Dean, one for all the Canons. Canning with me all eveng.

20. Sunday.

Chapel morng & aftn—sermon on occasion of Ordination from Ogilvie of Balliol in mg—good. It was a solemn service, & good to think that probably much prayer was ascending. Heard from T. and R.G., & from Mr Craig on prayer-meetings—spent the eveng with Harrison, from 8 to 11 in discussing that and other interesting religious topics. I seem to be more bold in theory, but am more cowardly in practice. therefore more guilty from both. And Oh for his godly meekness and remarkable candour and simplicity. Heard Paget preach well—Bible—Mant (finished) & Heber's J. T[aylor].

21. M.

Surplice Prayers. Adv. Learning. Canning & Steel had wine with me: asked Woodcock[2] & Sutherland.[3] Sutherland had been with me. he seems a nice fellow. Wrote over some of my Epistles—papers—Pindar with Harrison—Mathematics.

22. Tuesday.

Wrote over the rest of my Epistles—& gave them up. breakft with Sutherland—lunch with Dr Pett[4]—wine with Harrison. out. Adv. Learning, and Pindar. Paper—wrote to H.J.G.

23. Wednesday.

A Theme in Hall & few verses. Examined in Homer & Virgil in the Chapter-

---

[1] 'we ran through'.
[2] Charles Woodcock, b. 1809, vicar of Chardstock, Dorset, 1833–75, canon of Salisbury 1869.
[3] Alexander John Sutherland, 1811?–67, F.R.S., chief physician St. Luke's hospital.
[4] Phineas Pett, 1756?–1830, archdeacon of Oxford 1797, canon 1815; see 4 Feb. 30.

house.[1] Dined with Dr Barnes.[2] Adv. Learning. Wrote to Gaskell and Doyle. Shopping.

24. Thursday.

Christmas Eve—and the birthday of dearest Anne who will never count birthdays more but rejoices in the boundless expanse of eternity. Wrote to Mrs G—to Mr Craig—Breakfasted with Selkirk. Bill paying.
Made Student after Chapel, with Sutherland, Strangways,[3] Biscoe,[4] Canning, Mayo,[5] Steel & Jelf. For this may God make me thankful, & sensible too of the duties & obligations it involves. [6] Walked down to Cuddesdon & dined there very late & forgot to read the Bible at night. Backgammon. Beggar my neighbour.

25. Christmas Day.

Ch morng & aftn—Sacrament—Jacob Ley preached. Read Synge's Answer to all excuses,[7] and Adv. Learning. Christmas dinner. Saunders, 2 Leys,[8] Selkirk & Tancred. Saunders feasted the poor of the parish before.

26.

Finished Adv. Learning. a wonderful work, deserving of a more careful study than I have given it. Walked over to Wheatley & came up to town— read paper—& went down by Mail to Hallingbury[9]—arrived about midnight.

27. Sunday.

Set out to go to Church in morng but got wet & turned back from fear, having already a cold. Read the prayers in my room. Went in aftn. A fair sermon. Bible learning off & began Jeremy Taylor's Holy Living.[10] Also writing in verse & prose.

28. Monday.

went out to shoot. Began Lucretius parts of wh I have read before. Began Memoirs of Ld Liverpool.[11] wrote to T.G. Wrote up Journal. &c.

[1] See Morley, i. 49–50.
[2] Frederick Barnes, b. 1771?, sub-dean and senior canon.
[3] Stephen Fox Strangways, 1812?–39, of Maiden Newton, Dorset.
[4] William Archibald Biscoe, b. 1811?, brother of T. H. and F. Biscoe.
[5] Mayow Wynell Mayow, b. 1810?, d. after 1880, vicar of Market Lavington 1836–60. See Add MS 44246.
[6] Account in letter of 29 December to his brother John; in Bassett, 17–19.
[7] Edward *Synge, 'An Answer to all the Excuses . . . for . . . not coming to the Holy Communion', an S.P.C.K. tract (1744).
[8] Jacob Ley's brother John, 1805?–80?, fellow of Exeter 1831, rector of Waldron, Devonshire, 1851.
[9] The *Cannings' place near Bishop's Stortford.
[10] The Rule and Exercises of Holy Living (1650).
[11] Anonymous memoir of the second earl, prime minister 1812–27, written after his retirement but before his death.

29. *Tuesday*.

Memoirs of Ld Liverpool—Billiards with Canning—wrote a long letter to J.N.G.—Math—Hist. Greece[1] a little—& Lucretius—paper.

This is my birthday—now have I lived twenty years in this world, unprofitable in the sight of God and man—may I be made to feel permanently how great the shame of such a retrospect as mine is & convince myself how surely it is so.

With regard to the last year I have to thank God for many signal mercies. In one besetting sin there has been less temptation perhaps tho' not less readiness to be tempted—and though God has kept the temptation away there has been black sin on my part. Yet may I know who hath caused to be written " *The blood of Christ cleanseth from all sin* ".[2]

Miserably ignorant as I am, I have become persuaded of several things during the last year more strongly, as

1. That I must look for salvation from God.
2. That I am the chief of sinners.
3. That my wants are 1. Pardon through the blood of Christ.
            2. Sanctification through his Spirit.
4. That the main matter is, to eradicate the love of self, & substitute the love of God throughout—I mean after redemption.
5. That I cannot think a good thought, speak a good word, do a good deed.
6. That we are regenerate by Baptism & Baptism alone.
7. That we ought to love all men *as* ourselves.
8. That pleasure is identified with virtue. (i.e. perfect) and virtue is an abused & corrupted name for holiness. and holiness is included in the term "God", in the full extent of its signification.
9. And I am not to seek salvation for my own interest, but for the glory of God, for he may be glorified in the redemption of the meanest & worst of his creatures.
And 10. of all I think I am most certain of my own utter sinfulness.—and yet this certainty is not a pervading nor a living belief.

And may God be merciful to me a sinner & an hypocrite. Well it is good to think that a day will come when all my hypocrisy will be detected.

My mind has continued strongly inclined to the Church throughout.

My exertions & progress in temporal learning have been wretchedly deficient & my system requires amendment, & that radical, I fear it wants *a new principle*.

I am much too well thought of & yet have had some lessons to my pride for which I ought to be thankful.

And may blessing glory power & praise be to the Lord Most High.

30. *Wednesday*.

Out shooting from soon after breakfast till four. An Aunt of Canning's

---

[1] *Mitford.   [2] 1 John i. 7.

arrived.[1] read Ld Liverpool—Mathemat—Hist. Greece—& Lucretius: but not much of them. Heard from my Mother Tom & Helen.

31. Thursday.

The last day of the year. Billiards. Out. Memoirs of Lord Liverpool—looking over old pamphlets &c. wrote to Gaskell. Lucretius. Canning sat with me (always a good deal) more than usual. Heard from Doyle. Made up accts. Within the past year I think I have by God's grace made more advancement in temporal knowledge, in my modes of thought & notions of things, wretched as they still are, than in the last—would that I cd dare to affirm or believe myself *better* than I was. Yet my belief is that I have gained something in knowledge.

This year has brought us an awful loss in Anne's infinite gain.—but He who made her such can raise up another.

[1] George *Canning's half-sister, Joan Hunn.

Friday January 1. 1830. Hallingbury.

Memoirs of Ld Liverpool—paper. Billiards—out a good time with Canning, whom I like the more, the more I see of him—Lucretius and history of Greece.

Saturday 2.

Finished Memoirs of Ld Liverpool. Out shooting—billiards with Canning— History of Greece—Lucretius, and wrote to H.J.G.—Holy Living.

3. Sunday.

Church morng & aftn. Foster on Aversion of men of Taste to religion[1]— Taylor's Holy Living—Bible—& wrote in 'Selections'. heard from T.G.

4. Monday.

Fog. Out little. Billiards. Wrote to Pickering & Doyle. Lucretius—Hist. Greece—Denham & Clapperton[2] at beginning, cursorily—finished Foster's Essay.

5. Tuesday.

Finished Lucretius B.1.—packed up—Billiards—left at $12\frac{1}{2}$—arrived in London between 5 & 6—at George & Blue Boar[3]—paper—walked about the streets—Hist. Greece.

6. Wed.

Breakf with Uncle Divie, & dinner—saw Mr Larkins, Mrs Wadd, & Jane Cath[4] with whom I sat long—shopping & walking about—Hist Greece— moved to Berners Hotel.[5] Walked at night. Draughts.

7. Th.

Breakfast in Welbeck St—saw Mrs & Miss Wadd—shopping—at Temple— called on H. H. Joy & W. Ewart—papers—Hist. Greece—dined with Uncle D. again. Mr Mackay[6] there & his son.

8. Fr.

Packed—paper—left London by the Blenheim & got safely to Oxford about

[1] John *Foster, 'On Some of the Causes by which Evangelical Religion has been rendered less acceptable to Persons of Cultivated Taste', in his *Essays* (1805).
[2] H. *Clapperton, D. *Denham, and W. *Oudney, *Narrative of Travels and Discoveries in Northern and Central Africa on the years 1822, 1823, and 1824* (1826).
[3] Coaching inn in Holborn.   [4] Unidentified.
[5] In Berners Street, NE. of Oxford Circus.
[6] Possibly George Mackay of Strathkyle, 1757–1840, and his s. George, d. 1868.

4—sat some time with Biscoe—read papers—tea & sat with Tancred & Anstice—wrote home—wrote up Journal & accounts—unpack'd.

9. Sat.

Walk with Warter—heard from Mr G.—papers—wrote to Mr G.—going about, on the matter of rooms. Wine with Warter. At the Dean's in evg— a pretty large party—Lucretius & Hist. Greece—Companion to Almanack.

10. Sunday.

Chapel morng & aftn. Out, not very long. Breakfast with Tancred & Anstice —& sat conversing till 3½! on sundry subjects, a good deal on religion. At night, wrote on Conversion—extracts—began Short's Sermons[1]—Homilies —J. Taylor a little.

11. Monday.

Weather still very cold. Out. Looking at rooms—with Dean—talked with Mrs Albutt—Short & Paley—finished my paper on conversion—papers— Hist. Greece—Lucretius—Bishop at night with J. Ley.

12.

Left Oxford after breakfast & went by coach to Southam[2]—walked thence to Leamington—there found Mr & Mrs G, T.G. & H.J.G. & passed a very pleasant evening with them. Hist. Greece. Bp Sumner's Charge.[3]

13. Wednesday.[4]

remained at Leamington enjoying my short vacation—conversation. Hist Greece—Tales of a Grandfather—paper &c.

14.

Left Leamington about 10 & got to Oxford in 5 hours. remained at King's Arms[5]—went with my Father[6] to call upon the Dean. Lucretius.

15. Friday.

They[7] went, early in morng. Looking at rooms—moved into Canterbury rooms which require cleaning &c. &c. so that I shall be for some time un- settled, but [are] I think good & comfortable.[8] Very busy—my moving a formidable business. Hist Greece & Lucretius.

[1] T. V. *Short, *Sermons on some of the fundamental truths of Christianity* (1829).
[2] Seven miles ESE. of Leamington.
[3] J. B. *Sumner, 'A Charge delivered to the Clergy of the Diocese of Chester, at the Primary Visitation' (1829).
[4] Late entries till 21 January 1830 at least.
[5] Inn at Broad Street and Holywell Street.
[6] The words 'who was' here deleted.
[7] His parents.
[8] Rooms at the NE. corner of the Canterbury quadrangle of Christ Church, on the first floor. See Morley, i. 48–49. Sketch in Reid, G, 96.

16. Saturday.

With Biscoe a good while, talking about Lectures & degree &c. Engaged with Saunders for the Long Vacation in which I trust I have not done wrong. Went with Gaskell carpet-hunting. Debate with Quarterman the carpenter about bookcases. Hist. Greece—Lucretius.

17. Sunday.

Bible—Holy Living—Homilies—and writing. Chapel & sermon morng & aftn. Sat with Gaskell & had wine & tea in evening. heard from Mrs G & H.J.G.

18.

Ordered carpet—wrote home—paper—with Gaskell & Canning as on former days—no prospect of settlement [in rooms]—the former possessor's things not yet moved out—Hist. Greece & Lucretius. Dear John's birthday. God bless him.

19.

Dined with Canning at Dr Pett's. Stratfords[1] things at length moved out— but my laziness takes advantage of my confusion & I do nothing—Lucretius & Hist. Greece, but scant.[2]

20. Wednesday.

No more hope yet. Hist. Greece. Canning very ill with fever—sat with him & had coffee with Dr Pett in Evg and slept there. Sundries—for among other attendants of my move, I could not lay my hand on my Journal book, so I fear it will not be very accurate since Jan. 12. Wrote to Mrs G.

21. Thursday.

Coffee with Gaskell at Dr Pett's in Evg. Canning better. Up soon after 5— sat with him till Chapel—began Equites[3]—read a little Rhetoric. In utter confusion—absolutely turned out—wrote to Aunt E. Superintending & directing alterations. Slept again at Dr Pett's. papers—Lucretius.

22. Friday.

Had my new carpet put down—Ethics and lecture—with Canning—went to get a subscription or two in aid of those who are endeavouring to provide relief in the severe weather for the poor. dined with Dr & Mrs Hay.[4]—still

---

[1] John Wingfield-Stratford, 1810–81; high sheriff of Kent 1873; a gs. of 3rd viscount Powerscourt.

[2] 'but scant' substituted for 'about what they call "enough to swear by"'.

[3] Aristophanes, *Knights*.

[4] Thomas Hay, b. 1759, gs. of 7th earl of *Kinnoul; chaplain to house of commons 1790; canon of Christ Church 1795; m. 1786 Anne Bragge of Clevedale, Gloucestershire. See 29 Jan. 30.

directing alterations—with Doyle, Gaskell—breakfast with Seymer. Divinity Lecture.

23. Saturday.

Rhetoric Lecture—Shelley—began prickbillship[1]—long & interesting debate on Beauty & Taste—Anstice spoke remarkably well.[2] Elected President. wrote to Mr G. wrote out Debate—tried to get partially into order—discussion on beauty &c. priv[ately]. tried to get partially into order.

24. Sunday.

Sermon—morng—chapel mg & aft. unwell in aftn. with headache—tea with Dr Pett—Burnett[3]—conversation with Anstice, very good: with Gaskell not more painful than usual: afterwards with Doyle & Gaskell near two in the morng, exceedingly distressing especially as regarded Doyle.

25. M.

At Surplice prayers in mg—headach worse—staid in for my first time since coming here.

26. Tuesday.

In bed all day, and taking medicine—it is well to be reminded & especially so gently as I am how easily we are thrown off the pursuance of all our schemes.

27. Wednesday.

Better thank God & up, but not very long—attempted to read sundries—among the rest Arabian Nights. I believe I have doctored myself wretchedly.

28. Thursday.

My headach is almost gone—I am weak, probably from my mismanagement—Saunders & Biscoe both came & sat with me—read a little Burnet & part of the Epicurean[4]—wrote to Robertson—at Lyall's to wine—and at debate[5]—tea with Gaskell after.

---

29. Fr.

Poor Dr Hay died in the forenoon most suddenly & unexpectedly. I thought he seemed devout & trust his soul rests in his Redeemer.—out. finished Epicurean. Wrote to J.N.G. At wine with Seymer—went in again—read some of Mrs More's Tracts.—tradespeople's business &c.

---

[1] As one of the junior students, kept the roll of undergraduates attending chapel.
[2] T. D. *Acland on beauty; F. Cole on revolutions.
[3] Gilbert *Burnet, *Exposition of the xxxix Articles of the Church of England* (1699).
[4] Tale by Thomas *Moore (1827).
[5] A motion of *Manning's, replacing one of *Hanmer's, declaring parliamentary reform unnecessary was carried by 73 to 3.

30. Saturday.

Out. Essay Soc. Meeting—not very good—acted as President—named a subject with which I am not pleased.[1] read Mrs More's Tales[2]—paper—Lucretius—&c. &c. made up accts.

31. Sunday.

Chapel morng & aftn. sermon morng—sat with Harrison—sat after dinner & had tea too with Tupper—Bible—finished Mrs More's Tales which I have read with great pleasure—Two of Blomfield's Sermons—& Burnet.

February 1. Monday.

Burnet—and Divinity Lecture—Newton and Lecture—Ethics—Aristophanes—out—paper—wrote to H.J.G. & to Hagart.

2. T.

heard from & wrote to R.G.—papers—Notes to Queen Mab[3]—Burnet on the Articles—Equites—my book-cases partially put up. began to stow the contents.

3. W.

I continue to act as prickbill. Letters from Mr G., Mrs G & T.G. dear Helen I fear has suffered much. For four or five days now I have been in an execrably idle & discontented humour—I hope it may end by my having a clear idea for a time at least of my own sinfulness, if it please God. The weather continues intensely cold. Wrote to my dear Mother—getting my books put up. Burnet & Div. Lect, Newton & Lect. Ethics. Mitchell[4]—& Equites.

4. Th.

Poor Dr Pett died a little before 2. May we also be ready. Saw J. Wishlade.[5] Tried an Equation. Wrote to R.G. & to Farr—[read] Burnet—Mitchell—Rhetoric & Lect—Equites and Lect—putting away papers &c—early [Greek] history cursorily & little.

5. Friday.

Attended Dr Hay's funeral with the rest of the Students. At his house soon

---

[1] F. Cole on revolutions; O. B. Cole on equal distribution of happiness. *Gladstone's subject was 'The Comparative Rank of Poetry & Philosophy'.

[2] Tracts (1819).

[3] *Shelley.

[4] T. Mitchell's translation of Aristophanes, *Knights* (1820).

[5] James Emmanuel Wishlade, a poor cottager, object of *Gladstone's charity.

after 9—funeral & chapel at 10. Heard from Aunt E. read Burnet & Mitchell—Mathematics—papers—wrote to H.J.G.—out—how long I am to go on as idle as at present I know not—a little Logic at night with Gaskell.

6. Saturday.

Rhetoric & Lecture. Mitchell—Burnet—a little Ethics—Essay Soc. & sitting afterwards[1]—& 600 lines of Prometheus Vinctus (+)[2] with Doyle. A *just better* day tho' no great things—choosing prints.

7. Sunday.

Prickbill. writing impositions &c. in that capacity. Chapel as usual—sermon in morng—in aftn sleepy—Bible—Blomfield—Burnet—Homilies—heard from Mrs G. Thank God a great & happy change in the weather.

8. Monday.

Divinity & Mathematical Lect—Ethics & Lect—papers—Equites—Harris's Philological inquiries[3]—& read near four hours at Æsch with Doyle—finished Prometheus Vinctus & began ἑπτα (+).[4] Canning relieved me as prickbill.

9. Tuesday.

Rhetoric & Lecture. Aristophanes & Lecture. Burnet—papers—heard from & wrote home—heard from R.G.—called on Maurice[5] and Cunningham.[6] tea with Cole—read about half the ἑπτα with Doyle—print buying.

10. Wed.

Finished Septem & began Persae,[7] with Doyle—a little Burnet & Div. Lect—papers—out—dined with Tancred & had coffee with Acland—a little Aristophanes—debates on treason & sedition Bills[8]—heard from R.G. Newton & Lect—Ethics and Lect.

11. Th.

Poor Dr Pett's funeral. At Wise's Sale. Idle—talking with Gaskell &c—wine with Wilson[9]—cogitated a little afterwards—spoke at Debating Society on

[1] O. B. Cole on happiness; Gaskell on phrenology.
[2] Aeschylus.
[3] By James *Harris, 3v. (1780–9).
[4] Aeschylus, *Seven against Thebes*.
[5] Frederick Denison *Maurice, 1805–72, Christian socialist, professor at London 1840–53, and Cambridge 1866–72.
[6] Charles Thornton Cunningham, b. 1811?, s. of J. W.*; colonial governor.
[7] Also by Aeschylus.
[8] 1795; see next entry.
[9] Robert Francis Wilson, 1809?–88, of Oriel; canon of Salisbury 1870.

Treason and sedition bills, not well [1]—papers—Critic—Burnet—tea with Harrison, afterwards with Gaskell. Elected on Committee at fag end. [2]

12. Fr.

Burnett & Div. Lect.—Math & Lect. Ethics (not long) and Lect. At Wise's a little. Hanging pictures &c. Persae with Doyle. Read papers— & looked to sundries, Turning &c. for my Essay—but with no success—wrote a good deal of my Essay.

13. Saturday.

Burnet—Rhetoric and Lecture—print hanging & sundry kinds of time-killing—paper—preparations by neatifying &c. &c. for the Essay Soc. to meet in my room at night—finished my Essay hurriedly & read it [3]—an agreeable meeting & soiree afterwards—debate on Phrenology—my Essay a failure—finished Persae. [4]

15. Monday.

Burnet & Lecture. Newton & Lecture. Ethics. breakft with Menteith—busy about a requisition to Dr Tatham, [5] wh seems possible—wrote to R.G. —& to H.J.G.—paper—unpacking books from Eton—tea with Gaskell—Aristophanes.

16. T.

Burnet. Rhetoric & Lecture. Aristophanes & Lecture. A little Ethics—unpacking & arranging books—at length got into pretty good order—a wine party—Woodcock, young Cole, Joyce, Sutherland, Barnes, Cunningham, Scott, [6] Mayo, Steele, Jelf.

17. W.

Burnet—Div. Lect. Newton & Lect. Ethics & Lect. Whately on Sabbath—wine & coffee with Neale—a few Lent verses (initial)—paper—Aristophanes—Walk with Seymer.

18. Th.

Burnet—Blomfield—Rhet. & Lect. Aristoph & Lect. Walk with Wilson—

[1] Maiden speech at Union; see Morley, i. 63. *Hanmer and *Gladstone opposed *Moncreiff's motion approving *Fox's conduct on the treason and sedition bills; it was lost by 26 to 44.
[2] Ninth of ten members elected, headed by Sidney *Herbert the new president.
[3] Add MSS 44720, f. 34. Cp. 20 Feb. 30.
[4] *Gladstone omitted to make an entry on 14 February, and the pagination of the next five pages of MS—till 22 March—is confused.
[5] Edward *Tatham, 1749–1834, controversialist; fellow 1781, and rector 1792, of Lincoln.
[6] Robert *Scott, 1811–87, lexicographer; master of Balliol 1854; dean of Rochester 1870. Cp. Add MS 44295.

papers—dined with Pusey, with whom I had a good deal of conversation, & I liked him extremely. *Tomorrow if it please Almighty God I purpose to remember the removal of my beloved sister*—but I cannot promise; for my body has the mastery over my mind.

19.

I consider myself to have been leading a more unchristian life lately than for a long time before—and I attribute it to these two causes, mainly: the indulgence of bodily intemperance, and a grossly careless & sinful habit of saying my prayers when half asleep at night & half awake in the morning. The consequences alas! have been a greatly increased wordliness of feeling: more frequent ebullitions of a temper naturally & habitually hard, selfish, testy, imperious, overbearing: O that God would print deeply in my heart the truth, the reality of each word as I here write it; but while it is a general sin of mankind to pare repentance down to confession, I add to this the paring confession down to a mere written & secret acknowledgement, of that scarcely admitting the truth, at least practically avoiding its acknowledgement. O may God deliver me from *my* pride, *my* sloth, *my* lust, *my* covetousness, *my* envy, *my* greediness; for *mine* they are, & made mine by resistance to the Holy Spirit. He in whose inner man the image of God is restored, is happy. Would God I could perceive its beginnings.

> Mercy, good Lord, mercy I ask,
>   This is the total sum:
> For mercy, Lord, is all my suit;
>   Lord! let thy mercy come.

May I feel what I am, & what I ought to be, and may the love of God destroy utterly the love of self in me—the latter being now painfully predominant.
Burnet—Blomfield—Newton—Ethics—Lectures in Divinity & Ethics—paper—wrote to Mrs G.—walked alone—corrected Essay—tea with Tupper—after with Gaskell—wrote over about half of Essay.

Sat. 20.

Walk with Harrison. Burnet—Rhetoric & Lect—a little Aristoph—wine with Barnes—did & wrote over Lent verses—finished writing over Essay—Long debate—thrown out by 7 to 5.[1]

21. Sunday.

Chapel & St Mary's morng & aftn—walk with Maurice—sat with Seymer & with Gaskell—read Burnet & Blomfield—& Coleridge's Aids to Reflection.

[1] See Morley, i. 59. *Gladstone moved 'That the rank of philosophy is higher than that of poetry'; and *Doyle read an essay comparing English poetry with Greek.

22. M.

Burnet & Lect. Math Lect. Ethics & Lect. Out with Gaskell—tea with him —paper—wrote to T.G.—heard from R.G.—Aids to Reflection—Aristophanes—wretchedly idle, though the items seem enough: for there is no substance in them.

23. T.

Rhetoric & Lect. Logic with Gaskell. Aristophanes & Lect—a little again. with Doyle—at Mills's Lecture[1]—out with Moncreiff—paper—Burnet—a wine party—had Canning, Gaskell, Doyle, Rogers, Wilson, Wood, Harrison, old Acland, Anstice, Tancred, Bruce, young Grimston, Seymer.

24. Ash Wednesday.

Two Chapels. out with Rogers. letters from home, Newton,—Ethics— Burnet—a little Aristophanes—papers—greater part of Therry's memoir of Canning[2]—no lectures. Georgics—Lucan.

25. Th.

Rhet & Lect. Aristoph & Lect—paper—out—finished Memoir of Canning— Burnet—Blomfield—thought & wrote on Canning, but unconnectedly— spoke for him at the Debating Society[3]—Gaskell & Canning also spoke, with others.

26. Fr.

Blomfield—Burnet & Lect. Math & Lect. Ethics & Lect. wrote to J.M.G. Robertson. papers. Lucretius. Walk with Anstice. Dined with Mr & Mrs Gaskell at the Angel.

27. Saturday.

Rhetoric & Lect—finished it. Theme. wrote to J.N.G.[4] paper—out with Gaskell—Blomfield—began Heeren[5]—dinner with Doyle—wine with Tancred & Grimston—Essay Society.[6]

28. Sunday.

Chapel—St Thomas's (Mr Jones) & St Mary's (Dr Faussit)[7]—walking with

---

[1] William Mills, 1793?–1834, Whyte's professor of moral philosophy at Magdalen 1829.
[2] (Sir) Roger *Therry prefixed a memoir to his 6-vol. ed. of *Canning's speeches (1828).
[3] Vaughan's motion 'that Mr *Canning's conduct as a Minister is deserving of the highest commendation' was carried by 53 to 15. See Morley, i. 63; notes for speech in Add MS 44719, ff. 201–2.
[4] Part in Bassett, 19–20.
[5] A. H. L. Heeren, Sketch of Political History of Ancient Greece (tr. 1829).
[6] *Doyle again; and Grimston on emulation in education.
[7] Godfrey Faussett, 1781?–1853, fellow of Magdalen 1802, Margaret professor of divinity 1827 and canon of Christ Church 1840.

Cole. At Canning's to wine—Seymer there. This is a medium between what I allow & disallow—I knew not what it would be—finished Burnet and Blomfield—Aids to Reflection—Kaye's Eccl. Hist[1]—Opinions on Bapt. &c.

March 1. Monday.

Divinity Lecture—Aids to Reflection—Heeren, with Bell[2]—Ethics & Lect. Newton & Lect. Wrote to my Father—wine with Acland—tea with Cole—a little Aristophanes. walk with Seymer.

2. Tuesday.

Aristophanes & Lecture—Mills's Lect. paper—walk with Harrison—making up accts, thirds &c. wrote to Childers—read to Gaskell who is ill—wine with Moncreiff—Aids to Reflection—Potter and Heeren on early history &c. heard from R.G. notes to Ethics.[3]

3. Wed.

Div. Lect. Math. & Lect. Ethics & Lect. Greek history—in Potter &c. Aids to Reflection—paper—Selections—out with Doyle—a wine party—Seymer, Cole, Jodrell, young Acland, Moncreiff, Lyall, Pusey, Neale, Buller, Strangways, Kynaston, Nicoll, a very little Aristophanes. writing.

4. Th.

Aristophanes a good deal & lect. Potter's Antiq. Hor[ace] Ep[istula] ad Pis[ones],[4] part of. papers—out with Rogers—wine with Biscoe and Nicoll —at debate—good[5]—Thornton[6] made a very promising speech. Moved Quarterly Theological Review & thank God! carried it. I say thank God advisedly.

5. Fr.

Walk with Rogers. Div. Lect. Wrote out Deb. Soc. proceedings—Ethics & Lecture—Math (little) & Lect. Potter—writing in blue book—heard from T.G. wine & coffee with Moncreiff—papers—Aids to Refl.

6. S.

Th & verses. Aids to Refln. History &c. in Tytler and Potter—out with Tancred—conv. with Tupper—had Anstice, Acland, Maurice, Gaskell, to

[1] Bp. John *Kaye, *Ecclesiastical History of the Second and Third Centuries, illustrated from the Writings of Tertullian* (1825).

[2] James *Bell, tr. C. Rollin, *Ancient History*, 3v. (1828).

[3] Aristotle.

[4] Another name for the *Ars Poetica*.

[5] *Herbert's motion on landlords' duty to improve the state of the poor was carried by 56 to 34.

[6] Charles Thornton, 1811?–39, priest.

wine—Essay Soc—good deb. on Emulation—carried agst it[1]—Horace A[rs] P[oetica]—paper.

7. Sunday.

Sacrament—a good attendance. Sermon & Chapel mg & aftn. In aftn resumed being prickbill. Dr Burton preached in mg on the Atonement—I trust he was misunderstood in the idea formed. Tupper had wine & tea with me—walking with Coles, & with Anstice—Aids to Reflection—Mant Bible. Life of J. Taylor—Selections—Bible.

8. M.

Out with Gaskell. Calling. Wine with Joyce. papers. Wrote to Mrs G. Tea with Cole. Div. Lect. Math & Lect. little Ethics—Horace—Viger,[2] Potter &c. Busy in mg finding out at Dean's desire who go in for the Ireland, &c.

9. Tues.

Aristoph & Lect. heard from Mr G. Mills's Lecture. Wine with Tupper and Anstice. tea with Gaskell. Horace A.P. with notes, criticisms &c. Hermann de pron. αὐτός[3] & abstracting him. A good while at work, but very little done.

10. Wed.

A day of parties. breakfast with Staniforth—wine with Tyndale & Wood —refused Bernard—tea with Hanbury—introduced to Mr Sibthorp—out with Gaskell. Div. Lect.—Math & Lect. little Ethics—finished A.P. of Horace—papers—reading Hermann &c. &c.

11. Th.

Aristophanes, Finished Acharnenses. did a few Greek Iambics. out with Seymer. Hermann. Elmsley on Medea[4]—Ed. Rev. on Etruscans—Cramer[5] —papers.

12. Fr.

Ireland began—Latin into Greek 9–12. Cowper into Iambics 1–4. Out with Wood & Rogers. Wine with Kynaston and Buller—History maths &c. paper.

13. Sat.

Cicero into English with notes 9–12. Roman History questions 1–4. History

---

[1] Grimston again; and *Harrison on ancient and modern views of political science.
[2] Possibly Franciscus Vigerus, seventeenth-century editor of Eusebius and Plato.
[3] On the pronoun 'self'.
[4] Peter *Elmsley ed. Euripides' *Medea* (1818).
[5] Probably J. A. *Cramer, *Ancient Greece*, 3v. (1828).

again—wine with Pusey—out with Wood and Rogers—Essay Soc.[1] tea with Cole. Persius. dates.

14. Sunday.

Out with Harrison, & with Moncreiff. A very good sermon from Mr Anderson of Balliol[2]—also another from Woodgate,[3] but not so exclusively a *sermon*. Harrison had tea with me. Bible—notes—Lightfoot[4]—Aids to Reflection.

15. M.

9–12, $2\frac{1}{4}$—$5\frac{1}{2}$ Ireland. English into Greek, & Greek critical questions. Out. Greek History with Biscoe—wine with Parsons—tea with Gaskell—papers—Greek philosophy.

16. Tuesday.

9–12 Greek history questions. 1–4 Greek into English and Latin. Out with Rogers. Wine with Jodrell—and Gaskell—papers—Record—a long conv. with Gaskell on religious matters—Greek history in morning—a little Persius.

17. Wed.

A little Persius—9–12 Latin Sapphics—1–4 English Essay. out with Rogers afterwards. Wine & tea with Cole.—read Coleridge's Ancient Mariner & Three graves. papers. a little Persius with Saunders in evg—chiefly talking.

18. Th.

Setting matters to rights. papers. Ed. Rev. on Horsley.[5] Out watching for the news of the Ireland. Payne[6] the successful candidate—a little Aristophanes. Potter. debate—spoke on the Age[7]—wine with Sutherland. Tea with young Acland. Close.[8]

[1] *Harrison again; and *Leader on disposition of character.
[2] James Stuart Murray Anderson, 1800?–69; rector of Tormarton, Wiltshire, 1851, and canon of Bristol, 1856.
[3] Henry Arthur Woodgate, 1801?–74, fellow of St. John's 1817–38, canon of Worcester 1847.
[4] Perhaps John *Lightfoot, *Collected Works*, 2v. (1684), mainly commentaries on the gospels.
[5] *Edinburgh Review*, xvii. 465 (February 1811), on Samuel *Horsley's *Sermons* and controversy with Joseph *Priestley.
[6] Peter Samuel Henry Payne, 1810?–41, scholar 1827 and dean 1839 of Balliol, priest.
[7] The Union rejected, by 52 to 24, a motion 'That our criminal code is a national disgrace', and turned to private business. *Gladstone spoke against a motion that the *Age* newspaper should be discontinued, but voted for it (it was lost, 26–63); he also opposed the purchase of *Moore's life of *Byron (carried by 23 to 22).
[8] Probably F. *Close, *Nine sermons on the Liturgy* (1825) or *Miscellaneous sermons*, vol i (1829).

19. Fr.

Went on with Close wh I like much. Selections. A little Aristophanes beginning on Nubes (+). Potter. wine with Bernard & Rogers—dined with Rogers. with Biscoe. heard news about Ireland as regards my own position. Heard from home. began Abstract of Rhet. Sundries. Unable to sleep for some time at night from excitement. Papers. Wrote out debate & did Secretary's business, Gaskell being ill.[1]

20. Sat.

Out. dined with Gaskell. Debate—spoke as usual.[2] Coffee afterwards. Behaved ill. [Read] Close. Coleridge. Wrote to H.J.G. papers. a little Abstract. read over Lent verses. investigating some of the questions with Biscoe.

21. Sunday.

A long & very pleasant walk with Anstice. Chapel & St Mary's morng and aftn. Selections—writing—Close—Aids to Reflection—sat with Saunders —Macneil on Evangelical Idolatry[3]—Tiptaft[4] & Hewlett.[5]

22. Monday.

Close. Ethics. Rhet. Abstract. papers. Lempriere's Biog. Dict.[6] Wine with Moncreiff. Walk with him also. Ethic Lecture. Tea & sat with Gaskell.

23. Tuesday.

Close. Aristophanes,—writing notes to it—Lecture—had to go to Veysie about a most disgraceful disturbance in Chapel last night. papers. read a little & made notes about Tyre.[7] Walk with Hope and Leader. Rhetoric Abstract a little. Heard from T.G.

24. Wednesday.

Last night between twelve and one I was beaten by a party of men in my own rooms.—Here I have great reason to be thankful to that God whose mercies fail not. And this for two especial reasons.

1. Because this incident must tend to the mortification of my pride, by God's grace: if at least any occurrence which does not border on the miraculous can. Because I take it for granted that I shall be despised by some for it. I hardly know what to think of my own conduct myself. It is no disgrace

[1] Union minutes for 4 and 18 March were signed by *Gladstone for Gaskell.
[2] *Leader again; and *Moncreiff on logic.
[3] Probably Hugh *McNeile, 'Popery Theological' (1829), a salvo in a pamphlet war against Joseph Sidden, a Roman catholic priest.
[4] W. Tiptaft's sermon on Matt. i. 21. (1830).
[5] Probably John *Hewlett, Sermons, 4v. (1804–25).
[6] J. *Lemprière, Universal Biography (1808), 2 ed., by E. Lord, with American addenda, 2v. (1825).
[7] Current subject for Latin verse prize.

to be beaten for Christ was buffeted and smitten—but though calm reasoning assures me of this, my impulses, my habit of mind, my vicious & corrupt nature, asserts the contrary—may it be defeated.

2. Because here I have to some small extent an opportunity of exercising the duty of forgiveness. So long a time has elapsed since anyone has in any way injured me, that I have feared, in repeating the words 'forgive us our trespasses as we forgive them that trespass against us,' that I really had no practical knowledge of the nature and spirit of the words I was uttering. And I do not pretend to say that this is an offence serious enough now when a few hours have elapsed to weigh or remain in any way upon one's mind— independently I mean of principle, it is unimportant & unworthy consideration. But just at the time there was an opportunity—which would to God that I had better used.

I may condemn myself, for though I soon ceased to resist, I did not behave as I ought afterwards. It was suffering but it was not endurance.

And if this hostile and unkind conduct be a sample of their ways, I pray that the grace of God may reveal to them that the end thereof is death. Even this prayer is selfish. I prayed little for them before, when I knew that they were living in sin and had rejected Christ their Saviour—but this is but one small product and fruit of the state of mind which such rejection implies. I ought to [have] prayed before as much as now. But this consciousness is not to prevent me now from saying, may God of his infinite mercy and love make them wise and good and happy in this world and the world to come.

Close's Sermons. Ethics. Nubes. Abstract of Rhetoric. out with Harrison and Doyle. Had some men to wine. Aids to Reflection and Whately's Historic doubts on Nap. Buon.[1]

25. Th.

Surplice prayers. Out with Tupper. paper. dined & had wine with Hanbury. At debate.[2] coffee with Wilberforce. Aristophanes and Lecture. Scholarship. Ethics a little. talked with Doyle I trust plainly on religion—but the weapon is weak in such hands as mine. &c.

26.

Gaskell & I breakfasted together. Had a long & more satisfactory conversation with him regarding religion. Ethics & Lect. Close. Aristophanes. Persius. Went with Saunders in a fly to Hanborough,[3] to dine & spend evg. Had much conversation & interesting with him. Saw the Wadds. Returned little before 12.

---

[1] Abp. *Whately, *Historic Doubts relative to Napoleon Buonaparte*, anti-Humean pamphlet (1819).
[2] *Moncreiff's motion that Leeds, Manchester, and Birmingham should have M.P.s was lost by 12 to 14.
[3] Six miles NW. of Oxford.

27. Sat.

Out with Wilson—spent evg between wine with Gaskell, Chapel, & tea with Canning. Talk in morng, & household matters—my idleness is not on the wane. Close. Rhetoric Abstract. Selections. little Aristophanes.

28. Sunday.

Chapel & sermon mg & aftn. Moncreiff sat with me. Wine with Gaskell[1]— out with Seymer. wrote to Mrs G. [Read] Lightfoot—Hall's review of 'Zeal without Innovation'[2]—Aids to Reflection. Notes to Bible. Little done. Coffee. & sat with Wilberforce—liked him much.

29. Monday.

Breakfast with Mayo[w]. wine with Ward & Seymer. out. paper. R. Hall on Gisborne & Lindsey.[3] Close. Lightfoot and Rhetoric Abstract. tea with Gaskell. Worse than ever today.

30. Tuesday.

Breakfast with Tancred. worked a good deal but with pottering at Abstract of Rhetoric & examples. finished it. Wrote to J.N.G. Hall's Reviews & Aids to Reflection. &c. &c.

31. Wednesday.

Settling matters, paying Bills &c. finished Hall's Reviews & Aids to Reflection. Ex[amples] to Rhetoric—Ethics—finished Nubes—paper—heard from & wrote home—began a book of Excerpta[4]—&c.

April 1. Thursday.

Collections. Examined in Aristoph. Eth. Rhet. Div. Hor. & Æsch. & did some Latin—wrote two papers—made notes about Tyre from Univ. Hist. & Mant's Bible. wine with Harrison—paper—packed up—tea with Gaskell— travelled all night.

2.

Arrived in London between six and seven. Found Helen looking pale & thin —a day of conversation, pottering & a little reading—Tales of a Grand- father & Foster's Essays. Out at Tom's rooms. paper.

3.

Out with my Father making calls &c. Paper. Wrote to R.G. Forster's Vindication of 'Mahom. Unveiled'.[5] Iris[6] &c.

---

[1] The phrase '(not a party)' deleted.   [2] In Robert *Hall, *Reviews* (1825).
[3] Ibid.   [4] Perhaps Add MS 44815A.
[5] Charles Forster, *Mahomedanism Unveiled* (1829).
[6] Evangelical annual, ed. T. *Dale.

4. Sunday.

Called on Uncles Colin & Divie. Began to analyse Burnet.[1] St James's mg & aftn. Heard Bp of London, excellent, & Mr Ward[2] very good too. Short's Sermons—[Richard] Mant's Clergyman's Obligations. Sacrament at St James's.

5. Monday.

Wrote to R.G. paper. looking for material about Tyre. Out calling &c. Clergyman's Obligations. This will not do. copying into Excerpta.

6. T.

Wrote to J.N.G. Copied a short paper. Clergyman's obligations. Walked much. Called on Doyle. Papers. Excerpta.

7. W.

Bible. Excerpta. pottered about Tyre. Papers. Clergyman's Obligations. Walked much—in evg to House of Commons but found it nearly over.[3]

8. Th.

Bible. Excerpta. Clerg. Obl.—finished Huskissons Speech. Called on Doyle. A week of debasement, but alas not of abasement. Christian Knowledge Society Report.

9. Friday.[4]

At St James's in mg, St Pauls Covent Garden in aftn. Called on Mr Finlay. Paper. Bible—finished Mant. & went to Sacrament at St James's—but never went to it less as a feast, more as a medicine. God mend me.

10. Sat.

Excerpta. A little Æschylus. Dined at Sir F. Doyle's. A pleasant evening. Out with Gaskell. Paper. Foster's Essays. Westminster Review. Either my idleness or my intentions of writing for prize[5] must come to an end.

11. Sunday.

St George's Hanover Sq. in mg, & sacrament. Dr Hodgson[6] preached: able

[1] Add MS 44720, f. 44, on G. *Burnet, *Exposition of the xxxix Articles* (1699).
[2] John Gifford Ward, 1779–1860, rector of St. James's, Piccadilly, 1825–46, dean of Lincoln 1845.
[3] Miscellaneous debates before house rose for recess: *NSH* xxiii. 1414.
[4] In the MS, this entry follows that for the next day.
[5] On Tyre.
[6] Robert Hodgson, 1773?–1844; rector there 1803, and of St. Peter's, Eaton Square, 1827; also dean of Chester, 1815–20, and of Carlisle, 1820–44.

& his manner impressive. St James's in aftn. Gaskell dined with us. Out with him &c. Short's Sermons. little Burnet & Bible.

12. Monday.

Dined at Uncle Divie's. Out with T.G. shopping. Excerpta. Copied a paper for Mr G. paper. Westminster Rev. on Moore's Byron, Montgomery's Satan, & Channing.[1]

13. Tuesday.

Excerpta. Foster. breakfast with T.G. Scott's Bible on Tyre—Tyre—very slow & heavy—paper—out shopping. Mr Larkins dined with us.

14. Wed.

Virgil. paper. Westminster Review on Random Records.[2] wrote to J.N.G. dined at Uncle Divie's—called on Mr Finlay & drove out with him. Excerpta.

15. Th.

Papers. Quarterly Rev. Excerpta a good deal. Very little Tyre which has the best possible promise of being a failure. Much conv. with T.G. about Helen &c. At a Sale. Self disgusted & with reason. read to Mrs G.

16. Friday.

Breakfast with Uncle Colin. Dined at Sir F. Doyle's. Mr Wilmot Horton[3] there, Mr Hay,[4] & Mr Hart Davis[5] &c. Tyre—out—at Sale—paper—Foster—Excerpta—copied part of a paper for Mr G.

17. Sat.

Tyre—only my second day of work which can in any degree be called effectual. Foster. Excerpta. Virgil. Selections. index to ditto—papers—copying out, shopping &c.

18. Sunday.

French Protestant Chapel[6] in mg. very good sermon—St James's in aftnn —Bp of London, most excellent—St Margaret's in Evg—Mr Dodsworth,[7] very good—Short—Christian Knowledge Charges—part of Dairyman's Daughter.[8]

---

[1] xii. 269, 355, 472 (April 1830).   [2] Ibid. 386.
[3] (Sir) Robert John Wilmot-*Horton 1784–1841; M.P. Newcastle-under-Lyme, 1818–1830; kt. 1831; 3rd bart. 1834; governed Ceylon 1831–7; with Colonel Doyle, destroyed *Byron's memoirs.   [4] Robert William Hay, 1786–1861, of the Colonial office.
[5] Richard Hart Davis, F.R.S.   [6] In St. James's palace; services in French.
[7] William *Dodsworth, 1798–1861; priest at Margaret Street chapel, Cavendish Square, 1827–37, and at St. Pancras 1837–51, when he became a Roman catholic.
[8] A pious rural tale by Legh *Richmond (1816).

19. M.

Virgil. Excerpta. finished Dairyman's Daughter. Tales of a Grandfather. Tyre—more effectually than hitherto, but still nothing great. Saw Mr Finlay.

20. T.

Virgil. Excerpta. Wrote to Aunt J. Tales of a Grandfather—finished V 1 & began 2. papers. out in evg. Tyre, better than usual.

21. W.

Excerpta. Tales of a Grandfather. finished Vol 2. Out shopping, papers. Tyre—not very efficiently. Virgil. Foster.

22. Th.

Calling. Tyre. Excerpta. Foster—packed partially—Tales of a Grandfather. Heard from J.N.G. Maundrell[1] &c. for ref[erences to Tyre]. papers.

23. Friday.

Packed—finished Tales of a Grandfather & Foster. paper. Wrote some notes. Sat with Mrs & H.J.G. Left London at ¼ before 5. got to Oxford by 1 a.m.[2]

Jan. 1829. Books read. (List thus far ill kept.)

Tales of a Grandfather Ser.2.
Grimshaw's Legh Richmond.
More on St Paul, Vol.1.
Burrows's Letter to Marsh.
Burton on Gk Metres.
Terence Eunuch & Phormio.
Thucydides L.6.
St John Gk T.
Mitford, Vol 2. (+).
Soph. Antigone.
Georg I and 2 (+).
Thucydides L 7. & 8.
Terence Heaut Tim. Hecyra.
Juv. S[atires].
Carr.
Vince. [(Hecyra) deleted.]
Gk Theatre. [(Ajax) deleted.]

---

[1] Henry *Maundrell, *Journey from Aleppo to Jerusalem at Easter A.D. 1697* (1703).
[2] The book list that follows fills most of the last two and a half pages of this volume.

Hellen. 1.2.

Q. Rev. on Rec. of Creation—on Polar Ice &c—on Ld Selkirk &c—on Bp Watson—on Progress of Infidelity.

Lond Rev. Introd.—on Ch Reform—Transpn & Pollok. Walton's Donne.

Sumner's Apostol. Preaching.

Village Dialogues. 1.2.3.

Whateley's Essays on St Paul.

Sumner's Sermons on the festivals.

Whately's Logic.

Cicero's Tusculan Disputations.

Hor. Od. 2.3.4. (+).

Montgomery (R)'s Volume.

April &c. 1829

Jerram's Two Sermons & Appx.

Close's Sermons

Quart. on Parry Weddell Franklin.

Virg. Æn 1–6. (+).

Mr Canning in Const. Misc.

Quart. Elem. Teaching, Paley, Ireland.

Sketch of Old England.

Granby.

Slave Conv. ['Soc. Report' deleted.]

Head on early rising.

Quart. Rev. on Phillips.

   on Campbell.

Virgil Æn 7–12 (+)

Soph. Ajax Philoct +Œd Tyr+Œd Col+ & *Electra+.*

Wilberforce's Christianity.

Christian Student

Barrow's Sermons on Faith &c.

Le Bas's Sermons Vol.2.

Livy L 1–5.

Aristotle's Rhetoric. L 1.

Pamphlet on Convocation.

Shutteleworth's Consecrn Sermon.

Acts in Greek T.

Belsham's letters to Bp Howley.

Animadversions on Improved Version.

Dealtry's Serm. for Xtn Knowl & Prop Gosp.

Anne of Geierstein.

Life of Wesley (Southey's) V.1.

Livy. VI.VII.

Quarty on Ch in India, & Heber.

Hooker's Eccl. Pol. 1–4, & Preface &c.

Aug.

Livy 8.9.
Eccl. Pol. 5.6.
Life of B. Gilpin. Essay & Sermon.
Lond. Rev. on Heber.
Life of Wesley V.2.
Davy's Village Conv. on Ch Offices.
Memoirs of Martinus Scriblerus, & Works.
Horne Tooke's Life Vol.1.

Septr.

Horne Tooke's Life Vol 2.
Eccl. Pol 7 & 8. Hooker on Justif. & *Persev.*
Livy 10.
Jones on Trinity.
Gurney on Society of Friends.
Williams's Life of Alexander.
Inheritance V.1 (+). Ld Palmerston on Cath Quest & Portugal. Quart. on
    Southey's Colloquies & Portugal.
Ed. on Pestalozzi.

Oct.

Inheritance V 2 & 3 (+).
Heber's Sermons in England.
Ed. Rev. on Utilitarians—Signs of *Times–Drama—Sadler on Ireland.*
Conversations on the Parables.
Channing on Fenelon—Stanhope's meditations—Abrdgt of Law's
Serious *Call—Lives of Wilson & Hildesley,* &c.
Stonehouse's Admonitions.
Cowper's Correspondence Vol 1.

Nov.

Cowper's Correspondence Vol 2.
Shelley's Prometheus, Alastor, Cenci.
Byron's Cain, Manfred, Chillon (+) Mazeppa.
Pind Olymp. (some +) & Pythians.
Polyb. 1.2.
Laurence. Vindicns of Doct. Bapt.
Erskine on Freeness of Gospel.
Luke in G.T. "Faith & duty of a Christian". *Soldier's* Manual.

December.

Ld Bacon's Life & Adv. Learning.
Polyb 3. Pind. Nem & Isthm.

Mant's Bampton Lectures.
Rhetoric B.2.
Cic. Or. to Archias.
Friend Vol 2.
Othello + —Synge's Answer—Barrow on Crucifixion.
Shuttleworth at Sons of Clergy Festival.

January 1830.

Memoirs of Lord Liverpool.
Foster on Aversion of Men of Taste to *religion.*
Lucretius 1.2.
Xtn Knowl. Selection from the Cheap *Repository Tracts.*
Moore's *Epicurean.*
Bishop *of Chester's Charge.*

February.

Burnet on the Articles.
Blomfield's Sermons.
Ethics 1,2. Rhetoric 3.
Æsch. Pr (+) Sept (+) & Persae.
Therry's Memoir of Canning.
Notes to Queen Mab.
Whately on Sabbath—Ld Palmerston on Cuba.
Mitchell's Prelim. discourse.
Homilies Vol 1.

March.

Aids to Reflection.
Hall's Reviews.
Aristoph. Nubes (+) mostly—*Vespae—Acharnes.*
Ethics 6.7.
Hor. A.P. Hermann on αὐτός
Ed. Rev. on Etruscans & Horsley.
Coleridge's Anc. Mariner & Three Graves.
MacNeil on Evang. Idol. Tiptaft &
Hewlett, Whately on Nap. Buon.

[On the back inside cover also appear the following notes of addresses in south-west Oxford:]

[In pencil]   Adam Morton
              Shoulder of Mutton yard
              St Thomas's
              By Morrell's Brewery.

[In ink]   Poor House Yard.
              3d Door.
              Rachel Jones.

William Harris
   Friar Street
      St Ebbes.
at John Bailes.

[In pencil]   Archer
                 Mrs Tims's
                    St Thomas's.

[In ink]   St Thomas.
              a street, facing the red ox
                 person keeps a green
                 grocer's shop.

[There is also a small grotesque ink sketch of a man's head and shoulders.]

[VOLUME V.]¹

[Front outside cover:]

Private.
W. E. Gladstone
Ch: Ch: 1830.

No 5.

[Back outside cover:]

Private.
W. E. Gladstone.
Ch: Ch: 1830.

[Inside front cover:]

Private.
W. E. Gladstone
Ch: Ch;
Ap. 1830–Sept 1831

Christian Knowledge Society. +
Gospel Propagation Society.
Church Missionary Society.
Jewish Conversion Society.
Church Building Society.
Oxford Benevolent Society. +
Liverpool Mariner's Church Society.²

Saturday April 24, 1830. Christ Church.

I begin my new book and term together. Out with Tancred. Read papers—
& Theol. Rev. on Van Mildert's, Copleston's, & D. Wilson's Sermons.³
Busy unpacking—putting up pictures, & setting things to rights. In evg
with Seymer & Gaskell. Wrote to Mrs G.

---

¹ Lambeth MS 1419. 48ff.
² Notes for subscriptions.
³ *British Critic, Quarterly Theological Review and Ecclesiastical Record*, iii. 452 (1828), i.
482 (1827), and vi. 194 (1829).

Sunday April 25.

I wish I were duly convinced of the extreme importance of residence at Oxford, both as regards individual progress in religion, and influence exercised directly or indirectly on others: especially in a case where the individual has the reputation of possessing more than he actually has. For these things above all let me seek—a sense of sin, deep, painful, abiding—the faith & love of Christ, lowly, patient, strong in his strength—deliverance from the punishment of sin by his precious, precious blood—from its power by the energy of his Spirit, renewing the soul in the image of God: & all this for His sake & his sake alone, who loved us, & gave himself for us, & who—O may he make us kings & priest unto the God & Father. In practice, the great end is, that the love of God may become the *habit* of my soul—& particularly these things are to be sought 1. the spirit of love. 2. of self sacrifice. 3. of purity. 4. of energy. Amen Lord Jesus.

Chapel & St Mary's mg & aft. Walk & tea with Harrison. Close. Bible—notes—Heber's J. Taylor.

26. M.

Close. Breakft & tea with Gaskell. Wrote over what I had written of Tyre & laboured at improving but with little effect. Papers. Theol. Rev. on Arnold —Walker[1]—&c. Out with Doyle. Worked at Herodotus. Newton on Proph.[2]

27. T.

Finished my Tyre—& writing over a copy to give Biscoe. Close. Selections. Out. Breakft with Gaskell in my room. tea in his. Butler little & Herodotus. In Parker's shop long.

28. W.

Read Juvenal with Gaskell—he breakftd with me—papers—Univ. Hist. & Malte Brun's geogr.[3] about Afr[ica]n deserts. out with Harrison. Tea with Cole. Herodotus (little) Larcher, Close, finished Preface to Butler.

29. Th.

Herodotus & Larcher. Life of Butler & Introduction. Heard from home. Papers—society[4]—tea with Harrison—out with Doyle—Close—correcting Tyre—wine with Tupper—wrote some lines on Afr. des[erts].

30. Fr.

Breakf. with Gaskell, & tea. Sat in the schools—heard Harrison pass a very

---

[1] Ibid. vii. 257, 420 (1830).
[2] I. *Newton, *Observations upon the Prophecies of Daniel and the Apocalypse of St. John* (1733).
[3] Conrad Malte-Brun, *Précis de géographie universelle* (1810, &c).
[4] The Union held Navarino justifiable, by 23 to 10.

good exam, to my great joy. Some English Verses. Finished Close. Butler, Virgil. Wrote to R.G.

May First.

Saturday. Wrote over, (after making corrections) my Tyre & sent it in.[1] Tea with Cole, Gaskell breakfg with me. Sat with Canning a good deal in early part of day he having had a fit in morng chapel. At Essay Soc. meeting. spoke.[2] Began Arnold's Sermon.[3] &c. Conv at night about ghost stories.

2. Sunday.

Chapel mg & aft. St Mary's aft. Sacrament. Conversation with Seymer & Gaskell on Slavery—out with Tancred & young Cole. Tea with Cole. Prickbill. Arnold—Bible &c. Jeremy Taylor. part of Davys's Vill. Conv.

3. M.

Div. Lect. Lazy. Butler. Began an Analysis.[4] Out. at Wise's. papers. Record. Arnold. a little Herodotus &c.

4. T.

Ethics & Lect. More lazy than ever. Tomorrow please God I must set to—

all their yesterdays have lighted fools
The way to dusty death. . . .[5]

domestic matters. papers. wrote home. Virgil. Butler & D. Wilson on do.

5. Wed.

Butler—carried on Analysis, with D. Wilson's Essay. Arnold. Walk with Harrison, whose last day in the schools this was. A little Herodotus & Virgil Div. Lect. Ethics—papers—a large tea divan.

6. Th.

Ethics. Selections. Butler & Accompaniments. Virgil. Arnold. At debate.[6] papers. wrote to H.J.G. rode with Gaskell. Herodotus.

7. Friday.

Div. Lect. & Mathematical. Butler & Analyses. Bp of London's Letter. Herodotus. Arnold. papers. Virgil &c. Diary ill kept. read a very good tract called Husbandman's Manual.

[1] Add MS 44720, f. 224.
[2] *Moncreiff on uselessness of current academic logic (*Gladstone opposed him); *Rogers on philology.
[3] Thomas *Arnold, Sermons (1829), i.
[4] Add MS 44721, f. 149.
[5] Macbeth, V.v. 22–23.
[6] The Union held *Castlereagh's foreign policy to be 'most disgraceful' by 21 to 16.

8. Saturday.

Butler & Analyses. Herodotus. Theme. at Essay meeting—a good deal of private business.[1] Tea with Cole. Arnold. Ethics.

9. Sunday.

Chapel as usual—still prickbill—Bamp[ton] Lec.[2] tea with Cole—sat with Gaskell some time. Bible—wrote notes &c—commentaries—Arnold—Heber's Life of J. Taylor.

10. Monday.

Prospectively, I have the following work to do in the course of this term (I mention it now that this may at least make me blush if I fail.)

Butler's Analogy: Analysis, & Synopsis.
Herodotus. Questions.
St Matthew & St John. (Harmony: notes: perhaps)[3]
Mathematical Lecture. +
Æneid.
Juvenal & Persius. +
Ethics—five books. +
Prideaux (a part of: for Herodotus).
Themistocles Graeciae valedicturus.[4] +

& some things in Divinity &c.
Mathem. Lect. Breakft with Gaskell, who had the Merton men—papers—Ed. Rev. on Southey's Colloquies. Butler & Analysis—Ethics—a wretched day. God forgive my idleness. Notes to Bible.[5]

11. Tuesday.

Ethics. Butler and Analysis. Papers. Wrote to T.G. Notes to Bible. Arnold. Herodotus. At Wise's &c. &c.

12. Wed.

"Splendid Sins".[6] Math. & Lect. Seymer & Gas[kell] breakftd with me. At Wise's. wine with Pusey & Gaskell. Herodotus. Ethics. Butler & Analysis. Notes to Bible & Div. Lect.

13. Thurs.

Wrote to my Mother. At Debate. Elected Secretary.[7] Papers. Brit. Crit. on

[1] *Rogers again; *Doyle's essay not ready.
[2] Henry *Soames, 1784?–1860; rector of Shelley, Essex, 1812; chancellor of St. Paul's 1842; lectured on *Doctrines of the Anglo-Saxon Church* (1830).
[3] These words, bracketed in the original, are lightly crossed out. See 19 Oct. 30.
[4] 'Themistocles bidding Greece farewell', subject for a college prize.
[5] Version in Morley, i. 64.   [6] Presumably a tract.
[7] *Doyle's motion, that Napoleon's invasion of Russia was politically defensible, was lost by 6 to 28.

History of the Jews.[1] Herodotus. Ethics. Butler & Analysis. In the schools & convocation House, as the new Statute was in debate.[2] Arnold.[3]

14. Fr.

Div. Lect. Butler & Analysis. papers. Virgil. Herodotus. Juvenal. Mathematics & Lect. Walk with Anstice. Ethics—finished B.4.[4]

15. Sat.

Ethics & Lect. Began B 5. Breakft with Gaskell. Wrote over last week's theme to read. Did a Latin one, & verses. Herodotus & Butler, each little.[5]

16. Sun.

Chapel mg & aft. Paget morng, & Mills at St Mary's aftn. Liked both. Arnold—Bible—Leslie's "Truth of Christianity demonstrated".[6] Finished Heber's Life of J. Taylor & Davys's Vill. Conv. on Liturgy.

17. Monday.

Div. Lect. Juvenal. Math & Lect. Virgil. Worked at Debating Society Rules with Gaskell.[7] Hanging prints &c. wine with Acland. Out with Seymer.

18. T.

Heard from & wrote home. Arnold. Porteus's Evidences.[8] Ethics & Lect. Herodotus. Mathematics. papers. Berens's Poacher Tale.[9]

19. Wednesday.

Herod. Math. Berens's Smuggler.[10] Papers. Math Lect. Juvenal. wrote to Mrs G. wine with Gaskell. Tea & sat late with Acland. Received & read a good deal of Hallam's Poems. Div. Lect.

20. Th.

Surplice prayers—Sermon. Williams preached very well. Finished Berens's

[1] vii. 374 (1830) on H. H. *Milman, *History of The Jews* (1829).
[2] Creating a fourth class in the final honour schools; abolished 1967.
[3] Part in Morley, i. 64.
[4] Dated 13 May in Morley, i. 64.
[5] He also attended the essay society, voting for a motion of Gaskell's that ghosts were credible, and hearing an essay of *Abercorn's on republican government. James *Hamilton, 1811–85, 2nd marquess of Abercorn 1818; K.G. 1844; viceroy of Ireland 1866–8, 1874–6; cr. duke of Abercorn and marquess of Hamilton 1868.
[6] By C. *Leslie (1710).
[7] Gaskell was president of the Union that term.
[8] Beilby *Porteus *A Summary of the Principal Evidences for the Truth and Divine Origin of the Christian Revelation* (1800).
[9] In E. Berens, *Christmas Stories* (1823).
[10] Ibid.

Christmas Stories. Did a little Themistocles. paper. walked out. thought about Jews, & spoke at some length but not well.[1] Arnold.

21. Fr.

Div. Lect. Juvenal. Wrote out Debate, papers of sundry kinds & good deal of Secretary's work. Out. wine with Sutherland—Menteath—Allies[2]—Tea with Gaskell. [Wrote] Some Themistocles. [Read] Plutarch's Themistocles. Arnold.

22. Sat.

papers. walk with Anstice & Acland. two wine parties—Theme—little Ethics—an imposition—Essay Soc. meeting.[3] some English verses. My lethargy grows deeper. O that I cd say God deliver me.

23. Sunday.

Heard Mr Hill[4] preach at St Ebbe's. Arnold—Selections &c. much rain. long walk with Anstice—would I were worthy to be his companion—speaking of the generality of University Sermons he said "depend upon it such sermons as these can never convert a single person". Turn thou me O God & I shall be turned![5] J. Taylor. Bible.

24. Mon.

papers. wrote to T.G. out—Virgil Æneid—Juvenal with Gaskell. Arnold. Div. Lect. Themistocles.

25. T.

Finished Porteus's Evidences. Got up a few hard passages. Analysis of Porteus's Evidences. Sundry matters in divinity. Themistocles. Sat with Biscoe talking. Walk with Canning & Gaskell wine & tea. wrote to Mr G. papers.[6]

26. W.

Juvenal. Virgil. Div. Lect. Sundry modern Latin poems—worked hard at, finished & wrote over, my Themistocles.

27. Th.

Late for Chapel, owing to having sat up last night—Ethics & Lecture. Cd not go to debate in evg, being confined. read a good deal of Virgil. some divinity. & Herodotus. In Schools.

[1] He spoke against a motion of Lyall's 'That the civil disabilities of the Jews ought to be removed'; it was lost by 16 to 55.
[2] Thomas William *Allies, 1813–1903, of Wadham; classical first, 1832; tractarian; convert to Rome 1850.
[3] *Abercorn again; and A. H. D. Acland on general and particular knowledge.
[4] John Hill, 1786?–1855, vice-principal of St. Edmund Hall.
[5] Cp. Jer. xxxi. 18.   [6] In Morley, i. 64.

28.

Div. Lect. Herodotus a good deal & Lect. Juvenal with Gaskell, little. Persius with Canning, & Tea. Wine with Rogers, Cunningham, Scott— papers. wrote out Debate &c.

29. Sat.

Surplice prayers mg & aft. Leslie—Equation—little. Herodotus. Essay Society[1] papers—a *villainously* spent day—wine with Acland—tea with Cole—read Doyle's Tyre. I regret much to hear that Harrison will not get his Mathematical first—but he knows how to bear it.

30. S.

Sacrament. St Mary's mg & Aft. Mr Symons—good.[2] Walked to Kenning- ton in evg to a Charity Sermon. Bible—Taylor's Holy Living—Erskine's Evidences—Selections.

31. M.

Finished Clio. Writing on Evidences but confusedly. I am greatly puzzled as to whether Leslie's argument be demonstrative. Mathematics. read the new Statute.[3] paper. wrote to Hagart.

June 1. Tuesday.

Surplice prayers again. Herodotus & Larcher. I neither work as I ought, nor get on as I ought when I do. Butler &c. Introductory Essay & Preface to Thomas a Kempis. Juvenal. paper. wrote to Mrs G.

June 2. Wed.

Div. Lect. Breakft with Gaskell. Juvenal. Math. Lect & Math at nt with Acland—*conv. tea* and *addle* on abstruse subjects. Herodotus—with which I cannot manage to get on—wrote in Scrap book. wine with Jelf. wrote to Farr. paper.

3. Th.

At Debate.—and wrote it out.[4] Juvenal with Gaskell. Ethics. A Kempis. Math. questions.—Herodotus—papers—part of Article on Bp. Butler in Quarterly. Larcher's notes skimmingly.

---

[1] A. H. D. Acland again; and T. D. *Acland on evidence.
[2] Benjamin Parsons *Symons, 1785–1878, fellow of Wadham 1812; warden 1831–71; vice-chancellor 1844–8.
[3] See 13 May 30.
[4] *Brougham's proposal for county court judges was approved, by Gaskell's casting vote, on a tie.

4. Fr.

Div. Lect. Herodotus—notes to Bible. Hallam's Poems—paper—Sec's business at Society[1]—Juvenal with Gaskell—& Persius with Canning.

5. Sat.

Ethics & Lect. Latin Theme & verses. Herodotus, skimming Larcher, & Lect. At Essay Soc. Anstice's Essay very good.[2] Logic in evg. papers—out with Seymer. wine with young Acland—tea with Gaskell.

6. S.

Chapel mg & aft—at ord[ination]—heard imperfectly Clerke's sermon. long walk & interesting conversation with Childers. Arnold. Erskine. Blank verse. Two first books of "Course of Time".[3]

7. M.

Div. Lect. Ethics. Herodotus. Juvenal. Vince's Astronomy.[4] None very much. Heard young Acland in Schools—wine with Seymer—walk with Bruce. Cunningham's Sermon on Mr. Batten.[5]

8. T.

Ethics & Lect. Herodotus. Juvenal. Gave a large wine party—had Gaskell, Doyle, Canning, Lincoln,[6] Grimston, Bernard, Bruce, two Taylors,[7] Wood, Rogers, Lushington.[8] Arnold—papers—&c.

9. Wed.

heard from T.G. that they were gone to Leamington. Wrote to R.G. & H.J.G. I hope the move may be for good. Gave another wine party—Childers, Aclands, Coles, Gaskell, Doyle, Lyall, Tancred, Wilson, Maurice & one or two more. Herodotus—Juvenal—Div. Lect—Butler—Math & Lect. poor Harrison I grieve to say is very ill. Prickbills confined.

10. Th.

At Committee. Cd not go to debate being confined. Ethics. Herodotus—

[1] Correspondence and recording debate.
[2] T. D. *Acland again; *Anstice on civil and political liberty.
[3] By Robert *Pollok (1827).
[4] S. *Vince, *Complete System of Astronomy*, 3v. (1797–1808).
[5] On the death of S. E. Batten (1830).
[6] Henry Pelham Fiennes Pelham *Clinton, 1811–64; styled earl of Lincoln; 5th duke of Newcastle 1851; M.P. Nottinghamshire 1832–46, Falkirk burghs 1846—51; Irish secretary 1846; colonial secretary 1852–4, 1859–64; war secretary, 1852–5. See Add MSS 44262–3.
[7] Vernon Pearce Taylor, b. 1809, vicar of Pitcombe, Somerset, 1846–80; and William Taylor, b. 1808?, nephew of Charles Henry *Hall who was dean of Christ Church, 1809–1824.
[8] William Hurdis Lushington, 1808?–42, Eton and Oriel; rector of Eastling, Kent, 1836.

Juvenal—Butler—&c. wine with Tancred. finished Arnold—an admirable book.

11. Fr.

Surplice prayers. Math Lect. Herodotus. Persius with Canning. Cramming Logic with Gaskell. wine with Tyndale—wrote out Debate & did other Sec's business—at Bible Society meeting.

12. Sat.

Ethics & Lect. Did a theme so little to the purpose that I was ashamed & did another. Harrison thank God better. Herodotus, at night did Thucydides for two hours with Gaskell—papers—finished Article on Butler in Quarterly very clever & a most able analysis.[1]

13. Sunday.

Chapel mg & evg. Thomas a Kempis—Erskine's Evidences—tea with Mayo[w] & Cole—walked with Maurice to hear Mr Porter, a wild but splendid preacher.[2]

14. M.

Gave a large wine party. Div. Lect. Mathematics. Wrote three long letters —Herodotus began B.4. Prideaux[3]—papers—&c. T. a Kempis.[4]

15. T.

Another wine party. Ethics. Herodotus. A little Juvenal. paper—Hallam's poetry. Lecture in Herodotus. Phillimore got the verse prize.[5]

16. W.

Div. Lect. Herodotus—papers—out at wine &c—forgotten at time of writing up—wrote to T.G. a little Plato.[6]

17. Th.

Ethics & Lecture. Herodotus. Working at Rules. Spoke, or rather delivered my opinion. T. a Kempis—Herodotus, Excerpta—wine with Gaskell.[6] Wrote out debate.[7]

[1] Also at essay society, to hear *Anstice again.
[2] In Morley, i. 64. John Porter, Methodist preacher 1830, d. 1831.
[3] H. *Prideaux, *Connection of the Old and New Testament*, 2v. (1716–18).
[4] In Morley, i. 64.
[5] Ibid., i. 65.
[6] Part ibid.
[7] The Union approved by 19 to 15 'the establishing of Colleges in London for the education of the Middle Classes'; *Gladstone spoke against it.

18. Fr.

Nearly four hours at Rules—besides Sec's business. Ethics—& Lect—interesting conversation with Williams. Breakft with Gaskell—T. a Kempis Div. Lect. Herodotus—Wrote on Philosophy versus poetry—a little Persius —wine with Buller & Tupper.[1]

19. Sat.

T. a Kempis—Herodotus—papers—wrote out Report of Committee Meeting—breakft with Wilson—Gaudy day—acted as Bible Clerk, ill—a little Juvenal—out with Cole.

20. S.

St Mary's & Chapel mg & aftn. T. a Kempis—wrote on Predestination—read part of Homily on Rebellion, and some Pollok. Dined with the Dean.

21. M.

Herodotus, and Lecture, a little Juvenal. breakft with Childers. walked with Saunders over to Cuddesdon. Read a sermon of Townsend's & his dedication. &c.[2]

22. T.

Analysis of Herodotus a little. Walked back to Oxford with Saunders. paper. wine with Canning. Conversation with Doyle & Gaskell on religion &c. Heard Burton preach. Long & stormy debate about rules. Tea with Cole; introduced to Mrs C.[3] cd not stay long: wrote & wrote over a letter to Hallam. &c. Hallam's Poems. read the Prize Poems.

23. W.

Commem. Heard Rickards.[4] Wrote out debate. Papers. Prideaux—Rennel[5] —papers of Anstice's—endeavouring to get up some Herod[otean] history & geography—slow work. Wrote to H.J.G. Juvenal. Breakft with Anstice—calls.

24. Th.

Collections began. Herodotus again—read some papers of Anstice's from Rennell, &c. Persius finished. Juvenal finished as far as need be. T. a

[1] Part in Morley, i. 65.
[2] G. *Townsend, *Sermons on some of the most interesting subjects in theology* (1830).
[3] Jane Eliza, née Owen, of Co. Monaghan; m. Major Henry Cole of Twickenham who d. 1815; mother of F. and O. B. Cole.
[4] At the annual Encaenia, or commemoration of the benefactors of the university, the year's prizewinning poems are publicly read. *Rickards had won the *Newdigate.
[5] James *Rennell, *The Geographical System of Herodotus*, 2v. (1800).

Kempis. Heard Mr Grantham[1] preach. Tea with Cole again to meet his mother. Packing.

25. *Friday.*

Ethics. Collections 9–3. Among other things wrote a long paper on religions of Egypt Persia & Babylon—& on the Satirists—Finished packing books & clothes. Left Oxford between 5 & 6 & walked 15 miles towards Leamington —then obliged to put in, being caught by a thunderstorm. Comfortably off in a country In at Steeple Aston—read & spouted some Prometheus Vinctus there.[2]

26.

Started before 7—walked 8 miles to Banbury, breakftd there & walked on 22 to Leamington—arrived at 3 & changed. Found Helen something better. Gaskell came in Evg. Life of Massinger.[3]

27. *Sunday.*

Ch. mg & aft. Began "Times of Trial".[4] read a little Butler & some History of Enthusiasm.[5] wrote to Canning.

28.

Dear Helen's birthday. I know not what to say of all the things that are usually said on birthdays. διχα θυμος ἐην.[6] Gaskell went. Wrote a thing to Echo for Helen's Album. part of Virgin Martyr[7]—paper—saw Warwick Castle with Gaskell.

29.

began to copy out Debating Society Rules—paper—finished Virgin Martyr —read some of Bp Heber's Life[8]—very interesting. wrote long letters to Bp of Calcutta & J.N.G.—wrote also to Hallam and Aunt E.

30.

Finished Copying Debating Society Rules. Paper. wrote to T.G. Finished T. a Kempis. Times of Trial—Bishop Heber's Life—R.G. came from Lpool —happily for me. copied out my "Echo" about wh I am very dubious. Shelley.

[1] George Grantham, 1781–1840; demy 1798, usher 1801, fellow 1809, and bursar of Magdalen, 1812.
[2] Repunctuated in Morley, i. 65.
[3] Ibid. T. *Davies prefixed a *Life* to his ed. of *Massinger's *Dramatick Works*, 4v. (1779).
[4] Mary Ann *Kelty on the reformation (1830).
[5] [Isaac *Taylor the younger] *The Natural History of Enthusiasm* (1829).
[6] 'My heart was divided'.
[7] *Massinger.
[8] By his widow, 2v. (1830).

July 1. Thursday.

"Times of Trial" (a sort of Hist of Reformation) a good deal. Out in carriage. Beauties of Shelley. Eton Misc—papers—Mr G. went to Town.

2. Friday.

Shelley—papers—long & interesting debate[1]—Madden's Travels & made notes from them[2]—& made a list of the better pieces in the Eton Misc. Finished Times of Trial.

3. Sat.

paper. out with R.G. Notes on Egypt &c. from Madden. +. Began Life of Cranmer. Shelley. &c.

4. Sun.

Ch at Warwick in mg. Finished Sargeant's Life of Cranmer. Butler's Analogy. Ch at Leamington in aft. R.G. went by mail.

5. M.

a little Butler. put up things. left Leamington at $\frac{1}{4}$ bef 9. so ends my Long Vacation. At Oxford in 5 hours. Wrote letters to Mrs G., T.G., Gaskell, Farr. Walked down to Cuddesdon. Found Anstice & Hamilton. Unpacked books &c.

6. T.

Up soon after six. Began my Harmony of Gk Testament. D. Calc. &c. &c. in Mathematics, a good while but in a rambling way. Began Odyssey +. paper—walk with Anstice & Hamilton. Turned a little bit of Livy into Greek. Conversation on Ethics & Metaphysics at nt.[3]

7. W.

Gk Testament Harmony. & Math. before breakft. Began to translate Phaedo. Another little bit of Livy into Gk. Out with A & H. heard from Gaskell. Excerpta books &c. Began Old Testament with Anstice. O that God wd enlighten me in it. Saunders's organ put up. Butler. A little Thucydides at nt.

8. Th.

paper—Greek Testament—Bible with Anstice. Mathematics long but did little. Translated some Phaedo. Butler & construed some Thucydides at night. Making hay &c. with S, H. & A. Great fun. Shelley.[4]

[1] *George IV had died on 26 June. On 29 and 30 June both houses debated *William IV's message on the impending general election. *NSH* xxv. 699–828.
[2] R. R. *Madden, *Travels in Turkey, Egypt, Nubia and Palestine in 1824–27*, 2v. (1829): notes in Add MS 44721, ff. 116–20.
[3] In Morley, i. 65.   [4] Most in Morley, i. 65.

9. Fr.

Gk Testament—Lightfoot's Harmony—Bible with Anstice—Notes to it— and vague inquiries with some writing in my blank books—a Serm. of Short's—Butler—wrote something upon mediation—construing Thucydides at night—out with H. & A.—Mathematics.

10. Sat.

Gk. Testament. Lightfoot. Butler & writing a marginal analysis. Old Testament with Anstice & a discussion of early history. Mathematics— cricket with H. & A. A conv. of two hours at night with A. on religion till past 12. paper—Scholarship—in Thucydides &c. I cannot get anything done though I seem to be employed a good while. Short's Sermons.[1]

11. Sunday.

Church & Sunday School teaching morng & evening. The children miserably deluded. Barrow. Short—walk with S.[2] H. & A. Conversation of an hour and a half with A on practical religion particularly as regards our own situation. I bless & praise God for his presence here.

12. Monday.

Gk Testament. O.T. with Anstice & History.—Butler—Mathematics— Phaedo—heard from home & wrote home—cricket. Paget Puller & Acland dined here—a very pleasant evening.

13. Tuesday.

Gk Testament. Butler & Analysis. paper. Cricket with H. & A. Tea in the arbour. Old Testament &c. with Anstice. Thucydides at nt aloud—Mathe- matics—a little Phaedo into English & Fergusson[3] into Latin.

14. Wed.

out with S.H. & A. paper—received & began to read Tennyson's Poems.[4] Gk Testament—Butler & Analysis—O.T. with A—& worked at notes wh consume a great deal of time & show very little—but I think it is very use- ful & know it is very interesting—Mathematics—construed Thucydides— conversation with A. on religion &c—looked a little at Herodotus. Learnt a bit of Thucydides.

15. Th.

Butler & Analysis—O.T. with A. and notes—learnt a lot of Thucydides.

---

[1] Most in Morley, i. 65.
[2] Thus far in Morley, i. 65.
[3] Robert *Fergusson, Scottish pastoral poet, *floruit* 1770.
[4] *Tennyson's second book: see *DNB* lvi. 67.

mathematics—Tennyson—paper—cricket—read preface to Peacock's Algebra[1]—Herodotus.

16. Fr.

Butler & Analysis—O.T. with A & notes—Mathematics—Odyssey—Herodotus—paper—cricket—did some Livy into Greek & wrote it over—heard from T.G.—no seat yet.

17. Sat.

O.T. with A. & notes—much conv. too on religion, which is a great blessing. Wrote to Helen & to Gaskell. Herodotus—finished Butler—& Stewart—Mathem. paper—Odyssey.

Heard from T.G. of his standing for Queensboro. wish him success.[2]

18. Sunday.

Began Pascall's Thoughts[3]—& Romans with A. Went with him to hear Porter—very good—got wet through. At Garsington in aftn—Townsend's Serm. Much conversation with Hamilton & A. on religion &c. I like H. much.

19. M.

Walk & cricket. Heard from Mr G. & T.G. accounts good. Continued my marginal analysis of Butler. O.T. with A—Herodotus—Odyssey—Mathematics—D. Stewart's Appx on Necessity finished—I like not the subject & am sorry it should be one to get up.[4]

20. T.

Cricket. Saunders returned. Butler. Odyssey. Herodotus—Mathematics—a little construing Thucydides at night. O.T. with Anstice—paper—&c.

21. W.

Cricket. Wrote to T.G.—Butler & writing on him—Herodotus. construing Thucydides at nt—Diff. Calc. Questions—Odyssey—O.T. with Anstice & notes—paper—wrote to T.G.—translated a little Phaedo—little of all. learnt a bit of Thucydides.

22. Th.

Int. Calc. & questions—Butler—O.T. with A. Herodotus—Doyle came over at nt—walked to Bullingdon[5] expecting to meet him—Odyssey—Gk Testament—Learnt a bit of Thucydides.

[1] Treatise by G. *Peacock (1830).   [2] See 2 Dec. 30.
[3] Blaise Pascal, *Pensées* (1670).
[4] The appendix 'Of man's free agency' at the back of Dugald *Stewart's *Philosophy of the Active and Moral Powers*, 2v. (1828) was already a set text.
[5] Three miles WNW. of Cuddesdon.

23. Fr.

Butler—Odyssey—Herodotus, better than heretofore—some Math. Questions—construing Thucydides at night—Tennyson's Poems. We got a tent set up. Walked to Wheatley with Doyle & sat some time talking with him.

Sat. 24.

Butler. Odyssey. Herodotus. Doyle & Acland came over. Bagot[1] came. much cricket in evg. & Thucydides little. heard from T.G.—also letter from J.N.G. Math. Questions—writing in my Excerpta books. Turned a little Gk into Latin. Conv. with Anstice on rel[igion] at nt.—He talked much with Saunders on the motive of actions, contending for the love of God, *not* selfishness even in its most refined form. Had I loved God & my Saviour, wretch that I am, I should have been in ecstasy to hear such an avowal of grand & high truths: but as it was the working of my Satanic heart were far otherwise, as the day of judgment will show. Well, I trust God will teach me to bow to him.

25.

Prayers read on the green mg & aft. Walked to Newnham &c. with Anstice—Romans—Pascal—Townsend—Barrow—&c. little done. T.G.'s birthday but it passed unnoticed by me for I forgot the day of the month.

26. M.

Wrote to Father[2]—& to T.G. supposing it to be his birthday. Gk Testament—Pascal—Began Iliad—Herodotus—Math. Quest. I get on very ill.—a little construing Thucydides at night. weather very hot.

27.

Pascal—Herodotus—again very hot indeed, beautiful weather for ripening the corn. Iliad—Math Quest—Thucydides before dinner. Anstice went. began Paley's Moral Philosophy.

The main matters I wish to have done within this vacation are *as follows:* θεοῦ εὐδοκοῦντος:[3]

---

[1] Charles Walter, 1812–84, rector of Castle Rising 1846, chancellor of Bath and Wells, or his brother Lewis Francis, 1813–70, rector of Leigh, Staffordshire, 1846; both younger ss. of Richard *Bagot, 1782–1854, the new bp. of Oxford, bp. of Bath and Wells 1845, and both, like him, at Christ Church.

[2] Part in Bassett, 20, dated 25 July.

[3] 'God willing'.

Old Testament with Hist. &c. say to 1st B. of Kings.
Herodotus 5–9. +
Harmony of Matt & John: with notes on them.
Marginal Analysis of Butler. &c.   1
Analysis in verse or otherwise of Herod. & Thucyd.   1
Thucydides.
Half Odyssey—half Iliad.   1
Ethics.
Livy.
Paley's Moral Philosophy. +
Rennell's Geogr. of Herodotus.
Plato's Phaedo.
Smith's Moral Sentiments.
Townsend's Sermons.   1
Short's Sermons.
Four Gospels in Greek.
Pascal's & Beveridge's Thoughts.[1] +
In Mathematics, D. Calculus & I.
            Newton
            Mechanics.

entering Scholarship, characteristic Anecdotes &c. in my books of Excerpta.

Paradise Lost &c.

} chiefly

28. Wed.

Heard from & wrote home. Pascal—Herodotus—Paley's Moral Philosophy —Much retarded in Herodotus by writing in my Excerpta books, yet I do not do it at all completely. Sophocles & construing—Maths. Wrote home. Cholmeley & Paget here.

29. Th.

Long talk with S. on 2nd vol. of Herodotus. Pascal. Math. Questions. Herodotus. Paley. Sophocles. Tried to sketch a sort of map which may be useful to me.

30. Fr.

Herodotus (about 85 chapters) took up most of my day. Sophocles at nt— Pascal—Math. Questions—paper—cricket with Hamilton & Bagot— carried on my sketch.

31. Sat.

Another day of Herodotus—104 chapters. it is now very easy & there are few stoppages—Finished Pascal—paper—little Mathematics—Paley— Sophocles—did my monthly business.

[1] See 1 Aug. 1830.

August 1. Sunday.

Ch. mg & aftn. & teaching in school: would God I might do good there. Headach. Beveridge[1]—Barrow on Faith—Townsend—Selections.

2. Monday.

Herodotus &c. & my map. Had a good deal of headach, so walked into Oxford—had haircut &c. there. Walked back with Anstice. Conversed with him from ten to twelve on subjects of the highest importance. Thoughts then first sprung up in my soul (obvious as they may appear to many) which may powerfully influence my destiny. O for light from on high: I have *no* power, *none* to discern the right path for myself.[2]

3. Tuesday.

Finished Herodotus—Beveridge—map—Thucydides construing at nt— wrote to Mrs G. & Childers. Walked alone in garden two hours very uncomfortable. There is a fearful weight on my mind. I ask myself the question why I am slumbering & trifling over matters which have at best but an indirect connection with religion, while souls throughout the world are sinking daily into death? Ans[wer:] I am not old enough. Well God only knows: shall I be able to urge this as a plea in the last day? That God only knows: I am unable to answer that question or indeed any other. I declare I should be utterly miserable but for the persuasion that He will answer these questions for me and gently lead my mind to the right conclusion. And O that, whithersoever he calls, I may follow! Strange thoughts of my future life & of giving up home, friends, University, passed through my mind: that I can do little is no reason against it—no reason why that little (by God's grace) should not be done.

4. Wednesday.

Began Thucydides—also working up Herodotus—ἐξηρτυόμενος.[3] Construing Thucydides at night. Uncomfortable again & much distracted with doubts as to my future line of conduct. God direct me. I am utterly blind. Wrote a very long letter to my dear Father on the subject of my future profession, wishing if possible to bring that question to an immediate & final settlement.[4]

5. Th.

Less distracted, but I fear rather from smothering my inquiries than satisfying myself. Wrote over & slightly corrected my letter. Heard from Can-

---

[1] W. *Beveridge, *Private Thoughts Upon Religion,* or *Upon a Christian Life* (both 1709).
[2] See 8 Aug. 30.
[3] 'devising'.
[4] In Morley, i. 81; letter ibid. 635–40, explaining his wish to be ordained.

ning. Thucydides & construing Thucydides at nt. Integral Calculus. Working a very little at Herodotus.

6. *Friday.*

Thucydides. paper—wrote a good deal of verse at least if not poetry. Read my letter over again & sent it. Mathematics—Paley—Excerpta—construing Thucydides at night.

7. *Sat.*

Math. Paley—papers—Thucydides & construing him aloud at nt—verse again—excerpta—heard from T.G.—Saunders examined me in 90 chapters of Thucydides. Beveridge's Private Thoughts.

8. *Sunday.*

Ch & School morng & eveng. Out—alone & with Anstice: spoke to him about that awful subject which has lately almost engrossed my mind. They arose thus. On Monday when I was in Oxford and saw the people parading with flags & bands of music my first impulse was to laugh, my second to cry: & I thought how strangely men had missed of the purpose of their being. And then it occurred to me Why are not the men who pray for a truer view earnestly & incessantly busied in making them acquainted with it? If this exclusive devotion did but produce the salvation of a single soul, the addition of one sheep to our Redeemer's flock, would not the relinquishment of all the pleasures of intellect have been splendidly repaid? And why do the artificial chains and conventionalities of society blind us to these realities?

But at present I am come to a somewhat different state of mind: God only knows whether a sounder or a more desirable one. My own views indeed have not altered. But the idea which then threw me into doubt & perplexity with reference to the duty of acting upon them, is much modified. For I must not I think consider myself as a man exercising the unfettered judgment of a man: but as a being not yet competent for self-direction nor fitted to act upon his own uncorrected impressions, but under the guidance of others for his present course.
Bible—Barrow—Townsend—Beveridge—Selections.

9. *Monday.*

A day's work at Thucydides chiefly the summary. Heard from & wrote home. Construing Thucydides at night.

10. *Tuesday.*

Thucydides again—analysing & getting up the summary—also made a few memorial lines which I cannot remember & can scarcely wish to. construing at nt. A little Math. Paget dined here. Paley.

11. Wed.

Thucydides most of the day & writing in Excerpta—little Math. construing
at nt. Paley's Moral Philosophy [1]—& began to analyse & make notes upon
it.

12. Th.

Paley's Moral Philosophy. Had a most kind letter from my Father for wh I
ought to be very thankful. [2] Wrote to him & to Canning. Analysis & Notes—
Thucydides & construing at nt—Excerpta—Herodotus odds & ends. paper.
Math little.

13. Fr.

Paley's Moral Philosophy & Analysis with Notes. Thucydides History
finished B.2. Construing him at night. Heard from Farr. Math. Quest.
paper.

14. Sat.

Very kind letters from T.G. & Childers. Paley—Analysis—& a kind of
essay—wrote to R.G.—Excerpta—Thucydides construing him at nt—little
Math. Bishop came at last. [3]

15. Sunday.

Ch morng & evg. introduced to Bp. School mg & evg. Romans with Anstice.
Out with him, at nt read an S. of Arnold's aloud. Wrote a long letter to T.G.

16. Monday.

Thucydides—finished—construing his speeches aloud—Paley & analysis—
heard from Gaskell—paper—little Mathematics. &c.

17. T.

Very little Thucydides & some Paley—Confirmation—Bishop's address
very good. Went into Oxford to meet Uncle D[ivie] & hunted all over the
place but he was not come—a fatiguing day: wrote to Gaskell. read paper &
Brit. Crit. on Jebb & Blomfield. [4] Dennison came. [5]

18. W.

Laboured long at Mathematics, but very ineffectually as usual: I believe
unless my will or my power or my assistances mend, I shall not be fit to go

[1] W. *Paley, *Principles of Moral and Political Philosophy* (1785).
[2] In Morley, i. 640–1, counselling delay before choosing a career.
[3] See 24 July 30 n.
[4] viii. 169, 197 (1830).
[5] Henry Denison, 1810–58, student of Christ Church 1827; double first 1831; fellow of
All Souls 1831–40.

up in ten years. Paley—Thucydides—paper—Canning came—Excerpta—Hamilton went to Oxford, unwell.

19.

We all dined at the Bps. Liked him. Thucydides—Paley—Excerpta—paper—turned a bit of Paley into Greek. Letter from home.

20.

Little Paley and Thucydides. finished Book 3. Excerpta as usual, extracting some of (what seem) the Memorabilia. expedition to Newnham—Canning, Dennison, two Bagots & ourselves—a beautiful place: did not get above 4 hours' work—Mechanics a little.

21. Sat.

Canning went. Cureton,[1] & Saunders's Brother[2] here. Turned a bit of Paley into Greek. Thucydides & Excerpta. Analysis of Paley. Wrote to H.J.G. & cousin Edward.

22. Sunday.

School and Church mg & aft. Out, alone & with Anstice. Bible. Townsend. Beveridge. Barrow. Selections.

23. M.

Thucydides & Excerpta. Paley & Analysis. Math Questions. wrote over some Greek. Some Herodotus. Beveridge.

24. T.

Thucydides. paper. out with A.—Paley into Greek. Paley & Analysis. Beveridge. Math. & Questions. Excerpta.

25. Wednesday.

Thucydides Analysis & Excerpta. Virgil at night. turned a piece of Gk into Latin. Paley.—Beveridge—Math. questions. &c. paper—out with A. as usual.

26.

Patrick Smyth[3] came. out with A as usual. Thucydides began B 5. Beveridge—Paley—Excerpta—Math. Quest. &c. letter from T.G.

[1] William *Cureton, 1808–64, Arabist; priest, 1832; assistant keeper of MSS, British Museum, 1837; canon of Westminster, 1849.

[2] Saunders had five elder brothers.

[3] Patrick Murray Smythe, 1805?–72; Westminster and Christ Church; curate of Tamworth, 1829–47; rector of Solihull near Birmingham, 1847, and canon of Worcester, 1858.

24—I

27. Friday.

Two younger Dennisons[1] came. out with A. Paley—Thucydides—a bit of Robertson into Latin—Math Quest—paper—Commerce at night: lost: indeed I *never* won a farthing at cards. Saunders has a good rule of giving all to charities—P. Smyth extremely good natured: but I dread him as a clergyman.

28. Sat.

Hamilton returned.—Thucydides finished B.5. Analysis & Excerpta. Paley & Analysis. Townsend. Math. Questions. did a bit of Latin. out with Anstice.

29. Sunday.

Sacrament. Acland & Tancred here. Out. School & Church mg & aft. Communicants very numerous. Townsend—Beveridge—Barrow—began letter to J.N.G.

30. Monday.

Thucydides & Excerpta. Paley & Analysis. Beveridge. Mathematics. Doyle here in Evg. spent it mainly with him & talked much about religion. More satisfactory than usual thank God. Math. Wrote to H.J.G. finished to J.N.G.

31. Tuesday.

May God awaken me gradually at least to a sense of what I am. Finished Beveridge. Thucydides. Maps. finished Paley. Analysis. paper. Math. Questions. out with Dennison Hamilton & Anstice. Herodotus & Excerpta.

September. 1. Wednesday.

A long letter to T.G. Math. Quest. Excerpta. a little Odyssey. Thucydides—Analysis of Paley &c.

2. Thursday.

Newman, Wilberforce[2] & Horne[3] dined here. Thucydides (began B.7.) Odyssey—Excerpta. Analysis of Paley. Questions—Walker's Mechanics.

3. Friday.

same as yesterday & wrote a bit of Latin. Heard from Gaskell.

[1] Probably Stephen Charles 1811–71; at Balliol; classical first, 1832; barrister; and Frank, 1813–43, naval officer.
[2] Samuel *Wilberforce, 1805–73, 3rd s. of W.*; bp. of Oxford 1845, of Winchester 1869; notorious as 'Soapy Sam'. See Add MSS 44343–5.
[3] Thomas Horne, 1773?–1847, rector of St. Katherine Coleman, London, 1812; Bampton lecturer 1828.

4. Sat.

same as yesterday except Latin & questions. Heard from Mother. Paradise Lost. Dined with the Bishop. Cards at night. I like them not for they excite me & keep me awake. Construing Sophocles.[1]

5. Sunday.

Ch. & school morng & evg. The Bishop preached exceedingly well on Rom.8.28.—Out with Anstice. Wood & Bates[2] dined here. Barrow— Townsend—part of B.4 of Paradise Lost.

6. Monday.

Heard from R.G. Thucydides Analysis. Excerpta. Math &c. wrote to my Mother & part of a letter to R.G. Construing choruses of Sophocles. Od[yssey]. Anal[ysed] Paley.

7. T.

finished letter to R.G. Cricket. Odyssey. Finished Thucydides. Anal[ysed] Paley. construing Sophocles. Math. Quest. Examining each other in Thucydides at night for two hours. paper: read account of C. Grant's election.[3]

8. W.

Odyssey. Cricket. Walker's Mechanics. Anal[ysed] Paley. construing Sophocles. Began Hellenics.[4] Examining & examined in Thucydides.

9. Th.

Hellenics. finished B.1. Math. questions. &c. much as yesterday.

10. Fr.

As nearly as possible the same routine.

11. Sat.

Varied by a sort of half holiday & very pleasant game of cricket on Bullingdon. Finished Hellenics & Anal[ysis of] Paley.

12. Sunday.

Sunday school morng & evg—much with Anstice's class. Two boys have I do think *really* benefited by his instruction. no. one? Barrow—Bible—sat up till one & wrote a very long letter to Doyle on religion.

---

[1] Extracts in Morley, i. 66.
[2] John Ellison Bates, b. 1809?, Westminster and Christ Church.
[3] Charles *Grant, 1778–1866, b. at Kidderpore; wrangler 1801; M.P. Inverness 1811–18, and Inverness-shire 1818–35, when he was cr. Lord Glenelg; president of board of trade 1827–8, of control 1830–4; colonial secretary 1835–9; retired in disgrace to Riviera.
[4] Xenophon.

13. M.

A broken day. Tried to begin Livy in morng. Finished B.12 of Odyssey. Algebra & Walker's Mechanics. Construing Herodotus with Saunders. In Oxford with Hamilton. Introduced to Wriothesley.[1] Wrote to Farr. paper. Spineto.[2]

14. T.

Biscoe & Aug. Short dined here. Construing &c. in Herodotus. Iliad. Working at Prideaux & analysing—much addle & little fruit. Walker's Mechanics. Spineto & analysing.

15. W.

Continued Prideaux & Analysis. Spineto & Analysis. Began notes on St Matthew. Construing Herodotus. Iliad. Wrote home. Dined at Bp's. Cards.

16.

Mech. & D. Calc. questions. Construing &c. Herodotus again. Spineto & Analysing. Finished Prideaux B.2. & analysis. Iliad. Read Ed. Rev. on the Ministry.

17. Fr.

Herodotus. Mechanics. D. Calc. Question. Construing Herodotus. Spineto. Notes on Matthew. Iliad. &c. Much shocked in Evg to hear that Mr Huskisson[3] had been killed.

18. Sat.

Went down early to Wheatley for letters—found one from my brother:[4] it is indeed true & he poor man was in his last agonies when I was playing cards on Wednesday night. When shall we learn wisdom? Not that I see folly in the fact of playing cards: but it is too often accompanied with a dissipated spirit.[5] Iliad: finished Clio: read & abstracted Rennell on the Satrapies; wrote to T.G. read papers about the melancholy accident. Mechanics.

19. Sunday.

Out with A. School & Ch mg & aft. I think the Hymns succeed. Barrow. Townsend. Began Scougal's Life of God in the soul of man.[6]

---

[1] Walter Wrottesley, 1810–72; 4 s. of 1st Lord *Wrottesley; barrister; fellow of All Souls 1831–43.
[2] The marquis Spineto, *Lectures on the Elements of Hieroglyphics and Egyptian Antiquities* (1829). See p. xlv above. Notes in Add MS 44720, ff. 81–3.
[3] *Huskisson was struck down at *Wellington's feet at opening of Liverpool and Manchester railway on the 15th.
[4] Extract in Morley, i. 68.   [5] Thus far in Morley, i. 66.
[6] By H. *Scougal (1677); see *DNB* li. 120.

20. *Monday.*

Read a good part of Melpomene in English & made a kind of abstract. Talk on it at night. Math. & Questions a good while—but did little. Iliad—a little Livy. Townsend. Notes on Matthew.

21. *T.*

Rhetoric Lect. &c 10 to 12. Iliad. Spineto. Abstract of Herodotus. & of Livy: reading Baker.[1] Math. Townsend.

22.

Rhetoric & nearly all as yesterday. Townsend. Wrote to Helen & to Gaskell.

23. *Th.*

Nearly same as yesterday. Wrote to Mr. G. Blomfield's Sermon before the King.

24. *Fr.*

Rhetoric. Herodotus. Iliad. Livy. Tr & Abstract. Math. Question. Townsend. Gk Testament & Notes. papers. My Father may perhaps stand for Lpool.[2] poor Mr Huskisson's burial.

25. *Sat.*

Nearly as yesterday. Herodotus διχῶς.[3] papers.

26. *Sunday.*

Harrison here to my great joy looking pretty well & in good spirits. Ch. & school mg & aft. Out with H. & A. Woodcock, Kynaston, Mr Bishop, dined here. Townsend—Bible.

27. *M.*

Much as on most days of late. Spineto. papers. Walk part of way with Harrison to Oxford.

28. *T.*

As yesterday. A longer day's work than usual. no Rhetoric.

29. *Wed.*

A bad day. went to dine with Mr Cooke of Bakeley sadly against my will.[4]

---

[1] C. Baker tr. Livy's *History of Rome* (1814).
[2] See 29 Sep. 30.
[3] 'in two ways'.
[4] Theophilus Leigh Cooke, 1778?–1846, priest at Beckley, 4½ miles NE. of Oxford, 1803; and rector of Brandeston, Norfolk, 1815.

Did scarcely any Math. Otherwise much as usual. Wrote to T.G. (having heard from him) proposing to him that he should write & print a letter to the freemen of Liverpool. Began to write in case it should devolve on me.[1]

30. Th.

Finished Townsend. I like him very much indeed. Finished Livy B.4. Finished my English work at Herodotus & Analysis. Iliad. Martin of Exeter one of the examiners dined here.[2] Greek Testament & Notes. Walker. Questions.

October 1. Friday.

Began Ethics. Otherwise much the same as yesterday. Wrote home. Virgil at night.

Sat.

as before.

3. Sunday.

Ch & school mg & aft. Rose on German Rationalism. Short's Sermons. Finished Genesis with Anstice.

4. M.

heard from Mrs G wishing me to go home soon. Employments much as usual. Hannington[3] & Shuldham[4] dined here. Spineto.

5.

As Yesterday—Heard from T.G. to my great sorrow that Mr G. had offered to support Peel.[5]

6.

Same. Talking Thucydides at night; also on the Phaedo.

---

[1] *Gladstone was anxious that his father should succeed *Huskisson as M.P. for Liverpool. Unfinished draft letter to Liverpool electors, Add MS 44720, ff. 46–57.

[2] Richard Martin, 1803?–88, fellow of Exeter 1824–31; vicar of Menhenoit, Cornwall, 1831–83; canon of Truro 1878.

[3] Henry Hannington, 1798–1870; Montem 1817; fellow of King's, 1820; founded Cambridge University cricket club.

[4] John Shuldham, 1794?–1884, student of Christ Church 1813–46; rector of Wood Norton, Norfolk, 1845–79.

[5] But *Peel declined, on the previous day, to stand for Liverpool (letter in *Parker, ii. 162–3).

7. *Thursday.*

Saunders off to P. Smythe's. Wordsworth[1] dined here. pleasant evening talking with him together. As yesterday.

Friday 8 Oct to Thursday 14.

At Leamington. surprised at finding my Father in bed—but had the pleasure of seeing him improving as well as Helen when I left, and my dear Mother better than could be expected, except from the temporary though extremely severe ailment of toothach. I had intended to return on Tuesday but put it off on account of my Father's illness, as I wrote three or four letters for him every day, which he dictated. I read in this time two books of Odyssey, wrote out some Greek passages, continued my Abstract of notes on St John. Read Neele's Lectures on English Poetry,[2] with some of his tales: and sundry articles in reviews, with pamphlets & Mr Powys on Bible Soc.[3] Æschylus a little. Saw the Dean on Thursday. Wrote to J.N.G.

Friday 15.

Returned to Cuddesdon early: breakfasted there. Conv. with Saunders. called on Bp. Packed up my things. walked into Oxford. Wrote to Mrs G. Bride of Lammermoor. Finished my notes on St John &c.

16.

Prickbillship began. Much & hard work unpacking & arranging my concerns. Harmony. Sent Saunders a note without 10s. A little Phaedo. papers. &c. &c.

17. Sunday.

A powerful & admirable sermon from Shuttleworth.[4] Sat with Tupper. Harmony. Testament—Proverbs. Lightfoot. Pollok.

18. M.

Talk with Biscoe in evg about my plans. He is very kind. Continued my Harmony. Worked for an hour or more with Doyle in History. Odyssey.

19.

Heard from T.G. By a hard day's work finished my Harmony & sent it in

---

[1] Charles *Wordsworth, 1806–92; nephew of poet; second master at Winchester 1835–1846; first warden of Glenalmond 1846–54; bp. of St. Andrews, Dunkeld, and Dunblane, 1852. See Add MS 44346.

[2] H. *Neele, *Literary Remains* (1829).

[3] L. Powys, 'The Claims of the British and Foreign Bible Society on the Church of England' (1830).

[4] Philip Nicholas *Shuttleworth, 1782–1842; warden of New College 1822; bp. of Chichester 1840.

with a note of apology to Veysie.[1] Tea with the Coles: out with Gaskell: worked again at History with Doyle. paper.

20.

Breakfast with Mayow. Dined with the Coles: bade old Cole goodbye: he gave me a very nice Virgil as a κειμήλιον.[2] Polybius—Phaedo—extract books—a note to T.G.—tea with Doyle—&c. &c.

21. Th.

Polybius. Phaedo. Breakfast with Acland. Spent a good deal of time in discussing a paper about Slavery with him: & told him my position. Working a little with Doyle again. Writing out a rule in the Debating Soc's books, unfortunately omitted. Bland's Hydrostatics.[3] &c. &c.

22. Fr.

Polybius. Phaedo. A wine party: had Bagot, Phillimore, Bernard, Aclands, Anstice, Doyle, Gaskell &c. Bland's Hydrostatics & Math Lect. Papers: writing out rules: Œdipus Tyrannus. Lucretius.

23. Sat.

Looking over books at Parker's. Polybius. Sophocles Œd. Tyr. Papers. Longish Theme. Lardner's Outlines of History; Prometheus Vinctus.

24. Sunday.

Heard Shuttleworth: very able & philosophical, but I fear not calculated to be of general use like the last. Palmer in aftn. Chalmers in Evg at the Baptist Chapel: eloquent & admirable. Read Drummond's "Social Duties on Christian Principles"[4] &c.

25. Monday.

Hydrostatics, Lecture, Polybius, Sophocles, papers &c. Worked at Thucydides two hours with Gaskell in the evening. Learnt a passage in Lucretius. Wine with Acland.

26. Tuesday.

Sophocles and Lecture: Math. Quest. papers. Polybius. Learnt a passage in Juvenal. Thucydides with Gaskell.

27. Wednesday.

Wrote home.[5] Thucydides with Gaskell: we did the difficulties of a book a

---

[1] Add MS 44720. ff. 60–68; notes for it fill Add MS 44803F.
[2] 'keepsake'.
[3] M. *Bland, *Elements of Hydrostatics* (1824).
[4] By H. *Drummond (1830).   [5] Part in Bassett, 20–21.

day. Math. & Lect. Polybius: notes to Sophocles. Ld Palmerston's Portugal.[1]

28. Th.

Polybius. Sophocles & Lect. Math Questions. wine with Wordsworth. Read Lady Canning's able pamphlet:[2] wrote heads for a speech hurriedly, & spoke on the Foreign Policy of the Duke at some length. Beaten by two to one.[3] Wrote to R.G. wine with Wordsworth.

29. Fr.

Integral Calculus & Lecture. papers: wrote out the debate & sundries appertaining. Tea with Hamilton. talked Livy. Worked Homer with Doyle from 7 to 9. Heard Gaskell up for his littlego. Polybius: & a little Sophocles.

30. Sat.

Occupied the morning in part foolishly by making out a ministry: to be able to answer questions:[4] in part painfully by talking a great deal to James Wishlade on his temporal & external prospects & endeavouring to investigate his complaints: sad lies on one side or both. Polybius. Sophocles. Marmion.[5] Essay Society at nt in a queer way.[6] Much conv. with Acland, out with Anstice. Paper.

31. Sunday.

Missed Chapel oversleeping myself in morng, University Sermon twice. Tyler[7] very good. Refused an invitation from Hill but went to young Acland's to meet his brother Anstice & Hewitt.[8] qn. right? Jeremy Taylor. Pearson. Par[adise] Lost B.3. Bible.

November 1. Monday.

Again long busied & much troubled about this sad business of Wishlade's. I fear he does not tell the truth. Math & Lect. Gaudy day, dressing &c. bore decided. Sophocles. Polybius, a little Paley into Greek. breakft with Pusey. Wrote a letter for Wishlade to sign to Ld. Lilford.[9] Sat with Strangways in evg & had coffee.

---

[1] 10 March 1830, *NSH* xxiii. 76.

[2] 'A Brief Exposition of the Foreign Policy of Mr *Canning, as contrasted with that of the Existing Administration.' (anon., 1830).

[3] *Gladstone presided, as well as speaking for Gaskell's motion deploring *Wellington's foreign policy; it was lost, 24–48. Notes for speech in Add MS 44720, ff. 58–59.

[4] Perhaps stimulated by his father's letter, partly quoted in Morley, i. 69.

[5] *Scott.

[6] Only a few members turned up to hear F. Cole on national prejudice.

[7] James Endell *Tyler, 1789–1851, fellow of Oriel 1812–28; rector of St. Giles-in-the-fields 1826; canon of St. Paul's 1845.

[8] James Hewitt, 1811–87, 4th Viscount Lifford 1855; Irish representative peer 1856.

[9] Thomas Atherton Powys, 1801–61, succ. as 3rd Lord Lilford 1825; a Christ Church family.

2. Tuesday.

breakft with Cunningham. Sophocles & Lecture. Polybius. Out with Tancred. papers. Wrote letters to Mr G. & T.G. about my degree.[1]

3. Wednesday.

Hydrostatics & Lect. &c. Polybius. Sophocles and Notes. papers. Dined after
walking, with Rogers, & had wine with him. reading Shelley. Debates
interesting.[2]

4. Thursd.

Bad debate enough.[3] papers. wrote to Mr G. Sophocles & Lect. Worked
some time at Greek Iambics & did a good many. Polybius. Gaskell & Alston[4]
had tea with me. Outlines of history. Dined with Gaskell.

5. Fr.

Int. Calc. questions & Lecture. Long service. Sophocles. Polybius. papers.
Shelley & Milton—corrected & wrote over a long Theme to read tomorrow.[5]

6. Sat.

Did a long Latin Theme and verses. Meeting in Evg at Abercorn's rooms:
Bruce's Essay very good.[6] Acland chosen President. Bruce Sec.—heard
from Harrison. Prometheus, Sophocles, papers; read over Theme in Hall.
&c. D. Stewart.

7. Sunday.

A good sermon from Mills of Magdalen. Prickbill for Jelf. read Pollok: wrote
over some verse (q[uery] poetry?) I wrote in vacation. Began Whately's
Rev. on Future State.[7]

8. M.

Math. questions &c. & Lecture. papers. Shelley. Sophocles. read "Observations on two pamphlets"[8] &c. Wrote to Harrison & to Childers. Polybius:
Phaedo began to reperuse with a view to getting it up.

[1] See 9 Nov. 30 and Morley, i. 50.
[2] Long debates on address in each house of the new parliament, 2 November 1830.
H i. 8, 54.
[3] A motion that Napoleon II had had a better right to the French crown than Charles X
was lost without a division.
[4] Rowland Gardiner Alston, b. 1812?; contested Bury St. Edmunds, June, and Essex,
July 1841 as whig.
[5] Add MS 44720, ff. 70–71. And a poem on *Shelley: Add MS 44813D, ff. 32–35.
[6] F. Cole again; and *Bruce on national character.
[7] British Critic, vi. 130, reviewing T. Huntingford, On The Separate Existence of the
Soul (both 1829).
[8] Anonymous reply to *Brougham (see 9, 10 Nov. 30).

9. T.

Letter from Mr G. desiring me to give up Mathematics. So wretched a creature am I that now I have gained my wish I dare not act upon it! Alas alas. These are what people call the sweets of liberty. However it is my own fault. Biscoe wished me to wait a little. Wine with Tupper. Sophocles & Lect. Math. Qu. papers: "Country without a Govt".[1] Phaedo & Analysis. Prometheus Vinctus. Alastor.[2]

10. W.

Gaskell's antiGovt wine party. papers. "Result of the General Elections".[3] Prom. Vinct. Little Math & Sophocles & Phaedo. At night began to throw my heads of matter into order. Sat in the schools & had the pleasure of hearing Anstice do exceedingly well, thank God.

11. Th.

Perplexed a little by having my degree & debate both before me. Spoke to Saunders about it. Sophocles & Lecture. papers. Phaedo. Sat thinking after dinner. Opened debate & replied. Discussion long & interesting. Carried motion[4] by 57 to 56. Tea &c. afterwards.

12. Fr.

Talked more with Saunders & wrote to my Father. Math & Lect. Sophocles and Phaedo, papers &c. Out with Doyle. Herbert[5] rediscussed question with me. Wrote out debate &c. &c.

13. S.

Essay Society.[6] wrote to R.G. papers. Phaedo. Began Trachiniae.[7] Lucretius. wine with Cameron.[8] Tea with Cole. Theme. &c.

14. Sunday.

Chapel & St Mary's mg & aft. Admirable sermon from Majendie in aftn on the confessing Our Lord before men.[9] Whately. Paradise Lost. Cole Mon-

---

[1] Anonymous anti-tory pamphlet attributed to *Brougham (1830).
[2] *Shelley.
[3] Another anonymous pamphlet attributed to *Brougham (1839).
[4] 'That the Administration of the Duke of *Wellington is undeserving of the confidence of the Country'. He omits to mention that during the evening he was elected president. Minutes of debate in facsimile in Reid, *G*, 120.
[5] Sidney *Herbert, 1810–61; 2nd s. of 11th earl of Pembroke; Harrow and Oriel; tory and Peelite M.P. south Wiltshire 1832–60; minor offices 1834–5, 1841–5; secretary at war 1845–6, 1852–5; for war 1859–60; cr. Lord Herbert of Lea, 1860. See Add MSS 44210–1.
[6] Seymer on influence of drama.   [7] Sophocles.
[8] Charles Cameron, 1807–61, of Queen's, priest at Manchester 1844–53, and at Trusley near Derby from 1859.
[9] George John Majendie, 1795?–1842, Eton and Christ Church, fellow of Magdalen 1820–39, then rector of Headington, Oxford; canon of Salisbury, 1824; on Matt. x. 32–33.

creiff Tancred Gaskell Dodds [1] had tea with me. Read over again D. Wilson's Essay Introd[uctory] to Wilberforce.

15. M.

Sophocles little. Lucretius. Phaedo. Turned a little Shaksp[eare] into Greek. Wine with Ross & Cole. Tea with Mayow. papers. A very bad day.

16. T.

Little Lucretius. Little Phaedo. Little Sophocles. Lecture. did some Iambics. Anstice & Harrison with me a good deal. Read Horace Satire 1. Wrote a letter to the Standard. [2] Dined with Gaskell wine with Jelf & Moncreiff. papers. A very bad day.

17–19.

In these days, dined with Dean: had Harrison &c to Breakfast: acted as President at Society: had a good deal of Society business. repented not speaking on Thursday. [3] A little Sophocles & Lect. with Phaedo & Memorabilia. Wrote home. Read Mill's Sermon & Appendices. made out a list of votes on D. of Wellington, read papers. [4] Stanley—Gisborne—Shelley—Lancaster: [5] exceedingly desultory & alas exceedingly idle. Did a very few Lat. vss & Gk Iambb.

20. Sat.

Heard Hamilton throughout. [6] papers. Xenophon Mem. Latin Theme & Verses. Essay Society. [7] wine with Canning. Papers & letter from T.G. read them.

21. Sun.

Chapel & serm. mg & aft. Whately. Lancaster. sleepy. tea with Cole. Walk with Lushington & Colquhoun. [8] Read part of Selwyn's Essay on Types. [9]

22 Mon. to 28 Sun.

Chiefly busied in reading for my Essay: & wrote it: meeting held in my

[1] Henry Luke Dodds, 1810?–86, priest 1839; vicar of Glen- with Stretton-Magna near Leicester 1855.

[2] On 11 November debate; published, 18; by 'One of the Majority'.

[3] On 18 November the Union resolved in favour of free trade in principle, 52–28.

[4] A government crisis was raging; *Wellington resigned on 16 November, and *Grey began at once to form a new, more whiggish administration.

[5] T. W. *Lancaster, The Harmony of the Law and the Gospel with regard to the Doctrine of a Future State (1825). Notes in Add MS 44720, f. 80.

[6] In the schools.

[7] *Bruce again; and Gaskell comparing the state of Europe in 1815 and in 1830.

[8] William Laurence Colquhoun, 1810?–61, of Oriel and of Clathie, Perthshire.

[9] W. *Selwyn, The Doctrine of Types, and its Influence on the Interpretation of the New Testament (1829).

rooms.[1] papers. wrote home & to **T.G.** Encyclopedia Metropolitana Art[icle on] Socrates.[2] Xenophon Memorabilia about $2\frac{1}{2}$ books. Debating Society meeting interrupted by the proctor.[3] In the library, reading Apuleius, Priapeia! Stanley &c. Wine with Tupper. breakft with Lushington. wine with Allies &c. &c. Some Sophocles. and one Lecture. This has been a very bad week & it will not do. Class[ical] Journal. Read Mill's Plato[4] & Aristotle. A Theme &c. &c. Wine with Scott. Had Dunlop[5] to tea. A little Spineto & Phaedo.

Sunday 28.

Chapel mg & aft. St Mary's mg. Walk with Doyle. Had him, Anstice, Tupper, Cole, to tea. Finished Selwyn's Essay: read two B. of Paradise Regained & some Pollok. &c.

29. M.

Xenophon Memorabilia. Some Latin verses. Horace Satires 1 & 2. Breakft with Cole. Finished Whately. papers. Ld Holland to Shuttleworth.[6] Philpott's 2nd to Canning. Gally Knight to Ld Aberdeen.[7] Peel's Sp. on retiring from Office.[8] Wrote to H.J.G. &c.

30. Tuesday.

Sophocles and Lect. With Biscoe & Saunders, endeavouring to make an arrangement with Wordsworth.[9] Wine with Barnes & Menteith. At the concert. good, & amusing. Xenophon Memorabilia &c. &c. Made up accts. Had Canning & Gaskell to breakft. Walk with Canning.

I have read during the last month

Xen. Mem. 1. 2. 3. Polybius 2.
Whately on a Future State.
Œd Col. Antig. Trachiniae. Ajax.
Eight or ten political pamphlets: & reviews.
Selwyn's Essay on Types.

[1] On Saturday 27th. Gaskell's essay again; and *Gladstone on 'some of the systems of ancient philosophy, in reference to the Mind and Destiny of Man', Add MS 44720, ff. 91–101.

[2] Notes ibid. ff. 76–79.

[3] At the proctors' request, *Gladstone adjourned the Union's debate on 25 November over night lest, if it broke up at the usual time, it precipitate a town-and-gown riot. The house deplored a death penalty for forgery by 45 to 37.

[4] J. Mill, *Apology of Socrates* (1775).

[5] Andrew Dunlop of Kircudbrightshire, b. 1810.

[6] H. R. *Fox 3rd Lord Holland, 'A letter to the Rev. Dr. *Shuttleworth' (1827); on catholic emancipation.

[7] H. G. *Knight 'A Letter to the Earl of *Aberdeen, Secretary . . . for Foreign Affairs' (1829).

[8] 16 November 1830, *H* i. 561.

[9] For private tuition.

Enc. Metr. on Socrates (analysed).
Mills on Plato & Aristotle's belief &c.
Milton—Pollok—Shelley (parts).

December 1. Wednesday.

Wrote to the Rev. Mr Ridley[1] in answer to a very kind letter received from
him. Arranged with Wordsworth. Gave a wine party. Some Horace and
learning a bit of Cicero. Xen. Mem. Walk with Wordsworth talking. Persius
&c. &c.

2. Th.

A large wine party. made a vapid & declamatory speech at Debating Society
as also several on private business.[2] Wordsworth unwell & unable to begin
business. Heard from T.G. of his election. Wrote to congratulate him.[3]
Event of Lpool election unsatisfactory, nature of the contest still more so.[4]
Sophocles & Lecture—some Horace—Burke. &c. Sat with Hamilton.
Walk with Acland.

3. Fr.

Horace—Cicero into Latin. Horace with Wordsworth—dinner & wine with
Lyall. breakfasted at a party of Gaskell's. Wrote to T.G. & H.J.G. paper:
writing out passages. A sketch of Paley. "Parochial duties"—admirable.[5]
Drew out a scheme of the Deb. Soc. Speakers.—Poor Caroline Wadd: God
support her mother![6]

4. Sat. to 11 Sat.

Went on with composition—Horace—writing letters to T.G., Mr Ridley,
Seymer. Gave a wine party & a breakfast—bad debate on Pope[7]—row
about the letter in the Standard,[8] blew over for the present—almost wish
it had not. Finished Par. Reg.: little Lancaster & Memorabilia. Sophocles
with Gaskell, alone, & at Lectures. At Acland & Co's concert & Supper. Had
Baron (?) Friedel[9] to lunch. Wine with Mayow, Gaskell, Lincoln, &c. John

[1] Probably Henry John Ridley, 1788–1834, great-nephew of 1st bart.; Christ Church;
canon of Bristol 1816, Norwich 1832; rector of Newdigate, Surrey, 1814.
[2] *Acland's motion 'That the Declaration of Rights made by the National Assembly of
France in 1789, was founded on false principles' was carried without a division.
[3] Thomas *Gladstone, bottom of the poll at Queenborough, Kent, in the general election—though only fifteen votes behind the leading candidate—secured the seat on petition.
[4] In the by-election to replace *Huskisson, William *Ewart defeated J. E. *Denison by
twenty-nine votes out of 4,401 cast, after a particularly corrupt campaign; thereafter
Gladstones and Ewarts were no longer on speaking terms. John Evelyn *Denison,
1800–73, eldest b. of Henry; whig M.P. Newcastle-under-Lyme 1823–6, Hastings 1826–
1830, Nottinghamshire 1831–7 and 1857–72, Malton 1841–57; speaker 1857–72; then cr.
Viscount Ossington. See Add MS 44261.
[5] Probably *Parochial Letters from a Beneficed Clergyman to his Curate* (1829).
[6] The da. had d., aged 20, on 28 November.
[7] On 9 December; the Union held him not unequalled by 43 to 29.
[8] See 16 Nov. 30.   [9] Unidentified.

Law here—developed all the unhappy characteristics of the school. I endeavoured to speak to him a little but nor plainly nor forcibly enough. Abstracted Article on Plato in Encyclopaedia Metropolitana. Had a book very hansomely given me by Burton. Prickbillising, for the last time. Engaged with Wishlade's matters. Wine with Wilson. Wrote Essay on Plato & Aristotle, & read it &c.[1]

12. Sun. to 18. Sat.

Short's Serm. Heard Buckley. Lancaster. &c. &c. Finished Memorabilia & Sophocles. Collections: wrote on comparative credibility of Xenophon & Plato as recording ideas & notions[2] of Socrates. Read Merrivale's Essay[3]— the Bp of Calcutta's Journals, Charge, & Confirmation Adress.[4] Finished the Satires & Epistles of Horace. Wine with Cunningham. Had Laurence,[5] the Aclands, Scott, Strangways, to wine. Assisting in the removal of Union Soc's concerns & wrote to H.J.G., T.G., Edward Robertson, B. Harrison, Doyle twice (once in Latin) & Gaskell. Paid bills & packed: came to Leamington on Friday: much pleased with Helen's state. Read Barrow on W.I. question, having before read my Father.[6] Monthly Review on ditto[7] and Westminster Review on Coleridge,[8] &c. &c. Æneid B.1. & somewhat over. cards in evg of Sat. Wrote several notes to R.G. &c. Wrote a paper on Philosophy & Poetry.[9]

Sunday 19.

Ch in mg. very cold. Lancaster—& began to analyse him. Mr Jackson's poems.[10] Some of Arnold's Sermons. +. read them aloud. a MS sermon of Foster's. Bible.

20. M.

Began to read a little regularly: but up at $7\frac{1}{4}$ only. Æneid—Odyssey difficulties—Phaedo—Wordsworth's MS. Middleton & some turning.—papers.

21. T.

papers. Æneid—a good deal. Phaedo & Analysis. turned some [of Middleton's] Cicero into Latin. Odyssey as before. Cards.

[1] He re-read one paper to the essay society on 4 December, followed by Grimston on inferiority of modern to ancient eloquence; on 11 December, Grimston not appearing, *Gladstone read another, comparing the systems of Plato and Aristotle.
[2] Paper stained; these three words conjectural.
[3] H. *Merivale's 'Character of Socrates', university prize essay (1830).
[4] Either A. Heber ed. R. *Heber, *Narrative*, 2v. (1828), and his 'Charge' of 1824 or 1827, or MSS of J. M. Turner's, with his charge of 1830.
[5] William Rogers Laurence or Lawrence, 1811?–43; at Queen's, Oxford, 1829–33, and Trinity, Cambridge, 1833–6; priest at Whitchurch, Somerset, 1841.
[6] Sir J. *Barrow in *Quarterly Review*, xxxiv. 613 (December 1825). John *Gladstone, 'A Statement of Facts connected with the Present State of Slavery' (1830); see *DNB* xxi. 406.
[7] New series iii. 608–9 (December 1830); hostile.
[8] xii. 1 (January 1830).
[9] Add MS 44720, ff. 102–11.   [10] T. B. J[ackson], *Exodus and other Poems* (1830).

22. W.

papers. Walk to Warwick. Æneid & Eclogues. Finished Phaedo & Analysis.
Began Philebus.[1] Cic. into Latin. Odyssey. Cards.

23. Th.

paper. Lpool Squib book. Virgil. Cic. into Latin. Philebus. a very bad day
for work, from the same cause wh made it a very pleasant one—Robns
arrival. Cards.

24. Fr.

This was dearest Anne's day of birth in the human state: but it has passed
as a dream, whose close to her has been glorious, to us bitter: and felt now,
practically felt, & *but too* selfishly felt, scarcely less than when the first tears
were shed over her remains. This day I read some letters of hers to J.N.G.
which ought, in their mention of me, to cover me with the deepest sorrow
and shame. Half I believe what I have just written, half spurn it. My heart
at least—let me rather say I—for my heart, my nature, my disposition, are
all phrases which but too strongly tend to remove the direct and piercing
consciousness to something general & not appropriate to one's self—to common properties inherent in the race—to an abstract standard according to
which we suppose ourselves framed & from which unable to escape: instead
of the simple term I, which brings upon us immediate & undiluted all the
responsibilities of individuality. I then, I, who might by God's power have
escaped sin, I, the sinner, the twofold sinner, the sinner within & without,
sinner within my rankling passions, (passions which I dare not name—
shame forbids it & duty does not seem to require it—) and sinner without
in the veil of godliness and of moderation too which I have cast over them—
(and my moderation adds to my sin because it renders me much less sus-
pected than if I were a bold and manly character—) I, the hypocrite, and
the essence of sin, am indeed deceitful above all things and desperately
wicked, desperately wicked. Again I half believe what I write, half scorn it.
Half I do sometimes hope I see myself in all the completeness of its naked
deformities; yet even then in my best moments another & perhaps more
powerful voice rises from within assuring me that I am less sinful than my
neighbour. *If* I were, what then? but am I? I *know* how I ought to answer the
question: "No: ten thousand times more sinful, if at least the thoughts,
intents, desires of the heart are the seat of sin". Yet I feel that while I gave
the answer still my accursed self would be whispering a different belief. I
will leave the question then to the day of judgment: but O Lord God grant
that ere that time arrive I may have grown far deeper & far more practically
into the knowledge of those high & engrossing truths, the intensity &
inveteracy of my sinfulness, the measure and stability of the love of God
as shown forth in the sacrifice of God upon the Cross, of God upon the Cross,
true & very God.

[1] Also Plato's.

Perhaps even at this moment, I, the evil I, am encouraging myself, under Satan's guidance, in the use of these violent epithets, in order that thereby my hypocritical & forced self condemnation may spend itself in the war of words, and all practical self condemnation as leading to true self abhorrence, & all self abhorrence as leading to that faith which springeth low but riseth high, may be forgotten. *I* cannot believe: *I* cannot pray: *I* cannot repent: *I* cannot desire to believe or pray or repent: but the worship of Israel is still sure, the fountain is still open for sin & for uncleanness: behold my one and only, O Father may I add my abundant hope? If not abundant, why not abundant? In itself large & overflowing, in me perhaps debased & degenerate.

Read Virgil. Philebus. part of a brief sketch of the Phaedo. and some [of Middleton's] Cicero into Latin. papers. T.G. came. read "Mr Canning's Foreign Policy contrasted with D. of Wellington's".[1] Very able. walk with R.G.

Sat. Christmas Day.

Ch in mg & sacrament. Aunts dined with us & Helen downstairs. paper. Arnold's Sermons &c. cards. q. right?

26. Sun.

Ch mg & aft. Arnold. Began Miss Jewsbury's Letters to the Young.[2] Exodus.

27. M.

Wrote to Aunt M. Walk with T.G. Virgil. Dined at Dr Jephson's,[3] with Mr G., T.G. & R.G.—a fair quota for one family. Middleton Cicero &c. paper.

28. T.

Wrote to Wordsworth [4]—Gaskell—& notes. Papers—very interesting now.[5] Conv. with Mrs G. What a hypocrite I am. cards. Virgil a good deal, a little Odyssey. finished Analysis *of Analysis* of Phaedo, & did some Latin. The closing year: is its retrospect satisfactory?

29. Wednesday.

My birthday. Surely to me a day of pain in as far as it was a day of reflection: to others perhaps (God bless them) of joy. As to *idleness* one of my great foes, there has been *less* of it thank God during the past year: but the only redeeming portion was the Long Vacation—and then it was owing to my close contact with industrious persons.

[1] Cp. 28 Oct. 30.

[2] By M. J. *Jewsbury, later Mrs. Fletcher (1828).

[3] Henry Jephson, 1798–1878, fashionable Leamington physician, graduated at Glasgow 1827; went blind, 1848.

[4] In Charles *Wordsworth, *Annals*, i. 88–89.

[5] Christmas in Dublin was disturbed by massive demonstrations in favour of Daniel *O'Connell, 1775–1847, the Irish national hero.

25—I.

This has been my Debating Society year: now I fancy done with. Politics are fascinating to me. perhaps too fascinating.[1] Perhaps I have *less* to repent for the time spent at Cuddesdon (but how much every where!) than any other: most for the Easter Vacation.

I have thank God enjoyed much in Society. But as to real progress in religion: that is in the practical part of religion—the subjugation of the will & affections—I see no progress: though I may have clearer notions perhaps: which if so increase guilt.—

Virgil. Middleton & Cicero into Latin. papers. Heard from & wrote to Gaskell. Also to Wordsworth. A little Odyssey.—Cards singing, or trying, & wasting R's time.

May God keep me during the coming year & from day to day may I approach more a practical belief that *he* is my friend, I mine enemy.

30. Th.

Papers. Virgil. Cicero into Latin. A little Odyssey. a very bad day. Wrote however a long letter to J.M.G. also one to Doyle. Cards.

31. Fr.

Finish'd the Æneid. A little headache owing to myself. Paper. Xtn Observer on Drummond & Codrington estates.[2] Cards. Middleton & Cicero into Latin.

I subjoin the doings of the month.

Phaedo.
Æneid.
Philoctetes. Electra. Xenophon Mem 4.
Horace Satires & Epistles.
Tennyson's Poems. West Rev. on Coleridge. Foreign Policy of Mr Canning. Par. Regained. Parochial Duties illustrated. Bp. Calcutta's Journals, Charge & Address. Merivale's Essay. My Father & Barrow on W.I. question & Rev. in Monthly. Encycl. Metr. on Plato. Mr Jackson's "Crucifixion" &c. &c.

[1] These two sentences in Morley, i. 83; conflated with the entry of a year later.
[2] xxx. 697–708 (November 1830).

1831. January

1. Sat.

began Sumner's Records.[1] Eclogues. Homer. Cicero. Cards. &c. papers.

2. Sun.

Ch mg, & aftn out in the country. Miss Jewsbury's Letters. Sumner's Records of Creation. and read over again Heber on Moses. Heard from Gaskell.

3. M.

Cameron and Gooch dined here. papers—cards. Cic. into Latin. Homer—Eclogues (finished)—Sumner's Records. Conversation on Fasting &c. at nt. Awkward.

4. T.

Georgics, begun. Sumner's Records.

5. Wed–8. Sat.

parties at Mrs Cameron's & Mrs Hook's.[2] Jephsons & Gooch dined with us. Cards every night—papers every day—pretty ingredients of employment with a view to an Oxford degree. Did Cicero regularly, & Odyssey but too slow—read Sumner and the Georgics—Peter Schlimmel[3]—the Westminster on Tennyson, George 4, D. of Wellington &c.[4] wrote to Doyle. Aunts unhappily disgusted at the prospect of Aunt Mary's visit.

9. Sun.

Ch mg & afternoon. A very good sermon in mg from Mr Hopkinson[5] (I believe) a stranger. A most painful one in the afternoon. Miss Fry,[6] Miss

[1] J. B. *Sumner, *A Treatise on the Records of Creation*, 2v. (1816). Some notes in Add MS 44721, ff. 112–15.

[2] Mrs. Cameron, Charles Cameron's mother, was wife to C. R. Cameron, rector of Snaby, Lincolnshire. Anna Delicia Johnstone m. 1828 Walter Farquhar *Hook, 1798–1875, vicar in Coventry 1828, Leeds 1837; dean of Chichester 1859; uncle-in-law of Sir W. R. Farquhar. See Add MS 44213.

[3] J. *Bowring tr. Adelbert von Chamisso's *Peter Schlemihls Wunderbare Geschichte* (1814), the tale of the young man who sold his shadow.

[4] xiv. 210, 103, 232 (January 1831).

[5] Samuel Edmund Hopkinson, 1754–1831, vicar of Morton Lincolnshire, 1795.

[6] Possibly Elizabeth *Fry, *Observations on visiting female prisoners* (1827); more probably Caroline Fry (later *Wilson), *The Listener*, 2v. (1830), moral tales.

Jewsbury. Sat up late to carry into effect, partially at least, a wayward purpose of mine—to write a letter to Mr Crowther earnestly expostulating with him on the character & doctrines of the sermon he had delivered—and another to Mr Downes begging him to read & pronounce an opinion upon it. &c.

10. M.

Rewrote much of the letter to Mr Crowther—finished both & delivered them at their doors with my own hand.[1] Very long. Aunt Mary came. paper. Sumner—Odyssey *little*. Cic. into Latin.

11. T.

Cic. into Latin. Odyssey. At my Aunt's. called on Mrs Cameron. Began Analysis of Sumner. Finished Georgics. paper. West. Rev. on a book about Hannibal's passage—written, as I surmise, by my friend Todd.[2] Out with Tom.

12. Wed.

Out with Tom. paper. Odyssey—Sumner—Cic. into Latin. Finished Miss Jewsbury. A party in the evening at Miss Campbell's (senr).[3] Met Lady Morton,[4] the Pocklingtons[5] (I like both daughters much especially Miss Jane, with whom I got upon delicate ground about the Vicar's preaching) Miss Campbell, the Camerons &c. Cards—All this time I ought to be asking myself, do I mix in society (wretchedly capacitated for it as I am) for the gratification of self ?

My opinion of it has been in some measure changed: or rather I have had little opportunity previously of forming one. But it seems to me that female society, whatever the disadvantages may be, has just & manifold uses attendant upon it in turning the mind away from some of its most dangerous & degrading temptations.

13. Thursday.

Tom went early. Bestowed some time on learning "Friend of the Brave"[6] with that peculiar felicity in the choice of time & manner which charac-

[1] See Morley, i. 58–9, and 19 June 31. Samuel Crowther, 1802–79, was perpetual curate of Knowle, midway between Leamington and Birmingham, 1839–54.

[2] xiv. 42 (January 1831); ? by J. F. Todd.

[3] Perhaps related to Sir James Campbell of Inverneill, 1737–1805; lived in Leam Terrace.

[4] Frances Theodora Rose, d. 1879, who m. 1817 the 17th earl of Morton; or perhaps Susan Elizabeth Buller, d. 1849, widow of 16th earl 1827, later m. to Edward Godfrey.

[5] Roger Pocklington, 1775–1847, colonel, lived at Leamington; m. 1802 Jane, da. of Sir James Campbell; their 3rd s., Evelyn Henry Frederick, 1811–79, at Eton and in 52nd Reg., became a lieut.-general. Their elder da. Mary d. unm. 1873; Jane Augusta m. 1832 James Archibald Campbell of Inverawe, and d. 1842.

[6] A song from *Campbell's 'Pleasures of Hope' (1799); music by J. W. *Callcott.

terises me—for it can be of no use now that the vacation is over. Called on Miss Campbell—& on my Aunts—whist. papers—Finished Analysis of Sumner—Odyssey—Conversed a good deal with Helen.

14. Fr.

Odyssey—pack'd—bid goodbye to all—return'd to Oxford full of good resolutions but no stamen for performing them. Arriv'd about seven. Unpacked. Tea with Tupper. afterwards Wordsworth sat & had some with me.

15. Sat.

look'd over some difficulties in the Georgics & first Æneids. With the Dean & Biscoe—wrote home—&c.

16. Sun.

Chapel & St Mary's—Shuttleworth & Mills. Jerram's Sermon on Dr Good[1]—Christian Year—Bible—tea with Mayow—also sat some time with Cole & with young Acland.

17. Mon.

Breakfast with Denison, making a reading plan with him. Out with Gaskell. paper. Quart Theol Rev. on Bp of London's Charge.[2] Odyssey—ran over the difficulties in the Eclogues, &c. Tomorrow I begin: please God: for not even that can I do of myself, so much am I a slave to my propensities.

I am now looking forward to ten or eleven hours a day of work. At least if I do my duty & health permit, it cannot be much less. I am in that sort of dissatisfied humour with myself that I am sick of all my prospects & doings: but I lament to say it is not a humble but a morbid feeling. God be praised that other men are not such as I am! a hypocrite so deep, deceiving myself as well as others: so inconsistent, so wavering, so uncertain. A prevailing selfishness is almost the only fact or feeling which I can permanently recognise.

Where is my refuge? How am I to attain these two great objects, first to be nerved for the performance of those temporal duties, secondly to be saved from abusing them? How must I despair of either except for Him who was wounded for my transgressions & bruised for my iniquities. Through Him & Him alone can I hope for any benefit or blessing & by him I feebly and coldly pray for a fervent and energetic power of prayer that I may be delivered from the guilt & power of sin. O the loftiness and completeness of true Christian virtue, which sanctifies enobles & secures all to Christians? Let me not despair of attaining it knowing that he is faithful to promise & mighty to save, altho' I might well despair did I only look at the countless stains upon my soul, the grace of God with which I have dealt

---

[1] C. *Jerram, *Sermon occasioned by the Death of John Mason *Good* (1827), on 2 Tim. i. 12.

[2] *British Critic*, ix. 206 (1831), reviewing *Blomfield's charge of July 1830.

guilefully & the endeavours I have made & the wishes & [*sc.* that] I have felt to serve God & Mammon, & indulge in all sin, at the same time having an inheritance among the saints in light. O cursed thoughts, and cursed being to entertain them! But yet stands the immutable truth "The blood of Christ cleanseth from all sin".[1] Cleanse me then O Lord from mine for thou art gracious in will & abundant in power. And may I ever be near the cross.

18. Tuesday.

Dear John's birthday. May God crown him with every blessing, one particularly, amidst far lands and strange countenances.
Began fairly to read. Got up & went over with Denison part of Clio. Juvenal 1 & 2—Virgil difficulties—Adam[2]—Middleton Cicero—&c.—papers. shopping—out.

19. Wed.

Herodotus—& writing it with Denison—wrote home—paper—Harrison came—Juvenal—Adam—some Greek from Paley. Middleton &c . . .[3]

20. Th.

As yesterday, except Paley & letter home. Wrote to Moncreiff. Out with Harrison. Began the select orations.[4] Heard of my dear cousin Eliza Barlow's death.[5] May it be remembered.

21. Fr.

Herodotus & with Denison. Juvenal—Adams[6]—no lecture with Wordsworth—wrote to Mrs G. Adam. Out with Harrison. Arnold Appx III & Analysis. Wrote & sent to the printer my circular for the Debating Society.[7]

22. Sat.

Juvenal & Adams—with Wordsworth. read over again corrected & added to my Essay—read it to Society for 2nd time at Maurice's.[8] Tea with Erskine[9] & Bruce. Learnt a little Juvenal. paper. Called on Mrs Lloyd.[10]

23. Sunday.

St Mary's mg & aft. A good sermon on John 1.1. from Mr Walters, Mag-

---

[1] 1 John i. 7.   [2] Alexander *Adam, *Roman Antiquities* (1791).
[3] Diarist's dots.   [4] Probably an anthology from Cicero.
[5] Da. of Thomas Barlow.
[6] Abridgement of *Gibbon by J. Adams, 2v. (1789).
[7] Notice of meeting and subscription. Add MS 44721, f. 18.
[8] On Plato and Aristotle.
[9] Hay Macdowall Erskine, 1810–96, vicar of Woburn Sands 1868–74, then rector of Long Merton, Westmorland.
[10] Mary Harriett, née Stapleton, *Lloyd's widow.

dalen Hall.[1] Tea with Mayow. Long walk with Maurice. Bible—E. Neale's pamphlet[2]—D. Wilson's Pastoral Letter & 1st sermon.[3]

24. M.

Juv. &c. with Wordsworth, Adam; Uncle D[ivie] came—dined & spent evg with him—at [Union] reading room—heard from home & read a very pious letter from Cousin J.[4] to my mother. Some Greek prose &c. at night. Up late. Walk with Bruce.

25. Tuesday.

Surplice prayers. Lionising with Uncle D—saw the new Clarendon press: mechanically wonderful—how much more so morally! Juvenal &c: with Wordsworth. Herodotus with Denison—tea with Uncle D. Niebuhr's Geography of Herodotus[5] and some Iambics.

26. Wed.

Finished Juvenal; with Wordsworth. Middleton. out with Uncle Divie. dined & spent evening with him. paper—Greek Iambics—& scraps of history.

27. Th.

Edward matriculated. Uncle Divie went. They breakfasted, I fear very uncomfortably, with me: as did Gaskell. Cicero, Middleton, Iambics &c.[6]

28. Fr.

Wine with Alston. Work much as yesterday—add, history with Denison & began Nubes.[7]

29. Sat.

As yesterday. Wine with the Taylors. At Essay Soc. Spoke.[8] Tea with Harrison.

[1] Charles Walters, b. 1785?, rector of Bramdean, Hampshire, 1831.
[2] Erskine *Neale, 'Reasons for supporting the Society for the Propagation of the Gospel' (1830).
[3] Pastoral address on the duty of prayer and the financial crisis (1826); sermon on obedience as path to religious knowledge, John vii. 16–17, preached at Oxford (1810).
[4] J. M. G. Robertson.
[5] B. G. Niebuhr, the historian of Rome, *A Dissertation on the Geography of Herodotus, and Researches into the History of the Scythians, &c*, tr. (1830).
[6] *Gladstone also presided for part of the Union's discussion of private business, but not at this day's main debate: an anti-democratic motion by *Allies, set aside by a milder one of *Acland's.
[7] Aristophanes, *Clouds*.
[8] *Maurice read a paper against metaphysics. *Gladstone supported him generally.

30. Sunday.

Chapel & sermon mg & aft. Had Cole Morris[1] & Mayow to tea. D. Wilson on Sabbath[2]—Bible—wrote to H.J.G. at some length—and began a very extraordinary book of Erskine's[3]—which seems to bewilder me on some points & much instruct me on others; particularly the coincidence of suffering & sinning flesh in the crucifixion—and our Saviour's union with every human being from having no human individuality. But I am perplexed about his idea of pardon: he does not mention that which is to make us open our eyes to that light or favour of God in which we bask: & I tremble in defining the limits of our Saviour's humanity & its nearness to ours.

31.

Service morng & aft. Read Erskine—little Aristophanes—Middleton & Cicero—cards with Gaskell for a little, being locked out of my room. Wrote over &c. my Iambics—with Wordsworth. A bad day—sleepy.

February One. Tuesday.

Aristophanes—Cicero—Adam—with Wordsworth—Herodotus with Denison—wine with Anstice—called on Hughan[4]—Mayow came to tea.

2. Wed.

Aristoph—Adam—Cicero Orationes—out with Doyle. Herodotus with Denison. heard from R.G. Hamilton went. Wine with Dodds & with Mayow.

3. Th.

Work as yesterday, except Herodotus. Wrote to T. & R.G. Gave a wine party to Lincoln, Canning, Bruce, Doyle, Gaskell, Acland, Wordsworth, Wood, &c. Heard from Sir F. Doyle. At debate—spoke agst Westminster Review.[5]

4. Fr.

As yesterday: with Herodotus—little Aristophanes. an investigation about Ionians and by the help of B. Price & Pausanias I hope to get some light. Wrote a long letter to Sir F. Doyle, chiefly on the difficult subject of his to me:[6] God only knows whether I pursued at all the right course, for I don't.

---

[1] Robert Morris, 1808?–82?, rector of Friern Barnet, Middlesex, 1850.

[2] Daniel *Wilson, *The divine authority and perpetual obligation of the Lord's Day, asserted in seven sermons* (1831).

[3] Thomas *Erskine of Linlathen, *The Brazen Serpent* (1831).

[4] Thomas Hughan, 1811–79, Balliol; of the Airds, New Galloway; married 1836 a da. of 8th duke of St. Albans.

[5] In private Union business; the society ceased to take the review. In the main debate, the right to the throne of France of the duc de Bordeaux was upheld by 56 to 28.

[6] Of 2 February, asking *Gladstone to persuade young *Doyle to do some work (Add MS 44150, ff. 22–23).

At Brandreth's[1] to wine. Heard from my dear Father on the subject of J.M.G.R's letter.

5. Sat.

Work as usual. Saw Biscoe. paper. At Essay Soc.[2] wine with Rickards. Read part of Paterson's Essay. I am in much difficulty about my letter to Sir F.H.D.[3]—Walk with Doyle.

6. Sunday.

Bible—Erskine—& a long letter home, giving an account of Bulteel's extraordinary sermon.[4] It must rouse many & various feelings. God grant it may all work for good. May my proud heart never lose one jot of the truth of God through its prejudices & passions, & may all their strongholds be cast down, and may there be an absorption of my will in the will of God and a perfect prostration of my soul before him, through the one & only Mediator. But after having heard the remarkable sermon of this remarkable man, I cannot but still remember the words of St Paul, (in reference to the extent of redemption) For as by the disobedience of one *the* many were made sinners, so also by the obedience of one shall *the many* be made righteous.[5] Tupper with me in evg.

7. M.

Work as usual, but no Lecture. Called on Mrs Pett & out with Canning—wine with Pusey—began Thucydides with Denison. Bulteel's sermon is to be published.

8. T.

Work as usual—with Wordsworth. Harrison had tea with me. talked to both on Doyle's matters. Wrote a strange letter (anon.)[6] to Bulteel—& put it up to deliver at his house with Erskine's book.

9. W.

Work—no Lecture—Wine with Lushington—began Equites.[7] Thucydides with Denison—some Œdipus Tyrannus to improve myself, $\kappa\alpha\tau\grave{\alpha}$ $\tau\grave{o}$ $\delta\acute{v}\nu\alpha\tau o\nu$,[8] in Iambics. went to see poor Mrs Jones. Left my parcel at Bulteel's house.—

10. Th.

Wilberforce breakfasted with me & staid talking—I like his society, but all society is now awkward in morng. little of Aristophanes—Adams—Cicero—

---

[1] William Harper Brandreth, 1812?–85; s. of Dr. J. P. Brandreth of Liverpool; rector of Standish near Wigan 1841.
[2] Lushington read an essay on memory.
[3] The letter much pleased the recipient: Add MS 44150, f. 24.
[4] See 15 Feb. 31, &c.
[5] Rom. v. 19.
[6] Untraced.
[7] Aristophanes, *Knights*.
[8] 'according to my power'.

Sophocles—a wretched day. Anstice drank wine with me—out with Harrison—at debate, Bruce chosen President.[1]

11. Fr.

Breakfast & also wine with Gaskell. Work more as it ought to be, but still very deficient. Thucydides & tea with Denison—wrote briefly to Childers. &c.

12. Sat.

Out with Anstice. get on ill with Aristophanes. Dragging on as usual. At Essay Society an instructive subject.[2] Read papers. Did some Iambics, as also yesterday.

13. Sunday.

Chapel mg & evg. heard Buckley preach an excellent sermon, & Tyler in the afternoon. Read some Erskine—Bible—D. Wilson—&c. wrote home.

14. Monday.

Work as usual—& Denison with me in evg. Walk with Harrison.

15. Tuesday.

The same. Adam now gets on faster—but on the whole I flag sadly. Heard from home. Bulteel's serm. came out.[3] Much talk with Harrison on it.

16. Wednesday.

Work—Denison with me—wine with Hewitt and Lyall—met R. Montgomery[4] there—spoke at Debating Society on results of Catholic question, not satisfactorily[5]—Poor Osborne's appalling death at night. If this hath not a voice, all things are dumb to us.[6]

17. Th.

Work &c. out with Doyle—Inquest—'chance medley' the verdict. Wine with Harrison, & Gaskell. remained there long talking about education &c. did some Greek.

[1] The liberty of the press was affirmed by 81 to 35.
[2] *Rogers on the 'abolition of the nobility of blood' as the main cause of division between the ancient Greek republics.
[3] H. B. *Bulteel, *A Sermon on I Corinthians ii. 12*, on the church and the university; see 6, 8, 18 Feb. and 1 Mar. 31.
[4] Robert *Montgomery, 1807–55, the poetaster, was an undergraduate at Lincoln, 1830–3; ordained 1835.
[5] *Jelf's motion 'That the Catholic Relief Bill has not by its results justified the expectations which were held out by its supporters' was lost by 40 to 59.
[6] Lord Conyers G. T. W. Osborne, b. 1812, 2nd s. of 6th duke of Leeds, accidentally killed in a scuffle with some drinking companions in Christ Church.

18. Fr.

Aristophanes. Adams &c. Wrote over my Greek—wrote home—read paper
—Burton's 'Remarks'[1]—of which I much like some & am grieved at
others—&c.

Sat. 19.

Heard from & wrote to T.G. Osborne's death seems forgotten & none to
care a rush. Last night by 7 I saw B[os]c[awe]n drunk. Aristophanes—
Adam—Cicero—a few Iambics & a little of the politics.[2] At Essay Society
Meeting. Old Acland's Essay very good.[3] Talk with him— —tea with
Gaskell.

Sunday 20.

Long conversation with Doyle and earnest comparatively but I fear I have
not yet told him my mind. Had Tupper & Dodds to tea. Heard Buckley
and Faussitt.[4] Wrote a very long letter to Mrs G. also more or less to Aunts
M. & J. Bp of Calcutta, Mr Rawson[5] & Mr Hughes—made up a parcel for
Leamington.

21.

Work as usual. A few Homerics. history with Denison. Wine with Knatchbull.[6] Out with Wordsworth. Wrote to Hanbury about Lane End Church.[7]

22. Tues.

Aristoph—Adam—wine with Cunningham. Wrote to T.G. & to R.G. for a
horse—read long & kind letter from John—some Iambics—and Cicero.
Also Diog. Laert. Vit. Socr.[8] & Analysis of Aristotle's poetics.

23. Wed.

Out with Doyle & Lyall. Work as usual & hist. with Denison. Gaskell sat
with me. With Saunders in Evg about my degree &c. Wrote over Greek
verses & Iambics.

24. Th.

Finished Adam—began a part of Potter. Greek Theatre. a long letter from
my Father on politics &c.

---

[1] Pamphlet on *Bulteel's lately published sermon.   [2] Aristotle.
[3] On Grecian and Roman character.   [4] Faussett.
[5] Enclosing six guineas for Liverpool charities (Add MS 44352, f. 183).
[6] Henry Edward Knatchbull, 1808–76, of Wadham; 4th s. of 8th bart.; vicar of North
Elmham, Norfolk, 1833–67.
[7] St. James the Less, Lane End, Stoke-on-Trent, built 1833–4. (See VCH Staffordshire,
viii. 234.)
[8] Notes for the lives of the ancient philosophers, assembled by Diogenes Laertius in
the third century A.D., provide the principal source for their subject.

25. Fr.

As usual and history with Denison. I cannot now at all overtake my work. Out little. Wine with Mayow.

26. Sat.

Wrote sundry letters on compulsion—paper—had a kind letter from R.G. Ellison the third Examiner.[1] Plutarch's Life of Demosthenes—Potter. & other similar matters—Ranae[2]—Wasted some time in evg.[3]

27. Sunday.

Two University sermons. and heard Griffith the pro-proctor[4] preach an admirable sermon at St Peter's. Walking with Harrison &c. Finished Erskine. Bible.

28. M.

Work & with Wordsworth. Began History of Polybius with Denison—went to wine with Joyce, to meet Mr Cunningham,[5] to whom I was today introduced.

March 1. Tuesday.

Work &c. as usual. Had an interesting conversation with Mr Cunningham, about the state of religion here, and his son. I like him very much. Gaskell had tea with me: had a good deal of conversation with him on religion which went off I think far better than anything hitherto. O that God in his mercy may grant that the words which proceeded from my polluted lips may be purified and enlarged and so made the instruments of good to him.—I have not done my duty by young Cunningham: God enable me to amend in this particular. Read Bulteel's able reply[6] & two other pamphlets—paper.

Wed. March 2.

long letter from John with account of Wreck of Thetis. Had Mr Cunningham, his son, Anstice, & Harrison, to breakfast. Wordsworth's MSS—Cicero—some learning by heart—Polybius & with Denison—Wrote to Mr G. & T.G.—wine with Oaks[7]—out with Bruce.

---

[1] Noel Thomas Ellison, 1791?–1858, fellow of Balliol 1816–24, canon of Wells 1823, was examining for the *Ireland scholarship with *Symons and Vowler *Short.

[2] Aristophanes, *Frogs*.

[3] He missed an essay society discussion on Greek and Roman character, and a paper by *Bruce on 'history'.

[4] Charles Griffith, 1805?–86, rector of Talachddu, near Brecon, 1833–82.

[5] John William *Cunningham, 1780–1861, evangelical author; vicar of Harrow 1811.

[6] H. B. *Bulteel, *A reply to Dr *Burton's Remarks*, a closely argued pamphlet. (See 15, 18 Feb. 31.)

[7] Charles Henry Oakes, 1810–64, of Merton; barrister; 4th s. of 2nd bart.*

3. Thursday.

Began the Meidias[1]—Cicero—Wordsworth's MSS—wine with Bernard. At the debate for some time[2]—history of Polybius. Writing out passages &c.

4. Friday.

Meidias. four or five hours cramming [for Ireland] Scholarship. Wrote to Farr. paper a little. Wilson had tea with me—looked up some passages in Odyssey—Cicero and Middleton.

5. Sat.

Meidias—Scholarship—had Scott to tea—at Essay Society—a review of Tennyson by Anstice.[3] paper. out Cicero. &c.

7 [sc. 6].[4] Sun.

Chapel & sermon twice. Newman preached in the afternoon—much singular not to say objectionable matter if one may so speak of so good a man.[5] Bible—D. Wilson—Leighton's Praelect[6]—writing a little—heard Buckley preach most admirably—walked to Marsden[7] to see a poor man—heard a prayer at a Dissenting Chapel (standing at the door) on my way back.

[7]. M.

Work—Porson's Notes—Misc. Crit.[8] Demosthenes. Wine with Scott— Cicero.

[8]. T.

Work. Elmsley.[9] Leptines.[10] Adam & cram in general. Heard of J.N.G.'s arrival. out with Doyle.

[9]. W.

Finished Leptines—Heeren[11]—Elmsley &c.

---

[1] Demosthenes, *Against Meidias*, his personal enemy.
[2] A strong anti-reform motion of Sidney *Herbert's was carried by 80 to 56.
[3] Read in *Anstice's absence by *Harrison, the secretary.
[4] Down to 16 March each entry was originally dated a day late.
[5] Fragment in Morley, i. 58.
[6] Abp. Robert *Leighton, *Praelectiones Theologicae* (1693), which *Newton called 'a diamond set in gold' for purity of language and thought.
[7] Marston, now a NE. suburb of Oxford.
[8] T. *Kidd ed. R. *Porson, *Tracts and Miscellaneous Criticisms* (1815).
[9] P. E. *Elmsley on Socrates or Euripides.
[10] Demosthenes' speech *Against Leptines* (354 B.C.) and in favour of tax exemption for descendants of public benefactors.
[11] A. H. L. Heeren, *A Manual of Ancient History* or *Political History of Ancient Greece* (both tr. 1829).

[*10*]. *Th.*

Ireland Scholarship Exam began. 9–12 Latin from English.[1] 1–4—chorus
from Eumenides[2] which grievously dismayed me—Looked over some Latin
phrases & read some Sophocles, also some Adams at night. Out with Harrison. O that I may remember throughout this matter What shall it profit
a man if he shall gain the whole world and lose his own soul? Or what shall
a man give in exchange for his soul?[3] Would God I may follow these objects
solely and singly as means for a dear & high purpose. Wrote to T.G.

Symons.[4]

[*11*]. *Fr.*

9–12 Livy into Greek,[5] with notes—1–4, Latin History &c. A better day than
yesterday, I hope.—some phrases, Greek History &c.

Short—[4]

[*12*]. *Sat.*

9–12 Iambics. 1–4 Latin into English with some odd questions. Middling
day for me. Essay Society at night[6]—& out. Some Greek history—paper.
heard from Moncreiff, T.G. & Aunt Mary.

[*13*]. *Sun.*

St Peter's—heard Whately. St Mary's in aftn. wrote a letter to Harrison
on important matters. Tea with Cole—read Sumner &c.

[*14*]. *Monday.*

Latin Verse from Milton: & Critical questions—had prepared for History—
Disappointed—worked again at History in evg. Wine with Gaskell.

[*15*]. *T.*

Essay & Demosthenes. Wished for the end of examn till it came—then not
so.

[*16*]. *Wed.*

Read two Chapters of Ethics. Learned between 10 & 11 that Scott & I were
even—Brancker,[7] now at Shrewsbury the winner of the Scholarship. During

[1] Add MS 44720, ff. 134v.–135.   [2] Aeschylus.
[3] Mark viii. 36–37.
[4] B. P. *Symons, shortly (16 June) elected warden of Wadham, was one of the
examiners for the *Ireland. His name and *Short's, placed in gaps between entries, indicate that they had been invigilating.
[5] Add MS 44720, ff. 142v.–143.
[6] *Anstice compared the revolutions of 1688 and 1830.
[7] Thomas Brancker, 1813?–71; eldest s. of (Sir) T. Brancker of 61 Rodney Street,
mayor of Liverpool 1830; fellow of Wadham 1835–50; rector of Limington, Somerset,
1849.

this & the following days I gained much information about it—as from Short direct & through Biscoe—that taste won the Scholarship for Brancker —that Scott's answers, & mine in particular, were full of superfluous matter, —my essay (done on the same principle with that which mainly I think raised me last year) "desultory beyond belief". The least hint given to any of the three would have ensured his winning—it was quite a toss up which would have won if the examination had continued. Scott & I are to have books given us by the Vice Chancellor.[1]

From Symons &c. that Scott was a beautiful scholar, & my information (for wh I am indebted to Wordsworth) considered extraordinary. That Scott's papers were taken for mine & mine for Scott's up to the end of the examination, on Vowler Short's assurance!!!!! Alas for Vowler as examiner. That it had almost been determined to go on, & to set a paper of Homerics —tantalising intelligence—&c. &c. Wrote letters home[2] & to Wordsworth[3] —much conv. with Saunders, & Biscoe &c. communicated to them my long formed determination about postponing my degree in the event of missing the University Scholarship. I did it without hesitation as I thought I could see, particularly from the singular form of the examination, the Divine purpose pointing to the path I have now chosen, though this is perhaps not a thing to be noised abroad.

Thurs–Sat.

Wrote letters—read pamphlets, wrote over fair copies of some of my composition &c. Felt completely overcome by the reaction of my temporary excitement—in consequence Biscoe kindly asked & the Dean kindly gave me leave to come away. Wine with Lyall & Harrison, supped with Manning. Became acquainted with Boyle:[4] Arranged with Ward[5] for the binding of a large lot of books—perhaps 130 or 150—left Oxford on Saturday afternoon & walked to Deddington[6]—read some Æschylus & Shelley. Slept at Deddington. Middling inn.

20. Sunday.

Walked on to Gaydon.[7] read Testament—heard a very good sermon from the curate[8] at Deddington & an admirable one from Baring at Adderbury.[9] Delighted with his earnestness & twenty other things.

[1] John Collier Jones, 1770–1838; fought at Cape St. Vincent; rector of Exeter 1819; vice-chancellor 1828–32.

[2] Long extracts in Morley, i. 61–62.

[3] In Charles *Wordsworth, Annals, i. 89–91; Lambeth MS 1823, ff. 86–87.

[4] Richard Cavendish Townsend Boyle, 1812–86, 3rd s. of 8th earl of Cork and Orrery; rector of Marston Bigot, Somerset, 1836–75.

[5] Perhaps Thomas Ward of Paradise Square, St. Ebbe's.

[6] Small market town 17 miles north of Oxford on the road to Banbury.

[7] Village 10 miles NNW. of Banbury.

[8] John *Hughes, 1787–1860, celebrated evangelical preacher; vicar of Aberystwyth 1834, archdeacon of Cardigan 1859.

[9] Adderbury, 2 miles north of Deddington and 4 south of Banbury.

21. M.

Got to Leamington to breakfast. read papers, reviews, letters, &c. Glad to find Helen & my Mother pretty well, thank God.

22. T.

J.N.G. came early—went to meet him—read paper—& comedy of Errors.

to Th.

—heard from Wordsworth—Whist—calling on sundry—at Lubbocks[1]—heard with mixed feelings of the passing of the Reform Bill (2nd reading)[2]—took my first lesson in singing from Mr Marshall.[3] Wordsworth has behaved to me most admirably.

25. Fr.

Second lesson—& practising: a party at Mrs Hooks in evg: sang, in a way. whist. Shakespeare—Escott's pamphlet[4]—For. Pol. of Mr Canning—paper & debate—part of Article on Reform in Quarterly.

26. Sat.

Wrote to R.G. J.N.G. went to Liverpool. Whist. papers. Mrs G. headach. finished Article on Reform, & read Southey's on State of England.[5] After thinking & talking about Reform—since I came home, I trust in God the Bill will not be carried. Third lesson with Marshall.

27. Sun.

Swiss chapel mg—& at Lillington[6] Ch in aftn. Nat. Hist. of Enthusiasm. Two of Blomfield's sermons. Bible. From this time forth I purpose please God to commit to memory a passage of Scripture, say from four to eight verses, every Sunday: as I have found the good effects of this species of exercise in other respects.

28. M.

Singing—4th lesson. Out. Whist. Wrote to R.G.—T.G.—Gaskell—and Doyle. Shakespeare.

[1] Possibly Sir John William *Lubbock, 1803–65, astronomer, banker, S.D.U.K. supporter; treasurer of Royal Society, 1830–5, 1838–47; vice-chancellor, London University, 1837–42; 3rd bart. 1840.
[2] In the commons on 22 March, by 302–301; see *H* iii. 804–23, and G. O. *Trevelyan, *Macaulay*, 2 ed. (1877), i. 204–7.
[3] F. Marshall of Charlotte Street, music master and organist.
[4] B. S. Escott, *On the present state of the Reform Question*, attacked details of the current reform bill.
[5] *Quarterly Review*, xliv. 261 (January 1831).
[6] Now the northern suburb of Leamington.

29. T.

5th lesson. Whist. out with H.J.G. & Jane. Read 'King John". Copied out many passages, some in poetry & some in prose—particularly from the Alastor.[1] Call'd on Mrs Campbell[2]—as yesterday on Mrs Cameron with whom I had a long & very pleasant conversation. "Brazen Serpent".

30. W.

No lesson. J.N.G. returned and Mr G. came. calls—walked with H.J.G. & Jane—Read papers—part of Romeo & Juliet—"Real tendency of proposed Reform"[3] &c. Whist.

31. Th.

T.G. came—copying—at Warwick—whist—papers—called on Hope, come here for indigestion—singing, *6th* lesson—

April 1. Friday.

J.N.G. went to Portsmouth. Annoying, but necessary. At Ch & Sacrament.[4] T.G. & J.N.G. stayed. Too late for aftn Ch from seeing John off—but I should have gone had I expected a good sermon—was I right in keeping away? I wish I could see the rule on this subject.

As to general progress I would hope there is some against my besetting sins except one which returns upon me again & again like a flood. God help me for Christ's sake.

2 Sat.

H.J.G. more unwell. The Grants here—papers—Shakespeare—& Tacitus a little.

3. Sun.

Ch at Lillington in mg—in aftn, parish Ch. Sacrament—Bible—Nat. Hist. of Enthusiasm. More on St. Paul.[5]

4. M.

Spent good part of the day at the Warwick Reform meeting of which I think of writing an account.[6] papers—Shakespeare—Music lesson—wrote to J.N.G.

---

[1] *Shelley. Cp. Add MS 44813D, ff. 36–42.
[2] Mother of C. M. Campbell (see 5 Apr. 31).
[3] 'The Real Character and Tendency of the proposed Reform', penny pamphlet against the reform bill (1831).
[4] Good Friday.
[5] Hannah *More, *Essay on the Character and Practical Writings of St. Paul* (1815).
[6] County meeting favouring reform.

26—I.

5. T.

Music again. Copying. And wrote a long letter to Standard giving an account of Warwick meeting which with corrections & writing over occupied me nearly all day.[1] Hope & Campbell[2] dined with us—cards. Afterwards went to Miss Pocklington's & sang there. Out late. Shakespeare.

6. W.

Copying. Music—but no lesson. At Mrs Cameron's in evg. Sang there a little. Shakespeare—papers—a long ride.

7. Th.

Dined with M[ontgomer]y Campbells. An agreeable party. sang. a regular floor[3]—sang too at Mrs Hook's afterwards. Finished Romeo & Juliet—copying—practised some things with the Miss Pocklingtons.

8. Fr.

My letter is in yesterday's Standard.[4] Read Two Gentlemen of Verona—Tacitus—did a few Caractacus verses[5]—wrote to Childers & Mr Ridley—music lesson—cards—at Mrs Fallens[6] in evg—rode out.

9. Sat.

Copied 3 letters—wrote to J.N.G. & Wordsworth[7]—paper—read Milton—Dryden—Waller[8]—began 'Rectory of Valehead'[9]—singing at Pocklingtons'—in evg. at Miss Campbell's. Cards—stupidity—T.G. unwell.

10. Sunday.

Ch. mg & evg. A much better sermon from Downes in morng. Finished Natural History of Enthusiasm—Bible—&c. a good deal of copying, to my sorrow.

11. Monday.

Tom better.—Singing lesson. Out riding. Paying calls—Shakespeare—wrote query what? Alas an idle day—papers &c.

[1] Part in Morley, i. 70–71.
[2] Probably Charles Montgomery Campbell, junior to Gladstone at Eton, banker at Shrewsbury.
[3] A social disaster.
[4] Signed 'Spectator', on the Warwick meeting; part in Robbins, 96–97.
[5] Add MS 44720, ff. 240–5; for a college Latin verse prize, won by Charles *Canning.
[6] Possibly Celia Lynch, wife of Simon Fallon of Ballina House, near Athlone; he d. 1849.
[7] In C. *Wordsworth, *Annals*, i. 91–92; Lambeth MS 1823, ff. 88–89.
[8] Seventeenth-century poet.
[9] A novel by R. W. *Wilson (1830).

12. T.

Vaughan[1] dined here. Music in evg. Campbell called—long talk with him: Rode to Kenilworth. Wrote a few verses. copying—papers &c.

13. Wed.

A few verses. papers. Wrote to Bp. of Calcutta—Buying music—rode with Vaughan—Dined at Dr Jephson's. read Shakespeare &c. At nt much conversation with my Mother about Helen &c. Found her much afflicted & made her more so—unintentionally God knows: but it is a judgment that justly cleaves to my accursed & hardened selfishness.—Went to Aunts' to lunch.

14. Th.

Called on seven people—did a few verses—conversation with Mother— learned "Lord of all power & might"[2]—cards—at Miss Swinfens[3]—wrote to T.G.—and to Sir F. Doyle. &c.

15. Fr.

packed—practis'd the Collect I learned yesterday—came to Oxford safely thank God. This vacation has been worthy of the best days of my idleness, & unsatisfactory indeed. read Sir R. Inglis on Reform.[4] unpacked, & wrought vigorously to get my goods into order but without much success— made up my accounts &c.

16. Sat.

Calling on Dean, Biscoe, Saunders—out with Rogers—unpacking wine— read papers—Westminster Review on Reform[5]—most of Sir J. Walsh's pamphlet[6]—sat with Gaskell & Canning in evg—Gas[kell] with me in mg singing.

17. Sunday.

St Peter's—University Sermon—Chapel—Bible—D. Wilson on Sabbath— H. More's Spirit of prayer.[7] Began to write on the principles of social inter-course.[8] God help me. Read some of dearest Anne's letters to me. O is it possible that such a saint can have held communion with such a devil?

---

[1] Henry Halford *Vaughan, 1811–85; nephew of Sir Henry *Halford; at Christ Church; fellow of Oriel 1836–42; regius professor of modern history 1848–58; retired to Pembrokeshire to meditate.

[2] Collect for the seventh Sunday after Trinity.

[3] Perhaps sister or aunt of Samuel Swinfen, d. 1854, of Swinfen Hall, Lichfield.

[4] Against the bill, 1 March 1831, H ii. 1090.

[5] xiv. 440 (April 1831).

[6] Sir John B. *Walsh, tory M.P., 'Popular Opinions on Parliamentary Reform, considered' or 'Observations on the Ministerial Plan of Reform', long anti-reform pamphlets (1831).

[7] By Hannah *More (1825, often re-issued).   [8] Add MS 44815A, ff. 2–7.

Alas, I deceived her and many another. O merciful God, open unto me the fullest & largest views of mine own utter sinfulness—but lest my soul sink into despair open also the boundless treasures of thy love, and let those two truths make rapid but equal progress in subjugating my soul. May I know thee & in knowing love thee, & from loving serve thee. Here more especially enable me to glorify thee & raise up many other & worthier instruments— through Jesus the Mediator of the New Covenant & his precious blood.

18. M.

A bad day. Wrote to my Father, Tom, and John. Began Coddington's Optics[1]—finished Sir J. Walsh—some Caractacus—Virgil—Mus[ical?] Criticism—but all in a desultory way. dissatisfied. Busy about my books now binding.

19. T.

700 L. Virgil—& Optics, with which I get on miserably. Reform Debate[2]— Walk with Doyle—Wood & Lyall called on me. Read Mr Canning's 1822 Speech on Reform.[3] My work is heavy, but I can *hope*.

20. W.

Optics—& lecture. Miscellaneous Math—Moncreiff came—read 4th Æneid —'Notes on the Reform Bill by a Barrister'[4]—Reform Debate of last night[5] —a few verses.

21. Th.

Trigonometry—Virgil (read Æn. 2) breakfast with Gaskell—at Debating Society—spoke agst Westmr Rev.[6] papers—wrote to Mr G. & B. Harrison— began to throw Caractacus into shape; with somewhat better success.

22. Fr.

The excitement in politics is now too much for my reading. Spent much time in the reading room.[7] Mathematics and Lecture. Gaskell breakfasted with me. Virgil—began Æneid 1—papers—Ed. Rev. on Reform—wrote to Mr G. [8]& T.G.—& in consequence of a letter from my Father, to Mr Cunningham of Harrow, after a good deal of thought; about a public 'testimonial' for Mr Wilberforce. Sat with Biscoe & Saunders in evg.

[1] H. *Coddington, *A System of Optics*, 2v. (1829–30).
[2] First day in cttee, 18 April 1831; *H* iii. 1510.
[3] 25 April 1822, *NSH* vii. 106–39.
[4] A strongly-phrased pamphlet against reform by J. T. *Coleridge (1831).
[5] *H*. iii. 1605. *Gascoyne's amendment, that the total of M.P.s for England and Wales should not fall, was carried against government by eight votes.
[6] In private business the Union again rejected the *Westminster Review*. In public, emigration was held an incomplete remedy for distress by 31 to 11.
[7] Dissolution of parliament was believed imminent; and in the commons the opposition managed to reject a routine vote of supply late on the 21st, by 164 to 142. *H* iii. 1805.
[8] One sentence in Bassett, 21.

23. Sat.

read all the papers with harrowing interest.[1] Note from my Brother announcing dissolution.

Wrote two short addresses intended for placards on the subject. Consulted with Bruce and Lincoln about printing them—they were strongly for it—also Jelf—corrected them, & please God will have it done on Monday morng.[2] Read Girdlestone's twenty letters[3]—and others also—papers—at Essay Society & spoke[4]—long conversation afterwards with Bruce Egerton &c—a little Virgil—wine with Barnes[5]—walk with Moncreiff.

24. Sunday.

Letter from T.G. At Buckley's University Sermon. Bible—Spirit of prayer. —some Erskine aloud to Boyle and Tupper in evg. who had tea with me. Walk with Acland—wrote a few lines to Doyle. Lincoln came to me late at night about a placard.

25. M.

Surplice prayers—read some of Mr Canning's Speeches, & Pusey's pamphlet[6]—gave a wine party to Vaughan Ball[iol],[7] Vaughan Ch Ch, Knatchbull, Palmer, Rickards, White,[8] Gaskell, Moncreiff, Tait, Lyall, Jelf, Montgomery. Papers—at Wise's—busy getting my placards printed at Ham's.[9]

Saw in the paper the death of poor Doyle's sister[10]—got a letter from him from which he seemed to feel it much, and may God in his mercy make it the means of bringing him to a true and consistent religion—wrote a long letter but I fear a bad one to him in reply.

26. Tuesday.

Heard again from Doyle—wrote to him, to my Father,[11] Tom, & Robertson Saw Gaskell off for Yorkshire. My placards printed—they professed to have pasted them up but I suspect they lie. Heard much talk about them. Some Math—Forbes's India[12]—& a few lines for the English Verse—A wine party

---

[1] In scenes of unexampled confusion, *William IV in person prorogued parliament on the 22nd, to 10 May. See *H* iii. 1805–11. Next day, by order in council, he dissolved it.
[2] Drafts in Add MS 44721, ff. 20–21.
[3] An early version of Charles *Girdlestone, *Twenty Parochial Sermons* (1832).
[4] *Bruce argued that the historian's province is narrative, not speculation.
[5] George Barnes, b. 1813?, Westminster and Christ Church.
[6] Philip *Pusey, 'The New Constitution: Remarks' (1831) against the reform bill.
[7] James Vaughan, 1806?–86?, of Balliol; priest at Brighton 1838.
[8] John Tahourdin White, 1809–93, of Selborne; classicist; master at Christ's Hospital.
[9] A jobbing printer in St. Ebbe's?
[10] Frances Mary, *Doyle's second sister, d. in London on 23 April.
[11] Part in Bassett, 21–22.
[12] James *Forbes, *Oriental Memoirs*, 4v. (1813–15).

—Anstice Boyle the Tuppers[1] Cole Lushington Tancred Cameron Trower[2] Acland Cunningham &c.

27. Wed.

Heard from T.G. Found John had been seriously ill but was better, thank God. Electioneering news—papers—Math. & Lect.—tried to do some verses on Suttees[3]—Busy in raising subscriptions for an Antireform fund—at wine with Lincoln to bring in our proceeds—my quota amounted to £41.— Letters.

28. Th.

papers. Little Math—some few questions—again busy with the subscription, & at the printers about sundry matters. papers. wrote to J.N.G.—to Doyle—wine with Mayow & Tancred—tea with Dodds—spoke at Debating Society agst Cobbett.[4] few verses.

29. Fr.

Math. & Lect. breakf with Trower—busy closing the subscription.[5] heard from my Father. wrote to T.G. & to Doyle. Wrote some verses, but few. Music—& tried to copy some. Lincoln went off. Twice at St John's in evg without success.

30. Sat.

Settled with Ward & got my books arranged. Went to the Vice-Chancellor about my struggle. He delivered a gracious address. Wrote some placards. Worked hard & managed to cobble & patch up a Suttee poem.[6]

May 1. Sunday.

Saw the Doyles—all in much grief, struggling however against it—may they be supported. At Buckley's & Univ. Serm. Dined with Mayow in his rooms. Finished Sp. of Prayer—Pollok—D. Wilson—wrote.—wrote a letter to J.N.G.

2. M.

At Wise's buying books for Rn. Wrote to him, and to J.N.G.—paper.

[1] M. F. *Tupper's next b. Daniel, 1812?–69, at Brasenose 1830–4, later of the lord chamberlain's office.
[2] William Baker Trower, b. 1812?, of Exeter College; younger b. of Walter John Trower, d. 1877, bp. of Gibraltar 1863–8.
[3] See 30 Apr. 31.
[4] In public business, the Union approved the Manchester magistrates' conduct in 1819, without a division. In private, Lyall and *Gladstone failed by six votes to get the society to stop taking *Cobbett's *Register*.
[5] Jotting in Add MS 44721, f. 22.
[6] Intended for the *Newdigate prize. Result in Add MS 44721, f. 21.

Mathematics—Mr Campbell of Row's letter to his flock[1]—admirable. tea with Canning—sat also with Wordsworth—practised singing—my horse came—got it settled at Beasley's.[2] Work'd at my Caractacus, which will be but flummery.

3. T.

Packed up Robns large box of books—a troublesome business. papers. Tried my mare, and liked her much. Added to and corrected my verses—wrote them over (152) &c. and sent them in. Read Prior's Solomon B.1[3]—wrote to J.N.G.

4. W.

Made one of a cavalcade for mornings—afterwards hustled below the town hall—papers—wrote to J.N.G.—Gaskell—Mrs G—Bp of Calcutta. Wood Bruce and Herbert had tea with me—the first came about Homer—the two latter about a paragraph in the Times.[4] Tried to read some Optics—Fata obstant—a little Ethics—here there & everywhere—made an immense row & caught an immense cold.[5]

5. Thursday.

Quite hoarse and my throat sore from hollowing yesterday, with much cold and frequent nose bleeding. gave a wine party. tea with Joyce—read Math—papers—two or three Chapters of Ethics—rode out well clad—began to put together some materials for a Reform Speech or Essay—&c.

6. Fr.

Math & Lect. papers—wrote on Reform[6]—wrote to J.N.G.—Anstice, Lyall, Hewitt, Thornton, with me about Deb. Soc. matters—Stewart's Moral Philosophy—Ethics. At Amateur concert.

7. Sat.

heard from & wrote to my Father. Sorry to find my Mother has been suffering much. Wrote more on Reform. Ethics—Stewart. Rode—paper—at Essay meeting[7]—with Saunders.

8. Sun.

Staid in. At Buckley's & University Sermon in aftn. Majendie excellent: may God raise up many more such.—Had Harrison to dine with me—tea

---

[1] J. M. Campbell of Row (now Rhu) on Gareloch, 'A Letter Written as a Word in Season to his People' (1831).

[2] Beesley's livery stable in Bear Lane, on the north side of Christ Church.

[3] Matthew *Prior, *Solomon on the Vanity of the World* (1719).

[4] On that day, a letter appealed for money for the whig candidates for Oxfordshire; the tory candidate for Oxford City had withdrawn on 2 May. Cp. 11 May 31.

[5] See Morley, i. 71, and 9 May 31.   [6] See 17 May 31.

[7] O. B. Cole read an essay on the necessity of popular education.

with Tupper. Bible—Pollok—a pamphlet on the state of Cambridge[1]—
D. Wilson.

9. M.

breakfast with Mayow—tea with Bruce—paper—wrote to J.N.G.—out
riding—4 hours at election—argufying &c. a variety of adventures there.
twice narrowly escaped hustling. Parted good friends in general.[2]
Mathematics—Aristotle Ethics—and Stewart—but little.

10. T.

Much about the hustings again—walked at night to the Angel with the
procession, & shouted valourously.—Sat a good while with Wishlade who
is very ill. His mind is in a state which it is impossible to contemplate without much pain. Ethics and Lecture. Stewart. Out riding—got pelted—
almost a town & gown row—Lyall had tea with me. Wrote on Reform. &c.

11. W.

Mathematics & Lecture. Breakfast with Vaughan of Balliol. papers. On
hustings—lunched with Lyall. Rode with him. After dinner went in
N[orreys]'s procession & heard the speaking.[3] Gaskell came—we had tea &
sat together. wrote to T.G. Wrote on Reform.

12. Th.

Ethics & Lecture. finished 2nd Book. papers. wrote to my Father.[4] rode with
Gaskell & Brandreth. Talking about young Acland's matters. Wrote a
short Essay on Aristotle's Analytical Method. Music—but very hoarse.[5]

13. Fr.

A long ride with Wilson & Gaskell Math & Lect. singing. papers. Lincoln
with me talking over a plan which we have formed[6]—wrote on Ethical
subjects.[7] Westm[inste]r [Review]. wine. Bagot, Tea with Dodds.

14. Sat.

mending—Math. quest.—Ethics—wrote on Reform—preface to Butler's

[1] 'Remarks on the Actual State of the University of Cambridge' (1830), fifty pages on
the university's academic and moral deficiencies.
[2] Polling for Oxfordshire began this day, with a good deal of tumult in the streets of
Oxford.
[3] Montagu Bertie, 1808–84, Lord Norreys; Eton and Trinity, Cambridge; tory M.P.
Oxfordshire 1830–1, 1932–52, Abingdon 1852–4; succ. in 1854 as 6th earl of Abingdon
and 10th baron Norreys of Rycote. He m. 1835 Elizabeth Lavinia, only da. and heir of
George Granville Vernon-Harcourt, 1785–1861, who beat him in the 1831 election.
Norreys announced late on the 11th that he would no longer contest the seat; and Harcourt and Major Weyland, the reform candidates, were formally returned on the 12th.
[4] Part in Bassett, 22.
[5] The Union's reform debate proposed for this night was deferred, viewing the disturbed state of the town, to the 16th.
[6] See 21, 30 May 31.
[7] He began a notebook on Aristotle's Ethics, now Add MS 44814.

Sermons & Sermon 1.[1]—papers—rode with Wood whom I like extremely. Westminster [Review]—wine—singing—I am trying to learn "O Lord have mercy upon me"[2] without an instrument.[3]

15. Sunday.

Breakf. with Bruce. Rectory of Valehead—singing my friend Perg[olesi]. read Mr Campbell's letter aloud at night at Cole's where I had tea. At Buckley's [sermon], & heard Keble in aftn. A long discussion on slavery &c. &c. with Cunningham & Gaskell till ½ past one in mg.

16. Monday.

Sleepy. Math. few & shuffling, & Lecture. Read Canning's Reform Speeches at Lpool & made extracts. Rode out. At debate, which was adjourned[4]—I am to try my hand tomorrow. My thoughts were but ill arranged but I fear they will be no better then. Wine with Anstice. heard from R.G. Singing. Tea with Lincoln.

17. Tuesday.

Ethics—but no lect.—little Mathematics. A good deal exhausted in forenoon from the heat last night. Dined with White & had wine with him, also with young Acland. Cogitations on Reform &c. Difficult to *select* matter for a speech, not to gather it. Spoke at the adjourned debate for ¾ of an hour, immediately after Gaskell who was preceded by Lincoln. [5]Row afterwards & adjournment. Tea with Wordsworth.

18. W.

Math. & Lect. Tired. wrote to H.J.G. papers—Ethics—Butler's 20 Sermons tea with Bruce—rode with Lushington—wine with Palmer[6] & Buller. Tried to arrange matters for bringing men down tomorrow.

19. Th.

Ethics a little, & Lecture. Gave a wine party to Lincoln Herbert Canning Bernard Bruce Bruce Hewitt Denison Lushington Wood, W. Taylor, Alston, Thornton, Doyle, Wordsworth. Gaskell wd not come. Much engaged in canvassing men to come down through the University at Debate in evg. [James] Bruce made a very eloquent speech for us. Divided on the motion

---

[1] (1729, often reprinted.)

[2] English version of the 'Confitebor' by G. B. Pergolesi, 1710–36.

[3] He was also at an essay society discussion on geology and chronology.

[4] Knatchbull moved 'That the present Ministry is incompetent to carry on the Government of the Country'; after nine other speeches, the Union adjourned at 11.30.

[5] *Gladstone moved a rider, that the reform bill 'threatens not only to change the form of our Government, but ultimately to break up the very foundations of social order', &c. Rider in Selborne, I. i. 129. From this speech his career in politics derived. See e.g. *Doyle, *Reminiscences*, 114. Notes for it in Add MS 44721, ff. 23–41.

[6] (Sir) Roundell *Palmer, 1812–95, lord chancellor 1872–4, 1880–5; cr. baron, 1872, and earl of, Selborne, 1882. Cp. Add MSS 44296–8.

& rider, 94 to 38. Afterwards had some supper with Alston & tea with Lincoln. The result was delightful: Acland's Hostile [?] & Alston's conversion speech produced the best effect.

20. Fr.

Math & Lect. Ethics & Lect. papers. wrote a letter to Standard on the decision, wrote a clean copy & sent it.[1] rode with Gaskell. wrote to R.G. Tea with Gaskell & Canning.

21. Sat.

Much knocked up this week by the three nights of the hot room. Breakf. with Wood—ride with Gaskell—wine with Tyndale. At Doyle's for the Essay.[2] With Lincoln & Wordsworth concocting measures for a future coup d'état.[3] paper. Ethics—Harris on Happiness[4]—& a little Math. Surplice prayers in aft. Sat with J. Wishlade some time. He was in a better state of mind.

22. Sunday.

Chapel mg & aft. Buckley's—heard Blanco White[5] preach well. tea with Mayow—sleepy—read Scott on the Divine will[6]—rectory of Valehead—a serm. of Bulteel's in the Preacher,[7] &c. Miserable that I am, though happy beyond measure in external circumstances, having nothing but a retrospect of sins committed and duties neglected. God help me. received the sacrament. not less than 18 undergraduates.

23. Monday.

Surplice prayers. Breakf. with Thomas at Trinity.[8] papers. Wrote to J.N.G.[9] Math, Lect, & questions—Ethics—Harris on Happiness. Singing. Burke "Appeal".[10]

24. T.

Surplice prayers—Math questions. Ethics & Lect. wrote a good deal on Ethics—paper—wrote home—began an Essay on the Principle of Government[11]—conversation with Thornton concerning projected petition. rode. Gaskell had tea with me.

---

[1] Published in next day's *Standard*, p. 3; signed 'Alumnus'. Draft in Add MS 44352, ff. 190–1; extracts in Robbins, 101–2.

[2] *Doyle read a paper in praise of *Tennyson's poetry; *Gladstone supported him.

[3] See 30 May 31.   [4] In James *Harris, *Three Treatises* (1744).

[5] Joseph Blanco *White, 1775–1841; b. José Maria Blanco at Seville; ordained catholic priest 1800; lost faith; took name of *White on reaching England 1810; in anglican orders 1814; in Oriel common room 1826–31; retired to Dublin 1832, and Liverpool 1835.

[6] Perhaps Thomas *Scott, *The Rights of God* (1793).

[7] 12 May 1831, ii. 162; on John vi. 37.

[8] John Thomas, 1811?–83, vicar of All Hallows by the Tower, 1852; canon of Canterbury 1862.   [9] Part in Bassett, 23–24, dated 20 May.

[10] Edmund *Burke, *Appeal from the New to the Old Whigs* (1791).

[11] See 28 May 31. Essay in Add MS 44721, ff. 1–17.

25. W.

Breakfast with Anstice—met Baring. rode. paper.—Canning & Burke—Math Lect, & quest—Ethics little. singing. tea with Doyle—scheming with Thornton and others—wrote a good deal on "Principle of Government"—finished 1st part of it.

26. Th.

Breakfast with Harrison—met Baring again. Math. questions Ethics & Lecture—writing. talking with Herbert about political matters—rode out—wine with Mayow—Burke's Appeal. tea with Tancred, at debate.[1]

27. Fr.

Had Baring, Anstice, Harrison, Tancred, Gaskell, to breakfast. Burke—Ethics—writing on ditto—heard from & wrote to H.J.G.—on subject of printing (!!!) my speech which is out of the question—had Harrison Mayow, Gaskell, to tea. rode. paper. Integral Calculus &c.

28. Sat.

Did—next to nothing. little Math. less Ethics. wine with Gaskell—Essay Society[2]—rode—began to try to write out my speech. Burke.

29. Sunday.

Chapel mg & evg. Buckley's Church. Young Acland, Joyce, Cole, sat with me—also Parr—and Cunningham, concerning whom I was [I] think much, and fruitlessly [troubled?]: no wonder: how can one so lost as myself be fit to advise or in any way benefit friends? Gaskell had tea with me. Finished D. Wilson on Sabbath—Bible—Rectory of Valehead.

30. M.

Math. Questions. with Saunders. Ethics & Lect. Burke. threw into form some rough ideas drawn up for a petition, a charge committed to me at a meeting held in Wordsworth's rooms.[3] papers. heard from home. Seymer came. tea with Harrison. Walk with Anstice. R.G. to be here on Friday.

It has heppended to me of late since my speech to receive more compliments than usual. It has also happened that I have never had cause to feel my own utter & abandoned sinfulness before God more deeply. Oh who can look at these bitterly instructive contrasts & yet deny that there is a Providence wonderfully framing out of a seeming series of accidents the most appropriate & aptest discipline for each of our souls.

[1] The Union approved the East India Company's charter by 29 to 11.
[2] Gaskell read an essay on the Italian renaissance, and *Gladstone one on the principles of government.
[3] See Charles *Wordsworth, *Annals*, i. 83–4; and 4–14 June, 2 July 31. *Gladstone was the principal originator of an anti-reform 'Petition of Resident Bachelors and Under Graduates of the University of *Oxford*', printed in the commons' *Votes and Proceedings* for 1831, ii, appx., 51. Over two-thirds of the resident undergraduates signed it.

31. T.

Six hours in the schools ("sitting" for three of them) working Mathematica Questions.[1] had Gaskell to tea. Wrote to Mr G. paper. Ethics little. Burke. wrote over again & corrected petition. Breakfast with Tupper. Mathematics in general. began a 2nd part of my Essay on Govt.

1. Wednesday.

Math—Burke—rode—wine with Pusey & Brandreth—went to breakfast with Tupper—wrote on Ethical subjects—Ethics and Lecture—old speech —Burke (began Refl. on Fr. Rev.[2]) heard Armstrong[3]—tea with Cole.

2. Th.

At Debate—made a quiet & dull speech about W. India Slavery. Burke. Ethics. petition discussed with Thornton—wrote on Ethics—rode out— wrote to R.G. My amendment carried at Deb. Soc.[4] Read part of Beverley's letter to Abp of York.[5] &c.

3. Fr.

finished Beverley—it shows a horrid spirit. breakfast with Denison. talked to him about the petition which he undertook to alter and did it very well. also with Thornton &c. &c. about. rode with Cunningham. heard from & wrote to J.N.G. Ethics & writing upon them. a good deal. At Reform meeting in Town Hall—at court a short time—Burke—&c.

4. Sat.

Breakf. with Cameron—wrote a great deal at my Essay—and also at my Reform Speech, late at night. Harrison has got the Theological Essay[6] and Acland his Mathematics first—in commemoration rode with Canning to dinner at Cuddesdon after much permutation of arrangements since the Essay Society were to have met in my room in evg. Returned late at night. Got extremely wet. Read Burke. At a long meeting at Wordsworth's where with great difficulty we got a little & but little business done.

5. Sunday.

Missed morning Chapel & unhappily Sacrament. Read D. Wilson on B.

[1] Certificate of due attendance in Add MS 44721, f. 65.
[2] E. *Burke *Reflections on the Revolution in France* (1790).
[3] Henry William Gleed Armstrong, 1805?–77, vicar of Willesden 1854–63, then of Bierton, Buckinghamshire.
[4] *Gladstone's amendment, favouring religious education of West Indian slaves and their compulsory manumission, was made to a motion of *Moncreiff's calling for immediate emancipation and carried by 31 to 11 (text in Robbins, 168; and see A. Patchett Martin), *Sherbrooke* (1893), i. 16–17. Notes in Add MS 44649, ff, 29–33.
[5] R. M. Beverley 'A Letter . . . on the present corrupt state of the Church of England' (1831) attacked rich bps. and fox-hunting parsons.
[6] *Ellerton prize essay, on 'The Evidence deduced from Prophecy in support of the Truth of Christianity'.

Woodds' death.[1] Bible—At St Peter's. Heard Armstrong preach a sermon displaying extraordinary eloquence. Robn came—went to University Sermon heard Shuttleworth. At aftn Chapel—Rn dined with me—at New Coll afterwards. drank wine & had tea with Gaskell. Wrote a note to J.N.G.

6. M.

Rn & Canning had breakf with me. Saw Rn off. Then met Armstrong at Cole's—much delighted with his simplicity & talent & healthy tone of feeling. Math & Lect. Burke. rode out. finished my Essay. wrote copies of the Petition. Had Essay Soc. in my room—Tried to finish writing out my speech but could not.

[7].[2] T.

A meeting at Wordsworth's of about 25—should have been at least 40. Arrangements made, with some difficulty. Great zeal in some of our men: others very lukewarm. Rode with Gaskell. P. Pickering came at night. Preparing parchments—wrote an imposition, for skipping chapel—3d time in five days—of which I am really ashamed. It was however owing to a long & interesting conversation I had with Egerton which kept me up till late. Burke—&c. &c.

[8]. W.

Skimmed some Ethics & had lect. The grand day. Operations commenced on a large scale & parchments circulated through the University.[3] Matters proceeded prosperously—but it reached Veysie's ears and about six p.m. I was sent for as the petition had been lying in my rooms for signature. He was exceedingly kind and only stipulated for my telling men concerned in it of the danger awaiting them. Tea with Harrison—afterwards with Hewitt.

[9]. Th.

Rode to Cuddesdon with Canning & got very wet. Wine with Gaskell & Joyce. Hallam came with Fred. Tennyson[4] from Cambridge. Talking with him. & arguing with Vaughan about petition most of the night. Ethics & Burke—much interrupted.

[10]. Fr.

Ethics. Scott's letter. Wrote to J.N.G. & T.G. had Pickering to tea. Breakfast with Denison—worked hard in B.N.C. for signatures & with good success.

---

[1] Sermon on Acts xi. 24, preached on 24 April 1831 on the death of Basil *Woodd; notes appended on *Bulteel's controversy with *Burton (see 15 and 18 Feb. 31).

[2] Up to 18 June, every entry bore the date of the previous day.

[3] Drafts and organisational details in Add MS 44721, ff. 43–64.

[4] Frederick *Tennyson, 1807–98, Alfred's* elder b.; also a poet, close friend of Robert and E. B. *Browning.

[11]. Sat.

About, getting signatures—finished today—had 770. Hallam & Pickering breakfasted with me. Surplice prayers. Burke. Dined with the Dean.[1] Copied out "Breathe Soft" with the music.[2] Ethics—&c.

[12]. S.

Chapel—University Sermon & St Peters—heard Oakley—walk with Tupper & young Menteath. finished D. Wilson on B. Woodd & Rectory of Valehead. Biscoe sent for me about petition. Tea with Seymer. Porteus's Tracts.

[13]. M.

Gawday. Canning read his verses. Ride with Boyle—pleasant way & company too. Breakfast with Tupper—had 3 invitations for today, as many for tomorrow. Burke. Horace. tea with Bagot. Wine with Gaskell & Scott. Mathematics. Cogitating for the petition.

[14]. T.

Had Canning Boyle & Rogers to breakfast. Hallam, Tennyson, Gaskell and an umbra to tea. papers. Burke. Math. Quest. The Dean talked to me both sensibly & kindly about the petition. rode out to meet J.N.G. but he did not make his appearance having had a toothach. Wrote some additions for petition.

[15]. W.

John came. At Commem. & the Concert—heard Pasta,[3] Caradori,[4] Mrs Knyvett,[5] Phillips, Braham, de Begnis.[6] Burke. paper—Ethics—Had Gas[kell] to tea—& a little musical prodigy—wrote home.

[16]. Th.

Second Concert—much delighted—had Canning and Gaskell to tea. Essayed to get to Blenheim[7]—overtaken & wet to the skin in five minutes. Sir R. Inglis[8] kindly came to call on me. Returned the visit. Burke. Sat up till near four with Canning, reading the Ethics.—&c.— —

[1] This engagement again kept *Gladstone from discussing the principles of government with the essay society.
[2] Probably a song from G. F. *Handel's opera 'Muzio Scevola'.
[3] Giuditta Pasta, née Negri, 1798–1865, Italian soprano; then at her celebrated best.
[4] Maria Caterina Rosalbina *Caradori-Allan, 1800–65, soprano.
[5] Deborah Travis, d. 1876, second wife of William *Knyvett, 1779–1856, musician.
[6] Giuseppe de Begnis, 1793–1849, Italian bass. They sang Spohr's 'Last Judgement' and part of Haydn's 'Creation', in the Sheldonian Theatre.
[7] Palace of the dukes of *Marlborough, 8 miles NW. of Oxford.
[8] Sir Robert Harry *Inglis, 1786–1855, tory M.P. for Oxford university from 1829 when he defeated *Peel to 1854.

[*17*]. *Fr.*

In Collections till near three. got off better than I had any reason to hope—packed up—started with J.N.G. about five & got to Banbury about eight—capitally accommodated: my mare travelled well, & the weather held up—pleasant journey. Read some Æschylus.

[*18*]. *Sat.*

Started at 6½. Arrived at Leamington about 9. Found my Mother had been ill but was better. Mare somewhat lame—read the papers—had a long discussion with my Father about the Reform Petition—wrote out a copy of it—and wrote a very long letter to Herbert on the subject of some alterations in it. "Christian gentleman".[1]

19. Sunday.

Bible—'Christian Gentleman' & a [blank]. Church morng & aftn—happy to hear two sermons of good principle from Mr Crowther.[2]

20. M.

Called on Mr Hook & Miss Campbell. Paper—part of Article in Quarterly on Reform & Burke's Vindication of Natural Society[3]—finished writing out my speech—and put together a plan for a possible pamphlet.[4] Wrote to Mr Cunningham.

21. T.

Called on Mrs Proby, Miss Swinfen, Mrs Jephson. Rode. papers. finished 'Vindication'. Began 'Sublime & Beautiful'.[5] Finished (2nd) Article in Quarterly. wrote to H.J.G.—copied a letter—wrote a good deal myself in the form of a letter to C. Grant.[6]

22. W.

paper. 'Sublime & Beautiful'. continued my as yet imaginary letter. Rode to Baginton with J.N.G. and dined there. Met Parr.

23. Th.

Still at my letter. Wrote to Baring—announcing tomorrow for a threatened visit. Up late with John, talking. Burke. We rode a short distance. papers—Mr Wood & Mr Hay, of Leith,[7] dined with us.

---

[1] [W. Roberts] *The Portraiture of a Christian Gentleman* (1829), a discourse on godly behaviour.
[2] See Morley, i. 59, and 9 Jan. 31.
[3] Edmund *Burke's satirical imitation of *Bolingbroke (1756).
[4] See 1, 13 July 31.
[5] Another early work of *Burke's (also 1756).
[6] See 1 July 31.
[7] Christopher Wood of Hermitage Park and John Hay of Prospect Bank.

24. Fr.

Breakf. & morng alone with J.N.G.—Mr & Mrs G. having gone to Strat-ford.[1] papers. Old Mortality[2]—packed—called on Mrs Hook—dinner early —left, with a heavy heart at four—John very kindly came with me to Gaydon—mare almost down with me: very sorry to part from J.N.G.— rode on to Adderbury—saw my horse put up &c—and shook Baring by the hand: delighted with him and all about him—sat up till one with him talk-ing on interesting, very interesting questions. Slept at his house.

25. Sat.

Breakfast with Mr & Mrs B.[3] Pottered in consequence of weather. Read some Sumner's Evidences—and 'Plain reading for plain people'.[4] They have prayers night & morning, grace before & after breakfast, the form of godliness & the power too. Left soon after one—got to Oxford before four: calls—wine with Denison—he & Bruce came to tea with me—papers— wrote a little more of my letter—not very cheerful on my return—un-packed. Met Mr Churton[5] on my way.

26. Sunday.

Chapel mg & aft. heard Powell[6] at St Peters & Keble at St Mary's in aft. Are all of his opinions those of Scripture & the Church? Of his life and heart & practice none could doubt, all would admire.[7] Bible—Pearson on the Creed[8]—Doddridge's Rise & Progress[9]—wrote to Tupper.

27. M.

Wrote to Mrs G., H.J.G. on her birthday, and Herbert. papers. paid Bills &c. read Gray's answer to Beverley[10]—good. Lardner's Introduction to Algebraic Geometry.[11] Wrote a little at my letter. Tea with Denison &c. Rode down to see Saunders.

28. T.

Commenced reading according to arrangement: tho' not with good heart, trusting in God for a better. Conic S[ections]—D. Calc. applications—&

---

[1] Stratford-on-Avon, 11 miles SW. of Leamington.
[2] *Scott.
[3] C. T. *Baring m. 1830 his cousin, Mary Ursula Sealy, who d. 1840.
[4] Tract?
[5] Thomas Townson Churton, b. 1799?, fellow of Brasenose 1831; rector of Great Shefford, Berkshire, 1851–66?
[6] Thomas Powell, 1797–1865, fellow of Worcester 1828; or Baden *Powell, 1796–1860, F.R.S., Savilian professor of geometry 1827.
[7] Version in Morley, i. 57.
[8] (Bp.) John *Pearson, An Exposition of the Creed (1659), an Anglican classic.
[9] P. *Doddridge, Rise and Progress of Religion in the Soul (1745).
[10] J. H. Gray 'Remarks addressed to R. M. Beverley, Esq.', an earnest expostulation; see 2 June 31.
[11] By Dionysius *Lardner (1823).

Mechanics—with Denison. We have breakfast & tea together: read some Rhetoric & worked it together. rode out together too.—paper. Odds & ends. Dearest Helen's birthday—may God bless her.

29. W.

Surplice prayers, read a general equation to 2nd degree with D[enison]. Questions. Rhetoric. Odes of Horace. rode out. Wrote some more of my letter. S. Perceval's Sp. on Reform.[1]

30. Th.

Conic Sections before breakfast. read Theory of Asymptotes—(little understood)—rectification & quadrature of curves. Rode. dined with Churton at B.N.C. papers. Sp[encer] Perceval on Fast.[2] Odes. sat up to finish my letter which is longer than I ever thought it would be.

July 1.

Conic Sections. Equation to 2nd degree again—Mechanical questions—rhetoric & worked it with D—Odes—paper—rode a little. perused my letter for the last time corrected &c. and sent it off by coach with a letter to Hatchard.[3] Made up accounts for the last two months, and found a great surplus which I cannot account for.

Sat. July 2.

Ordered Standard which I am to take in with Denison. Walked and dined with him & Rogers—read papers—our petition presented last night in the House of Commons.[4] Wrote to J.N.G. read paper. Ethics—Rhetoric. Conic Sections. Mech. Questions.—and $\left(\dfrac{dy}{dx} = \dfrac{0}{0}\right)$ section in Lardner's Calculus.[5]

Sunday.

Chapel mg & aft. Heard Buckley preach a very good sermon in the morng & received the sacrament at his Church. Symmons in aftn at St Mary's gave a curious account of Jewish seminaries of education. Bible. Pearson—Christian Gentleman—wrote out some arguments on the Sabbath. Heard from T.G. about my speech wh he proposed printing.

---

[1] *H* iii. 256–68 (9 March 1831). Spencer Perceval, 1795–1859, a s. of his namesake the prime minister, was M.P. for Newport, Isle of Wight, 1830, and Tiverton, 1831.

[2] *H* ii. 541–6 (19 February 1831).

[3] Pamphlet, signed 'Alumnus', cast in form of letter to Charles *Grant; draft in Add MS 44721, ff. 66–99. *Hatchard would only publish it at *Gladstone's expense (Add MS 44352, f. 194). See 13 July 31.

[4] *Commons Journal*, lxxxvi. 600. See 30 May 1831 n and *H* iv. 580–2. It was presented by Philip Henry *Stanhope, 1805–75, historian; styled Lord Mahon 1816, 5th earl of Stanhope 1855; M.P. Wootton Bassett 1830–2, Hertford 1837–52; initiated National Portrait Gallery and Historical Manuscripts Commission; see Add MS 44317.

[5] Dionysius *Lardner, *Elementary Treatise on . . . Calculus* (1825), section xv; on the direction of curvature of a curve.

27—I.

4. M.

I now read responses in Chapel at Veysie's request & it helps to fix one's waywardness or at least to check it. Wrote to T.G. Conic Sections & Diff. Calc. multiple points &c. Rhetoric. Horace. papers—out—Our talk on the Rhetoric dwindles.

5. T.

Conic Sections. papers. D. Calc.—rad[ius] of curvature—wrote to my Father. Out. Rhetoric. Horace and construing at night with Denison & Phillimore.

6. W.

Conic Sections. papers. little Lardner—got into talking about our plans, wasted time & addled. Also had an interruption from my mare's lameness & seeing the surgeon. Also Ham[1] came to me about a place in the choir. Whately—Rhetoric—Odes—and construing ditto at night.

7. Th.

Conic Sections. Equations. Abstracted one or two Articles in Lardner, & addled the usual time at our Mathematics. Heard from and wrote to Tom. paper—an excellent speech of Peel's.[2] God help the country. Phillimore joined our mess. Rhetoric—Odes—& construing them.

8. Friday.

Saunders made his appearance. Walker's Mechanics. paper—Trigonometry questions—and questions in mechanics. Odes. Rhetoric. Construing at nt. Out.

9. Saturday.

Did little, not being quite well. Math—Odes—walked to St Clement's.[3] At market: got things ready in my room to have Helen and Tom to tea expecting them at 7. They came by 8 & I had tea with them at King's Arms. Talk with Tom about my pamphlet. Looked over it and cut out some of the latter part.

10. Sunday.

Had Tom & Helen to breakfast—went to St Peter's with Helen—heard an *excellent* sermon from Buckley—at Chapel in aftn. Read Pearson, and Christian Gentleman. Rode in carriage with them as far as Kidlington[4] & walked back.

[1] Perhaps a boy from St. Ebbe's.
[2] *H* iv. 871–93 (6 July 1831), against reform bill 2⁰.
[3] The suburb of Oxford at the eastern end of Magdalen Bridge.
[4] Five miles north of Oxford on the Banbury road.

11. M.

Walker's Mechanics—Lardner—questions—Rhetoric—Odes—papers—walk with Lyall—construing in the Satires at night—Dean entrusted to me the keys of the Library for the Vacation.

12. T.

rode. papers. Mechanics & questions. D. Calc. Algebraic Geometry. In Library. Rhetoric. Odes. construing Satires at night—stole half an hour for singing.

13. W.

A long letter from my Father, doing away with the idea of publishing my pamphlet, which therefore leaves me free. Mechanics. D. Calc.: questions—Rhetoric—Odes. papers. rode out. Construing Satires at night. Wrote letters to my Father, to Gaskell, & to Childers.

14. Th.

D. Calc. Formulae. Algebraic Geometry. Saunders came over. papers—part of Article in Quarterly on Reform. Horace. Rhetoric—talking on it, and construing Satires at night. Whately's Rhetoric.[1]

15. Fr.

Trigonometry & Calculus. Formulae. my book now grows.[2] papers. finished Article in Quarterly. Horace & Rhetoric—construing at night. Rode, as yesterday—In the Library some time—Hallam's Middle Ages.

16. Sat.

Trigonometry. Calculus. Mechanics: formulae. Horace, little. papers. part of Article in Quarterly on 'St. Simon'—finished Rhetoric to my great joy—talked it, & construed Horace, at night.

17. Sunday.

Chapel mg & aft. Heard an excellent sermon from Buckley & part of one at St Mary's in aftn. Out. Read in the Revelations a good deal, & notes in Mant. Heard from Bruce. Read Pearson, & Christian Gentleman. Wrote to T.G. on the subject of the latter part of my (would be) pamphlet. Denison & Phillimore had tea in my room. Oh that the Father of light would so order my conversation and footsteps, that his truth might be shown forth in my paths,[3] if perchance others might be led. My Sundays are I fear useless to others & unprofitable to myself.

---

[1] R. *Whately, *Elements of Rhetoric* (1828).
[2] Add MS 44813A, an eighty-page pocket-book.
[3] Ps. cxix. 105.

18. Monday.

Horace—construing at night—Began the Agamemnon. Walk with Lyall.
papers. finished Article in Quarterly on St Simon. Diff. Calc. & Analytical
Geometry—Conic Section Formulae. A pamphlet called "the left leg or the
right".[1]

19. T.

Horace. Max. & Min. questions. Formulae. Application of D. Calc. to
Curves. Wrote to Bruce. papers. Butler's Preface (+) and third serm. on
Human nature.[2] Walk with Phillimore. Began Andocides de Mysteriis.[3]

20. W.

Horace. Andocides. Quarterly Review on 'Subversion of ancient governments'. Max. & Min. questions. Analytical Geometry D. Calc. seem at a
standstill though labouring much as a man at the treadmill—finished Epodes
—went on with Epistles[4] at night—wrote a good deal on Governments,
their progress and decay.[5]

21. Th.

Horace & construing & logicising in Evg. Got up at nine! read paper—part
of Art. in Theol. Rev. on Locke.[6] Ethics. Andocides. A little Agamemnon.
wrote in common place book. D. Calculus. & addled with questions. heard
from H. J. G. of their safe arrival at Seaforth.

22. Fr.

Again D. Calc. and Mechanics. papers—Burke—Horace at night—wrote to
H.J.G.—Out, saw—q. imprudent? God knows.[7]

23. Sat.

heard from & wrote to T.G. D. Calculus & Algebraic Geometry. Horace a
good deal at night—finished Art Poet. Out with Phillimore. paper. part of
Article on Locke. Saunders in Oxford.

24. Sunday.

Chapel mg & aftn. Heard Buckley & Newman. The former better than ever.
the latter good too. I do not quite know what to do about evening church.

[1] 'The Left Leg *versus* the Right; a case tried in the Court of Common Sense', a
pamphlet against reform (1831).
[2] Joseph *Butler, Sermons* (1726).
[3] Speech by Athenian admiral and orator in his own defence against charge of violating
Eleusinian mysteries (399 B.C.).
[4] Also Horace.
[5] Addenda to opening paper in Add MS 44721.
[6] *British Critic*, xv. 1 (July 1830), reviewing Peter, 7th Lord *King's *Life of John
Locke, his collateral ancestor.
[7] See p. xxx above, and 7 Sept. 31.

There is little satisfaction in our Chapel. the service is scarcely performed with common decency: and the time prevents my going to hear Buckley whom I regularly attend in the morning. I can however come in for part of the sermon at St Mary's, but it is not altogether an agreeable arrangement. Read Bible—Pearson—Litterae Sacrae[1]—finished Christian Gentleman, which I like extremely: tho' deficient in the technicality of system—& arrangement.

25. M.

dear Tom's birthday: may God crown him with all blessings.—Began Div. Leg.[2] Mathematics as usual. Went through the marked passages of B.1. of Livy. papers. Cleared off an old score by finishing B 9. of Ethics.—Much pleased on receiving a message to say that Miss Benwell was in Oxford— went and saw her at her brothers[3]—met also Mr Hitchings[4] whom I had long wished to know, & Mr Ratcliffe.[5]—Sat & had a good deal of conv. there, & music: sang, but very badly.

26. T.

Divine Legation—Agamemnon—Went over the Livy with D[enison] & P[hillimore]—D. Calc. Alg. Geom. & Newton. papers. read last years reform debate, part of, & copied a curious list of names *then* as *now* in the majority. singing—finished Article on Locke.

27.

De Lolme.[6] Divine Legation. Mathematics. Mr Hitchins kindly called on me—papers—again (a little) practising i.e. learning "The Sea".[7] ran through marks in B.2. of Livy & did it with D. & P. at night—sat in too long and got a headache & knocked up.

28.

Divine Legation. Up late in consequence of yesterday. Math. with little success. papers. Wrote on the Hellenes &c. Livy B.3 and did it at night— wrote to Seymer: paid Bills.

29. Friday.

Papers. heard from T.G. He has given up his tour.—heard from Tupper.

---

[1] John *Pearson, *Praefatio ad Criticos Sacros* (1660), introduction to a 9-vol. commentary on holy scripture.

[2] W. *Warburton, *Divine Legation of Moses Demonstrated*, 2v. (1737–41), eccentric views on life after death by *Pope's friend. Notes in Add MS 44812, ff. 278–86.

[3] Perhaps Thomas Benwell, coal merchant.

[4] Perhaps James Hitchings, 1790?–1850, Oxford born; Christ Church; vicar of Wargrave, Berkshire, 1826.

[5] Possibly John Radcliffe, 1780?–1852, vicar at Radley, Berkshire.

[6] J. L. Delolme, *The English Constitution* (tr. 1772), which much influenced the *philosophes*.

[7] A song.

Mechanics and questions. Int. Calculus—Divine Legation. Livy B 4 & went through it with D & P. Wrote out some passages. A little Agamemnon.

30. Sat.

Saunders here—persuaded me to go to Cuddesdon with him: only got three hours or little more at Math—then went. wrote home. Bathed at Cuddesdon. Read "Observations on Friendly Adviser"[1]—and two Satires of Persius there—found Merriman[2] very hard at work.

31. Sunday.

Ch. morng and evg. taught in the school morng & evg. Out with S. and M. read Bible and nearly the whole of Davison on Primitive Sacrifice.[3]

August. 1. Monday

read Persius III, IV, V, VI. worked at Math. but not very profitably. dined with Saunders & then drove into Oxford: did Livy with Phillimore & Denison, Book 6. Warburton's Divine Legation.

2. Tuesday.

Newton—Mechanics—Warburton—Livy & doing it at teatime—, papers —read & abstracted part of Arnold's Article on Niebuhr in Quarterly[4] Agamemnon.

3. Wed.

Diff. Calc.—questions—Rogers sat with me some time—not sorry to lose it thus far, having a headache—wrote to Hamilton—Agamemnon—Livy and doing it—finished Article in Quarterly—Warburton.

4. Th.

Diff. Calc. Newton. Divine Legation. heard from home—they proposed leaving for Edinburgh today. Agamemnon. Livy B.9—very superficially. Jones on the Trinity.[5]

5. Friday.

Just as yesterday. Got through B.10 of Livy. papers. Spent some time in the Library reading in Abp Laud's trial. Sad news in the papers from the continent: but "the end is not yet", I think.[6] Trigonometry Questions.

---

[1] Untraced.
[2] Nathaniel James *Merriman, 1810–82; archdeacon 1847, bp. 1871, of Grahamstown; accuser of Bp. *Colenso.
[3] John *Davison, An Inquiry into the Origin and Intent of Primitive Sacrifice (1825).
[4] Thomas *Arnold on B. G. Niebuhr, Römische Geschichte, 2v. (1811–12, tr. 1827), in Quarterly Review, xxxii. 67 (June 1825).
[5] William *Jones of Nayland, The Catholic Doctrine of the Trinity proved from Scripture (1756).
[6] Hostilities between France and the Netherlands had just broken out, on account of the Belgian question. (See Webster, *Palmerston, i. 138–9.) Cp. 3–7 Feb. 32.

6. Sat.

Walk over Port Meadow[1] with Phillimore whom I like more as I see more of him. Newton & Mechanics. Trig. Quest. Archdeacon Lyall's Charge.[2] an idle day. A little Agamemnon. and part of Ovid Metamorphoses B.15 for Pythagorean doctrine.[3]

7. Sunday.

Chapel mg & aftn. Heard Buckley: he preached extremely well as usual. Recd the Sacrament there: perhaps eighty communicants. Finished Davison—began Molesworth[4]—wrote—read Bp Hall's Specialities,[5] a Sermon &c.

8. M.

Canning breakfasted with me. Read Mechanics & did some Newton questions. Warburton's Divine Legation read about half the Menexenus.[6] papers. wrote to Seymer. Phillimore went away for a few days.

9. T.

A very idle day: wrote however several letters, to Mrs G., R.G., & Gaskell—from the last I recd one announcing that he was canvassing Wakefield—eheu! nescius.[7] finished Mcncxcnus. finished 1st vol of Divine Legation. A little Mechanics—Woodhouse's Pref.[8] part of papers—questions.

10. Wed.

Papers. De Lolme—analysing Warburton. Agamemnon[9]—Newton Quest. Mechanics. Calculus. Odes of Horace with Denison at night. Sent for & saw Tuckwell[10] on the subject of a noise in my ear.

11. Th.

Heard from Seymer. paper. De Lolme. Analysis of Warburton. Newton—Mechanics—Questions—walk—Finished Horace with Denison in evening—Agamemnon.

[1] The great Thames-side meadow to the NW. of Oxford.
[2] W. R. *Lyall, 'The nature and true value of Church Property examined' (1831).
[3] The opening section of the book.
[4] J. E. N. *Molesworth, *An Answer to ... *Davison's Inquiry into ... Primitive Sacrifice* (1826).
[5] *Observations of some specialities of Divine Providence in the Life of Joseph *Hall, Bishop of Norwich* (1660), autobiographical.
[6] Plato.
[7] 'ignorant, alas'. Daniel Gaskell, the reforming candidate, was unopposed.
[8] Short preface to Robert *Woodhouse's treatise on *Isoperimetrical Problems* (1810), a work on the calculus, or to that on *Astronomy* (1812).
[9] Aeschylus.
[10] William Tuckwell, surgeon.

12. Fr.

Agamemnon. Prometheus with Denison. heard from H.J.G.—they had arrived safely at Ed[inburgh]—& from Childers. De Lolme. Newton— Mechanics—papers.

13. S.

Newton—Trigonometry—De Lolme—Rousseau Contrat Social[1]—Aga- memnon—went to Iffley & had tea with Rogers.[2] papers of *two days*. Phillimore came back.

14. Sunday.

Chapel twice. had Rogers to breakfast and go to Church—we went to St Peter's and heard as usual an admirable sermon; simple, earnest, scrip- tural. Many other things I might say—but his praise is of God. Walked to Woodeaton.[3] Read a sermon of Bp Hall's—Molesworth—J. Taylor & others on fasting. Poor Bulteel has lost his Church for preaching in the open air: pity that he should have acted so: and pity that it should be found necessary to make such an example of a man of God.[4] May He overrule all to the glory of his name—had some agreeable conversation with Phillimore.

15. M.

Began to go over Sophocles with D. & P. and also Odyssey with P. a little Agamemnon—& notes from Warburton. Mechanics, & Newton Questions. heard from R.G. grieved to find my Mother was suffering at Fettercairn:[5] wrote to H.J.G. Walked out and sang. wrote a sort of essay on the Neces- sitarian hypotheses[6]—paper.

16. T.

Wrote a draught of a letter to Herbert about an old epistle to the Standard —and also wrote to him. Homer—Agam[emnon]—Sophocles at night— Mathematics—Rousseau—my eyes I am sorry to say gave strong symp- toms detrectandae militiae.[7]

17. W.

Wrote to Doyle. Seymer came. in Library. walked with Seymer. paper. Mathematics—Odyssey—Sophocles—Agamemnon—Warburton Analysis.

[1] Jean-Jacques Rousseau, *Du contrat social* (1762), the confused basis of subsequent democratic theory.
[2] Cp. 20 Aug. 31.
[3] Four miles north of Oxford, east of the Cherwell.
[4] This sentence in Morley, i. 58, dated 'summer of 1830'.
[5] John *Gladstone had bought in 1829 the new great house at Fasque, Kincardine- shire, at the eastern end of Strathmore; some 27 miles SW. of Aberdeen and 11 north of Montrose. Fettercairn, the village by the park gates, is nearly a mile and a half south of the house; of which a sketch is in Reid, *G*, at 211.
[6] Headed '*Fatalism*' in Add MS 44721, ff. 100–7.
[7] 'of fighting shy of the struggle'.

18. Th.

Wrote to Gaskell. Heard from Herbert. in the library. Buckland[1] made me exhibit in my gown to a foreign Lady. Math—De Lolme—Warburton—finished Agamemnon—Wrote sundries—Sophocles at Night as usual.

19. Fr.

Wrote home—and heard from home. had Seymer & Villiers[2] to breakfast with us. papers. Mechanics. Odyssey. Sculled Rogers down to Iffley.[3] Sophocles at night—Warburton Analysis—De Lolme. Wrote sundries.

20. Sat.

An idle day. paper. had tea with Rogers at Iffley to meet Newman as he kindly asked me.[4] Mechanics. finished De Lolme. Odyssey. Sophocles—finished Trachiniae. Analysis [of] Warburton. Cole came.

21. Sunday.

Cole breakfasted with me. walked & had tea with him. Sumner—Pearson—Molesworth—and the Bible: heard Ball[5] preach an excellent sermon at St Peter's in morng & a good one from Powell in aftn, of the expository kind—sat long with Cole.

22. M.

Wrote a long letter & an angry one to the Standard, on some passages in Lardner's Cyclopaedia, & Cabinet Library, which are I think infamous.[6] Also a note to Liverpool, to go with a woman who is to emigrate—Mechanics & questions—Cudworth,[7] Analysis [of] Warburton & philosophy generally —walk with Cole—paper—going over Sophocles and Odyssey. in evening.

23. T.

My eyes more troublesome than they had yet been. Had a visit from a singular old man who brought the book of Joshua—I liked him. Newton Questions. walked out with Phillimore. paper. Sophocles. Homer—Cudworth. Went earlier to bed κατ᾽ ἀνάγκαν.[8] Choephorae.[9]

---

[1] William *Buckland, 1784–1856, geologist; fellow of Corpus 1808; canon of Christ Church 1826; dean of Westminster 1845.

[2] Henry Montagu *Villiers, 1813–61, younger b. of 4th earl of *Clarendon; extreme low churchman; rector of St. George's, Bloomsbury, 1841; bp. of Carlisle 1856, of Durham 1860.

[3] Now a SE. suburb, 2 miles from the centre of Oxford.

[4] *Newman's mother lived at Iffley; *Rogers, then his only pupil, had lodgings near by (*Letters of Frederic Lord Blachford* (1896), 6).

[5] John Ball, b. 1800?, fellow of St. John's; vicar of St. Lawrence, Reading, 1834–66?

[6] Untraced.

[7] Ralph *Cudworth, *The true Intellectual System of the Universe* (1678), attack on atheism by leading Cambridge Platonist; or perhaps his *Treatise concerning Eternal and Immutable Morality* (1731).

[8] 'of necessity'.   [9] Aeschylus, *Bearers of drink offerings.*

24. W.

Rode. my mare all the better for her run. Cudworth—Anal[ysis of] Warburton—Choephorae—Newton Questions—paper—Iliad with Phillimore—
Sophocles δημοσᾳ.[1]

25. Th.

Cudworth. Math. Questions. Unwell & unable to get on—wrote a letter to
the Record [2]—Tupper passed through Oxford—staid with me some time—
rode with him & Cole—Homer—at night found it useless to attempt anything. Wrote to Childers.

26. Fr.

Breakfast, tea, & ride with Cole—read Beverley's Tombs of the Prophets,[3]
Wild's reply to him,[4] and Burton's Church Reform,[5] in his room. paper &c.

27. Sat.

Self weak—weather uncertain. Cole breakfasted with me: at length determined to set off. Drove to Bicester, Cole kindly accompanying me as far as
that. Rode on to Childers's [6] & arrived about half past six. Spent the evening with him.

28. S.

Taught in the school. heard him preach very well morng & aftn—& perform the rest of the service too.—out a good deal—compelled to debar myself from books. A good deal of conversation which I enjoy. &c.

29. M.

Rode with Childers. Wrote home. Dared not read.

30. T.

Saw Mrs Childers—& came away. Rode about thirty miles across country to
Cuddesdon—not the worse for it thank God—Saunders received me most
kindly—I trust this little break will show me my helplessness and make
me think of him who was the giver of all my health and strength.

31. W.

At Cuddesdon. Wrote to T.G. Read Horsley's Dissertation on Prophecies of

---

[1] 'in public'.   [2] Untraced.
[3] A lay sermon by R. M. Beverley on Matt. xxiii. 29–33, again alleging corruptions in
the established church (1831).
[4] W. T. Wild, 'A letter to R. M. Beverley . . .', an earnest riposte (1831).
[5] *Burton, 'Thoughts upon the demand for Church Reform' (1831). a mild conservative pamphlet.
[6] Childers was rector of Mursley, near Winslow, Buckinghamshire.

Messiah among the Gentiles.[1] Read a Sermon on Resurrection. Much conversation with Saunders. returned to Oxford in evening.

1. Th.

Worked according to, certainly not over, my strength—so also on

2. Fr. & 3. Sat.

reading Montesquieu,[2] Choephorae, Homer with Phillimore, Sophocles with Phillimore & Denison—began Gisborne[3]—& on Friday & Saturday did some questions & began hydrostatics. rode. papers. heard from J.N.G.

4. Sunday.

Bible. Finished Molesworth. Shuttleworth Sermon at St Peter's—Sacrament. Pearson. Walk. Denison determined to go away.

5. M.

Thank God I continue to improve. paper. Gisborne's Mor. Ph. which I am sorry to say is wishy washy. Newton questions &c.—Saunders here—Horace with Phillimore. Rode out. Choephorae—Rousseau.

6. T.

Dined at Pusey's. Met Newman & Jenkins,[4] fellows of Oriel. Homer—Newton—Gisborne—Rousseau—Choephorae—Rode—paper.

7. W.

Ride—paper—some time occupied with Mrs Carter, who proposes to emigrate[5]—questions in Math—Hydrostatics—Choephorae—Homer. Gisborne. A bad day—overslept myself, which I have now certainly no right to do, as I am most liberal in my allowance of rest.

8. Th.

rode early to Cuddesdon. spent the day there—papers—Gisborne—Polybius—Richard III—Phillimore, Jeffreys,[6] & Thomas[7] came over—all three had narrow escapes returning in the evening.

---

[1] Prefixed to S. *Horsley's *Nine Sermons on the . . . Resurrection* (1815).
[2] *Reflections on the Causes of the Grandeur and Declension of the Romans* (tr., 1734), by the author of *De l'Esprit des Lois* (1748).
[3] T. *Gisborne, *Principles of Moral Philosophy* (1789).
[4] For Henry Jenkyns, 1795–1878, b. of the master of Balliol; professor at Durham 1833, and canon 1841; see G. Faber, *Oxford Apostles* (1954 ed.), 114–15.
[5] No other trace: unless on 22 Jul. 31.
[6] Henry Anthony Jeffreys, 1811–98?, vicar of Hawkhurst, Kent, 1839, and canon of Canterbury 1872.
[7] Richard James Francis Thomas, 1813?—73; headmaster of Bancroft's hospital, Stepney, 1860; vicar of Yeovil, Somerset, 1855.

9. Fr.

Finished Homer with Phillimore—for which I am sorry notwithstanding the press of business. Newton. Hydrostatics. paper. ride. part of 'Six Letters to the Farmers on Tithes'.[1] Choephorae. part of First Philippic.

10. Sat.

Finished 'Six Letters'. finished Choephorae. read some Gisborne—& a little of Polybius b.VI. Wrote to J.N.G. read papers. rode with Jeffreys. Sat some time with Biscoe. A sadly, sadly, idle day.

[The back inside cover contained the book list below.]

April 1830.

Tales of a Grandfather Ser.3.
Close's Sermons.
Mant's Clergyman's obligations.
Fosters three first Essays.
Forster's Vindic. of Mahom. Unveild.
Huskisson's Speech. West Rev.
on Moore's Byron, Montgom's
Satan. Channing—Random
Records &c. Theol Rev. on
Arnold & 3 or 4 more.
Dairyman's Daughter.

May, 1830.

"District Chapels"—"Splendid
Sins"—Bp of London's letter
Heber's Life of Jer. Taylor.
Herod. Clio. Virg. Æn. 4.
Juv 11–16.
Berend's Christmas Stories.
Davys's Vill. Conv. on Liturgy.
Husbandman's Manual.
Ethics B. 3, 4—Splendid Sins.
Ed. Rev. on Milman + Leslie's Short
Method. Porteus's Evidences.

June 1830.

Juv. 1.3.4.5.7.8.10.—Persius.
Herod 2, 3, 4 with &c.s.

---

[1] *The Farmers and the Clergy* (1831?); six letters to farmers on tithes and church property.

Ethics 5, 8, 9.
Arnold's Sermons.
Thomas a Kempis.
Quart on Bp Butler. Hallam's
Poetry &c. &c.

July 1830.

Times of Trial.
Sargant's Life of Cranmer.
Butler's Analogy.
Herod. 5, 6, 7, with &c.s.
Pascal's Thoughts on relig.
Od 1–5.
Some Heber and Madden.

Aug. 1830.

Herod. 8, 9. with &c.s.
Thucyd. 1.2.3.4.5. with &c.s.
Beveridge's Private Thoughts.
Paley's Moral Philosophy.

Sept. 1830.

Townsend's Sermons.
Thucyd. 6.7.8. & &c.s.
Odyss 5–12. Iliad 1–9.
Herod 1 in Greek. 2 to 7 in English.
Prideaux B 1. & 2.
Hellenics 1.2.
Livy (English) 1, 2, 3, 4.

Oct. 1830.

Livy English 5, 6, 7, 8, 9, 10.
Œdipus Tyrannus.
Genesis with notes. (some).
Matt & John in Gk Test. with notes.
Polybius Book 1.
Odyssey 13, 14.
Neele on English Poetry, & some Tales.
Drummond's Social Duties.

Ethics about three books.
Sundry pamphlets & reviews &c.

Excerpta

Æn. 6. 848[–53].	Excudent . . . .[debellare]	superbos.
Æn. 6. 870[–86].	Ostendent	Munere.
Æn. 9. 446[–9].	Fortunati	habebit.
Æn. 9. 481[–9].	Hunc ego	auiles.
Æn. 4. 174[–7].	Fama	condit.
Iliad 4. 440[–3].	Ἔρις	βαίνει.
Æn. 4. 206[–10].	Jupiter	miscent?
Æn. 4. 320[–30].	Te propter	viderer.
Moschus.[1]	αἰ αἰ	ὕπνον.

[1] *Idyll*, iii. 106–11.

[Front outside cover:]

Journal No 6.

1831–3.

[Fly–leaf :—]

PRIVATE.

Sept. 1831–July 1833. (No 6).
Journal.

W.E.G. Ch.Ch. 1831.

And Death shall wave his bony arm
And Slaughter he shall ride
O'er the valour of the bridegroom
And the beauty of the bride—
Aye Glory he shall trample down
And grind to dust the kingly crown.

In beneficiis ad ærarium referendi. Mrs H. J.C. . . .y.
J.M.G.R.—C.Ll..d.—T.G.—R.P.—J.²

O Death that in selfworship liest,
O Life that unto Virtue diest,
Death that endurest, Life that fliest
Where are ye now.

Sunday Sept. 11. 1831.

This little book may carry me through very eventful time! God send the
best.
Chapel mg & afternoon. Heard a good sermon at St Peters from a clergyman I did not know by sight. Breakfasted with Villiers. Cureton had tea
with me. Walk. Read Bible—Davison on Prophecy—Pearson—and a very

¹ Lambeth MS 1420. 76ff.
² 'To be remembered for financial kindnesses'. Diarist's dots.

able Discourse of Shuttleworth's on the Atonement.[1] Also wrote a few notes on "The fulness of Time".[2]

12. M.

Dined with Cureton at his lodgings. rode with Thomas. Expected Phillimore but he did not return. Cudworth.[3] Finished Gisborne. paper. Spent most of my morning in writing on Ethical subjects.—A few problems. &c. Wrote to my brothers.

13. T.

Phillimore returned & again went off home in the evening. Began Sir J. Mackintosh's dissertation.[4] rode with Thomas. Philippics—wrote to Denison—and to Hamilton—also part of a Latin letter to Doyle—Hydrostatics, & Newton questions.

14. W.

Wrote to Seymer. papers. Coleridge's 'Introduction'.[5] Philippics. Bland's Hydrostatics & Questions. Rode to Cuddesdon with Thomas. Translated some Æschylus.

15. Th.

Rode—papers—Hydrostatics & Questions. Coleridge's Introdn. Cud[worth]. Finished Select Or[ations]. Translated some Homer. Wrote to my Father. Phill[imore] & Jeff[reys] returned. A bad account of Denison.

16. Friday.

Indifferent accounts from Denison. Last ride with Thomas. Cunningham came. paper. Hydrostt. & questt. Translated some Odyssey. Finished Cudworth. Finished Montesquieu to death of Augustus Ch.13. dispatched a Latin letter to Doyle. Went over half the Nubes with Ph[illimore].

17. Sat.

paper. Newton Questt. young Acland came. translated some Agamemnon—killed off the Nubes—began Thucydides—wrote a sketch of Cudworth. rode.

18. Sunday.

Out with Acland—& with Cunningham. Heard Whately preach a controversial sermon at St Peter's. He is just made Archbishop of Dublin! Doubt-

---

[1] Perhaps on John iii. 17–18, reprinted in his *Sermons*, ii. 365.
[2] See Gal. iv. 4; Add MS 44722, ff. 159–66; and 18, 25 Sept. 31.
[3] R. *Cudworth, *The true Intellectual System of the Universe* (1678).
[4] Sir James *Mackintosh, *Dissertation on the Progress of Ethical Philosophy, chiefly during the Seventeenth and Eighteenth Centuries* (1830).
[5] H. N. *Coleridge, *Introduction to Homer* (1830).

less he is a man of much power & many excellencies—but his antisabbatical doctrine is I fear as mischievous as it is unsound.[1] Today Phillimore told me he had been convinced by it—and Jeffreys seemed half to agree with him.

Read Bible & Davison—rested on account of my eyes: wrote some notes on fulness of Time.

19. M.

rode with Cunningham. long letter from home. paper—Newton Questions —Thucydides—transl[ation] from Agamemnon—Knights[2] with Phillimore—[Rousseau] Contrat Social—part of an Article on Oxford in Ed. Rev.[3] There are nails to hit on the head, but I think they miss them.

20. T.

paper—ride—Thucydides—transl[ation] Hydrostatics & questions— finished Knights—Hallam.

21. W.

looked over some Greek of Phillimore's & turned it myself—Hallam— Hydrostatics—Thucydides—Phillimore unwell in the evening—spent some time talking with him—paper—rode.

22. Th.

Wrote to Denison. Rode with Acland to dine at Cuddesdon & foolishly staid some time—Thucydides—Mathematics—Algebraic Geometry Questions— paper—division on Reform Bill satisfactory enough under the circumstances.[4] Hallam. Translated some Agamemnon.

23. F.

Canning passed through. Rode with Pusey. papers—Analytical Geometry— Thucydides—two letters to the Standard[5]—a letter to my Father—some Juvenal with Phillimore—had coffee with Jeffries & wasted much time.

24. Sat.

papers—and rode—read "What will the Lords do"[6]—wrote to T.G.— Thucydides—Juvenal with Phillimore—and Hydrostatical Problems—

---

[1] Morley, i. 57. *Whately was consecrated on 23 October 1831.
[2] Aristophanes.
[3] June 1831, liii. 384, a sharp attack.
[4] *H* vii. 464–78; 3⁰ in the commons, by 345 to 236.
[5] One from 'Alumnus', quoting views on reform of *Burke and others, printed 28 September.
[6] Pamphlet by Sir Henry Rich (1831).

28—I.

learnt a little Virgil—looked over some Iambics for Cunningham: a poor day indeed.—My work is all sadly behind. News of the Dean's departure.[1]

25. S.

Bible and Davison. went to see J. W[ishlade].—Heard Newman preach a good sermon on those who made excuse[2]—heard Bulteel's service from a window in Mrs Albutt's house—congregation large & very attentive— some of his sermon interested [me]—but there seemed to be a soreness of spirit in him.[3] Thought much of coming events. Notes on 'fulness of Time'.

26. M.

paper. Thucydides. Hallam. rode. Newton. Algebraic Geometry. Juvenal with Phillimore. Dined at Exeter with Jacobson[4]—met Falconer,[5] a pleasant man: and Baugh.[6]

27. T.

Rode. paper. translated Virgil. Hydrostatics. Juvenal. Thucydides. finished B.II.—writing out phrases very laborious—heard from Denison—he will probably not return before Monday. read Apologia Academica which I opine to be Ingram's.[7]

28. W.

Rode little—my mare lame from bad shoeing. Canning came. Thucydides. Hallam. Hydrostatics & Algebraical Geometry. some time with the Dean who was very kind. No Juvenal in evg—talking with Canning. papers. Did some Greek.

29. Th.

Walked—heard from T.D. Acland—also wrote to him. His letter pleased me.—paper. Thucydides. Hydrostatics. wrote to R.G. Juvenal—translated some Virgil—had serious thoughts of an expedition to London next week for the Lords' debate. Canning promises to get me an order from Ld Clanricarde.[8]

---

[1] Dean Smith exchanged his deanery for a stall at Durham held by Thomas *Gaisford, 1779–1855, classicist; regius professor of Greek 1812; eminent as publisher, still more so as editor. See Morley, i. 49.

[2] Luke xiv. 18.   [3] See Morley, i. 58, and 15 Feb. 31.

[4] William *Jacobson, 1803–84, professor of divinity 1848, bp. of Chester 1865.

[5] William Falconer, 1802?–85, fellow of Exeter 1827; rector of Bushey, Hertfordshire, 1839.

[6] Folliott Baugh, 1809?–89?; fellow of All Souls 1832; rector of Chelsfield, 1849–88, and Farnborough, Kent, 1849–76.

[7] James *Ingram's reply to the *Edinburgh Review* (see 19 Sept. 31).

[8] Ulick John de Burgh, 1802–74, cr. marquess of Clanricarde and m. George *Canning's da. Harriet 1825; Anglo-Irish magnate.

30. Fr.

Thucydides. Hydrostatics & Alg. Geom. Finished Juvenal (going over pass-ages) with Phillimore. Translated some Agamemnon into prose, & some into verse.

Oct. 1. Saturday.

An order for Oct.3. came from Lord Clanricarde. Heard from R.G. & from Herbert—wrote to him—also wrote to my Father—Thucydides. Agamem-non as yesterday—Alg. Geom. began Virgil with Phillimore—called on Mrs Charriere—got leave to depart—Robinson's Antiquities.[1]

2. Sunday.

Breakfasted with Villiers—found more men than I could have wished—went to St Peter's with Grimston—heard Whately—received the Sacra-ment. Read Bible—Davison—Doddridge[2]—& wrote out some texts.

3. M.

Yesterday an idea, a chimera entered my head—of gathering during the progress of my life, notes & materials for a work embracing three divisions —Morals—Politics—Education. And I commit this notice to paper now, that many years hence, if it please God, I may find it either a pleasant, or at least an instructive reminiscence: a pleasant *and* instructive one, I trust, if I may ever be permitted to execute the design: instructive, if it shall perish while in embryo, and serve to teach me the folly of presumptous schemes conceived during the buoyancy of youth, and only relinquished on a dis-covery of incompetency in later years. Meanwhile I am only contemplating the gradual accumulation of materials.[3]

Monday 3 to Saturday 8.

Journey to London—from Henley in Blackstone's chaise—present at five nights debate of infinite interest in the House of Lords: [on] the first went forwards & underwent a somewhat high pressure: on the four others, sat on a transverse rail—very fortunate in being so well placed—had a full view of the Peeresses: there nine or ten hours every evening.[4] Orders from Ld Clanricarde on Monday & Tuesday—Ld Camden[5] on Wed, through

---

[1] J. *Robinson, *Archaeologia Graeca . . . chiefly Designed to Illustrate the Greek Classics* (1807).

[2] Philip *Doddridge, *The Rise and Progress of Religion in the Soul* (1750); or perhaps his *Family Expositor*, 6v. (1760–2), a paraphrased N.T.

[3] Version in Morley, i. 76–7.

[4] Thus far ibid. i. 75. The lords were debating the reform bill 2⁰.

[5] Sir John Jeffreys *Pratt, 1759–1840, 2nd Earl Camden 1794; viceroy of Ireland 1794–8; president of council 1805–6 and 1807–12; cr. Marquess Camden 1812.

Tupper—Lord Howard de Walden[1] & Lord Harrowby[2] on Th. & Fr, through the kindness of Evelyn Denison, to whom I (paullo audacius)[3] introduced myself having had my pocket picked of a letter which S[tephen] D[enison] gave me to him. Met Ryder[4]—Pickering—Tupper— Wellesley—Savile now Ld Pollington[5]—slept at the Albany & breakfasted in Bedford Square where I received the utmost kindness.[6] Read Peel's Speech[7] & sundry papers relating to King's Coll:[8] wh I went to see—also London Bridge—Read Introduction to Butler & one Ch.[9] Wrote to Saunders—much occupied in order-hunting during the mornings.

Lord Brougham's was as a speech most wonderful[10]—Lord Grey's[11] most beautiful—Lord Goderich's[12] & Lord Lansdowne's[13] extremely good— and in these was comprehended nearly all the oratorical merit of the debate. The reasoning, or the attempt to reason, independently of the success in such attempt, certainly seemed to me to be with the opposition—Their best speeches I thought were those of Lords Harrowby,[14] Caernarvon,[15] Mansfield,[16] Wynford[17]—next, Lords Lyndhurst,[18] Wharncliffe,[19] & the Duke of Wellington.[20] Lord Grey's reply I did not hear, having been compelled by

[1] Charles Augustus *Ellis, 1799–1868, 6th Baron Howard de Walden; *Canning's under-secretary 1824; minister in Lisbon 1833, and Brussels 1846.
[2] Dudley *Ryder, 1762–1847, 2nd Baron Harrowby 1803; foreign secretary in 1804; cr. earl of Harrowby 1809; president of council 1812–27; wavering tory on reform question.
[3] 'rather daringly'.
[4] George Dudley Ryder, 1810–80; *Harrowby's nephew, at Oriel.
[5] John Charles George Savile, 1810–99; Eton and Trinity, Cambridge; styled viscount Pollington 1830; last M.P. for Gatton 1831–2; M.P. for Pontefract 1835–7 and 1841–7; 4th earl of Mexborough 1860; convert to Rome 1894; last survivor of unreformed house of commons.
[6] Thomas *Gladstone had rooms in the Albany; Divie Robertson lived in Bedford Square. Version of rest of entry in Morley, i. 75.
[7] H vii. 435–58, commons 21 September 1831, opposing reform bill 3⁰.
[8] King's College had just been opened, in the Strand, as a denominational Church of England rival to the non-sectarian University College, founded in 1825.
[9] Joseph *Butler, Analogy of Religion (1736).
[10] H viii. 220–75, late in lords' debate on reform bill 2⁰.
[11] H vii. 928–69, opening the same debate. Charles *Grey, 1764–1845, Foxite whig; foreign secretary 1806–7; 2nd Earl Grey 1807; prime minister 1830–4.
[12] H vii. 1368–77. Frederick John ('Prosperity') *Robinson, 1782–1859; M.P. 1806; cr. Viscount Goderich, April, and prime minister, September, 1827; resigned, sooner than meet parliament, January 1828; colonial secretary 1830; cr. earl of Ripon 1833; privy seal 1833–4; board of trade, 1841–3, of control, 1843–6. See Add MS 44285.
[13] H vii. 1344–62. Sir Henry *Petty-Fitzmaurice, 1780–1863, whig grandee; 3rd marquess of Lansdowne 1809; in every whig cabinet from 1830 to his death; at the time, president of the council.
[14] H vii. 1145–76.
[15] H viii. 85–107. Henry George Herbert, 1772–1833, 2nd earl of Carnarvon 1811.
[16] H vii. 993–1013. David William Murray, 1777–1840, 3rd earl of Mansfield 1796; tory.
[17] H viii. 188–209. Sir William Draper *Best, 1767–1845, cr. Baron Wynford 1829; judge.
[18] H viii. 276–99. John Singleton *Copley, 1772–1863; b. in Boston, Massachusetts; wrangler; barrister; cr. baron Lyndhurst 1827; thrice tory lord chancellor 1827–46; *Disraeli's patron.
[19] H vii. 969–87, in reply to *Grey. James Archibald *Stuart-Wortley-Mackenzie, 1776–1845, gs. of 3rd earl of *Bute; Canningite; M.P. 1802; cr. Baron Wharncliffe 1826; privy seal 1834, president of council 1841; like *Harrowby, a leading waverer.
[20] H vii. 1186–1205. Arthur Wesley, later *Wellesley, 1769–1852, hero; fought in India, 1797–1805, Denmark 1807, Spain and Portugal 1808–14, low countries 1794–5 and 1815; cr. Viscount Wellington 1809, earl and marquis 1812, and duke of Wellington 1814; among many other appointments, tory prime minister 1828–30.

exhaustion to leave the house:[1] remained with Ryder & Pickering in the coffee room, or walking about, until the division—& joined Wellesley & Savile as we walked home—went to bed for an hour, breakfasted, and came off by the Alert; arrived safely thank God in Oxford—wrote to my Brother and to Gaskell—had tea with Phillimore, & spent the remainder of the evening with Canning.

The consequences of the vote may be awful—God avert them—but it was an honourable & manly decision, & so may God avert them![2]

Sunday Oct. 9.

St Peter's in mg—Chapel in aftn. read Bible—Davison—Shuttleworth.

10. M.

Made up accounts & got them into as forward a state as I could—calls & shopping—paper—Thucydides. a little Optics—Virgil with Phillimore. Translation and Hallam.

T. & W. Oct. 11, 12.

Rode—papers—Virgil—Thucydides—both days. Also some Optics— wrote a long letter home—read a chapter of Butler on each—Hume— breakfasted (10) with Canning to meet Lady C. She received me, I thought, with great kindness & spoke a great deal about Ld Grey's conduct with reference to her husband's memory, with great animation & excitement— her hand in a strong tremor. It was impossible not to enter into her feelings.[3]

Th. 13.

Rode with Canning. paper. Thucydides. Optics. Butler. Ben Harrison came, & had tea with me—heard from Bruce—having finished the Virgil, began to run over the Select Orations with Phillimore.

Fr. 14.

I think Lady[4] Canning[4] liked me ill, & with reason, at Hallingbury[4]—& did not mean to see me passing through Oxford;[4] but heard a fallacious account whence I was asked to breakfast.[4]—Optics. Thucydides. Cicero with Phillimore—a little Persae—Middleton. papers.

Sat. 15.

New Dean installed.[5] Students attended the accompanying service. papers:

[1] H viii. 311–338: 'The House crowded to suffocation—the thermometer at 85' (E. J. *Littleton in A. Aspinall ed., *Three Early Nineteenth Century Diaries* (1952), 147).

[2] The lords rejected the reform bill by 199 to 158 (H viii. 339–44). Riots followed. Extracts in Morley, i. 75.

[3] Version ibid., i. 77.

[4] Each of these words lightly scribbled over.

[5] See 24 Sept. 31.

rode—half with S. & H. Denison. Thucydides—Middleton—finished running through Cicero's Epistles. Breakf. with Phillimore—he had tea with me—afterwards Mayow.

16. Sunday.

St Mary's mg & aftn. Shuttleworth & Tyler—we are seldom so well off. Wasted I fear much time—had Cole Hope & Cunningham to tea—Davison —Paley's Evidences—Bible.

17. M.

Heard from T.G. Wrote to Gaskell. Heard from Hamilton. Had the Bruces to tea—rode with Mayow & Tupper—logic lecture with Biscoe—reading it also—Whately, Moberly,[1] Aldrich.[2]—Middleton Cicero—Herodotus history & went through most of B.1.—Optics.

18. T.

Middleton Cicero. Whately's Logic, and lecture. Optics—rode with Denison —Herodotus & did B.2—wine with Mayow—surplice prayers.

19. Wed.

Breakf. with Trower. Logic & Lecture. Optics & Lecture. rode with Cole & Ryder—who, & also White, called upon me. Some conversation with Churton. Middleton Cicero. finished Vol.1. Herodotus did Bk.3 & a little of B.4. Gaskell of age today. God bless him.

20. Th.

Breakfast with Acland. Logic—Roman History in Clinton, Heeren, &c. began a Synopsis. Arnold Appx—Herodotus and worked in it with Phillimore. Rode Cole's horse through his kindness, mine being lame for the fourth time. Optics. Logic Lecture. Heard from Seymer, who is in great spirits about the Dorsetshire election.[3]

21, Fr.

Breakf with Ryder. Logic Lecture. reading Duncan[4] & Whately. Synopsis of Roman Chron[ology] from Middleton & Clinton. Churton called on me and talked much and well about religion—rode. Herodotus & worked thereat with Phillimore. Seymer came late & had tea & we talked over Dorsetshire matters. Phillimore gave me a very nice Virgil which I fear I have ill deserved from him.

---

[1] G. *Moberly, Introduction to Logic (1838, so perhaps MS draft).
[2] H. Aldrich, Artis Logicae Compendium (1691).
[3] The whig candidate, William Francis Spencer Ponsonby, 1787–1855, cr. Baron de Mauley 1838, was beaten in a by-election by Anthony Ashley *Cooper, 1801–85, styled Lord Ashley 1811, 7th earl of Shaftesbury 1851, tory philanthropist. See Add MS 44300.
[4] William Duncan, Elements of Logick (1748).

22. Sat.

Interrupted by visits from Hamilton—Herbert—Cameron—Acland—Lushington—also called on Lincoln, & on Mrs Charriere whose daughter I was happy to find had wonderfully recovered from a two years sickness on Sunday last, by an apparently marked interposition of the mercy and power of God. May He in his wisdom grant, that those reports and pretensions now abroad be neither rejected by prejudice nor received upon caprice, but humbly and soberly investigated according to His will and word. Surely the actual signs of the times are such as should make us ready for the coming of our Lord.

Wrote to my Mother: Logic and Lecture. Roman History & Synopsis from Clinton, Heeren, and Middleton—Herodotus and working it with Phillimore.

23. Sunday.

At Sermon twice. Majendie in aftn: sound as usual. *Walked & talked* with Acland. also with Cameron and Tupper. Had tea with Harrison—finished Davison's admirable work—read Bible & some Paley's Evidences. wrote a letter to Helen on miracles &c.

24. M.

Optics & Lecture. Butler (looking over) & Lecture. Roman History. Thucydides—began B.6.—Seymer & Doyle had tea with me—rode—analysed Second part of Hallam's Chapter on the Feudal System.[1] Read Anstice's Introductory Lecture [2]—liked it very much. A gratifying letter from Helen. Got a paper from Gaskell with the account of his festivities.

25. T.

Ride with Doyle & Cole. Optics. Mitford. Hallam. Butler and Analysis. Harrison & Hamilton had tea with me.

26. Wed.

Optics and Lecture. Butler and Lecture. Finished Herodotus with Phillimore. Hallam. Rode. Put my name down.[3]

27. Th.

as yesterday nearly. Began Thucydides History. At Debating Society.[4] Tea with Wordsworth.

---

[1] Henry *Hallam, *State of Europe during the Middle Ages*, 2v. (1818). i. 141–229.
[2] *Anstice's inaugural lecture at King's College London, 17 October, in defence of classical studies.
[3] For the final honours schools.
[4] Debate on distress in Ireland.

28. Fr.

Rode with Lushington. Did some Choephorae with Denison who came over for his All Souls examination[1]—Butler & Lecture—Thucydides History—Optics & Lecture. Surplice prayers.

29. Sat.

Rode with Grimston, & talked two books of Herodotus. Thucydides with Phillimore—Butler & Lecture. Finished Hallam vol.1—had a letter from Tom, which gave me a caution concerning abstinence from religious speculations, kindly meant and kindly expressed. God knows it ought to be a reproach to me the other way: for in the turmoil and anxiety of rapidly multiplying employments, my thoughts have been too much on the means and too little on what is I trust the end: too little on Him who died for us all and in whom we ought all to live.

—went to wine with Murray.[2] wrote a letter to my dear Father giving explanation.[3]

30. S.

Missed Chapel in mg. A very able but speculative discourse from Shuttleworth—Miller[4] in afternoon. Paley's Evidences—Bible—Toplady on Necessity & some of his letters.[5] Lunch with Tupper. Tea with Cole.

31. M.

Butler and Analysis. Thucydides text, and history with Phillimore. rode with Mayow. wine with Lushington. Optics questions tried—read the last 400 l. of Prometheus Vinctus.

Tuesday Nov. 1.

Finished Thucydides B: 6. Worked at divinity. History of Thucydides with Phillimore. Butler Lecture and abstract. Walked—called on Maurice. Had some tea with Saunders.

2. W.

Gaskell came—had coffee with him at Angel—he afterwards spent a good deal of time with me. rode. Thucydides History. Butler abstract.—Ethics B.1 read through—& made a sort of abstract of an abstract.

3. Th.

Gaskell arranged to take his name off immediately—& took lodgings. Sey-

---

[1] Henry: see 3 Nov. 31.
[2] Henry Stormont Murray, 1812–63; gs. of 2nd earl of *Mansfield; barrister.
[3] Probably of his letter to Helen: see 23 Oct. 31.
[4] Probably Charles Miller, 1797?–1885, of Magdalen; vicar of Harlow, Essex, 1831.
[5] A. M. *Toplady, *The Scheme of Christian and Philosophical Necessity asserted* (1775).

mer Denison[1] & Acland all elected for All Souls—read Ethics B.2 & five Chapters of B.3.—went through my marks in the Persae—Hellenic History in Mitford &c—rode—had a delightful letter from my Father—Campbell's Rhetoric, on Evidence[2] &c.

4. Fr.

rode with Cunningham. spent most of the evening at Gaskell's rooms. wrote home. went through part of the Septem[3]—Ethics and abstract—Mitford on Ath[enian] & Lac[edaimonia]n constitutions, & Hellenic history.[4] finished.

5. Sat.

rode—'forgathered' with Herbert—worked hard to finish Ethics, of which I have read through 4½ books, parts of the others & their abstracts &c. Whately's Rhetoric—finished Septem. Livy odds & ends. Phillimore unwell.

6. Sunday.

a really idle day. Sacrament in mg—well attended—heard Burton in mg on 'Charity στέγει παντα'[5]—in evg Short on the meek inheriting the earth.[6] Bible. Paley's Evidences and Divers.

Monday 7 to Saturday 12.

In the schools or preparing—read most of Niebuhr—finished going over the Agamemnon—got up Aristophanic and other hard words—went over my books of extracts &c. read some of Whately's Rhetoric—got up a little Polybius—and the history out of Livy decade 1—In the schools Wed. Th. & Fr. each day about 6½ hours at work—or under. First—Strafford's Speech into Latin—with Logical & Rhetorical questions—the latter somewhat abstract—& wearying. Dined at Gaskell's—met Pearson: a clever & agreeable man.[7] On Th. a piece of Johnson's Preface in morng—in evg, critical questions, which I did very badly, but I afterwards heard better than *the rest*: which I could not & cannot understand. On Friday we had in morning historical questions—wrote a vast quantity of matter, ill enow digested— in evening, Greek to translate and illustrate.—Heard cheering accounts indirectly of myself: for which I ought to be very thankful. Wrote to T.G. —dined with Pearson at the Mitre—very kind in him to ask me—met Mackworth.[8] made Sat. in great measure an idle day—had a good ride with Gaskell—spent part of evg with him: read about 6 hours.[9]

---

[1] Henry.
[2] George *Campbell, *Philosophy of Rhetoric* (1776), i. 103–63.
[3] Aeschylus, *Seven against Thebes.*
[4] W. *Mitford, *The History of Greece*, 5v. (1784–1818), i. 192ff., 257ff.
[5] 'Endureth all things': 1 Cor. xiii. 7.   [6] Matt. v. 5.
[7] Possibly (Sir) Edwin Pearson, 1802–83; kt. 1836; F.R.S.
[8] William Harcourt Isham Mackworth(-Dolben), 1806–72; Westminster and Balliol; inherited a Northamptonshire estate in 1835; connexion of W. M. *Praed.
[9] Version in Morley, i. 77–78.

13. Sunday.

Chapel thrice. Breakfast & much conv. with Cameron—read Bible—some Divinity of a character approaching to cram—looked over my shorter abstract of Butler. Tea with Harrison. walk with Gaskell—wine with Hamilton: more of a party than I quite liked, or expected. Altogether my mind was in an unsatisfactory state, though I heard a most admirable sermon from Tyler on Bethesda,[1] which could not have been more appropriate if written on purpose for those who are going into the schools. But I am cold, timid, and worldly, and not in a healthy state of mind for the great trial of tomorrow: to which, I know, I am utterly & miserably unequal: But which I also know will be ruled for good. God grant that He who gave himself even for me may support me through it, if it be his will: but if I am covered with humiliation, O may I kiss the rod.[2]

14. M.

Spent the morning chiefly in looking over my Polybius, short Abstract of Ethics: and definitions—also some hard words. Went into the schools at ten, and from this time was little troubled with fear. Examined by Stocker[3] in divinity: I did not answer as I could have wished: Hampden[4] in science —a beautiful examination and with every circumstance in my favour: he said to me "thank you, you have construed extremely well, & appear to be thoroughly acquainted with your books", or something to that effect. Then followed a very clever examination in history from Garbett[5]—and an agreeable and short one in my poets from Cramer, who spoke very kindly to me at the close. I was only put on in eight books beside the Testament— namely, Rhetoric, Ethics, Phaedo, Herodotus, Thucydides, Odyssey, Aristophanes (Vespae), & Persius. Everything was in my favour: the examiners kind beyond any thing: a good many persons there, and all friendly—at the end of the science of course my spirits were much raised, and I could not help at that moment giving thanks inwardly to Him without whom not even such moderate performances would have been in my power.—Afterwards rode to Cuddesdon with the Denisons—and wrote home with exquisite pleasure. At Gaskell's—he & Brandreth had tea with me—paper—with Wordsworth in Evg.—partly talking about Lincoln.[6]

15. T.

Dearest Robn's birthday. God bless him evermore. An idle day with me:

[1] John v. 2.
[2] Version in Morley, i. 78, omitting last sentence.
[3] Charles William Stocker, 1794?–1870, vice-principal, St. Alban Hall, 1831–6; professor of moral philosophy 1841–2; rector of Draycot-le-Moors, Staffordshire, 1841.
[4] Renn Dickson *Hampden, 1793–1868; double first, 1813; fellow of Oriel, 1814–18; principal of St. Mary Hall 1833–48; violent opposition to his appointments as regius professor of divinity 1836, and bp. of Hereford 1847; exemplary in both posts. See 8 Mar. 36; 15, 22 Nov. 47.
[5] James *Garbett, 1802?–79, fellow of Brasenose 1825–36, professor of poetry 1842–52.
[6] Version in Morley, i. 78; omitting last sentence.

Stewart & Macintosh, and looking over passages previously written out—wine with Brandreth—rode—Doyle with me for some time.

16. Wed.

In morning, getting up Roman history: but on going into the schools, found a moral Essay on a very fine but very difficult subject.[1] Wrought hard for five hours, from 10 to 3—but how effectually I have not the least conception —sat with Wordsworth—& with Phillimore—had Brandreth, Lyall, Gaskell, to tea—putting matters in order.

17. Th.

Six hours in the Schools—with Latin prose, Greek verse, and Latin verse. My performances today by no means brilliant—though bulky enough. Close of the examination of my books.

I have been examined in	Not examined in
Butler	Hellenics
Phaedo	Livy
Rhetoric	Polybius.
Ethics	Select Orations.
Homer Iliad & Odyssey	Horace.
Virgil	Juvenal.
Persius	Æschylus
Aristophanes	Sophocles.
Herodotus	
Thucydides.	

I fear that unless they alter this, no one will get up his books—In evening, writing up Journal, putting my books away, &c. At debating society[2]—read a few pages of Lardner's vol. on Mechanics.[3]

18. 19. Frid. Sat.

Two very idle days—read a little Algebraic Geometry, in Powell[4] and Lardner. On Sat. dined with Gaskell—afterwards went to the Essay Soc.[5]—Had Cole, Ward, young Anstice,[6] & Dodds to breakfast. Wrote home.—On Friday wine & coffee with Harrison—afterwards sat and had tea with Lincoln, talking over his Cuddesdon plan & other matters.

20. Sunday.

Chapel mg & aft. Good sermons from Majendie—on Cholera—and Ball on

---

[1] Untraced.
[2] Triennial parliaments opposed, 61–8.
[3] D. *Lardner and H. *Kater, *Mechanics* (1830), in *Lardner's *Cabinet Cyclopædia*.
[4] [Baden *Powell] *Elements of Curves* (1828).
[5] Lushington on connexion between church and state; *Harrison on religion as foundation of political stability.
[6] Robert Richard, younger b. of Joseph, *Anstice; freshman at Christ Church.

"No man can come" &c.[1]—a good distinction between physical & moral inability. Gaskell had tea with me. Bible—Strype—Sumner's Lectures.

21. M.

heard Maurice—who they say will have his first: strange reports current about others. Rode with Jeffreys—had wine with him, & tea with Wordsworth. Alg[ebraic] Geometry & Lecture with Hill.

22. T.

heard from home. went to hear Phillimore's Divinity—also some of Paine.[2] Alg[ebraic] Geometry.—Conic Sections—Lardner's Mechanics—read corrected report of Ld Harrowby's Speech.[3]

23.

Alg[ebraic] Geometry: with Hill: Differential Calculus & Lardners (Cyclopædia) Mechanics. Phillimore up: did very well. rode.—Gaskell had tea with me. Some anxiety about H. D[enison].

24.

Mathematics—but much disturbed & excited. Rode. List out about 4½ P.M. Denison and I(!) in it. Also Payne, Cornish,[4] and Baugh. Phillimore and Maurice, I much regret to say, in the second. Chamberlain[5] in the third. Harris[6] & Herbert in the fourth. Wrote a long letter home. Phillimore came to see me in the evening, and heartily congratulated me: could I have done the same, if our circumstances had been reversed? how much he is my superior, even in his adverse circumstances. God help me.—Much kindness shown me by all.

25. Fr.

Breakfasted with young Bernard. a pleasant party. Business of various kinds. Wrote to Grimston. lunch with Gaskell. Rode to Cuddesdon with Bruce—to remain there for a fortnight. read Powell's Differential Calculus[7] in aftn & evg. Shook hands with Denison on his class.

---

[1] John vi. 44.

[2] Peter Samuel Henry Payne, 1810–41, don; fellow of Balliol 1831.

[3] H vii. 1145–76; see 3–8 Oct. 31.

[4] Charles Lewis Cornish, 1810?–70, fellow of Exeter 1830–41; vicar of Compton Dando near Bristol 1859.

[5] Thomas Chamberlain, 1810–92; vicar of St. Thomas's, Oxford, 1842; honorary canon of Christ Church, 1882.

[6] George Francis Robert *Harris, 1810–72; 3rd Baron Harris of Seringapatam 1845; governed Madras, 1854–9.

[7] Baden *Powell, A Short Treatise on . . . the Differential and Integral Calculus (1829).

26. Sat.

Rode with Denison—at Mathematics almost all the day—yet seemed to make less progress than ever. Lincoln & Canning met us & rode.

27. Sunday.

Oakley[1] preached for Prop[agation of] Gospel Society. walked, alone. Bible: teaching in the school a little: Chalmers's Evidences.[2] Lincoln & Canning dined here.

28–30. M–Wed.

Rode out with Denison every day, & spent this time with little interruption on the Calculus, Algebraic Geometry, Algebra, and Optics. Had letters from home—from Sir F. H. Doyle—& from Mr Denison: on the class, which got into the papers last week. Considering the slightness of my acquaintance, it was particularly kind [of] the latter to write.[3]

1–3. Th–Sat.

My work continued, and my reluctance to exertion increased with it.— Optics in Coddington & Brewster—Algebraic Geometry, Calculus, Trigonometry &c. wrote to J.N.G.—and to Pickering. rode every day with Denison & commonly met company on Bullingdon. Jeffreys came down on Saturday, in immense spirits; indeed none of us are below par. Most thankful should I be that all circumstances are favourable and there is no hindrance additional to those which must arise from my incapacity for the subject, of which I am more and more thoroughly convinced every day I read: I mean on comparing myself with Denison and Jeffreys. For them I have no misgivings but for myself God knows many: many as to the immediate success: none as to the ultimate issue.[4]

4. Sunday.

Teaching in the school morning and evg. Saunders preached well on "ye cannot serve God and Mammon".[5] Read Bible—& four of Horsley's Sermons.[6] Paid visits to old people—the Sanderses, the Bacons, and Hinton.[4]

Monday to Thursday.

remained still at Cuddesdon enjoying Saunders's kindness. Rode every day with Denison: commonly found company on Bullingdon. Read about ten

---

[1] Frederick *Oakeley, 1802–80; fellow of Balliol 1827; canon of Lichfield 1832; introduced ritualism at Margaret Street chapel, 1839–45; in that year seceded to Rome; Roman canon of Westminster 1852.
[2] T. *Chalmers, *The Evidence and Authority of the Christian Revelation* (1814).
[3] J. E. *Denison, the eldest b.; his f. had d. 1820.
[4] Extracts in Morley, i. 79.
[5] Matt. vi. 24 or Luke xvi. 13.
[6] S. *Horsley, *Sermons*, 2v. (1810).

hours daily in different branches of Mathematics. Hill came over to us for one evening. Greatly rejoiced when Thursday arrived—for such exertion is very irksome. We transported ourselves into Oxford and awaited the morrow. Wrote home.

Friday.

in the Schools six hours with two papers of Algebra & Geometry in wh I succeeded better than I had any right to expect—& yet it was nothing great. Examined vivâ voce by Powell.[1] Wine with Mayow. Read Wordsworth.

Sat.

Differential Calculus & Algebra papers: did the former but ill: the latter as well as any hitherto. Wine with Lyall. went to Tuckwell who prescribed me saline draughts to quiet me, my pulse being high and some excitement existing which hinders sleep. Read Wordsworth. Heard from J.N.G.

Sunday. Dec. 11.

God be praised for his day of rest. Chapel & Sermon morning & evening. Newman preached the latter; it was a most able discourse of a very philosophical character: more apt for reading than hearing. At least I in the jaded state of my mind, was unable to do it any justice. Tea with Harrison: & much conversation also with Lushington: some with Cunningham on himself. Also sat some time with Seymer & had lunch with him. Read Van Mildert's Charge:[2] and part of Sewell's address on the Cholera.[3] Also was with old Acland, and trying to raise some money for Mr Ridley's church. Wrote to my dear Father on his birthday: and to Mrs Charriere.[4]

12. M.

Cramming, between Chapel and the Schools. Had Differential Calculus & Hydrostatics. Did better than I expected in the latter, and worse in the former.—In the evening, had Lyall, Lushington, Cameron, Ryder, to tea: and did sundry matters of business. Also read some Optics and Mechanics.

13. T.

Same process repeated in the morning. Had Mechanics & Optics. Did but ill in the former: wretchedly in the latter. Went to see Mrs Charriere. Had the melancholy pleasure of reading some letters about the Bishop's happy

---

[1] Baden *Powell. The other examiners were A. P. Saunders and Robert Walker, 1802?–65, F.R.S., professor of experimental philosophy 1839.

[2] To the clergy of his diocese of Durham, on anomalies affecting church property and on the proper conduct of the clergy (1831).

[3] W. *Sewell 'An Address to a Christian Congregation on the Approach of the Cholera Morbus', a pamphlet on Ps. xci (1831).

[4] Extracts in Morley, i. 79.

and holy death. Wrote to J.N.G., to Wordsworth,[1] accepting a very kind invitation from his father—to Hallam, on his marriage.[2] Arranged to send off my mare. Walked with Bruce. Paying bills.

14. Wed.

Principia in the morning: considerably disappointed in my performances. Astronomy! (which I had crammed for about half an hour,) during a short time in aftn—then had the book shown me with my name in Classis I—and felt the joy of release. How much thankfulness was due, and how little paid!—It was an hour of thrilling happiness, between the past & the future, for the future was I hope not excluded: and feeling was well kept in check by the bustle of preparation for speedy departure. Saw the Dean, Biscoe, Saunders (whom I thanked for his extreme kindness) and such of my friends as were in Oxford—all most warm. The mutual handshaking between Denison, Jeffreys, & myself, was very hearty.[3] Wine with Bruce—met Douglas.[4] Settled many matters as far as was in my power—packed up my things— wrote at more or less length to Mrs G., Gaskell, Phillimore, Mr Denison, my old tutor Knapp, Sir F. Doyle, & Glynne. Had tea with Bruce—& left Oxford on the Champion.[5]

15.

After finding the first practicable coach for Cambridge, was just able to manage breakfast in Bedford Square. Left Holborn at 10—in Cambridge before five safe & sound thank God. Excellently lodged and most kindly received by the Master of Trinity[6] through my friend C. Wordsworth. At night endeavoured to find Hallam but failed.[7]

16. Fr.

Attended Service in Trinity Chapel, & heard Hallam recite his declamation.[8] Dined in Hall—introduced to Whewell[9] & Rothman[10]—& renewed my acquaintance with *old* Hallam.[11] I was under Wood's[12] kind auspices. In the Combination room after dinner. Then at Hallam's to tea & supper—

---

[1] In Charles *Wordsworth, *Annals*, 92–93; Lambeth MS 1823, ff. 90–91.
[2] *Hallam was betrothed to *Tennyson's sister Emily, but d. unm.
[3] All three had mathematical firsts.
[4] Perhaps Stair Douglas, 1802–74, canon of Chichester 1854.
[5] Coach to London. Extracts in Morley, i. 80.
[6] Christopher *Wordsworth, 1774–1846; wrangler; master 1820; and rector of Buxted with Uckfield, Sussex; f. of Charles* and Christopher* and b. of the poet.*
[7] Extracts in Morley, i. 80.
[8] Earlier in 1831 *Hallam had won a college essay prize of which the recipient was expected to deliver an oration upon another subject. See 4 Apr. 32.
[9] William *Whewell, 1794–1866; wrangler; Knightbridge professor of moral philosophy 1838–55; master of Trinity 1841, and benefactor.
[10] Richard Wellesley Rothman, 1798?–1856, fellow 1825; and registrar of university of London 1838.
[11] Henry *Hallam, a fellow-guest.
[12] A. C. Wood.

met his friends Blakesley,[1] Tennant,[2] Garden,[3] Menteith,[4] Spedding,[5] Tennant. read paper: lionised a little. read Malden's Lecture at London University: good, I thought, & bore very hard upon the principle of the institution.[6] Wrote home.

17. Sat.

Breakfast with Blakesley. Rode with him & Wordsworth, mounted on the Master's horse. Its owner I liked very much: there seems to be a high toned principle of religion about him. Had a very pleasant dinner party at the Lodge. Blakesley, Fitzherbert,[7] Wood, Hamilton, Pickering, Hallam were there. Continued lionising but on a small scale. Wrote a long letter to H.J.G.

18. Sunday.

This day I fear I reaped evil consequences from being without a home. Breakfast with Pickering. Went with Hallam to hear Mr Smith, a Millenarian—he preached much to my mind, & I trust well. Heard an University Sermon—& a beautiful anthem at King's—dined in Hall with Wood—introduced to Peacock,[8] also to Mr Webster[9]—afterwards at Grey's rooms: both the sons of Lord G. up here seem to be very agreeable men[10]—met Stanhope[11] an old Eton man. Heard the anthem in Trinity Chapel and *went* to hear Simeon[12]—but heard a man who seemed inferior, yet told me a truth I had not practically known—that there was much filthiness of the spirit. Read an M.S. sermon of Dr Wordsworth's & sundries similar. Saw Prof. Smyth.

19. Monday.

Breakfast with Martin[13] who was very kind to me. rode with Wood & Wordsworth. Dined at the Lodge—evening at Wood's, & supper—met the Greys, Cavendish,[14] Stanhope, Hallam, &c.—Hallam to my great joy

[1] Joseph Williams *Blakesley, 1808–85; wrangler and fellow 1831; vicar of Ware 1845; dean of Lincoln 1872.

[2] Robert John Tennant, 1809–42, Anglican minister at Florence.

[3] Francis *Garden, 1810–84; priest 1836; editor *Christian Remembrance* 1841; taught theology in London university from 1858.

[4] Perhaps Charles Granville Stuart Menteath, 1800–80, of Trinity; barrister.

[5] James *Spedding, 1808–81, scholar; edited *Bacon.

[6] H. *Malden's inaugural as professor of Greek (1831).

[7] Edward Herbert Fitzherbert, d. 1853; wrangler; fellow of Trinity 1830; barrister.

[8] Anthony Peacock, later Willson, 1812?–66, Lincolnshire gentleman.

[9] Thomas Webster, d. 1840; wrangler 1805; vicar of Oakington 1809, and rector of St. Botolph's, Cambridge, 1834.

[10] John, 1812–95, rector of Houghton-le-Spring 1836 and canon of Durham 1848; and Francis Richard, 1813–90, rector of Morpeth 1842 and canon of Durham 1863–82; 5th and 6th ss. of 2nd Earl *Grey.

[11] Charles Wyndham Stanhope, 1809–81, conservative; 7th earl of Harrington 1866.

[12] Charles *Simeon, 1759–1836, evangelical divine; fellow of King's and rector of Holy Trinity, Cambridge, 1782; founded Simeon Trust.

[13] Francis Martin, 1803?–68; fellow of Trinity 1825; vice-master 1862–6.

[14] (Lord) Richard Cavendish, 1812–73; b. of 7th duke of *Devonshire; styled lord 1858. See Add MS 44124.

invited a renewal of our correspondence—to my *very* great joy. I ought to be very thankful for it. Had a good deal of conversation with him. Bid my friends goodbye—much kindness have I met with in Cambridge—from no one more than Wood—copied a letter of Mr Pitt's.

20. Tuesday.

Travelled outside to Leicester. Had a pleasant companion, a Cambridge man who had many acquaintances in common with me, as far as Stamford.[1] Remained three hours in Leicester: had tea, read paper, & Wordsworth, and slept—got inside the Red Rover before eleven. Travelled all night.

21.

After a tedious but thank God a safe journey, arrived in Liverpool between 2 & 3 P.M. Greeted my Father, John, & Robn in town—rode Helen's mare to Seaforth, & with great joy completed the round of salutations. Mr Finlay still here—& on the whole in good spirits. Unpacked &c.

22–24.

Riding: in town: reading "Castle Dangerous".[2] Divers conversations with my Mother (Fasque) John (tour) and Helen (Metaph: Mir:). Mr Rawson called on me—I on him, & also on young Hulton[3] who is at Crosby.

25. Sunday.

Sacrament. T. & J. remained. Glad again to hear Mr Rawson. read Leighton on St Peter[4]—& began "Church of England & Dissent".[5]
On Thursday Mr Finlay went.
On Friday evening I saw poor old Pincher who at first did not know me, but seemed to do so afterwards: he died the same night: an old friend: & such it is always a pain, whether of greater or of less magnitude, to lose. I was sorry for him: how avaricious is the human heart in all its attachments, from the greatest down to the least. No abundance of friends can prevent one feeling the loss of one. The void closes more speedily: but it exists, and is felt. Much may perhaps be inferred from this as to the *indefinite power of expansion*, or capability of expansion, in the human sympathies. The more it has admitted, the more it can admit: and it embraces all with an intimate persuasion of the intercourse subsisting, therefore it doth not lose in fidelity what it gains in span, but is extended without limit.

26. M.

Finished Castle Dangerous. Though not devoid of interest, and exhibiting

---

[1] Forty miles NW. of Cambridge, and 25 east of Leicester.
[2] The last of *Scott's *Tales of my Landlord*, just published.
[3] William Ford Hulton, 1809?–79, saved diarist's life ca. 1818 (*Bolton Chronicle*, 12 November 1879).
[4] Abp. R. *Leighton, *A Commentary upon the First Epistle of St Peter* (1693).
[5] J. *Ballantyne, *Comparison of English and Dissenting Churches.* (2 ed. 1830).

in parts the original & proper power of its author, it indicates indeed a waning light. Mr & Mrs Grant came. A game at whist. In Liverpool, called on one or two persons.

27. T.

[Cousin] Robertson of Inches,[1] a singular person, dined here, with a pretty sister in law, Miss Paterson.[2] Read a little Hooker: finished "Church of England & Dissent"—music at night. Walk with J.N.G.—Much conversation with & most useful directions from Tom as to our intended tour. Paper.

28. W.

Wordsworth—Hooker—paper. Le Malade imaginaire[3] with John, reading aloud. Rode to town with him—saw my Uncle Rob[ert] & T. Finlay. Whist in evening.—And with this day ends the record of another year in my allotted term of discipline. Blessed be God for the mercies which have attended it.

29. Thursday.

Finished Le Malade Imaginaire with J.N.G. read Rogers (Italy)[4] and Hooker. Rode with T.G. & J.N.G. also walked with J.N.G. Made out as well as I could an inventory of clothes and books for the continent. Played cards for a short time in evg. Mr Blundell & Mr Silvertop dined here: the former in great force; the latter a highly finished man; my Mother laid up with one of her attacks, suffering as usual no small pain. Read Westminster Review on The Bill.[5]

The return of a birthday suggests much matter of severe and profitable thought. It invites me to examine the course of my life: and points significantly to its close. Looking back over the past year, I could indeed tell, amidst the recounting of numberless mercies, many of a very marked character, a melancholy tale of my own inward life: yet by the pain which such a retrospect *ought* to bring, my heart ought to be stimulated more powerfully towards the penitence and the faith which the Gospel requires.—In moral conduct, I would I could flatter myself there had been any improvement: there has been much matter for deep shame and humiliation—may it cut to the quick, and do its appointed and fruitful work. Industry of a kind, and for a time, there has been: but the industry of necessity not of principle. I would fain believe that my sentiments in religion have been somewhat enlarged and untrammelled, but if this be true, my responsibility is indeed augmented, but wherein have my deeds of duty been proportionably multiplied?

[1] S. of Joseph Robertson of Inshes.
[2] Sister of George Paterson of Castle Huntly, Dundee.
[3] Molière.
[4] Samuel *Rogers, *Italy* (1822, 1828; revised ed. 1830).
[5] xv. 149 (July 1831), on the reform bill in its second version, which the lords rejected in October.

Fearful things have passed in the world around me, and no small impression have they wrought within—may it issue for good! Old sentiments have been uprooted in some respects: more however matters of application than of principle. One conclusion, theoretically, has been much on my mind: it is, the increased importance and necessity and benefit of prayer—of the life of obedience and dependence and selfsacrifice. May God use me as a vessel for his own purposes, of whatever character and results in relation to myself. May I know now and ever that the Redeemer is still omnipotent to save them that call upon him: and even though the general deadness of my heart, the utter and odious deadness to things of highest concernment, & the blackness of my natural (& vigorous) tendencies might well strike despair in my soul, may the God who loves us all still vouchsafe me a testimony of his still abiding presence and still unexhausted longsuffering, in the protracted though well nigh dormant life of a desire which at times has risen high in my soul, a desire of higher aim than I could ever have imagined, a fervent and a buoyant hope that I might work an energetic work in this world, and by that work (whereof the worker is only God) I might grow into the image of the Redeemer. Would that I could feel in the particularity and clearness of detail all that these words imply! Would that feeling I might act accordingly. It matters not whether the sphere of duty be large or small —but may it be duly filled. May those faint and languishing embers be kindled by the breath of the everlasting Spirit into a living and a lifegiving flame, and with a heart and mind struggling continually upward, may I never, O never, leave the cross of Jesus Christ, nor forget its simplicity and power.

And not only am I bound to pray for the quickening of those loftier aspirations, but rather for the clearness of that coordinate perception, of greatest moment, that the will of God concerning me is to be found, and all the purposes of God through me are to be wrought or prepared for completion, by the patient and faithful resistance of ungodly will and appetite in the round of daily duty. Amen Blessed Lord! Amen.[1]

Friday. 30.

Wrote to Sir F.H. Doyle. In town. Called on Mrs MacCartney—Brandreth —& Molineux[2] to arrange for singing lessons. Read Westminster Review on Tory reaction. Rode my own mare, now sound, from town—at last. The Roses dined here. Read "Prospects from Tory reaction" and part of "Political Adventures" in the Westminster Review—Music.

Sat. 31.

heard from Gaskell. Called on Miss Benwell, Mrs Moss, Mrs Sandbach, Mrs Parker. read French with John: also with Tom. Cards in evening—paper— & writing in my notebook. Also singing & learning after a sort.

[1] Extracts in Morley, i. 83–84.
[2] John Molineux kept a music academy in Bold Street, Liverpool.

1832.

Sunday, Jan. 1.

Another year commenced, by the mercy of God, in prosperity, peace—and ingratitude.—An excellent opening to it in Mr Rawson's two Sermons, particularly the morning. Read some of Arnold's sermons & Hooker on Baptism.

2.

In town—called on Mr Jones—dined with T. Finlay. Copying, & unpacking crockery with J.N.G. most of the morng. Wrote to Canning and to Mr Hagart. Called on Mrs Myers[1] & Mrs Carson.[2] Practising some singing, alone.

3.

Copying. With Mrs Conway talking chiefly about her son.[3] In town—had a singing lesson from Molineux. Walked home. Read West. Rev. on Oxford.[4] Cards in Evg. Cousins Jesse & Susan here.[5]

4. Wednesday.

Went to Ince with J.N.G. to an early dinner—had much mixed conversation with Mr Blundell. Began "Pamela":[6] singing; & copied a letter. Cards.

5. Th.

Dined and slept at Uncle Robert's. Singing lesson—& reading Molineux's book.[7] Ed. Rev. on Westminster & Eton—and Pamela. Went to the Fawcett's Iron Foundry.[8] Cards.

6. Fr.

Miss Traill's came. Concocted a letter to the Albion, with Robert, on Paganini—hinting that he ought to give some of his money to the charities.[9] Sat two hours with Mr Jones. Finished Vol.1 of Pamela. read paper.

[1] Probably wife of William Myers of Ewart, Myers & Co, brokers.
[2] Probably Elizabeth Carson of Seaforth.   [3] See 11 Jan. 32.
[4] Probably xvi. 1 (January 1832), reviewing *Whately on *Political Economy*; but perhaps *Edinburgh Review*, liv. 478 (December 1831), a sharp attack.
[5] Hugh Gladstone's da. Janet Strong (Jessie), 1829–86, and James Gladstone's da. Susannah, 1816–44.
[6] Samuel *Richardson.   [7] Probably MS notes on voice production.
[8] Fawcett and Preston's Phoenix iron foundry, York Street, Edgehill.
[9] Niccolò Paganini, 1782–1840, violinist and composer. Letter untraced.

7. *Sat.*

In town. singing lesson. Pamela. The Miss Sandbaches came. Plenty of music—in which

> I did but little there below
> And did that little ill.

Sat up late writing a letter to my Father on my future profession.

8.

An unsatisfactory Sunday: but an excellent sermon from Mr Rawson on the signs of the times.[1] Did not contrive to read much. At night set to very late to complete my letter: finished it, but did by no means *complete* it.[2] Lucy Traill a "grig".[3]

9.

Began to pack the Library—with J.N.G.[4] Completed three boxes. Traills & Sandbaches departed. Pamela. Dined at Mr Grant's & went in the evening to hear Paganini whose mastery over his instrument is astonishing: & apparently over the feelings too when he chooses to exert it.

10.

Packing all the forenoon. Went into town with J.N.G. and had a singing lesson: had some conversation with Jones the bookbinder on political matters: interesting enough. In the evening read the papers: & an obituary on Bp Turner in Christian Observer:[5] went to bed early, having a bad cold.

11.

Still packing—got through five boxes, with J.N.G. who is a capital fellow workman. Out little, having still some cold. Sitting with Helen who is confined to bed with a bad attack of the same kind, but better. papers—singing —Had some conversation with John Conway, & gave him a Horace.

12. *Thursday.*

Packing in the forenoon. Singing lesson with Molineux: dined at the Town Hall, & had to return thanks for my health being drunk. Slept at Robn's. Wrote a note to Mr Jones. Called on Miss Maurice.

13. *Friday.*

Packing continued. paper. dined at Mr Staniforth's. Much pleased with young Swainson.[6] Pamela.

---

[1] Matt. xvi. 3.   [2] See 15–17 Jan. 32.
[3] Extravagantly lively.
[4] The family was preparing to move from Seaforth to Fasque.
[5] December 1831, 815–21.   [6] Unidentified.

14. Sat.

Dined at Dr Brandreth's—a large party, & an agreeable evening. Music lesson—called on Mrs Traill. read Pamela. Packing, in the early part of the day—Miss Benwell went. My mother better.

Looking at a very strange pamphlet by one "Francis Armstrong".[1]

15. Sunday.

Mr Legh of Newcastle preached morning & afternoon. Read some of Arnold's Sermons—and reconsidered what I wrote a week ago.

16. Monday.

Wrote to my Uncle Divie about his son: and to Gaskell. Occupied all the afternoon in hunting after little Ned—paper: read Mr Pilkington's curious pamphlet[2]—and at night again reperused and began to rewrite my letter.

17. T.

In town—called on Mr Bolton & the Brandreths. Singing lesson—Finished my letter:[3] gave it to my dear Father: and had the gratification, high indeed, of hearing from him, that it met his wishes and my dear Mother's. God be praised.

Finished Pamela Vol 2. Singing in the evening. Read Mr Scoresby's Journal—Extracts in the Mar. Ch. Report.[4] I cannot quite recognise their tone: God grant it be not from prejudice and a carnal heart.

18. Wednesday.

In town: inquiries about my place. Called on Mr Staniforth—on T. Ogilvy. Settling matters with Jones. Singing lesson. Read part of Walter's Letters from the Continent.[5] Tom went. Cards. My Mother very ill. Had some little conversation with her on yesterday's letter. Dear John's birthday. May the Everlasting God crown him with ten thousand mercies.

19. Thursday.

Read Cobbett's Regr of Jan. 7. very alarming.[6] paper. singing. Whist. My Mother better. Packing. Had a good deal of conversation with dear Helen; & found she felt a good deal the change in my plans. My thoughts being thus turned upon the subject, soon showed themselves not to be at rest: there is a weight of responsibility which I cannot support: a dread of self-

[1] The Trumpet of Armageddon (1820), masonic and chiliastic.
[2] G. Pilkington, 'The Unknown Tongues discovered to be English, Spanish, and Latin', an anti-Irvingite pamphlet (1831).
[3] Summary in Morley, i. 82–83: settled on public life.
[4] William *Scoresby, Journal of a Voyage to the Northern Whale Fishery (1823); he was chaplain of the mariners' church, Liverpool, 1827–32.
[5] Weever Walter, Letters from the Continent (1828).
[6] *Cobbett's Weekly Political Register advocated abolition of sinecures.

deception which I cannot escape from: a fear lest under specious names I should have veiled to myself a desertion of the most High God. May he by his Spirit help me: may he build me up in his faith and truth: and so dispose of this worthless vessel, that it may show forth his glory. O may he help me! Thus much I do trust: that at the very bottom of my soul, a more inward feeling than all my vanity, lies a sense of destitution: of utter destitution: for more whither shall I look except to his changeless love? He knows my soul is sore beset: though doubtless by my own accursed back-slidings. O may they be repaired, and so the light of His countenance shine upon me again.

What a confession is mine! that after all my anxiety (perhaps because it was carnal) I have come to a decision, & am utterly ignorant not only of the goodness of the decision, but of the purity of the motive! How helpless, & how degrading! Yet there is an ample hope, though one by me often profaned. Jesus Christ is still and for ever *Wisdom* and righteousness & sanctification & redemption.

Friday.

Packing &c. called on the Rawsons—had much conversation with my dear Mother on future matters—and took a really melancholy leave of old Seaforth. The recollection of it will be associated with that of many objects and circumstances dear indeed to us all. May God rule our leaving it for good to every one.

Went to Manchester by Railway. Read the Globe—full of combustibles —;[1] had tea: read Wordsworth, my pocket companion—& left for Birmingham by Mail. Travelled all night.

Sat.

Got on by Triumph. In Oxford between two & three. Seeing friends—began to pack books in paper at night. Dined at the master's table & went to the Common Room.

22. Sunday.

Gilbert[2] & Newman at St Mary's: the latter very able indeed.[3] At the Common Room. read Strype's Cranmer[4]—&c. Young Acland sat with me. Had tea and talked with Saunders: on matters on which I knew I ought not. Alas! for my unchristian sabbaths. Wrote home.

23. M.

Packing books: did four boxes. In no small confusion. Breakfast with

---

[1] The *Globe*, a London daily, strongly favoured the reform bill.
[2] Ashurst Turner *Gilbert, 1786–1870; principal of Brasenose 1822; bp. of Chichester 1842.
[3] Version in Morley, i. 86.
[4] John *Strype, *Memorials of Abp. *Cranmer* (1694). Notes in Add MS 44722, ff. 23–26.

Mayow. Young Acland with me to tea. Wrote to Tom. Called on Mrs Charriere.

24. T.

Packing still continued: in utter confusion. Called on Jacobson—paying Bills &c. &c. as yesterday. Wine with Hope: tea with Wood, and a conversation too long for my immediate occasions, though not for my inclinations. Also with Saunders: found from him a fact regarding the Mathematical Schools which surprised me very much: & was pleasing as far as it went.

25. W.

Almost finished my packing labours, of which I have had quite a satiety. Breakfast with S. Denison after surplice prayers. Saw W. Harris and J. Wishlade: the latter very ill. Wine with Mayow. Tea with Tupper. Also with Biscoe and Saunders in evening. Both extremely kind: wrote home: and to Selwyn. Heard from T.G.—Obliged to relinquish a plan I had vaguely conceived of visiting Eton, on account of time.

26. Th.

Read, or heard read, the Articles—and took my Bachelor's degree: also had numberless other matters to settle. Breakfast with Hewitt—lunch with Tupper—thirds,[1] bills, boxes, degree, epistles, farewells, all burst upon me en masse.

Got off by the Triumph: Bruce & Phillimore escorted me to the coach when I bid them farewell. Arrived in town about ten $\frac{1}{2}$. At Burlington.[2]

27 Friday to 31 Tuesday.

Days spent in a miscellaneous manner—calling on relatives; also on Ld Sandon,[3] Sir R. Inglis, Mr Backhouse:[4] writing letters: dining at Uncle D's, also Colin Mackenzie's,[5] and the Albany:[6] arranging money matters &c: & providing articles connected with our journey, occupied these days, at least the weekdays.

On Sunday heard Mr Ward & Bp of London.[7] Breakf with Andrew:[8] dined in Bedford Sq.

And now let me pause for a moment on the eve of departure, to offer my unworthy prayer, that in whatsoever country we may be, God himself may be our guide, and may direct our path so as shall most effectually conduce to the fulfilment of his purposes in us.

[1] Payment for furniture in college rooms.
[2] Burlington Hotel, Old Burlington Street.
[3] Dudley *Ryder, 1798–1882, Viscount Sandon 1803; double first 1819; 2nd earl of Harrowby 1847; protestant conservative; M.P. for Liverpool 1831–47; lord privy seal 1855–7.
[4] John Backhouse, 1783?–1845; permanent under-secretary, foreign office, 1817.
[5] Colin Mackenzie of Portmore, 1775?–1835.   [6] Where his b. Thomas lived.
[7] *Blomfield.   [8] Cousin Andrew Robertson.

[Entries for the next six months are from Add MS 44818 A unless otherwise specified.]

1832

Feb. 1.[1]

We left London with military precision almost as the clock struck twelve on the night of the 31st January: so our tour and the succeeding month of February came into the world almost simultaneously: it is to be hoped that the former will be the longer liver of the two.

Arrived at Dover about 10½ a.m.; and was detained, with the Ostend packet, upwards of three hours more, waiting for the results of Lord Palmerston's negociations: a strong proof of his incompetency to conduct the affairs of the country, that he should have kept us waiting thus long. Employed in "cramming" French phrases, and in dismal presages of sea-sickness.—When we did start for Ostend, if the steamboat were deep, it was not with the weight of the Ratifications obtained at the momentous meeting of last night.[2]

We left the white cliffs, which present to the good folks over the way a front of becoming reserve and almost of menace, and pursued our way rapidly in the Salamander,[3] Commander Lieut. Watson R.N., a fastsailing steampacket, with a fair wind and a degree of swell I fancy moderate enough, but quite enough to unsettle my affairs.—I attempted the use of a remedy which had been suggested to me—the adoption of a completely horizontal position—lying on a bench with nothing under my head. And I think this would certainly have succeeded, had I not left my post, compelled mainly by the cold. We made the passage, about 61 miles, in seven hours, with the tide against us almost all the way. Could not walk the deck.

Much trouble at Ostend, first in getting what a Belgian porter called "primmets" and other people call "permits" to release our luggage before morning: and then in using them. The examination at the Customhouse was sufficiently slight—but the porters attempted a monstrous imposition, in a charge of twelve francs for carrying up our own & our servant's luggage —and succeeded in a decent one—of eight & a half.

Slept at the Cour Imperiale: a cheap inn, and a comfortable one as far as beds were concerned, though the appearance of the coffeeroom was not promising.

[1] Late entries till 20 Feb 32.

[2] On 31 January 1832 the British and French governments exchanged ratifications of the treaty of 15 November 1831 from which Belgian independence stemmed (see *BFSP* xix. 92–93, 1413–14). Henry John *Temple, 1784–1865, 3rd Viscount Palmerston 1802 (M.P. 1807–34, 1835–65; tory minister 1807–28; foreign secretary 1830–4, 1835–41, 1846–51; home secretary 1852–5; prime minister 1855–8, 1859–65), presided at the great powers' London conferences on the Belgian question, 1830–9. See Add MSS 44271–3.

[3] Salamander [4], plying between Woolwich, Dover, and Ostend; still on her trials.

Feb. 2. Thursday.

Before leaving by the Diligence at 7. a.m., set out on an expedition to recover a small packet of John's from the Steamboat—and had very nearly
lost myself into the bargain.

Service was going on in the Catholic Chapel at the early hour of 6½
a.m.

The harbour of Ostend consists of a very long narrow slip, completely
sheltered. Buonaparte intended to have made great use of it in invading
England. The town is strongly fortified.

Passed through Bruges to Ghent. Distance 13 leagues, or near 40 miles.
Time about seven hours and a half. Country richly cultivated & extremely
populous. Pavè good but rather narrow. Diligence comfortable inside: an
enormous load for three horses. We at first thought that such could only be
practicable on a dead level, such as Flanders is from Ostend to Antwerp.
But we afterwards found that equally great feats were performed on the
other side of Brussels & in France.

Dined at the Hotel de Vienne: upon a great variety of dishes: at two
francs a head!

We remained at Ghent until 11 at night. In the interval, we saw the
Cathedral, and the Church[1] nearly over against our hotel: both very lofty
and imposing: both, particularly the former, adorned with a profusion of
rich marbles. In both, sermons in the Dutch language were being delivered:
with no small animation of manner on the part of the preacher. The pulpits
were rich beyond anything I had ever seen: of carved wood, in devices. The
Netherlands I believe are celebrated for such.

We saw a procession march through the streets, with the Host, to a sick
person's house: the men had their hats off: some of them, and all the women,
on their knees. We gazed without affronting them from the window. There
is something beautiful even in exterior devotion: let us hope that there was
more even true worship, offered in sincerity though not in knowledge. In
those who were more immediately concerned, there was not much appearance, I thought, of solemnity.

As to the images and dresses of the Blessed Virgin which we saw here and
elsewhere, to speak of them in point of *taste*, I should characterise them as
coarsely conceived and tawdrily executed.

This is not the place formally to discuss those other and graver charges
which have been brought against the worship of the Virgin Mary—and
against the worship of images in general.

One or two superficial remarks however may be made.

If I enter a temple decorated with images, and behold one image more
prominent than all the rest, in magnitude, in position, in the attention
directed towards it: I naturally conceive it to represent the deity of the place:
and other images less conspicuous, I readily take it for granted, belong to
his or her satellites. What conclusion then are we to form, when we enter
the temple of Jesus Christ, and (omitting for the present the general ques-

[1] of St. Nicholas.

tion of image worship) find that the Virgin is the prominent figure of the place, and the Saviour represented as an infant *in her hand*?

Secondly. If we grant that the form of Jesus ought to be kept thus visibly placed before the eyes of worshippers, still is there not a manifest incongruity in this systematic choice of his *infant* age? The ideas most closely connected with the destination of the building are those of his Atonement firstly, and secondly of his spotless righteousness of life: whereof the one is in no way connected with his childhood, and the other very indirectly. It was as man—in the full development of his human character—that he served, and that he suffered. The innocence of his childhood did not necessarily involve subsequent spotlessness: nor would the obedience of a child, who is under tuition, be the voluntary and justifying obedience which was necessarily required from him: because there would not be the same power of temptation on the one hand: nor the same strictly human exercise of will on the other. Hence we have no detail in Scripture of our Saviour's early life: and hence our Church with Scriptural exactitude commences its pleadings with His "Baptism, Fasting, and Temptation"—no earlier: since it was from the first of these that his especial commission took its date. Why then does the Church of Rome on the (false) plea of raising our souls to the contemplation of him who is removed beyond the reach of our senses, choose to represent him that character wherein he is least of all connected with those whom He had died to save? And why, in the very place where He is to be worshipped as God and Jehovah, does she exhibit Him as a child and a pupil?

To any exhibition of our Saviour under his human form, intended to assist us in worshipping him, there seems to be this objection, that he is not worshipped as man but more properly as God.

Again. If our minds cannot be raised to the contemplation of a *human* being in the other world, without the intervention of an image, much more must the *difficulty* be felt in realising the notion of God who is a spirit only: therefore the Church of Rome must confess a great defect in her means, if she can only supply aid to the mind for what is *less* difficult, and leave it unassisted in what is more so.

Lastly: as a question of metaphysical fact, I much doubt,[1] whether the exhibition of an image be calculated to answer the proposed professed purpose, *in* the act of worship.

For it is professed, that the image is to be to the mind a *step* between earth and heaven. There is then *another* step to make in order to the act of worship: and the whole use of an image is in its very nature *preparatory*.

To explain: what I mean is this. The image conveys to the mind, & paints in it, the *copy* of a sensible object. As long as the outward attention is on the image, so long its whole power and effect tends to keep the *mental eye* fastened on the *mental image* aforesaid. But, this mental image is *not* the true and very substance, which ought to be present to the mind *in* worship. That is wholly incorporeal and without material form. Now I appeal to the

---

[1] The diarist underlined in pencil 'I much doubt', and added in the margin: 'these arguments very open to exception WEG better in p. 38, 9 [i.e. 28 Feb. 32], but not well'.

testimony of every man for a *fact* which he will observe as taking place in the workings of his mind—and this fact is, that in order to fix the mental eye where indeed it ought to rest, you require a *distinct* and substantive effort, and you summon to your aid a new faculty, and transport your view into a new region—you leave the province of all perceptions founded upon sense: you are compelled to tear your mind altogether away from sense, and fix it upon *substance* considered apart from *sense*, and strive to realise this idea. And not small is the exertion required: surely it is incompatible with the full & *simultaneous* action of the mind in that kind of worship which has been characterised as strictly appropriate.

The truth is that it is exceedingly difficult to realise such an idea—but surely there is no course more philosophically unsound, or more practically dangerous, than to introduce, in the very moment of worship, a perception which hangs upon it and encumbers it like a dead weight.

Now it may perhaps seem, that when made strictly preparatory, and confined as it were to the vestibule of the sanctuary, sensible representations may have their use, and may[1] advance us a little nearer, and give us as it were a vantage ground from which to make our spring upwards.

But much more ought to be written on this subject, and by abler hands.—

The portico in front of the University of Ghent is very fine: and the town altogether affords a very excellent specimen of the ancient style.—public library. Ascend Cath. tower.[2]

The appearance of the peasantry is healthy and favourable—particularly that of the women about Bruges.

I know not whether the spirit of devotion supposed to possess the lower orders of R. Catholics be very general or not. The waiter at the Inn in Ghent said he had not been to Church above four times in his life—and another person afterwards in Paris, while showing a Church, incidentally told me that the number of commandments was seven.

I observed here and elsewhere that the Continental women eat much more ravenously than those of our own country—comparing of course those in the same rank of life.

We left Ghent by diligence at 11 a.m. choosing this hour chiefly on the recommendation of Mr. Hamilton a fellowtraveller who seemed disposed to pay us attention.

At the end of the first stage we had a specimen of Continental coach-travelling. The horses to go on were not ready—and all the people of the poste aux chevaux in the arms of Morpheus: lenibant curas & corda oblita laborum.[3] The postillion stood tapping at intervals upon the gate, with uninterrupted patience—not I presume the patience of effort, but of indifference. Meantime he was stimulated in his persevering course by cries from the *dilly* of "frappez, mon ami!" "Vous ne frappez point du tout!" "Il faut remettre les chevaux!" "Il faut tirer la diligence vousmême!" &c. &c.

---

[1] 'prepare and' deleted.
[2] Slight change of hand indicates break in entry here.
[3] Virgil, *Aeneid*, iv. 528: 'their hearts forgetful of their toils, they were soothing their cares' [in sleep].

However we made out the customary rate of five miles an hour—and after some waiting, we embarked in a boat Friday. Feb. 3. and found ourselves gliding quietly over the bosom of the Scheldt, a river here I should think near twice as wide as the Thames at London. We passed under the Dutch guns: saw the Dutch and Belgian sentries within two or three yards of each other—but with a good wall between[1]—landed at Antwerp and—took up our quarters at the best Inn, the Hotel de St. Antoine: very comfortable—expensive in fire: like others without redeeming points.

John and I breakfasted in company with a fellow traveller from whom we learned that he was a clergyman, and had been at Oxford—together with diverse particulars of his private affairs: a man apparently by no means void of talent.[2] We commenced lionising after breakfast, under the guidance of a commissioner, who got four francs for his pains. He was a staunch revolutionist, and maintained that the Belgian army would beat twice its number of Dutch in the field. Others of the common people with whom we came in contact were indifferent, and even friendly to the prince of Orange,[3] declaring that the revolution was a great misfortune to the country in so many words.

The chief matters we saw were 1. The fortifications. It was an extremely interesting, though a partial view of the lines which the Belgians have drawn.[4] The Dutch have flooded the country opposite Antwerp—and hold a fort opposite it, as well as the citadel to the South: they have too gunboats moored in the river. The Belgians have barricades in the streets: batteries opposite the fort: and counterfortifications under the citadel—but they are very jealous, and would show but little. A Belgian sentinel heard my brother speaking of the calibre of the guns—he shouted in a monstrous passion "Passez de vos chemins"! We did not clearly hear his words, and laughed at his blustering manner, or at least smiled: he repeated in a supererogatory passion, "Mon Dieu! passez de vos chemins!" and laid his hand on his firelock. So much for this "brave Belge".

We saw the artillerymen exercising with their cannon at the batteries: under every human likelihood that they would be summoned to exercise in earnest in a short period—and with no great presumption, then, against their being called upon to do so in a few days: the muzzles of the Dutch guns lay immediately opposite, and we saw their sentries distinctly.

Trade seemed well nigh dead in the city—there were no goods on the quays, excepting only in one place some hundred or two of casks of wine. Through the town, there were an immense number of houses to let: (we saw in Brussels a still greater proportion:) in one row, along the river and opposite the guns of the Dutch fort, it was partly ludicrous and partly

[1] The kingdom of the Netherlands established in 1815 included Belgium, which revolted in August 1830. Till December 1832 a Dutch force under general D. H. Chassé, 1765–1849, held the citadel of Antwerp, and occasionally bombarded the town.

[2] Joseph Berry King of Soho, b. 1804?; at Exeter College Oxford 1822–6.

[3] William, 1792–1849; commanded Dutch forces in civil war; king of the Netherlands in 1840, when his f., William I, 1772–1843, abdicated.

[4] A small sketch-map shows Antwerp, with Ghent to the WSW., the cities linked by a dotted line. The citadel is shown to the south of Antwerp, on the same side of the river; a Dutch fort is shown opposite Antwerp on the western bank.

melancholy to observe in I think every one "Maison a louer ou a vendre presentement", and "Een huys te hueren terstond"—which it required no great degree of skill to interpret without a knowledge of Dutch.

Neither here nor elsewhere did we think much of the evolutions of the Belgian troops: they were slovenly enough: and sometimes one might detect a man changing his feet to recover step. We were told there were 10,000 or 12,000 soldiers in the place.

2. The cathedral: a very extensive building: length 400–500 feet & breadth I think 200—in round numbers. An immense organ—disappointed in the sound. A good many worshippers. The altars numerous: many paintings: a profusion of marble: pulpits here and in the other churches sumptuously carved, as at Ghent. The tower is exceedingly lofty and beautiful: we could not ascend on account of its being now used as post of military observation.

3. Church of St. Jacques. Marble and altars as before—beautiful paintings, by Rubens, Van dyck, Van Homrigh, and others. The dead body of our Saviour on the cross by Vandyck was exquisitely true and fine.

4. Church of St. Dominique[1] or Le Predicateur. Splendid picture of the scourging of our Saviour by Rubens—and copy by Vandyck. The former preferable, in my mind, as being far more true.

These Flemish churches are extraordinary structures and well deserving attention.

5 Hotel de Ville—front very much wrought.

6. *Museum*—once a convent—grave of P.P. Rubens.[2]—Among many pictures, one by that great artist, entitled, Le Sauveur mort dans les bras *de son Pere*: a picture, I thought, so faulty in design, as to be irredeemable by any excellence of execution. To represent the paternal relation, where there is manhood on the side of the son, there must be a degree of age on the side of the father: and from this it is perhaps impossible to sever the notion of decrepitude and decay. Besides which, it involves the idea of priority and posteriority in time, where time has no place: and these incongruities were so strong as in my mind to overpower the impression from the power of the artist.

Dined, sumptuously according to an Englishman's notions, at the Hotel de St. Antoine—with our fellowtraveller Berry King.—

Saturday Feb. 4.

Left Antwerp at 8¼ A.M. Arrived at Brussels about one P.M. Passed a beautiful church at Mechlin.[3] One incident occurred well worthy of commemoration: our Diligence, under the influence of the spirit of opposition, changed its pair of horses in about a minute and a half!—Be it remembered however in extenuation of this extraordinary feat, that the harness consists only of bridle & reins, collar, backstrap, and traces—all alike rude: the two latter do not change at the commencement of a stage, and are attached to the collar with hooks only.

[1] St. Paul, formerly belonging to adjoining Dominican monastery.
[2] But Rubens was buried in St. Jacques.
[3] Malines, 14 miles south of Antwerp.

Brussels, Hotel de Suéde. We found this house both very good and very reasonable—sent there by Tom's recommendation.

Left our letter for Sir R. Adair[1]—also for Mr. Weston.[2] Called on Campenhowt about the carriage. Dined at the table d'hôte; exceeding plentiful; for two francs a head!

Sunday Feb. 5.

Having seen in the coffee room announcements of *two* English services, we set out in the morning for one, and, to our annoyance, found the church was now shut, only just in time to enable us, after another long hunt, to come in for part of Mr. Drury's[3] sermon at the other, in the Rue de l'Orangerie.

Congregation small—but it is to be expected, according to the accounts we hear, that the English have almost all been driven out of Brussels by the Revolution—Communicants about 22.—Returned in the afternoon—congregation miserable: and *this* cannot be accounted for by any reason equally unexceptionable.

Dinner in our room: a mode about twice as expensive as the other, or more so.—Had some reading.—Inklings of bile, remaining from my half stifled seasickness.

Brussels is exceedingly full of beggars—and great indigence is stated to prevail. There are symptoms enough of motion, on the road between this city and Antwerp—we met I think eight diligence.

Ghent and Antwerp contain 60 or 70,000 persons—Brussels more.

On this Sunday we went into the Cathedral, while low mass was in the course of celebration. There were a great many people with books: ringing of bells, and motions of a priest with one or two satellites about the altar—this I believe was all: and to me I confess it was an unmeaning and sorrowful ceremony.

Afterwards several thousands of Belgian troops were marched in and completely filled, standing, the body of the cathedral & the aisles: it must have been a fine *coup d' œil* from a commanding station, as their numbers were I suppose *at least* 5000.—The men were small—for both John and I could see over the heads of the whole mass with ease. Read a very good sermon of Mr. Blunt's on "the Sabbath"—&c.[4]

Sunday Feb. 5. at Brussels.[5]

While our ordinary transactions are committed to my journal, it may still be desirable to keep in this private record some occasional notices of that inner life which is should always be our first care to tend.

This day, being somewhat disordered with the remains of my sea-sick-

[1] Robert *Adair, 1763–1855; diplomat; friend of *Fox; K.C.B. 1809; 1831–5 engaged on a special mission to the Low Countries.

[2] See 6 Feb. 32.

[3] W. J. J. Drury, 1792–1878; chaplain to the King of the Belgians, and of the English Chapel at Brussels, 1829.

[4] Henry *Blunt, *The Lord's Day* (1832).

[5] This entry from Lambeth MS 1420.

ness, I was rather depressed in spirits: but hypocritically endeavoured to persuade myself and John, that it was the result of general uneasiness as to the manner in which my Sundays had been spent: and their grievous incongruity with that tenor of occupation and of thought which ought to mark this holy season.

It was however then, as indeed it has long been, a subject of much anxiety, though perhaps of a morbid and unfruitful kind, because coupled with an irresolute & worldly mind.

Another thought lay very heavy on my heart: it was the harrowing fear lest, in the steps which have lately been determined on in reference to myself, I should have betrayed the cause of God to my worldly ambition, and sold even the cross of Christ for the love of earth and the things of earth. My conscience is indeed unsatisfied. I should have more, far more confidence in reference to that subject, were I not conscious of my great offences against God, and sinfulness, in other respects: for the Most High will not hear the prayers which proceed from unclean lips.[1]

Would to God that as the Persian king had one to remind him daily of his projected vengeance against Athens, so a voice from heaven might continually ring in my ears, or a hand from heaven might seem to write on the wall before mine eyes, those words of Scripture, so awfully and deeply true "Love not the world, neither the things that are in in the world: for the friendship of the world is enmity with God".[2] And I pray that those who are near and dear to me, and have a clear-seeing concern for my best interests, may be enabled to open before mine eyes the path of duty, by shedding upon it the beacon-light of the will of God.

Monday Feb. 6.

Endeavoured to overcome my menaces of bile by lionising—but with very little success.

We went to Campenhowt's, where John settled for the carriage—which Campenhowt assured us was in excellent travelling condition. We went to the Chamber of Representatives, a very appropriate place of assembly, like the French Chamber which we saw afterwards. Also to that of the Senate, or "Ancients" as they are called which was a handsome room—the only question is, whether it is not wasted in its present application.

The park is fine: with statuary intermitted among the trees—which have been much injured by the firing of the Revolution.[3] We went through the apartments which suffered most in the Belle Vue Hotel,[4] and the cellar where the English remained—also to the Boulevards where the troops were exercising. It is said that King Leopold[5] has taken great pains in organising

[1] Cp. Isa. vi. 5.
[2] John ii. 15; Jas. iv. 4.
[3] From 23 to 26 September 1830, the park was a principal scene of conflict: it was occupied by the Dutch, while the Belgians advanced from the Place Royale, a hundred yards to the SW.
[4] An hotel in the Place Royale.
[5] Leopold of Saxe-Coburg, 1790–1865; b. of *Victoria's mother; m. 1816 *Charlotte, only child of *George IV, who d. 1817; refused crown of Greece, 1830; elected king of Belgians 1831.

them: and that he is much affected by the recent loss of General Belliard,[1] on this as well as on other accounts. Everyone speaks favourably of him as an individual: but shakes his head when you speak of the security of the tenure by which he holds his throne.

We saw Mr W[esto]n, a person I fancy of most respectable station, who told us in terms sufficiently intelligible, that he was, in consequence of the Revolution, bankrupt!

The front of the Hotel de Ville excells that at Ghent—and has a fine tower as well as a rich front. We saw a Church[2] by the Belle Vue—in middling taste within, handsome without. I say in middling taste, because it seemed liable to the same charge with some French works, of gilding even to tawdriness.—Read the English papers at Ewbank's readingroom.— John went to an opera in the evening. I was unwell and very glad to go to bed.

Tuesday Feb. 7.

I remained in bed all day, & physicked myself. Saw Dr. Tobin, an English (or Irish) resident physician and found myself getting round in the evening. —John took advantage of an order which I could not, and went to see the Prince of Orange's palace,[3] which he reported to be extremely beautiful.

Dr. Tobin liked the Revolution as ill as anyone, and said that half the army would not fight against the Dutch, in case of the war breaking out.

Wednesday Feb 8.

Tried a journey to Waterloo in a rough cab to ease my stomach—it succeeded à merveille. It is about ten miles distant from Brussels: the road pavé: and the jolt on the frame of the cab from the ascent and descent of the curve of each individual stone was transmitted to our persons with scrupulous fidelity on the part of the springs ('if springs they might be called which springs were none') of said cab. Forest of Soin for three or four miles of the road.[4]

We had a "commissioner" to guide us over the field so full of interest to Englishmen and to the world. He showed us the different monuments— the points to which the lines reached—the place where the Duke stood— where Sir Thomas Picton[5] fell—where 4000 Prussians were buried—and where the Guards lay sheltered previous to their last and decisive charge.

We ascended the monument erected by the King of Holland—an immense mound of earth 200 feet high, with a lion on the top. The design

[1] Auguste-Daniel Belliard, 1769–1832; French count and general, ambassador at the newly constituted court of Belgium, 1831–2.

[2] St. Jacques sur Caudenberg.

[3] Palais Ducal, erected at national expense and presented to the prince, afterwards William II, in 1829. After the revolution it became the property of the Belgian government.

[4] The Forêt de Soignes lies between Brussels and the village of Waterloo 8 miles south of the city.

[5] Sir Thomas *Picton, b. 1758, lieut-general; fought in peninsula, 1810–4; killed leading a charge, 18 June 1815.

is simple: and it has been executed in a manner to render it as imposing and conspicuous as it ought to be.

The sight of this field, especially under the present aspect of circumstances, suggests many recollections of an overwhelming interest. How dearly the honours and the benefits of that field were brought: and how does the very grandeur of the victory itself bear a melancholy witness to the intensity of the struggle. If indeed that battle were fought in a wrong cause, how painful has been our guilt: if in a right one, and if in accordance with the commands of God, yet with how much alloy of baser motives has the great enterprise been prosecuted! Yet after all, if the cause were good, this is indeed a spot where an Englishman's heart should beat high with exultation.

But what if the tide of our national destiny is turned, and if we are now about to go hand in hand with those alien principles, against which we once waged an implacable war? God forbid, and direct all for good. And indeed in the grand division of continental parties, it is very much easier to predicate evil of one side, than good of the other. It may be painful to see Church Establishments overthrown—but who would wish for the renewal of the Empire of Popery in all its pride? It may shock our feelings to see the kingly office first misunderstood and misdefined, and then degraded, yet who can say that the ancient despotism was a wholesome government for France?

We saw the Church, with the monuments of those who fell: in them there was much to feel yet something of omission to regret. We saw the Church-yard, and the place of the graves of 400 soldiers; also Lord Anglesea's boot and the spot where his leg lies.

On returning to Brussels, being tolerably convalescent, I was ready to set out. Accordingly we started for Mons[1] about two, in the carriage which my brothers used. Some hill—but the country did not deserve to be called picturesque.—We and our Brussels landlady parted with mutual satisfaction. Our horses carried a number of bells, and the postillions cracked their whips for us as lustily as if we had been travellers of the first water. Country very populous. We made out our seven postes to Mons in about five hours.

Mons, Hotel de la Couronne. A very good house: the waiter much inclined to the Dutch: complained of few guests and an empty stomach since the revolution, and was not duly alive to the value of political regeneration. The town strongly fortified: celebrated for a siege by the Duke of Marlborough.[2] There is a cathedral. Slept here.

Thursday Feb. 9.

Left Mons about eight, in a very thick fog. It continued till we had got some distance past Valenciennes.[3] Passed through the French custom-house without much difficulty. Before our entering Valenciennes, a parcel of

---

[1] Belgian town 32 miles SW. of Brussels.
[2] Who captured it in 1709.
[3] French town 20 miles west of Mons and 18 NE. of Cambrai.

fellows came out and felt the pockets of one illstarred postillion for contraband goods—they succeeded, after well rummaging his person, in extracting two packets of snuff, which they at once carried off, apparently for their own especial benefit. The postillion apparently stupified by misfortune, nearly drove us against a post in making our entry. Valenciennes is a good large town, ugly and dirty enough: fortified.

As we entered Belgium under cover of the night, so we left it in a dense fog—no inapt type of certain negotiations and ratifications. We passed through Cambray,[1] strongly fortified, to Peronne:[2] a day's journey of about fourteen postes. We got a hasty cold repast at Cambray: for such things as these they make *ample* charges on the continent.

Peronne. Our Inn had the impudence to call itself the Hotel d'Angleterre. It was indifferent, to say the best: and almost as dear as the very best: i.e. considering the difference of things, much dearer. It appears to be a general rule for the continent, to avoid inferior country Inns. Fire and candles, and matters chargeable separate from the meals, are the chief channels of imposition.—Slept in indifferent beds, with featherbeds *upon* us.

We had this day a fair specimen of the dishonesty of customhouse functionaries and the like. A man came out and demanded our passport. "Oh," said Louigi[3] "cà, voilà—c'est un officier de la marine royale Anglaise" and produced the passport enshrined in the smart green morocco pocketbook which he has purveyed for it. The fellow looked at it, and gave it back, saying "c'est bien—et—et—est ce qu'il y a quelque chose pour boire a sa santè,"—"Oh! rien, point du tout," we shouted univocally. "Humph!" quoth he—"mais, le passeport, est-il la dedans? voyons!" Accordingly it was again handed to him—and he inspected it. We drove laughing at, and disgusted with him: he sulky enough.

Friday Feb. 10.

Peronne to Paris is less than thirteen hours: according to Louigi, seventeen postes.

The journey as far as country was concerned, had little interest. About the middle of this day, we got into a fine forest. At least, one which appeared to be of great extent, but the timber all young. A beautiful Church at Senlis.[4]

The French pavè everywhere too narrow: about Valenciennes very rough: sides of the road ill dressed. Obliged for the most part to go off the road in meeting & passing—very trying to the carriage. Little water—Meuse at Peronne, and [blank].[5] Beggars at all the postes in very great abundance—some kindly offering to take our Belgian money which they said could be of no further use to us. It seems to the practice here for labouring people to

---

[1] Thirty-seven miles SSE. of Lille.
[2] Twenty-two miles SSW. of Cambrai, and 79 NNE. of Paris.
[3] Luigi Lamonica, the brothers' valet.
[4] Twenty-seven miles NNE. of Paris.
[5] The Somme at Peronne, and the Oise 7 miles north of Senlis.

beg. We saw a whole body with forks, spades &c, who, upon our carriage stopping, after exchanging a few words assailed us.

We left at 8 by Peronne time, 8½ by our own—by all means adopt the former, as more creditable to our hours. And we were landed at Meurices[1] before nine P.M. thank God well and safe, the road having been no small trial to the carriage.

Paris. Saturday Feb 11.

We found we had abundance of work on our hands for the time we proposed to spend in Paris.—In the forenoon we set out, and accomplished the delivery of our letters at the Embassy[2] and General La Fayette's,[3] and also divers matters in the shopping line. John also arranged for the making considerable repairs in the carriage. We walked through the Tuilleries gardens and about the river, but did not enter upon systematic lionising.

Found the dirty, slippery, and often rough pavé extremely disagreeable for walking: besides which it renders almost constant stooping inevitable, and thus robs mankind of his noble privilege—

> Os homini vultumque dedit, jussitque tueri
> Sidera, & erectos ad cœlum tollere vultus.[4]

Before I had been here many days, the bones of my feet ached with a new & unheard of dolour—and John's ditto.

We had a most excellent dinner at Vefour's in the Palais Royal, with lots of newspapers: including a bottle of wine—and ample pay to waiters it cost 8½ francs.

In the evening went to the Theatre Francais,[5] where the new tragedy of Louis XI was to be performed.[6] I got by mistake into the gallery instead of the parterre, and could scarcely hear a word, in a seat otherwise very inconvenient. After two hours and a half of patient endurance I made my escape. There was a very pretty procession and a kind of psalm sung nicely in it.

The French nation have the credit of going to at least *this* theatre for the sake of the pure drama. The decorations of the houses were almost none: the chandelier utterly unequal to purposes of display: there was not even an orchestra: and I for my part did not think that I saw any one who had

---

[1] Hôtel Meurice, Rue de Rivoli.
[2] See 12, 13 Feb. 32.
[3] Marie Joseph Paul du Motier de Lafayette, 1757–1834, French grandee; marquis; major-general in United States army 1777, in French army 1781; colonel-general of revolutionary National Guard 1789; survived. Leader of opposition, 1825–30. During revolution of 1830, resumed leadership of National Guard.
[4] Ovid, *Metamorphoses*, i. 85–86. The text is:
> Os homini sublime dedit cœlumque videre
> Iussit et erectos ad sidera tollere vultus.

'He gave to man a lofty aspect, and ordered him to watch the sky and to raise his uplifted looks to the stars'.
[5] Margin note: see Private J[ournal—i.e. second entry for 12 Feb. 32].
[6] By Casimir Delavigne (1832).

come there for anything but the play itself. The tone and spirit of it, as far as it incidentally reached me, was good. And yet with all this absence of particular and positive faults, I am far from thinking that French pleasures are untainted: or from forgetting that they are not only excessive in degree, but false in principle, and most pernicious in their practical results. Politics here seem to fill up the interstices of gaiety: and the same spirit of the nation, which indolently yields itself to the external titillation of the one, seems to display, particularly perhaps from the nature of this false and perilous excitement, the most restless inquietude in the other. It still displays the barren luxuriance of human nature, and remains essentially the same in its different moods, whether of frivolity or wildness.

And yet there is surely (though these remarks are here somewhat antedated) much to imitate in the French character: though of a superficial description. Their almost uniformly polite demeanour and obliging disposition—and their ease and playfulness of manner, might well be so attempered as to form an harmonious and beautiful combination with those stronger and sterner traits which are more essential to the production of the character of the good and great man.—*Under* the surface I fear there is much unsoundness everywhere: but here almost more than anywhere else that unsoundness has in many points been openly and daringly legitimatised, and perhaps, to quote a particular case, there is no country in the world where the false principle of individual honour bears more undisputed sway, than this.—

We found letters from England—one from Tom, giving a less satisfactory account of health at home than we could have wished.

In the evening began my long delayed Journal—which still however lagged behind for some time.

Sunday Feb. 12.

Went to the ambassador's to Church.[1] A large room extremely well filled. Bishop Luscombe[2] read prayers with an impressive voice, and preached on "For this purpose the Son of God was manifested, that he might destroy the work of the devil."[3] In the afternoon, with a good deal of inquiry, found out Marbreuf chapel[4] just after the service had begun. It is very pretty, and comfortable even to luxuriance. A Mr. Lovett officiated.[5] He preached without book, on John VI. 64–71.

Dined at Meurice's table d'hôte, very comfortably.[6] Some odd questions were discussed by the company, who were all English—nine or ten in

---

[1] Lord Granville *Leveson-Gower, 1773–1846, youngest s. of 1st marquess of *Stafford, tory M.P. Lichfield 1795–9, Staffordshire 1799–1815; secretary at war 1809; ambassador to St. Petersburg, 1804–5, 1807; the Hague 1823–4; Paris 1824–8, 1831–5, 1835–41; cr. viscount 1815, and earl Granville 1833.

[2] Matthew Henry Thornhill *Luscombe, 1776–1846, Scottish episcopal bp. to the continent of Europe and chaplain to the British Embassy in Paris, 1825.

[3] I John, iii. 8.

[4] Another anglican chapel, in the Avenue Marbœuf.

[5] Robert Lovett, minister of the Marbœuf chapel and chaplain to the earl of *Rosse.

[6] Marginal note: Charge 4½ francs, with*out* wine.

number. The propriety of suicide was one—it scarcely seemed decided any way. Another person was declaring that he did not go to the theatre on Sundays: not because he thought there was 'any harm' in it, but because "it was not what he had been accustomed to in England." What an infinity of mischief is done by "there's no harm in it." Another described his introduction at the Tuilleries, I think on the previous Sunday. A gentleman with whom we had some conversation after dinner said he had been in Paris fourteen years ago—that the non-observance of Sunday was sufficiently bad and glaring then, but that there was this difference—public works were not then, *as now*, carried on on that day. A proposition is now in the Chamber of Deputies to repeal an Act of 1814, long ago virtually abrogated, which exacts fines for the desecration.

Very many shops were entirely open: scarcely any shut: a good many with half closed windows. The city was indeed a painful sight: in England matters are bad enough, but by no means so far gone. It seems that the Bourbons wished to restore the observance, but proceeded slowly: and the theatres have *always* been open.

I believe there is no more exact criticism of the moral advancement of a people, than the sanctity which they accord to the Christian sabbath.—

Reading as usual—and Bp Hall.—

It is said that the English in Paris sadly deteriorate from their countrymen at home as regards Sunday: giving dinner and even evening and card parties. This is melancholy. Alas! Who ever heard of a want of facility in gliding into godless practices? The truth seems to be here. When the true principles of action have really taken hold of the heart, and struck a deep root into it, then either persecution or temptation do but tend to quicken its vigilance and fortify its determination. But if there be no abiding root: if our only defence consist in the forms of godliness and the name of Protestantism—then indeed the seed lies on the surface, and is scorched by the beams of the sun, or scattered to the winds of heaven.

Sunday Feb. 12. Paris.[1]

This city, on this day, is indeed a melancholy sight.—Had a good deal of conversation with John upon points connected with religion: particularly upon the general state and prospects of the world.

Sat night I went to the Theatre Francais: an action which after the course I have pursued and contemplate pursuing, in England, requires an explanation: and though I am averse to entering unnecessarily upon the subject of one's own conduct with others, yet *here* in private I would wish to record my reasons briefly.—The first is that I have always understood that the theatres here were not, as in England, inseparably allied with vice, and mainly instrumental in its advancement.—This understanding it was, which as I thought removed the bar.—Supplementary to this was the fact, that my object in going was rather general knowledge connected with the

[1] This entry from Lambeth MS 1420.

country, and particularly I hoped in reference to the language, than my own gratification.

The same considerations, a little modified, apply to the Italian Opera.

Monday Feb. 13.

Our first day of lionising. Found the Tuileries impracticable, as the King[1] was there. Visited

1. The Arch and place of the Carousal.[2] Through the former there is a very fine vista extending along the Gardens and Avenue de Neuilly up to the Arc de l'Etoile.

2. Contenting ourselves with front views of the Treasury and Admiralty (the latter exceedingly fine) we went to the Pont Louis XVI[3] and examined the very fine statues which adorn it.

3. Chamber of Deputies.[4] The shape is admirable, and the place handsome enough—but the new one, still in a state of preparation, which we saw, is much finer: very rich in marble: larger by the upper bench all round. Hall of entrance very beautiful—but the *exterior* of the projection, I thought, too narrow for its height. The same pile of building contains the apartments of the late Prince of Condé.[5]

4. Passed the Suspension Bridge and Chaillot Steam Engine—crossed the simple but handsome Bridge of Jena or the Hospital—and saw the Champ de Mars with Cavalry and Artillery exercising in it. Saw the exterior, and something of the courts, of the Ecole Militaire.[6]

5. Went through the Abbatoir of Grenelle—arrangement and cleanliness admirable. We took this as a specimen for all.

6. Hôpital des Invalides: founded by Louis XIV. Contains at present four thousand odd hundred. Library 18000 volumes: given by Napoleon. The part I pitched on was historical. Saw the kitchens & dining rooms. Officers and men apart. Church, and Dome particularly magnificent: I thought however a little gaudy. Decorated with many trophies. Ascended the Dome: we were told by 404 steps—and I think I verified the statement in my descent.

Before the Revolution of July,[7] the pensioners were expected to attend the Chapel—*since, not so*: and, in consequence, very few come. About three old men were there when we went in. I do not think there were seats for more than a small fraction of the entire number.

Panorama from the top very fine: though the day was not particularly clear.

Lunched at an inferior restaurant: as usual, indifferent and dear.

---

[1] Louis-Philippe d'Orléans, 1773–1850; fought at Valmy; émigré, 1793–1814; proclaimed King of the French 1830, abdicated 1848.

[2] Arc de Triomphe du Carrousel, erected by Napoleon in 1806.

[3] Now the Pont de la Concorde.

[4] The Palais Bourbon.

[5] Louis-Henri Joseph, Prince de Condé, 1756–1830.

[6] Then barracks and headquarters for National Guard.

[7] 1830: it replaced Charles X by Louis Philippe.

After our return we went to Place Vendôme. Its column[1] is very splendid. Called on Hagart in the Rue de la Madeleine—had some conversation with him on French matters—& saw something of the Boulevards.

Dined at the Ambassador's: a small party, but yet magnificently served. Found myself placed, unawares, between Miss Gower[2] and Lady Granville[3]—however, could not help it. Liked both. French fashions partly pursued.

Tuesday Feb. 14.

The Louvre nearly monopolised the lionising portion of the day. Went through the halls of statuary below—and the picture gallery above. Of the numberless beauties of these collections it is vain here to speak. I will only say[4] of the three schools of painting—French—Dutch, Flemish, German—Italian—I liked them in an inverted order: though all were beautiful. Here we have, all in extreme beauty, and most in rich abundance, Le Brun, Le Sueur, Poussin, of the French: Rubens, Teniers, Van Dyke, Rembrandt, of the next schools: Raffael, Titian, the Caraccis,[5] Tintoretto, Iulio Romano, Guido, Domenichino, Salvator Rosa, Correggio, Leonardo da Vinci, of the Italian schools. Of all I saw, I was most delighted with a small painting of Ludovico Caracci's, representing our Saviour dead, and his head on the knee of the Virgin.

We afterwards went to the showrooms of the Sevres porcelain, which is painted in a manner very soft and beautiful.—We wrote a joint letter home —and went to dine at the Café aux Mille Colonnes in the Palais Royal. Here we became acquainted with one of the wonders of Paris. A dinner consisting of "Potage, trois plâts au choix, un dessert, un demi-bouteille de Vin, & Pain" for *two francs*! The cookery and the material, were both excellent: and the only fault I had to find with the repast was, that it was too good.

In the evening John went out: I remained at home: crammed French, and read for the second time "Monsieur de Pourceaugnac".[6]

Wednesday Feb. 15.

Breakfasted at a restaurant, by way of experiment. Quite as dear as Meurice's, and not so good. Meurice's house is I think well arranged and comfortable. It is not now above one third full: the number of English in Paris being small. It is a good place for getting information: for meeting Englishmen: the waiters I fancy understand English more or less: as does Meurice:[7] and there are many conveniences.

[1] Erected by Napoleon, 1810, to celebrate his victories.

[2] (Lady) Susan Georgiana Leveson-Gower, d. 1866; elder da. of 1st Lord *Granville; m. 4th Lord Rivers, 1833.

[3] Lady Harriet Elizabeth Cavendish, 1785–1862, 2nd da. of 5th duke of Devonshire; m. 1809.

[4] 'that' deleted.

[5] Ludovico Caracci, 1555–1619, and his cousins, Agostino, 1557–1602, and Annibale, 1560–1609.

[6] Molière.

[7] The hotel-keeper; he had sold out by 1836.

On this day we made[1] progress as follows—besides visiting one or two Churches, which presented little worthy of note. As far as we can see, there are seldom more than two or three praying in the Paris Churches on week-days. In Belgium we saw more. The images again are very few in the streets here. In a week's lionising the town, I only saw one. At Antwerp they are in almost every street. In the *country* we saw crucifixes often enough—generally painted a light green or some similar colour, which was odd.

1. Grande Messagerie. Larger premises and better arranged than those of any English coach office I know. From 25 to 28 Diligences leave it daily. *Two* of these offices do all the business in Paris, except as concerns short stages.

2.[2] Market, and fountain of Innocents. Close by were interred some of the tués of Juillet—the frail monuments erected over them were adorned with wreaths—and bore inscriptions denouncing despotism—and a soldier kept guard. They were those who had fallen in the neighbourhood. One thus we saw under the Louvre.—Alas! such inscriptions as these, in a cause too not altogether void of question, are insufficient. In the first place, there is much *omitted*: and this apparently not in one case or another, but in all. And the zeal which animated their breasts, I much fear, is wasted: there are other more crying evils, and far more fatally menacing our present peace, than despotism. Yet these are perhaps hard reflections over those who at least defended their cause with their hearts' blood. Let us hope that they are in peace. But little indeed seems here to be known or to be thought of the way of peace.

Every care has apparently been taken by the French, to extirpate the recollection of the old Bourbons. The names of streets and galleries are changed: the tricolour waves in[3] every possible situation: paintings removed: the works and pictures of Napoleon reinstated (ominous enough for the friendship with England about which my Lord Palmerston talked glib and fair—): so that nothing may be remembered of the later Bourbons save the wrongs they did and the retribution they suffered: and that all objects may remind Frenchmen of the price they paid for their present condition, and of its tenure.

It is a melancholy event in the history of nations when they think themselves compelled to blot out a period from their history, even as Job cursed the day of his birth and wished it had never been.[4] The life of nations is given to be used like that of individuals: but this erasure tells that the fruit of a portion of it has been lost and is not. The days of nations like those of individuals should be "bound each to each by natural piety"[5]—but here we see a severing of those links which united us to other times, whereby we hold communion with the dead, and may hope to imbibe the rudiments of a kindred spirit. Painful it is indeed, if the extent of ancestral shame be so great, that, in order to hide it, we must hide with it ancestral glories, and do away with some of the tenderest sympathies of human nature.

[1] 'one or two' deleted.   [2] Marginal note: (Note 2. belongs to Feb. 16).
[3] Instead of 'suspended from'.   [4] Job iii. 1.
[5] *Wordsworth, 'My Heart Leaps Up' (1807).

Obsequies, we found had been performed over these tués by the curé, but the ground had not been consecrated.— —

2. Hotel de Ville—front fine—but not without its faults.[1]

3. Place de Bastile: and Fountain of the Elephant.[2] The latter was a fine conception: but is disfigured by a tower on the back: it does not spout water at present.—On the site of the old prison workmen are now engaged in erecting a monument to those who were killed in the last Revolution.

4. Pere la Chaise. This singular and interesting place demanded much more time and attention than we were able to give it. No place, of all we have seen, was I so sorry to be hurried away from. The number and variety of the tombs: the crowd of inscriptions, so much greater, in proportion, here than in England: the wreaths [with] which they were hung, and the anticipations previously formed, all contributed to add to the strength of those feelings, under which one ought to visit a repository of the dead.

The inscriptions over the gateway are promising. On the left of the gate, in Latin "He that believeth in me, though he were dead yet shall he live"[3] —and on the right "their hope is full of immortality".[4] After this it was a painful disappointment not to find among the scores I saw, one epitaph which involved the sentiments of sound Christianity. Of the expression of sorrow there was enough: and no symptoms of heartlessness, there at least, appeared: but there did not appear, I thought (yet it is fair to say that my examination was very partial,) in company with sorrowing Love, that Faith which ought to bear its burdens, and that hope which ought to elevate its glance. The most common of the short inscriptions seemed to be "priez pour son âme"—and one of, I thought, a very equivocal character "concession a perpetuité." It is liable to the same objection as the line in Gray's Elegy

"Each in his narrow cell *for ever* laid—"[5]

But it is more easy to fancy an expression escaping unsifted through one individual mind, than when it has become as it were *publici juris.*

Another epitaph on a husband described his widow, with his children as mourning incessantly[6] for him—and *her* as only constrained to survive him by her love for them.

Another was "Il avoit vecu trôp pour ses malheur, pas assez pour ses amis."

It is possible that epitaphs may be inscribed here, as in England, pretty much at the discretion of ignorant, unconcerned, and irresponsible functionaries: and it would be cruel indeed to visit their delinquencies upon the head of blameless relatives.—In this case the tone of the Père la Chaise Epitaphs only remains one evidence among many, to the superior purity of general sentiment produced by our reformed religion.

[1] Burnt 1871.
[2] The colossal fountain planned by Napoleon was never completed; the elephant seen by the diarist was a full size model, 72 feet high, kept in a shed near the site of the Bastille.
[3] John xi. 25.   [4] Cp. Rom. ii. 7.
[5] Thomas *Gray, *An Elegy Wrote in a Country Churchyard* (1751).
[6] Instead of 'everlastingly'.

If we analyse the sentiment of *this* epitaph, it is melancholy indeed. "He had lived too long for his misfortunes." Nay "whom the Lord loveth he chasteneth".[1] How much too long did our Blessed Saviour live, if the measure of life is thus to be adapted to human notions of its uses! How does this most unhappy sentiment involve the proposition, that the misfortunes of life nullify its purpose, when on the other hand we assuredly know, that *the* purpose of life is the renewal of the image of God in the soul of man, and that all things, be they sweet or be they bitter, are truly valuable and of[2] good to us, only in proportion to the efficacy with which they act in promoting this single end: in forwarding and fitting that system of discipline which God has ordained to be the instrument for completing his designs of mercy to mankind.

We were told that Jews and infidels were buried here with Christians.

I quitted Pere la Chaise with a deep and melancholy interest, and a hope to return thither. Yet it is melancholy indeed. A Christian burying ground, if it is to be indeed Christian, is a place for meditation not of a gloomy[3] cast: but of a mixed character: containing the elements both of melancholy and of joy: yet with a great preponderance (yet *still* a mixture) of joy. They are a joy and a grief which blend and harmonize: for the joy is built on the highest truths of revelation: and the grief springs from the best sympathies of human nature. But that joy is not small, if we are able to believe, that the spot we contemplate is, on one signal day, to be marked by the legions which shall then arise out of the bosom of the earth, to pass to everlasting glory.

5. Plate Glass Manufactory, Rue de Reuillet. We find the glass is not actually manufactured here: but we saw the polishing and the "etamage" or applying tin and quicksilver. It seems most wonderful, that this *single* manufactory should supply the immense number of mirrors used in France.

6. Jardin des Plantes—wild beasts (we did not however see the Giraffe)—and a Conservatory. There are other things attached to it.[4]

7. Halle aux Vins. The plan of this establishment seems excellent, and everyway worthy of a great city.

8. Notre Dame. The front is exquisitely rich and elaborate: and there are three very[5] fine painted windows: and also paintings in the Church. Some service was going on: the priest did not perform it in a very prepossessing manner.

Thus ended a pretty good day's lionising, which also had shopping intermingled.

I have observed the order in which we visited the objects, as I think it was *on the whole* a convenient one.—

The *cab-driver* may often supply the place and perform the functions of a *commissioner*: he should be hired by the hour.

---

[1] Heb. xii. 6.   [2] Instead of 'effective'.
[3] Instead of 'melancholy'.
[4] Botanical and zoological gardens, containing also a laboratory, a library and a number of collections concerning natural science.
[5] Instead of 'extremely'.

In the evening, wrought at French—read the papers and Molière, and went to the "Salle de Danse"!

Thursday Feb. 16

In today's work we went to

1. Egyptian museum and *cidevant* gallery of Charles Dix.[1] Cielings exquisitely rich: but some, I thought, quite overgilded.—Saw a representation, in one of the Greek rooms, of a banquet couch. A male and female were reclining upon it: its height was represented as considerably greater than that of wooden couches: and a small table with food upon it was before them: and it was *considerably* lower than the couch. A boy was by it, waiting. The whole person was on the couch.—The whole collection was extremely rich and beautiful.

2. Marine Museum.[2] For this I refer to John's journal: but I could admire, though with no professional knowledge.

An order was necessary to see these Museums.[3]

4. Morgue.[4] No bodies were there. A number of passersby came in to look for them, in the manner we call "dropping in," i.e. as habitually & a matter of course.

What inference can be drawn from the existence of such a place in Paris, as a public sight, while there is none in London?—I fancy there are many more lives wasted here: and the system of Coroner's Inquests in England elicits[5] information wherever it is to be found.

5. Halle au Blè. Of this I can only repeat what I said of the Halle aux Vins yesterday—and to add that the Dome is very fine.[6]

6. *Bourse.*—quite modern. The portico, and the whole exterior of the building are very handsome & I thought in good taste.—In the interior is a fine covered oblong, with a gallery on the first floor running all round it: to which the public repair. Where the roof closes in upon the skylight, there are painted imitations of basso rilievo, most admirable: the deception is perfect while one stands opposite, and can only be detected by looking along the side parallel to the line of view.[7]

The place was very crowded—and a public sale going on.

In the evening went with John to the Italian Opera—heard La Blache,[8] whose voice is magnificent—Mad. Raimbaux,[9] Sign. Bourgogni[10] and others, who were good. The audience was large; and the house[11] is handsome but not gaudy.

[1] Both in the Louvre.   [2] Also in the Louvre.
[3] In margin: 'for 3, see No 2 of the day before' [p. 423].
[4] On the Ile de la Cité; the corpses of unknown people drowned in the Seine, or who had otherwise perished, were exhibited there for three days, with their clothes suspended above them.
[5] Instead of 'finds'.   [6] Corn market, built 1622.
[7] The paintings are by de Pujol and Meynier.
[8] Luigi Lablache, 1784–1858; Italian bass singer.
[9] Adèle Raimbaux, née Gavaudan 1807, French cantatrice.
[10] Giovanni Bordogni, 1789–1856, Italian tenor.
[11] The Théâtre Favart.

Friday Feb. 17.

Morning occupied in reading &c. and at the *salle de danse*. Left by the twelve o'clock diligence for St. Germains,[1] a good conveyance[2] drawn by four small but well-fed horses. When the driver got down to let in a passenger, the horses began to turn about all manner of ways, after a sort which would have made one think an English stage coach in danger: we shouted to the conductor to mind his horses, but he took it quite coolly and said "hah! il n'y a point de danger, Messieurs"—by and bye he was down again, and the horses would not stop at all but continued their journey peaceably towards St. Germains even as if he had been on the box; so we e'en told him we could go without him as well as with.

Passed the Marly (steam?) engine which raises the water to Versailles—[3]

Shown through the deserted halls of St. Germains.[4] Saw the apartments of James II.[5] and of the mistress of Louis;[6] and the trapdoor by which he used to visit her. The chapel[7] is still partially embellished—the cieling has been fine, but is now spoiled. The shape of the building is fantastical: and the apartments are not large: but there is a fine prospect, a very extensive terrace, and a forest with shooting, of which Charles Dix was fond. The situation has much of the air which befits a royal residence.

Returned to Paris, inside, a distance of five leagues, for a franc each!

In the evening, at a brilliant part of Lady Granville's. Rooms & company both magnificent. Duke of Orleans[8] there, with heaps of ministers. I was a spectator only: John also. We neither of us made *any* acquaintances.

Saturday Feb. 18.

This day we heard from home—as thrice before since our arrival—and I wrote.

We visited

1. The Mint—well worth seeing. Our guide a regular *ouvrier*, who said he should like to hang anybody who introduced steam-engines: and endeavoured to get a *liberal* payment out of us for showing, by alleging that he had to divide with his comrades. But we neither of us like liberalism.

2. The Pantheon[9]—a most magnificent building: extremely rich, and chaste withal: dedicated "aux grands hommes." A church until the Revolution of July—now solely appropriated to the purposes of a place for burial—rather perhaps for monuments.—Surely there was no discrepancy between the two great purposes to which Christian temples are usually appropriated. The

---

[1] Saint-Germain-en-Laye, 12 miles WNW. of the centre of Paris.

[2] Instead of 'diligence'.

[3] Marly-le-Roi lies just south of St Germain. A huge steam engine, replacing an engine of 1684, supplied the fountains of Versailles 4 miles to the SSE.

[4] 'Versailles' deleted.

[5] *James II of England lived in exile at St. Germains from 1688 until his death in 1701.

[6] Françoise-Athenaïs de Pardaillan, marquise de Montespan, 1641–1707.

[7] The remains of the first château on this site.

[8] Ferdinand Philippe, duc d'Orléans, 1810–1842; eldest s. of Louis Philippe.

[9] Built in 1764 as the church of St. Geneviève; in 1791 the Convention renamed it the Panthéon, dedicated 'Aux grands hommes la patrie reconnaissante'.

tombs of Voltaire and Rousseau were brought here during the first revolution. The former has the inscription

"Poete, Historien, Philosophe,
Il aggrandit l'esprit humain,
Et lui apprit
Qu'il devroit être libre."

Another kind of freedom was taught before him, and will live after him.

Rousseau's tomb has "Homme de la nature et de la verité."

3. Eglise Val de Grace: a Church with a very fine dome and rich altar.

4. Gobelins.[1] This manufacture with that of Sevres porcelain must I suppose be perfectly unique. A single piece of tapestry takes four or five years to finish! The outlines are transferred from paintings, by means of tracing paper. The carpets are as extraordinary in their way as the tapestry. They are now weaving carpets for the Tuilleries. The tapestry excels most paintings, and rivals nearly all.

5. School of Deaf and Dumb.[2] Very interesting: chiefly as being the original institution. I saw an exhibition of the Deaf & Dumb in Edinburgh—where I imagine they have carried instruction much farther. There, they answered questions in religion admirably: here the master, who seemed a very intelligent man and beloved by his pupils, said they could only teach the idea of God as a Creator. Yet they had admirable prayers hung up, and marked 'for the use of the class;' not even involving any Romanism.[3]—

The only payment desired for the sight is, the the purchase of some trifle in turnery, executed by the pupils—& this is not demanded.

Read Moliere, wrote up Journal &c. John at Theatre.—Dined at cafe in Rue Castiglioni: good and gentlemanly: but not a prodigy of cheapness like the aux deux frères in the Palais Royal, where you have

une demibouteille de Vin, ⎫
un Potage,   ⎪
quatre plats au choix,   ⎬ for two francs!
Pain a discretion,   ⎪
un dessert.   ⎭

Paris. Sunday Feb. 19.[4]

Reading: Bible, Pascal's Provincial Letters,[5] Bp Hall's Balm of Gilead.[6] A good deal of conversation with John on the observance of Sunday—& on Calvinism. Unhappily my manner tends to turn every conversation into a debate.

Bishop Luscombe preached a sermon on "So God created man in his own

---

[1] Tapestry workshops, and carpet workshops known as La Savonnerie.
[2] Founded by Charles-Michel, abbé de L'Epée, 1712–1789.
[3] 'open at 3 p.m.' in margin.
[4] This entry from Lambeth MS 1420.
[5] Blaise Pascal's Jansenist attack on the Jesuits (1656).
[6] By Joseph *Hall (1660).

image"[1]—mainly on the necessity and means of regaining it now that it was lost. I thought it admirable: of a superior class in point of thought and talent: and sound and plainspoken in doctrine. May God prosper him and his labours: and his son[2] likewise. A Pure creed should indeed be precious here.

Sunday Feb. 19.

An admirable sermon from Bishop Luscombe at the Ambassador's on "So God created man in his own image". He dwelt with great soundness of doctrine, and power of exhortation, and no small degree of ability more-over, on the loss of that image, and the means of that loss: and on the neces-sity and manner of its recovery. In the afternoon I went to the Oratoire, which has then an English service: I suppose intended to be supplementary to that of the morning at the Embassy: the Bishop's son is minister: he seems a good and zealous man; the congregation respectable and attentive.

Monday Feb. 20.

Went to St Cloud[3]—saw the Palace, which though not a magnificent is a very handsome residence.[4] Crossed the Park to Sevres—saw the exhibition of porcelain there—everyway far more magnificent than that in Paris—where there are neither fine vases, nor pictures: which we saw here, beauti-ful beyond belief. To see the manufacture, an order is required, which we had not.

Went on by Diligence to Versailles.[5] The Ecuries for the army are very handsome.

We went through the Park Gardens: through the Orangery: where there is one tree "semé 1421"—through the Grand Palais de Trianon, built for Madame de Maintenon:[6] as the Petit was for Madame de Pompadour.[7] The jets d'eau in the gardens are innumerable: the variety of basins almost endless: and the store of marbles profuse. None of the trees, however, are old or well grown. The grand periods of resort to Versailles are at fêtes when the jets d'eau play—they are held I believe on Sundays. We saw also the Colonnade of Fêtes Champêtres.

We went through the Palace. Such a crowd of gilded apartments on such a scale I never saw. They call the façade 1800 feet. There are a great many paintings—Verney,[8] Paul Veronese, &c. and some ceilings by Le Brun.— The Chapel is I think exquisitely beautiful, and could scarcely be improved: some of the apartments, e.g. the "cabinets particuliers du roi" surely by

---

[1] Gen. i. 27.

[2] Henry Harmood Luscombe, president of Cambridge Union 1828; ordained deacon, 1830.

[3] A western suburb, 6 miles from the centre of Paris.

[4] Burnt 1871.

[5] Eleven miles WSW. of Paris.

[6] Françoise d'Aubigné, marquise de Maintenon, 1635–1719; mistress of Louis XIV.

[7] Jeanne Antoinette Poisson, 1721–64, marquise de Pompadour; mistress of Louis XV.

[8] Horace Vernet, 1789–1863.

far too much gilded. The apartments were dismantled during the first revolution.

They also showed us the salle d'opera. Returned to Paris. Had a long Etonian conversation with Hagart—and began to look to matters connected with our contemplated departure tomorrow: and wrote up my journal, which at last (Monday Night) has caught me up.

Tuesday Feb. 21.

We went to leave our P.P.C. cards at Lord Granville's—and after having prepared everything for our departure, went in a cab to the Palais du Luxembourg to behold the sitting of the Peers, relying on two tickets which Mons. Le Questeur had sent us, without any day inscribed upon them, but simply "Billet d'Entrée, Chambre de Pairs"—when we arrived there we found that they held good only for the day on which they were sent us. After much murmuring and divers attempts, we drove back to Meurices. I do not know that we lost a great deal, for I believe that this Chamber is in little request. Its proceedings are very rarely reported, and we had difficulty in finding out when it sat. However, for one reason it would have been desirable to see it: and that is, that it is at least a question whether it may be in existence at the period of any future visit.

I forgot to mention how regally the Royal Family are seated in the Chamber of Deputies. Opposite the Tribune, are the "gentlemen of the Press"—supported on their right by the ambassadors, as the representatives of royalty abroad, and on their left by the French King and his family! All three in separate boxes.

Left Paris about two—arrived at Fontainebleau[1] between 7 & 8.—Pavè. Accompanied more or less by the Seine.—Hotel de la Ville de Lyon—a very fair Inn, and not at all beyond the average of expense. Slept here.

Wednesday. Feb. 22.

After breakfast, went to see the Chateau. It is an immense pile of building, without much architectural beauty, but of a regal air. We were told it contained fourteen hundred and sixty-odd apartments! The great gallery very fine, and that of Francis I curious. In the roof of the ballroom the first unerased & undefaced fleur-de-lis that I have seen in France met my eye! They are now *repairing* this room, and doubtless the repairs will include this poor solitary fleur-de-lis.

We saw the apartments which Buonaparte assigned to Pius VII when his prisoner.[2] The concierge seemed to have a great respect for "Le Sainte Père"—we saw too the table on which Napoleon signed his Abdication in 1814. There is much splendour in the palace—some exquisite Sevres porcelain.

[1] Thirty-seven miles SSE. of Paris.
[2] When in 1809 Napoleon declared the papal states annexed to France, Gregorio Barnabé Chiaramonti, 1742–1823, Pope Pius VII 1800, excommunicated the invaders, and was held prisoner by the French until 1814.

We were told here that the exquisite quality of the Gobelines tapestry is in great measure owing to a spring there which imparts a peculiar brilliancy & delicacy of hue to the thread.

On starting we passed through more of the extensive and fine forest. No old *timber* yet. All the game was killed, here & at Versailles, in the Revolution of July.

We made out 14¼ postes in about 10½ hours from Fontainebleau by Fossard,[1] Sens,[2] and Joigny,[3] to Auxerres[4]—following for the most part the vale of the Yonne, & so having little hill[5]—road part pavè, part soft & heavy, pretty much *au naturel*. Stopped to see the Cathedral of Sens, which is fine, and contains a mausoleum of Louis XV and his queen. The country is picturesque and abounds in vineyards.

Auxerre. Hotel de Leopard. Very good beds, & altogether a very fair Inn. (We do not get good tea on this road, and find the cafè au lait, which they *do* give good, preferable.) If anything, *rather* dear. This town has Churches worth seeing.

Thursday, Feb. 23d.

7 ¼ A.M.—10 P.M. 16 ¼ postes: a good deal of hill: and also now as yesterday some *very bad* road and none decidedly good, except the last stage from Chissey[6] to Autun.[7] Country on the whole by no means uninteresting. Breakfasted at Vermenton[8]—Hotel de Notre Dame—unpromising outwardly—but provisions *very good*, and not dear. Fire, cafè au lait, two sheep's tongues, 6 eggs, bread & butter, & waiter, 6½ francs.

Passed the grottos of Arcy[9] unseen, as we were hurried this day. Avallon[10] a nice town. From Chissey to Autun, road picturesque. Autun a town in very antique style: gates[11] remarkable.

Hotel de la Poste at Autun. Tolerable: dear. Beds very good.

Friday Feb. 24.

8¼ A.M.—6½ P.M. 13¾ postes. Road hilly in parts. First stage, to St. Emilan,[12] very picturesque: & excellent road. On the whole, the road very much improved. Chalons[13] a considerable place. All the country through which we are now passing is rich and highly cultivated, and trades largely in corn, or cattle, or wine, or cloth and other manufactures. All the towns

[1] Forty miles SSE. of Paris.
[2] The French Scone; 61 miles SSE. of Paris.
[3] Fifteen miles NNW. of Auxerre.
[4] City ninety-three miles SE. of Paris.
[5] Note in margin: 'Fossard: Inn good in appearance. Sens. Inn very good by report.'
[6] Fifty-one miles SE. of Auxerre.
[7] Twenty-nine miles WNW. of Chalon-sur-Saône.
[8] Fourteen miles NNW. of Avallon.
[9] Stalactite caverns near Arcy, 11 miles NW. of Avallon.
[10] Twenty-seven miles SE. of Auxerre.
[11] Second century.
[12] Nine miles SE. of Autun.
[13] Châlon-sur-Saône; ninety miles SE. of Auxerre.

here have their Cafès du Commerce, which we did not observe in the North of France.—From one spot I counted fifteen villages in sight. The country is also richly studded with Churches.

Our weather has been very fine, and the road was enjoyable enough, though Nature had her winter garb on, particularly in the morning: between rocks, and streams, and graceful branches, and the hoar frost in dewdrops glittering with the rays of the sun.

The regulations about not passing vehicles in motion on the road, is I fancy obsolete: at Paris we were told it only obtained in the case of "long" Diligences and carriages travelling post—but today we passed a Diligence most triumphantly, and left it peacably accomplishing its poste per hour.

On the plain of Chalons we *tasted* the keen Alpine breeze: which we afterwards lost, getting among rising grounds.

At Sens we saw a public-house with the singular sign of the Holy Ghost.

Macon[1]—Hotel du Sauvage. Not an ill-provided Inn, nor an expensive one. The *class* of Inns most to be avoided I should say are those where public conveyances stop.—Our Savage was however brutally dirty in the passages &c—but the beds were good. We are now on the Saone. A steam-boat passes between Chalons and Lyons, each way daily.

Saturday. Feb. 25.

8½ A.M.–2 P.M. 8½ postes. Road for the most part very good: and divers tolerable looking Inns on it. But the exterior of an inn cannot be trusted for its interior to the same extent here as in England. During the last stage but one, we ascended to a considerable height, & then had an almost uninterrupted descent into Lyons: with a fine view of it: and, after entering, a long drive along the quay to the Hotel de l'Europe—which gave us an opportunity of appreciating the situation of the town and the views along the river[2] in it: these we afterwards thought its best features.

After dressing we delivered a letter of introduction: dined at a middling restaurant: and went to the Hotel de Ville: and looked at the antiquities in the court of the Palais des Arts. The Place of Louis le Grand is very fine, and the Hospital[3] a very handsome building—but the town generally is very filthy, though nature has done much for it.

There is to us a very perceptible increase of mildness in the climate since leaving Paris—and throughout the journey we have scarcely been able to discern a cloud.

Wrote a letter to Bruce. As to reading, such as I have been able to accomplish in the evenings & in the carriage (but *here*[4] my performances are very trifling from inability in my eyes) has been Moliere, Bourrienne[5] at intervals, Manuel du Voyageur,[6] French Grammar, Shelley and Coleridge—but very little of any.

---

[1] Forty miles N. of Lyon.
[2] The Hôtel de l'Europe was at 1, Rue de Bellecour, overlooking the Saône.
[3] Hospice de la Charité.   [4] Marginal note: i.e. in the carriage.
[5] L. F. de Bourrienne, *Mémoire . . . sur Napoléon* (1829, tr. in 4v., 1831).
[6] Milan (1818).

Sunday Feb. 26.

Read Hall and Pascal. Attended the Protestant Church, apparently Luthe-ran. A very good sermon, though almost without any doctrine, on "this is the will of God, even your sanctification ".[1] I think the name of the clergy-man was Martin. The congregation was ample and respectable: but there is only a single service, & this is the only Protestant Chapel in the place. We walked to the junction of the rivers. Both are beautifully clear, particularly the Rhone: it is blue and the Saone green. We went into a Church, filled almost exclusively with women and children—had little time to stay, and could not make head or tail of what little we heard—it was chanting. We saw advertisements of plenary indulgences on the Church Doors connected with particular seasons: & in the same place, advertisements of sales by auction &c. Exceedingly bad taste.—There is said to be little in the Lyons Churches worthy of notice: the finest is opposite our windows.[2]

Sunday Feb. 26.[3]

My waking thoughts—those thoughts which are instructive and in the adoption of which the will has no choice—were of my future prospects: and they brought with them as usual their own bitterness. God forbid that I should shrink from that bitterness: it may be very salutary, and may work a good purpose in me. But God also forbid that if it be sent as a warning, I should fail of attaining to its meaning.

Heard a sermon on sanctification at the Protestant Chapel. It was almost exclusively on the work to be done: and little mention of the means: but very good: only a series of exactly such would not I think merit the appellation.

Monday Feb. 27.

Wrote to Helen. Went with John to see the manufactory La Sauvagère. I had seen the same things, I found, at Macclesfield,[4] four years ago: but had the privilege of riding in one of the most incomprehensible and unbearable vehicles I ever saw. The bridges are very numerous: of iron, wood, & stone: discus suspension, or demi-suspension.

We went to see the Museum: the Gallery of pictures, which has paintings by Rubens, Poussin, Caracci, & a strange one of the Circumcision by Le Guerchin:[5] and the library: perhaps twenty feet longer than that at Christ Church; but not near so fine. We saw too the Chapel. There are 300 students at the College: they attend the Chapel once on Thursdays & once on Sundays.

$3\frac{1}{2}$–7 P.M. 5 postes to Bourguine.[6] *Hotel du Parc.* Comfortable—except

---

[1] I Thess. iv. 3.
[2] Cathedral church of St. Jean.
[3] This entry from Lambeth MS 1420.
[4] See 28 Jan. 28.
[5] Giovanni Guercino, 1591–1666.
[6] Bourgoin, 48 miles SE. of Lyons and 20 SW. of Chambéry.

in a point or two, where all French Inns seem to fail. Charges as usual Almost the best bread we had tasted on the Continent—owing, as our land-lady informed us, to the quality of the water.

We found the *Hotel de l'Europe* at Lyon very comfortable: and moderate in its charges.[1]

I did not bethink me, until we had left the city, of Juvenal's allusion to it—

Aut Lugdunensem rhetor dicturus ad aram.[2]

After we had got some four miles out of it, and ascended some hill, the first view of the Alps burst upon us: and it was worthy of them. It was com-paratively uninterrupted by the minor ranges whose relative magnitude increased so much as we drew nearer; and at the same time their majesty was tempered by the mellowing and harmonising effect of distance and of evening. I could look at little else. They were distant from us from 50 to 60 miles, in a direct line. It was easy to discern, even here, that they were different from anything one had seen in Britain, by the boldness of the out-line, and the scale of grandeur & magnitude to which it was adapted.

Road tolerable.—

Tuesday Feb. 28.

9 A.M.–4½ P.M. Bourgouine, by Beauvoisin[3] and Echelles,[4] to Chamberry.[5] Road generally good. Entered Savoy at Pont de Beauvoisin—on the Guiers, which flows through the magnificent pass of La Chaille.—Little delay.—

I have little to say on quitting France, and that little in very cursory remarks.—We never received an uncivil answer in answer to a request for direction. We, at least I, never saw a person drunk except two: both were soldiers.—The appearance of the women is very inferior to that of the men, with whom they seem almost equally to partake hard[6] labour. The latter form a fine peasantry.—The appearance of the provincial towns very de-cidedly inferior to what one sees in England.—No such thing as a pretty village on our route—I do not mean this to apply to advantages of situa-tion. Style of roads & carriages of all kinds far behind England.—Very bad pronunciation by the people in the South, of Languedoc and Dauphiny. Crucifixes &c very few in the towns, pretty numerous in the country: but many in bad taste. Priests, in appearance, altogether inferior to the English Clergy: but they have a business like air about them.

[1] Marginal note: rooms 10f.
Dinners 8f.
Breakf 4f.
Teas 3f.
12 logs 4f.

[2] Juvenal, *Satire*, 1, 44: 'or of one who awaits his turn to orate before the altar at Lyons'.

[3] Twelve miles SW. of Chambéry.

[4] Les Echelles; 10 miles SW. of Chambéry.

[5] Chambéry, a Savoyard city 28 miles NNE. of Grenoble.

[6] Instead of 'violent'.

In Savoy we saw numbers of priests and crucifixes—the latter in better taste than in France.—

For my own part I see nothing superstitious in the act of erecting crucifixes at different places in the country; although perhaps another objection might be brought. It may be questioned whether it does more to excite religious feeling, (independent of the superstition which they *harmonise* with & so augment,) or to cause a revulsion from it: constituted as human nature now is. Whether the heart of man can be successfully assailed by means partaking so much of a *mechanical* character. Again: whether the mind can at once and *instantaneously*, upon the suggestion of a crucifix, be led up from its ordinary level "to the contemplation of high and heavenly things." Having a strong bias one way, it is only by slow degrees it can be led the other. This mode by crucifixes &c. seems to be out of the range[1] of ordinary mental processes.—At least I think whatever is erected ought evidently to be of the grave and imposing, rather than the slight & familiar character. The human mind requires to be gently and delicately dealt with, and he that calculates on ends without adequate instruments will find himself disappointed.

Savoyards particularly civil. Many bowed: even a priest among them. I longed for that bow to[2] have been made an occasion for conversation. Children curlyhaired & pretty: costumes pretty & in good taste.

At two leagues from the Pont, we ascended the pass of La Chaille. It is indeed magnificent: and almost *too* safe. Yet I should not like to walk along the top of the barrier wall. The effect when you are once fairly inclosed & lose sight of France is most striking. Over you, you have more or less of precipice: beneath, a ravine of immense depth—opposite, huge column-like piles of rock built up one over another in careless[3] and disdainful strength, on the scale of the most gigantic workmanship. The road good— nothing extremely steep.

In the next stage we pass through Buonaparte's tunnel, 950 feet long, and ascend to a great height in a sinuous mountain pass[4] all the way, but most gradually, and without precipice. Road for the most part admirable. Beyond St. Thibault le Coux,[5] a singular little cascade, said to be 120 feet high, close to the road on the right: the volume of water is so small that it all seems dissolved in spray long before it reaches the bottom: it plays beautifully in the sun & forms all the colours of the rainbow.

Chambery: a very nice town of much cleaner appearance than most we have seen. Visited the Cathedral, Governor's Church, ruin beside it, Boulevards and Promenade, and house of J.J. Rousseau[6] on a hill about $\frac{3}{4}$ of a mile off. The situation of the town is very fine. In the Cathedral we saw two boxes: one "for the[7] support of the Church": the other "for the souls of purgatory."

---

[1] Instead of 'sphere'.   [2] Instead of 'that that bow might'.
[3] 'strength' deleted.   [4] Instead of 'defile'.
[5] St. Thibault de Coux, village 6 miles SW. of Chambéry.
[6] Who lived in Chambéry, 1731–42.
[7] 'repairs &' deleted.

Said to be 6,000 troops here. In Lyon, 15,000. In Paris 30 or 40, some said 50,000.

Hotel de la Poste. A comfortable house. There are others which look well: the Hotel de l'Union &c.

Wednesday, Feb. 29.

$7\frac{1}{4}$ A.M.–$7\frac{3}{4}$ p.m. Chambéry to Modane,[1] 14 postes. A considerable ascent in the first stage, and then some descent to Aiguebelle,[2] or Aqua Bella—arch there to Charles Felix[3]—ascent begins.—After a peep of the Isere[4] at Montmeillian,[5] we here joined the Arc,[6] and followed its banks, though in the opposite direction, and with some intermission, to the end of our day's journey. It lay through a vale of considerable width, almost however blocked up in parts by immense rocks: everywhere fine, and somewhat varied. Road generally fair—but in parts intersected very disagreeably by dry channels, which are sometimes torrents. The country now is remarkably dry. Snow on the tops of the hills & some way down—but not near us till we had passed St. Michel,[7] (said to have a good Inn, Hotel de Londres,) and during the stage from that place to Modane the country assumed a wider aspect, and the course of the torrent was more broken. We passed a petrifying steam on the last stage but one—it had formed a projection of stone for its own bed.

Modane, Hotel de Lion d'Or. Bread coarse, coffee thick, fowl tough, room smoky, furniture scant: a very indifferent Inn, and to be avoided. Like other bad Inns, it was very high in some of its charges; and this, *absolutely*: relatively, it was so in all.

Thursday, March 1.

$7\frac{3}{4}$ A.M.–5 P.M. 12 postes, professedly, including Cenis:[8] but we both felt quite sure, that the distances were greatly overcharged, in order to make the traveller pay for crossing the mountain. Its charges may be stated thus—

Horses, $\frac{1}{2}$ franc each per Poste extra—
15 francs at Savoy barrier—
Extra *number* of horses—
Fees to guides, if taken—and
Whatever may be given, additionally
to the usual pay, to postillions.

And after all, it is very little.

From Modane to Lans le bourg[9] we had a good deal of hill, but also a

[1] Forty-six miles SE. by east of Chambéry.
[2] Nineteen miles east of Chambéry.
[3] Charles Felix, 1765–1831; b. of Victor Emmanuel I of Piedmont, who abdicated in his favour in 1821.
[4] The Isère joins the Rhône above Valence.
[5] Montmélian, 9 miles SE. by east of Chambéry.
[6] Joins the Isère near Aiguebelle.
[7] Thirty-seven miles SE. by east of Chambéry.
[8] Pass of Mont Cenis, 6,835 ft.; 5 miles east of Lanslebourg.
[9] Twenty miles NE. of Modane.

good deal of descent: more however of the former. Lans le bourg is stated in Reichardt[1] to be 4300 feet above the level of the sea—it seems almost incredible. Our highest point was under 5000. The pull is from Lans le bourg to Cenis. We had four horses, and they could scarcely do their work. Our lowest point in view was so high, that there was little of apparent augmentation in the scale of the scenery on the Savoy side. The road however was however sometimes formidable in appearance, there being little parapet in the galleries by which the chief part of the ascent is effected. There was a good deal of snow, apparently suffered for the most part to lie unmolested: we wondered what the government road-keepers were about. Pestered with volunteer guides. From Lanslebourg to Cenis we were $3\frac{1}{4}$ hours. From Cenis to Molaret[2] $1\frac{3}{4}$. The Piedmont side is the finer. The galleries down the face of the precipitous rock which faces the plain of Niccolo, admirable; and most striking in their appearance. During the whole descent, we had no occasion to use the drag! Nothing can be more admirable, than its gradations. Eyes much dazzled by the snow, & at the top one's vision very hazy. We found ourselves little annoyed, or indeed not at all, by the cold. Yesterday however, we were almost suffocated with dust, & today had some of it between Verney[3] and Lanslebourg. Suse,[4] Hotel de la Poste. Good food and lodging: charges if anything under the average.

We went to the Churches: to the arch of Augustus:[5] and to the ruins which are on rocks commanding the valley. This was formerly the key of Italy, by means of the strong places just mentioned: now however the place is defenceless.—Between Modane and Verney we passed a strong fort with a Sardinian[6] garrison, which commands the road.

I never saw a more simple or striking instance of independence on external circumstances, than today in two Alpine dogs, which gambolled all the way up Mount Cenis with us from Lans le bourg in the snow, playing sometimes with one another, sometimes with a rope's end, a stone, or a snowball. A dry bone picked up at a "casa di ricovero"[7] raised the happiness of one of them to its acme!

Friday Mch 2nd.

$8\frac{1}{4}$ A.M.–1 P.M. $7\frac{1}{2}$ postes. Almost all down hill. Road fair. Passed the Castle of St Giorgio, and that (anciently) of St. Michel, now inhabited by Capuchins: on a most commanding station, 800 feet or more above the level of the valley; between (I think) St. Ambroggio[8] and Rivoli.[9] Road extends 8 or 10 miles in a straight line between Rivoli and Turin. Carters

---

[1] Heinrich Reichard, *Guide des Voyageurs en Europe* (1793 and many subsequent editions).
[2] Molaretto, Piedmontese village 10 miles SE. of the Mont Cenis pass.
[3] Village 6 miles SW. of Lanslebourg.
[4] Susa, 40 miles SE. of Modane and 30 west of Turin.
[5] A.D. 8.
[6] Instead of 'Savoyard'.
[7] Wayside shelter.
[8] Village 18 miles west of Turin.
[9] Town 8 miles west of Turin.

asleep in their carts—numbers of people looking at shows in Turin: & other indications of indolence. Goitres still manifest. Dresses more variegated than in Savoy. Appearance of women much improved upon France—complexion of lower orders an olive brown. Vines trained on frames. Saw numbers of ripe grapes, keeping even till now, in Turin.—It was not till we had entered Savoy that we saw the vines attached to other trees: a practice to which we have so many allusions—as for instance

> Ergo aut adultâ vitium propagine
> altas maritat populos . . .
> > > Hor. Epod. 2.[1]
> Et vitem viduas ducit ad arbores—[2]
> Stratus humi palmes viduas desiderat ulmos—[3]
> Illa tibi laetis intexet vitibus ulmos[4]   G.2—

and many others.

Turin, Hotel de l'Europe.
Dressed, and left our cards & letter at Sir Aug. Foster's.[5] Dined at restaurant in the hotel—very good; and cheap. The vin ordinaire *here* is really excellent. Went to the cathedral—a sermon was preached there which is called le sermon de la 'Sindone'—for which the chapel attached to the Cathedral is famed. We could not see the Sindone or Sudario—said to be that in which our Saviour's body was laid. It is only shown at certain times, when the bishop comes.[6] Chapel rich—we were there when the Host was shown all round—and were the only persons in the Chapel who did not kneel: which was disagreeable. I would have gone out if I could, but the crowd of persons kneeling, and busy crossing themselves, was too great— and the other alternative was of course out of the question. We saw the Queen of Sardinia[7] come in and go out. Music very good.

The number of Padres is immense: merely driving through one street to our hotel, we met 22. There are said to be 5000, including monks &c.

We went to the Palace,[8] but only saw the staircase & hall of entrance— also the same in the public building occupying the centre of this Piazza[9]— visited several Churches: particularly the beautiful one of the Virgin,[10] across

[1] 'And so he either grafts the tall poplars with a well-grown shoot of vines . . .', Horace, *Epodes*, ii, 9–10.
[2] 'And leads the vine to the unwed trees' Horace, *Odes*, IV, v. 30.
[3] 'The vine-shoot spread out on the ground yearns for the empty elms', Juvenal, *Satire*, viii, 78.
[4] 'That [land] will entwine thine elms with joyous vines', Virgil, *Georgics*, ü. 221.
[5] Augustus John *Foster, 1780–1848; diplomat, plenipotentiary to Washington 1811– 12, Turin 1824–40; cr. bart. 1831; a suicide.
[6] The chapel contains what is said to be the shroud in which Joseph of Arimathea wrapped the body of Christ.
[7] Maria Theresa, 1801–55; consort of Charles Albert, 1798–1849, king of Sardinia-Piedmont 1831.
[8] Palazzo Reale.
[9] Palazzo Madama, in the Piazza Castello.
[10] Gran Madre di Dio; erected in imitation of the Pantheon at Rome, to commemorate the return of Victor Emmanuel I in 1814.

the Po, fronting the Strada del Po—splendid pillars of marble within, and of granite without: apparently of one piece: yet we could not conceive, how they should be raised.—Bridge after the pattern of the Bridge of Jena at Paris. It was built by the French.[1]

Sir Aug. Foster most politely sent to ask us to dine *today*—but we had already dined.

The city is extremely fine, though the architecture is not chaste. A great deal of the brick is moreover unplastered—and coarse ungainly material does not give fair play to fantastic and overdone design.

Turin is at the junction of the Doria (whose course our road followed to-day down the valley) and the Po. The Doria is insignificant, but has a handsome bridge.

Saturday. March 3.

After finishing a letter to Biscoe, and some singing, lionising began. We went about to the Churches of Francesco Paulo—S. Filippo—and la Consolata—the palace of Carignano—the University court and library—and the Museum.

The Churches are all rich: but that beyond the Po is the only chaste one. At la Consolata we were Chaperoned by a very polite old Padre of 71—he took us to the chapter, and showed us an immense number of pictures sent by persons who had experienced the benefit of the Blessed Virgin's intercession. The palace is now used for public purposes, the Museum is very curious. We saw the Isiac table:[2] Mummies—having actual or apparent remains of flesh, and matted hair—Roman mosaic and statuary—and many *Etruscan remains*, very similar to the Egyptian in their general cast and character.

At the Library we saw an old Bible of 1573, very fine: and a Testament of 1569—on looking at it, it appeared that the text μετανοεῖτε[3] &c. was translated resipiscite[4]—but now I think they render it "do penance". We saw a beautifully illuminated "life of Christ." Figures of dogs had been introduced in many of the scenes, whimsically enough. There were pictures of Le Père Eternel! On examining the Catalogue, I found that there were some works of Protestant Divines there—a tract of Porteus's[5] on the benefits of Christianity—Pearson on the Creed[6]—and some works of Tillotson,[7] I observed. I remarked this to a keeper of the Library who went with us, and he said "Yes, they had them, but generally kept them locked up." I asked him whether they would not show them to a priest who desired it.

---

[1] Ponte di Po, erected 1810.

[2] *Tabula Isiaca*, found in the sixteenth century in Rome; of bronze, incised with hieroglyphics and figures portraying Isis, and inlaid with silver; proved a forgery made during the reign of Hadrian.

[3] 'repent'.

[4] 'be reasonable'.

[5] Beilby *Porteus, 'The Beneficial Effects of Christianity on the Temporal Concerns of Mankind, Proved from History and from Facts' (ca. 1804).

[6] John *Pearson, *An Exposition of the Creed* (1659).

[7] John *Tillotson, 1630–1694; abp. of Canterbury, 1691.

They said, that they would to an old priest, but certainly not to a young one!—I saw that Pascal's Thoughts were in the Library—but not his Letters—I inquired the reason, (having my suspicions, of course,) as he writes nothing against the R.C. Church. "parce qu'il touche les Jesuites", was the reply. He said however that the Jesuits had not controul over the Library. The education of the nobles is in their hands.

We saw the front of Courts of Justice, now erecting: very fine & I think in taste.

Dined at Sir Aug. Foster's. He is an anti-reformer. I find from him the Vaudois[1] are only 35 miles distant from Turin—and would rather see them than anything else on the Continent. We went, by Lady Foster's[2] kindness, to the ball at the French Embassy—I stood there like a fool, for an hour, & came away.—Rooms rich, and much beauty: at least, far, far, before France: no comparison.—I make but little time for Italian. The guide and tour books take up more. Sir A. and Lady F. have been remarkably kind, though the scale of a Sardinian Embassy differs from that of Paris. The young Fosters are Etonians.[3]

Sunday March 4.

Pascal. Hall. S[acred] S[criptures].—M[orning] S[ervice].—went to Protestant service at the Prussian Embassy. Performed by a minister from among the Vaudois.[4] At Lyon, the order was, I think—1 psalm, 2. reading Decalogue & Summary, 3. written prayer, 4. Psalm, 5. Extempore prayer, 6. Sermon, 7. Psalm, 8. Concluding (written) prayer. Here it was 1. Reading Decalogue and Summary, 2. prayer, 3. Reading a portion of Scriptures, 4. (I think) prayer, 5. Sermon, 6. Prayer. The Prayers were all written. Those I heard at Lyon were repeated I think here, mutatis mutandis. Sermon on John VI, 67, 68, & pleasing. Good attendance but not, apparently, from the Embassies. This minister, Sir A.F. told me, has now £120 per ann. as Chaplain to the Prussian, English, and some other, Embassy—formerly he had only £40 for the English. Having mentioned to John my idea about the Vaudois, he very kindly took it up: and after he had made enquiries at the Inn, we set forth and called on the Protestant Minister whom we had heard; from him we learnt how they were best accessible, and he promised to call the next day and settle matters.

Walk.—In the Afternoon, saw the carriages in the Piazza. A great

---

[1] The Vaudois or Waldenses were a small Christian community, still surviving in Piedmont, originating from 'the poor men of Lyons' lead by Peter Waldo in the twelfth century; persecuted for their attacks on the worldliness of the Church. In the sixteenth century they formally renounced all recognition of Rome. A particularly fierce attack on them by the Duke of Savoy, in the seventeenth century, aroused sympathy for them abroad, and inspired *Milton's sonnet 'Avenge, O Lord, thy slaughtered saints'. Napoleon granted them a constitution in 1805, abolished by Victor Emmanuel I in 1814. Not until 1848 did the Vaudois receive a guarantee from Charles Albert of religious and political freedom.

[2] Albinia, 1788–1867, da. of Vere Hobart; m. 1815.

[3] Frederick John, 1816–57, later attaché at Turin and then at Dresden; and Cavendish Hervey, 1817–1890, later a priest.

[4] M. Bonjour; see 6 Mar. 32.

crowd, and a very pretty sight. The Queen was in her state carriage: the princes[1] too were in the procession, and the King, but incog. Sunday may be & I think is the day for the King habitually to show himself among his people—but as George 3. did it at Windsor, on the Terrace: not amidst this glare of state equipages and the pomp of military display, and altogether in a manner which must entail the doing a vast deal of unnecessary labour on the day of rest, and therefore is a manifest breach of God's law.[2]—A quiet evening, with some reading.

Monday March 4 [sc. 5].[3]

The subject of balls and evening parties has been a good deal on my mind, and was one of conversation between John and me last night.

Besides a constitutional indifference or aversion, which it might be matter of duty to resist, I likewise feel unable to discern in them, particularly as conducted abroad, anything bearing the semblance of rational intercourse: or any purpose at all tending to improve as well as relax: at all rising above the character of mere amusement. As Christians I think we are at least bound to strive to preserve in our amusements, something better than amusement: and still to be busied more or less directly, in improving the moral, the spiritual, the intellectual, or the social man. If we admit what is *mere* relaxation, it seems to me that it ought to be private, and not of this mixed and indiscriminate character. On the whole then I do not wish to go to a ball to dance: and why go to do nothing? I am therefore minded, please God, for the future to endeavour to avoid them.

(A record of inconsistency which ought not to be erased.)[4]

Monday March 5.

Italian Grammar. Finished Bourgeois Gentilhomme—reading Lardner's 'Outlines'. And wrote to T.G.—Went with J.N.G. to call on the lady of the Fr[ench] Ambassador[5]—and to see the Capuchin convent over the Po.[6] It commands a most magnificent view of the Alps, the city & country. Monks VERY dirty. Many good texts inscribed on the doors of their dormitories, from S.S. & elsewhere. e.g. (in Latin) "man! remember that thou art earth, and be not proud! that thou art joined to God, and be not unthankful!"

The Protestant minister called and acquainted us, that he was going up to the valley tomorrow, and would readily accompany us. This appears a very happy opportunity. We engaged three places, and propose starting at six tomorrow morning, to return Wednesday Evg.

[1] Victor Emmanuel, 1820–1878, afterwards Victor Emmanuel II of Sardinia, and first king of united Italy; and his b. Ferdinand, 1822–55, duke of Genoa.
[2] Exodus, xx. 8–11.
[3] This entry from Lambeth MS 1420.
[4] Later entry.
[5] Césarine d'Houdetot, 1794–1877, religious philanthropist; m. 1811 Aimable Guillaume Prosper Brugière de Barante, 1782–1866, author, administrator, and diplomat; attached to Mme. de Stael, 1805; prefect, 1809–15; cr. baron 1819; envoy to Turin, 1830–5, St. Petersburg 1835–48.
[6] On Il Monte, to the east of the city.

In the evening went to a ball at Sir Aug. Foster's—for no other purpose than to count one, and eat some refreshment which certainly was not earned by my exertions. Came away in about an hour. Sir A.F. very kind: asked us to dine on Wednesday after our expected return from the Valleys. He introduced me to a Sardinian officer whose name I did not catch.—Packing.

Tuesday March 6.

Called at 5 A.M. Left Turin by the Diligence for Pignerol[1] at 6. Distance 20 miles or more: performed in $4\frac{1}{2}$ hours. M. Bonjour, the Vaudois minister who acts as Chaplain to the Protestant Embassies here, was our companion. I had a good deal of conversation with him, and should have had more, had I been more expert in speaking, and more particularly in understanding, i.e. following with my ear the words spoken. Most of what I heard in this and other conversations I propose detailing in a letter home.

We breakfasted at Pignerol: which lies S.W. of Turin. Inn kept by a Protestant. We continued our journey to La Tour,[2] still all three together, in a voiture driven by one of the people of the valley. The road became tolerably rough, but the appearance of the country was such, as to guarantee its beauty and richness during summer. On the road I saw the finest tree by much which has met my eyes on the continent, just at the entrance of the valley. M. Bonjour pointed out to me, near the boundary line by which their settlements are restricted, one of the ordinary Madonnas by the roadside: where, beneath the painting, on a space usually left blank, was a picture of the infernal regions, and several persons represented as burning in them. The meaning was but too clear,[3] and circumstantial evidence seemed to corroborate his statement, that the heads were meant to represent the Vaudois.—Afterwards we passed through the first village, that of St. Jean:[4] here the Protestant Church faces the Catholic, and a high wooden paling was erected, by compulsion, to hide the entrance of the former! John however understood that they were now at liberty to pull it down, if they would.

We arrived at La Tour at $2\frac{1}{2}$ P.M. and were well entertained in an Inn kept by Protestants. We saw the Church, the principal school of the parish, and the Hospital. They were all simple enough but well adapted to their purposes. There are I think eight other schools in the parish—and *every* child is taught to read and write.

We called on M. Pierre Bert, Pastor of La Tour, late Moderator of the Churches, and father in law to M. Bonjour. He apologised for not accompanying us as he was unwell: and we had a good deal of conversation with him. We saw also his daughter and niece, both pleasing, and the latter pretty. Speaking generally the old gentleman seemed very thankful for the degree of indulgence which the Vaudois at present enjoy: and said, if Providence did not give them everything, doubtless it was because they

---

[1] Pinerolo, 22 miles SW. of Turin.   [2] Torre, 8 miles SW. of Pinerolo.
[3] 'Clear' written over 'evident'.
[4] Luserna San Giovanni, 2 miles SE. of Torre.

were not fit for it. He seemed to feel much goodwill and gratitude towards the English generally, and particularly towards some who have taken a peculiar interest in the inhabitants of the valleys, as for instance Mr. Gilly and Col. Beckwith.[1] The latter gentleman has passed the three last winters among them, building schools and performing other acts of munificence, and it is easy to believe that as M. Bonjour told me "son nom est en benediction dans les vallées".—We were pressed to take food, but did not, and left them to pursue our way. Dined comfortably at our Inn. In the evening, read Pascal's eighth, ninth, and tenth, provincial letters. From such morality as is there exposed, what could we expect except the spirit of hostility to such persons as the Vaudois. Letter to [blank] dated [blank].

Wednesday March 7.

In the morning I walked out before breakfast, and saw something more of the valley. We went after breakfast again to Mons. Bert's—had more conversation with him, and parted when compelled by our time to do so, with many invitations to return.

On our walk we found violets in bloom, the earliest of the year that we had seen—indeed they blow, under particular aspects, much sooner in these valleys than in the plains. M. Bert said, in some places they had them during the whole winter. Aspect is everything in this country: we see one side of a valley and the plain which composes it, covered with snow, while the other is perfectly cleared. And in the open country, nearly the same thing may be observed in each furrow in a ploughed field.—To find nature putting forth her earliest buds in these valleys, among such shelter as the rocks afford, appears singular, though it may be physically accounted for: but it presents so striking and yet so simple an analogy to the moral condition of the valleys, that it is enough to make any man commit poetry on the spot.

We brought away, by way of remembrance from M. Bert, a little book he has written containing an abridged history of the Vaudois,[2] and other matters intended for their use. It afforded me interesting reading in the weary Diligence to Turin, and in the evening.

At present laws exist against them, but are not enforced, and the present King has shown himself favourable to them. Their numbers are from 20 to 25,000. Three Valleys—Loserne—La Perouse—St. Martin. There are a good many Catholics at La Tour—but in most of the parishes extremely few. M. Bert said he firmly believed that the Vaudois still cling, as ever, to the faith of their forefathers, with the same fidelity of adherence which led them as willing victims to the stake.

We left before one, and got to Pignerol before 3 P.M. We came down to

---

[1] William Stephen *Gilly, 1789–1855, vicar of Norham and canon of Durham, wrote a *Narrative of an Excursion to the Mountains of Piedmont and Researches Among the Vaudois or Waldenses* (1824). This book so much impressed John Charles *Beckwith, 1789–1862, who had lost a leg at Waterloo, that he was moved to settle among them.

[2] *Le Livre de famille, ou instructions familières sur l'histoire des églises vaudoises et sur la religion, avec quelques cantiques* (1830).

Turin in 4½ hours! 20 miles, road good, and chiefly down hill, horses part of the way five, and part six! M. Bonjour came with us, and we shook hands with him heartily on parting at Turin.—May He who hath preserved to himself this remnant, yet continue to preserve it: and as the Vaudois, taken as a body, have indeed received in this life their evil things, so may they be abundantly blessed in that which is to come.

One of their very best characteristics, to my mind, is, that though they have perhaps suffered more at the hands of Popery than any other men, yet they do not contemplate with satisfaction those revolutionary movements which are now threatening it with destruction, because they do not see in them a conflict between a pure religion and a perverted one, but between a perverted religion and no religion at all.

As far as *we* had experience of them, their honesty fully bore out the purity of their principles. All the charges made were of the most moderate description. At the Inn, for a sittingroom and doublebedded chamber—for dinner with no small variety of eatables & a bottle of *good* wine—for breakfast the next morning, and for fire, the whole charge amounted to ten francs, or eight shillings! At ordinary Inns we have paid twice as much for less and worse material. I am delighted to have paid even this rapid and inadequate visit to the valleys.

Thursday March 8.

On leaving the Hotel de l'Europe, we can give it the character of an Inn decidedly good: for eatables remarkably so, and very moderate: for apartments, rather expensive.

8 A.M.–4 P.M. Turin–Alexandria.[1] 12¾ postes. A *day* of rain: the first of that description which we have had. Roads rather heavy in consequence: but well made: and we got on remarkably well. Posting in Piedmont on the whole the best we have seen. Our road lay through Truffarello,[2] Poirino,[3] and Asti.[4] At first by the bank of the Po. Passed a royal chateau. Country flat for five postes—then broken.—We saw numbers of carts containing each a very long cask of wine, whose stopper was evidently pretty often displaced: the object seemed to be, retailing it about the country. Most of them carried hay to feed the oxen, or cows, or horses, which drew them. Our road lay through a corn rather than a wine country. Asti however (birth place of Alfieri)[5] is celebrated for wine.—Though abused by Reichardt, it seemed to me to contain more Palazzi than any provincial town we have yet seen.—Lunched on Vaudois cheese, which we brought away from the valleys yesterday. Near this place our road joined the course of the Tanari[6] a large river which flows into the Po below Alessandria.

After reaching Alessandria we went out and saw 1. The Palace—used as a

---

[1] Alessandria, 48 miles ESE. of Turin.
[2] Eight miles SE. of Turin.
[3] Thirteen miles SE. by south of Turin.
[4] Twenty-eight miles SE. of Turin.
[5] Vittorio Alfieri, 1749–1803, poet and dramatist.
[6] River Tanaro.

sleeping place between Genoa and Turin: as yet unfinished: cieling of the entrance worthy of remark. We went to 2. the Churches of the Jesuits and St Alessandro—3. the citadel under cover of a soldier with whom we scraped an acquaintance. He could not take us far: but we saw that it was extensive and strong, with large quantities of stores, and a double moat, fortifications passing between. They can fill the moat at any time by means of sluice gates at the bridge by which they can stop the course of the river. Our soldier friend took us into the "Cantine" and there we drank wine with him.—The bridge is covered, and curious. River large. Town indifferent. 'Place' had acacias round it, planted by the French.

Albergo dell' Italia. A Diligence Inn: but fair, at least—and cheaper than most.

Friday Mch 9.

8 A.M.–4 P.M. 11½ postes (excluding of course the ½ p[oste] royal[1] for entering Genoa.)

Crossed the plains of Marengo.[2] After Novi,[3] entered a hilly country. Prospect most wintery till we reached the summit of the Appenines: almost everything, both hill and dale, covered with snow. The scenery however was very interesting. Its most remarkable, at least most novel feature, was the richness of the rocks, which (at least as it appeared to our inexperienced eyes) were streaked and chequered with veins of marble in profusions. Even the stones laid down to make the road even, very often full of beauty. Two ruins of castles on the right on the ascending course— and many, in descending. Churches almost everywhere placed in the most prominent situations, through Piedmont. We saw today one in the midst of the snow on the very top of a well-grown Appenine. Character of the scenery romantic, sometimes after the British manner. It is on the British scale, which perhaps suggested the idea. Road generally very good: a noble[4] national work, taken as a whole. Last stage from Pontedecimo[5] through suburb almost all the way. Numbers of villas. Numbers of ever-greens here, new to me in that character: weather extremely mild, though very cold on the other side. Rejoiced to get a sight of the sea—it always reminds one of home: first, as an Englishman: secondly because it conveys the idea of direct & proximate communication with its country. Besides which it is I think the most glorious object in nature.

Drive into Genoa most interesting: road makes the circuit of the harbour,[6] after passing inside the lighthouse. Then the ampitheatre opens on your sight, and its extent affords some time to familiarise yourself with the many beauties of the scene.

[1] A tax on travellers.
[2] Three miles SE. of Alessandria; here Bonaparte and Desaix turned apparent defeat into victory over the Austrians in 1800.
[3] Novi Ligure, 14 miles SE. of Alessandria; Suvorov defeated Joubert there in 1799.
[4] 'a noble' instead of 'noble as a'.
[5] Seven miles north by west of Genoa.
[6] Instead of 'bay'.

Hotel de la Croix de Malte. Delightful prospect—ships in the harbour for the foreground, with the mole and lighthouses: the wide sea melting into the distance in front, and to the right a crowd of snowclothed peaks.

Walked out—discovered a reading room with English news. We have none since leaving Paris—and I need not say that the remainder of the afternoon was devoted to devouring it. It only served to excite a craving for more.

Saturday March 10.

Bought a map: investigated by our books the principal objects, at least a selection of them: traced them on the map, and numbered them to be visited in order, according as they lie. This plan we have found the best, both on this and other occasions.

1. Church of the Carmine. All the Churches here are rich—otherwise, this has nothing peculiar. We took it in our way from the Bank, Gibbs and Co's.

2. Church of the Annunziata. Extremely gorgeous. The walls, pillars and cieling, were of of marble, relieved only by paintings and gilding. Here in fact staircases, floors, fronts, are of marble—the two former even in the Hospitals.

3. After looking at the fine entrance and staircases of the Durazzo Palace,[1] we went to the University—now closed. Library—Hall of Examination Too much painting &c. for much examination to go on there, I should think —not like the severe (q. almost shabby) simplicity of the Schools at Oxford? Chapel—bas-relief of Michael Angelo. School of Law, altar piece by Guido. Other Schools &c. Fine marble lions in the vestibule.

4. King's Palace—formerly of Marcello Durazzo.[2] Many fine pictures. Paul Veronese's chef d'œuvre. I was most pleased with heads of the Madonna and our Saviour by Carlo Dolci. But I never had any discrimination in pictures, and fear the effect of viewing so hurriedly a profusion of them will be rather to destroy my "nihil illud" than to impart anything like a genuine taste. Yet I should love to learn.

Doria.[3] Going to decay. Its present (I suppose) degenerate possessor[4] has deserted the scene of the glories of his ancester, and the seat of his honourable repose, for Rome. Remains of art & splendour yet discernible. Statue of Doria as Neptune behind, in the gardens. We passed on our return through Piazza Acquaverde, and agreed in admiring much the modern exterior of the palace[5] now undergoing renovation there.

6. Albergo di Poveri. View from the entrance beautiful—and even now *scarcely* distinguishable from a summer prospect. Staircase and landing, and Chapel, all extremely fine. Statues of the benefactors, in marble like every-

---

[1] Palazzo Marcello Durazzo.

[2] Palazzo Reale, built for the Durazzo family, purchased by the Piedmontese royal family 1815.

[3] Palazzo Doria, presented in 1522 to Andrea Doria, 1470–1560, admiral of the Papal, Imperial, French and native fleets.

[4] Prince Giovani Andrea Doria Pamphili, 1779–1838.

[5] Palazzo Faraggiana.

thing else, the chief ornament. 1800 poor are harboured here. Tended if sick, taught trades if able to work. The children, and men, were importunate in begging: which seems to be a fault in the regulations.—The establishment however, as well as the Great Hospital, is noble—perhaps there is too much personal ostentation in the careful exhibition of the statues of the benefactors, since it seems to be systematic. But this is unfair.

7. We attempted to see Palazzo Brignole—but could not *sur le champs*, so went to the Serra,[1] and saw the gorgeous, though not very large, oval salon. It seemed about 40 f. by 27. Profusion of gilding, yet (to me) no idea of tawdriness suggested.

8. Ducal Palace.[2] Front worthy of attention. Two salles, petite & grande, are shown—The latter is a "has been". Its marble pillars are now wrecks, and its marble statues are not. Plaister stands instead. Both are very fine apartments. In hopes of seeing here a bonâ fide rostrum[3] of a Carthaginian vessel but it has been removed.

I ought now to put as No 9., our dinner, which was welcome after so much work. We were entertained chez Michel Restaurateur (*Grand'*) as he calls himself, after the manner of the Continent,) fairly enough.

9. Cathedral. Chapel to the left (entering opposite altar) reputed to contain ashes of John Baptist. Saw the case in which they are said to have been transported. This Chapel seemed to attract peculiar attention from the worshippers in the Church. The celebrated Emerald Vase[4] we cannot see till Monday. In another Chapel on the same side, altarpiece[5] by Canova.[6]

10. Church of St Ambroggio. Not unlike Annunciata. Evening came upon us. Too late for pictures in this 'dim religious light'.

11. Church of Remedio.

12. Church of St Stefano. The floor an inclined plane. Beautiful altarpiece, representing the stoning of the Saint. But the figures above—to omit the fundamental fault in design, which always attends, I think, the representation of God in a human form—are so like those beneath, that the picture did not convey to my mind the idea of the first being high and far away in heaven, the latter on earth. The upper part by Raffaelle, the lower by Julio Romano.[7]

13. Hospital. Admirably arranged: for 1000 patients, more or less—at present less. The Dispensary beautifully arranged. In it we saw a picture, most curious to behold. A line of wires at certain distances, vertically, over it. Viewing it in front, it appeared to be a man and child—from each side, a female face, but these different one from the other. And all, moreover, appeared beautiful.

---

[1] Palazzo Serra.

[2] Ancient residence of the doges, founded in the thirteenth century.

[3] Ship's ram.

[4] A grail reputed to have been captured by the Genoese at Caesarea, during the Crusades.

[5] Instead of 'statues'.

[6] Antonio Canova, 1757–1822; neoclassic sculptor.

[7] Giulio dei Giannuzzi, 1492–1546; also known as Pippi or Romano; architect and religious painter.

14. Promenade of Acquasole. Fine views of sea and city, but not quite panoramic.

I have numbered our day's work, because I think the arrangement of the objects would be found on the whole a convenient one.

Diary of an Invalid[1]—guide books. Journal and Blackbook—with finishing a letter to Saunders commenced yesterday, occupied the remainder of the day.

Sunday March 11.

We were pleased to find that there was not only a Protestant, but an English Church here: and we were also pleased to find it well served by a Mr. Battiscombe,[2] I fancy an Eton man and all but a contemporary of mine, brother to the regular minister.[3] His sermon contrasted the temptations of Eve & of our Lord.[4] Chapel neat and comfortable. About fifty persons.

Dined at Croix de Malte, and walked afterwards to the lighthouse. Reading &c. as usual.

Monday March 12.

Heard from home: and dispatched a letter thither.—Went to the Church of St. Filippo Neri—small but beautiful: & a Madonna by Puget[5] in the Oratory—to the Ciro,[6] large and as rich as any we have seen—to the Cathedral, to see the Green Vase, but failed—and to the Brignole Palace.[7] A beautiful collection of pictures. Carlo *Dolce* seems to deserve his name, judging from what we have yet seen of him: today, a beautiful picture of the Agony on copper. I must also record one picture which I disliked much: St. Thomas's unbelief, by Cappuccino[8] I think.

Left Genoa about 1. $5\frac{1}{4}$ hours—$6\frac{1}{4}$ postes, to Chiavari.[9] Road most interesting. On our left, the bold Appennines: on our right the blue and open Mediterranean: before and behind, for the most part, very extensive views of a magnificent coast, to Sestri[10] in front, and along the whole coast of the gulf of Genoa behind—Cape Fino being a prominent object, and worthy of its conspicuous station. Around & immediately beneath us, the rich and thickly peopled vales which lie between those many arms of the Appenine chain extending to the sea. Oranges and lemons in great abundance: olives

----

[1] Henry *Matthews, *Diary of an Invalid* (1820); the journal of a tour in Portugal, Italy, Switzerland, and France.

[2] Henry Battiscombe, 1802–1871; he later founded the Zion chapel in Cambridge, then rejoined the Anglican church and was minister at Kidbroke, Kent, 1865–71.

[3] Robert Battiscombe, 1799–1881; priest at Brompton, Middlesex, 1835–40; vicar of Barkway, Hertfordshire, 1840. Both brothers were at Eton and King's.

[4] Gen. iii. 1–16, Matt. iv. 1–11.

[5] Pierre Puget, 1620–94; French sculptor.

[6] S. Siro.

[7] Palazzo Rosso del Marchese Brignole.

[8] Bernardo Strozzi, 1581–1644; called il Cappucino Genovese.

[9] Twenty-two miles east of Genoa.

[10] Sestri Levante, 4 miles east of Chiavari.

cultivated everywhere in profusion, on stages from the tops of hills often to their summits. Churches abundant indeed: though their architecture is not always of the most strictly appropriate kind. Their bells were ringing in many places: effect very pleasing.—Road hilly but good. Towns along this coast the most pleasing we have seen: extremely clean, the buildings very pretty, and the situations also.

Chiavari. Hotel de la Poste. Good: and moderate. Pretty town. Close to the sea. Found high mass going on in the large Church[1] to the right of the Promenade. The building was everywhere lighted up: it is very rich in painting, gold, and marble: its pillars were all hung with rich crimson silk: and its floor was crowded with people, chiefly women, who wear here the pretty headdress of Genoa, a light muslin scarf, thrown back[2] on the head, and reaching below the waste—the best headdress, I think, by much, that we have seen. In this Church its effect was particularly beautiful. The people were all on their knees, and chanting, at the moment when I entered; and certainly a more imposing scene I never beheld. It was soon spoiled (partially at least) by the prostration of the priests before bringing out the Host.

Tuesday Mch 13.

$8\frac{1}{4}$ A.M.–6 P.M. Chiavari to Sarzana,[3] 11 postes. We passed Sestri, and then ascended the Bracco.[4] Our greatest height may have been 2500 feet. I walked a great deal, and hunted heath &c. upon the hills. The heath was in full bloom: the bushes were extremely fine, larger than most of the *firs* in the vicinity—but these were of course dwarfs. Road fine to Borghetto:[5] but one can scarcely conceive *why* they have taken it over these tremendous hills, instead of following the sea-coast: this we hear Napoleon intended too. The road is indeed admirably made: but it seems a waste of ingenuity and magnificence. At our greatest height it was mild and warm. An immense quantity of marble used in making the road. Before Mattarana[6] the road opens on a very fine view of about eight chains of hills, almost all lower than that on which it passes. After the descent, the road becomes indifferent, and winds among these hills. Opening on the bay of La Spezia magnificent. Saw Lerici, the place of Shelley's residence,[7] but the road does not pass close. Passed the Magra[8] in a *pont volant*.—Walk round ramparts at Sarzana. Hotel de Londres (late Luigiani). Pretty good. Evening employed as usual.

Wednesday, March 14.

$7\frac{1}{2}$ A.M.–$6\frac{1}{2}$ P.M. Eight Italian postes. Stopped two hours at Carrara,[9] which were employed, first in walking or scrambling over a break-shin path, com-

---

[1] San Salvatore di Lavagna. [2] Instead of 'over their'.
[3] Town 40 miles SE. of Chiavari; on frontier between kingdom of Piedmont and duchy of Modena.
[4] Six miles east of Sestri. [5] Village 25 miles SE. of Chiavari.
[6] Town 48 miles SE. of Chiavari. 'and Borghetto' deleted.
[7] In 1821–2; $7\frac{1}{4}$ miles east of Spezia.
[8] Ligurian river. [9] Thirteen miles ESE. of Spezia.

posed of pieces of white marble about and under the size of paving stones, and quite loose. (Before reaching Carrara one perceives that the stream which the road meets is of a dingy sickly white—it is from the dust of the marble.) After we had seen one of the quarries we went to two studij and bought some little things. Crossed a chain of hill to Massa[1]—finely situated. Hills and plain extremely rich. At Pietra Santa[2] we leave the sea-road, and again cross hills very rich in foliage, even at this season, until we descend upon Lucca,[3] crossing the Serchio.[4] Cathedral fine—the Palace we did not enter. From Lucca to Pisa[5]—leaning tower visible from a distance of three or four miles, but not in a point of view favourable for perceiving the inclination.—Road, the whole of today, very fine,—Passed, in all six customhouses.—On our right we left Via Reggio, where Shelley's body was found.[6]—The Duchess of Berry[7] was in the Palace at Massa, we were informed.

We saw no Sardinian troops from Genoa *eastward*, till we got to Sarzana, where, as being a frontier-town, we found there were some fifty. Curious contrast with the other side of the Sardinian dominians.

Today we had a violent battle with the Postillions, on the grand question of five, or six pauls per poste. The latter is exorbitant, but I suppose that, after making a gallant resistance, we must give in. The postillions grew more and more sulky, so we paid worse and worse, until at last we arrived at the "ne plus ultra" of 'cattiva paga'[8]—three pauls!

Walked along the river: quays particularly beautiful.—

Tre Donzelle. A very comfortable house: and decidedly reasonable in its prices.—

Thursday. March 15.

After breakfast, sallied forth to view the celebrated quaternion. First went to the Cathedral. Saw here paintings of the era 1300. Colouring faint, of course, and not bearing tokens of much absolute merit: yet very curious and interesting. This building boasts an immense *variety* of attractions. It is of marble, one may almost say of course. The front towards the Baptistery like what we have seen at Lucca and elsewhere. Here we have bronze doors, one professing to be brought from Jerusalem: columns of oriental granite: every kind of marble: verd antique, brocatello, porphyry, &c: pictures, sculptures, mosaic in stone and wood: combined with great dimensions. And yet of this cathedral as a whole it may perhaps be said that it cannot

[1] Four miles SE. of Carrara.
[2] Eleven miles SE. of Carrara, 15 NW. of Lucca; in an outlier of the grand duchy of Tuscany.
[3] City 38 miles west by north of Florence; seat of another formally independent duchy.
[4] A Tuscan river.
[5] Pisa, 11 miles SW. of Lucca, lay in the grand duchy of Tuscany.
[6] Port of the duchy of Lucca, 12 miles west of the capital. *Shelley was drowned in 1822.
[7] Caroline Ferdinande Louise, 1798–1870; da. of Francis I of Naples; m. 1816 Charles, Duc de Berry, 1778–1820, a younger s. of Charles X.
[8] 'bad pay'. A paul was worth about fivepence.

be called grand—in the same sense that Lord Brougham cannot be called a great man; it is a wonderful assemblage, but a defective combination. There is an immense accumulation of objects, but they do not harmonise as parts of a whole.—However, it is a most striking interior.

Leaning tower. Observe the very striking difference in the ascent of the stair, between the difficulty of one part of the circuit and that of the other. —Went to the top.—It might lean more, one would suppose, without danger. Inclination (of which the total is fourteen feet) begins to decrease at the *fourth* story: but scarce perceptibly. The eye however is immediately struck by the angle formed by the vertical of the eighth with that of the rest.

The supposition suggested by circumstantial evidence, strictly, would seem to be one removed from both opinions, and midway between them: that the soil began to give way when the architect had reached the third story: and that as the lapse progressed, he made nearer and nearer approaches to rectification—and perhaps the eighth story was added to make all safe.—It is liable to the general objection urged against the Cathedral.

The interior of the Baptistery appeared somewhat sombre, but striking: Echo remarkable: as was, particularly, that in the vaults of the Pantheon at Paris.

In the Cathedral, again saw an attempt to represent the Almighty.— There was a picture of a Greek bishop assisting at the Mass, and the 'commissionaire' dignified this with the title of the reconciliation of the Churches: and would have it that the Greek Church now owned obedience to the See of Rome.

Campo Santo. Gradation of the frescoes remarkable—a very large collection of remains: among the rest, those of two uncles of the man who showed it. Earth from Jerusalem.[1]

In an old fresco painting, representing the infernal regions, they profess to discover, in different parts of three separate countenances, an aggregate likeness to Napoleon!

The Cathedral, we learned, has forty canons and twenty eight Chaplains!—

Went to the Church di Cavalleri, adorned with trophies and a crucifix in silver. Found a priest preaching violently, nearly in the dark.

Went to Leghorn,[2] 2 It[alian] postes, in a caleche de remise. road flat— plain very highly and thoroughly cultivated. Women of Herculean frame:[3] carr[yin]g immense loads of wood.—Dined at Thompson's, Locanda di St Marco: very good: price full. Went to the Docks, Cathedral, English burying ground, and Jews' synagogue. The burying ground is appropriate and has some good epitaphs. At the synagogue the man who conducted us to the 'concierge' strove anxiously to get paid beforehand, and before we had discovered that he did not show it himself.

---

[1] Reputedly brought from Calvary by crusaders.
[2] Tuscan port 12 miles SSW. of Pisa.
[3] Instead of 'strength'.

Returned at night—but after having made our contemplated purchases of alabaster, with as much care and consideration as the time would allow, at Micali's, in the Via Grande. This is said to be one of the best places: not one of the cheapest.

Friday. March 16.

Left Pisa before half past ten A.M. and arrived in Florence[1]—six Italian postes—in a little more than six hours: having however yielded the point of six pauls. Beggars innumerable. Spring already making its appearance in many places. Kept near the Arno: which though muddy at Pisa we are glad to find is clear at Florence: it is discoloured by a tributary stream which joins it on the way. Country sufficiently broken.
Countenances of the peasantry prepossessing:—according with the general repute.
     Schneiderff's Hotel, Florence.
Went to the Post Office, & upon other matters—then content to spend the evening chez nous, reading and writing. Guide books—Journal—Revolt of Islam[2]—part of Hallam's Essay.[3]

Saturday March 17.

Expedition to discharge ourselves of our letters. Left those for Mrs M'Kenzie[4] and the Minister[5]—though the latter is now ἀποδημῶν [6]—at Rome. Could not find Hallam's Abbate.[7] Spent upwards of two hours very pleasurably in the Gallery[8]—where we hope to spend more. The collection of portraits in Corridors is most interesting. Much struck by the bold character of the Roman Imperial busts. Two altars: one triangular: both with hollows—but no aperture for the blood. This hollow is what Sophocles in a difficult passage calls the γύαλον[9] of the altar. Had only time to bestow a cursory attention on the Tuscan rooms—in what we saw, Carlo Dolce appeared to me to bear the bell.

Dined at Vigna's, Via della Porta Rossa; well, and moderately.

Went to see the Cathedral with its portraits of Dante and Hawkwood,[10] and last work of Michael Angelo.[11] Remained some time, to catch the effect

---

[1] Capital of Tuscany.
[2] *Shelley (1818).
[3] Arthur Henry *Hallam, *Essay on the Philosophical Writings of Cicero* (1832).
[4] Perhaps Anna Watson, née Fowler, d. 1854; who m. 1825 Thomas Mackenzie, 1797–1887, of Ord, Ross-shire.
[5] (Sir) George Hamilton *Seymour, 1797–1880, diplomat; knighted 1836; British envoy at Florence, 1830; Brussels, 1836; Lisbon, 1846; St. Petersburg, 1851–4; Vienna, 1855–8.
[6] 'away from home'.
[7] Paolo Pifferi; *Hallam's friend and teacher in Italy in 1827.
[8] The Uffizi.
[9] *Oedipus at Colonus*, 1492, in a passage so corrupt as to be meaningless.
[10] Sir John de *Hawkwood, d. 1394 in Florence; general, and joint-ambassador for England at Rome, Florence, and Naples. Fresco of him by Paulo Ucello, 1436, transferred to canvas 1845.
[11] *Pièta*, left unfinished.

and general character—so important in a building of this kind. An object however which one usually sacrifices altogether, for the sake of bestowing tumultuous glances on a multitude of minute objects. Well were it, if in these matters only we sacrificed wholes to parts.

Baptistery. Canvas drapery here and in Cathedral: indicates perhaps at least a questionable taste. Remark gates of bronze, and altar piece. The outer surface of the white marble is everywhere jaundiced: and the dark has lost its fresh and glossy blackness. We see sometimes carved stone in England, which appears to my eye (though I own neither competent nor unprejudiced,) more appropriate, more rich, and more imposing.

Saw two Baptisms administered: dissatisfied[1] with the matter, disgusted (I cannot use a weaker term) with the *manner* of the service. Much irreverent ministering of holy things have I seen in England: but never any to equal this. I got behind the priest's shoulder & looked over his book—but it was only by *jumping* that my eye could follow his voice.

Sunday March 18.

Greek Testament. Pascal—finished Vol.I and Hall—also finished. Went to the French or rather Genevan Protestant service, supposing it the English: and found a clergyman earnestly pleading the cause of the poor, in an expository sermon on the parable of Lazarus and Dives.[2]—Afterwards, English service was performed to a new set of persons in the same place. Both congregations respectable, and the first crowded.—Dined at home, i.e. at Schneiderff's.—On the whole, I am agreeably surprised at the number of Protestant, and of English places of worship, which one finds on the Continent. There seems to be little to hope from the Romish Church.

Monday March 19.

This day was the day of St Joseph—we were therefore precluded from seeing the lions in general. We went to St Joseph's Church, and found services in the course of performance there. It is painful to speak disrespectfully of any religious services—but certainly these seemed no better than mummery. A crowd of people—few had books, or seemed to participate more than ourselves in the services—which were chiefly carried on behind the high altar, out of sight. Every now and then an entry of priests, with gigantic candlesticks & paltry lights nodding before them—then an array round the chancel, and an exit. Bad music.

Church of Santa Croce. Extremely large—extreme length I should think upwards of 400 feet. Monuments of Galileo—Michael Angelo (who is buried here)—Dante, only erected in 1829—Alfieri, by Canova—and Machiavelli. A rare assemblage!

There is a good deal of sculpture in the Church besides these monuments.

Went to call on Mrs Mackenzie, who has been remarkably kind and attentive. Attempted the Pitti, but found it shut. Received letters from home

---

[1] Instead of 'disgusted'.   [2] Luke xvi. 19–31.

by post—dined very comfortably at the Restaurant "della Luna" near the Cathedral.

Wrote home—and also part of a letter to Phillimore: and one to Micali at Leghorn about our alabasters.

Tuesday. March 20.

Pitti Palace. It was most vexatious (tho' necessary, as there did not seem to be any catalogue forthcoming) to be encumbered with a guide, as the hour and a half which was all we could bestow on the entire of this magnificent collection, might have been well spent on a single room or two. Here are the chef-d-œuvres of Raffael and Carlo Dolce—two battle pieces by Salvator, the larger one of which contains more delineation of passion in countenances than I ever saw before in any such space—the Fates by Michael Angelo, a striking picture, in which the countenances are most legibly marked with the character & the genius of the artist—and works in short of almost every celebrated painter, or at least every first rate, of the Flemish and Italian schools, except Claude[1]—. The Palace itself is extremely splendid—and that I think without being gaudy: which cannot be said of all the Continental Palaces. Canova's Venus finished the exhibition. The turn of the limbs is indeed exquisite: but the fingers seemed to me unnaturally pointed—the attitude not wholly free from constraint— and the line of the profile as having less beauty[2] than one might conceive attainable.

Then we went to see a private collection in the House of an Abbate, opposite the Pitti: his name I have done him the injustice to forget. It contained, though small, divers fine pictures: and in particular one by Titian of his daughter, holding up a basket of fruit, which is very celebrated.[3]

The remainder of the lionising portion of the day we devoted to the Tribune[4]—and it was I think well bestowed.

It is difficult for an ignorant person to speak of the Venus de Medicis: because being accustomed to have his ideas on these subjects in great measure regulated by more authoritative opinions from others, in a case where he has heard much before seeing at all, he will not know, after sight, what portion of his impressions are fictitious, and what natural: how much he really owes to his own feelings and perceptions, and how much to those of others, with which, as an eyeglass he came prepared to see. Reserving then these inexplicable doubts, I did most warmly admire the Venus, when I had looked at her long enough to form any thing like a general idea; and the more I looked afterwards, the more & warmer admiration was excited. The conception, except that it is not perhaps strictly correct in point of fact—I mean, inasmuch as it does not correspond to the ancient ideas of Venus, is most exquisite. And this is no great objection, if the statue does

[1] Claude Gellée, 1600–42; French painter who worked in Italy.
[2] 'having less beauty' substituted for 'less beautiful'.
[3] In the collection of the Abate Celotti; bought 1832 by the Kaiser Friedrich Museum, Berlin; now held not to be Titian's da.
[4] A gallery in the Uffizi.

indeed correspond with the most minute accuracy to a far higher form of ideal beauty, constituting a far higher law to the true artist. Nor is it altogether so incorrect in point of fact, as has been said by Matthews. If we adopt the character of the goddess such as she is represented, for instance in the first Æneid;

> Virginis os habitumque gerens, & virginis arma
> Spartanae: . . .
> Namque humeris de more habilem suspenderat arcum
> Spartanae, dederatque comam diffundere ventis:
> &c. &c. &c. . . . —[1]

here we have a picture which I think suggests as great a degree of artlessness and modesty, as has been embodied in the celebrated statue. The vest[2] and circumstances are different, but I think the essential points of character, now constituting the question, are the same. Happier illustrations of what has been asserted might if I mistake not be adduced.

For the present it is enough to record the vivid feelings of delight which I enjoyed, like most men, in the Tribune. The turn of the limbs is grace itself, the attitude the same: and the marble, though discoloured, has a rich gloss upon it. With the ravishing merits of the statue, it has, I say not, defects, but disadvantages—in the discoloured surface—in the shape and attitude of the hands, which are modern—and in the many junctures: but the transcendant conception of the statue, in my mind, almost eclipses the former, and after a few moments[3] of gazing, totally annihilates the latter.

The Apollino[4] seemed entitled though in a minor degree to the praises of Venus. The head of the Fawn shows how wonderfully Michael Angelo took and made his own the conception of the figure. But of this and the other statues it may be said, that their merit, which is of the highest in its kind, consists in fidelity of *execution* only, and therefore does not ascend to the highest kind.

Of the pictures—though here it is invidious for any one and almost impertinent in me, to give a preference—Pope Julius II[5] and Raphael's Madonna seemed to me at least *of* the very best.

Dined at "the Moon"—went to the Cafè of the columns for ice and papers.

In the evenings I have Italian grammar and Journal—both of which lag —Lardner's Outlines of History, guidebooks & divers &c's.

Wednesday March 21.

We lionised little today—all in the gallery: some portion in the Tribune.

---

[1] Virgil, *Aeneid*, Book 1, 315–19. '. . . bearing the aspect and attire of a virgin, and the arms of a Spartan, as usual she had hung a light bow from her shoulders, [as a huntress,] and had given her hair to the winds to dishevel'.
Line 319 should begin 'Venatrix dederatque comam'. Diarist's dots.
[2] In ancient times, a loose outer garment.
[3] Instead of 'a short time'.
[4] Sculpture of the school of Praxiteles.
[5] By Raphael: his copy of the original in the Pitti.

Salle de Boraccio—Salles Venetiennes—Bronzes, Antique & modern—
Cabinets of Vases and of Gems—We were both delighted with Carlo Dolce's
Maddalena.

Dined at "the Moon". A long evening—with more reading and writing
than usual.

Wednesday. March 21.[1]

The Fast day appointed in England[2] and not wholly forgotten by me at
Florence, however imperfectly kept. Looking back to it after a time, and
to the course of the cholera in that & in other countries, one might perhaps
say without too much confidence, it had brought its blessing with it. I
doubt not many sincere prayers were offered and heard, and it is a great
mercy if their acceptance has been thus early manifested.

The appointment of this Fastday, so reasonable in itself, and so supported by the injunctions of Scripture and the practice of older days, was
a sign for good in the history of our country at one of its most critical
seasons. God be thanked for the spirit which called for it, which granted it,
and which sanctified it.—The principle has thus received a public acknow-
ledgment and ratification, which may have uses further and greater than
we are yet acquainted with.

How melancholy that Spencer Perceval to whom the great credit of this
national act is in no small measure due, should so speedily have changed the
tone of soberness in which he called for it, for that of the extreme excitement with which his speech on the Reform Bill was delivered. Religion can
ill afford the waste of the services of her friends, and, perhaps, can still
worse brook exhibition in such a guise.[3]

Thursday March 22.

Laurentian library[4]—9000 manuscripts. A Virgil, purporting to be of the
3d or 4th Century—and the celebrated Pandects of Justinian, dating from
the 6th or 7th, brought hither from Pisa, where they were deposited after
being found at Amalfi.[5]

We saw one very curious object here—an Atlas, after the system of
Ptolemy, in which the sea was painted Prussian blue, and the mountains
were of the colour of gold. I saw that it followed Herodotus in one of his
great errors—making the Palus[6] nearly or altogether as large as the Cas-
pian. I think too he had placed Africa as indefinitely extended towards the
South. The fountains of the Nile were here most felicitously explored, and
the river as broad at its source as at its mouth. Sicily equilateral. This
volume was, we were told, of the 14th century.

[1] Next three paragraphs from Lambeth MS 1420; a late entry, made early in April.
[2] On account of the prevailing epidemic of cholera.
[3] A visionary outburst at the close of the previous night's reform debate in the commons, a speech during which 'indescribable confusion prevailed' in the house (*H* xi. 581).
[4] Founded 1444; gradually enlarged by Medicis.
[5] Sixth century: the oldest existing MS of this collection, the chief document for the
study of Roman law. They were brought in 1135 from Amalfi to Pisa.
[6] The sea of Azov.

Gallery—finished. Saw the Hall of Niobe[1]—thought the *dress* of the child in her arms most unnatural—it was, or seemed to be, sitting very close, extremely fine, and yet crumpled, in a way which nothing could account for except her being well drenched: perhaps Niobe's fountain had wet her through. Saw the Halls of Inscriptions, the Hermaphrodite, painters' portraits, Tuscan, Dutch, French, and Italian schools. Dined at "della Stella"—went to the Boboli Gardens,[2] which are extensive—and seem scarcely to miss the spring. Its approach is however now perceptible. Here there is much statuary.

In the evening went to Mrs Buchanan's[3] and heard some admirable amateur music from [an] Italian gentleman, and a Miss Postan,[4] English, aged only 17, with a very rich and powerful contralto, of which she was perfectly mistress.

Called at Lady Lockes[5]—saw Chiesa di Firenze, where the Sexton told us "that the Pope was God in the world".

Friday. March 23.

Gabinetto Fisico.[6] Very extensive and curious. The room of the Plague is avoided by many, and it is indeed most painfully (as one may conceive) accurate—but not I think the most *avoidable* of all the rooms.

Academia Reale—a noble Establishment, where instruction, models, and every advantage are provided for Students in Painting, Engraving, Sculpture, and Architecture. All they require is permission. There are now 500—and our guide said "molti Inglesi". There is also a fine collection of old paintings—one said to be Greek, and to date about the year 1000, when it appears painters were brought from Greece to Florence: and here commenced the renovation of the art.—Cartoons in abundance. Disappointed in the show of prize-paintings. Benvenuto[7] is Director. We saw a painting of his containing two figures, which would bring him, the person said, about 800 francesconi. But we heard next day from Noechi the Engraver that a figure, by another portrait painter, costs 50 louis d'or only.[8]

Campanile. Ascended today, and enjoyed the view much. We fell in with a Padre of France, a Carlist, who told us Carlists abounded, and that in Marseilles and other southern parts there were thirty for one liberal—he said too, freely, that the main body of the clergy were Carlists.[9]

----

[1] A gallery in the Uffizi named from the statues showing Niobe weeping over her children, slain by Apollo and Diana.

[2] Terraced gardens, laid out in 1550, ornamented with antique and Renaissance statues.

[3] Possibly Janet, née Sinclair, d. 1867; 1st da. of 12th earl of Caithness; m. 1805 James Buchanan, who d. 1860; mother of Sir A.*

[4] Unidentified.

[5] Lady Matilda Jane, née Courtenay, 1778–1848; 10th da. of 2nd Viscount Courtenay; raised to rank of earl's da., 1831; m. lieut.-gen. John Locke, who d. 1837.

[6] Museum of medicine and natural history, with waxwork illustrations.

[7] Pietro Benvenuti, 1796–1844; director of the Academy from 1803. There is a self-portrait in the Uffizi.

[8] Francesconi were worth 5⅗ francs; a louis d'or was worth 20; so 50 louis d'or were worth less than a quarter of 800 francesconi.

[9] Adherents of Charles X of France, succ. 1824, expelled in 1830.

Dined at "the Moon". Tea with Mrs. Mackenzie, who has been extremely attentive and kind. Accompanied her to the Opera. Choruses *abominable*. Plot of the piece, Anne Boleyn,[1] & some scenes, interesting. Hugher (prima donna) sang very well—as did Salvadori & Merola. David[2] has entirely lost his voice, and has only the technical portion of what they say he has been, remaining. Audience very thin. Oftentimes reminded during the performance, of Coleridge's description of this kind of singing.[3]

Saturday March 24.

Intended to have made an expedition to Foesule,[4] of which we have only had the view from the Campanile: the weather however was not sufficiently promising.

We went to the Church of the Annuziata, and others. On this day and at other times I took opportunities of observing particularly the mode of performing mass, and got very near the priests, in order to endeavour to hear them as they read—but all in vain. As yet, I have not heard any one mass, I believe, read with common decency: and hearing their words, though in Latin, is to me out of the question, except when they turn round to the people with a "Dominus vobiscum" or something of that kind, which they articulate distinctly enough.

Went to see the manufactory of Pietra dura.[5] The work is very beautiful: yet I almost doubt whether on the whole the beauty produced is worth the labour bestowed.—A slab for a table, perhaps four feet and a half by two, but I think under, is valued at 18,000 scudi,[6] and takes eight persons three or four years!—Calls on Mrs Mackenzie and Mrs Buchanan.[7] Buying prints.[8] Dined at "the Moon".—Evening employed as usual.

Sunday March 25.

Went to Lord Wenlock's,[9] where we had heard service was performed—but found it was confined to his acquaintances. Went to the English chapel—a good sermon from the Chaplain,[10] chiefly on the doctrine of habits. Text, "Can the Ethiopian change his skin" &c.[11]—

Dined at Schneiderff's. Began Bossuet's Oraisons Funébres[12] and read some of Quesnel's condemned propositions[13]—Pascal, &c.

---

[1] Donizetti, *Anna Bolena* (1830).

[2] Giovanni Davide, 1789–1851; Italian tenor. Other singers unidentified.

[3] An Eton joke.   [4] Fiesole: 5 miles north of Florence.

[5] marble inlaid with semi-precious stones.   [6] A scudo was worth 4s.

[7] 'Walked in the Cascini' here deleted.

[8] 'and at Pisani's alabaster shop' here deleted.

[9] Robert Lawley, 1768–1834; whig M.P. Newcastle-under-Lyme 1802–6; cr. baron 1831.

[10] Mr. Apthorpe.   [11] Jer.xiii. 23.

[12] Jacques Bossuet, 1627–1704, Bp. of Condom and of Meux successively; the *Oraisons Funèbres* were funeral sermons preached in the latter part of the seventeenth century on, among others, *Henrietta Maria of England, Queen Marie Thérèse, and the Prince de Condé.

[13] Pasquier Quesnel, 1634–1719: French Jansenist theologian, who wrote *Le Nouveau Testament en Français avec des Réflexions morales* (1692), of which the papal bull *Unigenitus* (1713) condemned 101 sentences.

Monday March 26.

Again deterred from riding. Walked into the Cascini[1]—at Pisani's—calling —Dined and spent the evening at Mrs. Jackson's;[2] an English party—At Noechi's print-shop again—reading "History of the Jesuits"[3]—packed up.

Tuesday March 27.

Wrote to T.G.—Left Florence at 10 A.M. Arrived at Sienna at 6 P.M.—five posts. Road extremely hilly, and driving I thought indifferent. Country of course very much broken, and latterly barren. road good.

Sienna. Went to "Armes d'Angleterre", did not like the rooms or the prices, and went to the "Aigle Noire" which we found better but yet not good.

Of Schneiderff's I should say, its rooms were dear, its meals cheap and good—its arrangements generally convenient—rooms indifferently furnished.

Had just time to see the Cathedral of Sienna with daylight—the Graces[4] —the frescoes—the pulpit—the pavements, very curiously wrought—and the interior[5] generally, are all objects of interest. Visited the Amphitheatre.[6]

Wednesday March 28.

Sienna—San Lorenzo.[7] Nominally $9\frac{3}{4}$ posts. Twelve hours or more on the road. A great deal of hill. Country much broken, and cut up by the rain which wears for itself innumerable channels down the deep declivities of a loose and sandy soil, and often intersects them in such a way as to give the appearance of a mass of mountains, as they appear in a bird's eye or panoramic view.—Personal appearance of the people generally prepossessing. Road best after entering papal dominions—and country there most picturesque and interesting: particularly about Acquapendente.[8] Evil rumours of robberies on the road—we afterwards found them for the most part unfounded, though at the time it was thought advisable to have the pistols within reach. The Papal country is in a more unsettled state on the side of the Adriatic.—

'*Afloat*' from $7\frac{1}{4}$ A.M–$7\frac{1}{4}$ P.M—or there-abouts. Great imposition in horses.

Entered Pope's territories at a place called *Ponte* Centino,[9] perhaps because there is no bridge there: lucus a non lucendo.[10]

San Lorenzo. Inn indifferent.

[1] Park on the west side of Florence.   [2] Unidentified.
[3] By John *Poynder (1815); hostile.
[4] An ancient, pagan group of the Graces, found when digging the foundations for the cathedral.
[5] 'Interior' instead of 'building'.
[6] The Piazza del Campo, an elongated semicircle at the centre of the town, resembling an ancient theatre.
[7] Fifty-five miles SE. of Siena.
[8] Twenty-five miles NNW. of Viterbo.
[9] Thirty-eight miles NW. of Rome.
[10] 'light out of darkness'.

San Lorenzo by Bolsena,[1] Viterbo,[2] Baccano,[3] to Rome. Rain. Road often bad: very indifferent in fabric.

[*March 29th*].

5½ A.M.–5. P.M. 9½ Postes. Breakfast at Viterbo—Acquila Nera—very good Inn. Innkeeper complained grievously of stagnation in his lines.

Country remarkable for its number of caves. Traverse the old Cimminian[4] forest. It becomes less interesting on approaching the junction with the Terni[5] road, and continues so to Rome.

It bears every exterior mark of ill government. The land is often ill drained, and for the most part miserably tilled. Crops by no means so forward as about Lucca and Pisa—and they had a blotched appearance. Even the hedges in ruins—and in short everything bearing the most slovenly appearance. A great deal of ground utterly uncultivated.

There seems to be every absurdity involved in the idea of an ecclesiastical government—whether legislative or executive. Perhaps in that of an ecclesiastical sovereign. It seems on the one hand to entail inefficiency of protection, incomplete knowledge of the interests of the subject, and yet more incomplete power to advance them: on the other, to imply on the part of the governors, a manifest dereliction of those high and solemn charges to which, as Ministers of the Gospel, they are ordained?

Crossed the Ponte Molle,[6] and entered Rome by the Porta del Popolo. *Piazza del Popolo* is very striking, and worthy of either Papal or Imperial Rome—but the impression is diminished grievously when one merges into the Via del Babuino and burrows through it to the Piazza di Spagna. And this has no great beauty, though the steps to the Trinita del Monte, and the fountain,[7] are fine.

Casa Serny: opposite Hotel Serny. Here we are comfortably accommodated, having vestibule and anteroom, with the entire of a quiet old waiter to ourselves, besides good rooms: and at the very modest price of 12 pauls a day. Otherwise, the Inn is dear enough—except tea, only 2 pauls: everything very good.

Found our *lascia passare* after all no great charity, as our luggage in this way cost about two dollars: one of them a fee to the officer at Rome for which he gave a receipt.

On coming to Rome, speedily found a great change in climate, and, simultaneously, caught a bad cold and of a kind difficult to get rid of. Though at first surprised hereat, I soon found it was a very common incident. Mr. Bunsen[8] attributed it, as a general rule, in part, to the coldness of the floors, which causes a rush of blood to the head.

---

[1] Twenty miles NNW. of Viterbo.   [2] Forty miles NNW. of Rome.
[3] Eighteen miles NNW. of Rome.
[4] Ciminus Mons (Monte Cimino); a wooded range of hills in Etruria.
[5] Twenty-nine miles ENE. of Viterbo.
[6] A bridge a mile from the Porta del Popolo, on the Flaminian Way.
[7] 'La Barcaccia'; by Gianlorenzo Bernini, 1598–1680.
[8] Christian Karl Josias, Freiherr von Bunsen, 1791–1860, Prussian diplomat, orientalist, and theologian; envoy to the Vatican, 1823–38, to Bern 1839–41, and to London 1842–54. See Add MS 44111.

Friday, March 30.

A pretty laborious day of delivering letters to the Glasgows,[1] Mr. Bunsen, Mr. Dodwell,[2] Mr. Mence,[3] Mr. Earle,[4] and others. We called too on Miss Mackenzie—and arranged for a month's subscription at the readingroom, taking a fair sample of its merits on the first opportunity which our privilege afforded us.[5] Also made Mr. Earle's acquaintance. John at Mr. Bunsen's in the evening. We heard, when at Florence, dreadful accounts of robberies along the road. As we advanced their number was reduced—at last, they were all reported to have occurred in Rome—now that we have arrived here, the scene of action, or rather of rumour, is transferred to the Naples road. It appears however to be true that the police of this city is very defective, and the priesthood most unpopular.—Found that it had been correctly described to us, as presenting to view a singular mixture of splendour poverty and filth. When we had advanced further, and seen something of ancient Rome, other elements of a higher character were added to complete the notion—and one gradually felt the truth of Shelley's concise description. It is indeed "the queen, The grave, the city, and the wilderness".[6]

Saturday March 31.

Further arrangements: we thought of quitting the Casa for the hotel, but have changed our minds. Mr. Glasgow paid us a long and (to us) profitable visit.

Set out to view St. Peter's, and gave it a whole afternoon. Cannot help bearing a spite against the approach. Delighted with the Piazza—though it is not supposed wholly unexceptionable in execution. Could not, either at first or subsequently, reconcile myself to the *front*: on grounds which have often been taken up heretofore, and successfully maintained: and altogether independent of those more general principles on which, in Church architecture, my humble homage is reserved for that Gothic style, which prevails in our own English cathedrals. Those rest upon a notion of the primary idea of a Church, and of the subservient harmony which its architecture ought to exhibit. Separate from the notion of the building the recollection of its purpose, and the question is essentially changed. But as long as they remain conjoined, let the supremacy of the one over the other

[1] Robert Robertson Glasgow, d. 1845; assumed the name of Glasgow on succ. to the estate of Montgreenan, Ayrshire, on his marriage to Anne Glasgow in 1804.

[2] Edward *Dodwell, 1767–1832, explorer of Greek antiquities; who d. in Rome on 13 May 1832.

[3] Perhaps Samuel Mence, 1781?–1860, Rugby and Trinity Oxford; deacon 1803, priest 1808; reader at Highgate 1816; rector of Ulcombe, Kent. 1838.

[4] William Hamilton Biscoe Earle, of Everton, resident in Rome from about 1825.

[5] Margin entry: at Gibson's studio. See 1 Apr. 32.

[6] *Adonais*, xlix: Go thou to Rome,—at once the Paradise,
    The grave, the city, and the wilderness.

be acknowledged, and let the observance of its law be considered the very first essential to perfection in the architecture of a Church.—Yet still this is a question of degrees, and does not carry bigotry so far as[1] to interfere with the strong feelings of admiration and delight which the contemplation of the interior raises in us all—feelings which scarcely lose any thing, such are the admirable proportions, and such the general effect, of the fabric, upon discovering partial 'defects'—as for example, that the pilasters of the nave are of stucco: and that the Baldacchino is an incongruity in architecture, presenting enormous pillars without any adequate superincumbence. —Experienced the truth of the universal opinion, that St. Peters grows upon one's continuing contemplations: and thought it a most powerful exemplification of the law of harmony in the relative magnitude of its parts, whose effect is to create softness without detracting from magnificence.— The deviation from this harmony in the dimensions of Michael Angelo's 'Pieta', who, when contemplating such a work, can regret?—Of particular objects, delighted perhaps most with Canova's bas-reliefs on the Stuart monument,[2] and his Genius of Death—the latter perhaps at John's instance. —Lionised the Chapels, the Subterranean, and the Sacristies.

In entering such a Church as this, most deeply does one feel the pain and shame of the schism which separates us from Rome—whose guilt (for guilt I at least am well persuaded there always is where there is schism,) surely rests not upon the Venerable Fathers of the English Reformed Church, but upon Rome itself—yet whose melancholy effects the mind is doomed to feel, when you enter this magnificent temple, and behold on its walls the images of Christian saints and the words of Everlasting Truth, and yet, such is the mass of intervening incumbrances, that you scarcely own, and can yet more scantily realise, any bond of sympathy or union between yourself and those who are here it may be worshipping the same Redeemer in precisely the same inward form of faith & dependance as yourself. To us, when we live gaily and blindly in the life of self, this is a thought which has no point nor power: but when we look back and forwards on the snares around us, and inwards on those more formidable foes which nestle there, in the hour when the soul sickens under the sense of desolation and necessity and desire, how painful and how unnatural does it appear, that we ourselves should be so little alive to the value of those sympathies, which uniting man to man, make us present as it were a single front to the enemy, & lend the powerful aids of concentrated power & reciprocal encouragement. May God bind up the wounds of his bleeding Church.

Delighted with the mosaic pictures,[3] which were to me as new in kind as excellent in execution.

Dined at Mr. Earle's. Soon found how much we had reason to like him.

[1] 'as' instead of 'that'.

[2] Half-length portraits in mezzo-relief, erected in 1819, of *James Stuart, 1688–1766, the old pretender; his elder s. *Charles Edward, 1720–1788, the young pretender; and his younger s. *Henry, Cardinal York, 1725–1807.

[3] Perhaps Giotto's mosaic on Matt. xiv. 28–32, preserved in the atrium of St. Peter's.

Found Miss E.[1] ladylike & agreeable.[2] Met the Northeys[3]—the Lockers[4]—&c. Evening party of music at Mr. Milnes's.[5] Miss M.[6] very pretty. Sang beautifully. Glad to recognise in R.M.M.[7] an old acquaintance.

Sunday April 1.

Calls from Armellini[8]—Mr Mence & Mr Glasgow to pilot us to the English church. Found a most respectable congregation. Responses repeated by all. Sermon from Mr. Voules,[9] *locum tenens* for Mr. Burgess[10]—of whom I heard very flattering accounts.—Prayers only in the afternoon—very thinly attended: went after them to hear an English R.C. Sermon at the Church of Gesu in the Corso from a Dr Baggs[11] of the English college. Of a serious and practical character, with little popery, and inoffensively introduced.

Dined at home—read Bible—Pascal—Bossuet; Milnes sat with us for some time—Went at about 5½ P.M. to hear Vespers at the Trinita del Monte. The nuns' chanting exquisitely touching and beautiful.The priest's antiphony from the opposite end of the Church, though by no means the worst I have heard in this country, yet excessively harsh; an unnatural contrast to the response. Sorry to learn, that it was a Litany to the Blessed Virgin.— Speaking of the Virgin, surely we are as much too remiss, yet not the Church of England, but her members, in commemorations of saints, as the Romish Church is *officious and audacious.*—

Monday April 2.

First lesson in Italian from Armellini. Thought him a good master & agreeable man. Visit to Gibson's[12] Studio—for the second time. We were there on Friday and saw his works which of course we liked much. His subjects however are mythological to what I think an unfortunate extent. It is perhaps almost hopeless *now* to look for sublimity of conception within the limits of that class. Saw the commencement of the process of making a mould. Then comes the cast which is strengthened by iron. The subject, Proserpine surprised. Manfully assaulted the Vatican. It is almost in vain to mention the great objects of admiration there: the Laocoon, and Apollo: then the

[1] Presumably Earle's sister.
[2] 'Read papers' here deleted.
[3] Probably William Brook Northeys, 1805–80; Eton and Coldstream Guards; of Box, Wiltshire; m. 1829 Agnes Boreel, da. of a Dutch general and niece of a Dutch diplomat.
[4] Possibly Edward Hawke *Locker, 1777–1849; at Eton; in navy 1804–14; a commissioner of Greenwich hospital 1824–44, where he organised picture gallery; m. 1815.
[5] Robert Pemberton *Milnes, 1784–1858; M.P. for Pontefract 1806–18; lived in Italy from 1829 onwards.
[6] Henrietta Eliza, 1814–91, his only da. m. 1838 the 6th viscount Galway.
[7] Richard Monckton*, son of R. P. *Milnes.
[8] See 2 Apr. 32.
[9] J. P. Voules, 1800–34, sometime chaplain at Rome.
[10] Richard *Burgess, 1796–1881, educationist and author; Anglican chaplain at Geneva 1828, Rome 1831; rector of Upper Chelsea 1836–61 and of Horningsheath, Suffolk, 1869.
[11] Charles Michael *Baggs, 1806–45; rector of the English College 1840; bp. of Pella 1844.
[12] John *Gibson, 1790–1866; sculptor; worked mainly in Rome from 1817, under Canova and Thorwaldsen; carved *Huskisson.

Perseus, worthy as it seemed to me of its exalted station—the Antinous—
the Torso—the Minerva Medica—the Nile. The extent of the collection
here is perfectly bewildering. Baths most magnificent.

Went to the Capella Sistina. The frescoes here are much injured: but
Michael Angelo has written his own grandeur and boldness of design upon
them all, in very legible characters. The introduction of the Sybils seems
scarcely warranted by the extent to which the tales concerning them went.

Visited St. Peter's again: it seemed to have gained in magnificence, &
lost nothing in interest. Statue of Roman Co[n]s[ul] below ground taken as
model for that of St. Peter in his Chair.

Dined at Mr. Robertson Glasgows, in whose family I recognized old
acquaintances, having met them at Thornes House. Met Colonel Blair, &c[1]
Staid late.

Tuesday Ap. 3.

Second Italian lesson. Wrote home. Gibson kindly took us to Thorwaldsen's[2]
studio. The number of works he has on hand is amazing—in every kind and
on every scale. Beautifully designed baptismal font, of quadrilateral
exterior. A bas relief of immense length and labour—colossal horse—Our
Lord and his Apostles—and other works of very great beauty.—No fore-
shortening is now introduced in bassorilievo—and the size of men is allowed
to be[3] somewhat large in proportion to animals. Secondary marble always
used for larger works. None polished.

Forum Romanum. Saw here a great variety of objects. Church of St Martin
& St Luke—Academy of Arts attached to it with divers very good pictures
—Arch of Septimus Severus.—Remains of Temples of Jupiter Tonans and
Fortune—base of that of Concord by the Tabularium.—Colonna di Foca—
Comizio—Curia Hostilia—Tempio di Antonino e Faustina, e Chiesa di S.
Lorenzo in Miranda—Tempio di Remo della Pace—di Venere e Roma.
Arco di Tito, di Constantino. And the Colosseum. There is little here to
detail beyond the names, for particulars, and the general effect. There are
enough ruins in the Forum and its neighbourhood, to render it, as a scene,
of the most interesting and imposing character, were it not for the unseemly
additions of modern times. The restless ambition of Papal Rome has intruded
even on the repose of desolation, and forced an unnatural marriage between
elements in their characteristics discordant enough. The portico of Antoninus ill befits the Church of St. Lawrence, and the inscription of Pius on
the Arch of Titus is nothing less than execrable.

The Tempio della Pace is held by some to be the Basilica of Constantine
—by others to be neither.

As to the Colosseum, my tranquility was much ruffled in the course of
inquiry, by much ignorance on the part of the Custode: who contra[di]cted
all the statements I had ever heard, and his own, which was the worst,

---

[1] Thomas Hunter Blair, s. of *Burns's friend*; retired 1831.
[2] Bertel Thorwaldsen, 1770–1844, Danish sculptor, lived in Rome 1797–1838.
[3] Margin entry: (JNG).

among the number. This class of persons are, as it seemed to us, ill qualified enough, in general, for their duties. On comparing however the confused ideas I brought away with Burton's statement,[1] it appeared that we have now no remains of the third grand division of seats—or of that fourth, platform or whatever it was, which gave standing room to 20,000. Architecturally considered, the building is most faulty to even the uninstructed eye: on account particularly of the enormous load with which, on the external face, the upper story seems to overwhelm the lower ones. Dined at Restaurant (Lepre) as commonly, except when engaged out; and at home on Sundays.—Restaurant's here not fitted up with very much of comfort or cleanliness: yet their cookery even in plain dishes is blameless.—

Evening spent at the Concert of the Philharmonic Society, by the Piazza Navona. Instrumental music *capital*. The Italians seem admirable timists:[2] the chorus however seemed to be rough and harsh, and much inferior to what one would hear in England. Two good bass singers, one of them Signor Coligny, I thought *splendid*: deep, soft, and tender too. Two females, one professional. Great crowd & heat. One excellent tenor Conte [blank].

April 4. Wednesday.

Lessons in Italian continue every morning. Today too we had Hely's[3] first Lecture, which conveyed a good deal of information, to us very useful, on the elements of architecture. From those which followed, we learned less than we had expected: perhaps from the nature and difficulties of his undertaking, and its novelty to us.

Vatican Library. Range of apartments in one line about $\frac{1}{4}$ mile. 120,000 vols. Of these, 30,000 MSS. Custode declared there were no Protestant books there! and when I found in the room with open shelves the name of Calvin, said it must be another. There were also many other protestant names.— saw view as designed by Buonarrotti. They seem to have departed from it much, and generally for evil. In general effect I should think the loss can scarcely be calculated.

Presentation copy of Henry VIII's Book on the Sacraments. His[4] Letters to Anne Boleyn. An extremely early Virgil. Mexican Calendar, on squares joined or *hinged* together laterally, and so folding up by alternate turns.

Next went to the Loggie of Raffael, and Gallery of pictures: the latter is perfect luxury, because it contains the cream and essence of the art almost without alloy. People say and I think truly that in literature, as in animal food, too much nutrition kills, and you must have the incumbrance of a pulp: but here it is not so, or perhaps that which answers to it is, the inferior portion of each picture, since even in the masterpieces we are not to look for an equal degree of excellence on each square inch of canvass. Most of all

[1] E. *Burton, *Description of the Antiquities of Rome* (1831 ed.), ii. 56–64.
[2] i.e. keep good time.
[3] Antiquarian and dealer.
[4] 'ex' deleted.

pleased with the transfiguration and Maddona del Foligno. But I hoped to return.

In the grand works of art, the order of comparative interest, commonly assigned to a first & a second inspection, is reversed. There is more in them, than can be discerned in a short time, or without an attempered frame. And it is in fact only on repeated inspections that we begin to enter within the depths of the conception of the artist.

Could not help wondering at the attitude Raffael has chosen for an angel playing on the violin in the Coronation of the Madonna. It is precisely that of a dancing master teaching one of the elementary steps.

Went up to the ball of St. Peter's by favour of some Germans who admitted us of their party. The ascent is wonderfully easy. To the roof of the nave, you do not ascend a single *step*. It is said a carriage might drive up. The ball must be fearfully hot under a strong sun. All men's minds must revert to the audacity of Michael Angelo's architectural system when they look down the Cupola. Ball professes to hold sixteen persons—but I should not like to be one of that number.

Today spent the evening at home. Our time is abundantly occupied between forming plans for lionising & executing them—papers—books of the antiquities—Italian—Reviews (Ed. on Ev party[1]—Q. on Misgov.[2] &c—read too Hallam's Oration,[3] & some other matters—) Journal—Letters, &c. Calling too is an important item.

Thursday. 5 April.

Calling. Hely's Lecture. Got a Bill cashed at Torlonia's on purpose to be asked to his evening party[4]—and found it as dull as we deserved. Spent however most of the evening at Chevalier Bunsen's, the Prussian Envoys: found them very agreeable persons. Mr Bunsen was Niebuhr's[5] secretary, & is I fancy imbued with all his lore. Made acquaintance with his secretary.[6]

Taken by the Glasgows to the Vigna Palatina, which is beautifully situated on the hill whose name it bears. It belongs to Mr Mills.[7] Fine views of a sort of façade of ruins belonging to the ancient palace of the Caesars. And a very beautiful view of the Aventine and away on both sides of it. Mr M. has many antiques found on the property—and moreover frescoes purporting to be by Raphael—at least, [I] suppose, by his Scholars.—Went afterwards to the Foro Trajano.[8] All that remains is of a character such as to make one regret all that remains not. The triumphal columns seem to have

---

[1] 'The Drama brought to the Test of Scripture and found wanting: The Pretensions of the Evangelical Class'; *Edinburgh Review*, liv. 100–14 (August 1831).

[2] 'Progress of Misgovernment'; *Quarterly Review*, xliv. 544–622 (January 1832).

[3] A. H. *Hallam, 'On the Influence of Italian Works of Imagination on the Same Class of Composition in England' (1832); the text of his oration of 16 Dec. 31.

[4] The Prince Torlonia, Duke of Bracciano, owned a Roman bank, much used by English travellers.

[5] Barthold Georg Niebuhr, 1776–1831, historian of Rome; Prussian envoy to the Vatican 1816–23.

[6] Unidentified.

[7] An English resident in Rome.

[8] Second century A.D.

been the noblest architectural *invention* of the Romans. Even these are not wholly faultless, if examined upon the primary and rigorous theory of architecture. But the spirit of that theory is somewhat exclusive, and its canons of narrow application.

Torlonia's is anything but select. Princess of Denmark[1] (who was described to Mr Lark[ins?] as "the baddest vumman in the vole vurld"), Lady Coventry,[2] &c. &c. frequent it. A splendid mansion.

Friday April 6.

3d Lecture: & lesson of course. I like Armellini much. He gives nothing to prepare in his absence: for, he says, if he does the pupils don't prepare it.

At Mr Bunsen's by 11—Lionised his various prospects. Went with him and the Northeys to see the Castle of St Angelo,[3] now I believe somewhat difficult of access. It consisted formerly of a square basement—a circular superstructure of one story: & a smaller one of the same kind upon this: the whole surmounted with a cupola. Modern innovations, or rather those of the middle ages, have carried the building with undiminished periphery from the first story to the top. We descended, by the aid of torches, the singular corridor, lately discovered, through which wound the funeral processions to the sepulchral chamber on the second story. Their sullen glare is always picturesque, and was here most suitable to the associations connected with the spot. Fine mosaic discernible.

The Hall above contains arabesque & Fresco by Raphael or his scholars. At the top state prisoners are kept. The roof affords, or is considered to afford, a very good view of the Vatican.

Mr Bunsen showed us the part of the Tarpeian rock[4] now remaining—and over it a small piece of the wall of Servius Tullius: the only portion remaining. He computes the rock to have been 80 feet: taking what remains at 50—(I should have thought it less) and allowing thirty between the rubbish which has accumulated at the bottom, and the loss occasioned by the fall of a large piece some time back.

Pantheon[5]—now S. Maria ad Martyres. Intrinsically imposing, as well as most interesting by association. One must greatly regret the Attic—from the existence of which the pillars inside, noble as they are, seem utterly overwhelmed.

Piazza Navona—fountains and obelisk—Bernini concerned in the former. *Church of St. Agnes*[6]—and Lupanarium beneath. Fine sculptures in relief above: and beneath, St. Agnes miraculously covered by her hair, by

---

[1] Charlotte Frederica, 1784–1840, princess of Mecklenburg-Schwerin; m. 1807 to and divorced 1818 from Christian Frederick, 1786–1848, briefly king of Norway 1814, King Christian VIII of Denmark 1839.

[2] Mary, 1791–1845; da. of Aubrey Beauclerk, 6th duke of St. Albans; second wife of George, 1784–1843, 10th earl of Coventry and Tory M.P. for Worcester 1816–26.

[3] Hadrian's mausoleum, completed 140 A.D.

[4] On the southern height of the Capitoline Hill; hence traitors were thrown to their death.

[5] Late first century B.C.; consecrated as a Christian church in seventh century.

[6] S. Agnese fuori le Mura.

Alsardi[1]—said to be very fine: but it did not please me much, the figure seeming very clumsy.—St. Agnes in the flames, above, by Ercole Ferrata,[2] fine.

Chiesa di San Luigi di Francia. Frescoes of Domenichino. Catechising was in progress. Everything seemed carried on by means of drollery. I imagine few of the boys can read, or of the girls either.

In the evening at Mr Mences—a small musical & tea party. Miss Mence sang. (a choir soprano—not of the *most* melodious order, but admirable execution—) and Miss Pigott,[3] contralto, rich and good.

Saturday Ap. 7.

Fourth lecture. At Gibson's studio.
Palazzo Doria. Pictures very numerous, and fine. Splendid Claudes. And works of almost all the first masters. Orti Farnesiani and Palace of Cesars.[4] Our guide made little attempt to go into particulars: and it was melancholy enough, when he did. Colours in the chambers are finely preserved. But on the whole nothing can be more humiliating than this mass of ruins: nothing should bring home its lessons for more powerful: For amidst this utter wreck and desolation, we should remember, that it is on the ruins of no common tyranny that we stand, but of the most vast and most abiding empire that the world ever saw. Now, all its pride is level with the dust, and the remaining chambers of its palaces are buried under the fragments of their own ruins.

Dined at Mr. Earle's. Met among others Prince Musignano,[5] nephew of Buonaparte &c, I imagine, strikingly like him. He is a violent Liberal: & his conversation interesting. Milnes had tea & a discussion with us.

Sunday Ap. 8.

At the English Chapel, Mr St Quentin[6] preached an able Sermon on the nature of the repentance required by Christianity. Text—"I gave her time to repent of her evil deeds—and she repented not"[7]. Every one seemed pleased with it. Not an unequivocal test of merit this: but yet an agreeable adjunct to it.—Evening prayers wretchedly attended—Dr. Baggs preached again at the Gesu: on excellent principles: and he alluded to the importance of the differences between us and himself as affecting *our* state most materially; in a manly yet affectionate tone, such as could give no offence to us, but should conciliate our respect for him. *This* and no other course is likely to evolve truth in the end: how superior is even bigotry, when in this

[1] Alessandro Alsardi, 1602–54; sculptor, painter, and architect.
[2] Ercole Ferrata, 1610–80; sculptor.
[3] Unidentified.
[4] Gardens and ruins on the Palatine.
[5] Charles Lucien, 1803–57; Prince of Canino and Musignano; s. of Lucien Bonaparte.
[6] George Darby St. Quentin, 1803–72; rector of Broughton, Hants, 1827–41; chaplain to lord Salisbury 1847–72.
[7] Rev. ii. 21.

garb of manly kindness, to the morbid delicacy now become so fashionable. Chanting in Trinità del Monte: beautiful as before. Reading as usual—with Christian Year and an Italian catechism.

Monday April 9.

Fifth & last lecture. On the whole, somewhat disappointed. Mausoleo d'Augusto, now an amphitheatre: little to be seen there. Calls: precluded from further lionising. Mr Mence's in the evening: Miss Donelly,[1] (with a powerful and *very* deep voice,) added to the former performers.

Tuesday Ap. 10.

Wrote home. Gibson took us to Cammuccini's[2] studio. His drawing is considered very fine, but his colouring my eye for one cannot abide. Divers calls. Went out to lionise with Mills. 1. To the Baths of Titus, where the Laocoon was found. Arabesques remaining, still beautifully bright.[3] Hence 2) to St John Lateran. Tomb of Agrippa in the Corsini Chapel very fine: and Bernini's Pietà in the subterranean chapel struck me as exquisitely beautiful.[4] The facade though wanting in simplicity, yet seems far less open to objection than St Peter's, and its effect is very fine. 3. Baptistery of Constantine—4—Santa Croce in Gerusalemme: and Scala Santa:[5] here we saw many ascending the steps, perhaps peculiarly owing to the time of year. Indeed the Churches are far fuller now than we have observed them heretofore. 5. Ruins of a temple of Venus in a Garden hard by—not worth visiting.—6. Church of San Stefano Rotondo. Sickening pictures of the tortures inflicted on the ancient Saints—and also, fine specimens of antique Corinthian Columns. 7. Church of S. Gregorio whence came the present pope[6]—frescoes. At S. Croce, we saw in the tribuna the history of the finding of the true cross by the Empress Helena: three or four separate scenes painted in one piece, as is not uncommon. First, the finding three crosses—then, the miracle effected by the true one—then, the carrying of it in triumph.

We also saw some other Churches. Dined at Mr Glasgows, & met a large party: Pakenham we saw here for the first time; and Count [blank], a rigid & sincere Catholic: such a person is worth knowing nowadays.[7] Liked the family more.

Wednesday Ap. 11.

Mr Glasgow took us to the Exhibition. We found some very good paintings and sculptures, chiefly by Englishmen: and also some very bad, execrably bad, in which class, I think, we had no share.

[1] Unidentified. [2] Vicenzo Camuccini, 1771–1844; neoclassic painter.
[3] From Nero's palace, which lay below the baths. [4] Cp. 22 Dec. 38.
[5] Marble staircase traditionally believed to have been brought from Pilate's palace in the fourth century.
[6] Bartolommeo Alberto Cappellari, 1765–1846; abbot of San Gregorio 1805; cardinal 1825; Pope Gregory XVI 1831; patron of building and learning; reactionary in politics, anti-Jansenist in theology.
[7] See 14 Apr. 32.

We went to Desoulevay's[1] and Wilson's[2] Studios: liked both: but particularly the former: his colouring is deep and rich: Wilson's seems to partake[3] in *some* degree of the faults of the modern Italian school. *They* are at once weak and glaring: aiming probably at the production of stronger general effect, they have forgotten those laws of combination & opposition on which it depends, & have overshot the mark by producing an unmeaning flare, which bears no resemblance either to natural or ideal beauty. They appear to the greatest advantage, perhaps, in *copying*: and here too when conceived on small pictures, which do not afford the same occasion as large ones for this attempt at display.

Villa Borghese gardens: found Miss Robertson[4] painting there. Could not see the villa. Went to Palazzo Albani[5] to lunch: thence to S. Maria degli Angeli and the baths of Dioclesian. The design & proportions of the Church[6] most striking: eight antique columns: injured by the floor's having been raised & *false* bases put to them. Fine frescoes.

Fell in with Pakenham: went with him to S. Maria Maggiore—exceedingly beautiful: chapels in transept overdone with ornament: effect of the Ionic pillars (36 antique) spoiled by the smallness of the arches they support. But the size of the Church is not here lost, as at St. John's by the massive pilasters.

Temple of Minerva Medica. An interesting ruin: beautiful statue[7] in the Hall of the Nile at the Vatican found here.

Chiesa di S. Pietro in Vincolo. Michael Angelo's Moses: of magnificent execution: but conception scarcely answerable to the idea one entertains. Pendants designed by him. Picture by Guercino—and others. Fine specimens of antique Doric columns, fluted: flutings nineteen and twenty.— Here is shown the pillar to which Christ is said to have been bound in the judgement Hall.—We went to other Churches—and to the forum of Nerva, passing through arch of Gallienus.

Thursday Ap. 12.

A long day of lionising with Pakenham. Theatre of Marcellus—which appears to have been very fine, & in point of taste perhaps sufficiently inoffensive—Portico of Octavia—temples of Vesta and of Fortuna Virilis— Arch of Janus Quadrifrons, and that of Severus in the F[orum] Boarium by it—Cloaca Maxima,[8] and Ponte Rotto[9]—English burial grounds, with the graves of Shelley and Keats, and of John's friend Ryder[10]—and a fragment of the Ostian way, some 8 or ten feet below the present level—pyramid of

[1] T. Dessoulavy, English landscape painter.
[2] Andrew *Wilson, 1780–1848; Scottish landscape-painter who lived in Italy 1826–47.
[3] 'to partake' instead of 'rather'.
[4] Possibly Frances, d. 1851, 2nd da. of George Duncan Robertson of Struan, 1766–1842, maj.-gen. 1821.
[5] The Torlonias'.
[6] By Michelangelo.
[7] Of Pallas.
[8] The great drain, which crosses the valley in which the Forum lies.
[9] First stone bridge in Rome, 142 B.C.
[10] Charles Dudley Ryder, s. of Henry*; midshipman; drowned off Tiber mouth 1825.

Caius Cestius,[1] extremely picturesque however little one would have expected this beforehand from the shape. This scene is interesting, and its features appropriate. The ancient and time worn walls of the former[2] city aid in protecting one of the cemeteries—and a quiet grove protects them from the mass of the modern one.

Church of St Paul:[3] some portraits still remaining. Scaffoldings of enormous magnitude are erected, but the work of rebuilding seemed grievously to lag: as though they had a presentiment, that the days of the present system were numbered.

Church of St. Sebastian[4] (pictures) and catacombs: which are interesting. On the friar's showing us a tomb purporting to be of some Pope's children, we began to talk about the marriage of the clergy, and one friar gravely alleged that the passage "have I not power to lead about a wife even as Cephas",[5] was nowhere existing!

Tomb of Cecilia Metella.[6] Internal diameter about 22 feet—wall about thirty, exclusive of the outward casing with very large blocks!

Circus of Romulus—very interesting. Spina, metae, carceres (placed obliquely to prevent undue advantage, & at some distance from the course,) towers for trumpeters, seats of emperor &c. still easily discernible[7]—and the whole forming a very interesting monument of antiquity.

Temple, supposed of Romulus—of Bacchus—(supposed) grotto of Egeria[8]—Temple of Deo Redicolo[9]—tombs of Scipios[10]—and at length landed at the Campidoglio,[11] & parted from Pakenham. Went hurriedly through the statuary and busts, more leisurely through the pictures. Dined at Restt. My readings in Burton &c—or Shelley, & writings, scanty as they are, occupy all the disposable time which is rescued from lionising, always excepting a large percentage usurped by indolence. John went to Torlonia's.

Friday Ap. 13.

Calls on divers persons. Mr Case,[12] just come from Liverpool, called on us.— Lionising—Temple of Antoninus Pius, now Customhouse—Terme Antoniane—of immense and dreary extent: the most stupendous ruins, per-

---

[1] Caius Cestius, praetor and tribune, died ca. 20 B.C.

[2] Written over 'ancient'.

[3] S. Paolo fuori le Mura, founded in fourth century, much embellished since; burned 1823; rebuilding completed 1854.

[4] Fourth-century basilica, rebuilt in the seventeenth century.

[5] 1 Cor. ix. 5.

[6] The tomb, of the first century B.C., was in the thirteenth century made into a fortified tower.

[7] Romulus was the s. of Maxentius, emperor in the early fourth century. The *spina* was a wall erected along the centre of the arena, at an oblique angle, to equalise starting positions. The *metae* were goals and the *carceres*, barriers.

[8] The goddess of fountains and of birth.

[9] Rediculus was a divinity believed to have caused Hannibal to retreat as he neared the city gates.

[10] The third-century sarcophagus of the Scipios had lately been removed to the Vatican and replaced by a model.

[11] The square, by Michaelangelo, with museum, on the Capitoline hill.

[12] Of Huyton, near Liverpool.

haps, I ever saw:[1] some mosaics remaining: custode in the dark as usual.
Chiesa di S. Teodoro, *supposed* Temple of Romulus and Remus:[2] an antique
circular altar, with cavity as usual, in front of it.—Chiesa di San Pietro in
Vincolo & Mamertine prisons:[3] Sacristan recounted the miracles, and
showed the fountain and the trestle [?] with the image of a countenance on
the wall, with an air of much modesty & propriety.—Masonry of infant
Rome is indeed wonderful. She was as a Hercules even in the cradle: and
seemed even from the first to aim at immortality, and left her own character
of stability impressed indelibly on all her works.

Observed an arch of Sev[erus] in Velatro, the place whence the figure of
Geta had manifestly been erased.[4] Dined at Restt. in P[iazza] di Spagna.

Saturday Ap. 14.

Calls—Case[5]—introduced to Mrs. C.—Gibson. Lionising. Milnes with us.
Palazzo Sciana: exquisitely lovely Maddalena of Guido. His style is that of
ideal not natural beauty: and withal he combines amazingly chaste colouring, and appearance of simplicity. Raffael's portrait—Leonardo's Vanity &
Modesty—(q. true conception?)—Caravaggio's Gamesters—&c. &c.

Palazzo Farnese—statuary—and fine frescoes by Annibal Caracci. Also
some few pictures.

Chiesa di S. Andrea della Valle. Tribune and four figures in the quadrants
of the Cupola by Domenichino, Cupola by Lanfranco.[6] Went to the English
College, chiefly to see Mr. Spencer.[7] He was out. Saw Dr. Wiseman,[8] the
head, an agreeable and I believe able man: went over the College. Saw in the
Library a copy of *Fox*,[9] first Ed., with Father Parsons's[10] *marks* of the passages to be answered. There were some books of English Protestant Theology, which Mr. Spencer had possessed, and presented to them. We saw
also some Pope's Bulls, and old documents relating to the foundation, which
is very ancient, having been formerly an hospital for English pilgrims. There
was one book containing a list of martyrs to the Catholic faith in England.
Of all the men in the world whom should we find as a visitor in the Library

---

[1] Baths of Caracalla (Marcus Aurelius Antoninus, 186–217 A.D., emperor, 211).

[2] Church, first mentioned sixth century; it probably occupied the site of an ancient
temple.

[3] S. Pietro in Vincoli: built, fifth century, as a sanctuary for the chains that bound St.
Peter. The diarist has confused the whereabouts of this church, which he had seen on
11 Apr. What he visited on this occasion was two cells, in one of which St. Peter baptised
his gaolers with water from a miraculous spring. The church above the prison is not
S. Pietro, but S. Giuseppe: the prison is known as S. Pietro in Carcere.

[4] 212 A.D., Caracalla, successor of Severus, murdered his b. and rival, Geta, with most
of Geta's principal adherents.

[5] Thomas, 1811–87, s. of the Mr. Case of 13 Apr. 32.

[6] Giovanni Lanfranco, 1580–1647.

[7] George Spencer, 1799–1864; youngest s. of 2nd Earl *Spencer.

[8] Nicholas Patrick Stephen *Wiseman, 1802–65, rector of English College 1828–40;
papal envoy in England 1848–50; cardinal and abp. of Westminster 1850.

[9] John *Foxe, *Actes and Monuments* (1562); 'the Book of Martyrs'.

[10] Robert *Parsons, 1546–1610; fellow of Balliol 1568–74; jesuit 1575; in Spain 1588–97;
rector of English College 1597.

of the R.C. College, but the Protestant Clergyman of Rome, Mr Voules. We dined at Restaurant—reading Review and papers—in evening went to a party at Count Cini's—the Countess pretty & pleasing in her appearance. Miss Mence & some Italians sang.

(*Palm Sunday*) *Ap. 15.*

In the Sistine Chapel from 9 to past 12. Got into the side partition, by having had the luck to be so placed as to block up a doorway & render it impracticable for priests passing to and fro. Thought the Pope's appearance ordinary and undignified, but the expression of his countenance is benign, simple, & devout. Demeanour of the ecclesiastical functionaries in general less reverential than I had expected beforehand.—The chanting of the Lamentations, and the Passion, on the whole very good, and in parts particularly fine and impressive. The services seemed for the most part unexceptionable, excepting the very frequent and gratuitous introduction (as gratuitous as offensive, at least such it appeared to me,) of the term merit— for though always stated as *derived* and not proper to us, still it is I think a far purer taste, and a far sounder creed, which has rejected utterly and at once all notion of it in connection with the names & deeds of a fallen race.— As matter of sound, this service came up to my expectations: and the feelings it is framed to raise are in great measure such as all Christians should heartily participate in. But the fact of it *being* a sight—the crowd, the heat, the talking, the manifold interruptions, are all against this. As a *sight*, it came up not to my expectations of solemn splendour, but rather *down* to the idea one naturally forms of the present condition of popery, as a system of faded gauds whose vices and whose virtues are rapidly passing away, and which already is little more than a record of its own past existence. If one could but have *thought*, the scene presented inexhaustible materials. Before us, and on the platform of the very same apartment, moved an assemblage of beings in all the intricacies of the most august ceremonies of their Church: with little of interest or energy, but rather like men who did it simply because they had done it before, and under the influence of an impulse long ago communicated, the hand that gave it now for ever withdrawn, and its power and results waxing fainter and fainter: as in a machine that continues for a little space to work, though the hand of the machinist, its principle of life, has left it. Even so stood before us the great members of the papal system, as the cold and pale spectres of the highest and most powerful domination the world ever beheld. From all the windows proceeded masses of an un-religious light, sombre and yet not solemn, restricted and yet not softened: rather, dirty and dim as the apertures through which it passed. From before us stood forth the bold and powerful delineations of Michael Angelo, each one in strictest unison with the darkest and most terrific conception of the awful scene they represented. Above were the sublime figures of the prophets, some with expressions of expostulation, some of wrath, but all clothed in sternness, and seeming to denounce the unsubstantial shows beneath. So entirely did they harmonise with those symptoms which are now appearing in the moral and political and religious worlds, affecting the destiny of this falling Church: with the tone of those thunders which are approaching as they roll, and with the hue of those clouds whose darkness is gathering around us.

English Church immediately after the function was concluded.

More, than usually, disposed to appreciate the extreme beauty of its services. A Charity sermon from Mr. Voules.—Having had the pleasure of meeting Cole in the Sistine this morning, and shaking hands with him on his return from Naples, took a walk with him in the Borghese Gardens. Heard part only of the chanting at the Trinità del Monte: and dined at Mr Glasgows. It professed to be a family party—but we were six guests to four of the family. Paolo Pifferi was there.

Monday Ap. 16.

Gibson took us to Severn's[1] Studio: enjoyed the visit much both from the man & from his works. Two pictures of Ariel—one very large one, the chaining of the dragon, from the Revelations.[2] All his works are full of poetry: & of a higher *class* in this respect than any I have seen in Rome, either in painting, or Sculpture, except only Thorwaldsen's—if even those. Reading the papers and books on Rome. Wrote home. In the afternoon, at St Peter's and the Vatican: went to the room of the Biga,[3] the Stanze di Raffaello, the manufactory of Mosaics, & the Sculptures and pictures for a second time. Delighted with Guido's Madonna and Saints—particularly the figure of St. John. In the biga thought we saw manifestly enough what was meant by the ἄντυξ[4] of Homer.—curious to observe the difference in the tone of the heathen & Christian Epitaphs on the walls of the Gallery: and the fulness of hope substituted for the vacancy of mingled sorrow & doubt: doubt, which could not be relieved: & sorrow, which could not be elevated. The one was no exercise of faith: the other no discipline of the affections, in the case of the heathen. To us how different. It is difficult to translate "Dis manibus"[5]—why? not because it is difficult to realise the idea which ought to have been conveyed: but rather, to trace the idea which was entertained. How different is "requiescit in pace"!—Statue of Diana triformis (alii aliter)[6] illustrates the ancient idea.—In the Stanze, Raffael has ventured to give an astounding antiquity to the Pope's liveries!

Italian lesson as usual. Visited St Peter's again. Cole came to tea: [blank.]

Tuesday Ap. 17.

Left, not till past 8 in consequence of a man's having disappointed us, for

---

[1] Joseph *Severn, 1793–1879, painter; friend of *Keats whom he accompanied to Italy, 1820, till *Keats's death, 1821; lived in Rome 1820–41 and from 1860; British consul there 1860–72.

[2] Rev. xx. 2.

[3] Sala della Biga; named after a two-horse chariot preserved there.

[4] Rail round front of chariot.   [5] 'To the divine shades'

[6] 'threefold (according to the beholder's eye)'.

Tivoli[1]—with Pakenham and Cole. Stopped at Adrian's villa,[2] and went through that immense assemblage of ruins. It is full of spots for drawings; their number is almost infinite; the scenery is interesting, and the associations cannot fail to strike the traveller as he stands amidst those ruined edifices which the soul of luxury devised in its pride and then deserted in its darkness. Went on to Tivoli on foot, our horses being knocked up: dined at Regina, a tolerable Inn. Then went to the temples of Vesta and the Sibyl: descended to Neptune's grotto & were delighted with the waters dashing through the excavation in the rocks: Cole remained till he was almost drenched with the spray. Then crossed and made the giro, passing Horace's site, now tenanted by an ecclesiastic—the many views of the many waterfalls—the villa of Mecænas—&, in ascending again, the circular temple. On the whole Tivoli is extremely interesting and beautiful, from what it has been and what it is too: though its beauty in some respects falls short of the highest kind. The cascades—except perhaps that on which the exquisite temple of Vesta or Nymphæum looks down, bear the marks of an artificial position: and the foliage is deficient in warmth and variety of tint. Yet, much romantic beauty within the vale, and such a fine expanse and distance beyond it & seen from it, form a rare combination.

The chief objects on the way from Rome are, the petrifying lake (and most curious is the mark of the wheel &c. in the rock at Tivoli—"travertine"[3] is all fluviatile—), the sulphuric stream, and the burial place of Plautinus and his family: immensely massive.—Arrived in Rome after many delays and relays of horses and asses *de renfort* by nine P.M. But the expedition might be accomplished *well* in eleven hours. Supped with Pakenham at his lodgings in the Via Babuino.

The view of St Peters from a distance is inconceivably grand. I use the term deliberately: for one cannot *realise* the conception that an object so vast and majestic should be the work of man's hand. I think Madame de Stael says, it is the only edifice, which seems worthy to be classed among the works of the Creator himself[4]—and really in contemplating its cupola from a distance one can appreciate this strong but scarcely strained expression. On this evening too I felt for the first time how interesting was a return to Rome; even though after so short an absence. (statements as to matter of fact are of course here less to be depended upon). (From this paragraph, inclusive, down to Monday May 7., this Journal was not completed till after I had returned to England—and in beginning to fill up the gap (Torquay Sept. 17) I feel strongly the deep interest of the scenes in whose contemplation the period was spent, and the softening and gentle influences with which they dwell upon the recollection.)

Wednesday April 18.

Borghese Palace—collection of pictures very large—Correggio's celebrated

[1] Seventeen and a half miles east by north of Rome.
[2] Built 125–35 A.D. by the Emperor Hadrian.
[3] A kind of building stone.   [4] *Corinne* (1807), IV. iii.

Danæ—the notion of the golden shower adopted fearlessly by Guido with his marvellous picture of "The Conception"—When one compares the conception of a subject like this, with that which must have filled the spirit of Coreggio's when he painted one of his Holy Families or delineations of the Virgin & Child, one sighs for the mind that was successively inhabited by guests so different in dignity, perceiving at the same time the disparagement & degradation undergone by Art, when she is brought into contact with anything short of the noblest objects, and herein her strict alliance with Virtue and Truth.

Sibyl. Some Carlo Dolce's. His rank in my estimation is much lower now than some time back. This shows to how large an extent the faculties by which we judge are themselves the products of the influences exercised by the objects subjected to judgement.

Armellini & reading as usual—

We dined at Mr Earle's—met Mrs Wingfield,[1] sister to Portman[2] my contemporary at Eton & Christ Church, a very agreeable person. We went up with them to the Sistine—got inside the formidable (side) door by means of Mr Earle's uniform[3]—and heard the first Miserere—after the chanting of the Psalms. We were told that the thirteen lights did not refer to the Apostles and Virgin, but to the number of psalms to be chanted. Perhaps all three may be correlative.

I remember being struck with the first burst of the Miserere as plaintive beyond belief or expression. The music was of a character to us very new, strictly, I imagine, chaste and classical, and therefore requiring more practised ear and taste to enter into the full enjoyment of its beauties: although some passages would go to the heart of every hearer, and there were many perhaps who would feel its power as a whole when an object of memory to exist with a vigour and freshness, which affords a very strong criterion of merit.

Thursday April 19.[4]

We breakfasted at the Europa with Cole & Fitzroy[5]—& went with them up to the Sistine. Most of the day was occupied in different functions. Our party soon split, when the *rushes* commenced. 9–1. Mass in the Sistine Chapel. The Host carried in procession by the Pope to the Pauline Chapel, where it was deposited in a receptacle intended to symbolise the Sepulchre —and magnificently illuminated, after the design, it is said, of Michael Angelo. The Chapel was visited by people all day—many in prayer. Certainly it was a spot for noble reveries—but they are interdicted to those, to whom they would not be "of faith". "For whatsoever is not of faith is sin"[6]—will have, I should suppose, its application in such cases as these.

---

[1] Lucy, wife of George Wingfield-Digby, of Sherborne Castle, Dorset.

[2] Fitzhardinge Berkeley Portman, 1811–93, rector of Staple Fitzpaine, Somerset, 1840–89; fellow of All Souls 1831–40.

[3] Earle was a militia lieut. col.

[4] Maundy Thursday.

[5] Augustus Fitzroy, 1809–69; rector of Great Fakenham, Suffolk, 1834–57; a Cambridge friend of Monckton *Milnes's.   [6] Rom. xv. 23.

Is there not something very singular and anomalous in their thus antedating the ceremonies intended to represent our Lords Passion, Burial, and Resurrection, by an entire day? Neither are they correct in the time of the day.

After this function was over I went down into the covered gallery on the Vatican side, to hear the Benediction, which I did. The number of people in the Piazza, exclusive of troops, was very small, and despoiled this beautiful and innocent ceremony of its full effect, the space being so vast. The people I suppose do not now think it worth while to leave their occupations: but it was very different some time back. It is a very sad pity that the benediction is followed by an act both ludicrous and, as it seems to me, blasphemous —the dropping down indulgences from the Gallery in the front of the Church whence it is delivered, to be caught by those of the people who may chance to be successful in the scramble which ensues. How singular and perilous a notion of *sin* must a man have, before he can be persuaded any of its penalties, of its just penalties at least, can be mitigated by such means as these.

Hence I went with Cole to the staircase leading (I think) from the floor on which the Sistine stands, to the story above—where there was a tremendous squeeze. The Roman soldiers are no match for Englishmen even in such a conflict as this—party after party forced its way upwards, with more courage than propriety—none got more than a slap with the butt of a musket. The poor Papalins generally were very goodnaturedly disposed— far more so than the Swiss guards who keep order in the Chapel: but when they lost their temper they became very laughable: & seemed to have no notion of that calm selfpossession which results from a manly courage. Neither had they the smallest skill to make up for their want of strength— they were obliged to make very resolute charges to make the people yield (tho' downwards) a single inch—and it was soon regained. We waited patiently, like others, not thinking it fair to break through—till the Abate Prosperi came by, and goodnaturedly took up John, who had joined me by accident, & myself. It is not fair to abuse the soldiers: who are among the most unfortunate of this unfortunate country. One of them, about the most martial in appearance, in one of the intervals of comparative repose, calmly waved his hand over the hot & fuming crowd before & beneath him, cried from behind a decent pair of mustachioes, "Bella famiglia d'Inghilterra"! The satire was neither pointless nor unmerited. Ladies were fainting etc.

The washing of feet in this chamber did not appear at all *bonâ fide*—but it was an extremely curious sight, as a relic of other times. The pilgrims looked as well washed as the Cardinals. We went from hence to the Supper Chamber, where they sat ranged along one side of a long table, while the Pope walked along the other, and helped them all successively to a variety of the viands which lay before them, apparently a repast sumptuous enough, of course excepting meat. The Pope's manner was at once kind, easy, and *dignified*—though his countenance of itself has no claim to the latter epithet. Milnes & all those who had uniforms found the benefit of them to be very great—they procure admittance everywhere—& otherwise it is not always at all easy.

We dined at Restaurant—& had some reading in the middle of the day— In the afternoon the Miserere and Service, of which I have nothing to add to what is noted for yesterday.

The discomfort in crowds at Rome compared with crowds in England, arising from the difference in point of personal cleanliness, is very great. For bodily pressure they are of no consequence, except where mainly composed of English—for the Italians are too inert to exert themselves corporeally on such occasions—at least they have not the excessive & pertinacious restlessness of our own countrymen.

Sir W. Scott[1] arrived—but we could not find him out. Italian lesson &c.

Good Friday Ap. 20.

English Church and Sacrament. No afternoon prayers.

Third and last performance of the tenebrae and miserere in the Sistine. Afterwards a procession into St. Peters—the pope knelt down at a desk placed for him a certain distance in front of the Baldachino and remained with his hands over his face for some time in prayer. All the train knelt behind him—an imposing sight. The relics were afterwards shown in the small gallery above. S. Veronica (J.N.G.) They were showily encased & I for one could not discern the objects. After this was over, all the people began to lounge about St Peter's, discoursing apparently with indifference —although the service with the Miserere was going on in the Cappella del Coro—I did not understand this at the time but afterwards found it stated & commented upon in Madame de Stael's Corinne.[2]

Hence we went to the Trinità de' Pellegrini to see the feet of pilgrims washed. The entrance of females into the apartment where the men were was strictly forbidden—but Mrs Ashley[3] was there. By and bye came Bernetti,[4] Cardinal & Home Secretary, with other washers, dressed appropriately. Some of the people were attired in a manner intended to suit the pilgrim's character—others as simply poor persons of Rome—but all were professedly pilgrims. I was close by Bernetti & Milnes by me. He began to wash—and here the washing was more a matter of practical utility than at the Vatican—repeating the Creed, Ave, & Pater Noster all the time, & the "pilgrim" after him. Credo in Deum—(a scrub) Patrem omnipotentem (another scrub) &c. The old man's feet were sore—and when the Cardinal began to wash, he winced & shed tears—I thought, from the smarting— Milnes however maintained, it was from a deep feeling of shame at the humiliation & indignity which the Cardinal was undergoing. Afterwards a very long train sat down to a supper of an ordinary style enough—& were waited on by persons evidently of high station. They were all dressed like the poor of Rome, and it was impossible to believe it other than a gross imposition to call them pilgrims. John asked one of them flatly, & he named

[1] Sir Walter *Scott, 1771–1832, novelist and poet; cr. bart. 1830.
[2] Book X, chs iv and v.
[3] Unidentified.
[4] Thomasso Bernetti, 1779–1852; Vatican secretary of state from 1827.

I think some part of Italy as his country. On Saturday morning we met an Irish friar in the Church of St John Lateran who owned that they were merely the poor of Rome. Milnes & Cole at tea.

Saturday April 21.

In the morning we went up to St Giovanni in Laterano—but were late—the Baptisms were very nearly over. The people stood on chairs round the font in the Baptistery of Constantine. There were I think two young blacks & a Jew—the current rumour, but I suppose slanderous, is, that this was not the first time we had received it. In England I have heard of old women ambitious of being periodically 'confirmed'.

The ordination in the Church—long & complicated service—We were rather interested by a father, apparently of the condition of a small trades-man, who pointed out his son, receiving orders as a deacon, with much exultation. We conversed a great deal with an Irish friar, who was utterly ignorant of Protestantism—did not know that we received the new Testa-ment, nor, I believe, that we were baptised! His argument for purgatory was concise & remarkable, as showing how it clashes with the doctrine of atonement—"God is *just*".

There were I think eight different orders of ecclesiastical functionaries, including even the Sagristani & ostiarii[1] whose offices are I fancy only menial. There is however the policy of the Romish Church strongly marked in this profusion of favours which cost her *nothing*—which so much enhance the dignity of her appointments in the eyes of those on whom they are con-ferred—which so greatly multiply the number of those who are her pledged & inseparable adherents *ex officio*—and which extend her ramifications throughout all ranks & the entire fabric of society. And indeed it might be well if some of those connected with the Church, e.g. as Clerks and School-masters, were more brought into contact with its officers; though it would be contrary to our manner to venture upon anything so solemn as this without direct warrant.

It is only at a certain point (deacon?) that orders bind for life—and (priest?) celibacy is essential. John writes that one hand is laid on Deacons —both on priests. Also that their hands are rubbed with oil & bound up—the *ostiarii* touch the keys—others have 4 locks of hair cut off by the Cardi-nal—the tonsure is the mark of priesthood.

Heard from home—Rn G's election[2]—& departure for Torquay.

Rode with J.N.G. & Pakenham nearly to Veii,[3] furnished with hacks by Mr Brown.[4] We turned off to the right[5] over the Ponte Molle: & our road lay during the last four or five miles over delightful turf through a valley in parts remarkably pretty. Met Mr Greig.[6] Turned at the Isola Sacra & came home by the Baccano road. Distance perhaps 22 Roman mm.

---

[1] Sacristans and church-door keepers.
[2] As one of Liverpool's two bailiffs for the year 1832–3.
[3] Ruins of the ancient city, 12 miles NW. of Rome.
[4] 'of the' deleted.   [5] For 'left'
[6] Perhaps Robert Hyde *Greg, 1795–1875, antiquary; of Quarry Bank near Wilmslow.
34—I.

We dined with General Montresor[1] and in the evening went to a musical party at Mr Earl's.

Easter Sunday April 22.

9–12. Mass &c. in St Peter's. For the first time, I went in light trowsers—& found that for the first time they excluded the wearer from the space within the line of guards whence alone the service could be properly viewed. The Pope officiated in parts of it. Most of the English within the line knelt down when the Host was elevated—I believe this is not usual, with them, nor can it I think be justified. If it is *expected* that spectators should do it, their course seems clear—they should not be spectators—a very large number of the common people were in the Church: the men little cleaner than on common days.

The Benediction was delivered soon after 12 from the same place as on Thursday. I went to my old point, & saw well. There may have been, including troops, 20,000 persons present—enough to make the sight sublime —but what must it have been in the palmy days of the Papacy? Nothing can be finer than this scene to the eye—even now too it has many claims upon the mind—but admit the assumptions of Rome, and its grandeur transcends everything. The Vicar of Christ upon earth, in the metropolitan city of his universal Church, that city crowned with a thousand rays of glory, each bright enough to ennoble a nation's history—ascends the most gorgeous temple, peradventure, that the world ever saw, and calls down, while he authoritatively declares, the blessing of the Eternal Father upon the multitudes gathered from all quarters of the world at this holy season, crowding even the wide expanses before him, endless in variety as countless in number; essentially one fold, and visibly marshalled under one Shepherd. And how noble the terms "urbi et orbi".

Met Marsh[2] under the gallery.—The *martial* music which follows the blessing is not I think in good taste according to our notions, but probably suits theirs.

English Church at half past twelve, & Sacrament. Sorry to find no more English Sermons at the Gésu in the Corso.

No illumination—money applied to repair the damages at Foligno[3]— così si dice [4]—no fireworks—on account of the general poverty of the Government. On St Peter's day however the Illumination always takes place.

Mr. Glasgow asked us to dine. Cole with us.

Monday April 23.

We went with Mr Earle to see a very fine Mosaic Landscape of Poestum—

[1] (Sir) Thomas Gage Montresor, 1764?–1853; ensign in 2nd Dragoon Guards 1783; fought in Corsica, Egypt, India; col. of his regt., 1837; K.C.H. 1834; gen. 1841.
[2] Thomas Coxhead (Chisenhale-)Marsh, 1811–75; Eton and Trinity Cambridge; double first 1834; of Gaynes Park, Epping; extended surname on marriage 1846; some-time chairman of Essex Quarter Sessions.
[3] Twenty miles SE. by east of Perugia; greatly damaged by an earthquake in 1832.
[4] 'so it's said'.

also to con over Mr Hely's table composed of specimen marbles—(price 30 louis—circular—diameter perhaps 2½ feet?) We went to Gibsons, & with him to Wyatt's [1] Studio. He has some subjects sufficiently original— as, a shepherd boy & his dog in a storm. He is a pleasant & I believe very modest person—considered by some superior to Gibson. It is very gratify- ing to see the English lay claim to so large a share of the talent of Rome in the fine arts.

J.N.G. and I rode to Frascati [2]—12.30–8 P.M.—Some of the road exces- sively bad—it would be difficult to find one so much bearing the appearance of neglect between the most obscure villages in England. We met peasants with *guitars*. The distance back to Porta San Giovanni we did in 1¼ hour. J.N.G. calls it 12½ mm.

Dined indifferently at the 'Londra'. (A new Inn was opened a few days after our visit.) Got an intelligent Cicerone—he had served Buonaparte— much liberalised in his religious notions in consequence: but not inclined I thought to unbelief. He said to me—"Roma è una città maravigliosa per le antichità, per la bellezza, e per la birberia. Capisce sua eccellenza? Un popolo birbo vuol dire quel che non crede nella sua religione". [3] This agrees but too well with other accounts. This poor man seemed endowed with a lively and enthusiastic imagination: he would never cease telling us the ill usage received by Tusculum from Rome, and repeating poetry on the sub- ject—with intervals however of goading John's ass, & shouting the accus- tomed "Agh! Agh!"

We had remains of theatre, aqueduct, road, Academia & house of Cicero (as supposed)—and an extensive prospect from an elevation (J.N.G.) of 1900 palmi.—On our descent we went to the Aldobrandini villa, an excellent specimen I should imagine of the style of an Italian country place. It is on the slope of the hill which descends rapidly, and commands a very extensive view over the Campagna & to the sea, with abundance of air & in summer I should think a most refreshing coolness. There were frescoes by Domenichino, cav. d'Arpino [4] (& qy?) We had also all the *giochi d'acqua* [5] set a-playing for us, and though their machinery is now somewhat rusty from disuse, the sight was very fanciful & curious, & ren- dered almost magical by a whole troop of schoolboys, who overspread the stage before us in an instant, clad in their demi-ecclesiastical costume.

Cole came to tea—papers &c & wrote home.

Tuesday Ap. 24.

Arrival of newspapers with Lords' Debate on the second reading. [6] Gibson took us to Mr. Atkins's [7] Studio in the Corso, where we saw an admirable

---

[1] Richard James *Wyatt, 1795–1850; sculptor, lived in Rome from 1820.
[2] The ancient city of Tusculum, 12 miles SE. by east of Rome; birthplace of Cato; where Cicero and Marcus Brutus had villas.
[3] 'Rome is a city marvellous for antiquities, beauty, and rascality. Does your Excellency understand? Rascally people means that they don't believe in their religion.'
[4] Giuseppe Cesari, called Cavaliere d'Arpino, 1560 or 68–1640.
[5] Fountains.
[6] Of the reform bill, on 9 April: *NSH* xii. 1 ff. See 26 Apr. 32.
[7] James Atkins, portrait painter, d. 1834.

portrait of him—a picture of the Corpus Domini Procession &c. We called on Mr. Mence & dined at home.

We went out on a lionising expedition with Cole and Milnes. Chiesa di Sant' Onofrio—Tasso's tomb—his oak in the garden, and delightful view of Rome from it—*here* & in such spots one feels, that Italy has been, nay is, a fairy country, in which the imagination finds its rest and its home.— Celebrated frescoes[1] in the cloister or rather arcade.—Santa Sabrina— (Carlo Maratta)—Santa Maria in Campitelli. Corsini Palace. learned something from Cole's better[2] taste & criticism. A large collection & well worth the visit. Salvatori Prometheus. Went to the English College & were introduced to Mr. Spencer—with whom we had a conversation long & friendly: bearing much of course upon our differences in religion. Much of it touched upon himself, yet there was not the smallest appearance of egotism. He spoke in a very gratifying manner of Bp Blomfield's personal character— and said he did not look upon our Church or Clergy as rootedly hostile to "the truth"—thought many among us would be saved—but whether or not by the *un*covenanted mercies of God, did not appear clearly. He considered Wiclif, Luther, Cranmer, & all "Reformers", as "*abominable*". His own mind had passed through many varieties of sentiment: & he was in a *generally* unsettled state, before[3] he became a Catholic. He rested his defence of R.Cm. not on any single but rather on a constructive argument, founded partly on miracles and partly on historical testimony—for which he did not seem to have gone deep. He appeared *very ignorant*, considering the circumstances, of the true character of the Church of England on the question of private judgement. Spoke generally with clearness & good sense —&, whether in their communion or in ours, he is doubtless a singleminded and devoted servant of God.

Evening party at Mrs Blair's.—

Wednesday April 25.

Fitzroy & Cole came to breakfast—Hutt[4] & Cole to tea. Paid six or seven P.P.C. calls.

We also went with Cole to the Capitol & went through the statuary a second time. Admired Marius extremely—next perhaps to the Gladiator.[5] Some of the Emperors are *often* difficult to distinguish apart: e.g. Titus & Vespasian—the latter more brawny. The style of hair in which Lucius Verus is equipped is not dissimilar to our own—and does not betoken a manly age or character.

Went through the Palace of the Senator. Alas! how much bitterness is there *now* in the letters S.P.Q.R. But it accords with the policy pursued, to perpetuate the memory & associations of glory. We found here the cele-

---

[1] By Domenichino.
[2] Instead of 'superior'.
[3] Instead of 'when'.
[4] Possibly (Sir) George *Hutt, 1809–89; commanded Indian artillery in Persian war 1857; retired 1859; secretary, Chelsea hospital, 1865–56; K.C.B. 1886.
[5] Dying Gladiator: Greek statue of a wounded Gaul.

brated bronze wolf of Romulus & Remus—much pleased with the boy extracting a thorn from his foot—and the astonishing bust of Brutus— which almost reconciled me to having the eyes marked by white—in busts only however—which do not possess the entire character of Sculpture. Gibson puts a mixture to the hair of his Narcissus—but 'public opinion' seems to be against him.—Pictures of Polidoro da Caravaggio. &c.

Thursday April 26.

The news of the second reading in the Lords arrived.[1] Packed, one or two calls.

At mid-day left Rome—at 8 reached Velletri[2] 3¾ posts. Road often bad. Little interest in the country generally. At Albano[3] we stopped—& called on Mr Hely—a man who offered as cicerone, refused to go to the emis-sarium,[4] because it—not rained—but looked as if it would! Mr Hely very kindly conducted & arranged for us. The wood-walk high on the lake side is beautiful, and the view of the lake—with the site of Alba Longa[5] at one corner, the country seat of the pope[6] at that diagonally opposite—and Albano reaching dowards from a third. We walked a long way along the brink and saw in many places the massive remains of Roman constructions. —did they build into the water for coolness & air—or for the sake of the idea—or, (as at Baiae[7] for instance) with a view to convenience from the difficulty of the ground? The shape of the basin in which the lake lies is alone enough to mark it as formerly a volcano. We passed the recess sup-posed to have been a nymphaeum—or a drinking grotto—and came to the celebrated emissarium, so simple, and so small in the dimensions as an object of mere ocular view—but so interesting by association & so wonder-ful. It will surely last till time is no more, unless disturbed by human hands or by some great natural convulsion.—

We returned by the other side—Mr H. pointed out the site of Aricia[8]— and of other towns, Lanuvium[9] &c. towards the sea. We went to contem-plate the Via Appia where the valley is built across by an enormous massive causeway of (I think) 565 yards in length—and rejoined our carriage beyond the gates of [blank][10] whose walls bore the singular inscription in different places "viva il sangue di Gésu Cristo".—We again left our carriage at the entrance of the avenues,[11] and ran up the long one, to get the prospect of the lake from the extremity—it is extremely beautiful, & as rich perhaps to the painter as that of Alba to the historian.

[1] Reform bill carried by 184 to 175 on 14 April, after four days' debate: *NSH* xii. 454.
[2] Twenty-one miles SE. of Rome.
[3] Fifteen miles SE. by south of Rome, on the SW. side of Lake Albano.
[4] Duct which Romans pierced through rock to drain lake during siege, 396 B.C.
[5] Vanished city on east side of lake, founded according to tradition by Ascanius, s. of Aeneas.
[6] Castelgandolfo, on the western shore.
[7] Roman watering-place, 10 miles west of Naples.
[8] Ancient city 16 miles SE. of Rome.
[9] Another ancient city, 4½ miles west of Velletri.
[10] Genzano, 6 miles west of Velletri. Cp. 21 May 1832, p. 501.
[11] Of the Parco Chigi, just SE. of Albano.

Albergo Nuovo—fair, & reasonable. But most who travel post go to La Posta.

Friday Ap. 27.

Velletri to Mola[1]—10 posts—9⅓ hours. Arrived at 4½. The journey to Naples is two easy enough days—and might be done in less.—We felt like others very strong inclination to sleep on the Pontine Marshes—& indeed did: but checked ourselves.[2] Descent at Cisterna[3]—there are about five posts of them. Appearance of the country singular—hills to the left—flat extending thence to the sea—*rank* luxuriance of vegetation—one can now form some idea of jungle after the tangled wood & grass of these marshes: *partial* & imperfect drainage—a good number of cattle—buffaloes. Avenue of immense length—seaview when you come upon it very fine. Fine perpendicular cut in the rock at Terracina,[4] which is very well situated—Neapolitan boundary succeeds. For fear of cholera, the officer took our passport from Luigi with a pair of tongs!

Country excessively luxuriant with lemon groves &c. View from the Inn at Mola (we went to the new House kept by the old man, very fair not more) delightful—we did not go to Gaieta[5]—but lionised the ancient buildings, called a temple & part of Cicero's buildings on the shore[6]—our guide complained of the miserable state of the country from poverty & taxation, now & ever since the French came. Gardens (of lemon trees) delightful, & apt to promote sentiment strongly—the spot thoroughly Italian.

Saturday Ap. 28.

7½ A.M.–4½ P.M. 6 Posts to Naples.—road variable—country generally luxuriant, especially from Capua[7]—where the crowd of miserable objects is perfectly appalling. Posting poor. March of mind indeed! They are building a suspension bridge over the Garigliano[8]—whose placid & peaceful stream recalls the

> Non rura que Liris quietâ
> Mordet aquâ taciturnus amnis.[9]

Between this & St Agata,[10] passed the camp, where the King now was with his forces.[11] No decent Inn from Mola to Naples. In the Campagna here the usual mode of cultivation is, vines pendant from trees thickly planted above

[1] One and a half miles north of Gaeta.
[2] Mrs. *Starke, Information for travellers*, 266, advises strongly against it.
[3] Six miles SE. of Velletri.
[4] Seventeen miles WNW. of Gaeta.
[5] Gaeta, 72 miles SE. of Rome and 40 NW. of Naples.
[6] Villa Caposele.
[7] Thirty-three miles east by south of Gaeta.
[8] The ancient Liris river; enters the Mediterranean 9 miles east of Gaeta.
[9] Horace, *Odes*, I. xxxi. 7–8, 'not the regions which the still river Liris eats away with its silent stream'.
[10] Twenty miles SE. of Mola.
[11] Ferdinand II, 1810–59, called Bomba; King of the Two Sicilies 1830.

—& corn beneath which was already forward.—Entered by the Strada Nuova—view of the city, sea, mountain, & Campagna, splendid—must not forget the islands. Naples is curious to the eye of a stranger: its very dense population, multitude & variety of vehicles, & of costumes, crucifixes every where painted, as large as life, orange & lemon stands with Madonnas above &c.—Vittoria. Indifferent rooms—went to dine at Corona di Ferro—wh John remembered *in bonam partem*.[1] The Toledo,[2] whatever it is, cannot I think be called strikingly magnificent or beautiful.

Sunday Ap. 29.

English Church morning & aftn. Congregation respectable, & Minister also —Mr Bennet[3]—who I am informed has been mainly instrumental in establishing it on its present footing—found an *organ* at last: at Rome & elsewhere they have no music. The Govt I am told will not let the English have a distinct building—so they are under the same roof with Sir H Lushington.[4]—reading &c. walked out—dined well at home—saw Pakenham & in the evening Milnes, with whom we walked to the Crocelle,[5] whence we saw in the darkness the red glare of the slow broad stream of lava noiselessly descending the mountain side.

Monday Ap. 30.

Letters—dined at Albergo Reale—delivered letters of introduction—made divers calls about parcels &c. and engaged with a singing master in the Palazzo Leone (Sigr Luigi Billemi)—we were obliged to go to him having no instrument—and oh! as our Luigi said, che sporco palazzo![6] He always seemed master of his business. Took my first lesson—wrote home—& heard —The ordinary letters are detained in the Office three days, we hear, on account of smoking![7] the Minister's less.

Tuesday May 1.

Expedition with the Cases to the Bay of Baiae: immediately on arriving in Pozzuoli,[8] we were assailed by a crowd of beggars, ciceroni, and boatmen, all most indefatigable & swift of foot. This is the only country where I ever saw a blind man run full gallop.—No decent Inn. We engaged boats & asses —went across, passing the fragments of Caligula's bridge, to the centre of the bay: landed & mounted our asses. N.B. the boat might be dispensed with. Mrs Case took some sketches from the water & elsewhere with great rapidity of execution. My donkey picked his way along the stones while I

[1] Favourably.
[2] Main street.
[3] Probably Henry Bennett, 1795–1874; ordained 1822; rector of South Cadbury, Somerset, 1831–36, and of Sparkford, Somerset, from 1836.
[4] Sir Henry Lushington, 2nd Bart., 1775–1863; consul at Naples 1815–32.
[5] A fashionable hotel in Chiaja, the district west of the harbour.
[6] What a filthy palace!
[7] As a disinfectant against cholera.
[8] Seven miles west of Naples.

read the Aeneid on his back—the face of the country still corresponding in many particulars, notwithstanding the violence of volcanic action. (I should have said that we went to see the Temple (of Jup[ite]r?) in Pozzuoli—a very good specimen, as far as regards explaining the plane of the *floor* of such buildings.)[1] We had passed the hill of the Falernian wine,[2] & that called Monte Nuovo raised by an earthquake in 17[blank].[3] We pass the Lucrine Lake,[4] to the Avernian. The passage is now blocked up: but it is interesting to recur to the well known passages of Virgil, in the Georgics—

Quid memorem portus &c.
and of Horace in the Ep. ad Pis.[5]

We entered what is called the Sibyl's cavern—it appeared to me, that the coast on the Sorrento side may indeed very fairly be supposed to have suggested Virgil's hundred mouthed cave: much more so, than according to Forsyth's suggestion.[6] Locality he was not obliged to observe. We descended the narrow passage to the right to what are called the Sibyl's baths, on men's backs—the water tolerably deep—bad enough to ride, much worse to carry. Stories of the guides ridiculous. Our bearers called themselves *cavalli*.[7] They were of course discontented with the pay awarded. When we came to the light, we alleged they were the very same men who had just been rowing us as boatmen, & were to do it again: but they stoutly denied their own identity, or that they had any thing to do with the boat, till some time after we entered it again! These *cavalli* we may dub by the name of a fish commonly found in the Bay of Baiae, sea-horses.

We passed on among the ruins of Baiae, to Nero's baths, which Case & I descended, stripped to the skin upwards; the heat was most oppressive: he threatened to turn back, & if he had done it I fear I should not have had the courage to have gone on. Every one should go in dirty clothes, and then keep as near as possible to the ground. Do what you will, you come out in a filthy state, & almost dissolved. The action of such heat upon the muscles of the legs in their distended state from crouching all the way was such that when I came out they trembled under me, and they ached violently & were very stiff for a week. The passage is excessively narrow, & the descent very steep.—We went on to the three temples of Baiae, which are all simple & curious. At the Inn we took some refreshments, and then resumed our way, to see the Piscina Mirabile,[8] & took a view of the scene called by them

[1] Pavement declined towards the centre.

[2] The *Falernus Ager* produced some of Italy's finest wine, praised by Horace and Pliny.

[3] 1538.

[4] The Lucrine Lake and Lake Avernus were connected to each other and to the sea to make the harbour of Portus Julius, in the first century A.D.

[5] *Georgics*, ii. 161–4, slightly misquoted; and *Epistola ad Pisones* (*Ars Poetica*), 63–66.

[6] Joseph *Forsyth, *Remarks on antiquities, arts and letters during an excursion in Italy in the years 1802 and 1803* (1813), 311, suggests that Avernus was from remote antiquity dreaded as a passage to the nether regions, and that Virgil converted the grotto opening onto the lake into a mouth of hell.

[7] Horses.

[8] Piscina Mirabilis, a reservoir with a vaulted ceiling supported by massive columns.

the Elysian fields.[1] Their theory of the four infernal rivers I do not pretend to have comprehended: it was a strange jumble of fire & water, earthquake volcano & inundation, which has mangled the face of the country. The Piscina is very wonderful. Being hurried, we omitted the Cento Camerelle.[2] The prospects from different points in our day's work were alone worth the labour.

J.N.G. & I made great haste to get up to the Minister's Villa, sopra il Vomero.[3] A party of Gentlemen; Mr Falcunet[4] & the Rev Mr Bennett, & Sir Ch. Greville,[5] among them. He received us with great kindness—a sumptuous repast—he has a good many pictures, and a splendid situation —but the access to carriages is vexatiously circuitous. There is a short footway.

Wednesday May 2.

Singing lesson—calls—dined with the Cases. Papers—&c.

We spent the early part of the day among the statuary at the Studio. For my own part, of the very famous pieces, the Adonis & Flora struck me least. I cannot abide a colossal woman: at least excepting Helen MacGrigor and Meg Merrilies.[6] The equestrian Balbi[7]—the Aristides—the Venus Callipyga —the head of Plato—(& of Julius Caesar?) and the Torso, were all very interesting—but the fragment called Psyche appeared to me, I confess, both then & subsequently, the most thoroughly exquisite piece of sculpture I had ever seen—and, more than this, the most perfect realization of ideal beauty according to the Grecian standard, that imagination could desire.

The globe of the Atlas is surely ludicrously small. However, it was necessary to make facts bend a little. The corn & olive mills of the court are curious.

Dreadful accounts of cholera from Paris.

Thursday May 3.

Singing lesson—& dined at Mr Falconnet's. Met Irby,[8] an old Etonian schoolfellow. Mr F's rooms richly furnished & almost exclusively with English books and prints.

[1] A plain of gardens and vineyards, with numerous tombs, mainly of sailors of the Misenum fleet. Cp. *Aeneid*, vi. 637 ff.

[2] 'The hundred little rooms', a labyrinth of subterranean chambers in a height near Bacoli, 10 miles west of Naples.

[3] 'On Mount Vomero' a hill on the NW. outskirts of Naples. The minister was William Noel-*Hill, 1773–1842; 3rd Lord Berwick 1832; envoy at Turin 1807–24, Naples 1824–33.

[4] Falconnet, an Englishman resident in Naples, had been prominent for many years among the merchants there.

[5] Sir Charles Greville, 1786–1836; maj.-gen., col. 38th foot; 2nd s. of 2nd earl of Warwick; M.P. Warwick 1816–31, 1832–3, 1835–6.

[6] Rob Roy's wife in Walter *Scott's *Rob Roy* (1817), and the old gypsy woman in his *Guy Mannering* (1815).

[7] Equestrian statues of Balbus, praetor and proconsul at Herculaneum, and his father.

[8] Frederick William Irby, d. 1877; J.P.; of Boyland Hall, Norfolk.

Our morning was again spent at the studio. Among, firstly, the Egyptian antiquities. The point which struck me as most curious was, the representation of the Supreme Being, in the little antique images, similar to the Roman penates, in a triune form—three figures, attached bodily together: a father mother & son, I think. And such we learned was the general rule.

Hence to the ancient specimens of fresco painting found at Pompeii and Herculaneum. They differ exceedingly in merit—in some there was spirited and correct drawing. The perspective I think was generally wretched—but yet the assertion that the ancients were *ignorant* of perspective, may be too unqualified for the facts. It would seem indeed, from *these* specimens, that they had not studied it scientifically, but a greater or less degree of perspective nature will teach to artists according to the correctness of the eye. Else, whence came the science itself?

Representations of naval battles: but at this time I do not remember any thing more than a single bank of oars, & no light seemed to be thrown on the controverted points.[1] The subjects I think were almost universally Grecian. There may be a twofold reason given.
1. The Grecian origin of Pompeii & Herculaneum.
2. The Grecian & derived character of all Roman literature and art. We saw also the Mosaics—some of those from Pompeii very fine—a cat in particular. But the Alexander's triumph lately found there surpasses them.[2] Pieces of wall-side, with the scribbling of the guards off duty.

I think one might say, that some of the frescoes are worse done than any that could now be found?

Friday May 4.

Singing lesson—dined at Corona di Ferro—and removed to the Gran Bretagna, for the sake of an immense improvement in our rooms. We spent all the early part of the day at the Studio: among
(1) The Bronzes. In general better executed than the marbles? Many fine figures—Discoboli, sleeping & drunken Fawn, some very fine busts. The Herculaneum objects are far better preserved than those from Pompeii, owing to the more effectual exclusion of the air.
(2) The Pictures. The gallery on the 'Neapolitan' side was on the whole the most indifferent, I thought we had seen. Salvators scanty and not of his best,[3] although the school claims his name. Perhaps no great painter has been so little followed as this stern & wild genius. Among the specimens here was a representation of the man with the *beam* in his eye reproving his neighbour with a mote[4]—the artist no way abashed with the difficulty, has actually painted the reprover with a beam not indeed in—for that was physically impossible, but projected obliquely from his eye.—The German & Florentine rooms contained some very old specimens, otherwise nothing

[1] Over arrangement of oars in triremes and quinqueremes.
[2] Depicting the battle of Issus, 333 B.C. Cp. 21 Nov. 38.
[3] 'not of his best' substituted for 'indifferent'.
[4] Matt. vii. 3–5.

interesting. The drawing or rather carving of the German figures by far harder than anything I had ever seen—they seemed to be made of castiron well starched. In the Flemish rooms, one small Rubens, a head: (I think): two Vandycks & two by Mysveld,[1] exceedingly similar in style, to us indistinguishable. The other side of the Gallery is interesting. Here are some *studii* of Correggio, and the beautiful little originals. In the Roman room, a Raffael; specimens of Perugino & Pinturicchio close together, affording a good opportunity of contrasting them in the point of softness & expression wherein they differ—Carlo Maratta.[2] Here also we found many specimens of Parmeggiano & of different degrees apparently of labour, from the picture of his mistress[3] downwards. A large collection of Canaletti's scenes in Venice—very admirable portraits by Titian and Tintoretto, Philip I of Spain among those of (I think) the latter.[4] Among the capi d'opera—Guercino's Magdalen ([5] at Doria), Raphael's Holy Family. Giulio Romano's Madonna del Gatto are those which with the above have most fixed themselves in my memory—and a picture of Ann[ibale] Caracci's with all his power of *fancy* (which is I think his faculty as contradistinguished from that of imagination) and bad taste. But these are the scanty fragments of recollections four or five months old.

Saturday May 5.

Singing lesson—commenced keeping the accounts of our 'concern'—

We went pretty early to the Cathedral (Chiesa del Archivescovado) having heard the grand Neapolitan miracle, the liquefaction of the blood of its patron saint,[6] was to take place today. It occurs three times a year. We went over the Cathedral, & into the Chapel below where there is a kneeling statue by or after M[ichael] Angelo. We made enquiry of a vast number of ecclesiastics where & when the exhibition was to take place: they were however either unable or unwilling to tell—most of the accounts we got were contradictory, scarce any two agreed. We went to see some other Churches—the Trinità Maggiore,[7] in a subterranean chapel of which I saw a singular benefaction of one of the Popes, that for every mass said there, a soul should be released, at a venture as it were, from purgatory: how completely is the connection between guilt & punishment, even as placed by this erroneous doctrine, set at nought. *A* soul for a mass—no matter if the mass be not intended for anyone in particular by him who has it offered. The Gesù—These two are amongst the handsomest Churches in Naples—

---

[1] Michiel Miereveld, 1567–1641; Dutch portrait painter.　　　[2] 1625–1713.

[3] Margin entry in pencil: *Wife.*

[4] The painting is of Philip II of Spain, by Titian.

[5] 'Surely' [?] here deleted.

[6] According to tradition, St. Gennaro, bp. of Benevento, was thrown to the lions in the amphitheatre of Pozzuoli, in A.D. 305, but was unharmed and so was beheaded. When the saint was re-interred at Naples, a phial of his blood, brought to the bp., St. Severus, liquefied as he received it. This phial and the body of St. Gennaro were deposited in the cathedral of Naples in the fifteenth century. The liquefaction of the saint's blood is a great Neapolitan festival which takes place in May, September, and December.

[7] Also called the Gesu Nuovo.

very rich & solemn. In general the Churches here are not fine, & the paintings are by inferior artists.

Hearing there was a San Gennaro function at the Santa Chiara, we went there; & after waiting a long time, music by no means to our ears of a sacred character playing at intervals, we saw a demi-statue of the saint in silver most idolatrously borne at the head of a long procession in which walked an immense number of the State & other functionaries. The music was now wholly military. I forget whether it was here or at Venice I saw them demonstrate their contempt for the show by carrying their candles in many cases upside down & extinguished.—Well, San Gennaro was set upon the altar, with seven or eight candles burning round him.

I returned in the evening between six & seven. A number of people were still assembled—the common people placed behind a railing running along the sides of the Church—the band still playing in a manner much more enjoyable than appropriate. There were reserved seats inside for strangers, priests, & ladies—to which I got access, meeting with great civility from the soldiers. I found Sir C. Greville there. Waited a long time—at last all the silver statues, or "treasures", as they are called, were brought in an enormously long train, each having its procession of ecclesiastics: of whom the number seems to be beyond belief—all these were regulars. Each saint in succession was brought up to the rails; these his bearers set him down for a few moments to look at San Gennaro, and then took him on! At intervals a parcel of women, who had been selected from the mob for the purpose (I suppose)[1] & *packed* on one side of the altar, raised horrible & discordant cries which an Italian near me told me were Aves & Credos: but he admitted them to be unintelligible & senseless.

By and bye came a distinct procession with the blood of the saint: in a vessel shaped like those which hold the host: with in was a small flat & circular bottle, communicating apparently with another, cylindrical: they held up the vessel to show that the blood lay liquefied here—which I thought it did. The people now rushed in, and pressed round the altar & upon the Archbishop excessively. Why did they not leave it on the altar to liquefy there? But in place of this, he takes the small vessel of[f] the stand, and holds it in his hands, turning his face to the altar & his back on the crowd who pressed him, where I conceive no one, certainly only three or four, could get a sight *at all* of the motions of his hands. I was within two feet[2] of him or less, but could see nothing. In a very short time, he held it up, giving out that it was liquefied, as it was: the period was less I should think than a minute: the crowd renewed its turbulence, the women their horrible shrieks, the music struck up, and the devotees knelt down to kiss the vessel containing the blood, headed by Bishop Machale,[3] and numbering among them my fellow Protestants M[ilnes] & M[ars]h. The noise & squeezing round the altar (by priests, ladies, & foreigners,) were most indecorous.

---

[1] *Le zie di S Gennaro*, the saint's 'aunts', a body of poor and aged women chosen to attend all these ceremonies.

[2] 'Within two feet' instead of 'within a foot or two'.

[3] John *MacHale, 1791–1881; abp. of Tuam, 1834; friend of *O'Connell.

Sunday May 6.

English Church morning and afternoon—reading—a quiet day. J.N.G. had an affair with a pickpocket whom he licked. Milnes came in at night.

Monday May 7.

Called pretty early—wrote home, put up things, & left Naples about nine A.M. in a vetturino carriage for Paestum,[1] with Pakenham[2] & Count Orlowsky, a Russian Pole, aged only about 20. The road to Pompeii by Herculaneum & Resina,[3] skirting the bay and Vesuvius, lies through what is almost one continued town.

The sight of Pompeii was of course highly interesting: but the *facility* itself with which these visits are now performed, has brought them within the range of everyday objects, has given them a technical and common-place character, and has destroyed that illusion which constituted their highest charm. Pompeii would be indeed extraordinary if we could realise the ideas it conveys, and believe, practically believe, that we are walking amidst the very streets which were trodden by the ancient Romans, and in the very chambers which they inhabited. We went through the whole series of objects. About an hundred dead bodies have been found in the town. The temples and theatres seem to have been executed with great beauty: more however as it depends on magnificence than as it flows from taste. The method of painting the exteriors of the houses is not pleasing to our eyes. The apartments seem to have been exceedingly small. Houses generally comprised but one story. The wood destroyed while the masonry resigned. The new mosaic of Alexander's triumph magnificent: and many of the frescoes well executed. Yoke of oxen, with the harness &c. represented exactly as it is used in the present day.[4] The situation is still very beautiful: and it must have been delightful indeed when the sea, which receded at the time of the earth-quake, was near at hand. View from the extreme corner of the temple of Hercules, which is called triangular, very beautiful. Either there must have been immense general wealth, or this must have been a *pet* place. The Comic Theatre has a sunk passage to receive the aulaeum[5]—this and the amphitheatre are both very perfect, particularly however the former. In the lower parts, the steps are much wider & much lower—so that they seem to have been meant to receive chairs—as they are they could hardly be intended to sit upon!

Ride onwards to Salerno,[6] where we arrived about 5, extremely dusty, but generally beautiful: about La Cava[7] quite exquisite, and not less so on the descent into the magnificent bay of Salerno. Here during the evening we enjoyed the prospect excessively. The outline out of the mountains on the

---

[1] Greek-founded city, which became a Roman colony in third century B.C.; 50 miles S.E. of Naples.
[2] Arthur, b. 1810, 14th child of Admiral Sir Thomas *Pakenham.
[3] Four and a half miles SE. of Naples.
[4] In the MS there is here a smudged diagram of a yoke.   [5] Curtain.
[6] Thirty miles SE. of Naples.
[7] Three and a half miles NW. of Salerno.

right is extremely fine—and sky and sea were even brighter and clearer than we had yet seen them. Went to see the Cathedral which contains Mosaics from Poestum, said to be of the time of Constantine, and the monument of Gregory the Seventh.[1] besides, as it is said, the remains of St. Matthew.

Dined at slept at the Albergo dei Forestieri—where we were very fairly accommodated. Its situation on the quay beautiful.

Tuesday May 8.

Set out for Paestum after breakfast, somewhat late—through a tract considerably resembling, except near Salerno, the Pomptine marshes. The distant features[2] however of the prospect were very fine.

Avoiding Eboli we took the direct road for Poestum and arrived there about one. Spent three hours there, which time, except a little taken up in getting some scanty refreshment at the (so called) Albergo, was occupied, and very pleasurably among the ruins. However little associated with direct historical recollections, these monuments must always be interesting from their connection with the ancient religion of the country, and from their intrinsic beauty. Of the three great ruins, the order is Doric—the towers taper very much, particularly in the "Basilica"—and the capitals are overwhelming: so much so that [it] is extremely difficult to persuade one's eye that two, which lie on the ground, are not considerably larger than their brethren which retain their appropriate stations—so enormous do these masses (ovals & abacus, of a single block) appear when close. The temple of Neptune is much the most interesting, as it retains its unity & grandeur in a far greater degree than the others. Within we found a second story of pillars, which may have been one of the earliest 'attics': they are however simply *continuations* of those beneath them so there is no 'position *in falso*'. We saw the theatre, and the recent excavations, affording examples of the other orders of architecture. And after exhausting the slender stores of the albergo, Pakenham, my brother, and I walked out to the ancient gate —we found it & the walls characterised by true Roman solidarity: but enjoyed the spot most from the exquisitely beautiful view it gives of the temple of Neptune. From this spot, it appeared to receive additional elevation, which improves the appearance of the structure to the eye, and to *crown* the whole plain. In this lordly position, the rays of the sun descending obliquely upon it, fell, behind the massive pediment, upon each row of pillars, and thus illuminated them laterally; every part of the whole building was displayed with the utmost distinctness of relief, and an indescribable softness in the lights and shades. Certainly, I then saw Grecian architecture in perfection, and could duly appreciate its chastity and majesty.[3] Its triumph is complete, in realising the most imposing effect from the simplest combination.[4] The rank[5] vegetation of the plain is perhaps a mis-

[1] Hildebrand, pope 1073; excommunicated emperor Henry IV 1076; d. 1085.
[2] 'distant features' instead of 'outlines'.   [3] 'Until then' here deleted.
[4] 'Had Mrs Starke seen it, she would certainly have inserted it with a comment' [?] here deleted. Cp. *Starke, *Information for Travellers*, 340–1.
[5] Instead of 'exuberant'.

fortune, when one is actually among the temples. It is coarse: and takes away from the idea of desolation without conveying that of richness. On our return to Salerno, had a good deal of conversation with Count Orlowsky about his country &c. & found him very well read & well informed. He is a liberal Catholic—and yet a faithful one:[1] he does not think that the doctrine of Transubstantiation can be positively inferred from the words of Scripture. *This* would have burnt him 300 years back. Got to Salerno by dusk. A priest, who had taken Orlowsky to the Cathedral came in; we asked him to dinner & he acquiesced, with a "come volete".[2] Conversation about the two systems of religion—he seemed *exceedingly* ignorant. Speaking of prayer to the saints, the Pole (ironically as he said himself afterwards,) alleged as an argument that Abraham could hear Dives pray from out of hell[3]—that *hell*, being under the earth, was *farther* from heaven than the earth itself, and therefore that a fortiori the saints could hear us when we pray to them. For this notion, the priest seemed very thankful and readily adopted it. It then came out that *Vesuvius* was the mouth of hell: a doctrine supported by both landlord and priest.
Hotel des Etrangers, Good.

Wednesday May 9.

After breakfast, sailed for Amalfi[4]—arrived in a little less than 2½ hours. The coast was exceedingly fine and the water perfectly smooth. Every one who comes to Naples, ought to see the Gulph of Salerno, were there no Paestum. We found a comfortable Inn at Amalfi—but it is necessary in all matters hereabouts, whether of donkeys, boats, ciceroni, or inns, to *bargain* rigorously and beforehand. Went to the Cathedral. Pakenham and I went up the mountains a height of 1000 or 1200 feet to procure asses, wherein we failed, but enjoyed the expedition as the views were most magnificent on every side, though not extensive, and our path steep as it was, was bordered with myrtles & wildflowers. 2 piastres demanded for asses to go to Castellamare.[5]—We went by boat to Scaricatejo,[6] and then crossed the hills to Sorrento.[7] The view in ascending, when about two thirds of the way up, is glorious indeed, and the foliage of the mountain very rich, and varied like the scenery in England. In descending, the Pole, who had been unwell previously, & was excessively tried by the ascent, gave in, and we were obliged to get a mule to take him to Sorrento. We put up at the Albergo di Parigi, a comfortable Inn enough, though it does not exempt travellers from the necessity of bargaining. It is not mentioned by Mrs. Starke.

[1] 'for' here deleted.
[2] 'as you please'.
[3] Luke xvi. 19–31.
[4] Twelve miles WSW. of Salerno.
[5] At the eastern corner of the bay of Naples.
[6] Diarist here follows Mrs. *Starke (*Information for travellers*, 355) in mistaking a description for a name (*scaricare*, to go down or disembark). Spot near Positano is meant, 6 miles east of Sorrento, on the opposite, southern side of the peninsula that separates the bays of Naples and Salerno.
[7] Fifteen miles west of Amalfi, on the Bay of Naples.

Thursday May 10.

Left Sorrento by boat for Castellamare;[1] about two hours in performing it without wind. Enjoyed the trip, as the coast was most magnificent, and we sailed into one of those mysteriously communicating caverns, whose orifices are so numerous and varied, that they may well (if a groundwork be needful,) have been the groundwork of Virgils

> Excisum Eubiocae latus ingens rupis in antrumo,
> Quo lati ducunt aditus centum, ostia centum:
> Unde ruunt totidem voces, responsa Sibyllae.
> > Aen. 6. 42.[2]

One bit of coast strongly impregnated with sulphur—At Castellamare we hired donkeys for the return ride—found the road (a misnomer—it seemed only distinguished from the rest of the mountain by greater ruggedness—) rough and precipitous beyond belief, but the views magnificent: rich wood and brilliant flowers, tremendous precipices beneath, and the bay of Naples beneath stretching far away in its silent loveliness, with the city in the distance. How truly is this a fairy land, full to excess with all the elements of beauty, full to enchantment: what more could one desire in Paradise than its natural character, what more lamentable on this sorrowful earth than its moral condition? but for dreams of youth and enthusiasm—for imbibing the idea of natural & ideal beauty and engraving it deeply on the heart and rousing it to a strong adoration, what country can surpass Italy, everywhere impregnated with its essence and crowded with its forms? But the mind must awake to the realities of life, and must not be enervated in its slumbers.

Plain of Sorrento extremely rich—but views choked up by the high walls. Went to the cathedral and saw Tasso's house. Sailed for Capri about six— we all had a tedious and I a sick passage, of near four hours. Mounted to the town, and lodged ourselves at Giuseppe Pagano's.

Friday May 11.

After breakfast, a donkey cruise to the villa of Tiberius[3]—pharos—mosaics —and a smirking friar, who begged of us and was refused. In this small isle are forty priests. Want of timber. Coasts magnificently precipitous. Salto[4] of Tiberius awful. Found the boatmen most rascally—the innkeeper civil & respectable. After dinner, set out for Ischia.[5] I was very sick, or should have enjoyed it much. Orlowsky & Pakenham also sick. There being some

---

[1] Fifteen miles SE. of Naples.
[2] 'One vast side of the Euboean rock is hewn into a cavern, to which lead a hundred broad avenues and a hundred gateways, whence issue as many voices, the Sybil's reply.' The diarist has 'antrumo' for 'antrum'.
[3] Who lived on Capri A.D. 27–37.
[4] The rock, near Tiberius's villa, from which he is said to have had victims hurled into the sea.
[5] Island 17 miles WSW. of Naples and 15 WNW. of Capri.

sea, we were unable to enter the newly discovered cavern. Wind got round—
after some tossing and several hours sailing, it was found impossible to get
to *Isch,* as the boatmen call it (all the inhabitants here abscide the terminations, & mangle moreover; for Capri they say Crapi:) and we sailed with a
fair wind for Naples when we arrived about one A.M. on Saturday morning.
Delighted to get to rest.

Saturday May 12.

A day of rest & partial lay up after my seasickness. Wrote a long letter to
Gaskell—and read a good deal (according to my present measure of great &
small) of Wordsworth. Pakenham here.

Naples. May 13.[1]

Of late and today in particular, I have been employed in examining some
of the details of the system of the English Church, as set forth in the Prayer-
book, with which I was before less acquainted. To coming into Catholic
countries, and to some few books, I owe glimpses which now seem to be
afforded me of the nature of a Church, and of our duties as members of it,
which involve an idea very much higher & more important than I had previously had any conception of. Perhaps time, prayer, and mercy, may bring
out the same and turn it to good effect. How much would be gained, if we
could indeed interweave with the whole of life a pervading and equalised
spirit of religion.

Sunday May 13.

My appetite declared itself convalescent. Church. A very good sermon from
Mr Bennet—"if any man sin, we have an advocate with the Father".[2]
Walk in the Chiaja gardens. Employed some, but few, hours with pen and
book. *These* studies might indeed be interesting.

Monday May 14.

Duncan Milligan[3] came to breakfast with us, and afterwards we went to
the Studio, and saw the kitchen and other furniture, the articles in glass,
and those in the precious metals, with the preserved provisions: also the
papyrus, and the manner of unrolling it, dramatically represented, for the
piece on which they performed had been unrolled already. The process is
simple and the recovery beautiful. Much yet remains, exhibiting mere charcoal to all appearance. *Nearly* all the recovered stones are Greek hitherto,
thus illuminating the positive historical fact of the extreme poverty of the
Latin language up to (I suppose) the time when Herculaneum was destroyed:
as we know from Cicero and other sources that Latin literature was new

---

[1] This paragraph from Lambeth MS 1420. Cp. Morley, i. 87.
[2] 1 John ii. 1.
[3] B. 1793, s. of Robert Milligan, 1746–1809, West India merchant.

and that those who then studied, studied in Greek. And Lucretius[1] complains of his subject.

> Difficile illustrare Latinis versibus esse [, . . .]
> Propter egestatem linguae & rerum novitatem.[2]

Surprised to find, among the utensils, how many of the contrivances of convenience now resorted to were handed down from antiquity. Saw *styli* here, as at Florence, painted at one end and with a kind of button (but parallel)[3] at the other, illustrating

> Saepe stylum vertas[4] – –
> – – – – incomtis allinet atrum
> Transverso calamo lignem.   A. Poet.[5]

Heard from T.G.—Had a singing lesson as usual. We find Billemi a satisfactory master, though his situation is remote and his "Palazzo" otherwise objectionable. Woe be to him who, coming into this country and hearing of a palace, is so far misled by the term as to expect anything better than a pigsty.

Dinner at Corona di Ferro—and started, about 4½ A.M. for Herculaneum[6] —How lamentable it is, that the excavations cannot be continued, and supports for the town above provided. The theatre is still curious, but far less so than it should be, because the whole *effect* is lost where examination is only practicable in detail. The ancient wood in [deletion] masses of oak, to which the lava served as a moulding, is curious in the *nuove scave*.[7]

Surprised to find the ascent of Vesuvius so easy, up to the Hermitage:[8] performed it of course on donkeys. Put up with the hermit—metamorphosed partially into an innkeeper: partially, for, at an Inn, you receive accommodation & pay for it: here you pay (almost) without receiving. Fleas are bad in a soft bed, but worse on a stony one. The hermit conversible enough: thought the state of the world very bad; perhaps wrong in his reasons,[9] right in his fact. *Pakenham* scandalised him.—Lay down from 11 to 3 but did not sleep.

Tuesday May 16 [sc. 15].

In the evening the flame was fine & the summit clear—but the morning was dismally clouded. Howbeit, we pursued our way, and arrived upon the

[1] Margin entry: *A.D. 79.*
[2] *De Rerum Natura*, i. 137, 139; 'How difficult it is to explain in Latin verses, because of the poverty of the language and the novelty of the subjects'.
[3] 'parallel' instead of 'not at right angles'.
[4] Diarist's dashes. Horace, *Satires*, i. 10, 72: 'turn your stilus often'.
[5] 'Score out the ugly lines in black with a stroke of the pen'; 'lignem' should read 'signum' (Horace, *Ars Poetica*, 446–7).
[6] Five and a half miles SE. of Naples; a Roman town on the seashore overwhelmed during the eruption of Vesuvius in A.D. 79.
[7] 'new excavations'.
[8] Inn on the slopes of Vesuvius.
[9] Substituted for 'fact'.

plain formed by lava which has filled up the old grand crater about 4¼. The steep part took 40 minutes, but might be done without difficulty in 30. We wandered about the top from place to place in cloud, rain & despair: after much of each, the top was good enough to clear for a little, and we saw the showers of red hot stones and lava with great distinctness. The smoke of the crater, deeply tinged with a burning red, preclude's one's prying vision, and conceals its own horrors, but the sides of the orifice, and its issues are enough to raise strong feelings of wonder[1] & awe as to the interior. How fearfully near are the weapons of judgement in the armoury of heaven: and with how much longsuffering has punishment been suspended or abridged.

The mountain at present is in a state of perpetual change. Besides the fearful cracks, loud as thunder but more discordant, which issued from the small crater then open, immediately previous to each emission we heard continually reports from beneath & around us, betokening new fissures, and it was cloven at short intervals on the surface. In places, & particularly near the crater, the atmosphere was so sulphurous as to be all but insupportable. We trod on lava only a week old, and from which great heat was emitted, particularly when rain had just fallen.

A scene of more utter and hopeless desolation in appearance than that presented by this plain of lava, I cannot conceive. It is hard in substance, jagged in surface, dismal & monotonous, except where varied by the deadly hues of sulphur, in colour.[2] In many places the outward asperity of form is so great, that it seems as though it had been a sentient thing, petrified whilst in the sufferance of exquisite torture, and left as its own changeless monument. In some tracts it lay like rude masses of bark of trees piled together, but the variety of forms was infinite.—The lips of the old large crater are distinctly traceable.

The cone again gathered its mantle of clouds around it, and we descended —the steep part, whose perpendicular altitude is 900 feet, and whose inclined surface perhaps above twice as much, since the angle can hardly be 30°,[3] took my brother 3½ min. to descend. We then remounted and descended to Resina,[4] with no other accident than a collision between my brother's ass & mine which sent me sprawling & brought him less ignobly to the ground along with his ass. We brought pieces of lava down from the mountain, gave them to the cicerone to carry, & then forgot them.—

A day of determined rain. Wrote to Phillimore, & home. Made some calls —read Wordsworth & Forsyth: singing lesson. Milnes sat here in the evening—he is on the eve of departure for Sicily.

Wednesday May 16.[5]

Called on Mr Hill, and then pursued our way up to the Camaldoli Convent,[6]

[1] Instead of 'wonderment'.
[2] 'And' deleted.
[3] Margin entry: Sin 30° = ½.
[4] 'Resina', substituted for 'Herculaneum', is the modern city beside the latter.
[5] Date substituted for 'Ap. 17'.
[6] On the Camaldoli Hill to the NW. of Naples.

which calls itself 8 miles from the Mole, and may be six. It likewise pretends to an elevation of 375 passi, each $= 7\frac{1}{3}$ palmi.

This gives $7 \times 375 = 2625$

$$\frac{375}{3} = \frac{125}{2750}$$

and a palmo is rather > 10 inches. Taking it at 10, we have

$$12 | \underline{27500} \text{ in} \quad \text{feet for the height.}$$
$$2291.8$$

The view is panoramic and exquisitely beautiful: embracing the coast from the point of Gaieta to Campanella[1]—and a great extent of Campagna. The craters of volcanoes, now extinct, which may be discerned from hence, are very numerous. Astrone, Agnano, Solfatara, Averno, Ischia,[2] two basins on the slope of which Naples rests.—The friars fed us on fruits wine which they called particolare, and a sort of liqueur which *they* make from coffee— and on being paid, the acknowledgement was "Il Signor vi paga, per la carita,"[3] twice repeated.—The scenery between the convent & Naples very rich & picturesque. John met an old Acquaintance, the Papal Nuncio at Rio.[4]

Yesterday we went to see the silk worms feeding at Resina—they are kept in low flat open baskets: each set made so many pounds of silk: ten days feeding—they much resemble some of the caterpillars we have in England. The Camaldolite Church has one very good painting by Santa Fede,[5] and another opposite it worth notice. The friars are very polite and clean—but it is painful to visit men, the principle of whose establishment one must deprecate as well as deplore its general result. They showed us splendid sacerdotal vestments in the sacristy, given they said per elemosyna[6] —but how unnatural does this appear when one views the condition of the population of this country.

Dined at Mr. Thompson Pater's,[7] who has been very kind to us.

Thursday May 17.

Went to San Severino by a mistake—but found it a fine Church: hence to the *Cappella di San Severo* to see the veiled statues of our Saviour's corpse & of Modesty, & that of Vice in a net, all by different artists, our real objects, and extremely well worth visiting, as we both thought. They are by Corradini[8]—Giuseppe San Martino,[9] & Queirolo,[10] respectively. For my part I

---

[1] Twenty miles ESE. of Naples, at the southern extremity of its bay.
[2] Almost in a line, bearing WSW. from the convent.
[3] 'The Lord will pay you for your charity'.
[4] Peter Ostini, cardinal 1831, bp. of Albano 1843; d. 1849.
[5] Fabrizio Santafede, ca. 1559–1628.
[6] 'for alms'.
[7] Probably an uncle of Walter *Pater, 1839–94.
[8] Antonio Corradini, d. 1752; Italian sculptor.
[9] Giuseppe San Martino, 1723–93; Italian sculptor.
[10] Francesco Queirolo, 1704–62; Italian sculptor.

have not seen many pieces of sculpture, particularly of modern sculpture, more interesting than the recumbent body of the Saviour. It is a good idea of Mrs Starke's, that the sheet seems clammy with the damp of death.[1] The expression of the countenance is shown through it with exquisite effect and yet apparently without effort.—Royal Gardens—somewhat in English style. Saw Bancunas—a favourite promenade on Sunday, when they are thrown open.—Campo Santo. here bodies are inhumated without coffin or winding sheet, in deep holes. One for each day of the year. Saw two: and in the one indistinctly, three corpses from the hospitals just thrown in, in the other, the whitening bones of a year ago within a day.

Studio, 2nd visit to the statues. More and more delighted with the Psyche.—visited the bronzes—where nearly all the busts are fine, and Fauns, Discoboli, and others among the statues—and the apartment of the Tauro, for the second time. Saw too the Middle Age Farnese Collection, & the earthenware vases &c. for the first. In the former, one work of Michael Angelo's.—Prince Leopold's[2] picture's: one room of modern ones, many of them execrable: the other containing many fine ones. Thirteen Salvators: and others of Guercino—Titian—Vandyck—Annibal Caracci—Gherardo della Notte[3]—Sasso Ferrato—Claude—Baroccio[4]—and others.

Dined at Mr Hills. Sir C. Greville (who kindly brought us down—) Mr M'Carthy,[5] &c. Mr H seems to have good pictures.

Friday May 18.

Our last expedition. Tomb of Virgil: what a work to reach it! & when reached, nothing but uncertainty and a crabbed bad epitaph. Qui cimeres? Tumuli haec vestigia conditur, olim, Ille hic, qui cecinit pascua rura duces.[6] End of the first line abominably involved. It has been made a question by some, whether this is Virgil's? Lago d'Agnano—Grotto del Cane[7]— Cumae[8]—(Grotto of Sibyl, Gate, road, amphitheatre, Tempio dei Giganti—) Pozzuoli[9] amphitheatre—and Solfatara.[10] The material dug up is put into a pot of earthenware: the earthy part, two thirds of the whole, sinks, and the sulphur remaining above is drained off through a hole at a proper height in the side, & then hardens. Banker[11] lost at Pozzuoli: at last brought back with the whole population at his heels; *each* one had of course been the finder.—Singing lesson: writing up: and reading in evening. Count Orlowski had tea with me.

---

[1] *Information and Directions for Travellers on the Continent*, 295.

[2] Leopold II, 1797–1870, grand duke of Tuscany 1824–59; his mother, Louisa, d. 1802, was a Neapolitan princess.

[3] Gerard van Honthorst, 1590–1656.   [4] Federico Barocci, 1526–1612.

[5] Possibly Nicholas Twite *MacCarthy, 1769–1833, known as the Abbé de Levignac, Irish-born Jesuit preacher.

[6] 'Whose ashes are these? Whose these signs of a sepulchral mound? Here is buried he who once sang pastures, the country, and leaders in war.'

[7] A grotto whose ground and sides were so impregnated with carbonic acid gas that a dog sent in would be overcome by the fumes in a few minutes.

[8] Twelve miles west of Naples.   [9] On the coast, 7 miles west of Naples.

[10] Chemical works in volcanic crater west of Pozzuoli.   [11] John's dog.

Saturday 19 May.

Calling. Went over the Studio gallery (on the best side only) for the second time, and laboured to gather some ideas. Horridly addled about Parmeggianino.[1] His Inamorata is certainly extremely beautiful. Liked Schidone[2] much. Called with John on his Archiepiscopal friend the Nuncio—on Hoffman,[3] Falconnet, Galton,[4] &c. Singing lesson. Teatro de' Fiorentini with John in evening—"Il Protettore dell' Orfana"[5]—never knew a piece with a better moral tone; but it must have been dull to the Neapolitans, and seemed so—to us it was amusing because the *protettore* was Milord Inglese. The notions of England it displayed were in some respects odd enough, but somewhat flattering too. These nations conceive a *milord Inglese* quite a different being from one of their own half & half nobility— and they are right.—Lava shops.—

Sunday May 20.

English Church. A good sermon in a good tone, as usual, from Mr Bennet. Reading &c. as usual. In afternoon, went to hear a sermon in a neighbouring Church. The subject was, the[6] resurrection which we are in this life to undergo analogous to that of Christ. The groundwork was excellent, and the spirit good—but the manner humourous even, sometimes, to buffoonery. —There was much skill in the manner in which after having raised a laugh through the congregation, he would check them with an impressive touch.

Went also to the Mole, where the usual exhibitions were going on. Heard also a part of another Catholic sermon about St John the Baptist and some other saint, which was whining, ceremonial, & dull.—The people seem always attentive.

Monday May 21.

Wrote to Aunt J. Made some calls. Last singing lesson. Lava shops and dealings. Also visited shops for body-colour-prints of Vesuvius: and went up to the Chiesa di San Martino, which is extremely rich in marbles—has many fine pictures—the capo d'opera of Spagnoletto,[7] a dead Christ—a very beautiful though unfinished altarpiece by Guido—a fine baptism by Carlo Maratta—and others: and two splendid views. Formerly convent of Certosini: now a military hospital. A soldier told me mass was said every morning & all the soldiers went—but this seemed grievously belied by the appearance of the Church. Neapolitan army he says amounts to 50,000 men.

What a pity that the view of Naples from all points except the sea, is divided.

[1] Francesco Mazzola, 1503–1540; called Parmigianino.
[2] Bartolommeo Schidone, 1570–1615.
[3] Unidentified.
[4] Perhaps Samuel Tertius Galton, 1783–1844, banker, f. of (Sir) Francis,* 1822–1911, eugenist.
[5] Perhaps Buini's *Il protettore alla Moda* (1758), with Galuppi's music.
[6] 'benefits' here deleted.
[7] José de Ribera, called Spagnoletto, 1590–1652; Spanish painter and engraver.

Packing &c. in the evening. Wrote to Aunt J. Wordsworth. On the whole —unfortunate as we have generally been in our weather, Naples cannot but appear to be a place of many delights and attractions. The ancient and venerable ruins of Paestum—the scenery, both coast and land of the Amalfi & Sorrento peninsula—the terrors of Vesuvius—the familiar instruction of Pompeii, in its neighbourhood, and the concentrated beauties of the Studio within its bounds, form a rare assemblage. From the people you must expect almost universally, the attempt (I will not say, to cheat, but) to extort a high price: but as long as you preserve your good humour in the bargain you are certain, not withstanding vehemence of manner, of finding it reciprocal. A Neapolitan's principle seems to be, that he first asks you an exorbitant price, and then claims the praise of moderation for relinquishing it, and its reward too, in the shape of a miniature imposition, or of the humble 'bottle':[1] calculating on your yielding the minor in your joy at having escaped the major. In religion they seem to be very low: ceremonies in Naples are of a more idolatrous cast than I have seen or heard of elsewhere: & at the same time the city is (& I should believe it) said to be extremely lax in morals.—The country is luxuriant beyond belief—and has in general its vines above, on poplars—an union which we did not see in the N of Italy, but named by Horace—

> Ergo aut adultae vitium propagini
> Altas maritat populos[2]—

while corn or vegetables of some kind occupy the ground below. It is not however cultivated with such exactitude of economy as the plains of Lucca and Pisa. The costumes are picturesque enough, but perhaps inferior to the Roman, except where they assimilate to them. The women's dress has not so classical an appearance: but in both these countries, and particularly about Albano & Genzano in Romagna, there is much female beauty. The male dress of Romagna is almost exclusively a kind of purple velveteen or plush. Here, drab and brown also prevail: indeed few jackets are worn, except when cast over the shoulders: and one often sees dress approaching its minimum, and consisting only of an open half-shirt with a pair of short drawers attached. The people sleep all they can, as it appears: in the streets, amidst that extreme filth and wretchedness which seems to prevail: and in the fields beneath the shade of trees, where you constantly see a heap of clothes almost equally inanimate whether there be a bundle of flesh under them or not.—Their dialect seems to be extremely vicious: the terminations of all the words are dispensed with: and they cannot always understand you if you retain them. A Cicerone at San Germano said to me "Io non capisco mai la lingua de' Signori—"[3] though he did not pronounce the words as I have written them. It was an odd qualification for his place. Their habit of using strong expressions is sometimes exemplified oddly enough. "Is so and

---

[1] A tip.

[2] Horace, *Odes*, ii. 9–10: 'And so he either grafts the tall poplars with a well-grown shoot of vines'. See 2 Mar. 32.

[3] 'I never understand the gentlemen's language'.

so *sempre* the case"? "Si Signore, *sempre*". "Ma, c'è *sempre sempre*?" No, Signore, non sempre sempre, ma, generalmente!"

Neapolitan character may be studied everywhere, at all places, throughout the intercourse of daily life: the inquiry it invites is superficial, because the character is superficial too. Particularly it will come out in striking bargains: and, the sermons in the Churches—the exhibitions on the Mole—and the Puncinello entertainments, may perhaps be specified. I was surprised to find a good many ecclesiastics on the Mole, on Sunday evening. One would have thought there could be little to gratify them: and if they have not influence enough to raise the character of the Sunday evening's enjoyments, decency might at least prevent their making this public and ostentatious illustration of their own incompetency.

Tuesday May 22.

Again among the lava and pictures. Went to the King's Palace, but could not see it as he was there. Went to the Stamperia Reale,[1] and saw the printed papyri of Herculaneum, which are sold there.

Left Naples at mid-day, by Vetturino, for Rome, by the Monte Casino road. We were four hours & a quarter going to Caserta![2] road good, tho' dusty. When arrived there, we went to see the Palace, which is called the largest Royal residence in Europe. The staircase and grand landing-place are admirable. The large royal app [*sc.* apartments] very well proportioned, & the Chapel handsome, with pictures. The rooms in general bare. Here there is a theatre open at the back, so that they use the *country*, by means of the aperture, as a scene.—We then took a carriage & went to see the Aqueduct of Charles III,[3] seven miles off: roads still good: indeed this is the grand road of communication with the Campo Basso.—The Aqueduct is indeed magnificent. A carriage may drive over the top, within the barriers: but it is only permitted to the King. The length of the top I paced, and made about 530 yards. There are three stories of arches: and the extreme height I guessed at 1600 feet or more. The work is of brick & stone. Bears date 1753–1760.

On our way we had met Mr Hill & Sir Charles Greville, and returning to Caserta (where we were obliged to determine on remaining, from our voiturin's extreme slowness) we found them there: Mr H made us sit down with them to an excellent dinner prepared by his cook, and we discussed a report which was heard in Naples yesterday, and even so far believed as to depress the funds, of the defeat of the Reform Bill. Mr Hill hoped it might be true, ran over the names for a new Cabinet, declared himself a liberal abroad & an anti-liberal at home, and blessed the "dear good old souls" of Shropshire for their conduct on the late election.[4]

[1] Royal printing-house.
[2] Seventeen miles NE. of Naples.
[3] Charles III, 1716–88; King of the Two Sicilies 1734; and of Spain 1759.
[4] In 1831, the tory candidates for Shropshire, Sir Rowland *Hill and John Cressett Pelham, M.P. 1831–2 and 1835–7, were returned by handsome majorities.

La Posta seemed fair, but we were obliged to go to an Inn in a street opposite; where the fleas amused me all night.

Wednesday May 23.

Before four o'clock in the morning we were on our way: the air delightful. Stopped on the road to Capua[1] to see the amphitheatre supposed to have belonged to the ancient city, & near the road. The underground story, or the *cellars*, remain in much perfection: some of the pillars & wall which formed the outer circuit formed of stupendous blocks; and judging from the very numerous fragments remaining here, as well as the fine columns of Giallo[2] at Caserta taken hence, and the general aspect of the building, it must have been most sumptuous.

The gate too, which crosses the road, is double: its niches remain.

A long stage to San Felice.[3] The country extremely beautiful, and the foliage rich beyond almost any I have seen in this country. It is a very English style of beauty. The trees stand singly, but are very thickly spread over the face of the country: which near the road abounds in gentle & graceful undulations, and farther off the prospect is bounded by the hills. Few vines or olives. This tract is worth seeing for its beauty, & also for its novelty.—Inn at San Felice wretched. Lay down to read Wordsworth during the bait, after choking on the refreshment the place afforded.—A ride of less than three hours brought us to San Germano,[4] through a fine ironbound vale—excellent roads: Inn here too wretched and dirty.—Went up the hill to the Monte Casino Church & convent[5]—a good pull. View fine: not equal to what we have seen. Church marbles wantonly rich & elaborate, here as at San Martino. The skill of the stone cutters mars the work of the architect. The *parts* are provided for: the whole neglected. Delicacy becomes minuteness & then frivolity. A large theological seminary here. *Greek* is *not taught*, as I was informed on the spot—What do the friars do, I said—"read mass, and confess" was all the answer. (An ancient Chapel, & all of the disciples of St. Benedict.)

Thursday May 24.

Another early start. Passed Aquinum[6] on the left—Near San Germano, I should have said before, an ancient amphitheatre: a large mass of wall remaining. Stopped at Arce,[7] and mounted horses easily enough procured here to visit the Isola di Sora[8] and Arpinum.[9] Rocca d'Arce on a height to the right.—

Distance to Sora,[10] eight miles. (English—conjecture: called from 7 to 9 Neapolitan) Country fine—style somewhat English: road excellent. At

[1] Fifteen miles north of Naples.
[2] Yellow-veined marble.
[3] Eight and a half miles ESE. of Gaeta.
[4] Known from 1871 as Cassino; 30 miles NW. of Naples.
[5] Abbey founded by St. Benedict in 529; battlefield of 1944.
[6] Aquino, 30 miles west of San Germano.
[7] Fourteen miles WNW. of San Germano.
[8] An island in the Liris river, south of Sora.
[9] Five miles north of Arce.
[10] Eleven miles north of Arce.

Sora see the falls of the Liris: these, and the character of the river here do not answer to Horace's

> Non rura, quæ Liris quietâ
> Lambit aquâ, taciturnus amnis:[1]

the application must be sought lower down, where it becomes very still.

Sora to Arpinum, about four miles: road only for bridles—and scarcely that. Country very fine. Arpinum boasts ruins, in the town, I suppose of the middle ages—and at the Civita Vecchia, to which another considerable pull is required, they show a house they (impudently?) call Cicero's—and most interesting Cyclopæn remains. A stupendous wall, running up a very steep hill, of immense uncemented stones, not regularly hewn, but in shape sufficiently to give a kind of order to the structure: interstices sometimes supplied with small stones. There is too a quasi arch—no keystone nor concentric cuttings: large stones horizontally laid: the two sides approach by each jutting beyond his neighbour: inside shaped into a slight curve: topstones meet, and lean, more or less, one against the other. Size of stones immense. Distance to Ciprano,[2] whither we had sent our carriage, twelve Neap[olitan] miles. Joined the Arce & Sora road, & then leave it again to make what is *called* a short cut to Ciprano. I think the distance is not much short of fourteen English miles. The road good, until you enter the short cut for Ciprano.

The whole of this expedition may be accomplished without difficulty in less than six hours, if no halt be made for the sake of refreshment. We were little more: and made a breakfast (bacon & eggs) at Sora.

Enter the Pontifical territories before reaching Ciprano. The country gradually falls off in cultivation & in general appearance. Three hours ride to an Inn just beyond Frosinone[3]—better than those we have been at before, yet not very good: & disposed to cheat. But we have now learned to treat these fellows with nonchalance.—Balanced the accounts.

Friday May 25.

On the road soon after four. 26 (Roman) miles to Valmontone,[4] through a rather singular country. Valmontone is situated in a nook, very rich & well wooded. Made our dejeuner here. Six hours & a half in reaching it. Our horses, never fit for their work, and dreadfully knocked up. The voiturin walks & runs half the distance. Started again between one and two: presently on emerging from the hills, hailed the magnificent dome of St. Peter's in the distance. Arrived between 7 & 8 P.M. in the Piazza di Spagna, and took up our quarters again at Serny's. Some indifferent road between Valmontone and Rome. Passed between Tusculum & Præneste. Delighted at entering Rome again, for it is full of strong & manifold interest.

---

[1] Horace, *Odes*, i. 31; see 28 Apr. 32.
[2] Eight miles south of Frosinone.
[3] Thirty-five miles SE. of Rome.
[4] Fourteen miles SSE. of Tivoli.

An invitation from Miss Mackenzie, but did not go, having had quite enough in fourteen hours motion.

Found a good letter from Pakenham announcing the change of ministry.[1] Went to Monaldinis[2] and devoured his whole stock of Galignanis.[3] What to say to this intelligence I hardly knew. Glad that power had departed from hands which might and would I thought use it in a manner hurtful to the highest interests of my country—glad that the King had, by all appearances, shown much firmness of character and made a great sacrifice of popularity rather than do violence to the Constitution[4]—yet still apprehensive that under a Tory ministry a mischievous reform would be carried, and, upon my maturer thoughts, (for at first the news were stifling and confounding,) that if the Duke of Wellington were at the head such a Reform would not be adopted without much loss of character to the party. Could a Ministry have been formed of the moderate men who were avowed Reformers, and who should have carried a moderate measure by the votes of the violent Reformers, and then have stood upon the support of their own friends & the Tories, or a more Tory Ministry then have been formed, matters might have gone well. But this is demanding a calmness and disinterestedness which we must never look for in parties, least of all at such a period of excitement.

Surely the embarrassment has arisen from the fact that the H. of Lords sanctioned the second reading. After that, how could the Ministers, be they who they may, give up *the Bill*, without compromising King Lords and Commons? and how could the Duke, or even Ld. Caernarvon & Mr Baring,[5] carry a Bill against whose *principle*[6] they have voted? But the truth surely is that one half of them had a most inadequate idea of what was meant by the *term* principle as applied to the Bill: for it is a word that may be applied at any step in a long stage of propositions each one in series involving the succeeding, provided only *it* be applied to it with reference to its successors, which will then come under the denomination of detail. It is just the descending scale of *genus & species* in Logic over again. But this is not a journal of my travels.

Saturday May 26.

Called on Glasgows—Bunsens—Torlonia—Miss Mackenzie—wrote home, to T.G.—also wrote to Saunders—and read the fresh arrival of papers by

[1] See next note but two.

[2] Print and bookseller in the Piazza di Spagna, specializing in English books and papers.

[3] *Galignani's Messenger*, a newspaper published in English in Paris.

[4] On 8 May 1832, *Grey asked *William IV to create enough new peers to carry the reform bill in the lords. The king refused, and *Grey immediately resigned; he was re-called on 15 May, when *Wellington informed the king that he was unable to form an administration.

[5] Alexander *Baring, 1774–1848; M.P. for Taunton 1806–26, Callington 1826–31, Thetford 1831–2, North Essex 1832–5; cr. Baron Ashburton 1835; merchant; whig, but opposed reform bill; special ambassador to U.S.A., 1842.

[6] Margin entry: Great ambiguity in the term 'principle'.

this day's post. Dined at Lepri's. In the evening went to Mr Bunsen's to tea: and had much and interesting conversation. Politics: & the state of the study of theology, & ecclesiastical establishments in Germany & England. Met also a Roman count[1] who has a house at Ancona & is much scandalised at the encouragement afforded to outlaws by the presence of the French troops.—Called on C[hristopher] Wordsworth. Visited "S. Andrea del Monte Cavallo".

Sunday May 27.

Gesu Maria: a sermon on the resurrection: very vapid and Popish: terms I would not use without thinking seriously that the occasion warranted them. Conclusion a prayer addressed to a picture of the Virgin, which is displayed at this time, it being the Mese Mariano[2] a period of more peculiar devotion to the Virgin. She was pointed out as the grand conductress to salvation— the Intercessor with the Son, i.e. the Intercessor with the Intercessor! The Liturgy in the afternoon. How different. Dinner at Serny's. Reading as usual. In the evening, heard a better sermon at the Gesu—better, because it consisted of little more than a detail & paraphrase of a part of the Acts. Afterwards at the Trinità del Monte. That heavenly and exalting strain is vitiated by the words which bear it.

Monday May 28.

Wrote a letter to Mr Case. Took an early dinner with the Glasgows and went afterwards to the Vatican by appointment to meet Mr Bunsen. Dismayed (as was Mr B & the Glasgows too) at the English news.[3] God govern all for good.

A very interesting evening at the Vatican. We were joined by Wordsworth, and a learned German Professor named (I believe) Gherard,[4] who explained many monuments, and I heard too some good criticisms on the Perseus and other statues. Canova it seems had much to contend with, as when he appeared the arts had been vitiated by the school of Bernini. His Perseus is considerably far beneath the tone of conception, which the subject demands. There is little, it is said, of life or power in the figure. It is perhaps unfortunate that he should have chosen a subject, where the true conception, had it been attained, would have trenched on that of Apollo. But this ought to have had more wrath and energy, not less.

Mr Bunsen explained to me many of the symbols on the epitaph-stones. The *leaf* is only used as a punct.[5] The *dove* is that of Noah: with the olive branch very often: in one place Noah is drawn receiving it back. The *Lamb* is found—with a figure seated as for judgement, and a soul brought up.

---

[1] Unidentified. [2] Marian month.
[3] *Grey's reinstatement as prime minister.
[4] Eduard Gerhard, 1795–1867, Prussian archaeologist; worked in Italy 1822–37, then professor at Berlin.
[5] A mark of punctuation.

There are too some with a hammer & nails: alluding to the crucifixion, perhaps (Mr B.) but, the same seens to be found on epitaphs called Pagan. A
soul with the hands up, in the attitude of prayer, is common. A branch, that
of the olive. The sign ☧ for χιριστὸς.[1] The fish, signifying thirst for the living
waters of righteousness. The bunch of grapes: "I am the vine."[2] A man
carrying a sheep. "I am the good shepherd."[3] With the fish is connected a
sort of anagram, the name ἴχθυς also standing for I(ησους)X(ριστὸς) Θ(εοῦ)
Y(ιὸς) Σ(ωτήρ).[4]

A singular Pagan one is a wallet, inscribed "viator ad aerarium"[5] with a

ladle by the side. The common phrase here is D.M., Diis Manibus. Or to so
& so *bene merenti*[6]—this word also found in the Christian epitaphs. But the
former phrase is ordinarily exchanged for "In Deo" or "In pace" with or
without requiescit.—Among the Pagans too is the old "sit tibi terra levis":[7]
& some imprecating curses on those who molest—"ultimus suorum moria-
tur".[8] I have heard the like of Shakespeare's Epitaph[9]—and have *seen* one
at Thame[10] in Oxfordshire the last line of which is

> "But curst be he who moves these bones"!

These inscriptions go to the third & fourth century. How soon the passion
for symbols so natural to the human mind, asserted its sway. Mr Bunsen
says that *none* of these inscriptions favour the notion of purgatory: some
decidedly oppose it.

In the relief sculpture of a Roman father, mother, & son with the bulla,[11]
the son's toga is to all appearance the same with the Father's.

Bunsen pointed out the Demosthenes in the Braccio Nuovo, and a Venus
(?) near the Nile—Tiberius sitting—Cato & Porcia, & two in the Hall of
Statues, with others.

At night, read the papers and had a good deal of conversation with
Orlowsky, on religion. Gave him the articles of Church of England to read.
He gives dire accounts of the morals of the priests: and seems not to hold
with the Popish Church on the points of transubstantiation, worship of
saints, limbo, infallibility, or celibacy: but on the use of images, and extreme
unction.

Tuesday May 29.

Wrote up Journal. read Rogers's Italy. Church of San Girolamo. Called at
English College: we fear Spencer is gone. I saw him yesterday for a few

[1] Christt.   [2] John xv. 5.
[3] John x. 14.
[4] 'The name "fish" also standing for Jesus Christ the Son of God and Saviour', an
anagram in Greek.
[5] 'traveller to the treasury'.   [6] 'well-deserving'.
[7] 'may the earth be light upon you'.
[8] 'may he and his kin perish utterly'.
[9] '. . . Blest be he that spares these stones,
    And curst be he that moves my bones',
          on *Shakespeare's tomb at Stratford on Avon.
[10] Twelve and a half miles east of Oxford.
[11] Child's amulet, worn round the neck.

minutes in the street—and he expressed a desire that we might meet again. At Gibson's; also went through Thorwaldsen's studio with J.N.G. It is indeed a sight. Dined with D. Milligan at Lepri's. Went with Miss M'Kenzie to see Guerra's[1] horsemanship exhibition at the Mausoleum of Augustus— very good but too long. Some loose attempts at dramatic effect inter- mingled: some extremely well. Of course there was a *milord inglese*. Atten- dance not very large. Tea and a long conversation with Miss Mackenzie. Orlowsky went, late.

Wednesday May 30.

Finished "revolt of Islam". Journal. Rogers's Italy. Went for the second time to the Doria Gallery, where the pictures are admirable & the custodi intelligent. Murillo's (supposed) Maddalena, Salvator's Belisario—Claude's Landscapes, and *many* other attractions. Called on the Blairs—and then on the Glasgows: reports from England, said to have come by a carrier to Count St Aulaire.[2] Went hence with the Wilsons to the Churches of San Bernardo, Santa Susanna (frescoes) and Santa Vittoria—whose *body* was shown to us—at least 'si dice', bedecked in fine modern dress. Sculpture of Bernini's; overdone? and of Domenico Guidi's[3]—a pupil of the former. A fine painting and two frescoes by Domenichino—and two paintings (here the light was insufficient) by Guido.—Villa Albani. An excellent specimen of the Italian half town half country villa? Many of the Hermae well worth notice—and some Imperial statues—old Etruscan bas relief on the stair- case: Apollo, Faun on *his* right, Minerva & Jupiter in the gallery, and above all the celebrated basrelief of Antinous from Adrians villa. Spent the evening very pleasantly at Mr Glasgow's.

Thursday May 31.

Between nine & ten went with the Wilsons to St John Lateran. A short & rapidly enunciated sermon, in Latin, was preached in the middle of the function. The senses of sight and hearing were left to starve, but that of smell, by way of compensation, largely regaled, as is usual in Italian crowds. Processions much as usual: benediction very fine: I should think in all not much short of 12,000 people. Then went to the Glasgow's, and saw the Pope return in state to the Monte Cavallo. Festa dresses and decorations of the houses made the scene animated & pretty. Came down to get the papers and read the debate in the House of Lords[4] with many a thrill of horror— nothing less. May God deliver poor England. I hear, by Count St Aulaire's courier, that the French are in rapture with the conduct of the people of England! and I confess it aggravates, to me, the already overflowing bitter-

---

[1] Unidentified.

[2] Louis de Beaupoil, comte de Sainte-Aulaire, 1778–1854; writer and diplomat; French ambassador in Rome 1831, Vienna 1833, London 1841–7.

[3] Domenico Guidi, 1627–1701; sculptor and painter.

[4] *H* xii. 1375 (17 May 1832), angry explanations of *Wellington's failure to form a cabinet during the previous ten days' crisis.

ness of the intelligence. Attempted to see the Barberini Palace; but could not: called on the Miss Robertsons to sing, but they were out: visited three Churches. In one (Via Tritone, close by Miss Mackenzie's,) read a list of ten spiritual and four temporal benefits procurable by the right use of Holy Water: driving away evil spirits in the first list, and protection against pestilence in the second. The thing seems to *us* unreasonable: we do not see how the Church can possibly attach special, definitive, covenanted blessings to an act in its own nature indifferent, or recommend it on any other grounds than the large and general ones of its indirect and moral influence, in promoting a reverential habit of mind and communicating the influence of the same to exterior deportment.

After finishing the papers, went to tea at Col. Blair's, where we saw Mrs Blairs Indian Sketches, and also her paintings: both well worth more trouble.

Friday June 1.

Went to breakfast with Miss Mackenzie—read some Quarterly there—went to Pinelli's:[1] a bad dissipated man who makes figures of extraordinary merit in terra cotta at two louigis each. great power of grouping: bold and rapid workmanship. Hence to Finelli's:[2] Cupid & Psyche his principal work here: preferred apparently by the *savans* here to Gibson's Narcissus. by *much*— and *he* to Gibson. Hence, to Kessnels:[3] his great group of the Deluge, we could not see. A Christ bound to the pillar, very beautiful in expression. Hence to Weller's[4]—he paints Italian cottage scenes with great effect. Hence to Wolffs':[5] he is a German sculptor and stands well. Hence to the Barberini——saw the portion containing the most numerous collection, i.e. that highest up—but they are not generally very good. Eight Evangelists, four by C. Maratta & four by A. Sacchi,[6] a powerful sketch of a praying warrior by Salvator. Went to Camuccini's—but he was out. Among Fioppi's[7] Cameos. Dined at Lepri's. Read Ed. Rev. on German Rationalism. And went with Miss Mackenzie to Williams's Studio[8]—where we saw a beautiful painting of the bridge at Amalfi, and also a still more beautiful one of Rome in a golden sunset, from the Pincian.

Went to the Campidoglio, and through the picture gallery again. The number of paintings by great artists is extremely great: and the collection altogether very interesting. The Sibyls, Guernico's Esther, Guido's Sebastian, &c.—Sat and read Virgil (Aen. 6.) among the ruins of the forum, while *John* went to visit the Coliseum—then we went to Mr Bunsen's, and spent

---

[1] Bartolomeo Pinelli, 1781–1835.
[2] Carlo Finelli, 1786–1853; Italian sculptor.
[3] Matthew Kessels, 1784–1836; German sculptor.
[4] Theodor Weller, 1802–80; German painter.
[5] Emil Wolff, 1802–79.
[6] Andrea Sacchi, 1599–1661; Italian painter.
[7] A jeweller?
[8] Penry *Williams, 1798–1885; Welsh landscape and genre painter; lived in Rome from 1827.

a very pleasant evening. Their conversation is exhaustless, as their information which feeds it is. They talked politics applauding the Duke of Wellington most enthusiastically—classical divinity—and on our travels. Bid them farewell; with mixed gratitude and regret.

Saturday June 2.

Letter from T.G. Wrote at great length to H.G. Between 7 & 8 A.M. went to Camuccini's to see his pictures—which are most interesting. Particularly[1] pleased with Correggio's Maddalena & Guido's Crucifixion; Giov. Bellini's Carnival of the Gods is said to be one of the most admired. After breakfast went to see Mr Gott's[2] Studio—he has a statue of Mr Ewart, which he seems to us to be injuring by having departed from a bust of his own to follow two prints: tho' done by order. A beautiful figure of "infant piety"— somewhat like Sir J. Reynolds's Samuel—& much variety. Read the new arrival of papers—all news equally disastrous, except that I trust the King is now firmly attached to the Conservatives. In the afternoon, after dinner, went to the Palazzo Rospigliosi. Upstairs, an indifferent collection. Below & in a separate building, Guido's magnificent fresco of Aurora; her figure in front, a boy & torch for the sun, Apollo on the car, seven of the twelve Hours seen. This is indeed a delightful painting, and did not seem to fail, as I have often thought Guido's works do, in the drawing. The countenances are in a high style of ideal beauty. There is also a magnificent Banquet of Sampson by Ludovico Caracci, and Guido's Andromeda—it will never do to see that subject again, I think, in the hands of another artist. There are too the Saviour & twelve Apostles by Rubens, and the Paradise of Domenichino.

Colonna gardens. Two fragments: sculptured as belonging to a colonnade. But can they ever have been more than fragments? I measured them roughly with my umbrella, for want of a better standard. In lengths of it they are as follows—
The first—[blank.]
The second—[blank.]
Thunderstorm during good part of afternoon, continued till past midnight. Such a succession of vivid & almost blinding flashes of forked lightning, and such unintermitted torrents of rain, I never saw.—During an interval of partial relaxation, went to the Glasgows to tea. Music—Mr Severn & Miss Anne Robertson—and as usual a very pleasant evening.

Sunday June 3.

After breakfast went with John and the younger Wilson[3] to the Church of the Quattro Santi, between the Coliseum and St John Lateran, where there is a convent of Augustinian nuns, to see a lady take the veil. Her name was

---

[1] Margin entry: David & Saul of Domenichino.
[2] Joseph *Gott, 1785–1860; English sculptor.
[3] Probably Charles Heath *Wilson, 1809–1882, Scottish art teacher and critic, the eldest of Andrew *Wilson's four ss.

Anna Volpi. Cardinal Zurla[1] officiated. The Signora was decked out in full
dress: white sattin with silver lace, feathers and jewels: and beside her, on
one hand a lady acting as her sponsor: on the other, a child dressed out with
blue wings as an angel. The Cardinal commenced the service with an
impressive address, perfectly (as I thought) free from the peculiarities of
Popery. His discourse lasted perhaps near a quarter of an hour; and the
following is a sketch of it. "Glorious and happy was the Ascension of our
Blessed Lord, after the death of shame which he underwent for us. And as
he soared into heaven, so we are not to remain apart from him, but are in
heart and mind to ascend thither also, removing our desires and our whole
internal life from this world of sin and sorrow, to that place of blessedness
above—and hence it is that the Apostle says "Conversatio nostra in
cœlis est".[2] And hence it is that he says, "I live, yet not I, but Christ liveth
in me"[3]—as he lived not in his own natural life, but in the new life given
by Christ. Especially blessed then indeed art thou, who hast now determined
by renouncing the pomps and pleasures of this world, to make yourself in
a high degree the spouse of Christ and the object of his love. To you it is
given to realise the declaration of the Apostle "the world is crucified unto
me, and I unto the world".[4] And may the Spirit of God dwell in you and
bear your spirit to heaven, even before it has escaped from the prison of the
flesh, and seen that day which it will be your high privilege to anticipate".
This was in Italian. She sat opposite to him while it was spoken—in front
of an altar, over which was a double grating, communicating with the convent. Her age might be twentyfour: her looks were not plain, but without
decided beauty, and they wanted expression. All the time I, sitting within
two or three yards, could not detect one symptom of quickened pulse, or
beating heart, or failing[5] colour. In a few moments she completely dispelled
what would otherwise have been a most strong and fascinating illusion, as
she stepped briskly over to the cardinal and kneeling down replied to his
queries upon her future course with a voice of the most utter indifference:
never, it appeared, capable of expressing much feeling, and here having
none whatever to express.

The cardinal now rose and conducted her to the door of the convent:
she went in, and then appeared behind the grating. A Litany was now sung,
commencing with addresses to a long catalogue of saints and then proceeding to direct petitions—most of which are retained, if not all, in our own.
Then the Cardinal began to read a series of prayers for the novice—this
being the *white* veil—during which she was gradually stripped of all her
finery, her long hair cut away, and a dress of the order substituted for that
with which she entered, by two of the sisterhood. She spoke twice at intervals, with according symbolical acts, as follows—first—"Io renoncio a

---

[1] Giacinta Placido Zurla, 1769–1843; cardinal vicar of Rome, and writer on mediaeval
geography.
[2] Our conversation is in heaven: Phil. iii. 20.
[3] Gal. ii. 20.
[4] Gal. vi. 14.
[5] Instead of 'pallid'.

tutte le vane cose di questo misero mondo"[1]—then—"Io renoncio a questo mondo e a tutte le sue pompe"[2]—The words should have evoked a spirit of sympathy, but the voice which conveyed them paralysed their power. Two hymns were then sung, of which printed copies were handed round: the first addressed to her, the second as if spoken by her, and in her character. Her name was then declared changed, and a new series of prayers commenced—she appeared now in her nun's dress at the grating and remained, certainly wonderfully transformed in appearance by the change of dress, with her head on her hands. John thought he had seen her laugh before—and I saw her do MORE THAN smile at the close. Persons, apparently female friends, were seen in the background behind the grating. The prayers, beseeching grace and strength and favour for her who had just chosen the religious habit of St Augustin, and the special protection of that Father, came to an end: the cardinal put on his habit as a brother of the Benedictine order, and entered the convent. I left the Church, on the whole pleased with the ceremony, which be it what it may has more heart than most of them—which would have been, but for the circumstance which I have named, most highly interesting, since in its original design it was either perfectly unexceptionable—and *then* doubtless most noble and worthy of all praise, as in the case of the Soeurs de la Charitè, who enhance the *whole* of of St James's account of "pure religion and undefiled before[3] our God and Father"[4]—or even when falling short of this, at least an erroneous *form* of embodying a spirit involving the whole essence of Christianity, that spirit which St Paul powerfully felt and fully explained when he declared the world crucified unto him, and himself unto the world. And he who attends such a ceremony as this, even here where I hear it is usually profaned by being made a matter of more worldly arrangement and accommodation, yet wrongs himself and it, if he permits himself to forget, that he has to fulfil for and in himself, in the midst of the world, which these persons deem best fulfilled by going out of the world. If we are Christians, the world is crucified unto us, and we unto the world. We should strive both to practise and to understand it.—

Dined at the Glasgows'. Mr Lewis[5] was there. from him I endeavoured to get some information about ecclesiastical matters here. He[6] states the seculars & regulars in Rome at 1500 each—from statistical tables—without however vouching for perfect accuracy: and thinks the Church possesses perhaps near a third of the land: which is let at moderate rents, on short leases. We walked to the Maria sopra Minerva, where there is a Statue of our Saviour by Michael Angelo, to hear a sermon. It was on "ego sum vita"[7]—little matter; but good. Mr L says he thinks generally there is more

---

[1] 'I renounce all the vain things of this miserable world'.
[2] 'I renounce this world and all its pomp'.
[3] 'the' deleted.
[4] Jas. i. 27.
[5] Possibly Frederick Christian *Lewis, 1779–1856, or his s. John Frederick,* 1805–76; both painters.
[6] 'estim' deleted.
[7] John xi. 25: 'I am the resurrection and the life'.

matter in their sermons than in ours of England: and that they are very practical.

We went to the Gesu, and found a function to celebrate the last day of the Mese Mariano—tribune magnificently lighted—the Church which is very large was [1] much crowded—a sermon had been preached—there was music, and when the people all knelt the scene was very fine indeed. But it is painful to witness [2] devotions you cannot join.—Tea at home. English prayers— Bible reading and writing: and wrote the foregoing account—read a little of Augustin's confessions. [3] At the end of the Gesu sermon, a sort of rambling discourse was pronounced, of which we could only hear "la Madre Santissima", and "qualche piccola costa", [4] conjectured to be allusive to the *bags* which were then being carried round for a collection—till at last the preacher said, audibly even to us "viva"—"viva"—"viva"—and the congregation loudly responded from all quarters "viva, viva Maria"! The effect was singular.—At Genzano we saw everywhere on the walls "viva il sangue di Gesu Cristo". [5]—At S.M. Sopra Minerva, the preacher prayed that all his words might be made conformable to the will and word of God.

Mr. Lewis says the canons of St Peter's have ninety crowns a month— 300 men employed about the Church, exclusive of ecclesiastics, and 40,000 crowns annually expended in keeping it up.

Monday June 4.

The last day in Rome brings many regrets, half stifled by many cares. We had today to clear off all in shopping, calls, and sight-seeing. We read the papers—but there was little to invite one's appetite, for even terrible news is now becoming dull & common-place. Called at Mr Gott's, to compare Mr Ewart's statue & print [6]—I fear we have done more to perplex than enlighten him. Bid goodbye to Gibson—was just in time to see his drawings for Mr Huskisson's monument—and to take a last look at his Narcissus, before it goes to England. At Mr Severne's—his pictures lose nothing on a second visit. Ariel and the butterfly finished. At Mr Kessnel's—saw his admirable group of the Deluge—Gott has one, which seemed inferior to it, and even borrowed.—Church of Cappuccini—Guido's Michael—a picture of Camuccini's over the altar, which seemed very superior to his ordinary colouring—and others. Barberini Palace—room of capi d'opera contains almost everything worth seeing in the downstairs department: Guido's Beatrice Cenci, extremely beautiful: Adam and Eve by Domenichino. The former is a most interesting picture. Torlonia's—here no detail of circumstances is required. Protomotheca [7] at Campidoglio—endeavoured to grasp the idea of the principal poets and painters.—John remarked that

---

[1] One word deleted.
[2] Instead of 'see a'.
[3] St. Augustine of Hippo, *Confessions* (ca. 400): Migne, *PL*, xxxii. 657.
[4] 'any small sum' (piccolo costo).
[5] 'long live the blood of Jesus Christ'. Cp. 26 Apr. 32.
[6] Instead of 'picture'.
[7] A collection of busts of celebrated Italians, among the collections on the Capitol.

Bramante's[1] bust has a very strong resemblance to Mr Canning.—Vatican: visited the Stanze of Raffael, and the pictures, for the last time—when again shall I look upon countenances such as that of our Saviour in the Transfiguration, or St John in Guido's Madonna?—Went to St Peter's: took a cursory glance at the monuments and mosaics—it is sad that *here* alone Thorwaldsen should not have done himself justice. Gazed sorrowfully enough on the expanse of this magnificent temple, not only from doubts of again enjoying the contemplation of its majesty, but with questions too on the future and perhaps speedy fate of that dynasty with which are bound up the noblest ideas it suggests, and of that large part of the human race which at present sleeps within its shade.

Got my Plato—and a Marcus Aurelius for a wedded friend[2]—God bless him. Received too a magnificent present from J.N.G.

Went to Miss Mackenzie's in the evening, and on to the Palazzo Albani— to tea, music, conversation, and farewell. We have hopes of meeting these most kind friends in the Tyrol, but at any rate I trust we shall not forget them.—Night busy.

Tuesday June 5

Went to Wordsworth's to bid him goodbye—Left Rome at 8 A.M. My acquaintance with it has been short, but long enough to enable me to feel some of its fascinations. The scene of the two most extraordinary and most durable empires the world ever saw—now, even in her decay, the metropolis of a Church whose branches extend to the end of the earth—the depository of the noblest collections of the trophies of art in its golden periods, and the resort of its chief votaries in this not wholly degenerate period— crowded with the speaking monuments of the dead, rendered yet more effective by the lethargy and torpor of the living—clothed in Italy's softest hues, canopied with its most liquid sky, or reflecting back its deepest burning gold—who can visit such a place of "beauty and decay"[3] without feeling that it opens his mind to what[4] he never knew before and cannot hope to recal elsewhere?

Our road, from the *fork*, was beautiful: the old Cimmerian forest— Mount Soracte[5]—Nepi[6] and Civita Castellana,[7] both interesting: observe the fortifications and bridge at the latter—no wonder it detained Fabricius.[8] The foliage is very rich through this country; and it is somewhat like that about San Felice and San Germano in its character. We pass on through Borghetto[9]—Ortricoli[10]—and Narni.[11] Civita Cast. has good Inns. Narni

[1] Donato d'Agnolo Bramante, 1444–1514; architect.
[2] J. M. Gaskell, who m. 16 May 1832 Mary Williams-Wynn, d. 1869, 2nd da. of Charles Watkin Williams-*Wynn, M.P.
[3] *Shelley, *Adonais*, 55–56.   [4] Instead of 'feelings'.
[5] Twenty-three miles north of Rome.   [6] Twenty-five miles NNW. of Rome.
[7] Twenty-seven miles north of Rome.
[8] Georg Fabricius, 1516–1571; German poet, historian and archaeologist.
[9] Thirty miles north of Rome.
[10] Otricoli, 38 miles north of Rome.
[11] Five miles north of Otricoli and $7\frac{1}{2}$ SW. of Terni.

boasts of a singularly picturesque dell, and the ruins of a bridge built by Augustus over the Nera, which falls into the Tiber whose course we followed today. Half an hour is all the time required for seeing it. Here Luigi saw his brother, who is prior of a convent here: the meeting was curious enough. The prior was crying and laughing by turns. He came after us to Terni, and wanted Luigi to stay with him a few days and make a general confession.—A procession was just about to start from the Cathedral, to implore good weather of the tutelar saint. Road to Terni level and country fine. Passed [blank][1] on the left. Up to Foligno[2] we adhere to the Via Flaminia. Slept at Terni: found the *Europa* an excellent Inn—on the whole the best provincial Inn we have seen in Italy—and moderate enough. Our 8½ posts occupied 11 hours—besides ½ hour at Narni.

Wednesday June 6.

Up at 4. Expedition to the Falls—of the Velino into the Nera[3]—occupied 2¾ hours in all—in a carriage furnished, by monopoly, from the Post. Formidable hill. Morning delightful. Saw a curious stalactite grotto near the head of the fall—then descended to the different station. At different points, about a score of persons wished to be paid—one was custode of a door, another of a casina, another proprietor of a house, another of a garden —and at mid-day I believe there would have been another score. The grounds belong to the Count of Terni, whose desire it is that strangers should pass free. The Cicerone complained of the government of the *cardinals*: of the morals of the priesthood: of the taxes—but *most by much*, of the inequality of justice. He had served under Buonaparte. We saw the 'palace' whence the unhappy Queen Caroline set out for England: she was only there eight days.[4]—The falls are singularly beautiful, though perhaps I had overanticipated them. We had a *rainbow* there even at our early hour.— Left Terni before 8: to the Tolentino,[5] nine posts, thirteen hours and a quarter. Country to Spoleto[6] most beautiful, and the sky all that could be desired. All day the route was interesting—& the road thus far extremely good. Foligno upon its wooden legs is a curious sight—and a dreadful one too. I saw a *prayer* appointed on occasion of the earthquake, which seemed Christian without alloy. Saw the Cathedral—a fresco there ruined. Other places in the neighbourhood have suffered too. On the road to Case Nuove,[7] passed a town completely deserted. No good Inn from Foligno to Macerato[8] —we found the Post at Tolentino execrable as for food: beds decent.

Yesterday and today reading Wordsworth; a book the most profitable of all others in a carriage to one who cannot read there much or long.

[1] Nera valley.
[2] Twenty-five miles SE. of Perugia.
[3] Cadute della Marmore, 5 miles east of Terni.
[4] *Caroline of Brunswick stayed at the Villa Graziani, near the Terni Falls, 1820.
[5] Thirty miles SSW. of Ancona.
[6] Twelve and a half miles NNE. of Terni.
[7] Ten miles east of Foligno; the deserted town was perhaps Pale, between Foligno and Case Nuove.
[8] Twenty-two miles south by west of Ancona.

Thursday June 7.

Tolentino—Ancona[1]—six and a half posts—ten hours—We however breakfasted at Macerata—(La Posta—beds apparently good—eating tolerable—)
and staid a short time at Loretto,[2] where we saw the Church of the Casa
Santa:[3] the miraculous history is recorded in divers languages (one
English) on the walls & the statue of the Madonna, black, is unblushingly
stated to have been the work of St. Luke. The marble case and its ornaments boast many distinguished names among their devisers—Bramante,
Giac. della Porta[4] &c. Here is Balaam as one of the prophets—and ten
Sibyls above. A ledge runs round the lower edge—in which two distinct
ruts are worn by the knees of the faithful. The Sacristy has a beautiful picture of a school, by Guido.—The towns on this side of the Apennines are all
on high hills: which caused us much delay. Their appearance is much improved: and again the costume of the peasantry deteriorated: it has lost,
in a measure, its uniformity, and therewith its character. Ancona—French
frigate Artemisia, the largest here, 56 guns, we lionised.—also the arches:
Trajan's is beautiful[5]—the mole, the Cathedral & Church of S. Fil[ippo]
Neri & of the Jesuits. The situation of the town is pretty, its appearance
pleasing, its citadel commanding. The people seem unanimous, rather
against the Pope than for the French:[6] of whom there are 1800; besides
two frigates, a brig (16) and two corvettes de charge—no Papal troops remain in the town—but the Popes colours fly, and fly alone, from the citadel!
—Put up at Grande Bretagne—which we found a good Inn, and more
reasonable than the Pace, to which we first drove, and which has the sea
view.

Friday. June 8.

Walked to S. Domenico—where there is a crucifixion alleged to be Titian's
—to S. Francesco alle Scale, now dismantled. 8 posts to Rimini,[7] ten hours.
—9–7. But we stayed at Fano[8]—and saw the Cathedral—where there are
two fresco paintings by Domenichino—and the triumphal arch[9] a little
further: which must have been very fine. We staid too at Pesaro[10] & saw
the Cathedral & Chapel of the Sacrament—S. Girolamo by Guido: altarpiece by Conchi, in Guido's manner we thought—circumcision and Last
supper by Baroccio. Road crosses an antique bridge. Rimini—Church of
St Julian: picture by Guercino, & altarpiece by Paul Veronese. Bridge an
extremely beautiful remnant of antiquity—harbour good, for the Papal

[1] On Adriatic coast, 135 miles NNE. of Rome.
[2] Fourteen miles SSE. of Ancona.
[3] Built as a sanctuary for what was supposed to be the house of Mary, carried by
angels from Nazareth to Dalmatia in 1291 and on to Italy in 1294.
[4] Giovanni Battista della Porta, ca. 1542–1597.
[5] Second century A.D.
[6] Ancona was held by the pope 1815–60; and garrisoned by the French 1832–8.
[7] Nearly 60 miles NW. of Ancona along coast road.
[8] Some 30 miles NW. of Ancona.
[9] Of Augustus, second century A.D.
[10] Eight miles NW. of Fano and 20 SE. of Rimini.

States. Arch of Augustus on entering the city. Design of the interior front singular.[1]—Most of our road today uninteresting: being barred from the enjoyment of both sea and country. However we crossed the Metaurus:[2] & the coast views of Ancona & Rimini are fine. We found the *Tre Re* a comfortable Inn. La Posta is more attractive in appearance.

Saturday June 9.

5 A.M.–12¼. Exp. to San Marino[3] in an open caleche—for which, after some badgering, we had agreed at four scudi. The road is good till you enter the territory of the republic—the country rich—the distance I should think *good* 12 miles to the Borgo,[4] which is beneath the precipice—and then a tough ascent to the city. From the top the view is finely varied, and very extensive. There are in the way of sights, the fort containing the prison—the hall of the council and a picture in it by Giul. Romano opposite the princes' seats—the room of the archives, which we missed, being unable to find the director, though we caused search to be made for him almost through the whole republic—and the Tempio Nuovo, a Church fortytwo yards in length, which promises to be handsome, and is according to our Cicerone to cost the republic 50,000 scudi! The princes and council form the government, the people having no vote. The consent of both these powers necessary to a law—and the council must be unanimous. The princes are two: authority equal: chosen by the council: office lasts six months: eligible again after the lapse of three years. The council fills up its own vacancies—it consists of twenty *nobili*—twenty *cittadini*—and twenty *contadini*[5]—and these numbers must be preserved. Capital punishment is not used. The princes administer justice. At this time there are three prisoners. The *nobili* are the landowners. Corn is exported. There is no newspaper—but foreign ones are taken in by some individuals. Roman money is used. No printing press—but a manufactory of playing-cards. The bishop is appointed by the Pope. 40 priests—seventy monks and friars. No preaching, except in the six weeks of Lent, and a month at Christmas. Population, 7000. Churches nine. Schools three. One for nobili—who are sixty families: their school contains 20—but others are sent out of the country to be educated. The second contains thirty—and the third fifteen—and this I believe is the sum total of the education. The people are well contented with the government. There are however a good many poor. There appeared to be public spirit and a feeling of nationality—which does not exist in Italy generally. A labourer earns 15 to 30 bajocchi[6] according to the time he works. Some of their people are gone to work at Foligno where there is now a good deal of employment. No regular soldiers—but a sort of militia exists.—3½ hours going: 2 hours there: 1¾ in returning.

[1] Porta Romana, second century; decorated with sculptures.
[2] Hasdrubal was killed, not far upstream, in an attempt to force this crossing in 207 B.C.
[3] Twelve miles SW. of Rimini; one of the smallest and most ancient states of Europe.
[4] Town at the base of Mount Titano on which San Marino stands.
[5] Nobles, citizens, and peasants.   [6] Halfpence.

Visited S. Giuliano again. Left at 12½. Arrived at Ravenna,[1] six posts, at 7¾. Staid on the road at Forli[2]—where we saw the Cathedral, with Cupola by Cignani—Guido's Conception at S. Girolamo—execution as exquisite (J.N.G. however remarked the tallness of the figure) as the design is bold, nay rash—and at S. Filippo Neri Guercino's annunciation, extremely beautiful—a Carlo Maratta opposite it—and two Cignanis (I thought). There were other pictures—but the French are said to have carried them off.—At Savignano[3] we saw a Roman bridge—stone work *above*, and lower part of piers made of *brick*: which seems extraordinary. We inquire on all occasions, and of course many offer, about the priests and the government—and we hear I think almost uniformly ill. The bad morals of the former, and the corruption of justice, seem the most prominent subjects of complaint. Road and country fine: very flat: road from Forli to Ravenna bordered with houses at intervals all the way in a manner very uncommon in Italy—it gives an appearance of comfort and of a domestic character, which are too generally wanting. The towns in this part of the country are particularly airy, well built, and large—and the women particularly pretty. Crossed the Rubicon. In its present state it is little more than a brook.[4]

Ravenna—La Spada.

Sunday June 10.

Reading and writing much as usual.—Cathedral at half past ten—Whitsunday Function. Music very beautiful: numbers of ecclesiastics, and I never saw them appear more utterly indifferent. Read the prayers of the 14 Stazioni di Roma. Saw the service in the evening at S. Apollinari.[5] The priest kneels before each in succession, and a boy holds up a cross before him: a troop of people behind. The prayer is read: then come pater[6] and ave. In the former, I observed that the people left off at "debita nostra". This service is called Via Crucis. In the morning remarked how often they stand at prayers—while kneeling is only *imposed* for their own at least unwarranted 'elevation'. Heard a sermon—which I discovered with some difficulty—at S. Apollinari in evg from Fra Floriano. I fancy it was the only one preached today in the city. It was aimed wholly at the dangerous character of the conversazioni of society here: and the preacher spoke out pretty plainly. His principles seemed quite sound, if his facts were correct—but his audience appeared for the most part below the class he attacked. His last sentence was something like "e vi dirò per finire la mia predica, se si vuole conversarsi così, si vuole anche dammarsi così".[7] Then he looked round upon the people as much as to say "it's all true, depend upon it," and

[1] Thirty miles NW. of Rimini and 43 east of Bologna.
[2] Seventeen miles SW. of Ravenna.
[3] Nine miles WNW. of Rimini.
[4] Anciently, the Rubicon marked the boundary between Italy proper and Cisalpine Gaul.
[5] S. Apollinare Nuovo, already twelve centuries old.
[6] Instead of 'credo'.
[7] 'and I say to you to finish my sermon, if you want to talk like this, you also want to damn yourselves like this'.

bundled down the stairs. I respected him. In his sermon there was scarcely anything that savoured of Popery.

Monday June 11.

Went before seven to the Cathedral—saw Guido's picture of the manna,[1] and his cupola in fresco, also the fresco of the dreaming prophet:[2] the pulpit, with the lamb, dove, duck, fish, deer, &c. all doubtless intended to represent Scriptural figures: the Calendar[3]—known only to be anterior to the time of Pope Gregory[4] (A.D.) who reformed it: the ivory chair[5]— which one can scarcely believe not to be wood—covered with bas-reliefs of the history of Joseph &c. they seemed better executed than some of the early German paintings which one sees in the studio at Naples, though of (I think) the sixth century. The Baptistery—built in the *fourth* century late, and ornamented with mosaics about 430 according to an account[6] hung up there. *These* escaped the French who robbed the place of some of its antique columns. Fifteen feet of the ancient interior are now underground—it has been raised I suppose on account of the sea—which might seem to indicate, taken with other circumstances, that it has been on this coast at different times both lower and higher than it now is.—Walked 3½ miles to the Church Fuori di Classe.[7] In ancient times three towns were united—Classe, from the harbour which then approached in this quarter, Cæsarea, & Ravenna. The corresponding name Dentro di Classe is also preserved. Here there are very fine and ancient mosaics in the tribunae—(roof flat—) 24 columns of Greek marble with *vena transversa*, & of *nero & bianco orientale*, brought from Constantinople, and reported to have been from the temple of Diana at Ephesus: they are very fine, but the capitals are anything rather than classical. Ancient Sarcophagi of archbishops of Ravenna anterior to 846. And two fine paintings of Giotto's in the Sacristy. To reach this interesting church, leave the city by the Porta di Rimini, cross the bridge and strike off to the left. On the way to it may be taken the S. Maria del Porto, where there is a painting on the right of the martyrdom of St Mark by Palma Vecchio[8]—and the St Apollinarises—also the interesting tomb of Dante. Over it is a basso-rilievo of the poet whose deeply-marked countenance is rivetted on his work before him. There is an inscription as follows.

Iura monarchiae superos phlegethonta *lacusque*
Lustrando cecini, volverunt fata quo*usque*

[1] Exod. xvi. 14–22.
[2] The angel offering bread and wine to Elijah; 1 Kings xix. 5–8. Between this and the next line is a bracketed note: (q. wild!).
[3] A Paschal calendar on marble, calculated for the years 532–626.
[4] The Gregorian was substituted for the ancient church calendar by Pope Gregory XIII, 1582.
[5] The pastoral chair of St. Maximian, sixth century.
[6] 'still' here deleted.
[7] S. Apollinare in Classe.
[8] The painting is by Jacopo Palma il Giovane, 1544–1628, grand-nephew of Palma Vecchio.

Sed quia pars cessit melioribus hospita *castris*
Actoremque suum petiit felicior *astris*
Hic claudor Dantes, partriis extorris *ab oris*,
Quem genuit parvi Florentia mater *amoris*.[1]

I know not that much can be said for this epitaph: it seems to me didactic, spiritless, and obscure. I fancy the rhymes warrant one sufficiently in abusing it. But the tomb should by all means be visited—Although in a public street, yet it is appropriately environed with the silence and stillness of Ravenna.

These form one *giro* from the Inn.—A leaning tower should also be seen from the Corso.

Another journey may be made from the Inn to 1. The Cathedral—which we estimated at 120 or 130 feet in height, and its declension at 7 and 6: which is very considerable.—Hence to S. Vitalis[2]—a fine old octagon, with a tribune of magnificent and very old mosaics. I think one never sees in these mosaics of the 5th, 6th, or 7th century, the favourite design of the Virgin and Child—nor indeed the Virgin at all. If this be correct it is important.[3]—Hence the journey should be undertaken to the mausoleum of Theodoric,[4] through the Porta Nuova: to see the truly wonderful vaulted stone, which *singly* forms its roof. The internal diameter of this segment, horizontally, is 30 feet! and the thickness is stated in an account of the dimensions to add 7 Roman palmi. We estimated the vertical axis to be nine or ten feet. I fancy there are few greater architectural wonders. The porphyry urn, once on the top, may now be seen in the Corso—where I believe is supposed to have been Theodoric's residence.

Ravenna—Bologna[5] (by Faenza).[6] Six posts: $12\frac{1}{4}$–$8\frac{1}{4}$. Road flat: but country very rich: a beautiful line of rich rural hills to the left of the Via Emilia. Their outline is gentle and graceful, and their deep verdure is relieved by the light & shade falling on their prominent or receding points respectively: and by the number of cottages, villas, and Churches, which are interspersed throughout. The landscapes have that completeness which distinguishes those of England, and the soft lights of Italy to boot. The environs of Bologna must one would think be a delightful residence. The beauty of the women there seemed greater than even on the rest of this road. All the world was out when we arrived, it being the evening of a festa —and the appearance of the city in our drive was as striking as that of the people.—Near St Nicola a fine brick bridge. We did not stop at Faenza.

---

[1] 'I sang the laws of monarchy, the beings above, the fires and pit of hell, wandering wherever the fates turned me. But because my part withdrew to better regions, and sought its Actor more happily among the stars, here I Dante am shut in, an exile from my native shores; borne by Florence, a mother of scant love.'

[2] S. Vitale.

[3] There is a sixth-century mosaic of the Magi making offerings to the Virgin and Child in S. Apollinare Nuovo, but it is true that the motif is most uncommon in the Ravenna mosaics.

[4] Theodoric the Great, ca. 455–526, first Ostrogoth ruler in Italy.

[5] Forty-three miles west of Ravenna and 50 north of Florence.

[6] Seventeen miles WSW. of Ravenna.

Met Cardinal Albani,[1] with an escort of some 20 or more soldiers. We find the dialect of this part of the country corrupt enough: the people abbreviate like the Neapolitans. Towns still handsome and numerous—and country a garden. Immense quantities of grain—land in long slips intersected by rows of *elms* with vines. So here we have at last

Stratus humi palmes viduas desiderat ulmos

&c. &c.[2]

Locanda di San Marco. Very comfortably accommodated.

Tuesday. June 12.

Bought a map and laid out our lionising. Visited

1. S. Petronio—largest here: Gothic: but arches not all in the same proportion—and inner appearance somewhat motley: also somewhat bare. Intended to have been immense. Length now about 400 feet. Charles V[3] crowned here. Meridian[4]—Homo of A. Caracci: window, designed by M.A. Buonarotti.

2. S. Salvadore. Here became acquainted with Innocenzo da Imola (near Bologna) a scholar of Raffael, whose colouring assimilates much to that of Giulio Romano. Under 'cantoria' a painting supposed older than Giotto. Altar piece designed by Guido. Tiarini (a scholar of the Caracci) also a new acquaintance: most like Annibal.[5]

3. Palazzo Mareschalchi. A great many paintings of foreign schools. All are now to be sold. A pretty little Guido of our Saviour & the Samaritan woman: 30 louis demanded: Guido's St Peter: Teniers's banditti destroying a village, which I liked very much. Also a very fine fresco of Guido's, in the hall or anteroom.[6]

4. Hence to the Zambeccari palace: not on the whole a very interesting Gallery: a beautiful painting by Guido Cagnacci: and divers by a female of Guido Reni's school, Elisabeth Siri[7] (I think—) Also some of Giov. Bellini. Caffè della Barchetta—read Italian papers. Observed statue by Giovanni di Bologna[8] in the Piazza. No situation I think can be conceived more thoroughly impregnated with the manner and spirit of the middle ages, or a more lively image & memorial of them, than this open space. It bears away the palm I think *almost* from that of the Palazzo Vecchio at Florence.

5. Academia delle Belle Arti. The two rooms of Capi d'Opera the most beautiful—and the one next by no means contemptible. Custode intelligent. When he showed the Martyrdom of S. Peter the Inquisitor by Domenichino, I said an Inquisitor could hardly deserve to be called a martyr—he said

[1] Giuseppe Albani, 1750–1834; cr. cardinal 1801.
[2] See 1 Mar. 32.
[3] In 1530, the last crowning of an emperor in Italy.
[4] Meridian line laid down 1653 by the astronomer Cassini.
[5] Alessandro Tiarini, 1577–1668, Bolognese painter.
[6] The sentence 'Hence to the Caffe della Barchetta—read Italian papers.' here deleted.
[7] Elisabetta Sirani, 1638–1665.
[8] 1529–1608; a Flemish sculptor who settled in Florence, and carved the 'Fountains of Neptune' at Bologna.

"they must not say that in the Roman Catholic Church, for she held the Inquisition very dear." I said I trusted there were many things she valued more than that. We conversed with this custode on political matters. He named as the three great grievances 1. finanza 2. giustizia 3. Propaganda. now supported by Romagna alone. Delighted perhaps most with Guido's crucifixion. J.N.G. remarked on the extreme warmth of the mass of colouring which the rooms taken as a whole displayed. Here are capidopera of the Caracci's, Guercino, Guido—profuse & magnificent—Domenichino, Albano—Caverdone—Tiarini—Pietro Perugino—Francesco Francia—Giacomo Francia his son—Innocenzo d'Imola—and a S. Cecilia of Raffael considered quite first rate.

Had my first opportunity of appreciating an Austrian military band.

Chiesa SS. Agostino & Giacomo. In Chapel 10, S. Rocco of Ludovico Caracci.

Torre degli Asinelli[1] Ascent by a succession of stair ladders—Prospect rich beyond any thing—but to the N. & E impaired by the *flatness* of the country. About 450 steps. Effect of the snowy Apennines towering over the hills by Bologna remarkable. Landscape full of richness and repose.

8. Cathedral—a handsome Church in its kind, but that kind not what a Cathedral should be. Fresco of the Annunciation by L. Caracci How seldom one sees this subject designed & handled as it should be. Better I think by Guercino than any other.

Read "Outlines of History"—and wrote home.

Austrian troops much liked in most or all places—changed every six months—Papalini keep away.

Wednesday June 13.

Set out at our leisure for the remainder of our work. Bologna may be accomplished, should need be, in a day and a half, with tolerable completeness and comfort.

1. S. Bartolomeo. Fresco by Guido much admired: too high up to be well appreciated. A Guercino.

2. University—Biblioteca. MSS.7000. Books 100,000. Seemed in excellent order and preservation. Among "Theologia Heterodoxa" found curiously lumped Calvin, Pascal, Bayle,[2] and Molinæus[3]—poor Jansenius was here of course. Molinæus I fancy by accident: for the classification I was informed is not strict. We conversed much with a very intelligent Italian, who seemed connected with the management, and said if we staid in Bologna we might make use of the Library. He did not think Albani personally unpopular—said he was a just man—but few of the priests understood Greek—their *course* is of four years—a physic diploma of Bologna cannot practise in Milan—Students now 400 or 500—30 years ago 2000—diminished from the rigour of the priestly management: from which cause

[1] Leaning tower, erected 1109 by Gherardo degli Assinelli.
[2] Pierre Bayle, 1647–1706; French sceptic.
[3] Pierre du Moulin (1568–1658); French reformed theologian and author.

too few books are printed in Bologna—the University has no press—i preti fanno tutto[1]—much hoped from the passing of *the Bill* in England— "how many inhabitants has Bologna?" "Seventy thousand:" "Many Liberals?" "Seventy five thousand"—(J.N.G.)—Plato more read than Aristotle. This gentleman really seemed to feel for his country as a country —and said he meant soon to absent himself for [*sc.* from] it. He described the taxes as most unequally distributed.

3. University—astronomical instruments. Manufactured almost exclusively in London or Paris.

4. Academy: a second visit, well bestowed. How magnificent is Guido's Slaughter of the Innocents. Generally of the Caracci's: Annibal is the most *powerful* painter: Ludovico uses the greatest number of colours: Agostino's colouring is deficient both in *strength* and *variety*. Tiarini follows Annibal —but has less of life and force. Catalogue inconveniently arranged.

5.[2] Galleria Zampieri. Sketch of the upper portion of a beautiful Madonna of Guido's at the Academy: some fine dissegni, particularly two of Titians. These hasty performances from the hand of great masters are most interesting. Cielings in fresco *one* by each Caracci—very characteristic of their respective grades. *Two* by Guercino, very beautiful.

Dined at a good Restaurant, called "Della Vigna", Mercato di Mezzo— conveniently situated, close to the Piazza.

Began the *Piccolomini*:[3] and wrought at our money matters. In the evening, walked to the Church called "Madonna della Guardia"[4]—some 5 or 600 feet high: the hardness of the path very galling, particularly in descent. Arcades all the way. An early work of Guido's—and a Madonna which the priest, who alone could open the sanctuary (as it was called,) told us with perfect coolness was the work of St. Luke. "Is it well painted"? "very well for those times!" with the same imperturbable & even dogmatic countenance—yet he was perfectly polite. The work seemed respectable: but there is an odd botch under the right eye. "Why is this called the Madonna della Guardia"—"because it is written on it that she should be venerated on the Monte della Guardia"—"who wrote it?" "St Luke"!! It being too late to *see* the pictures at the Certosa,[5] we were contented with a view of it and the Campo Santo from the hill. The view is fine: and the contrast on the two sides remarkable. Writing, reading, Piccolomini, putting up our things, in Evg.

Thursday June 14.

$7\frac{1}{4}$ A.M.—$8\frac{1}{4}$ P.M. Ten posts to Padua:[6] including the crossing three rivers, and other delays. The road flat and generally good: a good deal of marshy

---

[1] 'the priests do everything'.
[2] 'Palaz' here deleted.
[3] Part ii of J. C. Schiller, *Wallenstein* (1799 tr. S. T. *Coleridge 1800).
[4] Madonna di S. Luca, on the Monte della Guardia, a fortified hill 2 miles SW. of Bologna.
[5] A former Carthusian monastery.
[6] Seventy miles ENE. of Bologna and 22 west of Venice.

country: and the oaks and elms which have brought us thus far along our road, are now changed for poplars and willows. The posting too seems on the whole inferior. The inhabitants of Lombardy have many beautiful faces among them, but of a different style, generally, from the beauties of Romagna and Legations—having flaxen hair and blue eyes. In Tuscany & Piedmont I could not find much that was remarkable, notwithstanding Mrs Starke's encomium on the appearance of the lower orders in the former state—but now I conclude that the Italian women bear away the palm from all others, and fairly distance them.

By this time one ought to be able to form an opinion of Italian scenery. On comparing it with English, it is evident that each has certain qualifications which the other wants. On the side of Italy, these perhaps are, first and foremost the exquisite softness and transparency of the lights—then the more picturesque and characteristic dresses of the people, and appearance too in some cases of the animals—lastly the exuberant vegetation which seems to spring from every pore of the soil. To this last property we owe the beauty and grace of the vine festoons waving over the wheatcrops: and the verdure which mantles over the hills to an astonishing height: yet it is not without certain disadvantages—as for instance, to my eye it appears sometimes to produce the effect of overlaid colouring—sometimes it conveys the idea of waste—and on the hills I think in particular it often has an unfortunate effect, for by breaking out in very small patches at extremely short intervals, it gives the whole a speckled appearance, and that way destroys the effect which is produced when the colours are well massed. England's landscapes too have their own beauties, which generally we do not find in Italy—the cattle feeding in the fields—the scene studded with stately mansions and with unobtruding cottages—the flowers that clothe[1] those cottages—the frequent lanes and pathways—all these communicate the appearance and still more the idea, of animated existence to the scene, and by suggesting and presenting to the mind man and nature in unison, they seem to form a more complete & harmonious whole. The country East of the Apennine generally is more like England than on the west: particularly in the architecture of the Churches and style of the towns.

The ferries over the Adige and Po are singular: a rope is made fast[2] a considerable distance up the river & carried down to the ferry boat, a considerable distance, supported upon a series of small boats: the ferry boat is so steered and contrived that the force of the current catches it obliquely each way, and so by means of this alone it performs *both* its peregrinations, the *rope* acting as radius to the circular arc it describes. The Po is half as wide again as Thames at London: the Adige half as wide again as Thames at Eton: after this the road passes along the *Brenta*, and is well lined with houses large & small: some fine Italian villas.

At *Ferrara*[3] we stopped and saw

[1] Instead of 'mantle'.
[2] These four words replace 'loop is wound'.
[3] Twenty-seven miles NNE. of Bologna.

1. The Cathedral—leaving our carriage before it arrived at the Poste. A Picture or two worth notice.

2. Hence to the University. Students now only 200. Library 80,000 volumes. Original letter of Ariosto & MSS. poem written as for the press— also editio princeps—Tasso's corrections written in prison and MS of Guarini:[1] who has affixed to Ariosto's tomb, now in this Library, the following Epitaph.

> Notus & Hesperiis jacet hic Ariostus & Indis
>   Cui Musa æternum nomen Hetrusca dedit.
> Seu Satiram in vitia exacuit, seu comica lusit
>   Seu cecinit grandi bella decusque tubâ.
> Ter summus vates, cui docti in vertice Pindi
>   Tergeminâ licuit ingere fronde comas.[2]

Scarcely worthy of an eminent name.

3. Tasso's prison. brought away a piece of a brick.—Disaffection universal: a disturbance last night. Since last year's tumults,[3] *Jews* no longer locked up alle due della notte[4] in their *ghetto*.

Kindly visited at Monselice[5] by the Postmaster to go and see relics of Petrarch in a *caleche* of *his*. It did not suit us.—Observed the mills on the rivers: why have they not been adopted in England? they cannot fail in summer like the small streams.—Austrian troops everywhere liked.

Friday June 15.

Padua, Stella d'Oro. A comfortable house & reasonable prices.—A horse fair going on—lasts 15 days: Sundays same as others.—Beware of the *Post* here. We were obliged to turn back, our horses evincing an invincible reluctance to take us to Dolo.[6]

Visited 1. The Cathedral. Tomb and picture of Petrarch. Numbers of domes in this and the other churches. These (and the spires) give a fine effect in the view from a distance, but quite the reverse I think, at least with their present arrangement, to the interior.

2. S. Antonio: specially worshipped here: very large fresco by Giotto. Crowd of unmeaning ornaments in marble.

3. Santa Giustina. More beautiful. Altarpiece by Paul Veronese. A painting of Tintoretto—here too we find Luca Giordano and Palma Giovane—a Pietà said to be very much admired, by a Genoese artist[7]—and the most beautiful reliefs carved in oak, by a Frenchman, that we have seen on the Continent.[8]

---

[1] Giovanni Battista Guerini, 1538–1612; poet.

[2] 'Ariosto lies here, known among western men and eastern, to whom the Etruscan Muse gave an eternal name; whether he whetted his satire against vices or played at comic verse or sang of war and glory on a great trumpet. Thrice highest poet, whose hair was crowned with a three-fold wreath on the peak of learned Pindus'.

[3] Abortive risings in northern and central Italy, in which Jews had played a large part.

[4] Two hours after sunset.   [5] Thirteen miles SSW. of Padua.

[6] Twelve miles west of Venice.   [7] Filippo Parodi, 1630–1702.

[8] Stalls by Richard Taurigny of Rouen, mid sixteenth century.

Four posts into Venice. Approach as curious and striking as we had expected, or could have wished—some 5 miles of open lagune.

Leone Bianco—on the Rialto. Well accommodated. Went to call on Mr Money[1]—and to tea there in Evg: where we found the Austrian commandant of Marino[2] here: & made an appointment to visit the arsenal tomorrow. —St. Mark's Place and the Cathedral. This Piazza is the most striking I have seen: indeed, can anything be more so? Who can stand there and believe he is living in the 19th Century? The Cathedral[3] is quaint beyond anything: and interesting from association: scarcely so from intrinsic beauty.— Pitt's Speeches.[4]—Papers. Letters from T.G.

Saturday June 16.

Lardner's Hist.—Piccolomini.—Papers—containing the disastrous but expected news, that the Reform Bill had passed the Lords:[5] I now only wait to hear of the King's consent. Galignani is taken at the Leone—and at the caffè Floriano whither we repaired for it.

Arsenal: the Archduke John[6] had taken our admiral by surprise at an earlier hour, and so spoiled our appointment. We went round however with an officer—and saw the frigate newly launched; which the British Naval authorities declared too narrow & too crowded with guns: the rope-walk, 1000 feet long—the armoury containing curious monuments of the old republic and early fire-arms: the model rooms, with models of the Venetian gallies worked by oars—one bank of oars, *seven* men to an oar, all sitting down: the stroke must have been very short. In the armoury is Canova's second work—a monument happily designed, but perhaps not powerfully executed. Here the Admiral had joined us. We saw too the modes of masts & pumps &c. 500 men said to be constantly employed. Principal arsenal of the Austrian Empire: Admiral has had its foundation: he was employed under Buonaparte.

Dined at "Il Vapore" a tolerable Restaurant. Mounted St Mark's Campanile with a map, and attempted to analyse the view which is curious and interesting: particularly Chioggia.[7] Counted the pillars on the *front* of St Mark's only: and found they amounted to one hundred and eighty-eight.

Sunday June 17.

At Eleven we were at Mr Moneys. he read prayers, and a sermon of *Mr* Lavington's.[8] About 20 or more present. Hymns sung: a collection by Mr.

---

[1] William Taylor Money, d. 1834; M.P. for Wootton Basset, Wiltshire, 1816–20; consul at Venice 1827.

[2] Amilcar Paulucci, marchese delle Roncole; dismissed, 1844.

[3] Margin entry, crossed through: 'counted the columns on the front alone: they amount to 188'.   [4] *The Speeches of William *Pitt in the House of Commons* (1806).

[5] On 4 June: *H* xiii. 350. Royal assent given on 7 June.

[6] Archduke Johann (Baptist Joseph Fabian Sebastian) von Habsburg, 1782–1859; b. of the Emperor Francis II (see 30 June 32); general of cavalry and director-general of fortifications; regent of Germany 1848.

[7] Fifteen miles south of Venice.   [8] Samuel Lavington, *Sermons* (1824).

Gipps of Hereford.[1] Dined at Leone Bianco: reading &c. as usual. Spent the evening at Mr Money's: Evening prayers at six: gondola and walk on the Porto Franco: tea afterwards—about fifteen persons—then hymns, reading Scripture verse by verse, with remarks made by divers of the company— and a prayer delivered by an artist present: some conversation afterwards with Mr Money. No comment here. Mr M. very kind. We were invited to dine.

Monday June 18.

Morning employed in writing to Mrs G.—A. Pakenham—and Cole.

Manfrini Palace. A very fine collection of pictures: particularly rich in the works of Giorgione, whose flesh seems almost to rival Titians. Two very good Carlo Dolces, a Maddalena & a Santa Cecilia. Many good Flemish paintings, and works of Paul Veronese and Tintoretto.

Dined and spent the evening at Mr Money's—read the paper and some of a book called "Political Disquisitions".[2]

After tea we went to a large party in Mr Money's gondola to hear an Austrian band on the Canal Grande: playing in honour of the Arch Duke John whom we saw in his plain gondola, and to[3] the pleasure of a large party who attended. We floated down to the bridge and then went gently up again. Time flew fast and pleasantly, and we were astonished to find it past twelve o'clock, when some of the party estimated it at nine: so far had it outstripped our calculations. The scene was very pretty. Lightning flashed rapidly in the distance, playful and innocuous: the figures stood boldly forth in the strong light of the torches, under the shade of the temples and palaces around us, themselves with the vessels near the Palace & Piazza of St Mark softly but distinctly marked under the light of the moon which gleamed at intervals in her passages from one deep blue mass of cloud to another. Many an illusion might one have woven in unison with the scene: but his imagination must be bold indeed who can plant his illusions amidst the stormy realities of this our time, and who does not rather incline to project them into a more peaceful futurity.

Tuesday June 19.

After breakfast, a *giro* recommended by Mr Money's kindness.—
1. Chiesa della Scalse.[4] Yields to none in the richness of its marbles. A Virgin and child by Giov. Bellini behind the altar: 12 Sibyls by Colonna a Venetian: a crucifix &c. by Torreti,[5] master of Canova. From the style of these which appeared to me rather ultra-Bellini, opinions may be formed of the real praise due to Canova.—On the way to this palace from the

[1] Henry Gipps, d. 1832; priest at Hereford 1824–32.
[2] Margin entry: E & C. Dilly Poultry
    1774 3 vols 8vo.
[James *Burgh, *Political Disquisitions: Or, an Enquiry into Public Errors, Defects, and Abuses*, 3v. (1774–5).]
[3] Instead of 'for'.　　　　　　　　　　　　　　　[4] Chiesa degli Scalzi.
[5] Giuseppi Toretti, 1694–1774.

37—I.

Bridge should be remarked the rich architecture of the Palazzo Pesaro on the left.

2. Chiesa dei Frari. Monument to Canova: from his own design and model for Titian—whose plain slab (did not see it) rests opposite. An Assumption Altarpiece by Titian: & another painting on the left where the Madonna is prominent, of Titian too. Monument of Doges.

3. Archives. There are said to be 250 rooms, (and some of them are very large,) filled with these records of Venetian History. I saw a treaty with the Emperor Charles (the Fat) dated 886—he reigned 884–888: and one with the Saracens, I think of the year 668. Among the correspondence with the English Kings I read a letter from Elisabeth, praying that certain duties newly imposed on articles in which some of her subjects had traded with Venice, might be taken off: or at least that they might be allowed to change their goods for a home cargo in Venice, without being subject to the impost. It was dated 1581.

4. Scuola di S. Rocco. One picture by Titian over the staircase—numbers both above and below by Tintoretto, involving an immensity of labour both in composition and execution: one very large, about 40 English feet by 20, of the Crucifixion. Their general effect powerful. Other artists had part in the work upstairs.

5. Barberigo Palace. The room where Titian painted to the last is now filled with pictures, many of them his, and of these some much celebrated: a Magdalen, Satyr, &c. Never observed a more offensive case of promiscuous collocation. A small Correggio—two heads of boys: *all* in miserable condition: the owner cares not for the arts: and he must indeed be indifferent, whom the actual *possession* of such treasures inspires with no pride or attachment.

6. Chiesa di SS. Giovanni & Paolo. Titian's magnificent picture of the "*Martyrdom of St Peter the Inquisitor.*" Domenichino now appears not to have been quite original in his manner of treating the subject.—Both the figures and the landscape in this picture are excessively admired: & it is considered to combine the grandeur of composition belonging to Raphael's school, and the richness of Venetian colouring. We met Mr Hasy[1] here, and got from him a good lecture on painting. Here also is a fine Tintoretto to the right of the choir—and a Pietà of Paul Veronese, very celebrated, near it.—In the sacristy are many pictures of Tintoretto and Palma—and bassi-relievi in Carrara marble. This is the biggest Church in Venice.

7. Academy. Here we found a room containing antiquities and small paintings by Titian, with a porphyry vase containing Canova's right hand, and a basrelief in porphyry—also casts of the Elgin marbles and most of the fine pieces of sculpture—besides the collection of pictures, which is extremely rich: but it is difficult to get an idea of it at a single visit, as the pictures are exclusively of the Venetian school. Here is an Assumption by Titian—which the custode, an intelligent man who had lived with Lord Byron,[2] maintained was considered equal & was superior to Raffael's

[1] Unidentified.   [2] *Byron lived in Venice, 1817–20.

Transfiguration: Paolo Veronese's masterpiece, a beautiful last Supper: where however the pillars seemed to interfere awkwardly: (and who would expect such pillars in that place? (?)) a magnificently drawn & coloured painting by Tintoretto, the Martyrdom of St Mark—and others by the rest of the Cagliari, Palma, and Bonifacio, extremely well worth observation: also the works of Carpaccio, a contemporary of Giovanni Bellini.—Today my only complaint is that we have seen too many good pictures.—Tea at Mr Moneys.

Wednesday June 20.

Another giro of Mr Money's arrangement.

1. Palazzo Pisani. Necessary to go between 10 & 11 A.M. A splendid picture by P. Veronese, of the family of Darius before Alexander—one opposite to it, not very Venetian.

2. Chiesa della Salute. A 'noble' work of Longhena, erected 1631 on the spot where the plague was stayed.[1] Il Redentore for a similar reason, earlier: in 1576—this was the plague to which Titian fell a sacrifice. In the octagon is one of Titian's pictures, not superior, and three of Luca Giordano: on the roof of the tribuna, eight heads by Titian, fine: including a portrait of himself. In the Sacristy, on the roof, are three magnificent Titians: Abraham & Isaac, Cain and Abel, David and Golia[t]h. They are full of the grandeur which is rare in the Venetian school. There is another Titian—Tintoretto—etc. Four magnificent columns of Parian marble at the high altar.

3. Il Redentore. Presepe[2] by Bassano. No painter, except perhaps Carlo Dolce, is so generally marked by his subjects, as Bassano.—In the sacristy a friar showed us the Madonna of Giov. Bellini: extremely soft & beautiful, & he said one of his best works. On offering him a "qualche cosa"[3] (& no more) he refused—but says he, give it to the young man of the Church, if you can find him. "Very well." Or says he "leave it here anywhere on the seat, and I will tell him"! I am sorry for the chance of "the young man of the Church."—Palladio's architecture.

4. Gesuiti. Incalculable labour unprofitably expended in inlaying Carrara marble & giallo with *verde*. The Martyrdom of S. Lawrence by Titian, a very fine painting in a bad light on the left, Presentation of the Virgin by Tintoretto. There is I imagine inexcusable absurdity in the design. When was a *woman*'s presentation heard of?[4]

5. San Georgio. Fine oak bassi rilievi in the presbyterio.[5] Pictures by two of the name Bassano, and Tintoretto. Sorry to find here a *statue* meant to represent God the Father[6]—this is an audacity for which we can scarcely entertain too strong a repugnance. The execution of the work, the four

---

[1] S. Maria della Salute, built 1631-82, in commemoration of the plague of 1630 by Baldassare Longhena.

[2] 'Stable' (at Bethlehem).   [3] 'something'.

[4] The Presentation of the Blessed Virgin Mary is a feast kept in the Western Church to commemorate the presentation in the temple of the Virgin, when three years old, as told in the apocryphal *Book of James* (second century). The diarist has confused this with the presentation of a cleric for a benefice by a patron.

[5] Instead of 'tribuna'.   [6] By Gerolamo Campagna, 1549?-1626.

Evangelists supporting a globe, on which stands the above mentioned mockery, seemed very fine. The Church is by Palladio: and has a kind of double pediment, one being truncated.[1]

6. Doge's Palace. 83,000 volumes in the Library. Admission to the use of it liberal, here & elsewhere. Try to keep clear of Ciceroni on the stairs.—Spot where Marino Faliero[2] was beheaded at top of the first staircase—& observe the blank in the list of Doge's portraits above, supplied by a black curtain with the words [blank].[3] The Leda was undergoing repair—the Ganymede we saw. On the roof of the great room (154 feet, but q. what feet, by 74) are three paintings by P. Veronese, Tintoretto, & Palma Giovane respectively. At one end Tintoretto's immense & hitherto I believe unravelled picture of Paradise. A gentleman is said to have lost three weeks in the unavailing attempt to count the heads. In the other room are curious pictures, one of the battle of Lepanto, Venice & Spain & the Pope against the Turks—and Palma Giovane's Last Judgement; the pictures here I suppose are his finest.

7. Prisons. The prisoners, as we understood, were first lodged in the building separated from the Palace by the Bridge of Sighs, which is covered, and unites I think the second stories of the two edifices. The state prisoners after condemnation were conducted into the vaults beneath, and we saw the grating where they were strangled, or, if life lingered, stabbed—and the old blood on the walls. Other prisoners were conducted back by the bridge into the opposite building, which is used at present for its original purpose. We saw the cells of the Inquisition, and one where when the republic was inclined to the Reformation,[4] the Romanist priests were confined. Of the terrible "Bocca di Leone"[5] the place alone remains: and the passage over the bridge is now stopped up.

After dinner we went to see a private collection of pictures at the "Casa di Ponte di Dio" belonging to Sig. Capilani Coaglizzi, who was most polite in showing them. A fine Canaletto of St Mark's on a *gala* day—a beautiful portrait of a Lady by Titian, and the Virgin learning to read by Vandyck, with many others, very interesting and in fine preservation. Here and at the Manfrini, alone I fancy of all the collections in Venice, are to be found good paintings of other schools than the Venetian.

We made a giro behind the arsenal and passing the leaning tower of St Peter on the left attempted to get to Lido, without success. Surely St Mark's has also a perceptible inclination? Met Mr Money and went home with him. Tea: and his hymns, reading & prayers as before.—Pitt's speeches. Walked in the Palace Gardens.

Thursday June 21.

Corpus Domini.[6] By the favour of our kind friend the Consul, had a window[7]

[1] In the margin beside this paragraph are two small pencil sketches of the church.
[2] Marino Faliero, 1279–1355, general; doge 1354; attempted coup d'état.
[3] HIC EST LOCVS MARINI FALETRI DECAPITATI PRO CRIMINIBUS.
[4] Early seventeenth century.
[5] 'Lion's mouth', an opening into which secret denunciations were thrown.
[6] Feast of Corpus Christi.   [7] Instead of 'place'.

in the Palace to view the almost interminable procession round the Piazza, passing under an awning erected for the purpose. The scene was animated and picturesque: not venerable or religious. Wax candles without number. At intervals baskets full of them were carried: we supposed for sale to such of the spectators as might be inclined to take a part—and there were a good many. The Government functionaries seemed to exhibit a studied indifference: most of their candles were extinguished & many carried head downwards. Every here and there were persons saving the wax which had sweated and then congealed, in great abundance, and which often reminded me of a cascade at Tivoli, to which, supposing it arrested in its course, they bore a strong resemblance. When the wafer was shown, the people kneeled —and at the close of this, which was done thrice, there was a heavy discharge of firearms. The Patriarch, an officer between the ranks of Bishop & Archbishop, carried it.

A conversation with Mrs Money.

In the evening we went to the Armenian convent: apparently a well ordered institution. The priest who showed us round a clever man, & acquainted with some eight or ten languages, English among the rest. His name is [blank] and he is much esteemed. We gave a trifle in aid of their education, & bought a copy of their Liturgy. Their priests may marry, *or* become monks, who do not marry—they use direct invocation of saints, and images as well as paintings. The appearance of their Church was just like that of a Roman Catholic one; they believe that Christ has only one nature, which is called the Eutychian[1] heresy: but said our conductor "this is only a question of words, for Christ was certainly both God and man." The Church contains a Virgin beautifully copied from Sasso Ferrato by a converted Turk. After this we went on to Lido, where we met Mr Money and his party. Found the seaward beach here exactly like that at Seaforth: a sufficient title to *our* attachment. In England however we rarely see such a fine contrast as was here exhibited by the distant clouds charged with a thunderstorm which presently overtook us, and the waves beneath, kindled into a green that rivalled the very highest emerald.—Sick as any one need wish to be.

Friday June 22.

Determined on not attempting Trieste, such a specimen of the extreme irritability of my constitution did last night's ripple (for it was nothing more) afford me. John goes alone in consequence.

Went to see the glass manufactures of beads, mirrors, and bottles. The latter extremely simple: the first very curious: and all beautiful. The workmen at the latter make we were told four to six swansigs[2] a day: those at the former, six, eight, and even ten. Two hundred men are employed in making these beads which go all over the world. John has seen *casks* of them in Rio. The *padrone* only knows the composition of the *pasta*. This when red hot is

---

[1] Eutyches (ca. 378–454), Monophysite heresiarch, denied that Christ's nature was partly human.   [2] Three to four shillings.

taken out in a small lump, attached to an iron rod, rolled into a cylindrical form, perforated, and drawn out into a tube of immense length. These are cut into lengths: each filled with a fine powdered composition of chalk & charcoal (we understood): put into an iron vessel with a quantity of fine sand to prevent coherence: by this friction, the glass being softened by heat, they become round, and the hole is contracted to a very small aperture, the interior still remaining filled with the composition: the beads are now put into a sack, and this is shaken out, being very fine and loose: the beads are then tried upon a board, to which a slight inclination is given, when all those which are found *true* run off: they are then put into a sack with sand, & shaken again: they come out polished: and are threaded by women in Venice.—The colouring matter is also prepared here, from lead &c.—At each step, the visitor must expect to be dunned: and should stop his ears as effectually as he can: unless indeed the workmen have done somewhat specially for his instruction.

We had tea at Mr Money's. J.N.G. went off by the steamer—I spent the evening there.

Saturday. June 23.

Finished "The Piccolomini" and read some of Pitt's Speeches. Shopping—bought a German grammar! Wrote. Dined at Mr Money's—afterwards out in Gondola—Tea & Prayers &c. Lady Malcolm[1] arrived in Evg—Mr Money read me some statements he had been drawing up on the Condition of the Lombardo Venetian Kingdom—and a report of a very curious and interesting conversation which passed between the Emperor[2] and him, on the "nouvelle politique" of England. The shortness of the days here at this time, as compared with those of England is very sensible.

Sunday June 24.

Reading &c. Church twice at Mr Money's: service and sermons by Mr MacLauchlen,[3] a young and zealous Irishman, of more decidedly Calvinistic views (I thought) than are strictly warranted by the tenets of the Church whose orders he bears. The outline of our evening Sermon was, that God was revealed to us as a God of Covenants: and the grand Covenant was between the three Persons of the Trinity: the Father, to elect "the Church": the Son to die for "the Church": the Holy Ghost, to save it. Went out in the Gondola after dinner, and unwell in consequence, in the evening, at prayers: when Lady Malcolm attended.

Monday June 25.

Left Venice at six: in every way satisfied with the Leone Bianco, except that in situation it is certainly inferior, *very* inferior, to Danieli's and the Europa. There is no recommendable Restaurant.

[1] Perhaps Mary, née Forbes, who m. 1809 Sir Michael Malcolm, d. 1829, 7th bart.
[2] Francis II, 1768–1835, emperor of Austria 1804; last holy Roman emperor, till 1806. Papers in PRO FO 7/237.   [3] Hubert M'Laughlin, 1806?–82, canon of Hereford 1857?

Venice on the whole is a place of much interest. All the part of it near St. Mark's has as much of the picturesque, and of that peculiar description of beauty which attaches to the picturesque in architecture, as the eye or mind could desire. St Mark's Tower is an eyesore, but not enough to spoil the sight. It has an inclination, perhaps best perceived in the direction of the Gardens. Many other towers have inclination. The number of edifices boasting architectural ornament in this city is extremely great: and had one the power of reassorting them all, much more beauty & magnificence of effect might be produced. But as they are, their appearance is motley: and they have in general little more than quaintness or profusion of decoration to recommend them, qualities which may answer their purpose in the city's youthful pride, but which avail nothing amidst an air of silent and sombre decay, which they do not relieve, and yet with which they cannot assimilate.—Cicisbeism[1] has been put out of fashion by the Austrian court here.—

We found a boat[2] hired by compact, a more eligible conveyance than the Post boat to Mestre,[3] & costing much less: it caused however a kind of search at the Customhouse, as we were probably taken for persons going by vetturino. Breakfast at Mestre: persons should not take anything for granted at the Inn here.—We did not stop till we reached Vicenza,[4] where Palladio lived. Here we saw his Theatre,[5] built in imitation of the ancient ones: scene immovable: three openings in the front, exhibiting streets which branch off: two at the sides. Roof (the present one quite new but on the plan of the former) made to imitate an extended awning. A profusion of statues, & bassirelievi, all in stucco. Surely to recall an ancient theatre, without recalling the ancient drama (and to do this, how many more changes would be required,) is only to[6] multiply anomaly, not to reduce it.

In different rooms of the public palace are pictures worth seeing, though out of condition: and in the Corona, an Adoration by P. Veronese, of which the colouring a little assimilates to Tintoretto: and a Baptism by Giovanni Bellino: worth seeing. There is also here (the second time only I had seen this profanation) a statue intended to represent God the Father, with our Saviour's dead body, and the Dove for the Holy Spirit.[7] The statue above-named was of no peculiar dignity, nor did it attempt it, but the artist seemed to have framed his conception with an audacity as careless as presumptuous. The high altar is worth attention, being Florentine *pietra dura* of about 160 years back.—Reichardt says the inhabitants from hence to Verona[8] are descendants of the Teutones & Cimbri. In many of the country portions of Lombardy, as well as here, one finds the flaxen hair, blue eyes, and fresh complexion, foreign to the proper Italian.

Nine land posts to Verona: 11 hours: besides ½ hour's delay at Vicenza.

[1] Flirting with married women.
[2] Margin entry: remember gondoliers of no. 307 327.
[3] Six miles NW. of Venice.
[4] Twenty miles NW. by west of Padua.
[5] Teatro Olimpico, completed 1564.
[6] 'create' here deleted.
[7] By Giovanni Battista Kron.
[8] Sixty-five miles west of Venice.

Posting indifferent. Obliged to take off a horse after starting. Road flat: but among the hills: country near Verona beautifully fertile: and the appearance of the town extremely fine.—Le Due Torri—a very comfortable Inn—but prices should be argued for. Found the Glasgows here, as we had expected from the accounts Mr Greig brought us to Venice. We sat some time with them in the evening—and wrote home.

Tuesday. June 26.

Very late up: aliquid humanitus accidit.[1]—I overslept myself. Went to St Anastasia St Euphemia & the Duomo: at the latter alone found matter worthy of notice, in Titians Assumpta, and early Veronese paintings. St Giorgio, on the Strada del Tyrol, is well supplied with paintings, but we did not go there: I hardly know why. We visited the Amphitheatre,[2] passing under the singular double arch,[3] a remnant of antiquity. There are two others. We passed Palladio's Theatre,[4] and went to see the ancient amphitheatre. Almost the whole outer wall is fallen—while the entire inner portion, of marmo di Verona, a reddish coarsegrained flaky stone, remains most wonderfully perfect. The original circumference I made out by measurement of an arch (there being 72 in the whole circuit) to be about 1450 feet. Every step I think is perfect. Here there is no projecting podium: but one single flat ledge, all the way round, I suppose for the provincial authorities. It scarcely appears how they were defended, the present area being only five feet lower. The custode wished to make out that the arena had been level with some pavement exposed to light in a partial excavation, and that the apparent substructions upon it, and under the arena, were of the middle ages.—Near this is said to be the tomb called of Juliet: nothing to see, we learned. We saw the monuments of the Scaliger family:[5] as profitably, I may warn others, to be seen without the custode as with him. Of custodi however I would say in general, that they are in this country very easily satisfied.—A strange mixture of materials and of styles.

Castel Nuovo[6]—1½ post round; to see Lake Garda: the old Benacus:

> te Lari maxime, teque
> Fluctibus ac fremitu assurgens Benace marino.[7]

This is only like meeting personally a man whom you have long known through a common friend.

Being scandalised[8] at the Postmaster's first demand of 1½ post for four

---

[1] 'something happened after the manner of men'.

[2] Probably first century A.D.

[3] Arco dei Leoni, one of two Roman gates. There is a pencil sketch in margin.

[4] Perhaps a confused recollection of the theatre at Vicenza, 25 June 32.

[5] The Scaliger, or della Scala family, were presidents of the Republic of Verona from 1262 to 1389.

[6] Twelve miles west of Verona.

[7] Virgil, Georgics, ii. 159–60; 'of thee, great Larius; of thee, Benacus, surging with the breakers and the tumult of the sea'.

[8] Margin entry: 1 post it seems is generally paid. The distance is called three miles.

miles (at most) to Peschiera,[1] including bringing us back, we made a walking expedition of it. There was a good deal of rain, and the hills were all wrapped in clouds: we thought it in vain to go on the lake: and could see little more than the general character of the hills on the western & the flats on the eastern side. Peschiera seems finely fortified: the houses little more than supplementary to the garrison.

The roads in this part of the country we find universally fine; annoyance is occasioned in the Legations and Lombardy by the number of fortified towns, where the passport is twice demanded: and, under the Pope, such would I suppose be as inefficient against an enemy in war, as they are against the smugglers during peace. The police system seems adequate to nothing beyond administering annoyance to travellers. The men however are civil. Dreadful cases of goitre in Lombardy. At Verona saw a sort of bandage employed to give support.

From Castel Nuovo to Roveredo,[2] $5\frac{1}{4}$ posts, occupies above six hours, Little hill. Country near Lake Garda seemed rich—the rest rather poor: crops very thin: land very stony. Indian corn, barley, mulberries, and vines. After rejoining the highroad to the Tyrol,[3] followed the Adige between walls of rock—which afterwards opened out. Entered Tyrol at Borghetto.[4] Corona at Roveredo comfortable. Found the Glasgows were here, detained by an accident.

Wednesday June 27.

Two posts to Trent, two and a half hours; we slept among the Euganean hills. We remained at Trent till past twelve: saw the Duomo and Maria Maggiore where the council was held:[5] a picture there illustrates it. The situation of the town is pretty.

5 posts to Botzen[6]—$6\frac{1}{4}$ hours. At Verona we began to perceive the indications of Germany's approaching: its language in the streets: and spitting boxes in the bedrooms. Now the language gains on Italian as we advance: three posts from Trent[7] it becomes victorious. Towns assume the characteristics of mountainous country. Number of crucifixes immense: also, once at least, that kind of Pietà which I saw at Vicenza, most horribly executed. The peasantry seem a fine race: more appearance of independance in their bearing: a degree of civility you do not meet with elsewhere: salutations almost universal. Horses much used for draught. Flowers at house windows. Valley opens out & the last two posts are exceedingly beautiful: mountains bold and well covered with low wood.

Botzen is a nice town. Shops nearly all shut by 7—long before dark: a handsome Gothic Church.

[1] Fourteen miles west of Verona, at SE. corner of lake Garda.
[2] Thirty-two miles north of Verona, 13 SSW. of Trent.
[3] Margin entry: 'Pont volant for Adige: similar to those crossed before'.
[4] Fourteen miles SW. of Roveredo.
[5] The œcumenical council, 1545–63.
[6] Or Bolzano; 33 miles NNE. of Trent.
[7] 'three posts from Trent' substituted for 'midway between Trent & Botzen'.

My books these days have been, German grammar, in which I am *roking*, blind as a mole: Lardner's hist.—finishing Pitt's Speeches, and the Death of Wallenstein,[1] which I like extremely, for particular beauties. Left the Glasgows behind.

Thursday June 28.

Nine posts: 5 A.M. to 10 P.M. stopping 40 min. for breakfast at the Elephant, Brixen[2]—where we had an excellent meal, at the moderate rates of the German Tyrol. The scenery of the first three posts is beautiful and stern in its character: the road runs low, ascending with the bank of this portion of the Adige. At Brixen the river again forks, and our road keeps to the smaller branch which it traces up to its original and elementary brooks, at Brenner.[3] After Brixen there is less of rock and precipice; the valley opens, and becomes more picturesque than grand, but extremely beautiful all the way. On the stage into Brenner, it closes, and is again very imposing. The descent is on the whole of a tamer character, but the last stage from Schonberg[4] to Innspruck,[5] is very fine.—The inns seem to be numerous, clean, and good, on this road. The posts are long, being on the German scale: horses good and well conditioned, but not very fast. Postilions at last carried the box by storm, at the strong instance of the postmasters: we kept them on horseback as long as we could. With some difficulty, we got into the Sole D'Oro for one night—and found it both comfortable and moderate. Provisions seem lower in the Tyrol than any other country we have been in. —Dear Helen's birthday. verses—Fox's Speeches[6]—A few lines to H.J.G.

Friday June 29.

Innspruck is most delightfully situated in a district at once cultivated and romantic: within, a remarkably cheerful & handsome town: around, rich in mountain, wood, and water. There is little direct ornament in the town, except the arch under which we passed in entering—the Churches are all at least respectable—pews, but without doors, are here used: the Church portals seem always open, and the interior never totally deserted. The Imperial Palace is large, and there are beautiful Gardens in the neighbourhood of the Inn, even here a fine river. The town is full on the occasion of the expected approach of the Emperor, and also with military, and the *Deputati* of the country, who determine the manner in which the taxes are to be raised, the amount being settled at Vienna.

We moved, perforce, to the Aquila d'Oro (Golden Adler.) an inferior house, where however all is still good, and the Landlord a great character, now almost an octogenerian (78) an old friend and Captain of Höfer's.[7]

[1] Schiller (1799); tr. S. T. *Coleridge (1800).
[2] Twenty-one miles NE. of Bozen.
[3] Thirty-eight miles north of Bozen, at the head of the Alpine pass.
[4] Fifteen miles NNW. of Brenner, 5 south of Innsbruck.
[5] Sixty-five miles south of Munich.
[6] *The Speeches of the Rt. Hon. Charles James *Fox in the House of Commons* (1815).
[7] Andreas Hofer, 1767–1810, Tyrolean national hero, shot at Mantua on Napoleon's orders.

Pictures of the hero seem to abound everywhere.—Walked to the Esel, where he posted his peasant army—and where you enjoy a delightful prospect. Verses—Germ. Gr.—Foxe's Speeches—&c.

Saturday June 30.

Wrote to Doyle on his class.[1] Germ. Gr. & Dict—Shelley & Coleridge's Poems—finished Verses & sent to H.J.G. Went out to see the Emperor's entrance. The Tyrolese peasantry all marched out in arms with their band, and looked very well: such a force consitutes a very strong bulwark to the country, however much more imposing may be the appearance of the Austrian regulars. Some of them have their medals, earned, under Höfer. The old Landlord pointed out to me all the localities of the first engagement, when the peasants captured the French invaders within the city.[2]— The reception of the Emperor was good—more perhaps if we consider the phlegmatic character of the people. His appearance is ordinary enough: that of the Empress[3] (I hope I am not belying the sex) ordinary more than enough. He did not bow in the carriage to the vivas, and afterwards at the Palace, where there was a very great concourse of people, nodded rather than bowed: a manner which has perhaps less grace and not more kindness.

Here every body smokes: ragged boys in the streets, and haymakers at their work. The appearance of German towns, hereabouts, is marked by their colours—almost exclusively black for the roofs and white for the walls. The people seem far better clothed & better fed, and have more appearance of comfort and content than those whom we have seen elsewhere.

Sunday July 1.

A day unmarked otherwise than by its usual employments. At the proper time, the domestics in our Inn were going to Church. Not a single priest has crossed my path since I have been in the Tyrol. Walked up the lower hills beyond the [river] Inn, and enjoyed the view of the grand ones above, and the beautiful city and fine vale before me. There is no greater reproach to man, than the beauty and peacefulness of outward nature, communicated in the influences it inspires.—

Monday July 2.

5 A.M.-8¼ P.M. 9½ German posts: as they are of nine and even ten miles, this was excellent work. We breakfasted at Ober Meimingen,[4] a very poor Inn. Postilions, now established on the box to their heart's content, go better. No French or Italian, that we could discover, spoken along this road. —The first two posts, regular ascent, by the Inn: *very* beautiful. Hay harvest was now everywhere going on. This with rye and Indian corn, and

---

[1] Classical first.
[2] In the risings of 1809.
[3] Charlotte Augusta, 1792–1873, da. of Maximilian Joseph, king of Bavaria; m. the emperor Francis as his fourth wife 1816; crowned queen of Hungary 1825.
[4] Ober-Mieming, village on left bank of Inn, 21 miles west of Innsbruck.

timber, seem to be the chief articles of produce. Towards Roveredo,[1] a great deal of silk is prepared: and sent to England, as I was informed.— The third stage, away from the river, still more beautiful: everywhere[2] orders of steep banks, thickly clothed in the graceful pendant foliage of the larch, above and among these the pine, up to the region of bold and rugged rock. From Ob. Mein. to Imst,[3] the valley is cold and sterile: here it joins the Inn again, and soon becomes finer. At Landeck[4] (6½ posts) we inquired for the Glasgows, & found they had been detained at Trent by indisposition. Hence to Stuben,[5] the road traces the Inn up to its very source: at least *one* of its component streams, for it forks twice above Landeck. The scenery is very wild: the road pursues the left bank, which is comparatively denuded, and so gives the full enjoyment of the scenery of the *right*, which is extremely fine, forests diversified by numerous little cataracts, and the huge rents which winter torrents had made in their banks. At last, we mounted far above the region of cultivation, and into that which is even at this season, tenanted by snow. Judging chiefly by the snow, we thought our altitude must be at least 5000 feet—considerably above the Brenner.[6] At the top. you soon come upon a magnificent mountain directly *en face*, which seems only an accumulation of spires and pinnacles of rock. Further off too, a mass of rugged and snowy tops, illuminated by the declining sun, was very beautiful.[7] Near Dalaas,[8] scenery becomes richer: still very fine. Road excellent all the way. This day we are fairly introduced to Alpine scenery, even if not before. Wooden bridges over the torrents abound. Immense labour seems to have been expended in defence of the road.—

Tuesday July 3.

The Inn at Dalaas is most beautifully situated: and we found it clean and comfortable, though unpretending. We also thought well of the Corona or Posta at Feldkirch,[9] where we breakfasted. An illomened day as to progress. Seven and a half posts, & long ones—from 6 A.M. to 9.40m. P.M. From Feldkirch to Tusis[10] our resting place, the driving very bad. It is I fancy advisable to go by vetturino here. At Balzers[11] J.N.G. after we had been kept waiting an hour for post horses, rowed the postmaster in a language which he had declared he did not understand: at this the Postmaster set upon him: I was reading in the carriage and heard a stamping of

[1] Cp. 26 June 32, *ad fin.*
[2] 'steep' deleted.
[3] Thirty-two miles west of Innsbruck.
[4] Forty miles WSW. of Innsbruck.
[5] Forty-six miles WSW. of Innsbruck; just over the provincial border, in Vorarlberg.
[6] 5,912 feet at head of Arlberg pass; 4,495 at head of Brenner.
[7] Valluga, 9,223 feet, north of the pass; and the main Rhätikon and Silvretta Alpine ranges, rising to 11,201 feet.
[8] Twenty miles ESE. of Feldkirch.
[9] Ninety miles west of Innsbruck.
[10] Thusis, in Switzerland, 11 miles SSW. of Chur.
[11] In Liechtenstein, 12 miles south of Feldkirch.

feet, came to the spot and found them engaged—I caught hold of the Post-master to pull him off, as J.N.G. was getting him back over the rails—An execrable Postilion who had brought us from Feldkirch then came out and set upon John, who was in a moment or two disengaged and able to look after him: I kept the Master of the Post company, and he did not seem inclined, after the specimen John had given him, to renew the contest. Luigi and a stable lad stood by. Tongue war took place of that which had seemed likely to be the order of the day—but not until John had shown his pistols. The master of the Post seemed inclined to refuse us horses, indeed did so, alleging they were just come back from Coire[1]—though we had seen some come in ourselves more than an hour before. However he thought better of this: and was contented with cheating us by telling Luigi he was to be paid by the Grisons tariff,[2] instead of the Austrian. At Coire we went to the Director to get some redress: he told us that the man belonged to another country, but was civil. He is a pluralist after a strong fashion: Landlord of the Inn: Master of the Post: and also *Director* to whom conse-quently strangers are to appeal on the subject of his own conduct!

The *country*, which all this time has been undeservedly forgotten, was beautiful. The descent to Feldkirch in the best style of the Tyrol: and a beautiful pass opens that town. On the next stage, our first view of the Rhine. Hill beyond Baldses,[3] where we entered Switzerland, extremely beautiful, & the scenery about the gate grand. All the remainder of our way, particularly till about eight miles beyond Coire, an exquisite combina-tion of what is grand and what is lovely in nature. The villages and their situations exquisite.—In the Tyrol, the valleys were thickly strewn with wooden sheds for the hay; and great numbers of stones upon them to pre-vent their being carried away by the storms. We enjoyed that country much: remarkable civility—a bow from almost every one who met us on the road. The men wear conical hats of felt—the women, partly round hats, and partly a bulging cone, black, and of a material like that of rugs.—Having finished Fox's Speeches, began Volney's ruins[4]—and continued to rake about in Germ. Gram. & Dict. Inn at Tussis clean and good.

Wednesday July 4.

$6\frac{1}{4}$ A.M.–$5\frac{1}{2}$ P.M. Five posts. We were well driven from Splugen[5] to Spoda Lunga[6]—ill all the rest.—The Grisons have no Customhouse—and the Austrian is a trifle to those who come our route. Posting is dear and bad in this part of the country: and vetturino advisable—but there is an objection, viz. being obliged to embark at Lecco[7] if you take the Splugen road properly

---

[1] Coire or Chur, 25 miles south of Feldkirch.
[2] i.e. a Swiss tariff.
[3] i.e. Balzers.
[4] Constantin François de Volney, *Les Ruines, ou Méditations sur Les Révolutions des Empires* (1791).
[5] Eleven miles SSW. of Thusis.
[6] On the Italian side of the Splügen pass, which lies 3 miles south of Splügen village.
[7] Fifteen miles ENE. of Como.

so called, & not the San Bernardino.[1] The latter is said to have more beautiful prospects: the former, to have the finer road.—The most magnificent feature in the whole passage, viz. the Via Mala,[2] is common to both: they fork at the Village of Splugen. Mrs. Starke's description of this passage is nothing less than a disgrace to her book. Amongst other varieties, she seems to confound the two roads: & I suppose has never travelled either. Nothing in her book, so generally useful, has met my eye, which can be compared to this mis-description:—except her Sonnets.[3]

Tusis to Andeer[4]—two hours: chiefly through[5] the Rheinwald called "schams" in Keller's map:[6] which is sublime at the entrance and throughout. Road generally one to two & perhaps three hundred feet above the river. The Pines are very fine—but we were not fortunate enough to see the one "said" (see Starke) [to be] "twentyfive ells round the trunk!" Beneath, the river is often enclosed within a space of very few feet—and hidden from view: above, rise rocks always bold, generally perpendicular, with pines clinging to them in situations where nourishment would appear impossible: some, withered by age, some with branches fantastically twisted & like *roots*—some, half precipitated from their stations by storms or torrents. The rocks are in great measure clothed, and the summits crowned with them. This extraordinary valley is above two leagues in length—it then opens, and the road reaches Andeer where there is a good Inn but bargains should be made.

Andeer to Splugen—also one post: valley closes again, and again opens. Still very fine.—Hay harvest going on in the open vales. The magnificence of the last stage suffers some abatement in this. The falls (I think) are a short distance above Andeer. But the Rhine all the way though here an infant, is an infant Hercules: and it hurries on its downward way as though it knew there was a long journey to perform before reaching the sea. At Splugen the scene changes, the nature of the road varies more—in general consisting of a long series of galleries, often with abrupt turnings. River forks again above Andeer. At length we got beyond the region of forests, into that of snow—but not the latter until we were within a few hundred feet of the top—& then only in patches. Ascent from Splugen occupied 1 hour & 50 min. Very near the top, I drank of the veritable Rhine, and jumped over it. From the summit, looking both ways, the advantage is decidedly with the Swiss side.

Indeed the descent is at first wholly uninteresting. Soon it comes on the brink of a very deep basin, having sides almost perpendicular. The view of this basin and the ravine downwards is extremely fine—because you do not from this point see the scenery in detail: which it will not, generally, bear. The descent into this basin down the side is by far the most wonderful

---

[1] Pass parallel to and SW. of the Splügen.
[2] A 4-mile defile in a tremendous gorge; begins a mile from Thusis.
[3] *The Beauties of Carlo-Maria Maggi, paraphrased: to which are added Sonnets: by Mariana *Starke*, (1811); and *Information for Travellers*, 480–2.
[4] Seven miles south of Thusis.
[5] Margin entry: Road forks above Tusis.
[6] These five words in margin.

work, in this kind, that I ever saw. And this, with the Via Mala, Rheinwald, and the interest of tracing a mighty river to its very source, are the points of interest. Except the cascades, which are numerous (one on the left, not quite but almost unbroken, of perhaps 300 or 400 feet) and the singularity of the masses of stone everywhere accumulated, there is little. The scenery is wild, but not of the sublime, nor (save the prospect of the Chiavenna valley) beautiful. All the way, it would seem, immense masses of stone must have been removed to make a passage. High up, are long grottoes of very solid and massive masonry: on the other side they are cut through the rock. The sides of the ravine,[1] which is very steep, are rude, but not sufficiently bold or precipitous, or, generally, clothed with wood: but everywhere are wonderful accumulations of fragments of rock, some large, some small. The finest, at least the most extraordinary feature of the other side is, I think, the profusion of firs or pines which seem to grow among and to feed only upon ragged fragments or actual precipices. The Moesa[2] accompanies the road on the Italian side.—The stage to Sponda Lunga occupied above 3¾ hours.—Chiavenna.[3] Conradi's. Prezzi fissi.[4] Everything good; some charges a little above par.—

Thursday July 5.

6 A.M.–7½ P.M. Post to Riva.[5] Wished to go to Colico,[6] but rather than submit to gross imposition (40 Sw[anzigs]) came to Domaso,[7] by Tariff. Wind agst us—much delay: hard work towing &c. for the men: at last the steamboat came and took us up. We came with it to Varenna[8]—landed, saw the grottoes near that place, and came on by vetturino to Lecco, having sent our carriage & servant to Como.[9] A boat worked by horses (or a horse) plies daily from Riva to Colico, which is the most eligible route: but today it chanced to be out of order. Off Bellagio[10] we had the view of the three branches: & coming off in the passage boat a breeze came down the lake: the effect upon the waves, which were backed by the dark sky of a distant thunderstorm, was very fine: and that on me not so bad as might have been expected, from rolling.—Shores seem to abound in stone containing ore. I forgot to mention that there are iron works high up the Splugen. The scenery is on the whole very fine: numbers of small towns & scattered houses: very lofty mountains (as Cotero and Legnano[11]): the chain gradually lowers as you go down the lake. New Austrian road a magnificent work. It

[1] 'are rude' here deleted.
[2] '(q. name?)' in margin. In fact the Moesa descends from the San Bernardino; the San Giacomo, from the Splügen.
[3] Six and a half miles north of head of Lake Como.
[4] 'Fixed prices'.
[5] Ten miles SSE. of Chiavenna.
[6] Twenty miles north of Lecco, on the eastern shore of lake Como.
[7] On the western shore, opposite Colico.
[8] Twelve miles NNW. of Lecco, on the eastern shore.
[9] Sixteen miles west of Lecco, at the head of the SW. branch of its lake; 25 miles north of Milan.
[10] Fifteen miles NNE. of Como, at the fork of the lake's three arms.
[11] Monte Legnone, 15 miles south of Chiavenna.

has even young trees planted on small platforms at intervals off the road, intended to afford shade to the travellers of future generations. Mira and Adda flow in at the two upper branches of the lake. An Englishman from Fawcett's[1] in Liverpool, is Engineer of the Lario (steampacket)—he gave me a good deal of information. The captain and clerk, who run her, pay 32,000 swansigs per ann. & he says she would answer, from the trade on the lake, if wholly unsupported by travellers. The company have a monopoly for 15 years.—He says there are schools in every commune: but the books chosen by government: the priest the master: reading & writing taught. He understands the priests generally to be considered the most depraved class: less so here. Great abundance: even for the lower orders: but discontent from partiality for Germans, in employments, & nontaxation.

The Austrian road seems as perfect a work as can be conceived.—Today Luigi gave me an account, when we were in the Riva boat, of what he could do with his hands, and how much more with a good stone or stick—excessively amusing.

Leone d'Oro at Lecco—very fair.—Situation pretty, but not to be compared to Como.

Friday July 6.

Lecco to Como by vetturino. Passed four lakes on the left—the two middle ones extremely pretty,[2] the banks being in the rich and picturesque style: the fourth we did not see. Four hours—not much short of eighteen miles. Country excessively fertile and well cultivated. Much corn cut—ground preparing for its second crop, of a species of Indian corn (called I believe grano Turco by the people) and other grain too.

Como—L'Angiolo—good Inn: bargains should be made. View of Lake very pretty. Boat to Villa d'Este[3]—situation and gardens pretty. Our boatmen acquainted us that the Queen was liked and did a great deal for the poor—Bergami[4] hated: made his fortune out of hers—and disgusted the persons whom he was employed to pay: always in attendance on the Queen, in boat and elsewhere. The English servants went off not liking the Italian appendages to the establishment: & the Milanese of the upper classes ceased to visit. Witnesses without knowledge of facts went off, for money, both for and against, to England. Majocchi[5] now lives in Milan, is a respectable man, and lived in the establishment as an artisan.—This end of the lake is very beautiful.—Distinguished from English lake scenery by the division into long narrow strips of land—by the different & to our eye inferior way in which the lines here are mixed, and the composition or masses of the landscape disposed—also by the relative (if not absolute) inferiority

[1] Fawcett and Prestons, Phoenix iron foundry.
[2] Lago di Pusciane and Lago di Sala.
[3] On an island in Lake Como, where *Caroline, Princess of Wales, stayed August–November 1815.
[4] Bartolomeo Bergami, d. 1845; employed at Milan 1814, by *Caroline, as courier; became her equerry and chamberlain; cited as co-respondent at her trial, 1820.
[5] Teodoro Majocchi, once a cook for Princess *Caroline, who gave evidence against her and Bergami at the trial.

of the trees in size, i.e. as compared with the height of the hills. Here they often appear like brushwood.

Duomo—handsome, particularly exterior. Interior filthy. $1\frac{1}{4}$–$5\frac{1}{4}$—three posts to Milan. Hotel de Ville—Tom's recommendation, on account of the convenience of the situation. Gran Bretagna & Albergo Reale more frequented by Englishmen. The plain of Lombardy at least in this part excessively fertile. Little appearance of poverty in the people. A decided brown the prevailing colour in dress—straw hats worn. An ordinary labourer can earn two francs a day: in harvest, three may be made. Land in small patches. —A ludicrous scene: Luigi got down and struck a pigheaded carter who ran against us. I almost split: John was more jealous of the honour of our concern.

Found a letter from Saunders at Milan: also another of extraordinary import from another quarter[1]—which gave our minds and pens employment most of the evening. Wrote to my Father—to Ld Lincoln—& pt of a letter to Saunders.

Saturday July 7.

Bought a map of Milan and an Ebel.[2] Inquiring in divers shops about books and other things. Saw the Director of the Post: J.N.G. stated to him our affair of the other day: he is beyond the reach of Austria: but we met with every politeness and disposition to do us justice. Cathedral—Exterior and interior very magnificent—but labour might be profitably spent in purifying the latter, and spared in decorating the former. The statues round the exterior of the windows, in the niche[s], I thought hideous: and the workmanship of the small statues in the pinnacles insanity: we should however consider that this roof is apparently in no small degree intended for promenading—& thus they may be appreciated. Odour from bodies in the Church. Did not choose to see the body of S. Carlo Borromeo[3]—as it was necessary to illuminate for him, and have a priest down to address prayers to him.— Biblioteca Ambrogiana[4]—open to all: what a liberal constitution: in England such as one would be too liable to abuse perhaps. MSS. Josephus[5] in papyrus—Petrarch's Virgil, &c.—Pictures—Raphael's cartoon of the School of Athens: a Crucifixion by Guido: portraits (very rare & precious) by Leonardo da Vinci, &c. Two Titians: a Holy Family by Luino, who imitates Leonardo apparently even to the obnoxious countenance, but seems inferior. Sketches by Breughel—&c. Some in pencil by Michael Angelo for his Last Judgement. A Bassano considered very good:

---

[1] From *Lincoln, offering influence on diarist's behalf at Newark, in impending general election, of his f., Henry Pelham Fiennes Pelham *Clinton, 1785–1851; 4th duke of Newcastle 1795; rigid conservative; founded Newcastle scholarship 1829; said to have lost six boroughs in schedule A of 1832 reform bill. See 6–8 July 32 below; and Add MS 44261.

[2] Johann Gottfried Ebel, *The Traveller's Guide through Switzerland* (tr. D. Wall, 1818, and many subsequent editions).

[3] St. Charles Borromeo, 1538–1584; abp. of Milan; cardinal and papal secretary of state under Pius IV.

[4] Library founded in the seventeenth century, the first in Europe to be open to all.

[5] Josephus Flavius, ca. A.D. 37–95; Jewish historian and military commander.

38—I.

(Giacomo).[1] Dined at table d'hôte—table d'hôte indeed—he sat down with us, and his wife too.—Much pleased with Milan.

Wrote to Mrs G.—to Lord Lincoln—& finished to Saunders.

Letter from Cole. Reading &c. as usual.

Sunday July 8.

Duomo bef. 12—found the morning sermon just over. Had a good deal of conversation there with two Englishmen named Clerk and Steele: half-brothers.[2] Found we had acquaintances in common.—Finished Bossuet.

At ¼ past two, went to attend S. Carlo Borromeo's Sunday School. Surprised to find them teaching writing and arithmetic. After some time, nominally an hour, they went to the second part of their work, Dottrina Cristiana, also in all an hour. First came prayers, which were Popish enough: but partly in *Italian*. I had however been reading, by permission, some prayers intended for the use of the pupils, entitled Atto di Fede, Atto di Speranza, Atto di Carità, Atto di Penitenza:[3] which were generally satisfactory. The first, the Creed we acknowledge, but with a sweeping clause of belief in all *the truths*—here is a loophole but no more—held by the R.C. Church.—I attended closely to one of the Classes, taught by an elderly layman—perhaps, judging by his appearance, a small tradesman. As in England, the boys were careless and unruly, and scarcely any of them displayed a capacity of answering more than formal questions. The class consisted of about thirty or forty. The teacher performed his part with ability and zeal: explaining what was involved in the being a Christian; not only the name, what more? Il Battisimo. What more? La Cresima. What more? La Confessione.[4] "Buona cosa anche questa—ma, n'en c'è niente di più?"[5] *They* had now run the length of their tether, or rather, when they had got to the end of the Sacraments: but he proceeded with much energy to show, that conformity to the mind of Christ, and imitation of his life, were essential to real Christianity, & without which we had only to expect eternal condemnation. Then, (knowing I believe that I was a Protestant,) as in duty bound, he proceeded to explain the absolute necessity of inclusion within the pale of the R.C. Church, and of obedience to the Pope as inheritor of the headship given by Christ to S. Peter, and as standing "in vece di Christo".[6] He exhorted them not to listen to the delusive notions of modern Christians, worldly men, who held an opposite opinion. But be not, he said, content with this. Then he inquired, how are we [to] know true from false? By the sign of the Holy Cross, was the answer. That is one, says he, but the most general. Is there no other? No answer. 'La Fraterna Carità'[7] —he was proceeding to dilate on this, when the bell sounded, and the

---

[1] i.e. Jacopo Bassano.
[2] Unidentified.
[3] Acts of Faith, Hope, Charity, and Contrition.
[4] Baptism, Confirmation, Confession.
[5] 'That's also good, but isn't there anything more?'.
[6] 'in Christ's stead'.
[7] 'Brotherly love'.

scene, which was interesting, closed.—A little boy then recited something I could not hear, and got a picture as a reward. A priest had now made his appearance, and, strange to say, delivered to this audience of children, a sermon wholly & solely on the necessity of paying tithes! As might have been expected, no attention was manifested.—He maintained them on the ground of the law both of nature and of God—seemed generally to speak of supporting the clergy & of this *mode* of support as identical—but allowed of the exception where a freedom had been bought, or law made other provision, or absolute poverty prevented payment. Otherwise, those who did not pay were worse than thieves. 'Even', said he, 'had God demanded *nine tenths* of the property of those able to pay, and left them but one, they would have been under obligation to pay—but now, that God has been so moderate in contenting himself (I use his own word) with *one tenth*, what excuse can be alleged?' On the whole, a most singular scene.—Some of the teachers made enquiries from me about the Protestant religion, and seemed pleased with what they learned. As far as our own Church is concerned, I think publicity is what we have to court.—The schools are curtained off from the Cathedral. Pax vobis over the entrances. Girls on one side, boys on the other. The *dottrina* is taught in all the parish Churches of Milan on Sunday, on S. Carlo Borromeo's foundation: arithmetic &c. in the Duomo only: surely much better left out. But how delightful it is to see so much doing at so remote a period, and with so little evil intermixed, owing to the piety and the benevolence of one man!

The master & director of our Inn, & a waiter are Protestants. The waiter, a pleasing young man, told us with much regret, that tho' there were 3 to 4000 Protestants in Milan, they had no Church—but only, twice a year, the clergyman of Bergamo came and administered the Sacrament to them in a room.

Stupid sermon in the evening at Duomo: contained however strictures on those who carried on the worship of saints otherwise than as subordinate to the worship of God.

Walked to the porta Orientale. Had not windows & balconies been crowded, one would have thought all the world was out of doors. Great display in equipages: and I think not a single pedestrian illdressed or in want, according to appearances, to be met with.

Milan. *Friday July 6, Sunday July 8.*[1]

Recalling on the latter of these days the thoughts which attended the former, I think I may call it the most remarkable of my life: it is one which may be fraught with the weightiest consequences, to me at least if not to others, and the proposal I received on it[2] constitutes an event in the life of any person at my years, much more in mine.—This stunning and overpowering proposal naturally left me the whole of the evening on which I received it in a flutter of confusion. Since that evening there has been time to reflect and to see that it is not of so intoxicating a character as it seemed

[1] Next three paragraphs from Lambeth MS 1420.
[2] See end of previous entry for 6 July 32.

at first. First because the Duke of Newcastle's offer must have been made at the instance of a single person,[1] that person young and sanguine, and I may say in such a matter partial.[2] Secondly because its having any material consequences is a distant & as yet an improbable contingency.

Had it devolved on me at once to send a reply to this proposal, how great & how insuperable my difficulties would have been. Happily, God, who established the order of nature, and who seals parental wisdom & experience by parental authority, did by this order relieve me. To learn his will, the first human means is to refer to my parents—and this was done. It remained to add earnest supplications to the throne of grace for defence and guidance on this arduous and delicate occasion: defence most of all from my own personal ambition, rashness, or vanity, or all—which would insinuate themselves under the plausible forms of suggestions that opportunities must be seized, and means of doing good must not be neglected: suggestions true in their meaning, but often destructively falsified by undue application.—Thus much at least became clear to me by the time I had recovered my breath: that decidedly more than mere permission from my dear Father would be necessary to authorise my entering on the consideration of particulars at all.[3]

And now, how far has my mind advanced? Let me be content for the present, if it is sound in the general principles which ought to direct me on such an occasion. It is right to be ready to forget the matter altogether on a moment's notice—it is also right to be prepared, should my Father urge me onwards, with some leading ideas for the settlement of the question. What then am I to ask myself? Simply whether, in the first form of the matter, whether my acceptance or the contrary will most contribute to forward those merciful purposes, with which God sent me and every other being into the world—and for the effectuation of which in us all Jesus Christ shed his precious blood upon the Cross. May the great gift of that sacrifice, even the presence of the heavenly comforter, be with me, support me, succour me, enlighten me, when the time shall come, if indeed it is to arrive, for deliberation on a subject of such weight. May I feel my weakness, mine utter and infantine weakness—and then indeed, and then only, there is hope that it may be made strength.

Monday July 9.

After breakfast went out and completed a purchase of Italian books. We went to the Brera Palace, or Royal Academy—saw the Library, where every one is admitted to read, persons being in attendance in all the rooms—and the pictures. Many Paul Veroneses. Bonifacios, not his best. Guercinos, good: Abraham dismissing Hagai, much celebrated. Rubens's Last Supper —a Guido in the *forte* style. A Last Supper of Paul V.s, in many respects resembling his Capo d'Opera at Venice: a Salvator, wild & powerful—a

---

[1] *Lincoln.
[2] These three sentences are given in Morley (i. 88) as part of a letter to his father.
[3] This sentence is treated in the same way (ibid.).

Raffael &c.—Not to be compared to the *great* Italian galleries, yet interesting. Frescoes by Luino: generally displaying that odious countenance which runs through so many works of Leonardo.

Letters from home of great importance, in consequence a resolution taken —God help us—a part of which is to return home immediately. Sat eight hours writing, with little interruptions only about money matters—no time to dine. We were to have seen the Maria delle Grazie—the S. Lorenzo—and the Marengo Arch—I missed all. John visited Leonardo's Fresco.[1] Wrote to the Duke of Newcastle & Lord Lincoln—three copies of each—also to my Father, and to Milnes Gaskell.

With what we have seen of Milan as a town, we are much pleased. It has an appearance of wealth, abundance, and activity: education is far more general than in other parts of Italy: the streets are very handsome and clean, and the paths in good order: the number of soldiers immense. I asked a bookseller with whom I was dealing the price of Martini's Bible[2] (with notes) when complete. He named a sum between one & two hundred francs. "Nothing cheaper?" "The cheapest Bible with notes costs 45 to 50 francs". "And is there no cheaper Bible to be had?" "Yes, Diodati's:[3] for 18 or 20." "Can this be easily procured?" "No: for it has no notes and is prohibited." I think when no Bible is purchaseable under 45 or 50 francs, we may without breach of charity say, that the Bible is, virtually, kept from the poor.

Satisfied with our Inn, decidedly.—

Tuesday July 10.

5.10 m. A.M.–8.10 m. P.M. $4\frac{1}{2}$ Italian Posts, and 10 French—$3\frac{3}{4}$ hours of stoppages.

Road to Sesto Calende[4] rich, one barren tract: harvest every where over: no decent Inn till this place: breakfast at La Poste: better than it looks: Tre Re more inviting in appearance. Crossed Tesino. A poor blind man plays the violin on board the *pont volant*: blind from two years of age: has no recollection of any form or colour. Piedmont customhouse wholly inoffensive. Fine ride to Arona:[5] walked (a mile from the Inn—which seems good —Sir A. Foster here, as we learned afterwards—) to statue of St Carlo Borromeo: statue alone 72 Paris feet. Proportions apparently beautiful: general appearance imposing and interesting. Rejoined carriage below. Came on to Stresa[6] on the banks of the Lake. Banks at lower end rich and picturesque in the extreme. The upper, judging by vista, somewhat in the style of Como. The branch to Baveno[7] presents by far the finest prospect I have enjoyed among the Italian lakes. The isles—the wooded banks thickly

---

[1] The Last Supper by Leonardo da Vinci, at the Dominican refectory by Santa Maria delle Grazie.

[2] Abp. A. Martini's Italian translation of the Bible (1769–77).

[3] Giovanni Diodati, Calvinist pastor; published Italian translation of the Bible (1607).

[4] Thirty-two miles WNW. of Milan, at SE. tip of Lago Maggiore.

[5] On SW. shore of lake, 6 miles WNW. of Sesto Calende.

[6] On west shore of Lake Maggiore, 43 miles NW. of Milan.

[7] Four miles NW. of Stresa, 18 SE. of Domodossola.

specked with towns and houses—the defile of the Simplon road, and Alp rising on Alp in receding rows, till the view was bounded by the grand and snowy ridge—all this, with Italy's bluest sky and softest lights constituted an enchanting scene, and forcibly reminded us it was our last. And on what occasion it is that I am quitting this lovely country! All tends to awaken affectionate remembrance.

Boat from Stresa to Isola Bella[1]—paintings, grotto rooms—storm on sea of Galilee in wood—inner view of the substructions on which the garden is raised—summit—and lower terrace towards Isola Madre[1] all worthy of observation, with much more. No one I fancy can have a better opportunity than here of appreciating the Italian Summer Villa in its best style. The prices Starke names for the *custodi* absurd.[2] The old man of the house was so pleased with a franc from my hand, that, besides a large allowance of thanks, he wished I might return soon, with my wife!—Isola Madre: gardens interesting: for their plants—their style, being less formal —a collection of pheasants of many kinds—& the points of views which have been much studied.

Baveno seems a delightful place. Road on to Domo d'Ossola beautiful: and scenery very fine: exceeding what one generally sees in the approaches to the Alps. The vale of the river beautifully green: the hills which skirt it at once rich and bold. We saw the tallest wheat today which ever met our eyes—J.N.G. called the longest straws 9 or 10 feet. La Poste at Domo d'Ossola: good: *tea* remarkably good. Trout.

Wednesday July 11.

5.10 m. A.M.–9.20 m. P.M. Domo d'Ossola to Sion,[3] capital of the Canton of the Valais. The distance charged is 18¾ posts—which constitute, any way, a very long day's journey. I am convinced however that the distances are much overstated, for the convenience of Postmasters. On the map indeed, not allowing for windings, the whole only amounts to between 18 and 19 leagues (of 25 to the degree): that allowance however would be considerable, on account of the mountain.

I think the Simplon does not give the idea of height so much as the Splugen. There was less snow near the road: but today for the first time we saw real & formidable glaciers. Taken altogether, this road is I suppose decidedly the more wonderful work: the management of the descent is exquisite: but I do not think it has any two single features so striking as the passage of the Rheinwald, on the N. of the Splugen, and the descent into the basin of Isola, on the south. Some parts however of the Italian side here correspond in a measure to the Rheinwald: but the vale is not so close at the top, nor are the sides so much covered with trees—and the road runs nearer its river. *There* the trees seemed to spring from among large frag-

---

[1] Two of a group of four small islands near by in Lake Maggiore; Isola Bella, formerly barren, was transformed in the seventeenth century into a garden rising nearly 100 feet, enclosing a palace.

[2] *Information for travellers*, 45 n.

[3] Forty-five miles west of Domodossola, but across the main range of the Alps.

ments of rock: here, to grow without soil out of the unbroken side. The grottoes and cuttings I suppose are scarcely matched by those on the Emperor's Como road: many of the cascades are very fine: the Italian side is full of savage magnificence, and the Swiss of Romantic beauty. The Swiss vale however from Brieg,[1] is far from being equal to the Italian beneath Domo d'Ossola. Less sensation of pressure on the lungs at the summit, than on the Splugen. q. because the day was much clouded when we were up, & with occasional rain, so that the air was less rarefied?[2]—The road on the Swiss side not so well kept. We saw two men in a hut, of very simple construction: the sides of wood: the roof, pieces of bark: four bits of *schist*[3] put up together formed a grate, where a cheerful fire was blazing. A wooden shoe used down to Brieg—I should think it might easily be dispensed with, and strains the perch of a carriage.

Sierre[4]—a beautiful village—has a new & nicelooking Inn—we came however on to

Sion, Lion d'Or. A comfortable Inn, but dear enough.

Thursday July 12.

6.10 m. A.M.–8¼ P.M. 14 posts.—Sion to Lausanne,[5] capital of the Vaud. Staid four hours at Bex[6] on account of heat: which was excessive: as great, almost, as the day before yesterday in Lombardy. Some of the Posts ludicrously short. Good Inn at Martigny,[7] where we breakfasted. Crossed the Rhone from the Valais into the Vaud. No customhouse annoyance whatever. An amazing improvement, in this canton, upon the last, in the richness and cultivation of the country. Saw most magnificent walnut trees all along the road. Passed the Pissevach[8]—and between the two mountains, so singular in their upper conformation, Dent du Midi,[9] & Dent du Morcle.[10] The former had far more snow (in the same aspect) yet the latter (on the right going down) is alleged to be much higher. A good Inn at Bex, & apparently much going on. Mounted the town for a view. Church contains above 1000: population of the district 3000. Doctrine Calvinistic—*but* they have a large organ. Service once every Thursday, at 9.30 A.M. Few, comparatively speaking, attend. Situation beautiful. Read a great deal of Daniel Wilson.[11] Stopped at Chillon:[12] saw the vaults: which are considerably handsomer than the upper part of the building. They are on the level of the lake. The drive round is enchanting: the sheet of water magnificent. Shoals in the S.E. corner caused by the deposit of the Rhone. Here there being no per-

[1] Brig, on the Rhone, 20 miles NW. of Domodossola and 30 east of Sion.
[2] The Simplon is not quite as high as the Splügen: 6,592 feet to 6,946.
[3] Rock.
[4] Nine miles ENE. of Sion.
[5] Forty miles WNW. of Sion.
[6] Twenty-six miles SE. of Lausanne.
[7] Sixteen miles WSW. of Sion.
[8] Pissevache, a cascade on the R. Sallenche, 4 miles north of Martigny.
[9] 10,696 feet, 8 miles NW. of Martigny.
[10] Grande Dent de Morcles: another Alpine peak, 9,777 feet, 6 miles north of Martigny.
[11] Daniel *Wilson, Letters from an Absent Brother, 2v. (1825).
[12] On east shore of Lake Geneva; castle once a stronghold of Savoy and a state prison.

ceptible current, the heavy matter sinks: and the river goes on to Lyon as blue as the lovely lake from which it issues. Relay *now* established between Bex & Vevey[1]. Road on to Lausanne is dreadfully exposed to the sun: & should not be travelled, except either late in the evening, or early in the morning.—Towns here abouts pleasing—pavements bad.

Friday July 13.

Before breakfast, went to the Cathedral. Its terrace has a fine view. The building is large & handsome. Not only statues outside the porch, but in the vestibule & over the principal door. A St. Sebastian—Two headless. The French used this Church as a barrack.[2] A monument to Sir Stratford Canning's Lady, designed & commenced by Canova[3]—A large organ. Two communion tables, wholly bare, in the tribune.

Made an attempt of dubious success to find Gibbon's[4] house.—He does not seem commonly known here. Children seem surprised even at being asked if they can read, & if there are Bibles in the houses of the Poor. At Bex we were told that there was little intercourse or friendliness between the Cath. & Prot. ministers.

Faucon a beautifully clean & most comfortable hotel: inclined to be dear.

Steamer for Geneva, a boat very comfortably fitted (Leman) with a restaurant (we dined on board), did not get fairly under weigh from Lausanne till near 11—professedly 10—Geneva at 3½. Saw Sir G. Palmer.[5] Great number of passengers. Found an Englishman who had resided in Switzerland some time & knew Tom Moss.—Regretted to change the E. for the W. scenery of the Lake. It is a magnificent sheet of water. The style of its scenery is much more English (except the vines on the N. bank) than that of the Italian lakes: much less formal than that of Como.

Situation of Geneva very fine: town handsome & *alive*. *Balance d'Or*—expecting to find Cole there—which we did. He started us on a walk—professedly for Ferney[6]—but we found it was 6 miles there & had not time. We enjoyed however the magnificent sunset view of Mt Blanc from the favourite point on the high road—just where a broken [jetty?] leads down to the edge of the lake which is close—and also, the full moon rising over the sharp angular peaks.—Letters from T.G., Gaskell, Phillimore. We had tea with Cole—excellently provided. Met Orlowsky too who is here with an aunt.—D. Wilson. Conversation with C[ole].

Saturday July 14.

7 A.M. a boat with Cole on the lake—we all had a delightful bathe & returned to breakfast. Business came afterwards—watchhunting &c. at Mr

---

[1] Eleven miles ESE. of Lausanne.   [2] 1798–1802.
[3] Harriet, née Raikes, d. 1817, first wife of Sir Stratford *Canning, 1786–1880, diplomatist; minister to Switzerland 1814–20, 1847–8; ambassador to Turkey 1825–9, 1831–2, 1842–7, 1848–58. The monument was not by Canova, but by Lorenzo Bartolini.
[4] Edward *Gibbon lived in Lausanne 1783–93.
[5] Sir George Joseph Palmer, 1811–66; 3rd bart., of Wanlip Hall, Leicestershire.
[6] Four miles NNW. of Geneva.

Bautte's—I kept clear. Made war with some success on Cole to get him to go home with us. In the evening, a carriage to Ferney. The environs of Geneva are singularly pretty and assimilate wonderful[ly] to the manner of English landscape. Voltaire's Villa is beautifully situated:[1] but loses the fine expanse of the lake. The pictures in his sittingroom accord with his character. The stone on his Church "Deo erexit Voltaire"[2] was destroyed by the French. He did it on account of the Papal thunders—having destroyed the old one. His old gardener told us long stories about the coquetting between him & Gibbon—the blasphemous lines of the latter—

> Dieu de génie
> Tu es comme Jesus dans l'Eucharistie
> Je te mange, je te bois, & je ne te vois jamais.[3]

His repartee when he had seen Voltaire against his will & the latter sent to demand 12 sous as the price of the exhibition of the monster. Gibbon sent 24, & claimed the privilege of a second sight. He showed Voltaire's last lines, declaring he was going to dissipate whatever prejudices he should find in the shades below—his collection of seals, inkstand, Catherine's[4] purse present, &c. &c. He said he was very benevolent: a most severe & exigeant master: seemed fully alive to the guilt & mischief of his opinions: spoke of them with horror: & of *him* said, c'etoit malheureux pour lui.

Sunday July 15. At Geneva.[5]

Since I last wrote, I have committed myself and am about to become, unless some exception arise on the part of the Duke, a candidate for the representation of Newark. Probability of success, considering the tone the Duke has taken, there is, surely: but there cannot be, I should think, anything approaching certainty, in a case where the constituency consists of 1600 voters.

But be that as it may, I stand pledged to this bold and terrible experiment: and it constitutes, considering the general unimportance of my being & life, a situation of no ordinary interest.

The resolution was taken, I trust, in a spirit not of utter forgetfulness of Him, who is the Author of all good counsels, all holy desires, and all just works.[6] And the strongest human warranty was afforded me, in the (I may say) unanimous advice of the members of our family, particularly of my Father. In such a case, I seem to feel, it is scarcely possible to overrate the weight of recommendations which proceed from such a quarter: and I trust before God, that here was the moving spring of the step I made.

---

[1] Voltaire lived at Ferney, 1755–78.

[2] 'Voltaire erected this to God'. The words appeared on an iron flag beneath the weather-cock of the church.

[3] 'God of spirit, you are like Jesus in the Eucharist: I eat you, I drink you, and I never see you'.

[4] Catherine the Great of Russia, 1729–96; admirer and correspondent of Voltaire.

[5] Next six paragraphs from Lambeth MS 1420.

[6] From the second collect at evensong.

One lesson I trust has been impressed with immense force and in indelible characters on my mind, by the considerations affecting my own conduct into which I have been called upon to enter, both at Christmas last, and on the present occasion. I am in my soul persuaded that by these opportunities I have been taught more than I had ever learned before, first of the childlike impotency of my understanding: secondly of the fiendlike deceitfulness of my heart. On other matters I have, God knows, pronounced dogmatically enough: but here at once I have found myself disarmed. I cannot raise an hypothesis or a hope as to my future destiny, but a thousand objections spring up from every quarter, and I cannot get rid either of them, nor yet of that to which they are objections: and again when after long and steady consideration, a proposition has become settled in my mind (I speak of those relative to my own individual condition in future) and I think that all is safe, in a moment when I look not for it comes some strong and fearful revulsion, threatening to tear up all by the roots. And all my planning & scheming is attended with a restless, selfish, and fevered anxiety.

Such is the melancholy picture of a mind now about to solicit a station in which it professes to act for others as well as for itself. To my paper at least, & for my own future instruction at a period when in retrospect I may at length be able to comprehend my own condition, I trust I have here told, with shame, the truth, the whole truth, & nothing but the truth.

But does not this blessed day bring with it anything but sorrowful and shameful contemplations? Is there no peace laid up, even for me, in the lifegiving Sabbaths of my God? Yes: they are my best instructors for the present: and my dearest hopes for that future and eventful period, on which I am about to enter. They may be an anchor to my soul, when there is no other: and even now they remind me to cast myself wholly upon my God, the mighty and the merciful God of my redemption and the redemption of the world. O holy, blessed, and most glorious Trinity, hold me up in the arms of everlasting strength: lay my pride level with the dust, sting my besetting sins even into utter extinction, conform my soul to thine image, my thoughts words and deeds to thy purposes of love: through the Crucified Redeemer. Amen, and Amen.

Sunday July 15.

Walked to M. Malan's[1] Church: & heard him catechise. It was chiefly exposition—and, what was odd enough, on the subject of paying tithes to God —the same subject, & to the same audience as that of the Cath. Pr. at Milan last Sunday. Both too made use of the same illustrative argument— what if God had demanded *nine* parts instead of one. Malan however did not appropriate his tithes to the clergy. His appearance is striking and venerable: his enunciation voluble: his style simple & clear: his sincerity &

---

[1] Caesar Henry Abraham Malan, 1787–1864; formerly a minister in the Swiss Reformed Churches, he founded his own chapel, L'Eglise du Témoignage, 1820, and was expelled from his Reformed Church ministry in 1823.

simplicity evident in every sentence: but from the middling attendance at his Church (not half full, morning or evg) & from what I have loosely heard, I should fear that his doctrines, in my mind strained beyond the spirit of Scripture, did not produce an abundant harvest. Yet surely is he a light, amidst the darkness of Geneva.—In the evening I went again—his times are nine & six—at the latter he delivers a sermon. He put his doctrine of assurance (so highly objectionable in form, yet with so much substantial & inoffensive truth involved,) closely home, by asking himself the question 'Est ce que j'attends les promesses de Dieu?'[1] and answering it in the affirmative himself. he next pointed it at the congregation whom he recommended to be ready to answer it individually before such an assembly as that, or before the whole world. He alluded pointedly to the apostacies of the German Church—and gave a part of his sermon, yet would it had been larger, to direct exhortation.—His music is touching & of a superior style to what one generally hears in conjunction with the French language. The books are marked "Eglise du temoignage". He has an organ—so have all the other Churches I have seen. He has separated from the Church—others of somewhat similar opinions remain in it, and have established an Academy for their purposes—an intelligent person with whom I walked named M. Gaussen[2] (I think) as one of the chief. They are forbidden to preach—but many espouse their cause on account of their continuing in the Church. He had a high opinion of Mr Burgess.—whom I heard in the English Church, near the hospital, at 11. His subject, the dying thieves:[3] he made an original & appropriate use of the case of the impenitent one, & was very good. Also I went to L'Eglise de la Fusterie, of the Establishment, and heard a M. Piccole[4] (I think). The service made me long for some Catholic ones which I have witnessed! Bold in the extreme. Church not quarter filled: could not sing. people would not. Minister prayed for the aid of the Holy Spirit—'in the name of thy Son Jesus Christ'—mentioned 'the Sacrifice he was to make for the expiation of our sins—' and addressed God as the God that had redeemed (rachetè) us—But these expressions were used in a very general way, appearing to import very little: they did not communicate any life to the body of the discourse (from which however I ought to have learned much) which was on the manner of interference in the conduct of others & of tendering advice. Walked round the ramparts, a delightful walk, with J.N.G. & Cole.

Monday July 16.

A scull and a bathe, early in the morning—also wrote to T.G. and packed: we breakfasted with Cole, and exhorted him to fulfil a half-formed plan, by which he was to meet us at Basle on Thursday, and go on with us down the Rhine. Left by the steamboat soon after nine. A pleasant passage, with a

---

[1] 'Am I awaiting God's promises?'.
[2] François Samuel Robert Louis Gaussen, 1790–1863; pastor at Satigny 1816–30; professor of systematic theology at evangelical college 1836–57.
[3] Luke xxiv. 39–43.
[4] Possibly Pierre Picot, professor of dogmatic theology 1795.

breeze and fine weather: could not help regretting so speedy a departure from this lovely and tranquil country, and contrasting the serene mood produced by the contemplations of the soft skies, majestic hills, deep blue waters, and shores whose scenery seems the very image of peace, with those of which I am about, please God, to be a witness, and, it is awful to think in such helplessness, perhaps more than a witness.

Arrived at Lausanne 2 P.M. Read some German vocabulary, and the French Charter of 1831[1] with Notes, on board.—Severe work among the voituriers. We were modestly asked by a person esteemed among the reputable, 200 francs besides buonamano,[2] for taking us to Basle! about 100 miles: we had not time to lose in waiting for chevaux de retour, which otherwise would have been advisable—and at last agreed with a man apparently very decent and civil, for the work to be done in 3 days with two horses—at 108 francs, besides B. M. & near 6 fr. for a mountain.—We are *much* pleased with the Faucon: situation good: food excellent: rooms extremely clean: prices of meals moderate: & apartment to be bargained for. Could not identify Gibbon's h[ouse] further than before.

4¾ P.M.–11 P.M. To Payerne:[3] 8 leagues. These leagues are very long—upwards, I should think, on the average, of 3½ miles. 1100 feet ascent from Lausanne. Evening fine, country highly rich and picturesque: resembling England beyond anything we have seen—so much appearance of what is domestic, comfortable, and cleanly, both here and further on—houses scattered through the country—gardens and domestic animals about the houses—ground carefully husbanded and cultivated—gentle hill and smiling dale—deep shades with varied and abundant foliage—are the characteristics of this part of the country. The road *opens* the Lake of Geneva, to a person reversing our route, as beautifully as could be desired. Read D.W[ilson].

Payerne—Hotel de Ville—beds *good*: feeding indifferent, compared with other Swiss Inns: and charges manifestly high.

Tuesday July 17.

5¼ A.M.–11 A.M. Payerne—Aarberg.[4] 8 leagues. Passed the column erected to commemorate Morat (1476)[5] in 1822 by Fribourg Canton. J.N.G. breakfasted at Couronne, Morat—found it clean and good: we made each a meal at Couronne, Aarberg, and can recommend it. Situation of Aarberg is pleasing. Our road skirted Lake of Morat,[6] which has little to boast of: and we got a glimpse of that of Neuchatel,[7] with the city. Settled a long account with Luigi—and read Daniel Wilson. 3¼–7½ Aarberg to Soleure[8]—six

---

[1] France was governed by the constitutional charter granted by Louis XVIII in 1814, as revised by the chamber of deputies in 1830–1.

[2] A tip.

[3] Twenty-five miles NNE. of Lausanne and WSW. of Bern.

[4] Twenty-two miles NE. of Payerne.

[5] Swiss victory over Charles the Bold of Burgundy; 16 miles west of Bern.

[6] The Murtensee, 16 miles NW. of Morat or Murten.

[7] 23 miles west of Bern.

[8] Or Solothurn, 19 miles north of Bern.

leagues, by the account of our voiturier. Country still rich and picturesque. Our road today lies through the Cantons of Friebourg, Berne, and Soleure: the first and last mainly Catholic: the second Protestant. The Jura mountains accompany the road all the way, at a considerable distance on the left. The houses are now genuine Swiss: a single chimney: high & steep thatch: often several stories, and communication between them apparently carried on by the galleries & balconies on the outside under the deep & long penthouses: the fabric being of wood. Fruit trees most abundant: the woods everywhere as rich and varied as those of England. In Berne, the women wear caps of black crepe, or something like it, with a sort of frill projecting at each side, having just the appearance of the extended wings of a butterfly—we afterwards found the same in white: the first may have been mourning.

Soleure—very well situated on the Aar, and fortified. Cathedral a handsome edifice: the pictures seemed very bad, but there was scarcely any of that tawdry finery which one sees in Italian Churches, even the poorest: and there were plenty of boxes for the poor, and none others. French seems a good deal spoken in the town, but German is the ordinary tongue. Couronne: extremely good. Taken as a whole, I know not where the Swiss Inns can be equalled: they are beautifully clean, well stored, & generally moderate. The Tyrol comes nearest to them.

Wednesday July 18.

$4\frac{3}{4}$-$11\frac{1}{2}$—Soleure to Wallenburg[1]—staid half an hour at Ballstall[2]—where J.N.G. breakfasted & found the Petit Cheval good & *very* moderate. The ascent of the Oberhaue[n]stein[3] from Ballstall is formidable—the descent much worse. The height is about 2840 feet. The views are very pleasing: and the opening of the mountains in which Ballstall lies, remarkably beautiful. Our view of the chain of Alps, coming from Soleure, was *magnificent* this morning about five: and enables one to conceive the splendour of the panorama from the top of the Weissenstein,[4] two hours distant.

La Clef, Wallenberg: dearer than the generality of country Inns in Switzerland. The ordinary prices are 40 and 30 sous respectively for breakfast and tea in the larger towns: 30 only for the first in the smaller.

It took more than four hours to bring us our five leagues into Basle—and the horses were so fatigued that we entered the town a perfect spectacle. With such prices as are paid to the Swiss voituriers, one has a right to be better served. The country rich & picturesque, the river on which we came some 2 or 3 miles from Basle is a magnificent stream, & the view of the city fine. The trois Rois is well situated and the view of the river from the salle-a-manger delightful. *Beds* begin to become dearer. Change of climate now very perceptible. Walked up to the Cathedral & its delightful terrace.

---

[1] Twelve miles NE. of Soleure and SSE. of Basle.
[2] Eighteen miles SE. of Basle.
[3] Mountain 10 miles NNE. of Balsthal.
[4] Mountain 12 miles WSW. of Balsthal.

Thursday July 19.

Cole joined us in the morning. Owing to delays with his luggage we did not get away till 10½ A.M. & travelled till ½ hour past midnight,[1] when we got to Offenberg:[2] happily we found and knocked up an active host at the Fortune, who spoke English, produced Galignani's paper, (a grievous injury to one's night's rest) and a good and plentiful repast. Visited the Cathedral of Freybourg: beautiful, and little bedaubed with mere finery, if compared with churches in purely Popish countries.[3] Change of climate today still more remarkable—but the wind was northerly. We are now four on the carriage, which has stood its work wonderfully well, and deserves our gratitude. About 18 miles from Basle, the country becomes flat, & continues so: fertile and well cultivated: crops heavy: the summer has been warm: wheat, & rye, Indian corn (which I do not remember to have seen in Switzerland) *hemp*, and potatoes—with great numbers of apple trees, and some fine woods, are the ornaments of the Grand Duchy of Baden. A decline in neatness, perhaps, as compared with the country we have been travelling through. Peasants wear shovel hats—horses admirable in make & condition: clean, plump, firm, & free action: but the postillions make little of them, & are phlegmatic & sulky.—We met numbers of young men, pedestrians, with knapsacks, very decently dressed, whom we afterwards supposed to be students—we were surprised to find them generally hold out their hats & run with the carriage like common beggars. John in retaliation held out his cap from the inside, and one of them put in a small coin, about one third of a kreutzer[4]—which I have kept as a curiosity. Cole's heart was touched—and he flung them a piece of silver.—By and bye the same thing happened again, & we got a kreutzer.—Country people everywhere very respectful—Here, as in the Tyrol, I cannot see a priest—and there is, on the other hand, much appearance of education.

Friday July 20.

8. A.M. to midnight. Yesterday we made nine posts—today nine & a half—some of them I am persuaded are 10 English miles—and we were delayed 1½ hours by Banker's being again lost. John had a great deal of trouble. Carlsruhe[5] is an extremely pretty place, & I should think very agreeable for a sojourn. Road hence for two stages a cross one, & bad. Country much as yesterday. A postillion who was desired to drive faster, threatened to belabour Luigi with his whip; Luigi made semblance of retaliation with my[6] umbrella, of which the stick was broken! The scene was ludicrous enough—and not less so that when complaint was made to the next postmaster. It might have been worse. It seems necessary in these countries to be well prepared to do yourself justice, at *least* defensively. On such cases as these I

---

[1] Margin entry: 'went into the Cathedral again'.
[2] Offenburg; 12 miles SE. of Strasbourg and 70 north of Basle.
[3] Freiburg-im-Breisgau, 35 miles NNE. of Basle.
[4] A kreutzer was worth about one-third of a penny.
[5] Forty miles NE. of Strasbourg.
[6] 'broken' here deleted.

look as often differing much from *personal* quarrels. Going from Como to Milan we had a very laughable exhibition: our zealous courier, indignant at two sleepy carters who were very stupid & clumsy & nearly did us material injury, got down, ran after them, and struck one on the arm, but with knowledge & ability so little proportioned to his will, that the result was suppressed laughter from us, & open from them.

Saturday July 21.

The Germans are excellent linguists—and more English is spoken here than on the French & Italian roads, in the proportion of ten to one—e.g. both our landlords at Offenberg and Mannheim[1] spoke English. At the latter we were at the Black Bear—a good house, and very moderate in its prices. It is the custom here to put up a variety of notices in German, French, and English. The latter is seldom at all correctly written. I copied the following announcement of the attractions of an Inn on our road. "A view of the new bathing house & hotel to the Roman bath &c. &c. of Io. Ik. Ioner—" so far well enough. "The excellent situation of this curing place is too generally "known, as to need some new recommendation.

"Cleanliness, equity, & quick attendance, will be always my strictest "point of view, and I shall endeavour with the utmost application to satisfy "that confidence of which I am begging for."—

My journey too gave me a long conversation with Luigi, on a subject hitherto little touched.

The whole morning was one of extreme hurry: John busy about bankers and the carriage—of which he contrived to dispose, it appears, very satisfactorily—but it could not be sold. I had boxes, packing, & payments, to look after. The town of Mannheim is regular & handsome—above 20,000 inhabitants. At three we embarked, after an excessive addle, in the steamer, where we dined, and had a long conversation with a German, belonging to one of the small states, who cried "a bas" for the Tories—abused Lord Palmerston as a Casimir Perier[2] man & a Tory! particularly on account of some ordinances lately published in Frankfort—applauded by Lords Grey, Brougham, Althorp,[3] Durham[4]—he hated the Tories because opposed to liberty in foreign states—particularly the Duke of Wellington: who he says was much beloved in Germany (he did not seem to speak of any but the

---

[1] Thirty-two miles north of Karlsruhe.

[2] Casimir-Pierre Périer, 1777–1832; French premier 1831; restored civic order in France and made France the protector of Belgium.

[3] John Charles *Spencer, 1782–1845; styled viscount Althorp 1783, till he succ. as 3rd earl Spencer 1834; Harrow and Trinity Cambridge; master of Pytchley 1805–18; whig M.P. Okehampton 1804–6, St. Alban's 1806, Northamptonshire 1806–34; m. 1814, widower 1818; lived in Albany ca. 1825–35; chancellor of exchequer and leader of commons 1830–4; 'the very model and type of an English gentleman' (Greville, v. 230).

[4] John George *Lambton, 1792–1840, whig M.P. Co. Durham 1813–28; m. 2ndly Charles *Grey's da. Lady Louisa Elizabeth 1816; mineowner, but called 'Radical Jack'; lord privy seal 1830–3; cr. lord Durham 1828, earl of Durham 1833; ambassador to Russia 1832, 1835–7; governor-general of Canada in 1838; lent name to 'Durham report' favouring more Canadian self-government (1839: see 12 Feb. 39); a brilliant failure.

small states) till he became English minister. Odillon Barrot[1] was his man among all the grades of French politicians. He said that the people of Germany were now become very friendly to the French and their opinions— and yet did not think there was any rebellious spirit spread through any considerable portion of the former, which however he considered to exist in the latter.

Weather cold. Banks uninteresting. Voyage to Mayence $4\frac{1}{2}$ hours: appearance of the city fine: fortifications the strongest in Germany: 15,000 Austrian and Prussian troops here.[2] The distance we came was seven German miles, 35 English: some stoppages, & a nominal search, at Worms.[3] The official man on board reported the distance 12 German miles.

Rhenisher Hof, Mentz. A good house—salle-a-manger presented, among other features in its character, musicians, a conjurer, and a newly married couple making manifest love at the public supper-table! There is a tariff here for carriage of luggage—but the faquins[4] attempted an overcharge— we offered to appeal to the police—they accepted it: we went, & came off with ease & in triumph—the award of the policeman being less than we wished to give & gave. "A bas" the faquins, say I.

Sunday July 22.

We were to have gone by the steamboat of this morning in order to get on by the Rotterdam Steamer to London on Tuesday—as there is no other boat all the week, but on Sunday next—and as the Cholera is out. This we found we could not do, and in consequence remained at Mayence for the day. I am not much disappointed, I confess, to have been able to avoid travelling today, for though I hope it was not on a trivial score, it is not satisfactory. Went into the Cathedral between six & seven A.M: it was very full: a great many soldiers: a tribune and altar at each end of the Church: all the people had books—which was a great novelty—and seemed very attentive. Walked three to four h. with Cole—and read a long time with him. All the shops are shut here, and Sunday seems comparatively well kept: but in our salle-a-manger at night we had a band of music and a juggler. Mentz. Rhenisher Hof—moderate & good: rooms small.

Monday July 23.

six A.M. to five & a quarter P.M. Steamer to Cologne—70 horse power: wind against us: stoppages at all the considerable towns. Rate of descent ten miles an hour, sometimes more. We breakfasted and dined very comfortably on board. Distance called from 90 to 100 miles. At Cologne we took up our quarters at the Mayntzer Hof, after we found there was no chance of

---

[1] (Camille Hyacinthe) Odilon Barrot, 1791–1873, French orator and statesman; a monarchist of the moderate left; briefly premier 1849.

[2] Mainz, 32 miles north of Mannheim. Cp. L. Hertslet, *Map of Europe*, i. 331 (1827).

[3] Eleven miles NNW. of Mannheim; over the frontier from Baden into Hesse-Darmstadt.

[4] Porters.

a steamboat from Rotterdam—this Inn being very distant from the river, but close to the Diligence office.

After all I had heard of the Rhine, I must confess I was most decidedly disappointed in its scenery. It has however very fine points: the majestic and powerful river, thus singularly secluded, and seeming to have high hills for its banks: the picturesque manner in which the ground is broken: the actual beauty of those numberless ruins which crown their heights, and the associations connected with them: the pleasing and romantic appearance of many of the towns, and of the huge timber rafts and vessels which we met: particularly the incessant shifting of the scene, by the rapid opening and closing of such a protracted succession of objects: are all singularly interesting. But the capital defect of almost the whole tract, want of wood, spoils the effect, at least to a person who has seen the Wye. The most beautiful part is from Coblenz[1] upwards half way to Mayence. The fortress of Ehrenbreitstein[2]—the town of Coblentz—the confluence of Rhine and Moselle,[3] each retaining its colour some time—and the seven hills of Bonn,[4] are among the objects of interest.—The bridges of boats at Mayence, Coblentz, and Cologne, are remarkable. From thirtyfive to forty boats are moored at intervals, alone or in pairs, across the stream—their horizontal position forming an arc, so as to resist the force of the stream by the principle of the arch. The superstructure seems extremely simple. At Mayence I should think the river is 5 to 600 yards wide—lower down, not more than two thirds of this, if so much. From Coblentz downwards the vale is more or less open—at length the hills retire altogether. We saw one pont volant such as those in Italy: and three or four of the rafts for conveying down the timber of which they are made—perhaps 200 yards long, or more.

Cologne[5]—58,000 inhab. 4000 soldiers. Purchased eau de Cologne & some German books. Took for our landlord a person who was extremely assiduous in getting us information & taking us about, at last discovered that he was a laquais-de-place. Went to S. Pierre, where is shown the font in which Rubens was baptised (near it, the house where he was born—) and the magnificent and highly finished picture of the Crucifixion of S. Peter. The colouring is rich beyond anything: but you look in vain, I think, for the *red* florid. The countenances seem to be the most remarkable part. A copy, executed by a man of Coblentz from memory, & as such extraordinary, tho' very coarsely executed & with very bad colouring—is shown first—then it turns round on a pivot, & the picture is revealed. It was done to supply the place of the original when the latter was in Paris. A baptism was going on: more decent than in Florence—and that is all.—A fixed sum is paid for seeing this glorious picture, & also the relics at the Cathedral—& applied to the uses of the fabrics. Great comparative simplicity in S. Pierre. Instead of

[1] Thirty-six miles NW. of Mainz.
[2] Twelfth century; rebuilt 1816–26, opposite Koblenz.
[3] Margin entry: 'the Rat Castle'.
[4] The Siebengebirge, some 12 miles SE. of Bonn across the Rhine. Bonn lies 35 miles NW. of Koblenz.
[5] Fifteen miles NNW. of Bonn.

the gorgeous ciborij[1] of Italy, a plain black box with lock & key, having "Emmanuel" painted on it.—At the Cathedral it is difficult to say whether there is more to admire or to lament. The work seemed to be going on: or at least, repairs. They say 700 feet is the entire length—and 560 meant to be the height of the two incipient towers when crowned with spires. We could not, by any liberality in our estimates, make out the former, or extend it much beyond 500—but one part was only to be seen through the glass, and may have deceived us.—

Tuesday July 24.

Our comfortable travelling—of which few I fancy have had a greater share —may now be considered at an end. Today we came in a kind of mail-post to Aix-la-Chappell or Achen.[2] We were 8¼ hours—and the distance may be forty miles. 6½ A.M.–2¾ P.M. Country generally flat: grows an immense quantity of corn: of which a good deal was cut & on the ground. The manner of cutting it is odd. The reaper or mower in one hand holds a short & sharp scythe, with which he cuts, by a sort of dashing motion, & in the other a pole equipped so as to catch what he has cut & prevent its falling: by means of the two he lays it down regularly, & without stooping. Pavè generally. Towns uninteresting of red brick. Gardens however & other characteristics of the villages, like England. Had to pay greatly for luggage: the conveyance being a malle-poste.[3] At Aix, we took up our quarters at the Hotel of the Diligences, called Hotel d'Hollande, and arranged to go to Brussels tomorrow. The whole disposition of the steamers seems as much against us as it could well have been. Hotel d'Hollande good: landlord reported a most bitter hatred between the people of Aix &c. & the French: they would rather have the Turks!

Went to the Cathedral: followed with a crowd into a small Chapel, when the official people were giving out that all the exhibition of the day (a grand festival of relics at Aix[4]) were over. But the people would not go, so by and bye they shut the door and exhibited a long series—collecting money, as they could, the while. They moved me little. The octagon part of the Church in whose centre Charlemagne[5] lies with the simple inscription "Carlo Magno" reminds one much of the antique Church of S. Vitalis at Ravenna— but here there are two stories of arches. *This* seems the old part. The tribune, in tall narrow Gothic, appears much more modern.

Wednesday July 25.

In the morning went to the "Pump-room" as I suppose it would be called

---

[1] Pyxes.
[2] Aachen, nearly 40 miles WSW. of Cologne.
[3] Mail-coach.
[4] Relics of Charlemagne and sacred relics presented to Charlemagne, supposedly such items as the Virgin's robe and the cloth on which the head of the Baptist was laid. They were shown only once every seven years, from 15–27 July.
[5] Ca. 742–814.

in England. Here are the springs, room, & promenade: & the building on a very large scale. This town is most largely supplied with Hotels.

9 A.M.–5 P.M. in the Diligence from Aix to Liege, two (German) posts & three quarters—about 25 miles.[1] Country rich, well wooded, generally pasture. Pave: much rise & fall, though without decided hill. Detained nearly 1½ hours at the Belgian Douane: all our things rummaged, books pulled out & weighed, and duty paid for carrying them through the country—they refused to plumb.[2] This is abominably bad, although the amount was under thirteen francs.

Liège, on the Meuse, in a dale—strong citadel—& fort on the opposite eminences, intended as a Belgian in the coach told us, to keep off the enemy *from Prussia*. He thought Liège had not suffered from the Revolution— perhaps because its manufactures (ironwork, particularly muskets and fowling-pieces, and cloth) are such as have been employed in furnishing the Belgian army: which now amounts (as a Belgian officer told me) to 120,000 men: the Hollanders about the same. This officer reported the Dutch cavalry better, & infantry inferior: said he did not know whether there were Polonese officers in the Belgian cavalry.

Dined well enough at Hotel des Diligences—and left at seven P.M. for Brussels, a distance of nearly seventy miles: which we accomplished in twelve hours. J.G's birthday was but unworthily kept in a diligence day & night. This[3] was however admirable for a diligence.

Thursday July 26.

Brussels looked brisk and well—we drove only through a line of principal streets: and left it for Ostende in less than an hour, which was well employed in inquiring (though very fruitlessly) for steamboats, and breakfasting at a Cafè. We left for Ostende at eight—stopped an hour at Ghent to dine—and arrived at our destination about 9.20 P.M. The Cour Imperiale was the first Inn we entered on the Continent, and we chose it as our last. Our travelling has been extremely good—80 miles in under 12½ hours. Pavè admirable—long avenues of beech, popular, & oak—struck by the amazing number of beer and spirit houses—our drivers stopped to drink in the middle of every stage. Harvest in progress: crops heavy. In general, they cut very low leaving barely any stubble, & seem to turn up the ground again immediately: in some places, a long stubble, and "privative jagt". (private shooting) written up. Ghent and Bruges appeared even more attractive, as towns, than they did before.

Friday–July 27.

A day at Ostende—as there is no steamer till tomorrow. The difficulty of obtaining information about steamboats before arriving at the immediate vicinity of the place whence they start, is immense. The country appeared

---

[1] To the WSW. of Aix; 54 miles SE. of Brussels.
[2] To put a leaden seal on the luggage.
[3] 'dis[tance]' deleted here.

to wonderfully greater advantage than in February, but still it is anything rather than beautiful in the vicinity of Ostende.—The military are now fewer on this side of the country than when we started hence. At present they are chiefly concentrated upon Brussels, Antwerp, Liege, Ghent, Louvain,[1] & towards Masstricht.[2] Their general appearance is that of extreme youth. We passed a regiment near Bruges, of which I should have said there was not a man in it, of the rank and file, who was over twenty years of age: and a good many as low as fifteen.

Our employments chiefly indoors, for Ostende is as devoid of attractions as any place can well be—except indeed that it has the sea, which here however is of a dingy brown. The town is clean, & the streets airy. We observed in the (principal?) Church abundance of worshippers: one man, decently dressed, keeping his arms fully extended but with a slight upward inclination for a considerable time; I never saw this but once, in the case of an old woman at St Peter's. I made a feeble and fruitless attempt to recover the duties we had paid: and learned that the proper course is, to engage the director of the diligence to be your surety and take over your effects into his possession till you quit the territory—but this I suppose forces you to keep to the same establishment for coaches all through the country. A foreigner would probably rather pay a sum if at all moderate than take the trouble which might be necessary.

Saturday July 28.

About 10¾ A.M. we left Ostende—and in less than eight hours arrived at Dover, in the Salamander, Capt. Mudge[3]—tide against us nearly all the way, a gentle breeze in our favour. Walked energetically up and down the deck most of the passage, as did Cole, to keep down seasickness, and succeeded, tho' not wholly unaffected by the feelings which usually precede the catastrophe.

Dover has as bad landing when the tide is low as can well be conceived: and the boatmen are extortioners, some among them too, insolent ones: but I believe exceedingly brave. Got rapidly through the customhouse, under the auspices of Mr Birmingham the Comm[issionai]r[e] of the Ship Hotel—where we had tea—our box however had been left behind by Luigi's carelessness, and we had subsequently some difficulty in regaining it. "Always look after your luggage yourself" is a wise precept even when we had a servant whose special business it was to do so. After making numerous payments (prices of porterage most exorbitant) we started for London in the[4] Mail. It seemed like magic after the Diligences—but I did not sleep a wink, voilà la difference—a straight & hard back instead of an inclined an easy one.—We found the Customhouse officers civil, reasonable, & expeditious—and of a genus infinitely superior to the foreign doganieri. No winking nor cheating, little bowing and scraping.

[1] Fifteen miles east by north of Brussels.
[2] Nineteen miles NNE. of Liège.
[3] Zachary *Mudge, 1770–1852; capt. R.N. 1800, admiral 1849.
[4] 'Liverpool' lightly deleted.

We arrived in London about seven on Sunday morning, after a journey as free, thanks to God, from indisposition and from accident, as any man could desire.

The country (when day broke, very early) well cultivated and the towns along the route beautifully clean.—

I may here put down opinions upon several of the books much used by Tourists.

Mrs Starke attempts too much by striving to compress all into one volume. She is often diffuse, and has many broad blanks—as for instance Switzerland. She appears in an unfavourable light, whenever she leaves the plain track of detail. Her description of the Italian antiquities is perhaps the best part of her book, (which we have had an opportunity of putting to proof) account of the Splugen road absolutely disgraceful. Much useful information in her appendix, and elsewhere too. Distances frequently incorrect.

Ebel's Germany—very concise and contains a vast deal of information in a very small space. It wants however the *description* of the routes.

Ebel's Switzerland—seems to deserve its reputation: but we had not time to try it fairly.

Dan. Wilson ought never to have been published. His religious information is very valuable, his spirit excellent: but the work is extremely hasty: style diffuse: descriptions overdrawn: statements frequently erroneous.

Forsyth's Italy I think as to moral tone demands no very high commendation. But he has taste & accomplishment & information in abundance: is wonderfully spirited & acute, & happy in the choice of his expressions: though perhaps he would sometimes sacrifice exactitude for pointedness.

Matthews I think enjoys much more reputation than he deserves. Though his remarks are often clever and his descriptions lively & amusing, his book is, as a whole, incomplete: he does not seem to have fixed and regulated principles of taste, nor to have duly educated the faculty.

Burton's Rome is faithful and full of information, commonly I fancy to be relied on: but dry & hard: seems only [to] view that [most] wonderful of city as a collection of sights—certainly it has many nobler aspects.—

In England again,[1] safe & well thank God, and having enjoyed many opportunities of mental advancement in a short space, however little they have been turned to account.

Sunday July 30 [sc. 29].

We took up our quarters at the Burlington Hotel early in the morning. St Philip's Church in the morning. Mr Repton[2] preached: addressed himself pretty closely to his Congregation—and spoke of the cholera. Went between services to see my Uncle & Aunt Divie who received us with their wonted kindness—and we dined there. In the afternoon I went to St James's and heard as usual a very good sermon there, much on the cholera. It is no small matter to have regained the stated ordinances of our beloved Church.—I found Tom waiting in Town to go with me to Newark if need should be.

Monday July 31 [sc. 30] to Tuesday Aug. 14.

These days were spent in an amphibious state between that of candidate and of ἰδιώτης.[3]

My Brother having written to the Duke [of Newcastle] on Sat. we thought an answer might arrive on Tuesday—but as none came, I wrote then my-self to announce my being actually arrived: & received in answer on Satur-day a letter from the Duke written in a very kind and friendly tone: and inclosing one from Mr Godfrey, President of the Red Club,[4] recommending my writing an Address &c—I took a copy of this letter, and spent the day in the occupations consequent. Made three draughts of addresses & at length got one into what we considered a practicable form: dispatched it to Newark, & a copy to the Duke.[5] A letter from Mr G[odfrey] came by return of post, announcing that he had made some trifling alterations and that the Address would be published as [sc. on] Monday. He also gave me another day's work, in writing letters, to Lord Winchilsea,[6] Ld Middleton,[7] Mr Holden,[8] Rev. T. Manners Sutton,[9] and Mr Tallents[10]—all electioneering—

---

[1] Lambeth MS 1420 resumed.

[2] Edward Repton, 1783?–1860, a s. of Humphry *Repton the gardener; priest at St. Philip's, Regent Street, 1820; canon of Westminster and chaplain to the house of commons 1838.

[3] 'private person.' Version in Morley, i. 89.

[4] Edward Smith Godfrey, chairman of *Gladstone's election committee; copy of letter in Add MS 44261, f. 2.

[5] Drafts in Add MS 44722, ff. 2–4. Text in Robbins, 118–19.

[6] George William *Finch-Hatton, 1791–1858, extreme protestant tory; succ. as 11th earl of Winchilsea and 5th of Nottingham 1826; fought duel against *Wellington 1829.

[7] Henry Willoughby, 6th baron Middleton, 1761–1835, tory; succ. 1800; voted for reform bill 1832.

[8] Robert Holden, d. 1844, of Nuthall Temple, near Nottingham; local magnate.

[9] Thomas Manners-Sutton, 1795–1844; nephew of abp.; canon of Lincoln.

[10] William Edward Tallents, 1780?–1837; eminent country solicitor; town clerk of Newark 1806–33, later *Gladstone's agent there.

of which some were dispatched that day and some the next. An answer came from Mr Tallents—and I had further letters to write putting more specifically the question whether I should go to Newark or not, as a letter had come from my Father declaring his opinion that the point was not sufficiently cleared by what had come from the Duke. Mr Godfrey being absent from Newark his answer on this point did not reach me till Monday the 13th, but was then so decisive as to set me wholly at Liberty: I then received the Nottingham paper with my Address, & a short favourable paragraph:[1] also a letter from Lord Winchilsea acceding to my request of his support. On Tuesday I found myself denounced in an advertisement of the Antislavery folk, published in the Guardian, as a person who they were persuaded would not cooperate in the promotion of their objects—which were, I thought, described in most Jesuitical terms. Lord Sandon was also, like me, in "Schedule A".[2] I had occasion to call upon him in the course of the morning, and, apparently without personal soreness, he spoke in strong terms of their conduct. All I say is, God help the poor slaves, whose interests I fear will be torn in pieces between the contending parties. In my soul and conscience, as I shall answer at the day of judgment, I do not feel that I have any bias on that question: nor is this at all laying claim to superior impartiality: for I think I could account for it intelligibly enough to any moderate person.

My own employments have been almost summed up in writing to Torquay, to Liverpool, to various friends, to Newark &c—& in copying my own electioneering letters—reading the papers & Mirror of Parliament[3]— 'Letters on Ireland'[4]—Wordsworth—Christian Knowledge Tracts, e.g. Facts & Assertions, Man created & renewed &c., The unfruitful Fig Tree, Cheap Repository—beginning Evans's Sermons[5] & Le Bas' Life of Wiclif:[6] making calls, closing our accounts for the journey, and shopping of various kinds. I had to lay in a stock of books for Torquay. About every other day I dined at my Uncle Divie's: with Tom until, Sat. Aug. 11, he went down to Liverpool, in consequence of a summons from Portarlington.[7] John left us for Torquay on Tuesday July 31—The large box left, as we found to our dismay when Luigi came up to London, at Ostende, only reached us on Wed. Aug. 8. On Friday Aug. 10 we heard of the truly distressing death of J.M.G. Robertson in Bombay: but his soul is in peace. On Saturday my cousin Will[ia]m[8] arrived from New York—and on Sunday I heard from

[1] *Nottingham Journal*, 11 August 1832; address on p. 1, five lines on p. 3. Cp. Robbins, 120.

[2] *Gladstone and *Sandon were among nineteen candidates listed by the Agency Anti-Slavery Committee in a schedule of strong supporters of slavery in a *Guardian* advertisement of 14 August 1832.

[3] Verbatim reports of speeches, ed. J. H. Barrow (1828–41).

[4] Perhaps the anonymous *Letters from an Irish Student in England to his Father in Ireland*, 2v. (1809), gossip about English customs.

[5] Caleb Evans, s. of John *Evans of Islington; his *Sermons* published posthumously with an introduction by his f. (1822).

[6] C. W. *Le Bas, *Life of *Wiclif*, vol. i in H. J. *Rose and W. R. *Lyall, *Theological Library*.

[7] His prospective Irish constituency, in Co. Kildare.

[8] William Gladstone, 1809–73, London merchant; Robert Gladstone's 3rd s.

Robn to my sorrow but not surprise, of the death of my cousin Thomas[1] in Demerara. How we are spared, even in the midst of a destructive epidemic!

Saturday, Aug. 4.

I saw Harrison & went down in the evg. to stay Sunday with him. His family appeared admirably regulated. At Clapham Church on Sunday I heard Dr Dealtry[2] in the morning, and Mr Murray, once a Scotch barrister[3] in the afternoon. Monday mg I went to see the Pickerings & came to town with Mr Harrison,[4] who was good enough to take me over Guy's Hospital, on which he as Treasurer has gratuitously conferred inestimable services. The cleanliness of everything I saw was beyond belief—in this it appeared far to surpass the immense Albergo dei Poveri at Genoa.[5] There are 530 inpatients—6000 regular *out*—and from 100 to 150 (more or less) come for temporary relief daily. There is also a refuge for 20 incurable lunatics. The patients attend prayers in the Chapel every morning, & on Sundays twice. None are excused but either those who, as Jews, have strong & decided objections, or those who are too unwell to attend, in which case they are also accounted too unwell to go out & visit their friends.—I then went to do some business in the city & call at the Charterhouse for Saunders, of whose expected arrival I had heard from Colin Larkins. I missed him but he came to see me at the Albany next day, and I wrote by him to Lincoln, as again in a day or two by post. That evening we went to Mrs Alexander's in the Regent's Park,[6] where there was a small party & very good music— particularly from the Miss Spottiswoode's,[7] who sang many songs together, particularly "The Rhine".[8] Their style not elaborate, but extremely spirited and captivating. Miss Marg. Spottiswoode both in face & form came quite up to the descriptions I had heard of her.

Monday Aug 13 I called on Mr Russell a barrister[9] to ask for his support— and did not find him: but afterwards went through a visit very singular & dangerous of which the consequences I would hope may be good to all the parties concerned.[10]

On Wednesday Aug. 1. Tom in the morning detailed to me at great length all the particulars of an affair which had concerned him nearly, in a

[1] Stewart.

[2] William *Dealtry, 1775–1847, Cambridge divine, professor of mathematics at Hailey-bury; rector of Clapham 1813–30. Clapham, long since swallowed up by London, was then a Surrey village some 3 miles south of Westminster, famous for the 'Clapham sect' of evangelicals.

[3] David Rodney Murray, 1791–1878; nephew of 7th Lord Elibank; rector of Brampton Brian, Hereford, 1826.

[4] Benjamin *Harrison, 1771–1856, succ. his father as treasurer of Guy's hospital 1797; had a villa on the edge of Clapham Common

[5] See 10 Mar. 32.

[6] Either Mrs. Alexander of 12 Hanover Terrace, or Mrs. Robert Alexander of 16 Sussex Place.

[7] Das. of John Spottiswoode of Great George Street.

[8] J. T. Craven 'The Rhine the Rhine your own sweet river' (1825).

[9] George Lake Russell, 1802–78, 5th s. of Sir Henry *Russell, bart.,; of Lincoln's Inn; later Bloomsbury county court judge.

[10] Untraced escapade.

manner such as to make him appear then, I thought, though under circumstances of most peculiar difficulty, more manly highminded & judicious than ever. I accompanied him then to [Grea]t G[eorg]e St, and also twice afterwards—would that I could have been of more use to him, and that the issue of all may conduce to his eternal good.[1]

On Wed. Aug. 8. we dined with Sir R. Inglis at Battersea Rise & had a very pleasant evening. Met Dr Dealtry, Mr Sp. Perceval, Mr & Mrs Northcote,[2] the Thorntons[3] &c. The grounds behind the house are remarkably pretty.

Tuesday night—I went to Mrs Macleod's[4] in great Cumberland Street, where there was very good music ("the Rhine" again) and dancing which seemed to pass off ill. Mrs M. & her daughter[5] agreeable.

Wed. Aug. 15.

Breakfast in Bedford Square—wrote to T.G. packing and shopping—enough to do. Left town at 4¾ by the Subscription Exeter coach, outside from necessity—an excellent conveyance: beautiful night, which I enjoyed exceedingly. country rich and towns everywhere pleasing till evening closed in. Letter from D. of N. to T.G.

Aug 16.

Again in the morning we had an opportunity of enjoying & admiring English domestic scenery. Arrived in Exeter about 1¼ P.M. came on by the two horse [post-chaise] at (past) 1½—arrived in Torquay at 6. Country beautiful: fully realised all my anticipations. Found all as well as I could have ventured to hope—and relished heartily my first evening at home.

Friday. 17.

J.N.G. & H.J.G. went in the yacht & had a gale at night. Read papers—& began Bp Sandford's Memoir.[6] Reading divers letters &c. & settling accounts. Out in phaeton, with my Father & Mother.

Saturday. 18.

Yacht returned—all had been sick. papers. finished Bp Sandford's Memoir —read part of Ld Henley's Church Reform[7]—& began Thaddeus of Warsaw.[8] Rode Helen's mare. Long conv. at night with my Father & John chiefly—about her.

[1] Untraced escapade.

[2] Henry Stafford Northcote, 1792–1851, eldest s. of 7th bart., and his wife Agnes Mary Cockburn, d. 1840.

[3] Orphan children of Henry *Thornton: see *DNB* lvi. 303.

[4] Anne, neé Stephenson, m. 1809, John Norman Macleod, d. 1835, M.P. for Sudbury [Eatanswill] 1828–30, of Dunvegan Castle, Isle of Skye.

[5] Emily Sarah, d. unm. 1896.

[6] John *Sandford's *Remains* of his f., the bp. of Edinburgh, 2v. (1830).

[7] R. H. *Eden, 2nd Lord Henley (*Peel's brother-in-law), *A plan of Church Reform*, a pamphlet against non-residence and for more bps.

[8] Jane *Porter's romantic novel of a Polish count in English society (1803); see *DNB* xlvi. 182–3.

Sunday. 19.

Church very well attended & very good music. Mr Clark[1] preached twice. sound, earnest, & intelligible. My Father, John, & Helen, went off to Cowes in the Evg. Read "a Diss[enting] M[iniste]r's fourteen reasons "[2]—Evans—and began Mr Meek's Reasons for conformity.[3] Copied a letter.

Monday 20.

Finished Ld Henley's Plan of Reform in the Church. Read Preface to my Charles I.[4] Tracts. And began Corinne.[5] Called with my Mother on Mr Clark and Mrs Leigh[6]—and drove her to Mr Ley's beautiful rustic residence, where I met a brother of Jacob's.[7] Paper.

21.

A letter to T.G. A good deal of conversation with my dear Mother. Heard from P. Handley. read papers—an admirable article in the Standard of the 18th. Read Corinne and the First Part of May's Breviary.[8] Abstract &c.

22.

2nd Part of May's Breviary, & abstract. Ch Miss[ionary Society] meeting—heard Mr Woodroffe,[9] Sir H.M. Neale,[10] &c.—rode beyond Newton[11]—paper—wrote to F.B. Cole—read most of Ivimey's Tract[12]—Cholera Service at $6\frac{1}{2}$, and sermon by Mr Gee, the Rector.[13] Congregation large & apparently attentive. May many hearts be opened by this manifest visitation, and the kingdom of the Redeemer enlarged.

23.

Finished Ivimey, and Breviary. Read Lilly's observations on Ch[arles] I, and D. of Newcastle's Address. Began Plato's republic, of which I intend

[1] Probably John Clarke, 1805?–70, of Harberton, 9 miles west of Torquay.
[2] Untraced tract.
[3] Robert Meek, *Reasons for attachment and conformity to the Church of England* (1831).
[4] W. *Lilly the astrologer, *Several Observations upon the Life and Death of Charles late King of England* in his *Monarchy or No Monarchy* (1651); notes in Add MS 44722, ff. 12–14.
[5] By Mme. de Staël (1807).
[6] Wife of Clarke's curate Peter Leigh.
[7] Jacob Ley, f. of Jacob Ley of Christ Church, rector of Ashprington, 5 miles SW. of Torquay, since 1796. His 2nd s. John, fellow of Exeter 1831, was rector of Waldron, Devonshire, from 1851.
[8] Thomas *May, *A Breviary of the History of the Parliament of England* (1650).
[9] Nathaniel George Woodroffe, 1765?–1851, vicar of Somerford Keynes, Wiltshire, 1803.
[10] Sir Harry Burrard *Neale, 1765–1840, admiral; 2nd bart. 1791; helped quell Nore mutiny; tory M.P. Lymington 1800–35; c.-in-c., Mediterranean, 1823–6.
[11] Newton Abbot, 5 miles NW. of Torquay.
[12] Joseph *Ivimey wrote many tracts; perhaps his 'Triumph of the Bible in Ireland' (1832).
[13] Robert Gee, 1786?–1861; wrangler 1807; rector of Thornton-in-Craven, Yorkshire, 1813; vicar of Paignton by Torquay 1832.

making an analysis.[1] papers. Heard from Mr Godfrey, & wrote a long account of my views about slavery, in answer to queries which have been put to him. Drove Mrs G. & Mr & Mrs Leigh out.

24.

Wrote a draught & copy to Mr Godfrey. Corinne—Began D. Hollis's memoirs[2]—papers—a little Plato—rode—Mr Gwillym[3] called—Mr Canning's Memoirs. Our sailing folk returned.

25.

Wrote draught & copy to the Duke of Newcastle. Wrote to Aunt E.[4] heard from F.B. Cole.—Plato—Hollis's Memoirs—Article in Quarterly called "Stages of the Revolution"—Corinne—and papers. Walk with J.N.G.

26. Sunday.

Church mg & aftn. Walked over & about the hill behind our house. Copied a letter. Read Evans, and Le Bas's Life of Wiclif.

27.

Corinne. Resumed an old practice—reading the Bible with Helen. May God grant it be not without its fruit in amended tempers & a heavenly conversation. Blackstone[5] Sect. 1. Analysis, & writing on Liberty—Analysis of Lilly—and Plato. Papers.

28.

Corinne. Plato & Analysis. A long article in the Quarterly Review on Lord Nugent's Life of Hampden: some important citations, & impartial, as well as partial, remarks. Out in the yacht, & among Sir P. Malcolm's Squadron.[6] Went over the Vernon,[7] attended by two of J.N.G.'s acquaintances on board. She is a magnificent frigate of 50 guns, having the tonnage of a 74—upwards of 2000 tons. Guns all 32 pounders. All the improvements are concentrated in this vessel. A beautiful stern, much rounded beneath, square above. Height on the maindeck above six feet under the beams. She beats the whole squadron. Dined at Mr Legh's[8]—met Mr Gwillym, & in the

---

[1] Add MS 44722, ff. 27–50 and 292–7; not completed for sixteen months.

[2] Denzil *Holles, *Memoirs 1641–1648* (1699). Notes in Add MS 44722, ff. 14v.–16.

[3] John Gwillim, 1783?–1859; All Souls 1805; rector of Bridenbury, Hereford, from 1810.

[4] Described as to his aunt Joanna in Bassett, 25–26.

[5] Sir William *Blackstone, *Commentaries on the Laws of England* (1765–9, often reprinted), long the standard work.

[6] Sir Pulteney *Malcolm, 1768–1838, fighting sailor; c.-in-c., Mediterranean, 1828–31 and 1833–4.

[7] Commanded by (Sir) Francis Augustus *Collier, 1783?–1849; capt., R.N., 1808; suppressed piracy in Persian Gulf 1819–20; kt. 1830; rear-adm. 1846.

[8] Peter Leigh.

evening a clever man, the Rev. Mr Strong[1] (I think). Read Denzil Hollis's Memoirs. Heard from Seymer. Bible with H.J.G. in morning.

29. Wed.

Corinne—Plato (began 2nd book) papers—Quarterly Review on Todd's Cranmer: a little Blackstone—& Analyses. Bible with H.J.G. Drove with Mr G. to Marychurch[2] &c—Wrote to Gaskell.

30. Th.

Yacht went to sea again. Rode. Wrote to Childers. Blackstone—Plato Republic (began B.2)—and abstracts. Corinne—Bible with H.J.G.—and paper.

31. Fr.

Corinne—Blackstone, Plato, & Abstracts. walk—partly with Mrs G, on the shore & about Tor Abbey.[3] It is a lovely spot, and such as one might well conceive an exiled religion would select to pour consolation into the wounds of her afflicted children. But I do not know that its possessors[4] are of this description. Papers: & in the evening, a long and interesting conversation with my dear Mother on the subject of the religious state of this family. Alas! it is a topic full of anxiety.—Made up my monthly accounts.

Saturday September 1.

Plato & Analysis. Finished B.2. Wordsworth—Corinne—wrote a few lines —called on the Gwillyms & Dr Scully.[5] Disposed of some Christian Knowledge Tracts to poor & chiefly old people. Papers. yachters returned. Wrote a long letter to Tom; & ventured upon a solemn subject. May God's mercy neutralise the errors & effectuate the truths if truths there be, of that which was written. Copied a letter. Letter from Jephson opened.

2. Sunday.

Scriptures with H.J.G.—Copied a letter. Is this as Naaman bowed down before Rimmon?[6] Scripture alone. Life of Wiclif, & Evans's Sermons—a splendid book. This day the Sacrament was administered, and we all knelt together at the Altar. May the Father of Mercies bless his own ordained mysteries, and may we attain to more than an outward unity. At present I dare not rely much here. I do not feel that [we] are on a sound footing as a Christian family, which is a Christian Church: but the Lord reigneth.

---

[1] Thomas Strong, 1770?–1860, rector of Clyst St. Mary, 15 miles north of Torquay, 1795, and of Theberton, Suffolk, 1819; res. 1841.
[2] The northern suburb of Torquay.
[3] Norbertine monastery, founded 1196; extensive ruins remained.
[4] George Henry Carey; his family had had its seat there since 1662.
[5] William Sculley, graduated at Edinburgh 1801–3; Irish origin; Torquay physician.
[6] II Kings v. 18.

3. Monday.

Called on Mr Legh who gave us some geological account of Kent's Cavern.[1] Out with Helen in the Schooner. Paper. Saturday Mag.[2]—Plato & Abstract: a little Blackstone: finished Vol 1. of Corinne: looked over Mr Wilks's "Church Establishment Lawful &c".[3] & had some conv. with Raby[4] on board to whom I gave a copy of it. Bible with H.J.G. Copied a letter.

4. T.

Bible with H.J.G.—Began 2nd Vol. of Corinne. Drive with Mr & Mrs G. An interesting morning at Mr MacEnery's (the R.C. Priest)[5] seeing the fossil remains from Kent's Cavern: read Plato—& papers—Blomfield's (+) Duty of Family Prayer[6]—heard from Gaskell.

5. Wednesday.

Scripture with H.J.G. Corinne—of wh I have read much yesterday and to-day, being a good deal interested. It is not however a satisfactory book in the subject of religion, tho' not devoid of the feeling by any means.—Plato & Abstract. Papers. A long ride with Mr Gwillym to Greenway &c—beautiful views of the river Dart.[7] My Father John & Helen left us for Leamington —I *hope* soon to return but am not confident.

6. Th.

Notes to Testament. Finished 3d Book of Republic & abstract—[read] Corinne, very interesting & much to be learned from it—paper—renewing some of my old poetical extracts in my memory—drove my Mother out— wrote to my Father & copied him part of a letter from Uncle D.

7. Fr.

Read a great deal of Corinne & little of anything else. Plato & Abstract— paper. Wrote to my Father. rode—Mrs G unwell with headach—dined at Mr Leighs—a pleasant evening—Mr Waldie,[8] Mr Strong, Mr Gwillym.

8. Sat.

Finished Corinne. It is as regards power over the feelings indeed a masterly work—I at least felt it to be such, as it was vain to resist. It is painful to see that it takes a very partial & therefore fallacious view of that religion which has often soothed in real life sorrows as deep & inward as those with which she has charged the destiny of her Corinne.

[1] See 19 Sept. 32.
[2] Weekly S.P.C.K. publication, begun in July.
[3] S. C. *Wilks, *Correlative Claims and Duties* (1821).
[4] Local yacht proprietor.
[5] John McEnery, priest at Tor Abbey.
[6] C. J. *Blomfield, *Manual of Family Prayers* (new ed., 1831).
[7] South-westward from Torquay.
[8] Probably Richard Waldy, 1795–1868, vicar of Affpuddle, Dorset, 1824, and canon of Salisbury 1849.

Wrote to Seymer—& in Italian! to Luigi Lamonica. read Plato. paper. Mrs G. better. account from H.J.G. they had had an escape in the bad weather. thank God! read Mr M'Ghee's letter to the Record[1]—wrote some notes & quotations to my Testament—rode out—and dined at Lord Sinclair's. Much pleased with him & his Lady[2]—& Mr Waldie too with whom I had a great deal of conversation.

Sunday 9 Sep.

A perplexing letter calling me to Newark in a few days time grievously broke in upon this day of rest. With my Mother's aid made the best arrangements I could, & wrote, there being no time to lose, to the Duke of N., Mr Godfrey, my Father, & Robertson.

Church morning & afternoon—Two very good sermons from Mr Clarke whose frank earnest & sincere manner proves I trust winning to many a heart in his crowded & attentive congregation. Even so, O Lord Jesus, may thy sheep be reclaimed from the power of the adversary.

Read Evans's—Le Bas's Wiclif—& Meek's Reasons for conformity.

10. M.

(Little) Plato & Abstract. Blackstone & Hollis's Memoirs, without, papers. wrote to T.G. & to Ld Lincoln. At Lady Sinclair's & went with their party to Mrs Johness place:[3] much labour & taste, & views lovely—rode out, with the phaeton—Notes to Greek Testament—Singular sensations while going to bed at night.

11. T.

Called on Dr Scully—drove my Mother & Mr Waldie to Whetcombe Rocks,[4] where also Ld Sinclair came with his lady & family. Capital exercise running about the cliffs & hills. A very idle day, for a particular reason: i.e. the idea of the continuance of the same sensations. Clem. Walker's "Mystery of the two Juntoes"[5]—began Behemoth:[6] Bible: &c. Bp Sandford's Diary.

Wed. Sept. 12.

Read papers, & Bp Sandford's Diary—wrote to Robn—much against my will had this day wholly cut up by an expedition to Teignmouth & Dawlish[7]

---

[1] A letter from R. J. M'Ghee on Irish education filled over four columns of *The Record*, 12 July 1832.

[2] Charles St. Clair, 1768–1863, 13th lord Sinclair 1775; Scottish tory representative peer 1807–59; m. 1816 Isabella Mary Chatto, who d. 1875.

[3] Woodbine Cottage, described as 'most elegant' in a local guide (*Panorama of Torquay* (1830), 19).

[4] Rocky valley by Watcombe Head, 2 miles north of Torquay.

[5] Clement *Walker, 'The Mystery of the Two Juntoes, Presbyterian and Independent' (1647), an acrimonious attack by one of its members on the long parliament's system of government. Notes in Add MS 44722, f. 17.

[6] T. *Hobbes, *Behemoth: History of the Causes of the Civil Wars of England* (1681). Notes ibid. ff. 20v.–21.

[7] Seven and 10 miles north of Torquay, on the coast.

with Mr Waldie & Mrs G—(agst my Mother's will too). Mr Waldie dined with us. Equivocal account from Leamington.

13. Th.

Account from Leamington rendering it I think pretty certain that they will go there forthwith & for the winter. Wrote briefly to Mr Godfrey in consequence—as I got a letter from him yesterday recommending my drawing near. Wrote to the Duke of N.—Plato Republic & Abstract. finished B.4. Also Bp Sandford—paper. a long ride on the side of King's Kerswell & Abbot's Kerswell.[1]

There appears to be little doubt that the Cholera is now in Torquay & not very far removed from our own dwelling. One person, or two, have died: said to be bad livers. May God here & elsewhere sanctify this awful instrument of his will to the general softening of our obstinacy, & the salvation of many souls.—My Mother read the Church prayer in the evening, & in a very impressive manner.[2]

14. Fr.

Plato & Abstract—Bp. Sandford's Letters. heard from R.G.—rode out—papers—B. Harrison's Essay on Language—[3] does him great credit me jud[ice]—writing fragments.[4]

15. Sat.

Wrote to J.N.G.—to Mr Kitson. Heard from Lincoln. from Mr Godfrey. Determination for instant removal to Leamington announced—& Mr G. arrived by steamer. Drove my Mother & Lady Sinclair—rode home—grey mare threw me—papers—Plato—that singular & monstrous part of his 5th Book de Republica in which he explains in detail the doctrine of community of women & children &c. &c. What a melancholy exhibition it is! Yet it generally consists, like many popular reasonings of this day, not of absolute falsehoods, but of half truths.—Bp Sandford—& writing fragments.

16. Sunday.

Church morning & afternoon. began to write on the subject of Baptism—God prosper it.—Mr Meek—Life of Wiclif—& 2 Sermons of Bp Sandford. Copied a short Letter. Heard from the Duke of Newcastle.

17. M.

Most of the forenoon occupied in an interesting conversation with my Mother, mainly on the nature of Baptism, & embracing family concerns. It

[1] Four and 5 miles NW. of Torquay.
[2] Special collect circulated for the service of 21 March 1832, and used thereafter in places threatened by the disease.
[3] B. *Harrison, 'The Study of Different Languages, as it relates to the Philosophy of the Human Mind', chancellor's prize essay, Oxford 1832.
[4] On *Harrison's essay; Add MS 44820, ff. 18 and 96v.

is painful, but I feel when speaking on any religious question that I am always at bottom seeking to glorify myself.—papers—Orlando Furioso[1]—ample work for my Dictionary. a ride—forgathered with Lord Sinclair—Mr Gwillym called & we appointed Wednesday for Kent's Cavern—wrote to Gaskell—& began to write up my Journal[2]—& Scraps.

18. T.

Wrote to Harrison (chiefly on subject of his Essay)—J.N.G.—& Ld Middleton in answer to a letter from him. Walk. read Sir J. Berkley's Tract[3]—Orlando Furioso—papers—worked at Journal, & wrote in Black Book.

19. W.

Wrote to A. Pakenham & T.G. Heard from J.N.G. Journal—Orlando Furioso—Fairfax's Short Memoirs & Huntingdon's reasons[4]—paper—Athenaeum—spent some hours at Kent's Cavern—in digging & hammering, with Mr Gwillym & Hegarty the guide. We brought home some specimens. It has already been much knocked about. No good stalactites remain. I should suppose a great proportion of its geological treasures hitherto unexplored. Extent said to be 500 yards—I think considerably less. Distance from the sea, & elevation above it considerable. None of the chambers very large: passages narrow, particularly the oven. People should go in old clothes & a cap.—Much packing—J.N.G's things.

20. Th.

Orlando Furioso. Finished Vol 1. of Masares's Collection of Tracts—Journal—wrote to London on business—papers—scrubbing & gumming my geological specimens, not I fear to their advantage. Packing—dined at Mr Leighs—met Ld Sinclair, Mr Dawson,[5] & Mr Strong.—besides themselves & Miss Stewart.[6] My Mother not well. *We* had a pleasant evening. Yesterday a second case of Cholera occurred. The man is dead—he had been tipsy on Monday & Tuesday. This sad fact will at least go to diminish apprehension. God be praised for his mercy to us.

21. Fr.

Copied some letters—read Orlando Furioso—the first book of the Excursion[7]—part of Sir A. Edmonstone's Leonora[8]—Journal—writing in verse &

---

[1] Ariosto.
[2] Cp. 17 Apr. 32, p. 75.
[3] *Memoirs of Sir John *Berk[e]ley* (1699); notes in Add MS 44722, f. 18.
[4] F. *Maseres, *Select Tracts relating to the Civil Wars in England*, 2v. (1815), included *May, *Lilly, *Holles, *Berkeley, *Fairfax, and *Huntington. Notes on the last-named in Add MS 44722, ff. 19–20.
[5] Perhaps George Dawson, b. 1804?, fellow of Exeter 1827–41, then rector of Woodleigh, Devon.
[6] Aunt or sister of Robert Stewart of Torquay, gentleman.
[7] *Wordsworth (1814).
[8] Sir A. *Edmonstone, *Leonora* (1832), romantic verse tragedy.

prose—papers—walked up to the ancient Chapel beyond Tor—the prospect thence is of luxuriant beauty.

22. Saturday.

Wrote to Duke of Newcastle. reading as usual, in quiet & now settled expectation of departure with them on Monday. Finished my Journal. Walked to Babbicombe over the hill,[1] & much enjoyed the excursion. Farewell call on Mr Leigh & saw Mr Clarke too who was extremely kind.

23. Sunday.[2]

I lay half dosing between 7 & 8 in the morning, & contemplating nothing else than a tranquil day—my Father burst in (at 7¾) & said there was a summons from Leamington, I must get up immediately—the Canvass was going on and my presence necessary. I rode dressed & breakfasted speedily, with infinite disgust—I left Torquay at 8¾, and devoted my Sunday to the journey. Was I right? I thought so at the time—yet when hurry and bustle are added to the urgency of convenience, one stands but a poor chance of judging impartially.

My Father drove me to Newton [Abbot]—chaise to Exeter—there near an hour: went to the Cathedral, and heard a part of the prayers—mail to London—conversation with a Tory countryman who got in for a few miles, on Sunday travelling, which we agreed in disapproving, at least under all ordinary circumstances—gave him some tracts. Excellent mail—dined at Yeovil: read a little of 'The Christian Year'.[3]

24. M.

6½ A.M. arrived in Piccadilly—18½ h. from Exeter. Went to Fetter Lane—washed—breakfasted—and came off at 8 o'clock by the Highflyer[4] for Newark. The sun lowered red and cold through the heavy fog of London sky, but in the country the day was fine—found the road flat; much of the country well wooded. Tea at Stamford. arrived at Newark at midnight—the details of my visit I propose to write elsewhere.[5] Found R. & J.N.G. & affairs in prosperous condition.

25. Tuesday.

Wrote home—after breakfast, speech, canvass from 9½ till about 6—speech again—dinner—short speech again—meeting with some 30 Methodists & others on Slavery—speech, on that subject again. conversation with my Brothers & writing letters at night.

[1] One and a half miles NE. of Torquay.
[2] Late entries till 9 Oct. (see 12 Oct.) 32.
[3] Extracts in Morley, i. 90.
[4] The York coach.
[5] See 17 Oct. 32, end. Cp. also Cornelius Brown, *Annals of Newark* (1879), 274ff.
40—I.

26. Wed.

A quiet day, on account of a cheese fair[1]—private canvassing principally in the outskirts: went to see the Assembly & reading rooms—Letters.

27. Thursday.

Canvass till about four—wild meeting—partial collision in the market place—speech afterwards—Dinner—speech afterwards—Club, and speech. Mr T. Godfrey[2] also spoke there; went to Mrs Corden's[3] by her invitation— Mr Tallents also spoke from our window—published an Address.[4]

28. Friday.

A day of private canvassing—duller work than the public—Robertson went away early in the morning—during all this period, I was corresponding with the Duke and home—wrote also to T.G.—Lincoln—Doyle—and others. We now likewise began to enter into discussions or inquiries about the expences. The private Canvass gave some opportunity of verifying the promises made on the public one.—A Club at night.

29. Saturday.

Another day of private canvassing—partly in Mr Tallents's Carriage—a Club at night. I had little time on my weekdays for reading, except the paper now & then & some accounts of Newark elections.

30. Sunday.

Bible—Evans—Christian Year—sat by the Mayor[5] at morning Church— an excellent sermon from Mr Simpson[6] addressed to him, on the duties of office, which he has just entered. Walk with J.N.G.—In the evening sat with Mr Caparn[7]—tea afterwards at Mr Tallents's.

October 1. Monday

Monday—private canvassing continued—dinner at Mr Tallents's—got some lessons in the figures, by way of refreshing my memory, and went to a ball where the trades' people's daughters were enjoying themselves heartily & without affectation. we had tea, with plenty of laughter—sat up as usual writing—I have had extremely little sleep for the last week, and the excitement which carried me through now begins to flag.

---

[1] Held annually on the Wednesday before 2 October.
[2] E. S. Godfrey's brother Thomas.
[3] Wife of William Corden, linen draper.
[4] Reproduced in Reid, G, 161.
[5] James Thorpe, merchant.
[6] Robert Simpson, 1796–1855, curate at Newark 1832; priest at Christ Church, Newark, 1837–44.
[7] Robert Caparn, attorney; *Gladstone's assistant agent; later succeeded Tallents as agent;? s. of Thomas Caparn, druggist, mayor of Newark 1837.

Tuesday 2.

John went off early—private Canvass still continued—in the evening went out with Mr G. Hatton[1] to dine and sleep at Mr T. Godfrey's[2]—Mrs T.G. is a remarkably ladylike person—& we had an agreeable party—I relished its quiet.

3. Wed.

Returned in the forenoon—and this day finished the private canvass to my great joy. The time however has been well spent. Dined privately at Mr Tallents's—he is a cultivated & very agreeable man. A Club at night—Called on Mr Williams.[3] long conversation.

4. Thursday.

Saw divers individuals—rode out to Aynham [sc. Averham?] & called on Mr Manners Sutton[4]—then went out to Stoke to dine with Sir R. Bromley[5]—met the Boothbys[6] &c. Sir R. Lady & two Misses Bromley[7]—music—an excellent house: some good pictures: an extremely valuable Vandyk of Charles 1. in three different positions[8]—Sir R. is a zealous & kind friend of our cause. Writing an Address.

5. Friday.

returned before midday—and called on near 100 of those who had been absent on previous visits—dined at Mr Tallents's—a Club in the evening—gave my Address to Mr T.

6. Saturday.

Paid 12 or 15 calls, which finished off the list—sat some time with Mr Simpson (grocer)[9] on the Slavery question. Altered and amplified my Address. Rode to Ossington[10]—and then also called on the Pocklingtons and Huttons at Carlton. Philip Handley rode with me as far as Muskham.[11] Called on Mr

---

[1] 'An active friend' (Add MS 44777, f. 2); lived at Carlton on Trent, 6½ miles north of Newark.

[2] At Balderton, just SE. of Newark.

[3] Charles Williams, 'a thoughtful opponent' (Add MS 44777, f. 8), and a nonconformist minister.

[4] John Manners Sutton, b. 1779, lived at Kelham Hall, near Newark; eldest b. of Thomas (see i. 564).

[5] Sir Robert Howe Bromley, 1778–1857, admiral; succ. as 3rd bart. 1808; of East Stoke, on the Trent some 4 miles SW. of Newark.

[6] Charles Boothby, 1786–1846, 3rd s. of 8th bart.; lost a leg at Talavera; canon of Southwell 1818, and vicar of Sutterton, Lincolnshire, 1819; m. Marianne Beridge 1820.

[7] Anne, née Wilson, m. 1812, d. 1873, had four das., Caroline, Elizabeth, Mary, and Sophia, as well as six ss., the youngest b. 1831.

[8] Perhaps a copy of the one in the royal collection.

[9] An opponent.

[10] Seven and a half miles NNW. of Newark; the *Denisons lived there.

[11] Three miles north of Newark.

Robinson[1]—dined at Mr Godfrey's—sumptuously entertained—Club in the evening.

7. Sunday.

Corporation seat in morning—Mrs Tallents found me a place in the evening. Two acceptable discourses from Mr Simpson. News of Lord Lincoln's arrival, to be tomorrow. Tea with Mr Tallents. Long walk alone—reading as last Sunday—received the Sacrament at the Church—perhaps 90 persons —my thoughts are terribly dissipated.

8. M.

Shopping—getting Christian Knowledge Books—Letters. with Lincoln, who arrived in the morning. Dined with Mr Tallents—From eight to half past ten at a great Red Club meeting, of perhaps 200—a longer speech than usual.[2] heard from T.G., Mr G., Harrison, & Childers.

9. Tuesday.

Breakfast with Mr Godfrey—conversation on money matters with Mr Caparn—heard from Lincoln. Settled Bill—paid our electioneering call— corrected the press for my Address (which I wrote over & sent yesterday) & got some copies in time to go with me in the chaise to Clumber[3]—fine drive—most kindly received by the Duke, who was better—a good deal of conversation with him. Dinner at three—walk afterwards—music in the evening—found four Lords and four Ladies Clinton.[4]

10. Wednesday.

Wrote to T.G. and to Mr G.—long conversations with the Duke—dinner at 3—walk before & after—escaped upstairs & wrote out, at some length memoranda of my conversations with him[5]—music. All are very polite & kind—wrote to Mr Tallents.

11. Th.

Further conversation. read some "Cure for Ministerial Gallomania"[6]—and

---

[1] John Robinson of Winthorpe Hall, 2 miles NE. of Newark, a property of *Middleton's.

[2] Cp. C. Brown, *Annals of Newark*, 275.

[3] Draft in Add MS 44722, ff. 59–64: printed in C. Brown, *Annals of Newark*, 276–7. *Newcastle's seat at Clumber, in a park some 11 miles round, lies 25 miles NNW. of Newark.

[4] Children of the 4th duke of *Newcastle: Lord Charles Pelham Clinton, 1813–94, M.P. for Sandwich 1852–7; Lord Thomas Charles, his twin, d. 1882, 1st lifeguards; Lord William 1815–50; Lord Edward, 1816–42, R.N.; Lady Georgiana, 1810–74; Lady Charlotte, 1812–86; Lady Caroline Augusta, 1818–98, m. 1852 Sir Cornwallis Ricketts, 1803–85, 2nd bart.; and Lady Henrietta, 1819–90, m. 1859 Admiral E. C. Tennyson-d'Eyncourt who d. 1903.

[5] Add MS 44777, ff. 15–22.

[6] Sub-title of [B. *Disraeli, d'Haussez, and de Haber] 'England and France' (1832); see Blake, 85.

left Clumber for Retford[1] in a carriage of the Duke's—read a pamphlet of his on R.C. Claims on my way[2]—Retford to Doncaster per Mail—on per coach to Wakefield. most heartily welcomed at Thornes,[3] which I reached in time for dinner—introduced to Mrs Milnes Gaskell: and my first evening passed in company with her was in no way disappointing. Found all well— Mr & Mrs Ainsworth, Prof. Smyth, and Miss Brandreth[4] in the House— Whist, paper, &c. in evening—Found Ld Winchilsea's letter.[5]

12. Fr.

Long "screed" with Gaskell—wrote to Robn G. Billiards—whist in Evg. Mrs Trollope's Sketches[6]—paper—writing up my Journal from Torquay to Clumber. Mr Sharp dined here—spoke of the Beer Bill.[7]

13. Sat.

Wrote to E. of Winchilsea & Mr Tallents—also some verses. paper— billiards—écarté—ride with Mrs M.G., Miss B., & Mr Ainsworth—Lord Morpeth[8] came to dinner—Mrs Trollope & paper—spoke for some time & seriously to Robert[9]—may God in his mercy grant that the effect may be good, and that the matter in so far as it was good, may not suffer loss thro' fault of the speaker.

14. Sunday.

Mr T. Brandreth[10] came. Prof. Smyth read an account of his intercourse with Mr Sheridan—I did not go: tho' very sorry to be obliged to absent myself—and the rather, because I know that no small portion of Sunday time is spent in conversation perhaps less profitable than such matter as this. As regards reading however, & hearing by parity of reason, it is perfectly practicable, & I conceive most desirable, to observe a rule strictly. Milnes read in Evg. a Sermon of Bp Porteus's—& prayers as of old. Read Bible—Evans—Blunt on Abraham[11]—& wrote some verses on the subject of Sunday Septr 23.[12]

[1] Ten miles east of Clumber on the great north road.
[2] The duke wrote a number of short, strong, protestant pamphlets, collected in his *Thoughts in times past* (1837).
[3] Thornes House, Wakefield, 20 miles NW. of Doncaster, the Gaskells' seat.
[4] Mrs. Benjamin Gaskell's sister.
[5] *Winchilsea wrote to *Gladstone on 6 October that steps had been taken to insure that his tenants at Newark would vote for the duke's candidates. Add MS 44352, ff. 281–2.
[6] Frances (mother of Anthony) *Trollope, *Domestic Manners of the Americans* (1832).
[7] Samuel Sharp, b. 1773?, vicar of Wakefield 1810–55. Under 'the duke of *Wellington's act', any ratepayer who gave sureties could, between 1830 and 1869, sell beer without a justices' license.
[8] George William Frederick *Howard, 1802–64; styled Lord Morpeth 1825; M.P. for Yorkshire 1830–41, 1846–8; Irish secretary 1835–41, viceroy 1855–8, 1860–4; 7th earl of Carlisle 1848.
[9] His manservant. See 23 Oct. 32.
[10] Thomas Brandreth, Liverpool cabinet maker, uncle or brother of Mrs. Benjamin Gaskell.
[11] H. *Blunt, *Twelve lectures upon the History of Abraham* (1831).
[12] Add MS 44722, ff. 57–58.

15. Monday.

wrote to Mr G.—T.G.—and B. Harrison. Heard from home: a letter to me personally most gratifying: may the Almighty Father enable us to reap fruit herefrom. read Mrs Trollope—& Lady Morgan's account of the Massaniello Revolution[1]—rode with Milnes G[askell] & Mrs M[ilnes Gaskell]—our party broke up—the Ainsworths, the professor, Lord M[orpeth], Mr Brandreth, & Mr Calvetti[2] all went off—whist in the evening.

16. Tuesday.

Mrs Trollope—Scrapbook—paper—whist. drove Mrs G[askell], Mrs M.G., & Miss B. to Leeds—learnt a passage of Burke by heart—Dr Gilby dined here.

17. Wed.

Breakfast with Dr Gilby—& afterwards got & forgot a lecture in mineralogy from him. He was, as also yesterday, in better spirits than when I saw him before:[3] but there is something to excite uneasiness in the state of this amiable & I believe religious man. Heard from Aunt J. a serious account of Tom's illness—thank God that it is now mitigated—How am I spared, and how is my cup, speaking individually, made to overflow with blessings! O God, may my heart escape the deadening influence of prosperity.—Walked to Mr Leathom's of Heath[4] and saw Miss Maurice who is governess there. On learning my altered destination she said "I am sorry to hear it". I should be sincerely thankful for this honest opinion.—Lord Morpeth came to lunch & went on. He is kind & courteous to all.—At night read Dumont[5] aloud & played whist—also read Mrs Trollope, & began "A visit to Newark".[6]

18. Thursday.

Continued writing my "visit to Newark". Mrs Trollope—a little Blackstone —paper—billiards with Milnes—walk, learning poetry by heart—We all dined at Lupseth.[7] Met the Ainsworths, Capt. & Mrs Foote,[8] & Goodenough.[9] Mr D.G. is mild & pleasing in his manner. Mrs D.G.[10] had a long conversation with me, continually on the brink of very serious questions which I

---

[1] In S. *Morgan's quasi-fictional *Life and Times of Salvator Rosa*, 2v. (1823), i. 365–405.
[2] Unidentified.
[3] See 12 Sept. 29.
[4] William Leatham, banker, lived at Heath Hall, a mile beyond the eastern outskirts of Wakefield.
[5] P. E. L. Dumont, *Recollections of Mirabeau* (1832).
[6] Add MS 44777, ff. 1–14; cp. 27 Nov. 32.
[7] Cp. 17 Sept. 29.
[8] Probably John Foote, d. 1854; entered navy 1797; wounded and captured near Gibraltar, 1806, soon exchanged; capt. R.N. 1827; m.; drowned in Baltic.
[9] Robert William Goodenough, 1809?–80, student of Christ Church 1826–36, vicar of Whittingham, Northumberland, 1835.
[10] Mary, née Heywood, m. Daniel Gaskell 1806.

endeavoured to avoid, but stated broadly a hostile principle on education. Her activity and benevolence ought to shame many who profess a purer creed.—Tea at Thornes, late: and a conv. upon Shelley & Wordsworth.

19. Friday.

Milnes's birthday. Miss Brandreth thrown at the gate from Mrs M's horse. Providentially not hurt. Billiards with Mrs M. Whist in evening, rode with Milnes. Finished Mrs Trollope—and read the Review of her in the Edinburgh. The book is I think unfair: the review still more so: & personal. Heard from Mr G. & J.N.G. Wrote to Helen & Uncle Divie.

20. Sat.

Wrote to Aunt Johanna. Drove Mrs M.G. & Miss B[randreth] to Lupseth & Horbury[1]—billiards with Miss B. Walk with Wordsworth—whist—read Ed. Rev. on It[alian] Republics—& Art. on Ld Henley aloud—began "England & France"—Internal evidence I think strongly supports Gaskell in ascribing it to Croker—in some respects at least.[2]

21. Sunday.

Thornes Ch. mg & aft. Milnes read a sermon in Evg.—Conv. with Mrs Gaskell on "world" & "final separation"[3]. Walk. Read Bible—notes—Evans—Keble. Finished Blunt on Abraham.

22. M.

Mr & Mrs G. with Miss B. went to visit the Walker Ferrands.[4] Ride—papers—whist—billiards—read "England & France"—& began Etienne Dumont. Wrote in Scrap Book. Summons from home.

23. T.

I am now on the eve of closing what has been a very delightful visit—against my will, but I am certain I should do wrong if I yielded to the kind solicitations I receive—In Wakefield taking my place &c. Announced to poor Robert his departure & wrote to his Father.—Whist in the evening—paper. Most of the day spent in finishing "England and France" and in reading Lady Cannings half volume supplementary to Ed.1. of Stapylton.[5] I do not think, from her account, that the old Tories acted in concert—the Duke of W. seems to have made frivolous objections to the wording of Mr Canning's letter—but to have been borne out in asking who was to be Premier—to have given up the Cabinet on account of the Catholic Question, the Army because of the tone of the note. Lord Melville's conduct was the

---

[1] Village 2½ miles SW. of Wakefield; where John Francis Carr lived at Carr Lodge.
[2] *Croker corrected the proofs. Cp. 11 Oct. 32.
[3] Further reflexions on this in Add 44722, ff. 151–8.
[4] See 13 Jan. 29. Harden Grange lies 20 miles NW. of Wakefield.
[5] Unpublished.

most bare. The contrast of Ld Grey's policy in 1808 and 1823 speeches regarding Spain, is very powerfully put.[1]

24. W.

Milnes up to breakfast with me at 5¼. Left Wakefield by the six o'clock coach. Had some political conversation, about Milnes &c., on the way— Finely wooded country almost all the way to Derby—by Barnsley, Sheffield, Chesterfield. The coach good—Vale running up to Matlock very beautiful. Arrived in Birmingham at 8¼—120 miles—went to Mr English[2]— could not find him. Paper & Wordsworth—met Stone[3] in the Hen & Chickens Coffeeroom.

25. Th.

Arrived in Leamington per Crown Prince to breakfast: found dear Helen looking as well as I could have hoped here. Much conv. Began Basil Hall's Travels in U. States[4]—wrote to Mr G.—to Mr Tallents twice—and to D. of N. on the subject of a new visit to Newark now proposed to me: which I am most anxious to avoid; for the time on my hands is little enough, & I am sure it is a duty to husband it. I find Dear Tom's illness has been even more severe than I thought.

26. Fr.

Bible with H.J.G.—Basil Hall—Wrote to T.G.—to Childers—to Pakenham —papers—rode to Kenilworth—Wordsworth—Read aloud to H.J.G.

27.

Improved accounts from Liverpool. Rode. Called on Mrs Proby & Mrs Jephson—papers—Wordsworth—finished Vol.1. of Hall—read aloud to H.J.G.—and Bible with her. Analysis of D. Hollis.

One remarkable similarity prevails between Wordsworth & Shelley: the quality of combining & connecting everywhere external Nature with internal & unseen mind. But how different are they in its application! It frets & irritates the one—it is the key to the peacefulness of the other. Even as that mighty River of America at one time & one character "spreads into successive seas", broad glassy & tranquil—at another fumes over the Rapids & thunders down the precipices of Niagara, so this same Power fulfilling its course through the channels of different minds, becomes an emblem & cause of peace or of war in each respectively.

---

[1] Cp. A. Aspinall, *Formation of *Canning's Ministry* (1937), esp. ca. xli.
[2] John, father of Charles, English (Charles, 1810?–67, was up at Trinity with *Hallam; priest at Sydenham 1843); or possibly Thomas English, surgeon dentist, of Colmore Row.
[3] John Spencer Stone, b. 1810?; Derbyshire family; Eton and Christ Church; studied law.
[4] 3v. (1829); by Captain Basil *Hall, R.N.; much annoyed Americans.

28. Sunday.

Charity Sermon in mg—Mr Riddell "Of such is the kingdom of heaven".[1] The point is, I think, the trustfulness of the child, who walks by faith. The Curate in aftn. Read a serm of Sandford's to the servants—& one of Evans's to H.J.G. two short tracts of Malan's & his "Temoignage"—which must I should think be interesting to all.[2]

29. Monday.

Called on Miss Swinfen. Mr Lane called here[3]—Bible with H.J.G. B[asil] Hall. began Vol 2—copied a Letter—read Wordsworth aloud to H.J.G. & proceeded in writing "A visit to Newark".

30. T.

Bible with H.J.G. A long conversation on the principle of Ethics. Heard from Mr G. & J.N.G.—Tom progresses slowly—Basil Hall—& making some Abstract. read Wordsworth aloud—papers—rode to Baginton. Read Ed. Rev. on Working of Reform.

31. W.

Bible with H.J.G. Finished Hebrews. Rode beyond Kenilworth hoping to meet Mr & Mrs G.—they came soon after—to dinner. paper—called on Mr Lane. Basil Hall—Notes from him—& "Visit to Newark".

Thursday November 1.

Wrote to Mr Tallents and the Duke of N. Bible with H.J.G. Began Philippians. Basil Hall & Notes—Quart. Rev. on Count Pecchio's Osservazioni.— Papers: Bristol Evidence[4] &c. Walk, & learning some Shelley.

2.

Basil Hall—and Notes therefrom. Rode. Bible with H.J.G.—Heard from Mr Tallents—I am actually let off my visit. Papers—part of Quart. Rev. on Prince Polignac. Went over the Prospectus of Liverpool paper, endeavouring to insert some verbal corrections.

3.

Finished Basil Hall. Analysis of Denzil Hollis. Wrote to J.N.G. Indifferent

[1] James Reddell, 1795?–1878, rector of Easton, Hampshire, 1816–36; vicar of Hanbury, Staffordshire, 1836–63; on Matt. xix. 14.

[2] [C. H. A. Malan] *Témoignage rendu à l'Evangile* (1813). Cp. 15 July 32.

[3] Charles Newton Lane, vicar of Alveston, eight miles SW. of Leamington.

[4] Charles *Pinney, 1793–1867, was on trial for neglect of duty as mayor of Bristol during the riots of October 1831; he was acquitted. One of the crown counsel against him was Thomas *Wilde, 1782–1855, *Gladstone's opponent at Newark; defended *Caroline 1820; serjeant-at-law 1824; king's serjeant 1827; whig M.P. Newark 1831–2 and 1835–41, Worcester 1841–6; solicitor-general 1839–41; attorney-general 1841 and 1846; chief justice of common pleas 1846–50; lord chancellor 1850–2; cr. Lord Truro 1850.

account of Tom. Rode. Bible with H.J.G. Q. Rev. on Polignac—papers. read Wordsworth to H.J.G.

4. Sunday.

Better accounts from Liverpool. A very good sermon from Mr Wells of Barford "For many are called but few are chosen".[1] Mr Downes on Daniel in aftn. My Father read one [sermon] of Arnold's at night. Bible—Evans— Life of Wiclif—and Malan's "Le Chrétien soumis aux Puissances".[2]

5. Monday.

Analysis of D. Hollis. Bible with H.J.G. German Grammar—if I do not attempt to secure an idea of German now, I know not when I may have the opportunity. Read "Proceedings at a Public meeting of the W. Indians" &c. made some notes from it.[3] Quart. Rev. on B. Hall.—very good, I thought, in general.[4] Letter from Gaskell, who is at Wenlock[5]—wrote to him—& also to the Standard, on divers matters.[6]—Newark Treat today.

6. T.

Pursued the Analysis of political Tracts—Bible with H.J.G.—Quart. Rev. on Flint's Ten Years.[7] Began Sarrans' Memoirs of La Fayette[8]—Part of the Reform Bill[9]—German Grammar—Rode out—Heard from J.N.G. (Womens' tea at Newark.)

7. W.

Memoirs of La Fayette—Analysis of Political Tracts—part of Quarterly Review on Fashionable Novels. Bible with H.J.G. Wrote to J.N.G.— Papers.

My State at present is one of danger: & that danger is of a singular kind. With personal blessings my cup overflows—except godliness and the mastery over my sins, I know not what to desire. While at the same time there are circumstances affecting us as a family, operating through the persons of others of its members, of a very different character. God Almighty has thought fit to overrule with the arm of His strength many plans & prospects which had been entertained—&, by clothing his visitations in the form of sickness, perhaps to touch the tenderest point. We have been

[1] Probably Giffard Wells, 1802–76; headmaster of Stourbridge school, 1833–55; on Matt. xxii. 14. Barford is four miles SW. of Warwick.
[2] Another tract (1824?).
[3] Perhaps *The Record* of 16 August 1832, nine-column report of meeting in Exeter Hall, on previous day, of friends of Christian missions in West Indies. Notes untraced.
[4] xlvii. 133 (March 1832), on Basil *Hall's autobiography.
[5] J. M. Gaskell was M.P. for Wenlock, 1832–68—unopposed after 1835.
[6] Untraced.
[7] xlviii. 201 (October 1832), on Timothy Flint, *Recollections of the Last Ten Years, passed in ... the Valley of the Mississippi* (1831).
[8] B. Sarrans *Memoirs of General Lafayette and of the French Revolution of 1830*, 2v, one of two translations just published of a work by Lafayette's secretary.
[9] 2 William IV cap. 45, 58 folio pages.

singularly dealt with—once snatched from a position when we were what is called entering society, & sent to comparative seclusion, as regards family establishment—and now again prevented from assuming the situation which seems the natural termination of a career like my Father's. Here is a noble trial: for me personally, to exercise a kindly & unselfish feeling, if amid the excitement & allurements now near me, I am enabled duly to realise the bond of consanguinity, and *suffer with* those whom Providence has ordained to suffer: and for us all, if we look through these matters & onward to their use & purpose, and never rest in our supplications to the throne of Grace, until that the messengers of God have done their work.

8. Th.

Sarran's Memoirs—Bible with H.J.G.—Finished Analysis of Vol 1. of Maseres—arranging papers &c.—finished Quarterly Review on Fashionable Novels. Good accounts from Liverpool. Read Foreign Quarterly on Translation of Milton.[1]

9. Fr.

Sarrans—and Analysis of him.[2] Bible with H.J.G.—Foreign Quart. on Works of Chateaubriand[3]—papers—part of the Reform Bill—as obscure, to me, in the letter, as it is awfully legible in spirit.

10. Sat.

Sarrans—began Vol 2. For. Qu. Rev. on Louis Philippe's govt papers.[4] Wrote to Mr Tallents—& heard from him. Copied two letters. Bible with H.J.G. Wrote and wrote over an "Address" on the subject of the Dutch war[5]—also went over my Father's (written to go to Liverpool) with him suggesting some modifications.[6]

11. Sunday.

Again Mr Wells morning. Mr Downes afternoon. Read Evans. Finished Life of Wiclif—& Meek's reasons for conformity. My Father read a Sermon at night. Good accounts from Liverpool—Walk.

12.

Papers—including Roman diplomatic Correspondence—important.[7] Sarrans—& Analysis. Bible with H.J.G.—Germ. Grammar—For. Qu. Rev. on Gouverneur Morris.[8]

[1] x. 508 (October 1832) by A. H. *Hallam.
[2] Add MS 44722, ff. 67–74.
[3] x. 297; by T. H. *Lister.
[4] x. 514; by H. *Southern; reviewing Sarrans.
[5] To the king: Add MS 44722, f. 65.
[6] Untraced.
[7] *The Times* for 10 November carried British protests to Austria at political conditions in the papal states; see *BFSP* xx. 1366–75.
[8] x. 411; also by *Southern.

13. Tuesday.

Bible with H.J.G.—German Grammar—Sarrans & Analysis thereof—divers writings—paper—walk—whist in the evening—Thornely is to stand in Lpool—J. Wortley against him—God speed the right.[1]

14. Wed.

Wrote to T.G.—R.G.—and Gaskell. Bible with H.J.G.—Sarrans & Analysis. Finished reading Vol 2.—papers—walk. Paradise Lost.—Whist in evening.

15. Th.

Wrote to W. W. Farr. Bible & conv. with H.J.G.—papers. German Grammar—finished Analysis of Sarrans with some notes from "England & France"—began Bourrienne—whist—an autograph letter from T.G.—R.G's birthday—May God's blessing be with him.

16. Fr.

Bourrienne and Analysis—but I find so much the want of knowledge in detail of the French Revolution, that I began Scott's account of it,[2] putting off Bourrienne: read a good deal of both. Bible with H.J.G. German Grammar—rode—papers—whist.

17. Sat.

Bible with H.J.G. Also (as on 17 [sc. 16]) conversation with Mrs & H.J.G. on some questions of schism &c. Analysis of Bourrienne, Scott—& Analysis.[3] German Grammar—papers—whist—walk: called on Mr Lane.

18. Sunday.

Mr Wells & Mr Downes. H.J.G. not so well. Heard from R.G. & Gaskell. Walk. Notes in Testament—Evans—Sandford—& Christian Year. Made a feeble commencement of an intended tract.[4]

Monday Nov. 19.

Finished I of Scott's Napoleon—began II. Analysis of the same. It is eloquent & the descriptions are most graphic.—Bible with H.J.G.—German Grammar—Wrote to R.G.—& to the Standard about Shepherd's Speech[5]—Papers—whist—walked to Warwick to find a poor woman but could not. Pakenham expected.

[1] Thomas Thornely, Liverpool merchant and nonconformist, stood with *Ewart next month; but lost to *Sandon, whose unsuccessful partner was Sir Howard *Douglas (see 8 Dec. 32). James Archibald *Stuart-Wortley, 1805–81, was Peelite M.P. for Halifax, 1835–7, and Buteshire, 1842–59.
[2] In *Scott's *Life of Napoleon* (1827), i.
[3] Add MS 44722, ff. 75, 77.
[4] Untraced.
[5] Letter unpublished. William Shepherd, Wesleyan minister at Edge Hill, made main speech in favour of *Ewart at Liverpool meeting on 12 Nov. 1832.

20.

Finished Analysis of I of Scott's Napoleon—reading II. Wrote to Mr Tallents—& copied a letter of my Father's, conveying a guarantee—Bible with H.J.G.—German Grammar—papers—whist—Pakenham again expected.

21.

Scott's Napoleon—& Analysis. Bible with H.J.G. Tom & John arrived. Tom quite as well as we could hope. Pakenham came in the evening. Papers. Heard from Mr Tallents. Rode to Kenilworth. My Mother ill.

22. Th.

Called on Bp of Oxford & Mrs Lister.[1] My Mother's attack very severe.— Finished II of Scott—Analysis—wrote to Mr Tallents—Bourrienne resumed—papers—whist in evg. Walking some time with Mr Lane.

23. Fr.

My Mother still very ill. Bourrienne—Analysis of Scott. Walked with Pakenham & J.N.G. to Warwick, & went over the whole—with more relish for the pictures than previously—Magnificent Earl of Arundel by Rubens —and Machiavelli by Titian. The feudalism of the entrance is perfect.— Pakenham went. Met Ryder & walked with him. Heard from Mr Tallents— papers.

24. Sat.

Analysis & Bourrienne—but little of each. My Mother thank God better. Bad news of the Liverpool Standard & of Liverpool Election.—wrote an Article on the Dutch war to offer for it[2]—wrote to R.G. & Mr Tallents— walk with Ryder & whist.

25. S.

J.N.G. went off 2 P.M.—My Mother better. Read Evans—Sandford and Bible &c.—Church—Mr Wells & Mr Downes.

26. M.

Papers—Bourrienne—Analysis of Scott. (finished it for Vol.2) continued my "Visit to Newark"—out with Ryder &c. At Mrs Lister's in the evg— met Lord & Lady Ribblesdale[3] & heaps more, most of whom I knew not. Heard from Mr Tallents.

[1] Perhaps (Lady) Maria Theresa *Lewis, 1803–65, authoress, sister of 4th earl of *Clarendon, m. T. H. *Lister 1830, Sir G. C. *Lewis 1844.
[2] Article published on 27 November 1832, p. 16.
[3] Thomas Lister, b. 1790, 2nd baron Ribblesdale 1826, d. suddenly 10 December 1832. He m., 1826, Adelaide Lister, 1807–38, who re-m., 1835, Lord John *Russell, 1792–1878; prime minister 1846–52, 1865–6; cr. earl Russell 1861; see Add MSS 44291–4.

27. T.

Papers—Mr Boyton's Speech, extremely fine.[1] Finished "A Visit to Newark". German Grammar &c—finished Bourrienne Vol 1—began Scott III—Whist in Evg—my work is sadly scanty!

28. W.

Bible with H.J.G. Wrote a paper supplemental to 'a visit to Clumber'.[2] Scott's Napoleon—wrote to Doyle—Bible with H.J.G.—papers—whist— walk with Ryder—Newark letters at night—addled.

29. Thursday.

Bible with H.J.G. Analysis of Scott & Bourrienne—read Scott—papers. In the evening at Lady Eastnorr's—Ld & Lady E. unaffected & agreeable:[3] introduced to Lady Farquhar,[4] Lady St Germans[5] & Miss I forget what her niece[6]—with whom I (!!) danced. Walked out with Tom.—Wrote to Mr Tallents—and heard from him at night.

30. Fr.

Called on Mrs Hook—Lady Eastnorr—Mrs Lister—Mrs Proby—Mrs Lane (met Lady Lucy Grant[7] there—very unaffected & conversible)—Ryder dined with us. Determined, that I should proceed to Newark forthwith. finished Scott's Napoleon Vol.III.—Wrote a long article for the Liverpool Standard[8]—commenced another—arranging letters & making up accounts —papers—& packing.

December 1. Saturday.

Left Leamington soon after 8. By Warwick to Coventry—Leicester—& Nottingham, whence I posted, after remaining near an hour—to read the paper—call on Mr Hicklin at the Journal Office[9]—and make acquaintance with Mrs Ward of the Geo: the Fourth.[10] Glad to find Mr Gordon[11] there on

[1] Charles Boyton, Belfast clergyman, on the Dutch war and its Irish implications; at meeting in Dublin of the Protestant Conservative Society of Ireland, 20 November 1832.
[2] Add MS 44777, ff. 13–14.
[3] John Sommers Cocks, 1788–1852, soldier and sportsman; styled Viscount Eastnorr 1821; tory M.P. for Hereford 1818–32, for Reigate 1812–18 and 1832–41 when he succ. as 2nd Earl Sommers; m. 1815 Caroline Harriet Yorke, 1794–1873, 4th d. of 3rd earl of *Hardwicke.
[4] Sybella Martha Rockliff, d. 1869, m. 1809 Sir Thomas Harvie Farquhar, 1775–1836, 2nd bart. 1819, banker.
[5] Harriot Pole-Carew, 1790–1877, m. 1819 *Pitt's nephew John Eliot, cr. earl of St. Germans 1815, who d. 1823.
[6] One of the Misses Pole-Carew of Antony, Cornwall.
[7] Lady Lucy Bruce, d. 1881; 3rd da. of 7th and half–sister of 8th earl of *Elgin; m. 1828 (as his 2nd wife) John Grant, 1798–1873, of Kilgraston, Perthshire, to whom she bore thirteen children.
[8] On church reform (11 December 1832, p. 48).
[9] Robert Hickling, printer of the Nottingham Journal, conservative weekly, founded 1769.
[10] Elizabeth Ward, landlady of the posting inn in George Street.
[11] Edward Herbert Gordon, agent.

his Canvass. Read Bp Law on Tithes.[1] arrived at Newark between 8 & 9—
our conveyances had been good tho' often changed—John the groom with
me—Met Mr Tallents—Mr Caparn—Mr Bramston[2]—most hospitably received at Mr T's where I took up my quarters.—Finished my Article for the
Liverpool Standard.

2. Sunday.

Bible. Sandford: writing—prose & verse. Church morning & evg—large
congregations. Sermon & Lecture from Mr Simpson. Sacrament. Conv. with
Mrs T[allents] &c.

3. M.

Wrote to J.N.G. Began Scott's Napoleon Vol 4, & Analysis thereof—
attended Committee Meeting—spoke briefly—arrangements made with
readiness & despatch. walked out & racked my brain for compliments to
the ladies tomorrow. Mr Godfrey—Mr & Mrs T. G[odfrey], Dr Morton,[3] &
Mr Caparn came to dinner—whist—paper—Fenelon—Memoirs of Dante &
Kosciusko.[4]

4. T.

Wrote to Mrs G—to the Duke of N.—and to Lord Lincoln congratulating
him.[5]—Scott's Napoleon & Analysis—papers—whist—dined at Mr. Godfrey's—Presentation of a flag to the Red Club—excellently attended. Spoke
perhaps 20 minutes[6]—Lady Bromley & her daughters there. Called on Mr
Simpson: gratified much: also on Mrs Harvey,[7] the Miss Becketts,[8] & Mrs
Caparn, who got up the flag. Began Miss Kemble's Francis the First.[9] Met
Mr Freeth.[10]

5. W.

Read Francis the First—which astonishes me. A little inexactitude in some
similes &c. for poetry has its laws of congruity, & strict ones.
Heard from Gaskell and Uncle Divie—wrote to Robn G. and Uncle D.
Walk—some calls—Wilde arrived in the morning—read Liverpool Stan-

[1] G. H. *Law, *Reflections upon Tithes* (1832).
[2] Branston, Newark alderman.
[3] Hugh Morton, Newark physician.
[4] Presumably in a biographical dictionary.
[5] On his marriage (on 27 November) to Lady Susan Harriet Catherine Douglas, 1814–
1889, da. of 10th duke of *Hamilton (see 11 Feb. 34); divorced, 1850; she re-m. M.
Opdebeck of Brussels, 1860.
[6] See C. Brown, *Annals of Newark*, 277–9.
[7] Probably wife of George Harvey, maltster.
[8] Sisters of Thomas Becket, draper in the market place.
[9] A verse drama by F. A. (da. of Charles*) Kemble, later Butler.
[10] Possibly Charles or George Freeth; both London gentlemen.

dard No. 4. almost through—Wrote out an abstract of yesterday's Speech. Good news of the S. Country Eln.[1]—Talked with Hackerby[2] about Slavery.

6. Th.

Wrote to my Father—and to Gaskell—Made a dozen or so of calls on voters —conv. with Mr Fisher,[3] who seems a clever man. Scott's Napoleon and Analysis. Reading carefully my Father's pamphlet,[4] in consequence of a placard assailing it and turning it agst me—and wrote an Address embracing that and other matters at some length.[5] Dined at Mr Caparn's—whist.

7. Fr.

Wrote a long letter to H.J.G.—wrote over and altered my Address.— Scott's Napoleon and Analysis. J.N.G. expected—did not come—Divers calls. papers. five Eton first classes.[6]—Wrote to Lushington (late at night) to congratulate him.[7] Heard from Uncle D. Read Mr Peart &c.[8] Mr Cook[9] & others dined here. Mr Bartlett[10] & his family came in the Evg. Mr Cook a clever man.

8. Sat.

Occupied most of the day in canvassing and visits. Some time with the Dysons[11]—thought them both pious and sober. wrote to E. Denison—and to T.G.—Read Sir Howard Douglas's dinner & Lord Sandon's Exchange Speech: both admirable: the former on Belgium—the latter on Slavery— the former too had a very fine passage about the Church.[12] Consultations &c. touching the Election. My address out. Paper—Scott. made very little of it.—J.N.G. came.

9. Sunday.

Christian Year—Bible—writing "Remarks on the present state" &c[13]— Bp Sandford's Sermons—and Chr. Knowl. Report. Morning Serm. Mr Harris[14]—Serj. Wilde in Church—Evening Mr Simpson—both good.

[1] Parliament was dissolved on 3 December; elections took place from the 10th to the 20th. Anti-reform prospects in SE. England were reasonable.
[2] Francis Huckerby, Newark maltster.
[3] Probably Richard Fisher, mercer.
[4] 'Facts relating to slavery' (1830).
[5] Draft in Add MS 44722, f. 87.
[6] Morley, i. 96.
[7] On his classical first.
[8] Robert Peart, Newark ropemaker; an untraced MS.
[9] Probably James Cook, victualler.
[10] William Bartlett, vicar of Newark 1814–35.
[11] James Dyson, Newark wine merchant.
[12] Delivered in Liverpool on 5 and 2 December respectively. Sir Howard *Douglas, 1776–1861, gunner, fought in Spain and Flanders; 3rd bart. 1809; contested Liverpool 1832, 1835; tory M.P. for it 1842–7; governed New Brunswick 1823–9, and Ionia 1835–1840; wrote on tactics.
[13] Perhaps Add MS 44722, f. 90.
[14] Possibly Robert Harris, 1764–1862, wrangler 1786, vicar of Preston from 1797.

10. Monday.

Much occupied in calling upon voters—removed to the Clinton Arms—dined at Mr Godfrey's. went the circuit of about 13 Clubs in the evening, making a short speech at each—some whist. Sat up reading my Father's pamphlet, Ld Sandon, Capt. Marryat,[1] Mr Peart, & certain notes of my own on Slavery.—&c.

11. Tuesday.

Nomination at 10—stood between six & seven hours, with some pressure, on the hustings, questioned for two or three of them, and allowed to speak at the close about 15 minutes perhaps. A stormy scene. The yells rung round my head—but wrought little effect. Show of hands carried against us. I was most powerfully escorted to the Clinton Arms.[2] Dinner afterwards— and whist. All in good spirits. Papers—up late. Wrote letters to T.G.—my Father[3]—R.G. and Leamington. Heard from R.G.—and Lushington.

12. W.

First day of polling. We took the lead from the first. It lasted 9–4. Numbers at close.

G. 667 ... plumpers. 151
H. 612 ... ----------. 7
W. 532 ... ----------. 316

I went from booth to booth. The Serjeant looked disgusted—& no wonder. He has been induced to follow a mistaken policy from the first. Much talk with Mr Humphreys.[4] Mr Basil Montagu[5] likewise introduced himself to me in the kindest manner. Spoke very briefly from the window—stone thrown —thank God missed—man detected. Dinner—papers—whist. Wrote to my Father—T.G.—R.G.—Doyle. Heard from Doyle. Wrote a short Address.[6]

13. Th.

The Serjeant made a push, which induced many to split upon Handley.[7] I remained at the Town Hall during the forenoon. Polling 8 A.M.–4 P.M.

Final numbers—G. 887
H. 798
W. 726.

Spoke briefly from the window. "Spencering"[8] in the market place, &

---

[1] Probably F. *Marryat, *Newton Forster*, his latest three-decker novel; two others, *The Naval Officer* (1829) and *The King's Own* (1830), were in print; possibly *Marryat's pamphlet on naval impressment (1822).   [4] Unidentified.

[2] Speech and details in C. Brown, *Annals of Newark*, 280–2.

[3] Part in Bassett, 26.

[5] Basil *Montagu, 1770–1851; author; lived a few doors from Divie Robertson in Bedford Square.

[6] Reproduced in Cornelius Brown, *History of Newark* (1904), ii. 250.

[7] i.e. vote for *Wilde and Handley.

[8] A local word meaning hustling.

throwing stones. Dinner &c—Many Ladies with us. Wrote to the Duke of N—and two letters to Leamington.[1] Papers. Note to Mr Tallents.

14. Fr.

Town Hall at 9. Return made—I am now member for Newark.[2] May the Almighty give me strength to perform the duties of this solemn office.

Spoke for an hour or more—Serjeant [Wilde] procured me a hearing—but a cold one. Handley seemed unpopular. Remarkable speech of the Serjeant. He is an enigma to me.—Left the Hall between one & two—large Escort to my Inn—spoke briefly from the window, the Red Flag waving over my head, beneath a bright sun & lovely sky.—Heard from & wrote to Gaskell—wrote to Harrison—to Leamington. Wrote an Address.—Scott's Napoleon.

Near fifty Reds dined together. The utmost enthusiasm was displayed. I spoke perhaps near half an hour.[3] Too much wine drunk by some of the party. Heard from Liverpool.

15. Sat.

Rose too late for Post matters—called on Mrs Caparn & Mrs Godfrey—dined with Mr Tallents—whist—papers—at night, wrote to Mr G., T.G., R.G., Pakenham, & the Duke of N. Called at Stoke & Farndon[4]—Lincoln arrived past midnight—sat talking with him two hours. Saw Mr Gordon.

16. Sunday.

Church morning & Evg. Morning Mr Bartlett—could not be heard—Evg. Mr Simpson. Lincoln there in morning. Walk.—Mr Caparn called on for an explanation[5]—Read Bible—Christian Year—some of Arnold's letters on the Church.[6]

17. M.

Ill with sore throat. Up just in time to see Lincoln's procession & witness the election in the Town Hall.[7] He hesitated in speaking but his matter was good. At two we had a dinner—he spoke well after it. I had to speak—about 15 m.—mixed company of town & country. Portarlington 10 & 10.[8] —Wrote to Leamington—received divers letters. In the evening (after Lincoln had gone) at Mrs Godfrey's—reading Arnold's Letters—whist—Mr Tallents off to Lincoln.

[1] One paragraph from letter to his f. in Bassett, 27.
[2] Morley dates this the day before (i. 93).
[3] Version of speech in Add MS 44649, ff. 32–33.
[4] Farndon, 2½ miles SW. of Newark, on the road to the Bromleys' place at Stoke.
[5] See 18 Dec. 32, 7 June, 17 July 33, etc: disputes about election expenses.
[6] [Thomas *Arnold] 'Thirteen letters on our social condition' (1832).
[7] *Lincoln and J. E. *Denison were returned unopposed for south Nottinghamshire.
[8] Thomas Gladstone and G. D. L. Damer his opponent were reported to have ten votes each on 14 December.

18. T.

Sore throat. J.N.G. too—made about 35 calls: the line is, Committee, Corporation, & Clergy. Mr Caparn's explanation—Dined at Mr Godfrey's—finished writing out my recollections of an after dinner Speech on Friday last. Whist.

19. W.

Ten calls—finished Arnold's letters. paper—packed &c. Came in evg post to Nottingham. Obliged to speak at a dinner party of Mr Houldsworth's[1] friends.—& also at the Constitutional Club. Wrote to Lincoln from Newark (under my first frank, given for tomorrow & addressed to the Countess) & from Nottingham to my Father—to Tom, & to Robn.

20. Th.

6¾–2¾ reached Coventry. Unfortunately we had booked through—& so had to wait in Coventry. Arrived at Leamington about 5¾. Found my dear Mother better—my Aunts with them. Conversation, nearly filled up the evening.

21. Fr.

Scott's Napoleon. Called on Ryder & Mrs Proby.[2] Papers. God knows, the news is in general melancholy enough.[3] Wrote to Uncle D—to Harrison (from whom I found a Letter here)—Childers—Seymer—Farr—and wrote an article intended for the Liverpool Standard—whist.

22. Sat.

Papers. Read Stanley's Speech at Lancaster[4]—rode—wrote to Robn—to Canning, Phillimore, & Mayow—disgusted with last night's article, wrote & sent another.[5] Cold still upon me—but how thankful should I be that I am as I am, in point of bodily health.

23. S.

Mr Downes and Mr Willis.[6] Went to the Baptist Chapel: Mr Cole[7] was preaching for adult Baptism by immersion. I stood at the door. Read out of Sumner to the servants at night. Bible. Writing "Thoughts"—Read Evans. Politics intruded into my thoughts today & worse.

---

[1] Thomas Houldsworth, strong conservative, M.P. north Nottinghamshire 1832–41.
[2] Isabella, née Howard, d. 1836; gd. of 1st Viscount *Wicklow; m. 1818 G. L. Proby, 3rd earl of Carysfort 1855.
[3] Whigs and radicals combined numbered about 300 more than tories.
[4] E. G. *Stanley at Lancaster, 17 December, returning thanks for election.
[5] Draft of first in Add MS 44722, ff. 92–93; revision untraced.
[6] Perhaps Thomas Willis, 1801?–57, of St. John's, Cambridge; priest 1825; never beneficed.
[7] Probably A. A. Cole, baptist minister at Walsall, Staffordshire, from 1832.

24.

Dearest Anne's birthday—when days were known to her. Wrote to T.G.—
to R.G.—to R. Williams—to Pakenham—read papers—finished Vol.4. of
Scott's Napoleon—wrote articles for the Liverpool Standard on the Dutch
War[1]—Mr Stanley's Speech[2]—the Church & Dissent.[3] In Evg, wrote to
R.G. again—whist.

25.

Christmas day. Sacrament. Mr Downes preached in afternoon. Before many
years, we may not be permitted to celebrate this festival as now. Bp Sandford's Serm.—Paradise Regained, two books. Very objectionable on religious grounds?—Part of Mrs Stevens's "Bread of Deceit"[4]—Papers. Ld
Henley's Union of his own & Dr Burton's Plans.[5]

26.

Antwerp gone! God help the poor oppressed Hollanders.[6]—read "The navigation of the Scheldt". papers—cards. Scott's Napoleon began Vol 5.—
Wrote two articles for Liverpool Standard—on Bribery, and the position of
the country.[7] Wrote to Robn—to Gaskell—and to Saunders—also Scraps.

27.

Wrote over a Speech of the 14th—Wrote to Phillimore—to Mr G.—to
Tallents—to Caparn. Heard from Mr G., R.G., Phillimore, Farr, Mr Finlay.
Wrote an Article on Political Unions for the Standard.[8] Scott's Napoleon &
Analysis. Whist. called on the Lanes.

28.

Wrote to Mr G. and Uncle Colin. Heard from Uncle D., D. of N. (very kind),
T.G., F.B. Cole. At Mrs Hook's to tea. Mrs Davidson,[9] Ld & Lady Eastnorr,
Lady Farquhar &c. Read Scott's Napoleon—& wrote Analysis of ditto.
Papers. rode & walked with J.N.G. Cold now better thank God.

December 29.

Heard from R.G.—Saunders—Pusey—Childers. Wrote to R.G., Saunders,
Pulford.

---

[1] Possibly leading article of 1 January 1833.
[2] Anticipated by article on 25 December 1832, p. 80.
[3] *Liverpool Standard*, 28 December, 88.
[4] Untraced.
[5] 'A Plan of Church Reform' (1832).
[6] Late on 23 December, after the citadel's walls had been breached by the French,
Chassé capitulated honourably.
[7] 28 December 1832, 88; and 1 January 1833, 96.
[8] Untraced.
[9] Perhaps Elizabeth Diana Macdonald, 1804–39, eldest child of 3rd Lord Macdonald,
who m. 1825—as the first of his five wives—Duncan Davidson, 1800–82, of Tulloch, Co.
Ross; M.P. Co. Cromarty 1826–30, 1831–2.

Finished Vol.5 of Scott's Napoleon. Finished a classification (imperfect) of the English members—melancholy indeed.[1]—Papers—an American one with the S. Carolina decree.[2] An Article for the Liverpool Standard[3]—Franking & arranging for it, occupies more time than I should have supposed.

On this day I have completed my twenty third year and the first duty its recurrence entails is one of rendering my hearty thanks to that Merciful Father who has during the course of the year preserved me, in spite of myself, from so many dangers, & crowned me with so many blessings.

The exertions of the year have been smaller than those of the last: but in some respects the diminution has been unavoidable. In future I hope circumstances will bind me down to work, with a rigour which my natural sluggishness will find it impossible to elude.—I wish that I could hope my frame of mind had been in any degree removed from earth and brought nearer to heaven, that the *habit* of my mind had imbibed something of that spirit which is not of this world.

I have now familiarised myself with maxims sanctioning and encouraging a degree of intercourse with society perhaps attended with much risk, nay perhaps only rendered acceptable to my understanding by cowardice and a carnal heart. Yet still I do think that mirth may be encouraged, provided it have a purpose higher than itself: it may be a humble minister to recruit that strength which is necessary to sustain exertion at all, but which cannot sustain it without remission. Nor do I now think myself warranted in withdrawing from the practices of my fellow men, except when they really *involve* the encouragement of sin: in which class I do certainly rank races[4] and theatres. But if I have incurred danger by too lax a creed, I hope by God's mercy it may find a counteracting principle and power in the *necessity* of painful and chastening exertion which now lies before me, and under which I hope to lead a severe life, and no life *of mine* that is not severe can be godly. May that exertion be made up to the full extent of the means which may be given; however small they are, I cannot say I deserved to be trusted with larger. The future is as full of interest, as the past of shame. May my aim be, to cut off *every* merely selfish appetite and indulgence, and to live with my best energies uniformly and permanently bent towards the great objects for which even I, mean as I am, am appointed to live—the promotion, O Holy Father, of thy glory, and the establishment of thy Kingdom upon earth.

30. Sunday.

Communion—about 90. Mr Downes in afternoon. Read Bible. made notes

---

[1] Embodied, still incomplete, on his copy of *Webb's List of the Members of the House of Commons* (1833), now Add MS 44817.

[2] On 24 November the state legislative of South Carolina forbade the levying within the state of a federal tariff.

[3] Untraced.

[4] But see 1 June 70, his only appearance on a racecourse.

—a Serm. of Sanford's aloud—Smedley's Ref[ormation] in France[1]—two of Hook's Lectures, with the notes.[2] Heard from R.G.

31. M.

Wrote to Cole and Pusey. Occupied in reading the Liverpool papers and writing several articles for the Liverpool Standard. Scott's Napoleon and Barclay's "Present State of Slavery"[3]—Whist—walked. Conv. with J.N.G. at night.

And so ends an eventful year: eventful to this poor country at large— eventful to my own prospects. May the mercy of God be upon its sins and failings, and may His Wisdom provide against their recurrence in that which now lies before us: any [sc. and] may the stormy elements of agitation which are now aroused, be overruled by Him to the glory of His name & the good of his creatures.

[1] E. *Smedley, *History of the Reformed Religion in France*, 3v. (1832–4), vol. i.
[2] W. F. *Hook, *The last days of Our Lord's Ministry* (1832).
[3] A. Barclay, *A practical view of the present state of slavery in the West Indies* (1826), seeking to refute at length James *Stephen's *Slavery of the British West India colonies* (1824–30).